OPTIMISM & PESSIMISM

OPTIMISM & PESSIMISM

Implications for Theory, Research, and Practice

Edited by

Edward C. Chang

American Psychological Association
Washington, DC

Published by
American Psychological Association
750 First Street, NE
Washington, DC 20002

Copies may be ordered from
APA Order Department
P.O. Box 92984
Washington, DC 20090-2984

In the U.K., Europe, Africa, and the Middle East, copies may be ordered from
American Psychological Association
3 Henrietta Street
Covent Garden, London
WC2E 8LU England

Typeset in Goudy by World Composition Services, Inc., Sterling, VA

Printer: Edward Brothers, Inc., Ann Arbor, MI
Cover Designer: Naylor Design, Washington, DC
Technical/Production Editor: Eleanor Inskip

The opinions and statements published are the responsibility of the authors, and such opinions and statements do not necessarily represent the policies of the APA.

Library of Congress Cataloging-in-Publication Data

Optimism & pessimism : implications for theory, research, and practice / Edward C. Chang, editor.
    p. cm.
    Includes bibliographical references and index.
    ISBN 1-55798-691-6
    1. Optimism. 2. Pessimism. I. Title: Optimism and pessimism. II. Chang, Edward C. (Edward Chin-Ho)
    BF698.35.O57 O68 2000
    149'.5—dc21

                                                                        00-031310

British Library Cataloguing-in-Publication Data
A CIP record is available from the British Library.

Printed in the United States of America
First Edition

To my parents, who always have believed in me and who taught me that anything was possible as long as I worked hard enough.

CONTENTS

Contributors xi

Foreword
Lisa Miller, P. Scott Richards, and Roger R. Keller xiii

Preface xix

Acknowledgments xxi

Introduction: Optimism and Pessimism and Moving Beyond the
Most Fundamental Question 3

PART I: PHILOSOPHICAL, HISTORICAL, AND
CONCEPTUAL FOUNDATIONS

Chapter 1   Optimism and Pessimism From a
             Historical Perspective
             Brian Domino and Daniel W. Conway 13

Chapter 2   Optimism, Pessimism, and Self-Regulation
             Charles S. Carver and Michael F. Scheier 31

Chapter 3   Optimism, Pessimism, and Explanatory Style
             *Jane E. Gillham, Andrew J. Shatté, Karen J. Reivich,
             and Martin E. P. Seligman* 53

Chapter 4   Defensive Pessimism, Optimism, and Pessimism
             Julie K. Norem 77

Chapter 5   Optimism and Hope Constructs: Variants on a
             Positive Expectancy Theme
             *C. R. Snyder, Susie C. Sympson, Scott T. Michael,
             and Jen Cheavens* 101

PART II: PHYSICAL–BIOLOGICAL FACTORS

Chapter 6   Optimism and Physical Well-Being
Christopher Peterson and Lisa M. Bossio 127

Chapter 7   Optimism, Pessimism, and Daily Life With
Chronic Illness
Glenn Affleck, Howard Tennen, and Andrea Apter 147

Chapter 8   Optimism and Pessimism: Biological Foundations
Marvin Zuckerman 169

PART III: PSYCHOLOGICAL FACTORS

Chapter 9   Optimism, Pessimism, and Psychological Well-Being
*Michael F. Scheier, Charles S. Carver,
and Michael W. Bridges* 189

Chapter 10   Understanding How Optimism Works:
An Examination of Optimists' Adaptive
Moderation of Belief and Behavior
*Lisa G. Aspinwall, Linda Richter,
and Richard R. Hoffman III* 217

Chapter 11   Great Expectations: Optimism and Pessimism in
Achievement Settings
Jonathon D. Brown and Margaret A. Marshall 239

PART IV: SOCIAL–CULTURAL FACTORS

Chapter 12   Cultural Influences on Optimism and Pessimism:
Differences in Western and Eastern Construals
of the Self
Edward C. Chang 257

Chapter 13   The Optimism–Pessimism Instrument:
Personal and Social Correlates
William N. Dember 281

PART V: CHANGES AND TREATMENT

Chapter 14   Building Optimism and Preventing Depressive
Symptoms in Children
*Jane E. Gillham, Karen J. Reivich,
and Andrew J. Shatté* 301

Chapter 15   Optimism, Pessimism, and Psychotherapy:
Implications for Clinical Practice
James L. Pretzer and Chaille A. Walsh 321

PART VI: THE FUTURE

Chapter 16   A Very Full Glass:
              Adding Complexity to Our Thinking About the
              Implications and Applications of Optimism and
              Pessimism Research
              Julie K. Norem and Edward C. Chang 347

Author Index   369

Subject Index   383

About the Editor   395

CONTRIBUTORS

Glenn Affleck, PhD, University of Connecticut Health Center, Farmington

Andrea Apter, MD, University of Pennsylvania School of Medicine, Philadelphia

Lisa G. Aspinwall, PhD, University of Maryland, College Park

Lisa M. Bossio, BA, Petaluma, CA

Michael W. Bridges, PhD, Carnegie Mellon University, Pittsburgh, PA

Jonathon D. Brown, PhD, University of Washington, Seattle

Charles S. Carver, PhD, University of Miami, Coral Gables

Edward C. Chang, PhD, University of Michigan, Ann Arbor

Jen Cheavens, MA, University of Kansas, Lawrence

Daniel W. Conway, PhD, Pennsylvania State University, University Park

William N. Dember, PhD, University of Cincinnati, OH

Brian Domino, PhD, Miami University, Middletown, OH

Jane E. Gillham, PhD, University of Pennsylvania, Philadelphia, and Swarthmore College, Philadelphia

Richard R. Hoffman III, PhD, University of Maryland, College Park

Roger R. Keller, PhD, Brigham Young University, Provo, UT

Margaret A. Marshall, MS, University of Washington, Seattle

Scott T. Michael, MA, University of Kansas, Lawrence

Lisa Miller, PhD, Columbia University, New York

Julie K. Norem, PhD, Wellesley College, MA

Christopher Peterson, PhD, University of Michigan, Ann Arbor

James L. Pretzer, PhD, Case Western Reserve University, Cleveland, OH, and Cleveland Center for Cognitive Therapy, Beachwood, OH

Karen J. Reivich, PhD, University of Pennsylvania, Philadelphia

P. Scott Richards, PhD, Brigham Young University, Provo, UT

Linda Richter, PhD, University of Maryland, College Park

Michael F. Scheier, PhD, Carnegie-Mellon University, Pittsburgh, PA

Martin E. P. Seligman, PhD, University of Pennsylvania, Philadelphia

Andrew J. Shatté, PhD, University of Pennsylvania, Philadelphia

C. R. Snyder, PhD, University of Kansas, Lawrence

Susie C. Sympson, PhD, University of Kansas, Lawrence

Howard Tennen, PhD, University of Connecticut Health Center, Farmington

Chaille A. Walsh, PhD, Behavioral Health Associates, Inc., Beachwood, OH

Marvin Zuckerman, PhD, University of Delaware, Newark

FOREWORD

LISA MILLER, P. SCOTT RICHARDS, AND ROGER R. KELLER

The authors of this volume have made an important contribution to our understanding of optimism and pessimism and the implications of these constructs for human development and personality, mental health, and the process of therapeutic change. They have also made it clear that much remains to be learned about optimism and pessimism.

The contributors reveal the psychological necessity of both optimism and pessimism. Ideally, optimism and pessimism work in confluence, shifting to meet the inherent vicissitudes of life. It is the dynamic balance between the two antithetical attitudes that bring people into good commerce with their daily lives.

The authors have rigorously examined the adaptive qualities of optimism and pessimism through a range of diverse conceptual paradigms. Optimism and pessimism are investigated in this volume as traits, cognitive styles and strategies, biological dispositions, culturally shaped processes, and philosophical positions. The diversity in psychological paradigms used to explore optimism–pessimism highlights, in the consistency of the findings, the necessity of balance.

As scholars interested in the contributions of the world's great religious traditions to the understanding of human behavior and functioning (Keller, 2000; Miller & Lovinger, 2000; Richards & Bergin, 1997), we found the theme of balance intriguing. The necessity of balance between optimism–pessimism reflected in the empirical findings of this volume may be found across all of the major world religions, potentially reflecting a fundamental truth. To illustrate more fully what we mean, we will briefly consider optimism–pessimism within five major religious belief systems: Buddhism, Confucianism, Judaism, Christianity, and Islam.

Buddhism holds that all things are transitory; nothing is permanent. By attempting to grasp things of the world, people constantly reap disappointment in their desires, thus creating suffering. This somewhat pessimistic view constitutes the First of the Four Noble Truths of Buddhism. In his first sermon following his enlightenment the Buddha stated the second of the Four Noble Truths:

> Now this, O Monks, is the noble truth concerning the origin of suffering. Truly, it is the thirst or craving, causing the renewal of existence, accompanied by sensual delight, seeking satisfaction now here, now there. It is the craving for the gratification of the passions, or the craving for a future life, or the craving for success in this present life. (Dhammacakkappavattana Sutta 1-8, trans. 1879)

In contrast, optimism in Buddhism is rooted in the third Noble Truth, which states that suffering ceases when desire ceases. Cessation of desire opens the way to Nirvana (literally a going beyond). Thus, the third Noble Truth states,

> Now this, O Monks, is the noble truth concerning the destruction of suffering. Truly, it is the destruction, in which no passion remains, of this very thirst. It is the laying aside of, the getting rid of, the being free from, the harboring no longer of this thirst. (Dhammacakkappavattana Sutta 1-8 trans. 1879)

In Theravada Buddhism (practiced in southern Asia) this process is achieved through the fourth Noble Truth or the Eightfold Path, a path of moderate asceticism and meditation. Mahayana and Vajrayana Buddhism (practiced in northern Asia) hold that through faith and specific spiritual disciplines persons can access enlightened beings, who have turned back from Nirvana, to assist them in their liberation from desire.

Diametrically opposed to the detached stance of Buddhism is the emphasis in Chinese Confucianism on earthly relations. In Confucianism, humanity's goal is to acquire virtue and act accordingly. Right action between humans is seen optimistically to proceed from their inherent nature. On a somewhat more pessimistic note, however, only through strenuous training can that nature be realized. The dialogue between Confucian philosophers Kao and Mencius reflects this paradox of optimism–pessimism. Kao says, "Man's nature is like a ke willow, and righteousness is like a cup or bowl. The fashioning of benevolence out of man's nature is like the making of cups and bowls from the ke willow." To which Mencius responds, "Can you, leaving untouched the nature of the willow, make with it cups and bowls? You must do violence and injury to the willow before you can make cups and bowls with it" (Mencius 6.1.1–4,6, trans. 1983). Suffering is the process of being *forced* into alignment with right action. Joy is fulfilling our inherent nature and *willingly* filling societal roles.

Judaism, much like Confucianism, views conduct as relevant to this life, although it adds the dimension of a world beyond. The divinely created world surrounding humanity is a source of great optimism, as reflected in the frequently recited prayer, "Holy, Holy, Holy is his Name. Who set out the waters and established the earth. Whose glory is revealed in the heavens above" (*Gates of Prayer, New Union Prayerbook*, 1975). Further optimism lies in the possibility that we can more fully experience the glory of this world, if we follow the gift of G-d's Law (Mitzvot). The Torah states, "Be mindful of my Mitzvot and do them: so shall you consecrate yourselves to your G-d. . . . Its ways are ways of happiness and all its paths are peace" (*Gates of Prayer, New Union Prayerbook*, 1975). To ensure that each generation benefits from Torah, the responsibility for its transmission is placed on the previous generation: "Set these words which I command you this day, upon your heart. Teach them faithfully to your children; speak of them in your home and on your way, when you lie down and when you rise up" (Deut. 6:6–7, Authorized King James Version). Ultimately, however, despite the help of Torah, appreciation of the world is based on a struggle within each human being for clarity.

> We pray to break the bonds that keep us from the world of beauty; we pray for opened eyes, we who are blind to our own authentic selves. We pray that we may walk in the garden of a purposeful life, our own powers in touch with the power of the world. Praised be the G-d whose gift is life, whose cleansing rains let parched men and women flower toward the sun. (*Gates of Prayer, New Union Prayerbook*, 1975)

Islam, like Judaism, views the world as good, but pessimism lies in the fact that Muslims believe human beings have fallen from a pristine state before G-d. This fall is predominantly a product of human choice. However, humans may choose to repent of their evil ways, and G-d out of his mercy and goodness responds graciously with forgiveness. The Qur-an states, "Say: O my Servants who Have transgressed against their souls! Despair not of the Mercy of Allah: for Allah forgives all sins: for He is Oft-Forgiving, Most Merciful" (Sura 39:53). Herein lies the optimism of Islam, and each Sura of the Qur-an underlies it as each begins, "In the name of Allah, most Gracious, Most Merciful."

Christians see the created world much as do Muslims and Jews. It is good. But many Christians pessimistically believe human beings are warped by what is called "original sin." Human beings are not good and cannot be good, apart from a divine act of intervention. That act comes in Jesus Christ who is willing to shoulder the sins of all those who turn to him.

> And just as Moses lifted up the serpent in the wilderness, so must the Son of Man be lifted up, that whoever believes in him may have eternal life. For G-d so loved the world that he gave his only Son, so that everyone who believes in him may not perish but may have eternal life. (John 3:14–16, Authorized King James Version)

Thus, G-d, through Jesus Christ, ultimately overcomes that which separates humans from himself. In Jesus Christ lies the fullness of Christian hope.

As has been seen, the sources of optimism and pessimism, and the tension between the two, vary across these religions due to different views about humanity's place in this world and the next, their purposes in living, and their capacity for growth. Accordingly, it is the significance people ascribe to life events, perceived through the optimism–pessimism of belief systems, which elicits emotion. For instance, a career success or failure might be immaterial to Buddhists, reflect the need to observe and perfect the self for Confucianists, be viewed as cause to seek G-d's guidance through prayer and Torah by Jews, or as a Divine test or opportunity by Christians or Muslims. Gladness or sorrow naturally follows from the religious meaning given to events.

During the past two decades, numerous empirical studies have provided evidence that people who are religiously devout and committed to their tradition, but not extremists, tend to enjoy better physical and mental health (Benson, 1996; Koenig, 1997; Larson & Larson, 1994; Pargament, 1997; Richards & Bergin, 1997). These findings have led researchers and theorists to speculate concerning the mechanisms through which religion may promote health. One possible explanation is that religious worldviews, doctrines, communities, and practices may do much to promote feelings of hope, faith, and optimism (Benson, 1996; Levin, 1995; Richards & Bergin, 1997). Certainly religion for many people informs a deep and optimistic (or pessimistic) worldview (Smart, 1983).

We agree with Campbell (1975) that the principles and values of the great world religious traditions are "recipes for living that have been evolved, tested, and winnowed through hundreds of generations of human social history" (p. 1103). During the past several millennia, religious writings about optimism and pessimism have provided considerable insight into the importance of these two constructs. The present volume illustrates how scholars, using the tools of behavioral science, can add immeasurably to our understanding and appreciation of such time-tested, health-related constructs. We view this book on optimism and pessimism as a welcome and valuable addition to the literature. We applaud the editor and authors for their contributions to this important domain of positive psychology scholarship.

REFERENCES

Benson, H. (1996). *Timeless healing: The power and biology of belief.* New York: Scribner.

Campbell, D. T. (1975). On the conflicts between biological and social evolution and between psychology and moral tradition. *American Psychologist, 30,* 1103–1126.

The Gates of Prayer. The New Union Prayerbook. (1975). New York: Central Conference of American Rabbis.

Keller, R. R. (2000). Religious diversity in North America. In P. S. Richards & A. E. Bergin (Eds.), *Handbook of psychotherapy and religious diversity* (pp. 27–55). Washington, DC: American Psychological Association.

Koenig, H. G. (1997). *Is religion good for your health? The effects of religion on physical and mental health.* New York: Haworth Press.

Larson, D., & Larson, S. (1994). *The forgotten factor: Review of research on religion and health.* Rockville, MD: National Institute for Health Research.

Levin, J. S. (1995, April). *Epidemiology of religion.* Paper presented at a conference of the National Institute for Healthcare Research, Leesburg, VA.

Miller, L., & Lovinger, R. J. (2000). Psychotherapy with conservative and reform Jews. In P. S. Richards & A. E. Bergin (Eds.), *Handbook of psychotherapy and religious diversity* (pp. 259–286). Washington, DC: American Psychological Association.

Pargament, K. I. (1997). *The psychology of religion and coping: Theory, research, practice.* New York: Guilford Press.

Richards, P. S., & Bergin, A. E. (1997). *A spiritual strategy for counseling and psychotherapy.* Washington, DC: American Psychological Association.

Smart, N. (1983). *Worldviews: Crosscultural explorations of human beliefs.* New York: Scribner.

PREFACE

As I have learned over the years, failure is often a necessary condition to success. About 2 years ago, I sat down in my office one afternoon to consider writing an article that attempted to integrate several lines of research focusing on the study of optimism and pessimism. After gathering several key references, I quickly realized that my efforts to provide an exhaustive review of the literature would be futile. In a rare moment of inspiration and foolhardiness, I considered the simple possibility of contacting leading experts in the area to see if they would be interested in contributing to a book on optimism and pessimism. Although I had some clear ideas about what the edited book would look like, I had strong doubts that a young scholar like myself would be able to solicit the assistance of individuals who have been my mentors and role models. No doubt, I was surprised to find that many of those I contacted were enthusiastic and willing to contribute to such a book. Accordingly, I remain indebted to them for their trust in me and for their contributing to any success this volume may obtain.

Optimism and Pessimism: Implications for Theory, Research, and Practice has evolved considerably from the manner in which I first conceived of it, and I think in many ways for the better. The contributors have focused on the topics they know best—given their respective expertise. They also have made a concerted effort to consider the implications of their work for both research and practice. As a clinical psychologist by training, I felt that it was essential to go beyond a survey of basic research findings and theoretical models to make an effort to bridge scientific knowledge with practice. Because the concepts of optimism and pessimism have strong philosophical roots, I also felt that it was important to provide an opportunity for philosophers to be involved in our efforts to understand optimism and pessimism. Clearly, this book is not exhaustive, nor does it attempt to be. Yet, I believe it provides fertile ground for anyone who is interested in gaining an understanding and appreciation of how optimism and pessimism influence human behavior.

Recently, I was fortunate to have been asked by then President of the American Psychological Association, Dr. Martin E. P. Seligman, with Dr. Mihaly Csikszentmihalyi of the University of Chicago, to attend a conference with other young as well as some more experienced scholars to consider the development of a Positive Psychology. Although a bit hesitant, I chose to attend. Among the many visions and concerns that evolved from the group was a sense that a significant cultural shift was needed, from the traditional focus on identifying and treating illnesses to identifying and promoting human strengths, a quest that quickly brought to mind my earlier readings of Plato's *Republic* and Aristotle's *Nicomachean Ethics*. Although the contributors to this volume have not necessarily made it their goal to address questions regarding the search for excellence or how to live the good life, their works no doubt have strong bearing on identifying and understanding when and how an optimistic and pessimistic attitude can serve to promote the best that we can be. As I look to our new millennium, I have become uncharacteristically optimistic about what people might be able to accomplish. It is my hope that this volume will help inspire not only the experienced, but also—maybe more importantly—the next generation of researchers, scholars, and practitioners who will continue to study the power of optimism and pessimism in the hopes of furthering the welfare of humankind.

ACKNOWLEDGMENTS

I thank the many individuals who have played a valuable role in assisting me with this volume. Several of my colleagues have been helpful in providing me with support and encouragement throughout this project, especially Bill Dember and Julie Norem. It may be of interest to note that it was Bill's work on the partial independence of optimism and pessimism and Julie's work on defensive pessimism that first inspired me to study the potential power of optimism *and* pessimism, as they continue to do so. I especially thank Julie for giving me the wonderful opportunity to work with her. I must also express my deepest thanks to Kah-Kyung Cho at the State University of New York at Buffalo who allowed me many years ago, when I was an undergraduate student, to participate in his graduate seminar on Martin Heidegger. I also thank the production and developmental editors at APA, especially Anne Woodworth, who helped ensure that the book was complete and ready for publication, and the many students who offered their assistance with this project. Last, I thank Margaret Schlegel at APA for giving me the opportunity to edit this volume and for her patience throughout this project.

OPTIMISM & PESSIMISM

INTRODUCTION:
OPTIMISM AND PESSIMISM AND
MOVING BEYOND THE MOST
FUNDAMENTAL QUESTION

Carpe diem, quam minimus credula postero.
"Seize today, and put as little trust as you can in tomorrow."

Horace

As philosophers long have noted, humans are cognitive beings (*res cogitans*). We are able to define ourselves by our quintessential ability to question the truth and meaning of our own existence. But what is the meaning of being? More than half a century ago, Martin Heidegger (1927/ 1962) raised this question of fundamental ontology in his magnum opus *Being and Time*. Considered by some as the most important and influential thinker of the 20th century, Heidegger raised to social consciousness a way of understanding human being as Dasein. As *Dasein* or "being-there," humans are not merely what they are (actuality), but more importantly are what they are not yet but can be (potentiality).[1] This idea has been prominently

---

[1]The distinction between actuality and potentiality as a means for understanding being was first made by Aristotle.

reflected in the subsequent writings of notable philosophers (Camus, 1942/ 1955; Merleau-Ponty, 1945/1962; Sartre, 1943/1956), theologians (Marcel, 1935/1965; Tillich, 1952), and psychologists (Allport, 1955; Frankl, 1946/ 1962; Maslow, 1962; Rogers, 1961). Accordingly, it is the power of possibility that represents an important determination of who and what we are and how we exist in the world. Among the range of possibilities that influence our existence, two stand out, namely, (a) expectations that good things will happen (*bonum futurum*) and (b) expectations that bad things will happen (*malum futurum*)—or in more lay terms, optimism and pessimism.

While the question of the meaning of being has continued to remain a central point of inquiry for philosophers and theologians since the publication of Heidegger's (1927/1962) seminal work, psychologists since have begun to actively examine the power of optimism and pessimism on our lives. No doubt, this is a direct result of Scheier and Carver's (1985) pioneering research on generalized outcome expectancies and Seligman's (1975) influential work on learned helplessness. Together, their groundbreaking contributions to understanding the significance of optimism and pessimism have led to an explosion of studies over the past quarter of a century. On that account, selecting contributions for the present volume was by no means an easy task.

In putting this volume together, I sought to promote a balance in breadth and depth by seeking the contributions of leading scholars, researchers, and practitioners who could best speak about the potential value of optimism and pessimism. In doing so, I also hoped to offer a volume that could appeal to a broad and diverse readership. For instance, students and new investigators will find many of the chapters a great resource for quickly acquainting themselves with the rich historical and scientific literature associated with the study of optimism and pessimism. Even well-seasoned researchers are likely to find some of the chapters informative, if not useful, for planning future studies or for developing more complex models of optimism and pessimism. Practitioners and educators alike will also find thoughtful and practical chapters on theories and techniques related to modifying optimism and pessimism in both children and adults, as well as probing discussions on the sociocultural context of optimism and pessimism. And even for those of us who simply wonder why it appears to be better to be optimistic than pessimistic, this book will help clarify why this is so (at least most of the time).

Yet, it is important to recognize that the significance of optimism and pessimism should be seen beyond individual goals and projects and be seen in light of how we live our lives both as individuals and as part of collectives. As Bailey (1988) noted in framing the definition of optimism and pessimism in this broader context:

Pessimism and optimism—can have perfectly respectable mundane meanings which refer to people's shared judgements about the supposed direction of social change on criteria which can be made explicit. These judgments have powerful social and cultural effects in that they lead to the formation of social movements and social organizations to affect these issues, or, alternatively, to justify apathy and inertia. That they have moral and emotional resonances is a signal of their salience in our social life, not a reason for avoiding them. . . . (p. 5)

Accordingly, this volume represents converging and collaborative efforts to directly examine the *value* of optimism and pessimism in our lives, broadly defined. Optimism is generally good. Expecting that good things will happen to us often can lead to positive outcomes, both personal and social. However, expecting that bad things will happen to us does not necessarily have to be associated with doom and failure. Just as always expecting the best may have its disadvantages (e.g., maintaining the status quo, overlooking important opportunities), so too can expecting the worst have its advantages (e.g., initiating social reform, identifying potential weaknesses and problem areas). No doubt, given our social proclivity to think that optimism is good and pessimism is bad, especially in the West, it may appear to some that the relative value of optimism and pessimism is a foregone conclusion. In that regard, several chapters in this book should offer some interesting, if not challenging, insights for assessing the value of optimism and pessimism.

A COMMON DEFINITION WITH
MANY OPERATIONALIZATIONS

Commonly defined, *optimism* reflects an expectation that good things will happen, whereas *pessimism* reflects an expectation that bad things will happen. Hence, although likely to be interrelated, optimism should be distinguished from other notable psychological variables such as internal control and self-esteem. Likewise, pessimism should not be confused with expressions of lack of control and self-effacement. Although most researchers are not likely to have strong disagreements with this conceptualization of optimism and pessimism, there is less agreement regarding the measurement of these variables.

Because the assessment of psychological variables typically depends on the theoretical framework from which they are derived, even subtle differences in theoretical models can lead to significant differences in their operationalization. This has been no less the case in studying optimism and pessimism. Consequently, researchers holding different theoretical views have developed different instruments to assess for optimism and pessimism. On the one hand, this has helped promote a richer and more pluralistic understanding of optimism and pessimism. On the other hand, it has also made it difficult for researchers to compare and contrast findings based on different measures of optimism and pessimism. For this reason, I strongly urge readers to first become familiar with the measures of optimism and pessimism before moving on to the chapters.

Optimism and Pessimism as Generalized Outcome Expectancies

One of the most popular measures used to assess for optimism and pessimism has been Scheier and Carver's (1985) Life Orientation Test (LOT), as referred to in many of the chapters in this volume. The LOT is an 8-item measure (plus 4 filler items). Four of the items are positively worded (e.g., "In uncertain times, I usually expect the best"), and another 4 are negatively worded (e.g., "If something can go wrong for me, it will"). Scores on the negatively worded items are typically reversed and summed with scores on the positively worded items to obtain a single summary score. Although the LOT is typically considered to be a unidimensional measure of dispositional optimism, some studies have found that it has a bidimensional structure (e.g., Chang, D'Zurilla, & Maydeu-Olivares, 1994; Marshall, Wortman, Kusulas, Hervig, & Vickers, 1992). It is noteworthy that Chang, Maydeu-Olivares, and D'Zurilla (1997) found that a two-factor model was also more appropriate than a one-factor model for their extended version of the LOT, the Extended Life Orientation Test (ELOT). The ELOT is composed of 15 items (6 items assessing for optimism and 9 items assessing for pessimism). Although the ELOT has been found to have good psychometric properties and slightly higher internal consistencies than those typically reported for the LOT (Chang et al., 1997), it has received much less attention by researchers. Nonetheless, the ELOT has been used by some researchers (see Chang, chap. 12, this volume).

Recently, Scheier, Carver, and Bridges (1994) introduced a briefer version of the LOT, the revised Life Orientation Test (LOT–R), a 6-item measure (plus 4 filler items) of dispositional optimism. Three items are positively worded and three are negatively worded. The LOT–R essentially eliminated some of the content overlap with coping that existed in the original LOT. However, there is considerable overlap between the LOT and LOT–R ($r = .95$, reported in Scheier et al., 1994). Also similar to the LOT, the LOT–R is generally considered a unidimensional measure of dispositional optimism. It is noteworthy that the LOT, LOT–R, and ELOT are all based on Scheier and Carver's (1985) definition of optimism and pessimism as reflecting generalized positive and negative outcome expectancies, respectively (see chap. 2 and chap. 9, this volume). In that regard, these measures provide the most direct assessment of optimism and pessimism as we commonly understand them.

Optimism and Pessimism as Attributions for Positive and Negative Events

Still another popular measure of optimism and pessimism that has been used by researchers (and is referred to also in many of the book's chapters) has been Peterson et al.'s (1982) Attributional Style Questionnaire (ASQ). The ASQ is composed of 6 negative event items and 6 positive event items. For each event (e.g., "you have been looking for a job unsuccessfully for some time"), respondents are asked to write down one major cause for why that event occurred. In addition respondents are asked to provide ratings across scales assessing for internality, stability, and globality. Individuals who perceive that good things (i.e., positive events) happen to them because of *internal* (something about the individual), *stable* (happens all the time), and *global* (happens in all situations) factors are considered to have an optimistic explanatory style. Conversely, individuals who perceive that bad things (i.e., negative events) happen to them due to internal, stable, and global factors are considered to have a pessimistic explanatory style. However, it is worth noting that research using the ASQ typically has focused on responses to negative events only.

More recently, given some concerns about the low reliability of the ASQ scales, Peterson and Villanova (1988) introduced the Expanded Attributional Style Questionnaire (EASQ), which is composed of 24 negative events (there are no positive events). Both the ASQ and the EASQ are based on an explanatory style framework for understanding optimism and pessimism (see Gillham, Shatté, Reivich, & Seligman, chap. 3, this volume). In addition, it is worth briefly noting that several other measures and techniques for assessing explanatory style have also developed, such as Peterson, Schulman, Castellon, and Seligman's (1992) Content Analysis of Verbatim Explanations (CAVE; see also Peterson & Bossio, chap. 6, this volume) and a children's version of the ASQ (see Gillham, Reivich, & Shatté, chap. 14, this volume). Generally speaking, in contrast to expectancy-based measures (e.g., LOT), attributional measures provide a more indirect assessment of optimism and pessimism. That is, expressions of optimism and pessimism are typically inferred by researchers based on the specific pattern of attributions presented by individuals to positive and negative events.

Other Measures of Optimism and Pessimism

Two other measures of optimism and pessimism are also worth briefly noting. Dember, Martin, Hummer, Howe, and Melton (1989) developed the Optimism–Pessimism Instrument, which is composed of 18 optimism items (e.g., "with enough faith, you can do almost anything"), 18 pessimism items (e.g., "as time goes on, things will most likely get worse"), and 20 filler items. This instrument provides separate measures of optimism and pessimism and is based on a definition of these constructs in the broadest sense possible (see Dember, chap. 13, this volume, for details). Norem's Defensive Pessimism Questionnaire (DPQ) is composed of 17 items that assess for defensive pessimism (e.g., "I go into these [academic/social] situations expecting the worst, even though I know I will probably do OK") and reflectivity (e.g., "I often think about how I will feel if I do very well in these [academic/social] situations"). More detailed information regarding research related to this scale is presented by Norem (see chap. 4, this volume).

Finally, a related measure of optimism is Snyder et al.'s (1991) Hope Scale, a 12-item bidimensional measure of hope consisting of a 4-item agency subscale (e.g., "I meet the goals that I set for myself"), a 4-item pathway subscale (e.g., "I can think of many ways to get the things in life that are important to me"), and 4 additional filler items. More detailed information regarding research related to the Hope Scale is presented by Snyder, Sympson, Michael, and Cheavens (see chap. 5, this volume).

AN OVERVIEW OF THIS BOOK

The present volume is divided into six parts. Part I focuses on the conceptualization of optimism and pessimism from different philosophical, historical, and conceptual perspectives. As noted by Bailey (1988), "the origins of optimism and pessimism lie in philosophy" (p. 26). Accordingly, Domino and Conway start chapter 1 of this volume by providing readers with a broad survey of the philosophical and historical contexts associated with the emergence of optimistic and pessimistic thought in the West. Spanning two centuries, they begin with the writings of René Descartes in the 18th century and conclude with the writings of William James in the 19th century. In chapter 2, Carver and Scheier provide a review of their self-regulation model of behavior as it pertains to dispositional optimism and pessimism and consider the operation of these variables in light of recent work in catastrophe theory. Chapter 3 by Gillham, Shatté, Reivich, and Seligman provides readers with a critical review of the theoretical and empirical literature associated with the study of optimism and pessimism from an explanatory style framework, with attention to important conceptual and methodological issues. In chapter 4, Norem presents readers with a fascinating counterpoint to the notion that optimism is always good and pessimism is always bad. Reviewing studies on defensive pessimism and recent works drawn from social cognition, Norem focuses on the potential advantages of using a pessimistic strategy to harness motivation. Chapter 5 by Snyder, Sympson, Michael, and Cheavens reviews research and theory related to the study of hope and distinguishes hope from optimism.

Considering humans as biopsychosocial beings (Engel, 1977), the next three parts examine the role of optimism and pessimism across biological/physical, psychological, and sociocultural dimensions. Specifically, Part II focuses on physical and biological factors associated with optimism and pessimism. Beginning with chapter 6 by Peterson and Bossio, readers are introduced to a critical appraisal of the empirical literature linking optimism to health, with particular attention to works drawn from the explanatory style literature. In chapter 7, Affleck, Tennen, and Apter acquaint readers to their daily process research paradigm and review their findings examining the link between dispositional optimism and chronic illness. Chapter 8 by Zuckerman provides a scholarly review and discussion of the possible biological foundations of optimism and pessimism as they relate to traits such as extroversion and neuroticism.

Part III focuses on psychological factors associated with optimism and pessimism. Chapter 9 by Scheier, Carver, and Bridges offers readers an up-to-date review of the theoretical and empirical literature involving studies linking dispositional optimism to psychological well-being and a discussion on the role of coping in understanding this link. In chapter 10, Aspinwall, Richter, and Hoffman continue to look at factors that may help account for the link between dispositional optimism and well-being, including flexibility in behaviors, beliefs, and selective attention. In chapter 11, Brown and Marshall consider results from a series of recently conducted studies examining the relative importance of low, medium, and high expectancies on performance and psychological well-being. The findings they present are interesting and serve to challenge any simple notion that greater optimism always renders more benefits to individuals.

Part IV focuses on sociocultural factors associated with optimism and pessimism. Chapter 12 by Chang reviews some of the notable findings obtained in recent studies of optimism and pessimism between different cultural groups (Easterners and Westerners) and discusses some of the implications of these reviewed findings for practice. As this chapter emphasizes, the notion that optimism is good and pessimism is bad may not be useful for understanding all cultural groups. In chapter 13, Dember discusses the development of the Optimism–Pessimism Instrument and provides a thoughtful review of findings linking optimism and pessimism with an array of important personality and social correlates using this instrument. This chapter is also of historical importance in that it was in developing the instrument that Dember and his colleagues made one of the first explicit arguments for considering optimism and pessimism as partially independent constructs.

Part V focuses on the modification of optimism and pessimism in children and adults. In chapter 14, Gillham, Reivich, and Shatté review the literature on treating and preventing depression in at-risk children, with particular attention to promoting resiliency in children by transforming their explanatory styles. In chapter 15, Pretzer and Walsh provide readers with a broad review of the clinical and empirical literature associated with efforts to modify optimism and pessimism in adults and suggest techniques and recommendations for intervention.

Finally, Part VI concludes this volume with a focus on the future of optimism and pessimism scholarship and research. Specifically, in chapter 16, Norem and Chang argue for greater complexity in the way that people think about optimism and pessimism. They highlight a number of important issues and concerns that will need to be addressed if we are to obtain a better means for evaluating the significance of optimism and pessimism in our lives.

CONCLUDING THOUGHTS

As mentioned in the Preface, this book was by no means intended to be comprehensive or exhaustive in its coverage of optimism and pessimism. To do so simply would have been well beyond the practical scope of the present undertaking. Nevertheless, some readers may find noticeably absent, for example, a chapter examining optimism and pessimism from a religious/ spiritual framework or a chapter critically reviewing the importance of optimism and pessimism from a developmental standpoint. To be sure, there has been a long-standing connection between religious thought and expressions of optimism and pessimism (see foreword by Miller, Richards, & Keller in this volume). Surprisingly, however, one will find that direct studies on this matter have been sparse over the past several decades. A similar problem emerges in considering a developmental examination of optimism and pessimism. Specifically, published studies on optimism and pessimism have been almost exclusively based on young to middle-aged adult populations, and only a handful of studies exist that have looked at these variables in children and in the elderly population. Clearly, the absence of such topics in this volume should in no way imply their lack of importance in the study of optimism and pessimism. On the contrary, their conspicuous absence may help stimulate greater research and scholarship on optimism and pessimism in these and other important areas of human concern and interest.

In closing, congruent with the Chinese notion of yin and yang, it may not be important for us to only appreciate the value of optimism and pessimism, but to also appreciate the value of their balance in our lives. To accomplish the latter, a fundamental shift may be necessary from the conventional way of thinking of optimism and pessimism as antagonistic processes (e.g., optimism vs. pessimism). Consider the quote by Horace at the beginning of this Introduction illustrating how optimistic and pessimistic expressions may harmoniously co-exist. That is, by expecting the best but preparing for the worst, we may all be able to live more fuller and satisfying lives. Indeed, it is my hope that the critical works presented in this volume will help illuminate to readers the significance of this balance between optimism and pessimism for determining our fullest potentials for being.

REFERENCES

Allport, G. (1955). *Becoming: Basic considerations for a psychology of personality*. New Haven: Yale University Press.

Bailey, J. (1988). *Pessimism*. New York: Routledge.

Camus, A. (1955). *The myth of Sisyphus and other essays* (J. O'Brien, Trans.). New York: Knopf. (Originally work published 1942)

Chang, E. C., D'Zurilla, T. J., & Maydeu-Olivares, A. (1994). Assessing the dimensionality of optimism and pessimism using a multi-measure approach. *Cognitive Therapy and Research, 18*, 143–160.

Chang, E. C., Maydeu-Olivares, A., & D'Zurilla, T. J. (1997). Optimism and pessimism as partially independent constructs: Relations to positive and negative affectivity and psychological well-being. *Personality and Individual Differences, 23*, 433–440.

Dember, W. N., Martin, S., Hummer, M. K., Howe, S., & Melton, R. (1989). The measurement of optimism and pessimism. *Current Psychology: Research and Reviews, 8*, 102–119.

Engel, G. L. (1977). The need for a new medical model: A challenge for biomedicine. *Science, 196*, 129–136.

Frankl, V. E. (1962). *Man's search for meaning: Introduction to logotherapy* (I. Lasch, Trans.). Boston: Beacon Press. (Original work published 1946)

Heidegger, M. (1962). *Being and time* (J. Macquarrie & E. Robinson, Trans.). New York: Harper & Row. (Original work published 1927)

Marcel, G. (1965). *Being and having: An existentialist diary* (K. Farrer, Trans.). New York: Harper & Row. (Original work published 1935)

Marshall, G. N., Wortman, C. B., Kusulas, J. W., Hervig, L. K., & Vickers, R. R., Jr. (1992). Distinguishing optimism from pessimism: Relations to fundamental dimensions of mood and personality. *Journal of Personality and Social Psychology, 62*, 1067–1074.

Maslow, A. (1962). *Toward a psychology of being.* New York: Van Nostrand.

Merleau-Ponty, M. (1962). *The phenomenology of perception* (C. Smith, Trans.). London: Routledge & Kegan Paul. (Original work published 1945)

Peterson, C., Schulman, P., Castellon, C., & Seligman, M. E. P. (1992). CAVE: Content analysis of verbatim explanations. In C. P. Smith (Ed.), *Motivation and personality: Handbook of thematic content analysis* (pp. 383–392). New York: Cambridge University Press.

Peterson, C., Semmel, A., von Baeyer, D., Abramson, L. Y., Metalsky, G. I., & Seligman, M. E. P. (1982). The Attributional Style Questionnaire. *Cognitive Therapy and Research, 6,* 287–299.

Peterson, C., & Villanova, P. (1988). An Expanded Attributional Style Questionnaire. *Journal of Abnormal Psychology, 97,* 87–89.

Rogers, C. (1961). *On becoming a person.* Boston: Houghton-Mifflin.

Sartre, J.-P. (1956). *Being and nothingness: An essay on phenomenological ontology* (H. Barnes, Trans.). New York: Philosophical Library. (Original work published 1943)

Scheier, M. F., & Carver, C. S. (1985). Optimism, coping, and health: Assessment and implications of generalized outcome expectancies. *Health Psychology, 4,* 219–247.

Scheier, M. F., Carver, C. S., & Bridges, M. W. (1994). Distinguishing optimism from neuroticism (and trait anxiety, self-mastery, and self-esteem): A reevaluation of the Life Orientation Test. *Journal of Personality and Social Psychology, 67,* 1063–1078.

Seligman, M. E. P. (1975). *Helplessness: On depression, development, and death.* San Francisco: Freeman.

Snyder, C. R., Harris, C., Anderson, J. R., Holleran, S. A., Irving, L. M., Sigmon, S. T., Yoshinobu, L., Gibb, J., Langelle, C., & Harney, P. (1991). The will and the ways: Development and validation of an individual-differences measure of hope. *Journal of Personality and Social Psychology, 60,* 570–585.

Tillich, P. (1952). *The courage to be.* New Haven: Yale University.

I

Philosophical, Historical, and Conceptual Foundations

1

OPTIMISM AND PESSIMISM FROM A HISTORICAL PERSPECTIVE

BRIAN DOMINO AND DANIEL W. CONWAY

The psychological accounts of optimism and pessimism delineated in this volume represent the most recent attempts by humankind to determine its place in the world. The roots of these contemporary accounts are found, we believe, in the various treatments of optimism and pessimism that have been advanced by leading philosophers of the modern period. In this chapter, we trace the historical development of philosophical understanding of optimism and pessimism from their emergence in the writings of Descartes; through their articulation by protopsychologists such as Schopenhauer and Nietzsche; and finally to their evaluation by two eminent psychologist–philosophers, Sigmund Freud and William James.

In philosophy, *optimism* and *pessimism* designate competing, antithetical positions. Philosophers are regarded as optimistic if they treat the cosmos as generally hospitable to the aims and aspirations of human beings; they are regarded as pessimistic if they treat the cosmos as generally indifferent or even hostile to the flourishing of human beings and civilizations. As philosophical positions, both optimism and pessimism presuppose the capacity of (some) human beings to arrive at an accurate forecast of the future. This capacity to forecast the future usually depends, in turn, on a reliable interpretation of the salient events of the past and present, such that the forecasted future might be presented as following naturally (or logically) from the general trends that characterize the past and present. Philosophical statements of either optimism or pessimism typically assume one of two forms: (a) Through the use of a priori reasoning (i.e., speculative), philosophers attempt to defend a particular forecast of the future by appealing to various general principles that are held as unchallenged truths, for example the existence of God, or (b) through the use of a posteriori reasoning (i.e., empirical), philosophers attempt to defend a particular forecast of the future by appealing to verifiable patterns found in nature. Although statements of the first form are perhaps more prevalent in the history of Western philosophy, statements of the second form are generally held to be more persuasive.

17TH AND 18TH CENTURIES

Descartes

The historical emergence of optimism and pessimism as identifiable philosophical positions is usually associated with the inception of the modern period of philosophy in the 17th century. In this period, it became increasingly common for philosophers to maintain that the successful application of reason to the cosmos warranted a philosophical outlook characterized by either optimism or pessimism. The formulation of an optimistic philosophical position can be traced to the writings of the French philosopher René Descartes (1596–1650). Widely recognized as the father of modern philosophy, Descartes contributed significantly to the transition from the Catholic Church–influenced philosophy of the Middle Ages to the more secularly oriented philosophy of the modern period. An accomplished mathematician and scientist, Descartes keenly understood the need for philosophers to escape the shadows of dogma and superstition. Where the Church had largely failed to improve the material conditions of human life, he believed, science would succeed in delivering a secularized world devoid of fear, scarcity, and disease. The source of Descartes's optimism can therefore be traced to his conviction that a methodical application of human reason can unlock the mysteries of the natural world (Descartes, 1628/1985). This conviction informs all of his writings, from the early *Rules for the Direction of the Mind* (Descartes, 1701/1985) to his final treatise, *The Passions of the Soul* (Descartes, 1649/1985), wherein he asserted, "There is no soul so weak that it cannot, if well-directed, acquire an absolute power over its passions"

(§50, p. 348). From an enhanced understanding of the natural world arises the power to blunt the ill effects of nature on the welfare and progress of humankind. In general, Descartes concluded, the continually improving state of the world warrants the optimism that pervades his philosophy.

Descartes also contributed significantly to the emergence of a distinctly moral sense of optimism and pessimism by his insistence that human beings are fully capable of improving the state of the world by their own efforts. In his "Discourse on the Method," Descartes (1628/1985) famously asserted that science will enable human beings to become the masters and possessors of nature; they will thereby enjoy the fruits of the earth and maintain their health. Although this claim may strike us as innocuous, it was considered daring, and perhaps even blasphemous, by many 17th-century philosophers and scientists. According to Descartes, human beings should be seen as participating creatively in the ongoing improvement of the material conditions of human life; they need not resign themselves to destinies determined solely by divine will and inscrutable fate. In particular, Descartes expressed hope that medicine would eventually prevent illness and the enfeeblement of old age. Because ill health caused a variety of social problems, he hoped that the scientifically fortified practice of medicine might deliver us to an Eden of our own making.

Pope

A similar optimism is expressed by Alexander Pope (1688–1744) in his highly influential *Essay on Man* (1733–1734). Unlike Descartes, however, Pope derived his optimism from an a priori insight into the goodness and interconnectedness of the cosmos. He thus challenged the meaningfulness of the claim that humankind could be better off than it is. Any such claim, he maintained, expresses the misguided wish that human beings become embodied gods. Indeed, for Pope, to insist that the human intellect could (and should) be more formidable is to forget that we are not divine. Pope appeals persuasively to the integrated imagery of the "Great Chain of Being," wherein each creation is appointed (and must maintain) its own unique place. To complain, for example, that our senses could be more acute is to deny our enduring nature. In many cases, he maintained, an increase in sensitivity would only bring about our own destruction. For example, if our sense of smell were to become substantially more acute, then we might "die of a rose in aromatic pain" (Pope, 1733–1734, VI). In fact, he concluded, our senses are as perfectly acute as is consistent with our obligation to maintain the unique station to which we have been appointed. Humankind is located precisely at its optimal position in the Great Chain of Being; to change our status even in the slightest would trigger a disruption throughout the entire plenum of nature. Or, as Pope famously concluded, "One truth is clear, Whatever is, is right" (1733–1734, I, p. 10).

Leibniz

As a technical philosophical term, *optimism* has its roots in the writings of Gottfried Leibniz (1646–1716). In particular, his *Theodicy* (Leibniz, 1710/1996) offers a more rigorous proof of the optimistic conclusions reached by Pope. Leibniz used the term *optimum* to name the unique maximum or minimum instance of an infinite class of possibilities. In particular, he argued that God followed the principle of the optimum in the creation of the world. Although he admitted that God alone can perform an infinite analysis, Leibniz held that the human mind is capable of comprehending proofs involving the infinite (1710/1996, §69). It is perhaps not surprising, then, that Leibniz's demonstration that this is the best of all possible worlds bears a distinct resemblance to a mathematical proof. According to this influential demonstration, God's infinite knowledge includes the ideas of all possible universes. God's moral perfection caused Him to choose to create the best of these possible universes—namely, the one that exists, which Leibniz famously described as "the best of all possible worlds." That this is the best of all possible worlds, however, does not entail that it is also perfect. As Leibniz argued, all things in the cosmos are interconnected; to change one part in the whole is, therefore, to change the whole. Although another possible world (one like ours but lacking some particular evil) might appear to be better than our world, this appearance arises from the mistaken belief that the elimination of a particular evil is a discrete, self-contained event. Our belief in a possible world better than ours thus proves not that such a world exists, but that we are unable to complete an infinite analysis. Leibniz argued, for example, that the elimination of one evil would entail the absence of the good produced by that evil, which would then yield a world worse than the present one. Once we are able to comprehend this analysis, he believed, we will agree that this is, in fact, the best of all possible worlds.

Voltaire

Leibniz's *Theodicy* is ridiculed by Voltaire (1694–1778) in *Candide, or Optimism* (1759/1959). The characters in *Candide* suffer all manner of torture, tragedy, affliction, and reversal of fortune. Throughout these misadventures, the unflinchingly optimistic Pangloss maintains that, indeed, all is for the best. Under the Leibnizian tutelage of Pangloss, Candide dutifully parrots his teacher's optimism. As a result, he habitually fails to learn from his impressive travels and diverse experiences. Toward the end of the book,

Candide announces that he has finally learned his lesson: He and the others should renounce the speculative philosophy practiced by Pangloss, as well as the false optimism that he preaches. They should busy themselves instead with the practical labor involved in "cultivating a garden," which will enable them to remain productive as they resist the blandishments of philosophical speculation (Voltaire, 1758/1959).

On a superficial level, Voltaire's specific charges against philosophical optimism could easily be answered by Pope and Leibniz. Neither thinker maintains that anyone's (much less everyone's) life is perfect. Voltaire's point, though, is not only to present a narrowly philosophic refutation of optimism, but also to demonstrate that optimism sanctions a numbing indifference to human suffering. In fact, he wishes to criticize both optimism and pessimism insofar as they rest on general, speculative principles that do not admit of empirical verification. For example, the purported interconnectedness of the cosmos, to which many philosophical optimists appeal when constructing their theodicies, is not confirmed by an empirical investigation of the cosmos. According to Voltaire, if reason is properly (i.e., empirically) applied to the world, it warrants neither optimism nor pessimism as a general philosophical outlook. He consequently portrayed the character Martin, an inveterate pessimist, as no less ridiculous than the optimist Pangloss.

In his *Philosophical Dictionary*, Voltaire (1764/1962) again marshaled his rhetorical powers against the view that "all is good [*tout est bien*]". Dropping the satirical excesses of *Candide*, Voltaire observed that optimism seems plausible only to young aristocrats, whose lives are indeed pleasurable. Such optimism is easily refuted as a general philosophical principle. A critic need merely "stick his head out the window, he will see unhappy people enough; let him catch a fever, he will be unhappy himself" (Voltaire, 1764/ 1962, p. 420f). Against Leibniz, Voltaire charged that the claim "all is good" means nothing more than "all is governed by immutable laws" (p. 425). That is, Leibniz failed to consider a sufficiently wide range of examples in presenting his defense of philosophical optimism. Voltaire suggested that he add the following illustration of the immutable laws of nature:

> When a stone is formed in my bladder, it is by an admirable piece of machinery: gravelly juices pass little by little into my blood, filter into the kidneys, pass through the urethras, deposit themselves in my bladder, assemble there by an excellent Newtonian attraction; the stone is formed, grows larger; I suffer evils a thousand times worse than death, by the most beautiful arrangement in the world; a surgeon. . .comes to thrust a sharp and pointed iron into the perineum and seizes my stone with his pincers. It breaks under his efforts by a necessary mechanism; and, by this same mechanism, I die in horrible torments. All this is

good, all this is the evident consequence of unchangeable physical principles; I agree, and I know it as well as you do. (1764/1962, pp. 120f, 425f)

Hume

Like Voltaire, Scottish philosopher David Hume (1711–1776) challenged the reasonableness of philosophical optimism. In his witty *Dialogues Concerning Natural Religion* (1775/1980), Hume debunked the popular claim that a robust appreciation of God can be derived from an experience of the order and beauty of the natural world. Showing that any appeal to natural religion must trade on some version of the *argument from design,* also known as the *argument from analogy*), he proceeded to demonstrate just how little we can actually infer about the designer of the cosmos. Speaking through the skeptical character Philo, Hume insisted that no general truths about the cosmos can be derived from the argument from design.

Restricting oneself to an empirical investigation of the beauty, order, and complexity arrayed throughout the natural world, one can infer at best that the universe was created by something bearing a remote resemblance to human intelligence. Whether the designer of the universe possesses any innate moral or aesthetic qualities, however, cannot be conclusively determined, nor does an empirical survey of the natural world establish whether this creator still exists. Rather than support a full-blown philosophical optimism, natural religion at best sanctions a modest commitment to deism. If an optimistic position is to be maintained, Hume skeptically concluded, it cannot rest solely on the evidence provided by natural religion. Relying solely on an analogy with human design, philosophical optimists cannot claim to have evidence of the complexity and necessity that they attribute (and Hume denied) to the cosmos as a whole. According to Hume, in fact, an application of a posteriori reasoning to the cosmos leads us neither to optimism or pessimism, but to skepticism. From this skeptical position, we may choose to invest our faith in optimism or pessimism, but in no event will we do so with sufficient reason (Hume, 1775/1980).

Kant

Like Voltaire, Immanuel Kant (1724–1804) dismissed the optimistic claim that the existence of evil mysteriously contributes to God's larger plan. In his aptly entitled essay "On the Miscarriage of all Philosophical Attempts in Theodicy," Kant rejected this claim as "need[ing] no refutation; surely it can be freely given over to the detestation of every human being who has the least feeling for morality" (1791/1996, p. 38). Beginning with his *Critique of Pure Reason* (Kant, 1781/1965), he thus maintained that both optimism and pessimism are metaphysically indefensible positions. Just as human beings can never know that God exists, so is it "impossible to prove that God is impossible" (1817/1966, pp. 335–452).

Kant nevertheless wished to claim that optimism holds great value as a practical position, warranted by the "postulates of pure practical reason" (Kant 1788/1956, p. 12). The following summarizes Kant's reasoning: Kant called the *summum bonum* the convergence of virtue and happiness. Philosophers have long sought to establish a basis for anticipating the *summum bonum*. This anticipation has been notoriously difficult to foster, however, especially in light of the widespread belief that immoral people are often happier than moral people. It is not surprising, then, that many religiously inclined philosophers have attempted to locate the convergence of virtue and happiness in an afterlife or afterworld. Kant himself acknowledged that if the *summum bonum* were unattainable, "then the moral law which commands that it be furthered must be fantastic, directed to empty imaginary ends, and consequently inherently false" (1788/1956, p. 118).

To avoid the contradiction involved in believing the moral law to be false, Kant recommended that we postulate the existence of God and the immortality of the soul as necessary conditions of the *summum bonum*, even though we cannot objectively determine that its realization in fact depends on them. A rational faith in these postulates of pure practical reason, although objectively insufficient, thus facilitates the pursuit of happiness. In fact, only by virtue of one's belief in these postulates can one avoid what Kant called the *absurdum practicum*—namely, the life of the scoundrel who chooses to disobey the moral law (Wood, 1970, p. 33). If we assume that God exists and that this world supports the possible convergence of virtue and happiness, then we will have sufficient motivation to act morally and to maintain our desire to do so. Such assumptions are, Kant admitted, matters of faith rather than of knowledge. But the faith invested in them is nevertheless rational, because both the existence of God and the optimality of this world are logically possible; that is, they do not contradict reason. As a practical matter, then, it is better to believe that God exists and that perfect virtue can coincide with earthly happiness than to believe otherwise.

19TH AND 20TH CENTURIES

Hegel

The most influential figure of 19th-century philosophy was Georg Wilhelm Friedrich Hegel (1770–1831), who is equally famous for his optimistic account of history and his pessimistic understanding of the development of human consciousness through conflict and domination. To describe the teleological mechanism by which human consciousness has developed, Hegel referred to the operation of the "cunning of Reason" (1837/1953, p. 89). Working "behind the scenes" of human history, Reason has orchestrated the various collisions between forms of consciousness that have collectively sparked the spiritual progress of humankind. In Hegel's view, then, the teleological progress of human consciousness, as facilitated by the "cunning of Reason," is the cause for great optimism. Even the seeming disasters of world history, wherein entire nations have been bent to the will of emperors and dictators, are recuperated within this teleological frame. All that has befallen humankind along the way has contributed to the freedom that characterizes the modern epoch. Although Hegel's optimism is more sophisticated than Leibniz's, it is similarly vulnerable to Voltaire's charge of insensitivity toward human suffering. According to Hegel's developmental account, historical atrocities are merely the necessary, if unpleasant, consequences of the articulation of increasingly more adequate conceptions of freedom. Had countless peoples not been sacrificed on the "slaughter-bench of history," the modern world would never have developed the mature notion of freedom that now informs our laws and institutions (Hegel, 1830/1975, p. 69). One could, as Voltaire warned, easily dismiss the myriad horrors of world history as the inevitable growing pains of the human spirit.

Hegel's world-historical optimism is balanced by his account of the development of consciousness, which many critics see as inherently pessimistic. Hegel understood humans as social beings who acquire their sense of identity through the recognition of others. He thus traced the origins of civilization to the inescapable battle for power and recognition between individuals. Stated briefly, each individual wants both to master his or her environment and to command recognition of this mastery from others. By risking one's life in the absence of any biological threat or justification, one asserts one's independence from nature, but one also requires a witness of this assertion, for one's identity is dependent on the recognition of others. This desire for recognition by the Other, which the Other shares reciprocally, leads to a struggle to the death, from which only one party can emerge as master. For any individual, the optimum outcome of this primal struggle involves the voluntary submission of the other, from which one receives recognition and confirmation of one's mastery over nature. Thus emerge the polar positions of "lordship" and "bondage," which are mutually defined in terms of the master's demand that the slave embody the master's independence from nature—that is, by working on the world and bestowing on the master the fruits of this forced labor (Hegel, 1807/1977).

According to Hegel, this original arrangement of lordship and bondage eventually reverses itself. The existence of the master is now dependent on the labor of the slave. The erstwhile master has become merely a consumer, whereas the former slave has become a creator. The master is now enslaved to a slave, while the slave now masters the master (Hegel, 1807/1977). Such tensions and reversals, developed more fully by Freud and other depth psychologists, lie at the very origins of human civilization. Although Hegel envisions an optimistic resolution to this drama whereby the slaves eventually inherit the earth, the pessimism inherent in his account of the development of human consciousness is difficult to ignore. If identity is dependent on recognition, and if recognition is achieved only under conditions of struggle and domination, then it is not immediately clear how human civilization might someday outgrow, as Hegel optimistically promised, its well-documented thirst for blood, sweat, and tears.

Schopenhauer

As gloomy as it may be, the pessimism suggested by Hegel's account of social development pales in comparison to that of the pessimist *par excellence*, Arthur Schopenhauer (1788–1860). In his major work, *The World as Will and Representation* (1818/1958), Schopenhauer argued not merely that this is not the best of all possible worlds, but that it is demonstrably the worst of all possible worlds. Schopenhauer began this famous argument by defining a *possible world* as one that could endure (as opposed to one that could exist only for a brief moment). This definition thus precludes any appeal to ostensibly worse worlds that simply could not endure (e.g., a world like ours, but in which all means of producing oxygen were suddenly to vanish; Schopenhauer, 1818/1958). If our world is not the worst of all possible worlds, then it must be possible to describe a worse world. Citing example after example, Schopenhauer argued that our world teeters on the brink of destruction. Any changes we might imagine that would demonstrate the possibility of a worse world would either cause our world to collapse, thus making it an impossible world, or create a better possible world. Schopenhauer thus concluded, "Consequently, the world is as bad as it can possibly be, if it is to exist at all" (1818/1958, Vol. 2, p. 584).

One might attempt to counter Schopenhauer's pessimism by noting that some people in this world are happy, even if they are exceptional in this respect. A worse world would therefore be one in which fewer people were happy. According to Schopenhauer, however, it would be a mistake to assume that even some people are happy. By his account, human beings cannot be happy, and aspiring optimists are merely ignorant that this supposedly worse world is indeed our own. According to Schopenhauer, human beings are motivated primarily by a blind, unconscious force that he called the *will*, which is nothing but an incessant striving for a goal that cannot be adequately identified. Indeed, the will's object is never chosen, because the will is even more basic than reason itself. The absolute freedom of the will, or so Schopenhauer claimed, is therefore illusory. Instead, he explained, the will blindly desires but is never satisfied. If happiness is understood in terms of the satiation of desire, as Schopenhauer maintained, then in this world no one is happy. What some people mistakenly take to be happiness is simply the transient illusion of satisfaction, which Schopenhauer attributed to a temporary reduction of pain. The only way to mitigate the will's constant strivings is by means of an ascetic abrogation of the will within oneself.

Nietzsche

The influence of Schopenhauer's pessimism is most evident in the writings of Friedrich Nietzsche (1844–1900). Both philosophers share the view that human beings blindly follow their unconscious impulses as they attempt to derive immanent meaning from lives devoid of transcendent meaning. Both also agree that typical human beings cannot resolutely embrace this truth and must instead invest their faith in the saving fictions of religion and philosophy. From this common misanthropic ground, however, the two philosophers part company. Whereas Schopenhauer recommended his brand of pessimism as constituting the only honest response to the blind strivings of the will, Nietzsche apparently promoted a joyful, affirmative response to the absurdity of human existence. This difference of philosophical opinion stems from their widely divergent accounts of the psychological disposition of those individuals who can bear the truth of the meaninglessness of life. In the symptomatological terms that Nietzsche preferred in his later writings, in fact, Schopenhauer's vaunted pessimism signifies the decline of life, whereas the spontaneous affirmation expressed by Nietzsche's *Übermensch* bespeaks the ascent and plenitude of life.

In his first book, *The Birth of Tragedy* (1872/1967), Nietzsche presented his most sustained discussion of the psychophysiological states represented, respectively, by optimism and pessimism. Influenced by Schopenhauer's claim that the world presents itself to us as both "will" and "representation," Nietzsche attempted to account for the "birth" of Attic tragedy in the synthesis of the Apollinian and the Dionysian impulses (Nietzsche, 1872/1967). The *Apollinian impulse* signifies those accomplishments for which the Golden Age of Greece is justifiably famous: measure and harmony in aesthetics, the clarifying light of reason, and a celebration of the dream world of myth and appearance. Yet, Nietzsche conjectured, the Apollinian impulse arises only in response to a more powerful, countervailing impulse that Attic tragedy also expresses; namely, the Dionysian impulse toward dissolution and disintegration. The *Dionysian impulse* engenders the ecstatic bliss that occurs when human beings surrender their illusory individuality and are once again subsumed within the eternal stream of life (Nietzsche, 1872/1967). The Dionysian impulse thus represents both the terror and joy that one feels at the destruction of one's self; it is the painful truth that lies beneath the Apollinian illusions.

By virtue of its dual allegiance to Apollo and Dionysus, Greek tragedy thus reflects a pessimism that Nietzsche initially interprets as indicative of great health and strength of will. Tragedy is pessimistic, he explained, insofar as it squarely confronts the inevitable demise of even the greatest human exemplars and accomplishments. Rather than promote a nihilistic resignation, however, tragedy encourages human beings to strive for greatness and excellence in their transient individual existence, enticing them with the grand illusions and fine appearances crafted under the aegis of Apollo. The "pessimism of strength" expressed by Attic tragedy thus manifests an affirmation of life itself, including the dissolution and demise associated with the Dionysian impulse.

Nietzsche's articulation of this diagnosis evidences the extent of his departure from the so-called existential claims that support Schopenhauer's pessimism. In the process of conducting his "genealogy of morality," Nietzsche (1887/1989b) observed that for much of Western history, the twin forces of Socratic hyperrationality and Christian asceticism have all but destroyed the type of humans who could give life meaning. He also believed, however, that these destructive forces are gradually withering and that new, creative superhumans may yet emerge to redeem the meaninglessness of human existence. The question that dominates his later writings is whether humankind has become simply too enervated to produce any creative geniuses of the magnitude necessary to warrant its future. In *Thus Spoke Zarathustra* (1883–1885/1983), he called this fatal condition the reign of the "last man," and he entrusted his character Zarathustra with the task of rousing humankind from its moribund condition. It is not clear whether Nietzsche intended *Thus Spoke Zarathustra* to serve notice of his own (guarded) optimism concerning the future humankind, or if he intended to engender in others an optimism that he himself could not muster. In any event, *Zarathustra* is widely regarded as a stirring attempt to find meaning even in the aftermath of the "death of God."

In the writings from his final year of sanity, 1888, Nietzsche largely abandoned the bombast of his *Zarathustra* and defended an optimism predicated on the teaching of *amor fati* (love of fate). The highest human beings are those who are able to affirm the cosmos as a whole, understood as a grand, interconnected network of fatalities. Against this fatalistic backdrop, any wish to change even the smallest element of one's life is understood in Nietzsche's scheme to harbor the nihilistic wish that the whole of one's life—and the cosmic totality in which it inheres—be different. Having a genuinely optimistic affirmation of life would mean that "one wants nothing to be different, not forward, not backward, not in all eternity. Not merely bear what is necessary, still less conceal it—all idealism is mendaciousness in the face of what is necessary—but *love* it" (Nietzsche, 1908/1989a, p. 258).

Freud

Like Nietzsche, Sigmund Freud (1856–1939) is neither an optimist à la Leibniz, nor a pessimist à la Schopenhauer. He too believed that civilization could be improved if the proper sort of individuals were to emerge, but his hopes for this emergence were even more tepid than Nietzsche's (Freud, 1927/1961a, p. 8). Although best known for his pioneering work in depth psychology and psychoanalysis, Freud endeavored late in his career to develop the sociological and anthropological implications of his basic principles of analysis. It is with respect to this latter enterprise that we may best appreciate his contributions to the philosophical treatment of optimism and pessimism.

Freud's considered opinion on the future of humankind can be gleaned from his response to Albert Einstein's letter concerning the necessity of war (1933/1961b). On the one hand, Freud emphatically dismissed any attempt to annul humankind's aggressive inclinations. On the other, he noted that whatever furthers the growth of civilization simultaneously frustrates the outbreak of war. At bottom, then, civilization is riddled with tensions for which there is little hope of resolution. This tension can also be located in Freud's depth-psychological model of the soul, which figures the (civilized) soul as the site of an unavoidable, internecine battle that ends only in death. Indeed, if happiness is defined in the ideal terms that Freud proposed, comprising the spontaneous outward expression of one's unconscious drives and impulses, then no civilized human being can be deemed happy. It is in this sense that Freud presented himself as a pessimist. If, however, happiness is defined in the more restricted terms favored by civilization itself, involving a delayed (but not pathological) gratification of one's unconscious drives and impulses, then it is possible for some human beings to secure for themselves a modicum of happiness (albeit only with the help of psychoanalysis). It is in this sense that Freud presented himself as a guarded optimist.

Continuing a long philosophical tradition, Freud asserted that human beings naturally strive for happiness. This pursuit takes two forms: Humans wish both to avoid suffering and to experience extreme feelings of pleasure (Freud, 1930/1961c). Two of the three sources of suffering are the superior power of nature and the frailty of our own bodies. Although we cannot eradicate either of these sources of suffering, we can minimize their impact by banding together for mutual support and protection—by doing so the first families and communities were formed. This banding together granted the additional benefit of providing an ostensibly secure means of regularly obtaining sexual satisfaction (at least for the male), which is the highest form of pleasure. By making one person the source of his happiness, however, the individual actually places his happiness at risk, for his lover may withdraw, abdicate, or die. Fearful of this inevitable loss, the individual then instinctually sublimates erotic urges and engages in "aim-inhibited love" or nonsexual relationships with others (Freud, 1930/1961c, pp. 102ff). To carry on its business, civilization encourages the individual to have such relationships, thereby directly confronting Eros and deflecting its advance. Civilization further encourages such relationships because they assist in its project to control the individual's aggressiveness. Thus individuals are drawn toward civilization for the security it offers in the face of a potentially hostile natural world, but they simultaneously rail against its enforced restrictions of their sexual and aggressive instincts. The best the individual can hope for is the formation of relatively small groups of people who visit their aggressions on people outside the group. In other words, there is no hope of eliminating the pains of life, only of redirecting them.

Of course, civilization would quickly expend its resources if it were obliged to enforce its prohibitions in every instance. Pursuing a line of interpretation developed by Nietzsche, Freud described the psychological mechanism by which civilization deputizes each individual as his or her own enforcer: The individual internalizes the founding taboos of civilization and consequently follows its dictates under the threat of self-punishment, or guilt. Guilt arises as the super ego deflects onto the ego the aggressive energies intended by the individual for outward expression (Freud, 1930/1961c).

Yet no matter how successful individuals become at policing their sexual and aggressive impulses, civilization ultimately fails in its mission to protect them from nature and from each other. Thus the individual remains a child in that he or she continues to require protection from superior powers. It is not surprising, then, that humans lend these powers fatherly attributes. Indeed, the comforting illusions created by religion have significantly furthered the advance of civilization, much as a devoted father contributes to his children's progress toward adulthood. Just as a paternalistic father can imprison his children in an arrested state of adolescence, however, so does religion now harm both individuals and civilization. As Freud saw it, religion has largely outlived its usefulness as a means of accommodating individuals to the demands (and benefits) of civilization. Particularly in "The Future of an Illusion," Freud argued that the psychic energies of humanity are best spent forwarding the project of science. The new god Freud wished to install is Logos. Although Logos cannot make promises on the order of those made by religious gods, it actually fulfills many of the promises that it does make. Although science lacks the emotional components of religion, Freud believed that civilization will eventually shed its infantile need for such comforts. Although our instincts often overpower our reason, this victory is only temporary:

> The voice of the intellect is a soft one, but it does not rest till it has gained a hearing. Finally, after a countless succession of rebuffs, it succeeds. This is one of the few points on which one may be optimistic about the future of mankind, but it is in itself a point of no small importance. And from it one can derive yet other hopes. . . . [The intellect] will presumably set itself the same aims as those whose realization you expect from your God . . . namely the love of man and the decrease of suffering. (Freud, 1927/1961a, p. 53)

Written only a few years after "On the Future of an Illusion," *Civilization and Its Discontents* closed Freud's distinguished career on a pessimistic note. Although he officially refused in this book to comment on the future of humankind, his gathering pessimism is nevertheless manifest. As the unprecedented slaughter of World War I made painfully clear, science has empowered humankind to annihilate itself. This grim realization apparently shatters the hopeful picture of science that informs Freud's earlier work. Like religion, science merely furnishes saving illusions, which only temporarily distract humankind from the discontents legislated by civilization. When the scientific illusion fades, human beings find themselves in full possession not only of their discontents, but also of weapons of mass destruction. Freud thus hypothesized that we have nearly reached a point of world-historical crisis: The psychic demands placed on us by civilization may soon exceed both the benefits that we receive and the native pains of a pre- or postcivilized existence. Whatever net value humankind has heretofore derived from civilization is now virtually exhausted.

Alarmed by the success of Hitler's Nazi party in the 1930 parliamentary elections in Germany, Freud added a new, final sentence to *Civilization and Its Discontents*. This sentence effectively deflates the optimism with which he had originally intended to close the book. Eros may in fact "assert himself in the struggle with his equally immortal adversary," as Freud had originally concluded. "But," he now skeptically adds, "who can foresee with what success and with what result?" (1930/1961c, p. 112). Throughout the 1930s, Freud's skepticism gradually yielded to a full-blown pessimism. Forced to emigrate from his home in Vienna by the recrudescence of nationalism and anti-Semitism and slowly dying from a painful throat cancer, Freud now foresaw the final victory of Thanatos over Eros. At the time of his death in 1939, in fact, Freud was well aware that the animosities that would precipitate World War II were inexorably gathering force. Having apparently learned nothing from the atrocities of World War I, humankind was preparing itself for yet another bloodletting of global dimensions. Could the demise of civilization itself be far off? These deathbed sentiments thus edged Freud closer to Schopenhauer than to Nietzsche, for unlike Nietzsche, Freud reserved little hope for the future of humankind.

James

A similarly pessimistic conclusion is reached by Freud's American contemporary, William James (1842–1910). A fellow pioneer in the new science of psychology, James shared several of Freud's greater doubts about the prospects for human happiness within the walls of civilization. James also shared Freud's concern about humankind's increasingly uncritical reliance on science to deliver the material conditions of happiness. James lent a far more personal—and therefore more ominous—voice to the possibility of the utter disruption of the self:

> Whilst in this state of philosophic pessimism and general depression of spirits about my prospects, I went one evening into a dressing-room in the twilight to procure some article. . .; when suddenly there fell upon me without any warning, just as if it came out of the darkness, a horrible fear of my own existence. Simultaneously there arose in my mind the image of an epileptic patient whom I had seen in the asylum, a black-haired youth with greenish skin, entirely idiotic, who used to sit all day on one of the benches, or rather shelves against the wall, with his knees drawn up against his chin, and the coarse gray undershirt, which was his only garment, drawn over them inclosing his entire figure. He sat there . . . moving nothing but his black eyes and looking absolutely non-human. This image and my fear entered into a species of combination with each other. That shape am I, I felt, potentially. Nothing that I possess can defend me against that fate, if the hour for it should strike for me as it struck for him. There was such a horror of him, and such a perception of my own merely momentary discrepancy from him, that it was as if something hitherto solid within my breast gave way entirely, and I became a mass of quivering fear. (James, 1902, pp. 160ff)[1]

As James's anecdote demonstrates, medical science exerts a democratizing influence on humankind. The difference between sane and insane, for example, is no longer understood as a difference in kind, but rather as a relatively small organic difference. Although science creates the possibility of a cure, and thus gives us reason to be optimistic, it simultaneously elides the perceived difference between oneself and the diseased other.

It is important to note that James radically shifted the topos within which discussions of optimism and pessimism can occur. The combined forces

---

[1] Although James presented this example as drawn from an anonymous source, his son claimed that the narrator is James himself (see Allen, 1967, pp. 164ff.).

of Kant's critique and scientific materialism render metaphysical questions otiose. The rise of empirical science might lead one to expect that the debate between Pope and Voltaire could be definitively answered, at least in theory. Yet as both James and Nietzsche argued, albeit in very different ways, science can never capture (or banish) the inescapably subjective element of human experience. Thus for James, the philosophical question of optimism versus pessimism can be decided not at any metaphysical or anthropological level, but only at the level of the individual.

If the choice between optimism and pessimism ultimately lies with each individual, then it is difficult at first to see why anything like a profound decision must be made. All things being equal, it seems far preferable to go through life with a Leibnizian or Popean attitude than a Schopenhauerian one. Indeed, one might argue that James's designations for these competing attitudes, "healthy-mindedness" and "the sick soul," merely reiterate our customary preference for happiness over unhappiness (James, 1902, Lectures IV). Nevertheless, James does not lapse into the bourgeois optimism of which Voltaire accused Leibniz and Pope. Optimism resembles a veil that shields us from the inequities of life. Like a veil, it may be blown away by a sudden gust of wind, or pushed aside by our own curiosity. One might be able to lead an optimistic life, James conceded, but this is unlikely given the insecurity of natural goods and the virtual certainty that one will fail at something meaningful to one's sense of flourishing.

REFERENCES

Allen, G. W. (1967). *William James: A biography*. New York: Viking.

Descartes, R. (1985a). Discourse on the method. In J. Cottingham, R. Stoothoff, & D. Murdoch (Trans.), *The philosophical writings of Descartes* (Vol. 1, pp. 111–175). New York: Cambridge University Press. (Original work published 1628)

Descartes, R. (1985b). Rules for the direction of the mind. In J. Cottingham, R. Stoothoff, & D. Murdoch (Trans.), *The philosophical writings of Descartes* (Vol. 1, pp. 9–78). New York: Cambridge University Press. (Original work written 1628, published 1701)

Descartes, R. (1985c). The passions of the soul. In J. Cottingham, R. Stoothoff, & D. Murdoch (Trans.), *The philosophical writings of Descartes* (Vol. 1, pp. 326–404). New York: Cambridge University Press. (Original work published 1649)

Freud, S. (1961a). *Civilization and its discontents*. (J. Strachey, Trans.). New York: W. W. Norton. (Original work published 1930)

Freud, S. (1961b). Letter to Albert Einstein. In J. Strachey (Ed. and Trans.), *The standard edition of the complete psychological works of Sigmund Freud* (Vol. 22, pp. 203–215). London: Hogarth Press. (Original work written 1933)

Freud, S. (1961c). The future of an illusion. In J. Strachey (Ed. and Trans.), *The standard edition of the complete psychological works of Sigmund Freud* (Vol. 21). London: Hogarth Press. (Original work published 1927)

Hegel, G. W. F. (1953). *Reason in history.* (R. S. Hartman, Trans.). Indianapolis, IN: Bobbs-Merrill. (Original work published 1837)

Hegel, G. W. F. (1975). *Natural law.* Philadelphia: University of Pennsylvania Press. (Originally published 1830)

Hegel, G. W. F. (1977). *Phenomenology of spirit.* (A. V. Miller, Trans.). New York: Oxford University Press. (Original work published 1807)

Hume, D. (1980). *Dialogues concerning natural religion,* (R. H. Popkin, Ed.). Indianapolis, IN: Hackett Press. (Original work published 1775)

James, W. (1902). *The varieties of religious experience.* New York: Longmans, Green & Co.

Kant, I. (1956). *Critique of practical reason.* (L. W. Beck, Trans.). Indianapolis, IN: Bobbs-Merrill. (Original work published 1788)

Kant, I. (1965). *Critique of pure reason.* (N. K. Smith, Trans.). New York: St. Martin's Press. (Original work published 1781)

Kant, I. (1969). Lectures on the philosophical doctrine of religion. In A. Wood (Trans.) & G. DiGiovanni (Ed.), *Religion and rational theology* (pp. 335–452). New York: Cambridge University Press. (Original work published 1817)

Kant, I. (1996). On the miscarriage of all philosophical attempts in theodicy. In A. Wood & G. DiGiovanni (Trans. and Eds.), *Religion and rational theology* (pp. 19–38). New York: Cambridge University Press. (Original work published 1791)

Leibniz, G. (1996). *Theodicy.* (E. M. Huggard, Trans.). La Salle, IL: Open Court. (Original work published 1710)

Nietzsche, F. (1967). *The birth of tragedy.* (W. Kaufmann, Trans.). New York: Vintage. (Original work published 1872)

Nietzsche, F. (1983). Thus spoke Zarathustra. In W. Kaufmann (Trans.), *The portable Nietzsche* (pp. 115–439). New York: Penguin. (Original work published 1883–1885)

Nietzsche, F. (1989a). Ecce homo. In W. Kaufmann (Trans.), *On the genealogy of morals and ecce homo* (pp. 215–335). New York: Vintage. (Original work published 1908)

Nietzsche, F. (1989b). On the genealogy of morals. In W. Kaufmann (Trans.), *On the genealogy of morals and ecce homo* (pp. 31–163). New York: Vintage. (Original work published 1887)

Pope, A. (1994). *An essay on man.* New York: Dover. (Original work published 1733–1734)

Schopenhauer, A. (1958). *The world as will and representation* (Vols. 1–2; E. F. J. Payne, Trans.). New York: Dover Publications. (Original work published 1818)

Voltaire, F. (1959). *Candide, or optimism*. (L. Bair, Trans.). New York: Bantam Books. (Original work published 1759)

Voltaire, F. (1962). *Philosophical dictionary*. (Vols. 1–2, P. Gay, Trans.). New York: Basic Books. (Original work published 1764)

Wood, A. (1970). *Kant's moral religion*. Ithaca, NY: Cornell University Press.

2

OPTIMISM, PESSIMISM, AND SELF-REGULATION

CHARLES S. CARVER AND MICHAEL F. SCHEIER

Optimists are people who expect good experiences in the future. Pessimists are people who expect bad experiences. These concepts have a long history in folk wisdom, as well as in early attempts to categorize people according to their qualities of personality (see chap. 1, this volume). It has long been believed that this fundamental difference among people is important in many, perhaps all, facets of life. In the past 15 years or so, this belief has been supported by a good deal of systematic research on the correlates and consequences of this individual difference variable. Later chapters of this book describe some of that research.

In this chapter we provide some conceptual background to this topic. More specifically, we describe the theoretical principles that underlie our own use of the concepts of optimism and pessimism. The colloquial definitions of these terms (and those found in dictionaries) turn on people's expectations

Preparation of this chapter was facilitated by grants CA64710 and CA64711 from the National Cancer Institute.

for the future—positive and negative, respectively. Scientific approaches to these ideas (including ours) also turn on expectations for the future. In so doing, these scientific approaches link the concepts of optimism and pessimism to a long tradition of expectancy–value models of motivation. This link means that the optimism construct, although rooted in folk wisdom, is also firmly grounded in decades of theory and research on motives and how they are expressed in behavior. Our approach to understanding behavior, an approach that is identified with the term *self-regulation*, is one variant within this broad tradition.

We begin by briefly exploring the elements of the expectancy–value approach to motivation, to better understand the dynamics that underlie optimism and pessimism and how they influence human experience. We then turn to a description of the specific self-regulatory model within which *we* address these qualities of personality in our own thinking and writing.

EXPECTANCY–VALUE MODELS OF MOTIVATION

The expectancy–value viewpoint on motivation begins with the assumption that behavior is organized around the pursuit of goals. Goals provide the *value* element of the expectancy–value approach. Goals are qualities that people take as desirable or as undesirable (you might think of the latter as "anti-goals"). People try to fit their behaviors (indeed fit their very selves) to values they see as desirable, and people try to keep away from values they see as undesirable. The more important these goals and anti-goals are to the person, the greater is the element of value in the person's motivation with respect to those goals. Without having a goal that is valued to at least some degree, people have no reason to act.

The second conceptual element in this approach is *expectancy*—a sense of confidence or doubt about the goal's attainability (or the anti-goal's avoidability). If the person lacks confidence, again, there will be no action. That's why a lack of confidence is sometimes referred to with the phrase "crippling doubt." Doubt can impair effort both before the action begins and also while it's ongoing. Only if people have sufficient confidence will they move into action, and only if they retain sufficient confidence will they remain engaged in effort. When people have confidence about an eventual outcome, their efforts will continue, even in the face of enormous adversity.

SELF-REGULATION OF BEHAVIOR

Our particular version of the expectancy–value approach to motivation also uses another idea: that behavior embodies feedback control processes.

The basic unit of analysis in this view is the discrepancy-reducing feedback loop. This is a system of four elements in a particular organization (cf. MacKay, 1966; Miller, Galanter, & Pribram, 1960). The elements are an input function, a reference value, a comparator, and an output function (see Figure 2.1). An *input function* brings information in. This function is equivalent to perception. The *reference value* is a second source of information (i.e., apart from what's in the input function). The reference values in the loops we're interested in are goals. The *comparator* is a device that compares input and reference value. The comparison yields one of two outcomes: either the values are discriminably different from one another or they're not. Comparators can vary in sensitivity, however, so some can detect very small discrepancies, whereas others can detect only much larger ones.

Following this comparison is an *output function*. We treat this as equivalent to behavior, although sometimes the behavior is internal. If the comparison yields "no difference," the output function remains whatever it now is. This may mean no output, or it may mean that the ongoing output continues. If the comparison yields "discrepancy," however, the output function changes.

There are two kinds of feedback loops, corresponding to regulation of present states with respect to goals and to anti-goals. In a discrepancy-reducing loop, the output function is aimed at diminishing or eliminating discrepancies between input and reference value. This is seen in attempts

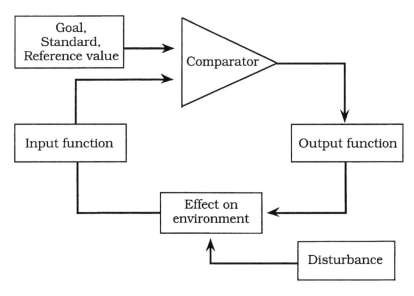

Figure 2.1. Schematic depiction of a feedback loop. In such a loop, a sensed value is compared to a reference value, or standard, and adjustments are made in an output function (if necessary) to shift the sensed value in the direction of the standard.

to approach or attain a valued goal. The goal can be a relatively constant one (e.g., being an honest person), or it can be more of a "moving target" (e.g., developing through the stages of a career). In either case, a discrepancy-reducing system tries to make reality match the goal value.

This isn't behavior for the sake of behavior, but behavior to create and maintain conformity between input and standard. That is, the value sensed by the input function depends on more than the output (see Figure 2.1). Disturbances from outside can change conditions adversely (increasing a discrepancy from the reference value) or favorably (diminishing a discrepancy). In the first case, recognition of a discrepancy prompts a change in output, as always. In the second case, though, the disturbance preempts the need for an adjustment in output, because the system sees no discrepancy.

The second kind of feedback loop is a discrepancy-enlarging loop. The value here isn't one to approach, but one to avoid. It's an anti-goal. Psychological examples of anti-goals are receiving traffic tickets, being subjected to public ridicule, and being fired from your job. A discrepancy-enlarging loop senses present conditions, compares them to the anti-goal, and tries to enlarge the discrepancy between the two. To use another example, a rebellious adolescent who wants to be different from his or her parents (thus treating the parents' values as an anti-goal) senses his or her own behavior, compares it to the parents' behavior, and tries to make his or her behavior as different from theirs as possible.

The action of discrepancy-enlarging processes in living systems is typically constrained in some way by discrepancy-reducing loops (see Carver & Scheier, 1998). To put it differently, avoidance behaviors often lead into approach behaviors. An avoidance loop creates pressure to increase distance from the anti-goal. The movement away occurs until the tendency to move away falls within the sphere of influence of an approach loop. This loop then serves to pull the sensed input into its orbit. Rebellious adolescents, trying to be different from their parents, soon find a group of other adolescents to conform to, all of whom are remaining different from their parents.

Feedback Loops and Goals

The view we take on behavior may be viewed by some as somewhat esoteric in its reliance on the feedback loop as the essential building block of behavior. In its reliance on the goal concept, however, this view is very much in accord with contemporary personality–social psychology. That is, the reference value functions very much as a goal (or anti-goal) for the operation of that feedback process, and today's personality–social psychological theory and research incorporates a great many discussions of goal constructs (e.g., Austin & Vancouver, 1996; Carver & Scheier, 1998; Elliott & Dweck, 1988; Pervin, 1982, 1989). Our position is that when these various goals are being used, they are serving as reference points for feedback processes involved in the creation of the resulting behavior.

A variety of labels are used in the literature of goals, reflecting differences in emphasis among various writers. Theorists who use different terms have their own emphases (for discussions, see Austin & Vancouver, 1996; Carver & Scheier, 1998), but many of the points they make are the same. All the theories include the idea that goals energize and direct activities (Pervin, 1982). They implicitly (and sometimes explicitly) convey the sense that goals give meaning to people's lives. Each theory places an emphasis on the idea that to understand a person means understanding the person's goals. Indeed, in the view represented by these theories, it's often implicit that the self consists partly of the person's goals and the organization among them.

Hierarchical Organization

An issue to be addressed in this context stems from the obvious fact that some goals are broader in scope than others. How to think about the difference in breadth isn't always easy to put your finger on. Sometimes it's a difference in how much time is involved in the pursuit of the goal. Sometimes, though, it's more than that. It's a difference in the goal's level of abstraction.

The notion that goals differ in their levels of abstraction is easy to illustrate. For example, you might have the goal, at a relatively high level of abstraction, of being a self-sufficient person. You may also have the goal, at a lower level of abstraction, of preparing dinner for yourself, or of replacing the spark plugs in your car. The first goal is to be a particular *kind of person*, the second set concerns completing particular *kinds of action*. You could also think of goals that are even more concrete than the latter ones, such as the goal of slicing vegetables into a pan, or the goal of turning a wrench to a particular degree of tightness. These goals (which some theorists would call strategies) are closer to specifications of individual acts than were the second set, which were more summary statements about the desired outcomes of intended action patterns.

You may have noticed that the examples we used to illustrate concrete goals relate directly to our example of an abstract goal. We did this to point out that abstract goals connect to concrete goals. In 1973, William Powers argued that the self-regulation of behavior occurs by way of a hierarchical organization of feedback loops. Because feedback loops imply goals, Powers's argument also constituted a model of hierarchical structuring among the goals involved in creating action.

Powers's general line of thinking ran as follows: In a hierarchical organization of feedback systems, the output of a high level system consists of resetting reference values at the next lower level of abstraction. To put it differently, higher order or superordinate systems "behave" by providing goals to the systems just below them. The reference values are more concrete and restricted as one moves from higher to lower levels. Control at each level regulates a quality that contributes to the quality controlled at the next higher level. Each level monitors input at the level of abstraction of its own functioning, and each level adjusts output to minimize its discrepancies. One processor is not presumed to handle functions at various levels of abstraction. Rather, structures at various levels handle their concerns simultaneously.

This hierarchical model per se has not been tested empirically. However, Vallacher and Wegner's (1985) action-identification theory strongly resembles the Powers hierarchy in some respects, and their theory has been tested. The Vallacher and Wegner (1985) model is framed in terms of how people think about the actions they're taking, but it also conveys the sense that how people think about their actions is informative about the goals by which they're guiding the actions. Work done within the framework of action-identification theory has developed considerable support for the notion of hierarchicality as proposed by Powers.

Hierarchicality and the Complexity of Behavior

Although the hierarchy we're discussing is in some ways simple, it has implications for several issues in thinking about behavior (see Carver & Scheier, 1998). Implicit here is that goals at any given level can often be achieved by a variety of means at lower levels. This permits one to address the fact that people sometimes shift radically the manner in which they try to reach a goal, when the goal itself has not changed. This is common when the quality that constitutes the higher order goal is implied in several different kinds of lower order activities. For example, you can be helpful (fulfilling an abstract goal) by writing a donation check, picking up discards for a recycling center, volunteering at charity, or holding a door open for someone else.

Just as a given goal can be obtained by way of multiple pathways, so can a specific act be performed in the service of diverse goals. For example, you could buy someone a gift to make him feel good, to repay a kindness, to put him in your debt, or to satisfy a perceived holiday-season role. Thus, a given act can have strikingly different meanings, depending on the purpose it's intended to serve. This is an important subtheme of this view on behavior: Behavior can be understood only by identifying the goals to which it is addressed.

A related point made by the notion of hierarchical organization concerns the fact that goals are not equal in their importance. The higher you go into the organization, the more fundamental to the overriding sense of self are the qualities encountered. Thus, goal qualities at higher levels appear to be intrinsically more important than those at lower levels.

Even two goals at a lower level aren't necessarily equivalent in importance. In a hierarchical system there are two ways for importance to accrue to a concrete (lower level) goal. The more directly the attainment of a concrete goal contributes to the attainment of a valued abstract goal, the more important is the concrete goal. Second, a concrete act that contributes to attaining several higher level goals at once is more important than an act that contributes to the attainment of only one such goal. With respect to the *value* aspect of the expectancy–value approach, then, value accrues (a) as one considers goals higher in a person's hierarchy of goals, (b) as a concrete goal relates more directly to the attainment of a higher level goal, or (c) as a concrete goal represents a step to satisfying multiple higher order goals simultaneously.

Feelings

The model described in the preceding sections addresses control of action. We have also suggested a way of thinking about how feelings arise in the course of behavior, by way of another feedback process (Carver & Scheier, 1990). This process operates along with the behavior-guiding one and in parallel to it. One way to describe what this system does is to say it's checking on how well the behavior loop is doing at reducing its discrepancies. Thus, the perceptual input for the affect-creating loop is a representation of the *rate of discrepancy reduction in the action system over time*. (We focus first on discrepancy-reducing loops, turning later to enlarging loops.)

We find an analogy useful here. Because action implies change between behavioral states, consider behavior as analogous to distance (change from one physical position to another). If the action loop deals with distance, and if the affect loop assesses the *progress* of the action loop over time, then the affect loop is dealing with the psychological equivalent of velocity (change in physical distance over time).

We don't believe the "velocity" input creates affect by itself, because a given rate of progress has different affective consequences under different circumstances. As in any feedback system, this input is compared to a reference value (cf. Frijda, 1986): an acceptable or desired rate of behavioral discrepancy reduction. As in other feedback loops, the comparison checks for a deviation from the standard.

We suggest that the result of the comparison process at the heart of this loop (the error signal generated by the comparator) is manifest phenomenologically in two forms. One is a hazy and nonverbal sense of confidence or doubt. The other is affect, feeling, a sense of positiveness or negativeness. Several studies have yielded evidence that tends to support this view (for review see Carver & Scheier, 1998).

It took us a while to realize it, but this is essentially a "cruise control" model of affect and action. That is, the system we've argued for functions much the same as the cruise control on your car. If you're going too slowly toward some goal in your behavior, negative affect arises. You respond to the situation by putting more effort into your behavior, trying to speed up. If you're going faster than you need to, positive affect arises, and you coast.

The car's cruise control is very similar. You come to a hill, which slows you down. Your cruise control responds by feeding the engine's cylinders more gas, to bring the speed back up. If you come across the crest of a hill and are rolling downhill too fast, the system pulls back on the gas and drags the speed back down.

When we began this section we said we'd restrict ourselves at first to discrepancy-reducing loops. Thus far we've done that, dealing only with the context of approach. Now we turn to attempts to distance oneself from a point of comparison, that is, discrepancy-*enlarging* loops.

As indicated in our earlier discussion, behavior toward anti-goals is just as intelligible as behavior toward approach goals. But what are the affective accompaniments to avoidance loops? The affect theory described above rests on the idea that positive feelings arise when a behavioral system is doing well at *doing what it's organized to do*. The systems we've considered thus far are organized to reduce discrepancies. There's no obvious reason, however, why the principle shouldn't apply just as well to systems organized to increase discrepancies. If the system is doing well at what it's organized to do, the result should be positive affect. If it is doing poorly at what it's organized to do, the result should be negative affect.

That much seems the same across the two types of systems, but we see a difference in the affects involved (see Figure 2.2). For both approach and avoidance systems there's a positive pole and a negative pole, but the positives aren't quite the same, nor are the negatives. Our view of this difference derives partly from insights of Higgins (Higgins, 1987). Following their lead, we suggest that the affect dimension relating to discrepancy-reducing loops is (in its purest form) the dimension that runs from depression to elation. The affect dimension that relates to discrepancy-enlarging loops is (in its purest form) the dimension running from anxiety to relief or contentment.

As Higgins and his colleagues note, these two dimensions capture the core qualities behind dejection-related and agitation-related affects. The link between affect quality and type of system shown in Figure 2.2 is compatible not only with the Higgins model, but also with other theories. For example, Roseman (1984, p. 31) has argued that joy and sadness are related

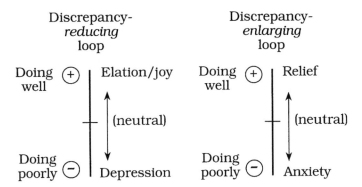

Figure 2.2. Two sorts of affect-generating systems and the affective dimensions we believe arise from the functioning of each. Discrepancy-reducing systems are presumed to yield affective qualities of sadness or depression when progress is below standard, and happiness or elation when progress is above standard. Discrepancy-enlarging systems are presumed to yield anxiety when progress is below standard, and relief or contentment when progress is above standard. From *On the Self-Regulation of Behavior*, p. 138, by C. S. Carver and M. F. Scheier, 1998, New York: Cambridge University Press. Copyright 1998 by Cambridge University Press. Reprinted with permission.

to appetitive (moving-toward) motives, whereas relief and distress are related to aversive (moving-away-from) motives. Davidson (1992, 1995) has argued that the left frontal cerebral cortex is part of the neural substrate for approach and for feelings of eagerness and depression, and that the right frontal cortex serves as part of the neural substrate for avoidance and for feelings of anxiety and relief.

Confidence and Doubt

In describing our view of the origin of affect, we suggested that one mechanism yields as subjective readouts both affect and a hazy sense of confidence versus doubt about the immediate future. This immediate sense of confidence and doubt can have an important influence on subsequent action. However, its influence usually doesn't occur in a psychological vacuum.

We've often suggested that when people experience adversity in trying to move toward their goals, they periodically experience an interruption of their efforts, to assess in a more deliberative way the likelihood of a successful outcome (e.g., Carver & Scheier, 1981, 1990, 1998). In effect, people suspend the behavioral stream, step outside it, and evaluate in a more thoughtful way than occurs while acting. This may happen once, or often. It may be brief, or it may take a long time. In this assessment people presumably depend heavily on memories of prior outcomes in similar situations, and they consider such things as additional resources they might bring to bear or alternative approaches to the problem.

How do these thoughts influence the expectancies that result? In some cases, when people retrieve "chronic" expectancies from memory, the information already *is* expectancies, summaries of products of previous behavior. These chronic expectancies may simply substitute for those that were derived from immediate experience, or they may blend with and color those immediate expectancies to a greater or lesser degree.

In some cases, however, people think more expansively about possibilities for the situation's potential evolution. For these possibilities to influence expectancies, their consequences must be evaluated. The possibilities probably are briefly played through mentally as behavioral scenarios (cf. Taylor & Pham, 1996), leading to conclusions that influence the expectancy (e.g., "If I try approaching it this way instead of that way, it should work better." "This is the only thing I can see to do, and it will just make the situation worse.").

It seems reasonable that this mental simulation engages the same mechanism as handles the process that creates the sense of affect and confidence during actual behavior. When your progress is temporarily stalled, playing through a scenario that's confident and optimistic yields a higher rate of perceived progress than is currently occurring. The confidence loop thus yields a more optimistic outcome assessment than is being derived from current action. If the scenario is negative and hopeless, it indicates a further reduction in progress, and the confidence loop yields further doubt.

Variations in Breadth of Expectancies

The fact that goals vary in specificity—from the very concrete and specific, to those that pertain to a particular domain of life, to the very general—suggests that people have a comparable range of variations in expectancies (Armor & Taylor, 1998; Carver & Scheier, 1998). To put it differently, you can be confident or doubtful about tying your shoes, about finding healthy food for dinner, about winning a particular tennis match, about performing well in socially evaluative circumstances, or about having a good life.

Which of these sorts of expectancies matter? Probably all of them. Expectancy-based theories tend to imply that behavior is predicted best from expectancies when the level of specificity of the expectancy matches that of the behavior. To predict a specific performance, you measure a specific, focalized expectancy. To predict an index of many kinds of performances in a given domain, you measure a broader sort of expectancy. This logic also suggests that to predict behavior over the broadest ranges, you should measure a generalized expectancy. This is what we think of as dispositional optimism versus pessimism: the generalized expectancy of good versus bad outcomes in life (Scheier & Carver, 1985, 1992).

Many outcomes in life have multiple causes. People also often face situations they've never experienced before, or situations that unfold and change over time. In circumstances such as these, generalized expectations may be particularly useful in predicting behavior and emotional reactions (Scheier & Carver, 1985).

The principles that apply to a focused sense of confidence versus doubt also apply to the generalized sense of optimism and pessimism. The difference between these cases is simply the breadth of the goals and the sense of confidence or doubt. When we talk about generalized optimism and pessimism, the sense of confidence at issue is more diffuse and broader in scope than when we talk about specifics such as test anxiety or social anxiety.

Thus, when confronting a challenge or threat, optimists should tend to take a posture of confidence (even if progress is presently difficult or slow). Pessimists should be more doubtful and hesitant. This divergence should also be displayed—and maybe even be amplified—under conditions of serious adversity. Optimists are likely to assume the adversity can be handled successfully, in one fashion or another, whereas pessimists are likely to anticipate disaster.

Our basic conceptualization of behavioral self-regulation addresses both approaching goals and avoiding anti-goals. This suggests that both approach and avoidance processes should involve expectancies (as well as affects). We have done no work that explicitly addresses this distinction, but this distinction may well bear on a measurement issue that has arisen in this literature. Our measure of optimism (the Life Orientation Test, or LOT) typically forms two factors. One factor is composed of items referencing good outcomes, the other is composed of items referencing bad outcomes (see, Marshall, Wortman, Kusulas, Hervig, & Vickers, 1992; Scheier & Carver, 1985, 1992; Scheier, Carver, & Bridges, 1994). It may be that one component of the measure reflects confidence about attaining positive outcomes, and the other component reflects confidence about avoiding undesired outcomes. This is an interesting possibility for future exploration.

Behavioral Consequences of Confidence and Doubt

As indicated earlier, the expectancies that people hold while attempting to attain goals can be influenced by many sources of information, an important source being the consolidated set of expectancies they have in memory. Whatever their source, the expectancies with which people return to action are reflected in subsequent behavior. If expectations are for a successful outcome, the person returns to effort toward the goal. If doubts are strong enough, the result is an impetus to disengage from effort, and potentially from the goal itself (Carver & Scheier, 1981, 1990, 1998; Klinger, 1975; Kukla, 1972; Wortman & Brehm, 1975).

This theme—divergence in response as a function of confidence versus doubt—is a very important one, applying to a surprisingly broad range of literatures (see chapter 11 of Carver & Scheier, 1998). One of the more obvious of these literatures is that of stress and coping. The differences in how people approach stressful circumstances have important implications for the manner in which people cope with adversities. Optimists take a goal-engaged approach to coping, whereas pessimists tend to show signs of coping in ways implying disengagement (e.g., Carver et al., 1993; Scheier et al., 1989).

Sometimes the disengagement that follows from doubt is overt, but disengagement also can take the form of mental disengagement—off-task thinking, daydreaming, and so on. Although this can sometimes be useful (self-distraction from a feared stimulus may permit anxiety to abate), it can also create problems. If there's time pressure, mental disengagement impairs performance, as time is spent on task-irrelevant thoughts. Further, mental disengagement often can't be sustained, as situational cues force a reconfronting of the task. In such cases, the result is a phenomenology of repetitive negative rumination, which often focuses on self-doubt and perceptions of inadequacy. This cycle is both unpleasant and performance-impairing.

Is Disengagement Good or Bad?

A question that needs to be considered is whether the disengagement tendency is good or bad. The answer is that it depends. On the one hand, disengagement (at some level, at least) is a necessity. Disengagement is a natural and indispensable part of self-regulation. If we are ever to turn away from efforts at unattainable goals, if we are ever to back out of blind alleys, we must be able to disengage, to give up and start over somewhere else.

The importance of disengagement is particularly obvious with regard to concrete, low level goals: People must be able to remove themselves from literal blind alleys and wrong streets, give up plans that have become disrupted by unexpected events, even spend the night in the wrong city if they've missed the last plane home. The tendency is also important, however, with regard to some higher level goals. A vast literature attests to the importance of disengaging and moving on with life after the loss of close relationships (e.g., Cleiren, 1993; Orbuch, 1992; Stroebe, Stroebe, & Hansson, 1993). People sometimes must even be willing to give up values that are deeply embedded in the self, if those values create too much conflict and distress in their lives.

The choice between continuing effort and giving up presents a variety of opportunities for things to go awry, however. It's possible to stop trying prematurely, thereby creating potentially serious problems for oneself; it's also possible to hold onto unattainable goals for too long, and prevent oneself from taking adaptive steps toward new goals (Carver & Scheier, 1998). But both continuing effort and giving up are necessary parts of the experience of adaptive self-regulation. Each plays an important role in the continuing flow of behavior.

More specifically, giving up is a functional and adaptive response *when it leads to the taking up of other goals*, whether these are substitutes for the lost goal or simply new goals in a different domain. Giving up thus can provide an opportunity to re-engage and move ahead again. In such cases (which appear to include all of the examples in the preceding paragraph), giving up is occurring in service to the broader function of returning the person to an engagement with life (Scheier & Carver, in press).

Thus, giving up a goal because of doubts about its attainment can be adaptive, when doing so leads to engagement with another goal. This principle appears to apply to goal values and doubts that extend fairly deeply into the sense of self. It probably does not extend, however, to the sense of generalized pessimism. Generalized pessimism is a sense of doubt that focuses not on just a single behavioral goal or even a broader behavioral domain, but on one's entire life space. A person who feels a deep sense of pessimism about all of life is a person who has nothing else to turn to. If this person gives up on that life space, there is nothing else to take its place. This absence of substitute goals—which seems to exemplify this person's situation—is a very serious problem (see chap. 18 of Carver & Scheier, 1998; Scheier & Carver, in press).

ENGAGEMENT VERSUS GIVING UP: EXPLORATION IN A NEW DIRECTION

An issue that bears further discussion is the divergence we postulate among responses to confidence and doubt. We've long argued for the existence of a psychological watershed between two sets of responses to adversity (Carver & Scheier, 1981). One set of responses consists of continued comparisons between present state and goal, and continued efforts. The other set consists of disengagement from such comparisons, and quitting of efforts. Just as rainwater falling on a mountain ridge ultimately flows to one side of the ridge or the other, so do behaviors ultimately flow to one or the other of these sets.

Our initial reason for taking this position stemmed largely from several demonstrations that self-focused attention creates diverging efforts on both information seeking and behavior, as a function of confidence versus doubt about success (Carver & Scheier, 1981). We aren't the only ones to have emphasized a disjunction among these two classes of responses, however. A number of other theorists have done so, for reasons of their own.

An early model incorporating such a disjunction in behavior was proposed by Kukla (1972). Another is the integration by Wortman and Brehm (1975) of reactance and helplessness: the argument that threats to control produce attempts to regain control and that perceptions of loss of control produce helplessness. Brehm and his collaborators (Brehm & Self, 1989; Wright & Brehm, 1989) have more recently developed an approach to task effort that resembles that of Kukla (1972), although their way of approaching the conceptual problem is somewhat different.

Over the past several years, we have become interested in the possibility of relating the dichotomy between effort and giving up to the principles of catastrophe theory. Catastrophe theory is a mathematical model that addresses the creation of discontinuities, bifurcations, or splittings (Brown, 1995; Stewart & Peregoy, 1983; Thom, 1975). A catastrophe occurs when a small change in one variable produces an abrupt (and usually large) change in another variable.

Although several types of catastrophe exist, the one that's been examined most frequently regarding psychological issues is the *cusp catastrophe*, in which two control parameters (variables that change the dynamics of the system—roughly akin to the independent variables of an experiment) influence an outcome. Figure 2.3 portrays its three-dimensional surface. The control parameters are x and z, y is the outcome. At low values of z, the surface of the figure expresses a roughly linear relationship between x and y, such that as x increases, so does y. As z (the second control parameter) increases, the relationship between x and y becomes less linear. It first shifts toward something like a step function. With further increase in z, the x–y relationship becomes even more clearly discontinuous—the outcome is either on the top surface or on the bottom. Thus, changes in z cause a change in the way x relates to y.

An important feature displayed by a catastrophe is *hysteresis*. A simple characterization of hysteresis is that in some range of z there's a foldover in the middle of the x–y relationship. At some range of z, a region of x exists with more than one value of y. The upper level and lower levels of possible values of y can be seen at the front of the surface of Figure 2.3, between points a and b. (The area where the fold goes backward is unstable; only the top and bottom surfaces have meaning.)

Another way of characterizing hysteresis is captured by the statement that the system's behavior depends on the system's recent history (Brown, 1995). That is, as you move into the middle zone of the front of the catastrophe surface, it matters which side you're coming from. If the system is moving from area c into the zone of hysteresis, it stays on the bottom surface until it reaches point b, where it jumps to the top surface. If the

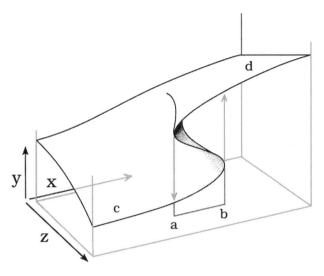

Figure 2.3. Three-dimensional depiction of a cusp catastrophe. Variables *x* and *z* are control parameters, *y* is the system's "behavior," the dependent variable. A cusp catastrophe exhibits a region of hysteresis (between Points a and b), in which a given *x* has two values of *y* (the top and bottom surfaces). Entering the zone of hysteresis from area c results in an abrupt shift (at Point b on the *x* axis) from the lower to the upper portion of the surface (right arrow). Entering from area d results in an abrupt shift (at value a on the *x* axis) from the upper to the lower portion of the surface (left arrow). Thus, the disjunction between portions of the surface occurs at two different values of *x*, depending on the starting point. From *On the Self-Regulation of Behavior* (pp. 267, 279), by C. S. Carver and M. F. Scheier, 1998, New York: Cambridge University Press. Copyright 1998 by Cambridge University Press. Adapted with permission.

system is moving from area d into the zone of hysteresis, it stays on the top surface until it reaches point a, where it jumps to the bottom surface.

Earlier in this section we said that several theories assume a disjunction between engagement of effort and giving up. In those models (including ours), there's a point at which effort seems fruitless and the person stops trying. Earlier we simply emphasized that these models all assumed a discontinuity. Now we look at the discontinuity more closely and suggest that the phenomena addressed by these theories may embody a catastrophe.

Figure 2.4 shows a cross-section of a cusp catastrophe, similar to the "front" edge of Figure 2.3. This figure displays a hypothesized region of hysteresis in the engagement versus disengagement function. In that region, where task demands are close to people's perceived limits to perform, there should be greater variability in effort or engagement, as some people are on the top surface of the catastrophe, and others are on the bottom surface. Some people would be continuing to exert efforts, at the same point where others would be exhibiting a giving-up response.

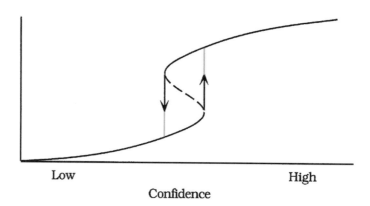

Figure 2.4. A catastrophe model of effort versus disengagement. From *On the Self-Regulation of Behavior* (p. 291), by C. S. Carver and M. F. Scheier, 1998, New York: Cambridge University Press. Copyright 1998 by Cambridge University Press. Reprinted with permission.

Recall that the catastrophe figure also conveys the sense that behavioral history matters. A person who enters the region of hysteresis from the direction of high confidence (who starts out confident but confronts many cues indicating the confidence is unfounded) will continue to display efforts and engagement, even as the cues imply increasingly less basis for confidence. A person who enters the region of hysteresis from low confidence (who starts out doubtful but confronts cues indicating the doubt is unfounded) will continue to display little effort, even as cues imply more basis for confidence.

This model helps indicate why it can be so difficult to get someone with strong and chronic doubt about success in some domain of behavior to exert real effort and engagement in that domain. It also suggests why a confident person is so rarely put off by encountering difficulties in the domain where the confidence lies. To put it more broadly, it helps show why optimists tend to stay optimistic and pessimists tend to stay pessimistic, even when the current circumstances of these two sorts of people are identical (i.e., in the region of hysteresis).

We have suggested elsewhere that the Wortman and Brehm (1975) model, the Brehm and Self (1989), and the Kukla (1972) models can be fit to this curve (Carver & Scheier, 1998). Although none of those authors proposed that their models have a region of hysteresis, we think a plausible case can be made for the presence of that feature in the phenomena addressed by their theories. We should acknowledge, however, that our position on this matter is speculative. No one has studied the processes of effort and disengagement in a truly parametric manner that would allow careful investigation of this question.

In contemplating such studies, it's important to keep in mind that the catastrophe cross-section (see Figure 2.4) is the picture that emerges under catastrophe theory *only once a clear region of hysteresis has begun to develop*. Further back, the catastrophe model more closely resembles a step function. Even further back, the relation is more linear (see Figure 2.3). An implication is that in trying to show a catastrophe, researchers need to engage the control variable that's responsible for bringing out the bifurcation in the surface (that is, Axis z in Figure 2.3). If this isn't done, the hysteresis would be less observable, even if the research procedures were otherwise suitable to observe it.

What *is* the control variable that induces the bifurcation? We think that in the motivational models under discussion—and perhaps much more broadly—the control parameter is *importance*. The subjective sense of importance has several sources. As we noted earlier, the more deeply an activity connects to the abstract sense of self, the more important the activity. The sense of importance also arises from social pressure from others (Tesser, 1980), from time pressure, and from self-imposed pressures. There's a common thread among important events: They demand mental resources. We suspect that almost any strong pressure that demands resources will induce similar bifurcating effects.

This hypothesis has a number of interesting implications. For example, it suggests that when a person is currently pessimistic about outcomes in some domain of life, that pessimism will exert a more profound influence when the situation is experienced subjectively as important. When pressure is high, when the behavior is important (when z is large), a region of hysteresis emerges. For the person on the bottom part of the surface, effort is potentially possible, but for it to happen *now requires a high degree of confidence* (see Figure 2.5). That is, as importance increases (the bottom portion of Figure 2.5), the region of hysteresis spreads increasingly wider, causing its edge (where the shift to effort actually takes place) to be more extreme on the confidence dimension.

Many problems in living seem to fit this picture, including a variety of all-or-none, black-and-white thinking. Of greatest importance at present is the fact that people who are crippled by doubts in an important domain of life would appear to live out that domain of life on the lower portion of the front of the catastrophe surface. Given their doubt, it's hard for them to make efforts in whatever domain the doubts exist *precisely because that domain matters so much*. That is, they're facing a huge challenge. To get to the point of real effort (the point where they jump from the lower to the upper surface), they need to be *very* confident (see bottom of Figure 2.5). Because they're not, the effort doesn't happen. They've lost the sense that they can make their lives better, and feel stranded miles away from the possibility of re-engagement with life.

Near the back of the surface, the relation between the other two variables is more gradual and more linear. At the back, a slight increment

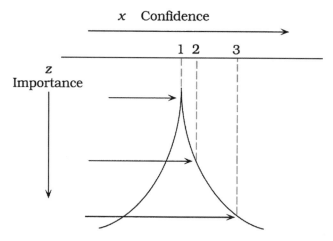

Figure 2.5. The so-called bifurcation set of the cusp catastrophe in Figure 2.3. This is essentially a "downward" projection of the two edges of the hysteresis onto a flat plane. It shows that as importance increases and the degree of hysteresis increases correspondingly, a person on the lower surface must move farther along the confidence dimension in order to shift to the top surface. With relatively low importance, the person must reach only Point 1, but as importance increases, the confidence needed continues to increase (Points 2 and 3). From *On the Self-Regulation of Behavior* (p. 298), by C. S. Carver and M. F. Scheier, 1998, New York: Cambridge University Press. Copyright 1998 by Cambridge University Press. Adapted with permission.

in confidence gains something in engagement. The cost of a doubt is gradual rather than precipitous. The person is able to stay engaged in the process of goal-pursuit, and staying engaged is a critical determinant of success.

The key to handling some kinds of problems, then, may be to reduce the pressure, to get some psychological distance. We think that creating distance, or reducing pressure, implies moving toward the back of the catastrophe plane. This diminishes the emotion-evoking potential of the event. It also ameliorates the impact of doubts on actions, by making the impact of doubt less abrupt.

CONCLUDING COMMENT

In this chapter we've provided a brief overview of the broad model of behavior from which our own interest in optimism first grew. Certainly thinking about optimism and pessimism per se does not require all of the complexities of that model (for example, the notion of feedback control of action). However, we want to make apparent the fact that our view of optimism connects to a dynamic and very broad model of the creation of behavior and feelings. This connection means that optimism need not be a topic that stands apart from the rest of psychology. This connection also provides a broader context for studies of behavioral and emotional consequences of optimism and pessimism, topics that are pursued in later chapters of this book.

REFERENCES

Armor, D. A., & Taylor, S. E. (1998). Situated optimism: Specific outcome expectancies and self-regulation. In M. Zanna (Ed.), *Advances in experimental social psychology* (Vol. 29, 309–379). San Diego, CA: Academic Press.

Austin, J. T., & Vancouver, J. B. (1996). Goal constructs in psychology: Structure, process, and content. *Psychological Bulletin, 120*, 338–375.

Brehm, J. W., & Self, E. A. (1989). The intensity of motivation. *Annual Review of Psychology, 40*, 109–131.

Brown, C. (1995). *Chaos and catastrophe theories* (Quantitative applications in the social sciences, No. 107). Thousand Oaks, CA: Sage.

Carver, C. S., Pozo, C., Harris, S. D., Noriega, V., Scheier, M. F., Robinson, D. S., Ketcham, A. S., Moffat, F. L., & Clark, K. C. (1993). How coping mediates the effect of optimism on distress: A study of women with early stage breast cancer. *Journal of Personality and Social Psychology, 65*, 375–390.

Carver, C. S., & Scheier, M. F. (1981). *Attention and self-regulation: A control-theory approach to human behavior.* New York: Springer-Verlag.

Carver, C. S., & Scheier, M. F. (1990). Origins and functions of positive and negative affect: A control-process view. *Psychological Review, 97*, 19–35.

Carver, C. S., & Scheier, M. F. (1998). *On the self-regulation of behavior.* New York: Cambridge University Press.

Cleiren, M. (1993). *Bereavement and adaptation: A comparative study of the aftermath of death.* Washington, DC: Hemisphere.

Davidson, R. J. (1992). Anterior cerebral asymmetry and the nature of emotion. *Brain and Cognition, 20*, 125–151.

Davidson, R. J. (1995). Cerebral asymmetry, emotion, and affective style. In R. J. Davidson & K. Hugdahl (Eds.), *Brain asymmetry* (pp. 361–387). Cambridge, MA: MIT Press.

Elliott, E. S., & Dweck, C. S. (1988). Goals: An approach to motivation and achievement. *Journal of Personality and Social Psychology, 54*, 5–12.

Frijda, N. H. (1986). *The emotions.* Cambridge, UK: Cambridge University Press.

Higgins, E. T. (1987). Self-discrepancy: A theory relating self and affect. *Psychological Review, 94*, 319–340.

Klinger, E. (1975). Consequences of commitment to and disengagement from incentives. *Psychological Review, 82*, 1–25.

Kukla, A. (1972). Foundations of an attributional theory of performance. *Psychological Review, 79*, 454–470.

MacKay, D. M. (1966). Cerebral organization and the conscious control of action. In J. C. Eccles (Ed.), *Brain and conscious experience* (pp. 422–445). Berlin, GDR: Springer-Verlag.

Marshall, G. N., Wortman, C. B., Kusulas, J. W., Hervig, L. K., & Vickers, R. R., Jr. (1992). Distinguishing optimism from pessimism: Relations to fundamental dimensions of mood and personality. *Journal of Personality and Social Psychology, 62,* 1067–1074.

Miller, G. A., Galanter, E., & Pribram, K. H. (1960). *Plans and the structure of behavior.* New York: Holt, Rinehart, & Winston.

Orbuch, T. L. (Ed.). (1992). *Close relationship loss: Theoretical approaches.* New York: Springer-Verlag.

Pervin, L. A. (1982). The stasis and flow of behavior: Toward a theory of goals. In M. M. Page & R. Dienstbier (Eds.), *Nebraska symposium on motivation* (Vol. 30, pp. 1–53). Lincoln, NE: University of Nebraska Press.

Pervin, L. A. (Ed.). (1989). *Goal concepts in personality and social psychology.* Hillsdale, NJ: Erlbaum.

Powers, W. T. (1973). *Behavior: The control of perception.* Chicago: Aldine.

Roseman, I. J. (1984). Cognitive determinants of emotions: A structural theory. In P. Shaver (Ed.), *Review of personality and social psychology* (Vol. 5, pp. 11–36). Beverly Hills, CA: Sage.

Scheier, M. F., & Carver, C. S. (1985). Optimism, coping and health: Assessment and implications of generalized outcome expectancies. *Health Psychology, 4,* 219–247.

Scheier, M. F., & Carver, C. S. (1992). Effects of optimism on psychological and physical well-being: Theoretical overview and empirical update. *Cognitive Therapy and Research, 16,* 201–228.

Scheier, M. F., & Carver, C. S. (in press). Adapting to cancer: The importance of hope and purpose. In A. Baum & B. L. Andersen (Eds.), *Psychosocial interventions for cancer.* Washington, DC: American Psychological Association.

Scheier, M. F., Carver, C. S., & Bridges, M. W. (1994). Distinguishing optimism from neuroticism (and trait anxiety, self-mastery, and self-esteem): A reevaluation of the Life Orientation Test. *Journal of Personality and Social Psychology, 67,* 1063–1078.

Scheier, M. F., Matthews, K. A., Owens, J. F., Magovern, G. J., Sr., Lefebvre, R. C., Abbott, R. A., & Carver, C. S. (1989). Dispositional optimism and recovery from coronary artery bypass surgery: The beneficial effects on physical and psychological well being. *Journal of Personality and Social Psychology, 57,* 1024–1040.

Stewart, I. N., & Peregoy, P. L. (1983). Catastrophe theory modeling in psychology. *Psychological Bulletin, 94,* 336–362.

Stroebe, M. S., Stroebe, W., & Hansson, R. O. (Eds.). (1993). *Handbook of bereavement: Theory, research, and intervention.* Cambridge, UK: Cambridge University Press.

Taylor, S. E., & Pham, L. B. (1996). Mental stimulation, motivation, and action. In P. M. Gollwitzer & J. A. Bargh (Eds.), *The psychology of action: Linking cognition and motivation to behavior* (pp. 219–235). New York: Guilford.

Tesser, A. (1980). When individual dispositions and social pressure conflict: A catastrophe. *Human Relations, 33,* 393–407.

Thom, R. (1975). *Structural stability and morphogenesis.* Reading, MA: Benjamin.

Vallacher, R. R., & Wegner, D. M. (1985). *A theory of action identification.* Hillsdale, NJ: Erlbaum.

Wortman, C. B., & Brehm, J. W. (1975). Responses to uncontrollable outcomes: An integration of reactance theory and the learned helplessness model. In L. Berkowitz (Ed.), *Advances in experimental social psychology* (Vol. 8, pp. 277–336). New York: Academic Press.

Wright, R. A., & Brehm, J. W. (1989). Energization and goal attractiveness. In L. A. Pervin (Ed.), *Goal concepts in personality and social psychology* (pp. 169–210). Hillsdale, NJ: Erlbaum.

3

OPTIMISM, PESSIMISM, AND EXPLANATORY STYLE

JANE E. GILLHAM, ANDREW J. SHATTÉ, KAREN J. REIVICH, AND MARTIN E. P. SELIGMAN

Dictionary definitions of optimism encompass two related concepts. The first is a hopeful disposition or a conviction that good will ultimately prevail. The second broader conception refers to the belief, or the inclination to believe, that the world is the "best of all possible worlds." In psychological research, *optimism* has referred to hopeful expectations in a given situation (Scheier & Carver, 1988) and recently has referred to general expectancies that are positive (Scheier & Carver, 1993). This more generalized expectancy, or *dispositional optimism*, is related to a variety of indices of psychological and physical health. Individuals who score high on measures of dispositional optimism report fewer depressive symptoms, greater use of effective coping strategies, and fewer physical symptoms than do pessimistic individuals (for reviews, see Scheier & Carver, 1992, 1993).

Perhaps consistent with the second, broader definition of optimism, the terms *optimism* and *pessimism* have recently been applied to the ways in which people routinely explain events in their lives (Seligman, 1991).

People are optimistic when they attribute problems in their lives to temporary, specific, and external (as opposed to permanent, pervasive, and internal) causes. An optimistic explanatory style is associated with higher levels of motivation, achievement, and physical well-being and lower levels of depressive symptoms (for a recent review, see Buchanan & Seligman, 1995).

Psychologists interested in optimism tend to reside in one of two parallel universes. In each, similar terms apply and similar findings are obtained. Until recently, however, there has been surprisingly little discussion of the relationship between dispositional optimism and explanatory style. Scheier and Carver (1993) argued that dispositional optimism and explanatory style theories are conceptually linked. However, several researchers caution that causal attributions and predictions can be unrelated (Abramson, Alloy, & Metalsky, 1989; Hammen & Cochran, 1981; Zullow, 1991). Given these conflicting views, it is important to clarify the link between explanations and expectations both theoretically and empirically.

Research on dispositional optimism is reviewed in chapter 2 of this volume. In this chapter, we describe the explanatory style construct of optimism, present some of the major research findings from this literature, and discuss the theoretical relationship of explanatory style to dispositional optimism. Research exploring the association of these constructs is reviewed. Finally, we discuss questions for future research and ways in which the investigators from one research tradition can learn from the other.

EXPLANATORY STYLE THEORIES

Reformulated Learned Helplessness Theory

When events, particularly negative ones, occur in our lives, we search for an explanation. According to the reformulated learned helplessness theory (RLHT; Abramson, Seligman, & Teasdale, 1978), the manner in which we routinely explain events in our lives can drain our motivation, reduce our persistence, and render us vulnerable to depression. Alternatively, our explanatory style can inspire us to problem solve and make us resilient in the face of adversity. The RLHT describes three dimensions on which explanations can vary: (a) internal versus external, (b) stable versus unstable, and (c) global versus specific. Pessimistic explanations for negative events are those that are more internal, stable, and global, that is, adversity is attributed to characteristics of one's self, factors that are likely to endure through time, and circumstances that affect many domains of our lives.

Optimistic explanations show the reverse pattern. Negative events are ascribed to environmental or situational factors that are temporary and affect few domains of one's life. In explaining a conflict in an intimate relationship, for example, a pessimistic person might tell himself or herself, "I'm not loveable" (internal, stable, and global), whereas an optimistic person may speculate along the following lines: "We've both been under a great deal of stress at work lately" (an external, unstable, and specific attribution). When explaining positive events, pessimistic and optimistic patterns reverse. Pessimistic explanations for positive events are external, unstable, and specific. That is, the source of success and good fortune is seen as fleeting, of limited influence, affecting few areas of life, and as caused by other people or circumstances. In contrast, optimistic explanations are internal, stable, and global.

The RLHT predicts that pessimistic and optimistic explanations will lead to different expectations about the future. Individuals who attribute negative events to stable and global causes will expect outcomes to be uncontrollable in the future. These individuals will be vulnerable to helplessness in the face of adversity. In contrast, individuals who attribute negative events to unstable or specific causes will expect to exert control in the future, and hence, will be more resilient. The RLHT proposes that the stability of the cause is related to the duration of helplessness symptoms, the pervasiveness (globality) of the cause is related to the generalization of helplessness across multiple situations, and the internality of the cause is related to the occurrence of self-esteem deficits in depression.

Hopelessness Theory of Depression

Abramson et al. (1989) argued that the stable and global dimensions of explanatory style have a stronger impact on motivation and depression than does the internal dimension. Thus, blaming the conflict described above on the belief that "love never endures" (an external, stable, and global attribution) also will lead to helplessness. According to the hopelessness theory (HT), a revision of the RLHT, three types of interpretations can put one at risk for depression following a negative event. First, the event may be attributed to stable and global causes. Second, negative or catastrophic consequences of the event may be inferred. Third, negative characteristics about the self may be inferred. When these interpretations are made frequently, they lead to negative expectations about the occurrence of highly valued outcomes (a negative outcome expectancy) and to negative expectations about one's ability to change the likelihood of these outcomes (a helplessness expectancy). According to the HT, these negative expectations are the proximal cause of a subtype of depression characterized by retarded initiation of voluntary response, sad affect, lack of energy, apathy, psychomotor retardation, sleep disturbance, difficulty in concentration, negative thinking, and suicidal ideation.

Several hundred published studies have investigated the relationship between explanatory style and various aspects of psychological and physical health. We present some of the major findings from this literature (for a recent review of research on explanatory style, see Buchanan & Seligman, 1995).

Measurement

As noted in the introduction of this volume, researchers interested in explanatory style have used several measures in their investigations (see also Reivich, 1995). The majority of studies of adults have used the Attributional Style Questionnaire (ASQ; Peterson, Semmel, von Baeyer, Abramson, Metalsky, & Seligman, 1982; Seligman, Abramson, Semmel, & von Baeyer, 1979). The ASQ yields composite scores for explanatory style for positive events (CP) and negative events (CN), as well as scores for 6 subscales (internal, stable, and global for positive and negative events). An overall composite (CP–CN) is calculated by subtracting the negative-event composite from the positive-event composite.

Over the past 10 years, investigations of explanatory style have frequently used one of the two expanded ASQs (E-ASQ; Metalsky, Halberstadt, & Abramson, 1987; Peterson & Villanova, 1988). The E-ASQs have been the favorite measures in investigations of the HT (Metalsky & Joiner, 1992; Metalsky, Joiner, Hardin, & Abramson, 1993). These scales contain more negative events, and are, therefore, more reliable than the original ASQ. Because the Extended-ASQs do not sample positive events, only explanatory style for negative events can be assessed with these instruments. Recently, Abramson, Alloy, and Metalsky (1998) developed the Cognitive Style Questionnaire (CSQ) to assess the tendency to infer stable and global causes, negative consequences, and negative characteristics about the self.

The Children's Attributional Style Questionnaire (CASQ; Kaslow, Tannenbaum, & Seligman, 1978) is the most widely used measure of explanatory style in children. The CASQ presents 48 hypothetical events (24 positive and 24 negative events) in a forced-choice format. This instrument yields the same composite and subscale scores as the original ASQ.

All of these measures are self-report measures. However, some studies have assessed explanatory style by analyzing speeches, statements, journal entries, and other written materials using the Content Analysis of Verbatim Explanations (CAVE) technique (Peterson, Bettes, & Seligman, 1985). In CAVE, causal explanations for positive and negative events are extracted and then coded for their internality, stability, and globality (for additional discussion of the CAVE technique, see chapter 6 in this volume).

Depression

Researchers have evaluated two hypotheses regarding the link between explanatory style and depression. The weak hypothesis, that a pessimistic explanatory style is associated with depressive symptoms, is supported by many studies of adults (for a review, see Robins & Hayes, 1995) and children (for reviews, see Gladstone & Kaslow, 1995; Joiner & Wagner, 1995a).

The stronger hypothesis, that a pessimistic explanatory style is a risk factor for depressive symptoms, has met with conflicting findings. Several studies have investigated the ability of explanatory style to predict changes in depressive symptoms over time. In some of these studies, CP–CN and CN scores predict depressive symptoms, with pessimistic explanatory style predicting increases in symptoms over time (e.g., Golin, Sweeney, & Schaeffer, 1981; Seligman et al., 1984). In other investigations, however, explanatory style does not significantly predict changes in symptoms (e.g., Bennet & Bates, 1995; Hammen, Adrian, & Hiroto, 1988; Tiggemann, Winefield, Winefield, & Goldney, 1991).

Few studies have investigated the link between explanatory style and clinical depression. Recently, Abramson, Alloy, Hogan et al. (1998) found that episodes of clinical depression in college students were predicted by their scores on the CSQ and a measure of dysfunctional attitudes central to Beck's theory of depression (DAS; Weissman, 1979).

In adults, recovery from depression during cognitive therapy is linked to improvement in explanatory style (Seligman et al., 1988). In addition, a pessimistic explanatory style predicts relapse following the termination of therapy (DeRubeis & Hollon, 1995; Ilardi, Craighead, & Evans, 1997). Programs that improve explanatory style help prevent depressive symptoms in adults and children (Gillham, Reivich, Jaycox, & Seligman, 1995; Seligman, Schulman, DeRubeis, & Hollon, 1999).

Most studies investigating the relationship between explanatory style and depressive symptoms have examined the overall (CP–CN) composite or the CN composite. Explanatory style for positive events is less consistently related to depressive symptoms (Peterson & Seligman, 1984; Robins & Hayes, 1995). For example, Seligman and colleagues (1984) found that the CN but not the CP composite predicted depressive symptoms in children.

Achievement and Productivity

Optimistic explanations for negative events are linked to higher academic achievement in college students and increased job productivity (for a review, see Schulman, 1995). Students who explain events in an optimistic manner are more likely than those who explain them in a pessimistic one to exceed the level of academic performance predicted by their high school class rank, SAT scores, and achievement test scores (Schulman, 1995). In children, attributions of academic failure to stable and global factors, such as lack of ability, are associated with decreased persistence and more negative expectations for future success (e.g., Dweck, 1975). In contrast to these findings, however, Satterfield, Monahan, and Seligman (1997) found that law students with a pessimistic explanatory style actually outperformed those who were considered optimists.

Physical Health

Explanatory style also appears to be linked to physical health (for a review, see Peterson & Bossio, 1991). Optimistic college students report fewer physical illnesses, make fewer doctor visits, and feel more able to prevent health problems than their pessimistic peers (Peterson, 1988; Peterson & De Avila, 1995). Explanatory style in young adulthood has been found to predict physical health in middle age (Peterson, Seligman, & Vaillant, 1988). More recently, Buchanan (1995) found that explanatory style predicted long-term survival among men who had had one heart attack.

Improving explanatory style may enhance physical well-being. Seligman and colleagues tracked visits to a student health center by university students who participated in a program designed to improve explanatory style. Compared to control participants, these students made more preventative health care visits and fewer illness-related visits (Buchanan, Gardenswartz, & Seligman, 1999).

Other Life Arenas

An optimistic explanatory style has also been linked to many other outcomes. For example, studies suggest that explanatory style is linked to athletic performance (Rettew & Reivich, 1995; Seligman, Nolen-Hoeksema, Thornton, & Thornton, 1990). Basketball teams whose members gave more optimistic explanations for losses were more likely than those with pessimistic explanatory styles to come back from a loss by winning the next game (Rettew & Reivich, 1995). In another study, members of a university varsity swim team were given false feedback after they performed their best event. Each swimmer was given a time for the event that was slightly longer than his or her actual time (Seligman et al., 1990). Although the actual discrepancies were small, they were large enough to make the difference between good and bad times. An optimistic explanatory style was associated with greater resilience and predicted greater performance following this negative feedback.

Explanatory style is also linked to marital satisfaction. Couples who attribute marital events to factors that are external to their spouse, unstable, and specific report higher levels of marital satisfaction than those with the reverse explanatory style. An optimistic explanatory style for marital events also appears to predict future marital satisfaction (e.g., Fincham & Bradbury, 1993)

Finally, explanatory style has been linked to political victory (Zullow, 1995), and military assertiveness (Satterfield & Seligman, 1994). For example, Zullow and Seligman (1990) content-analyzed (using CAVE) nomination acceptance speeches made by presidential candidates from 1948 to 1984. They found that defeat in the presidential elections was predicted by a combination of explanatory style and rumination (the tendency to dwell on negative events). Specifically, in 9 of the 10 elections, the candidate whose style was scored as more pessimistically ruminative lost the election.

Related Findings From the Dispositional Optimism Literature

For the most part, findings from the dispositional optimism literature parallel those from the explanatory style literature. For example, dispositional optimists report fewer depressive symptoms (Carver & Gaines, 1987) and fewer physical health problems than pessimistic people (Scheier & Carver, 1992). Dispositional optimism predicts greater psychological well-being and faster physical recovery after coronary artery bypass surgery (Scheier & Carver, 1992).

A few discrepancies exist across the literatures. For example, dispositional optimism predicts postpartum depression (Carver & Gaines, 1987). In contrast, Manly, McMahon, Bradley, and Davidson (1982) found that explanatory style was not related to postpartum depression. Cutrona (1983) found that explanations regarding daily events and child care stress were not related to postpartum depressive symptoms, but causal attributions for so-called "maternity blues" were significantly related to depressive symptoms.

EXPLANATORY STYLE AND OPTIMISM

Expectations about the future are a crucial component of both the RLHT and HT because they provide the link between causal explanations and helplessness deficits. Thus, according to Abramson and colleagues (1978), "the attribution merely predicts the recurrence of the expectations but the expectation determines the occurrence of the helplessness deficits" (p. 58).

Research on Explanatory Style and Expectations

Despite their theoretical importance, few investigations of explanatory style have assessed expectations. One recent exception is a study by Metalsky and colleagues (1993). Among students who received a low grade, those who attributed negative achievement events to stable and global factors expected to perform poorly in the future. These expectations predicted changes in mood.

A handful of studies have assessed both explanatory style and dispositional optimism, using the Life Orientation Test (LOT; Scheier & Carver, 1985). These studies have yielded inconsistent findings. Scheier and Carver (1992) reported correlations between the ASQ CP–CN composite and the LOT that are in the high teens and low twenties. Kamen (1989) reported a correlation of –.25 between the LOT and the ASQ CN composite. In contrast, Hjelle, Belongia, and Nesser (1996) reported a correlation of .41 between the LOT and the ASQ CP–CN composite. Gillham, Tassoni, Engel, DeRubeis, and Seligman (1998) found correlations of .63 and .41 between the LOT and the ASQ CP–CN composite in a sample of college students at two assessment points. These correlations rose to .77 and .49, respectively, after they were corrected for attenuation. Thus, across these studies, correlations have ranged from below .20 to .77. Clearly more research is needed that directly examines the relationship between explanatory style and dispositional optimism.

Relationship Between Explanation and Expectation

How strong a relationship should we expect to find between explanatory style and expectations? Several researchers have pointed out that the inferred consequences of an event may be quite negative even when an optimistic explanation is given (Abramson et al., 1989; Hammen & Cochran, 1981; Zullow, 1991). For example, Abramson and colleagues (1989) gave the example of a college student who performs poorly on the graduate record exam. This student could attribute his poor performance to noises in the testing room (an unstable and specific cause) while making catastrophic predictions (e.g., "I'll never be admitted to a graduate program."). Similarly, Zullow (1991) suggested that a person who suffers permanent injury in an automobile accident can give an optimistic explanation for the event (e.g., "The other driver was distracted.") and still make bleak predictions about his or her future. According to the HT, a pessimistic explanatory style is only one of several pathways to hopelessness. Individuals who catastrophize and blame themselves following negative events are also vulnerable to hopelessness, even if they do not have a pessimistic explanatory style.

Interaction With Other Variables

Explanations and expectations may interact with other cognitive variables in predicting psychological well-being. For example, explanations and expectations should affect us the most when they concern events that are important to us (Feather & Tiggemann, 1984; Turner & Cole, 1994). Zullow (1991) argued that explanatory style and expectancies may interact with rumination. The combination of an optimistic explanatory style, optimistic expectancies, and rumination may be particularly motivating. That is, individuals may be most motivated when they attribute setbacks to unstable specific factors and expect their efforts to pay off, but focus on the negative consequences that they are trying to prevent. Consistent with this hypothesis, Zullow (1991) reported that optimistic rumination was associated with vigorous campaigning in political candidates who were behind in the polls.

Zullow (1991) also indicated that motivation will be affected by the magnitude of the difference between two types of expectancies: (a) outcome expectancies given action and (b) outcome expectancies given inaction. A large difference in these expectancies may be especially motivating for individuals with an optimistic explanatory style who are optimistic about their ability to control outcomes. These individuals may pursue goals arduously when the perceived consequence of inaction is stable and global. Zullow (1991) illustrated this point using an environmental example. He suggested that the belief that deforestation of the rain forest will imperil the entire planet is more motivating than the belief that deforestation will deplete "the Amazon basin's soil of nutrients, which will take years to replenish" (p. 48).

BRIDGING THE RESEARCH LITERATURES

In the remainder of this chapter, we review some of the newer research questions within the explanatory style and dispositional optimism literatures. Although some questions are common to both research traditions, in many cases researchers within each tradition can benefit from considering the questions posed by the other. Further research is needed to clarify and better define the constructs of optimism, to understand the mechanisms by which optimism produces its effect on physical and psychological well-being, and to understand its origins.

Clarifying the Optimism Construct

Although explanatory style and dispositional optimism have been described and researched extensively for the past 20 years, fundamental questions about the definition of these constructs still remain. For example, are pessimism and optimism opposites? What are the important dimensions of optimism? What is the relationship between optimism and control?

Optimism vs. Pessimism

In the dispositional optimism literature, optimism and pessimism are often viewed as two poles of the same continuum. The terms *optimism, pessimism, hope,* and *hopelessness* are often used interchangeably. The underlying assumption is that the more individuals expect positive events, the less they expect negative events to occur. The explanatory style literature is similarly confused. Researchers using the CP–CN composite assume that people who give negative explanations for problematic events will also give negative explanations for good events. This assumption is complicated with regard to explanatory style, because pessimistic explanations for negative and positive events reflect opposite patterns of attribution (the former are internal, stable, and global, whereas the latter are external, unstable, and specific). To make matters more confusing, within the explanatory style literature, the term *optimism* is used to refer to several measures of attribution, including the CP–CN, CP, CN, and hopelessness composite scores.

Some researchers have suggested that by regarding optimism and pessimism as poles on one continuum, important distinctions between these constructs are blurred (Chang, 1998; Chang, D'Zurilla, & Maydeu-Olivares, 1994; Nunn, 1996). An individual who expects his or her wishes will go unfulfilled does not necessarily expect catastrophes to occur. Chang and colleagues (1994) suggested using the term *pessimism* to refer to expectations of negative outcomes and *optimism* to refer to expectations of positive outcomes. Thus, individuals can be high or low on optimism and high or low on pessimism.

Recently, researchers have begun to explore differences between dispositional optimism and pessimism. Chang and colleagues (Chang, 1998; Chang et al., 1994) found evidence that measures of dispositional optimism contain two factors: one that includes positive expectancy items and a second that includes negative expectancy items. Positive and negative factors were correlated, however (with rs ranging from $-.43$ to $-.60$).

In the explanatory style literature, relatively little work has been conducted on the distinction between attributions for positive versus negative events. Peterson (1991) noted that in several investigations, explanatory style for positive events is weakly or not significantly correlated with explanatory style for negative events. Clearly, further research is needed that explores the distinction between explanatory style for positive versus negative events. As in the dispositional optimism literature, more thoughtful and precise use of terminology is needed.

One important reason for distinguishing between expectations for good versus bad events (optimism vs. pessimism) and explanatory style for good versus bad events is that these constructs may have different correlates and may be related to different outcomes. Within the explanatory style literature, for example, explanatory style for negative events may predict increases in depressive symptoms, whereas explanatory style for positive events may predict reductions in symptoms. Consistent with this hypothesis, Needles and Abramson (1990) found that the interaction of positive life events with a "hopeful" explanatory style (stable and global explanations for positive events) predicted recovery from depressive symptoms in college students (see also Edelman, Ahrens, & Haaga, 1994). Similarly, Johnson, Crofton, and Feinstein (1996) found a hopeful explanatory style interacted with positive life events to predict symptom reduction in psychiatric inpatients with depression.

Optimism vs. Explanatory Style

Another obvious area of confusion results from the use of the terms *optimism* and *pessimism* to refer to explanatory style. Peterson (1991) presented the following arguments for the use of these terms by researchers investigating explanatory style: First, optimism and pessimism are terms from ordinary language. Second, it is optimistic to view the causes of negative events as external, temporary, and affecting few areas of life. Finally, explanatory style is associated with many outcomes, which are linked to pessimism, such as depression, lowered expectancies, passivity, poor achievement, and poor health.

In contrast, other researchers have argued that the use of *optimism* and *pessimism* to denote causal attributions is potentially misleading, because our intuitive notion of optimism concerns expectations (Abramson, Dykman, & Needles, 1991; Zullow, 1991). Although *optimism* and *pessimism* may be useful modifiers of terms such as *attributions* and *explanatory style*, we agree with the suggestion by Abramson and colleagues (1991) that these terms in isolation be reserved for the expectational components of the RLHT and HT. This suggestion also applies to the terms *hopeful* and *hopeless,* which have recently been applied to explanatory style (Abramson et al., 1989; Needles & Abramson, 1990).

Although explanatory style and pessimism are associated with many of the same outcomes, this does not mean we should equate the constructs. In most studies, measures of explanatory style are only weakly to moderately correlated with measures of dispositional optimism (Hjelle et al., 1996; Kamen, 1989; Scheier & Carver, 1992). Explanatory style also is correlated with self-esteem, extroversion, and neuroticism (Gillham et al., 1998) and is associated with many of the same outcomes (Clark & Watson, 1991). However, few researchers advocate using these terms interchangeably.

Dimensions

Most research on explanatory style uses composite scores that sum across three dimensions (internality, stability, and globality) of explanatory style. There is considerable debate among researchers regarding the validity of this practice. Correlations between the different explanatory style dimensions, particularly correlations between the internal dimension and other dimensions, are often quite low. This raises questions about whether these dimensions (a) reflect a single construct (explanatory style), and (b) should be weighted equally (Carver, 1989; Perloff & Persons, 1988). In contrast to measures of explanatory style, measures of outcome expectancies (such as the LOT) do not assess dimensions of optimism. Instead, these measures simply yield a composite score (or sometimes one score for optimism and one for pessimism). Nevertheless, there may be important dimensions of expectation that predict psychological and physical well-being. Further research is needed on the use of dimensions within the explanatory style and dispositional optimism literatures.

The Role of Control

An important component of the RLHT and HT of depression is the expectation that one can control events in the environment. Individuals who feel powerless are more vulnerable to motivational deficits and depression. Despite the importance of control to explanatory style theories, few investigations of explanatory style investigate perceptions of control. Peterson (1991) observed that perceptions of control are usually inferred from the causal attributions people give. Thus, when attributions for negative events are internal, stable, and global, the event will arguably be regarded as uncontrollable. Few studies have investigated this assumption, however. Peterson (1991) found that the stability and globality of explanations did not load onto the same factor with perceptions of control.

The relationship of control to dispositional optimism is also confusing. Scheier and Carver (1993) wrote that their approach to optimism intentionally de-emphasizes the role of personal efficacy or agency. At the same time, they propose that people's actions are greatly influenced by their expectations about the future (Scheier & Carver, 1992). If individuals perceive desired outcomes to be attainable, they continue to strive toward those outcomes. Conversely, if outcomes are perceived to be unattainable, effort is withdrawn. "We have assumed that positive expectancies cause the person to continue to work toward the attainment of goals. Implicit in this view is the notion that the optimistic person views the positive outcome as at least *partially* contingent on continued effort" (Scheier & Carver, 1992, p. 218). Thus, the dispositional optimism construct blurs two distinct types of expectations that are differentiated in the HT: (a) expectations of positive outcomes (or hopeless expectancies) and (b) expectations of control (or helpless expectancies). An optimistic score on the LOT could reflect either of two different outlooks: (a) the belief that the world is a benevolent place or (b) the belief that one possesses the skills to achieve one's goals. Research that investigates the interrelationship between these two types of expectancies and that investigates the relationship of each of these to psychological well-being is needed.

The relationship between beliefs about control and well-being is likely to be complicated. First, the relationship between control and motivation may not be linear. Motivation may be highest when individuals have some—but not complete—control over an outcome. Zullow (1991) argued that the most motivating situations are those for which the perceived probability of success is high but not 100%. In other words, challenges are motivating. This hypothesis is consistent with writings on the flow experience (e.g., Csikszentmihalyi & Csikszentmihalyi, 1988), which propose that people are highly motivated (and experience "flow") when the challenges of a task closely match (or are slightly above) the skills that they bring to it. When the challenges exceed skills, people feel anxious. When the challenges are too low, people are bored. Second, in some situations, a belief in control may actually be harmful. Seligman (1993) and Weisz and colleagues (Weisz, Rothbaum, & Blackburn, 1984) proposed that psychological health requires the ability to accept that which cannot be controlled. Third, the perceived controllability of past events may differ from that for future events (e.g., Brickman et al., 1982). Finally, there may be important individual and cultural differences in the need for perceived control and the relationship of perceptions of control to hopefulness about the future (Nunn, 1996; Weisz et al., 1984).

Consistency

Several researchers have questioned whether an explanatory style exists. That is, are explanations consistent enough across time and situations to warrant the designation *style?* The same question can be asked of dispositional optimism. Research suggests that there is some stability in explanatory style over time. Tiggemann and colleagues (1991) measured explanatory style in young adults across 3 years and found a moderate correlation ($r = .44$) between CP–CN scores across this time period. Burns and Seligman (1989) found explanatory style during late adolescence and young adulthood was related ($r = .54$) to explanatory style 50 years later. Cutrona, Russell, and Jones (1984) found that explanatory style was not highly consistent across situations. Abramson and colleagues (1989) suggested that explanatory style may be consistent within domains (e.g., interpersonal, achievement).

Overlap With Other Psychological Constructs

Recently, researchers have become interested in the uniqueness of optimism as a psychological construct. Watson and Clark proposed that several seemingly diverse personality and cognitive constructs actually reflect facets of two broad underlying constructs: positive affectivity (PA) and negative affectivity (NA) (Clark & Watson, 1991; Watson & Clark, 1984). Thus, constructs such as neuroticism, self-esteem, optimism, and explanatory style may correlate with each other and "predict" depressive symptoms simply because they each reflect NA. In support of this view, Smith, Pope, Rhodewalt, and Poulton (1989) found that the correlation between optimism and depressive symptoms disappeared when NA was partialled out. In contrast, Chang, Maydeu-Olivares, and D'Zurilla (1997) found that optimism and pessimism remained significant predictors of psychological well-being even after controlling for PA and NA. Lucas, Diener, and Suh (1996) found that optimism could be discriminated from negative affectivity and life satisfaction using a multitrait–multimethod matrix analysis. More research is needed to evaluate this hypothesis with regard to both optimism and explanatory style.

Mechanisms

Over the past decade, the focus on the pathway between optimism or explanatory style and well-being has increased. Three questions receiving increasing attention are (a) How do life events interact with optimism (or explanatory style) to affect adjustment? (b) Why does optimism (or an optimistic explanatory style) lead to greater well-being? And (c) Does optimism (or explanatory style) interact in important ways with other variables?

Diathesis–Stress Models

The RLHT and HT are diathesis–stress models of depression. According to these models, individuals with a pessimistic explanatory style (the diathesis) are more likely than those with an optimistic style to become depressed when they experience negative life events (stress). Most studies of explanatory style have examined the link between pessimistic explanatory style and depressive symptoms, without considering the role of negative life events. Several researchers have argued that these studies are, therefore, inadequate tests of the RLHT and HT (Abramson et al., 1989; Metalsky et al., 1987; Robins & Hayes, 1995).

A few studies explicitly test the diathesis–stress component of explanatory style theories. For example, Metalsky, Halberstadt, and Abramson (1987) studied depressive affect in students following receipt of a poor exam grade. These researchers found that most students who received poor grades reported immediate depressed mood, but only those students with a hopeless (stable and global) explanatory style for negative events continued to report depressed mood several days later. Thus, enduring depressed mood was predicted by the interaction of a pessimistic explanatory style with the experience of a negative life event. In general, studies of the diathesis–stress model have produced mixed results. Some show a significant interaction between negative life events and explanatory style (Hilsman & Garber, 1995; Houston, 1995), whereas others show that this interaction is not significant (Follette & Jacobson, 1987; Hammen, Adrian, & Hiroto, 1988; Tiggemann et al., 1991).

The diathesis–stress model also may be applicable to dispositional optimism or pessimism. Dispositional pessimists may be particularly vulnerable to making catastrophic predictions about the future when adversity strikes. This may further increase their hopelessness and render them vulnerable to depression. In support of this hypothesis, Dixon, Heppner, Burnett, and Lips (1993) found the interaction between stress and hopelessness was associated with depressive symptoms. Hopelessness was more strongly related to depression scores under high levels of stress.

Coping

Although optimism and explanatory style are related to a variety of psychological, behavioral, and physical outcomes, relatively little is known about the mechanisms involved. Steps have been made recently within both literatures to delineate the pathway from optimism or explanatory style to outcome. A major prediction of the RLHT is that an optimistic explanatory style enables individuals to maintain their motivation in the face of adversity and, thus, allows them to cope more effectively. Despite this prediction, few studies have explored the relationship between explanatory style and coping strategies. Follette and Jacobson (1987) found that contrary to the RLHT students who made internal, stable, and global attributions for poor exam performance reported more plans to study for the next examination than did their optimistic peers.

More research exists on the relationship between dispositional optimism and coping. Dispositional optimism correlates positively with problem-focused coping, the positive reinterpretation of a problem, and the attempt to accept the reality of situations that are perceived to be uncontrollable. In addition, optimism correlates negatively with the use of denial and the attempt to distance oneself from problems (Amirkhan, Risinger, & Swickert, 1995; Aspinwall & Taylor, 1992; Scheier & Carver, 1993).

Origins of Optimism and Explanatory Style

Little is known about the origins of explanatory style or dispositional optimism. Within the explanatory style literature, a variety of environmental causes have been suggested. Negative life events, particularly the experience of abuse (Kaufman, 1991; Gold, 1986) or parental conflict (Nolen-Hoeksema, Girgus, & Seligman, 1986), are linked to a pessimistic explanatory style in some studies. Seligman, Reivich, Jaycox, and Gillham (1995) proposed that parents can influence their children's explanatory style through modeling and through the attributions that they make for events in their children's lives. A child who is continually criticized as "stupid" or "lazy" following mistakes may internalize these internal, stable, and global explanations in the future. Thus far, research on the relationship between parent and child explanatory style has yielded conflicting results (for a recent review, see Joiner & Wagner, 1995b). Similar environmental theories have been proposed for dispositional optimism. For example, Scheier and Carver (1993) suggested that the development of dispositional optimism in children is influenced by experience with success and failure, optimism and pessimism modeled by parents, and coping strategies taught by parents.

There is some evidence for a genetic component of dispositional optimism and explanatory style. Schulman, Keith, and Seligman (1991) found that explanatory style was significantly correlated in monozygotic twins. In contrast, the correlation in dizygotic twins was not significant. Plomin and colleagues (1992) estimated the heritability of optimism and pessimism to be about 25%.

Understanding the origins of optimism and explanatory style is one of the most interesting and potentially valuable goals for future research. There is growing evidence that depressive symptoms, anxiety, and perhaps even physical health problems can be prevented with interventions that focus on improving explanatory style (Gillham et al., 1995; Seligman et al., 1995; Seligman et al., 1999). Knowledge about the origins of explanatory style will enable clinicians to develop even more powerful intervention programs. Eventually, such knowledge may lead to techniques that prevent a pessimistic explanatory style from developing in children.

CONCLUSION

Explanatory style is related to a variety of psychological and physical health indices, including academic achievement, depression, and physical illness. Although findings in the explanatory style literature parallel those from the dispositional optimism literature, these two constructs have largely been studied in isolation from each other. We know surprisingly little about the relationship between explanations and expectations. Studies that bridge these separate research traditions are sorely needed. We have learned a tremendous amount about optimism and explanatory style over the past 20 years, but important questions remain. Optimism and explanatory style must be more precisely defined and differentiated from each other and from other constructs. The mechanisms through which optimism and explanatory styles affect well-being need to be identified. The sources of optimism and explanatory style need to be discovered. These questions are particularly fascinating because of their practical value. If optimism and explanatory style are causally related to well-being, the answers to these questions may enable clinicians to improve the quality of life for many people.

REFERENCES

Abramson, L. Y., Alloy, L. B., Hogan, M. E., Whitehouse, W. G., Cornette, M., Akhavan, S., & Chiara, A. (1998). Suicidality and cognitive vulnerability to depression among college students: A prospective study. *Journal of Adolescence, 21*, 157–171.

Abramson, L. Y., Alloy, L. B., & Metalsky, G. I. (1989). Hopelessness depression: A theory-based subtype of depression. *Psychological Review, 96*, 358–372.

Abramson, L. Y., Alloy, L. B., & Metalsky, G. I. (1998). The Cognitive Style Questionnaire: A measure of the vulnerability featured in the hopelessness theory of depression. Unpublished manuscript. University of Wisconsin-Madison.

Abramson, L. Y., Dykman, B. M., & Needles, D. J. (1991). Attributional style and theory: Let no one tear them asunder. *Psychological Inquiry, 2*, 11–49.

Abramson, L. Y., Seligman, M. E. P., & Teasdale, J. D. (1978). Learned helplessness in humans: Critique and reformulation. *Journal of Abnormal Psychology, 87*, 49–74.

Amirkhan, J. H., Risinger, R. T., & Swickert, R. J. (1995). Extraversion: A "hidden" personality factor in coping. *Journal of Personality, 63*, 189–212.

Aspinwall, L. G., & Taylor, S. E. (1992). Modeling cognitive adaptation: A longitudinal investigation of the impact of individual differences and coping on college adjustment and performance. *Journal of Personality and Social Psychology, 63*, 989–1003.

Bennet, D. S., & Bates, J. E. (1995). Prospective models of depressive symptoms in early adolescence. Attributional style, stress and support. *Journal of Early Adolescence, 15*, 299–315.

Brickman, P., Rabinowitz, V. C., Kaurza, Jr., J., Coates, D., Cohn, E., & Kidder, L. (1982). Models of helping and coping. *American Psychologist, 37*, 368–384.

Buchanan, G. M. (1995). Explanatory style and coronary heart disease. In G. M. Buchanan & M. E. P. Seligman (Eds.), *Explanatory style* (pp. 225–232). Hillsdale, NJ: Erlbaum.

Buchanan, G. M., Gardenswartz, C. A. R., & Seligman, M. E. P. (1999). Physical health following a cognitive-behavioral intervention. *Prevention and Treatment, 2*, 10, journals.apa.org.

Buchanan, G. M., & Seligman, M. E. P. (1995). *Explanatory style*. Hillsdale, NJ: Erlbaum.

Burns, M. O., & Seligman, M. E. P. (1989). Explanatory style across the life span: Evidence for stability over 52 years. *Journal of Personality and Social Psychology, 56*, 471–477.

Carver, C. S. (1989). How should multi-faceted personality constructs be tested? Issues illustrated by self-monitoring, attributional style, and hardiness. *Journal of Personality and Social Psychology, 36*, 1501–1511.

Carver, C. S., & Gaines, J. G. (1987). Optimism, pessimism, and postpartum depression. *Cognitive Therapy and Research, 11*, 449–462.

Chang, E. C. (1998). Distinguishing between optimism and pessimism: A second look at the "optimism-neuroticism hypothesis." In R. R. Hoffman, M. F. Sherrik, & J. S. Warm (Eds.), *Viewing psychology as a whole: The integrative science of William N. Dember* (pp. 415–432). Washington, DC: American Psychological Association.

Chang, E. C., D'Zurilla, T. J., & Maydeu-Olivares, A. (1994). Assessing the dimensionality of optimism and pessimism using a multimeasure approach. *Cognitive Therapy and Research, 18*, 143–160.

Chang, E. C., Maydeu-Olivares, A., & D'Zurilla, T. J. (1997). Optimism and pessimism as partially independent constructs: Relationship to positive and negative affectivity and psychological well-being. *Personality and Individual Differences, 23*, 433–440.

Clark, L. A., & Watson, D. (1991). General affective dispositions in physical and psychological health. In C. R. Snyder & D. R. Forsyth (Eds.), *Handbook of social and clinical psychology: The health perspective* (pp. 221–245). New York: Pergamon.

Csikszentmihalyi, M., & Csikszentmihalyi, I. S. (1988). *Optimal experience: Psychological studies of flow in consciousness*. New York: Cambridge University Press.

Cutrona, C. E. (1983). Causal attributions and perinatal depression. *Journal of Abnormal Psychology, 92*, 161–172.

Cutrona, C. E., Russell, D., & Jones, R. D., (1984). Cross-situational consistency in causal attributions: Does attributional style exist? *Journal of Personality and Social Psychology, 47*, 1043–1058.

DeRubeis, R. J., & Hollon, S. D. (1995). Explanatory style in the treatment of depression. In G. M. Buchanan & M. E. P. Seligman (Eds.), *Explanatory style* (pp. 99–112). Hillsdale, NJ: Erlbaum.

Dixon, W. A., Heppner, P. P., Burnett, J. W., & Lips, B. J. (1993). Hopelessness and stress: Evidence for an interactive model of depression. *Cognitive Therapy and Research, 17*, 39–52.

Dweck, C. S. (1975). The role of expectations and attributions in the alleviation of learned helplessness. *Journal of Personality and Social Psychology, 31*, 674–685.

Edelman, R. E., Ahrens, A. H., & Haaga, D. A. F. (1994). Inferences about the self, attributions, and overgeneralization as predictors of recovery from dysphoria. *Cognitive Therapy and Research, 18*, 551–566.

Feather, N. T., & Tiggemann, M. (1984). A balance measure of attributional style. *Australian Journal of Psychology, 36,* 267–283.

Fincham, F. D., & Bradbury, T. N. (1993). Marital satisfaction, depression, and attributions: A longitudinal analysis. *Journal of Personality and Social Psychology, 64,* 442–452.

Follette, V. M., & Jacobson, N. S. (1987). Importance of attributions as a predictor of how people cope with failure. *Journal of Personality and Social Psychology, 52,* 1205–1211.

Gillham, J. E., Reivich, K. J., Jaycox, L. H., & Seligman, M. E. P. (1995). Prevention of depressive symptoms in schoolchildren: Two year follow-up. *Psychological Science, 6,* 343–351.

Gillham, J. E., Tassoni, C. J., Engel, R. A., DeRubeis, R. J., & Seligman, M. E. P. (1998). The relationship of explanatory style to other depression relevant constructs. Unpublished manuscript, University of Pennsylvania, Philadelphia.

Gladstone, T. R. G., & Kaslow, N. J. (1995). Depression and attributions in children and adolescents: A meta-analytic review. *Journal of Abnormal Child Psychology, 23,* 597–606.

Gold, E. R. (1986). Long-term effects of sexual victimization in childhood: An attributional approach. *Journal of Consulting and Clinical Psychology, 54,* 471–475.

Golin, S., Sweeney, P. D., & Schaeffer, D. E. (1981). The causality of causal attributions in depression: A cross-lagged panel analysis. *Journal of Abnormal Psychology, 90,* 14–22.

Hammen, C., & Cochran, S. (1981). Cognitive correlates of life stress and depression in college students. *Journal of Abnormal Psychology, 90,* 23–27.

Hammen, C. L., Adrian, C., & Hiroto, D. (1988). A longitudinal test of the attributional vulnerability model in children at risk for depression. *British Journal of Clinical Psychology, 27,* 37–46.

Hilsman, R., & Garber, J. (1995). A test of the cognitive diathesis-stress model of depression in children: Academic stressors, attributional style, perceived competence, and control. *Journal of Personality and Social Psychology, 69,* 370–380.

Hjelle, L., Belongia, C., & Nesser, J. (1996). Psychometric properties of the Life Orientation Test and Attributional Style Questionnaire. *Psychological Reports, 78,* 507–515.

Houston, D. M. (1995). Vulnerability to depressive mood reactions: Retesting the hopelessness model of depression. *British Journal of Social Psychology, 34,* 293–302.

Ilardi, S. S., Craighead, E. W., & Evans, D. D. (1997). Modeling relapse in unipolar depression: The effects of dysfunctional cognitions and personality disorders. *Journal of Consulting and Clinical Psychology, 65,* 381–391.

Johnson, J. G., Crofton, A., & Feinstein, S. B. (1996). Enhancing attributional style and positive events predict increased hopefulness among depressed psychiatric inpatients. *Motivation and Emotion, 20,* 285–297.

Joiner, T. E., & Wagner, K. D. (1995a). Attributional style and depression in children and adolescents: A meta-analytic review. *Clinical Psychology Review, 15*, 777–798.

Joiner, T. E., & Wagner, K. D. (1995b). Parental, child-centered attributions and outcome: A meta-analytic review with conceptual and methodological implications. *Journal of Abnormal Child Psychology, 24*, 37–52.

Kamen, L. P. (1989). Learned helplessness, cognitive dissonance, and cell-mediated immunity. Unpublished doctoral dissertation, University of Pennsylvania, Philadelphia.

Kaslow, N. J., Tannenbaum, R. L., & Seligman, M. E. P. (1978). The KASTAN: A children's attributional style questionnaire. Unpublished manuscript, University of Pennsylvania, Philadelphia.

Kaufman, J. (1991). Depressive disorders in maltreated children. *Journal of the American Academy of Child and Adolescent Psychiatry, 30*, 257–265.

Lucas, R. E., Diener, E., & Suh, E. (1996). Discriminant validity of well-being measures. *Journal of Personality and Social Psychology, 71*, 616–628.

Manly, P. C., McMahon, R. J., Bradley, C. F., & Davidson, P. O. (1982). Depressive attributional style and depression following child birth. *Journal of Abnormal Psychology, 91*, 245–254.

Metalsky, G. I., Halberstadt, L. J., & Abramson, L. Y. (1987). Vulnerability to depressive mood reactions: Toward a more powerful test of the diathesis-stress and causal mediation components of the reformulated theory of depression. *Journal of Personality and Social Psychology, 52*, 386–393.

Metalsky, G. I., & Joiner, T. E. (1992). Vulnerability to depressive symptomatology: A prospective test of the diathesis-stress and causal mediation components of the hopelessness theory of depression. *Journal of Personality and Social Psychology, 63*, 667–675.

Metalsky, G. I., Joiner, T. E., Hardin, T. S., & Abramson, L. Y. (1993). Depressive reactions to failure in a naturalistic setting: A test of the hopelessness and self-esteem theories of depression. *Journal of Abnormal Psychology, 102*, 101–109.

Needles, D. J., & Abramson, L. Y. (1990). Positive life events, attributional style, and hopefulness: Testing a model of recovery from depression. *Journal of Abnormal Psychology, 99*, 156–165.

Nolen-Hoeksema, S., Girgus, J. S., & Seligman, M. E. P. (1986). Depression in children of families in turmoil. Unpublished manuscript, University of Pennsylvania, Philadelphia.

Nunn, K. P. (1996). Personal hopefulness: A conceptual review of the relevance to the perceived future of psychiatry. *British Journal of Medical Psychology, 69*, 227–245.

Perloff, J. M., & Persons, J. B. (1988). Biases resulting from the use of indexes: An application to attributional style and depression. *Psychological Bulletin, 103*, 95–104.

Peterson, C. (1988). Explanatory style as a risk factor for illness. *Cognitive Therapy and Research, 12,* 117–130.

Peterson, C. (1991). The meaning and measurement of explanatory style. *Psychological Inquiry, 2,* 1–10.

Peterson, C., Bettes, B. A., & Seligman, M. E. P. (1985). Depressive symptoms and unprompted causal attributions: Content analysis. *Behavior Research and Therapy, 23,* 379–382.

Peterson, C., & Bossio, L. M. (1991). *Health and optimism.* New York: Free Press.

Peterson, C., & De Avila, M. (1995). Optimistic explanatory style and the perception of health problems. *Journal of Clinical Psychology, 51,* 128–132.

Peterson, C., & Seligman, M. E. P. (1984). Causal explanations as a risk factor for depression: Theory and evidence. *Psychological Review, 41,* 253–259.

Peterson, C., Seligman, M. E. P., & Vaillant, G. E. (1988). Pessimistic explanatory style is a risk factor for physical illness: A thirty-five year longitudinal study. *Journal of Personality and Social Psychology, 55,* 23–27.

Peterson, C., Semmel, A., von Baeyer, C., Abramson, L. Y., Metalsky, G. I., & Seligman, M. E. P. (1982). The Attributional Style Questionnaire. *Cognitive Therapy and Research, 6,* 287–299.

Peterson, C., & Villanova, P. (1988). An Expanded Attributional Style Questionnaire. *Journal of Abnormal Psychology, 97,* 87–89.

Plomin, R., Scheier, M. F., Bergeman, C. S., Pederson, N. L., Nesselroade, J., & McClearn, G. (1992). Optimism, pessimism and mental health: A twin/adoption analysis. *Personality and Individual Differences, 13,* 921–930.

Reivich, K. (1995). The measurement of explanatory style. In G. M. Buchanan & M. E. P. Seligman (Eds.), *Explanatory style* (pp. 21–48). Hillsdale, NJ: Erlbaum.

Rettew, D., & Reivich, K. (1995). Sports and explanatory style. In G. M. Buchanan & M. E. P. Seligman (Eds.), *Explanatory style* (pp. 173–186). Hillsdale, NJ: Erlbaum.

Robins, C. J., & Hayes, A. M. (1995). The role of causal attributions in the prediction of depression. In G. M. Buchanan & M. E. P. Seligman (Eds.), *Explanatory style* (pp. 71–98). Hillsdale, NJ: Erlbaum.

Satterfield, J. M, Monahan, J., & Seligman, M. E. P. (1997). Law school performance predicted by explanatory style. *Behavioral Sciences and the Law, 15,* 95–105.

Satterfield, J. M., & Seligman, M. E. P. (1994). Military aggression and risk predicted by explanatory style. *Psychological Science, 5,* 77–82.

Scheier, M. F., & Carver, C. S. (1985). Optimism, coping and health: Assessment and implications of generalized outcome expectancies. *Health Psychology, 4,* 219–247.

Scheier, M. F., & Carver, C. S. (1988). A model of behavioral self-regulation: Translating intention into action. In L. Berkowitz (Ed.), *Advances in experimental social psychology* (Vol. 21, pp. 303–346). San Diego, CA: Academic Press.

Scheier, M. F., & Carver, C. S. (1992). Effects of optimism on psychological and physical well-being: Theoretical overview and empirical update. *Cognitive Therapy and Research, 16,* 201–228.

Scheier, M. F., & Carver, C. S. (1993). On the power of positive thinking: The benefits of being optimistic. *Current Directions in Psychological Science, 2,* 26–30.

Schulman, P. (1995). Explanatory style and achievement in school and work. In G. M. Buchanan & M. E. P. Seligman (Eds.), *Explanatory style* (pp. 159–171). Hillsdale, NJ: Erlbaum.

Schulman, P., Keith, D., & Seligman, M. E. P. (1991). Is optimism heritable? A study of twins. *Behavior Research and Therapy, 31,* 569–574.

Seligman, M. E. P. (1991). *Learned optimism.* New York: Knopf.

Seligman, M. E. P. (1993). *What you can change and what you can't.* New York: Knopf.

Seligman, M. E. P., Abramson, L. Y., Semmel, A., & von Baeyer, C. (1979). Depressive attributional style. *Journal of Abnormal Psychology, 88,* 242–247.

Seligman, M. E. P., Castellon, C., Cacciola, J., Schulman, P., Luborsky, L., Ollove, M., & Downing, R. (1988). Explanatory style change during cognitive therapy for unipolar depression. *Journal of Abnormal Psychology, 97,* 13–18.

Seligman, M. E. P., Nolen-Hoeksema, S., Thornton, K. M., & Thornton, N. (1990). Explanatory style as a mechanism of disappointing athletic performance. *Psychological Science, 1,* 143–146.

Seligman, M. E. P., Peterson, C., Kaslow, N. J., Tannenbaum, R. L., Alloy, L. B., & Abramson, L. Y. (1984). Attributional style and depressive symptoms among children. *Journal of Abnormal Psychology, 93,* 235–238.

Seligman, M. E. P., Reivich, K. J., Jaycox, L. H., & Gillham, J. (1995). *The optimistic child.* New York: Houghton-Mifflin.

Seligman, M. E. P., Schulman, P., DeRubeis, R. J., & Hollon, S. D. (1999). The prevention of depression and anxiety. *Prevention & Treatment, 2,* 8, journals.apa .org.

Smith, T. W., Pope, M. K., Rhodewalt, F., & Poulton, J. L. (1989). Optimism, neuroticism, coping, and symptom reports: An alternative interpretation of the Life Orientation Test. *Journal of Personality and Social Psychology, 56,* 640–648.

Tiggemann, M., Winefield, A. H., Winefield, H. R., & Goldney, R. D. (1991). The prediction of psychological distress from attributional style: A test of the hopelessness model of depression. *Australian Journal of Psychology, 43,* 125–127.

Turner, J. E., & Cole, D. A. (1994). Developmental differences in cognitive diathesis for child depression. *Journal of Abnormal Child Psychology, 22,* 15–32.

Watson, D., & Clark, L. A. (1984). Negative affectivity: The disposition to experience aversive emotional states. *Psychological Bulletin, 96,* 465–490.

Weissman, A. N. (1979). The Dysfunctional Attitudes Scale: A validation study. Unpublished doctoral dissertation. University of Pennsylvania, Philadelphia.

Weisz, J. R., Rothbaum, F. M., & Blackburn, T. C. (1984). Standing out and standing in: The psychology of control in American and Japan. *American Psychologist, 39,* 955–969.

Zullow, H. M. (1991). Explanations and expectations: Understanding the "doing" side of optimism. *Psychological Inquiry, 2,* 45–49.

Zullow, H. M. (1995). Pessimistic rumination in American politics and society. In G. M. Buchanan & M. E. P. Seligman (Eds.), *Explanatory style* (pp. 21–48). Hillsdale, NJ: Erlbaum.

Zullow, H. M., & Seligman, M. E. P. (1990). Pessimistic rumination predicts defeat of presidential candidates, 1900 to 1984. *Psychological Inquiry, 1,* 52–61.

4

DEFENSIVE PESSIMISM, OPTIMISM, AND PESSIMISM

JULIE K. NOREM

The term *defensive pessimism* was coined in the mid-1980s by Nancy Cantor and her students (Norem & Cantor, 1986a; Norem & Cantor, 1986b) and refers to a cognitive strategy in which individuals set low expectations for an upcoming performance, despite having done well in similar situations in the past. Theoretically, setting low expectations helps "cushion" the potential blow of failure. People using the strategy then mentally rehearse or extensively reflect on what might happen—with special attention paid to potential problems that they might encounter. They play through various mental scenarios, including all of the possible things that might go wrong, and work hard to prepare for the upcoming performance or situation. Typically, individuals who use this strategy initially feel anxious and out of control. The strategy seems to help them gain a feeling of control and to "harness" their anxiety as motivation. Individuals using the strategy perform quite well, contrary to their dire predictions.

A prototypical example of defensive pessimism would be an expert public speaker who is anxious before every speech, who repeatedly asserts that he or she is going to embarrass himself or herself terribly in the next talk, despite a multitude of previously successful talks. This individual can enumerate in detail all of the potential pitfalls that might mar the performance, from the forgotten note cards to the spilled water pitcher on the podium, to the humiliating trip over the microphone cord. Having envisioned the pending disasters in such vivid detail, however, the anxious speaker can also plan carefully to prevent them: He or she requests two copies of the notes for the speech, that the water pitcher be moved out of range, and that electrical tape secure the microphone cord to the floor. Although these precautions cannot ensure rousing applause at the end of the talk, they can at least alleviate anxiety about the worst possible outcomes.

Defensive pessimism has a reputation as a gadfly in the world of optimism and pessimism research, because investigation of the construct started with the hypothesis that this kind of pessimism served positive functions for those who used it. This position seems contrary to most research, in which pessimism is almost invariably related to more negative outcomes (see Isaacowitz & Seligman, 1998; chap. 16, this volume). In this chapter, I compare and contrast the construct of defensive pessimism with other constructs of optimism and pessimism, review past and ongoing defensive pessimism research, and discuss remaining research questions and promising future directions. I conclude with consideration of the implications defensive pessimism has for how people think about pessimism and optimism.

STRATEGIES AS UNITS OF ANALYSIS

The construct of defensive pessimism as a cognitive strategy derives from a social–cognitive approach to the study of personality and behavior. Cantor and Kihlstrom's (1987) social intelligence theory discusses strategies as units of analysis that describe how people go about pursuing their important goals, or life tasks. Strategies describe coherent patterns of expectations, appraisals, planning, effort, and retrospection as individuals pursue personally relevant goals (Norem, 1989).

There are several implications that follow from the description of defensive pessimism as a strategy. First, strategies are developed in the context of particular goals, which implies that the same individual may use different strategies over time and across situations as he or she pursues different goals. Thus, although strategies describe important individual differences, they are not assumed to be stable over time and consistent across situations in the same way as traditional traits, motives, or styles. Theoretically they are potentially malleable. Individuals may develop a repertoire of strategies for different goals or situations, and they may change strategies as their appraisals of relevant situations or goals change. This implies that there is considerable domain specificity in the use of these strategies. In other words, an individual may use defensive pessimism in one type of situation, strategic optimism in another, and some other strategy in a third.

Second, strategies describe processes that unfold over time. For defensive pessimism, for example, the deployment of the strategy begins with setting low expectations in response to anxiety. The strategy then continues as the individual plays through different scenarios. This implies that components of a strategy may have different effects separately than they do together. For example, pessimism by itself and increased reflectivity by itself tend to increase anxiety, but for people accustomed to using defensive pessimism, they tend to decrease anxiety. Furthermore, an individual's specific vulnerability to disruption of the strategy will vary according to when that disruption occurs during its use.

It is important to make clear what is *not* implied by the use of the term *cognitive strategy*. We do not assume that people are necessarily conscious of the strategies they use, although they may be. Just as with other defensive or self-protective strategies, defensive pessimism and strategic optimism may be used without awareness of the process, the motivation, or the consequences. People may also be aware that they use a particular strategy without necessarily being aware of when or why they are using that strategy. Thus, for example, many people recognize themselves in the description of someone using defensive pessimism but maintain that using the strategy was not what they were doing in the particular laboratory performance or situation under discussion, even though data or observation suggests otherwise. Other times, individuals will recognize in retrospect that they used a strategy, but they were not aware of using it at the time.

Describing processes as strategic means only that they are done in the context or in reference to a particular problem or goal. It does not mean that a particular strategy will necessarily be effective or lead to success (Norem, 1998). People may use ineffective strategies, or they may use strategies inappropriately. Few strategies are inherently effective, independent of when, where, and how they are used. Strategy effectiveness needs to be evaluated in terms of the costs and benefits most likely to be associated with particular strategies, with sensitivity to needs of the individual using the strategy, and by the appropriateness of the strategy to specific goals and situations.

Strategies are cognitive in that they capture the way that people think about or construe situations, but they are not *cold* in the sense of connoting rational processes that are untouched by affect or motivation. Quite the contrary, their purpose is to regulate emotion and behavior, and they have emotional and motivational antecedents and consequences. Strategies emphasize what Adler (1935/1979) called "the creative power of the individual" (p. 67) in adapting to one's own temperament and the influence of the environment.

This chapter focuses on defensive pessimism and frequently contrasts it with strategic optimism. *Strategic optimism* refers to a strategy used by individuals who do not typically feel anxious in a particular domain. Instead, they feel in control of their own outcomes, and they set high expectations that are generally congruent with their perceptions of themselves and their past experiences. People using this strategy actively avoid thinking about negative possible outcomes. Indeed, they generally avoid thinking about upcoming tasks, although they do tend to do what is necessary to prepare (e.g., they will study for a test, but they will avoid thinking about what grade they might get, what trick questions the test might contain, and so forth). Strategic optimism offers an informative contrast to defensive pessimism, as the research discussed below illustrates.

Focusing on these two strategies, however, does not assume that they are the only two strategies that people use, or that everyone is either a defensive pessimist or a strategic optimist. In the research conducted with college student samples, up to 40% of the respondents may be classified as "aschematic" with respect to defensive pessimism. That means that they do not appear to use either defensive pessimism or strategic optimism consistently within the domain or situation being assessed. There are potentially any number of strategies that people may use in different situations. Among the most studied by psychologists are various self-handicapping strategies, which can be distinguished from both defensive pessimism and strategic optimism (Martin, 1999). *Self-handicapping* involves adopting or claiming an impediment to performance (e.g., drinking too much at a party, not practicing before a big game) to obscure attributions in the case of failure and thereby protect one's sense of self-esteem (see Berglas, 1985; Higgins & Harris, 1988). It is important to note that although both those who use self-handicapping and those who use defensive pessimism generally report high anxiety, defensive pessimists do not withdraw effort or adopt handicaps in response to their anxiety. Instead, they defend themselves from the negative impact of failure by lowering their expectations so they are neither surprised nor as severely disappointed if failure occurs. They then cope with or "harness" their anxiety through extensive reflection about possible outcomes and plans to avoid negative outcomes and to approach positive outcomes. This contrasts sharply with the effort withdrawal or self-sabotage characteristic of self-handicapping.

Defensive pessimism and strategic optimism, construed as strategies, can thus be differentiated from other constructs of optimism and pessimism by their connection to goals, their domain specificity, and their temporal frame. Strategic optimism is perhaps most closely related to the kinds of "positive illusions" described by Taylor and Brown (1988). Indeed, early research referred to "illusory glow" optimism instead of strategic optimism, and demonstrated that individuals using this strategy would reliably resort to self-esteem-protecting attributions after failure, whereas defensive pessimists seemed to cushion the impact of failure by way of their protective expectations (Norem & Cantor, 1986a, 1986b). In contrast, however, to Taylor and Brown's emphasis on the adaptive advantages of positive illusions, work on defensive pessimism and strategic optimism has focused on the costs and benefits of each strategy, and on how each strategy makes sense given the psychological situation faced by those using it, that is, by emphasizing "copers" as individuals, as opposed to "coping" as an abstract process.

Defensive pessimism is also different from the pessimistic attributional style described by Seligman and his colleagues (see chap. 3 in this volume). Defensive pessimism does not correlate strongly with an internal, global, and stable attributional style, nor do defensive pessimists typically make different attributions for success and failure. Defensive pessimism describes a strategy used to prepare for stressful events, not a reaction after those events, and thus is further differentiated from attributional style. Showers and Ruben (1990) found that defensive pessimists did not use the avoidant coping methods found among people with depressive disorders, nor did their anxiety and rumination persist after stressful events. Similarly, Ronan and his colleagues have shown that individuals using defensive pessimism use more effective, confrontive problem solving than do mildly depressed individuals (Cuddihy & Ronan, 1990; Hammontree & Ronan, 1992).

Defensive pessimism and strategic optimism are also different from the trait optimism and pessimism explored by Carver and Scheier (see chap. 2 in this volume). Trait optimism describes a stable tendency to hold positive expectations and should generally influence expectation setting consistently across situations and over time. As already noted, strategic optimism and defensive pessimism are domain specific and are hypothesized to be relatively malleable. They also describe specific processes that include both expectation setting and subsequent cognitions. The description of the strategies also includes an explicit statement of the function of those processes.

MEASUREMENT OF DEFENSIVE PESSIMISM AND STRATEGIC OPTIMISM

Early attempts to measure defensive pessimism relied on a 9-item, face-valid questionnaire—the Optimism–Pessimism Prescreening Questionnaire (OPPQ; Norem & Cantor, 1986a). When the items were generated, the research team focused on elaborating the description of defensive pessimism. Six of the items on the early questionnaire thus referred to the two hypothesized components of defensive pessimism: pessimistic expectations and negative thinking, and their presumed "opposites." That is, there were two questions about expectations intended to measure pessimistic and optimistic expectations within whatever domain was studied and two questions each about negative and positive thoughts and feelings. There were also two questions that referred to feelings after a performance, which reflected the hypothesis that defensive pessimists may feel more relief than satisfaction after having done well. In other words, although their defensive expectations may cushion the impact of failure, defensive pessimists may also "water down" enjoyment of success (Showers, 1992).

Our initial theorizing about defensive pessimism focused on the negative thinking that we had observed among people using defensive pessimism. We somewhat blithely assumed that, just as optimistic expectations seemed the "opposite" of pessimistic expectations, thinking about positive outcomes was the natural opposite of thinking about negative outcomes. For example, one question stated: "I often think about what it will be like if I do poorly in an academic situation," and another stated "I often think about what it will be like if I do very well in an academic situation." Our initial scoring of the questionnaire (which was used to categorize prescreened research participants as defensive pessimists or optimists for subsequent experiments) was theoretically, not empirically, driven: We considered thinking about doing poorly to be a defensive pessimist item and thinking about doing well to be an optimist item.

Subsequent research has shown that this initial conception of defensive pessimism was mistaken in that the people who tend to reflect extensively about possible negative outcomes also tend to reflect extensively about possible positive outcomes. In contrast, people who report that they do not tend to think about possible negative outcomes do not tend to think about possible positive outcomes either. In other words, thinking about positive outcomes correlates positively with thinking about negative outcomes, and both are part of the "thinking-through" process by which defensive pessimists increase their feelings of control and decrease their anxiety. The current version of the Defensive Pessimism Questionnaire (DPQ) contains several items designed to index this thinking-through process, as well as items designed to measure pessimism (see Exhibit 4.1). Factor analyses of the scale show that although all the items load satisfactorily on one major unrotated factor, oblique rotation also produces two correlated factors that I have labeled *Reflectivity* and *Pessimism*. Exhibit 4.1 indicates which items load on the Reflectivity factor and which items load on the Pessimism factor (it also includes filler and experimental items).

In current research, I continue to use a single defensive pessimism score computed by summing both the pessimism and reflectivity items (with appropriate reverse scoring). In addition, however, I also compute separate

Exhibit 4.1.
The Revised Defensive Pessimism Questionnaire

When you answer the following questions, please think about how you prepare for and think about (academic/social) situations.[a] Each of the statements below describes how people sometimes think or feel about these kinds of situations. In the blank space beside each statement, please indicate how true it is of you, in (academic/social) situations.

1--------2---------3---------4---------5---------6---------7
Not at all   *Very true of me*
true of me

_____ 1. I go into these situations expecting the worst, even though I know I will probably do OK. **(PESS)**

_____ 2. I generally go into these situations with positive expectations about how I will do. **(PESS–R)**

_____ 3. I've generally done pretty well in these situations in the past.[b]

_____ 4. I carefully consider all possible outcomes before these situations. **(REFL)**

_____ 5. When I do well in these situations, I often feel really happy. **(Filler)**

_____ 6. I often worry, in these situations, that I won't be able to carry through my intentions. **(PESS)**

_____ 7. I often think about how I will feel if I do very poorly in these situations. **(REFL)**

_____ 8. I often think about how I will feel if I do very well in these situations. **(REFL)**

_____ 9. When I do well in these situations, it is usually because I didn't get too worried about it beforehand. **(Filler)**

_____ 10. I often try to figure out how likely it is that I will do very poorly in these situations. **(REFL)**

_____ 11. I'm careful not to become overconfident in these situations. **(Experimental item)**

_____ 12. I spend a lot of time planning when one of these situations is coming up. **(REFL)**

_____ 13. When working with others in these situations, I often worry that they will control things or interfere with my plans. **(Experimental item)**

_____ 14. I often try to figure out how likely it is that I will do very well in these situations. **(REFL)**

_____ 15. In these situations, sometimes I worry more about looking like a fool than doing really well. **(PESS)**

_____ 16. Prior to these situations, I avoid thinking about possible bad outcomes. **(REFL–R)**

_____ 17. Considering what can go wrong in academic situations helps me to prepare. **(REFL)**

Note. PESS = Item loads on Pessimism factor; REFL = Item loads on Reflectivity factor; R = reverse-scored item.
[a]The domain of interest should be specified here.
[b]This item is included to differentiate between those who are realistically pessimistic and those who are defensively pessimistic, on the assumption that those who report having done very badly in the past are realistic when they anticipate doing badly in the future. In college student samples, typically fewer than 20% of respondents rate themselves below 5 on this item.

pessimism and reflectivity scores for further exploration of the roles of those two processes. Recently, Martin (1999) found that expectations and reflectivity show somewhat different relations to other variables over time, and it will be important to continue to examine how these processes work separately and in conjunction.

The revised version of the scale correlates at $r = .65$ with the original OPPQ and has a higher reliability (Cronbach's alpha = .78). The Reflectivity and Pessimism subscales have comparable reliabilities (average Cronbach's alphas = .74). In a recent longitudinal study of women at Wellesley College, the DPQ showed a 3-year test–retest reliability of $r = .55$ ($N = 67$) from the first year to the senior year of college.

Much of the research using the DPQ has been experimental, and it has shown good predictive validity when used to prescreen research participants. For prescreening purposes, those who score in the upper tertile or quartile (depending on sample size and particular distributions) of the DPQ are classified as *defensive pessimists*, those in the lower tertile or quartile are classified as *strategic optimists*, and those in the middle of the distribution are considered *aschematic* with respect to these two strategies. When using the scale for prescreening, Item 3, which asks about previous performance, has been used to distinguish realistic pessimists from defensive pessimists. The assumption has been that those people who have done badly in the past are realistic when they predict that they will do badly in the future, whereas those people who report having done well in the past are being defensive if they predict that they will do poorly in the future. This is also congruent with theorizing that defensive pessimists do not misinterpret objective success, but that their strategy follows from their subjective experience, an experience that includes considerable anxiety and uncertainty and that is likely to have a negative influence on construction of future situations. This item also allows some discrimination of those who appear unrealistically optimistic, that is, those who report having done badly in the past but nevertheless expect to do well in the future. In most college samples fewer than 20% of the participants responding rate themselves lower than a score of 5 on this item. Both optimistic and pessimistic individuals who score low on Item 3 tend to have lower grade point averages and tend to perform more poorly on experimental tasks than do those who score higher.

Other data attest to the convergent and divergent validity of the DPQ (see Table 4.1; Illingworth & Norem, 1991; Norem & Crandall, 1991). Theoretically, defensive pessimism is motivated by the need to manage anxiety. Thus, it is not surprising that it is positively correlated with trait anxiety and neuroticism measures, as well as with other measures that include a strong anxiety component, such as the Fear of Negative Evaluation scale (Watson & Friend, 1969), the Impostor Phenomenon scale (Clance, 1985), and the Self-Handicapping scale (Jones & Rhodewalt, 1982). The DPQ is

Table 4.1.
Divergent and Convergent Correlates of the Defensive Pessimism
Questionnaire (DPQ)

	DPQ Academic version	DPQ Social version
Coed Sample 1[a]		
NEO–FFI Extraversion	−.29	−.36
NEO–FFI Neuroticism	.22	.27
NEO–FFI Conscientiousness	.23	.11
NEO–FFI Agreeableness	−.24	−.20
NEO–FFI Openness	.05	.04
Need for Cognition (n Cog)	.13	.09
Need for Structure (n Struct)	.15	.32
Fear of Negative Evaluation (FNE)	.22	.36
Beck Depression Inventory (BDI)	.18	.22
Self-Handicapping scale (SHS)	.27	.49
Repression–Sensitization (R–S)	.26	.29
(high score = sensitizing)		
Optimism (LOT)	−.23	.30
DPQ Social version	−.38	
Coed Sample 2[b]		
ASQ–Internal	.23	
ASQ–Stable	.12	
ASQ–Global	.17	
Female sample[c]		
BFI–Extraversion	−.33	−.46
BFI–Neuroticism	.46	−.49
BFI–Conscientiousness	.10	−.02
BFI–Agreeableness	−.18	−.15
BFI–Openness	−.27	−.19
Self-Attributes Questionnaire (SAQ)	−.31	−.27
Self-Clarity (SC)	−.28	−.43
Impostor Phenomenon scale (IPS)	.48	.64
Optimism (LOT)	−.35	−.30
DPQ Social version	.48	
RRQ–Rumination	.38	.52
RRQ–Reflection	.02	.17

Note. NEO–FFI, Costa & McCrae, 1992; n Cog, Cacioppo, Petty, & Kao, 1984; n Struct, Neuberg & Newsom, 1993; FNE, Watson & Friend, 1969; BDI, Beck, 1976; SHS, Jones & Rhodewalt, 1982; R–S, Epstein & Fenz, 1967 (this version of the R–S scale was developed to minimize its correlation with anxiety); LOT, Scheier & Carver, 1985; ASQ, Peterson et al., 1982; BFI, John, Donahue, & Kentle, 1991; SAQ, Pelham & Swann, 1989; SC, Campbell et al., 1996; IPS, Clance, 1985; RRQ, Trapnell & Campbell, 1999. The Defensives Pessimism Questionnaire (DPQ & R–DPQ) copyright 1994 by Julie K. Norem. Reprinted with permission.
[a]For Sample 1, $N = 189$ except for LOT where $N = 400$.
[b]$N = 180$.
[c]$N = 87$.

also clearly related to, but far from redundant with, measures of other constructs that include aspects of negative thinking, such as Repression–Sensitization (Epstein & Fenz, 1967), and the RRQ–Rumination (Trapnell & Campbell, 1999).[1] The DPQ does not appear, however, to be correlated with measures of more general motivations such as need for cognition or need for structure, or, as a domain-specific strategy for pursuing personal goals, should it correlate with those general motives.

Also not surprisingly, defensive pessimism correlates negatively with self-esteem and with self-clarity (Campbell et al., 1996). Given a willingness to think about negative aspects of both situations and themselves, defensive pessimists include those negative aspects of self in their self-evaluations, and they then score lower in self-esteem. Defensive pessimism, however, may provide individuals experiencing low self-esteem with a way to work effectively toward raising their self-esteem and increasing their sense of clarity about themselves (Norem, 1996; chap. 16, this volume).

The DPQ is intended for use as a domain-specific measure of strategies, and the specific wording of the items should reflect the domain under study. As mentioned above, people may use different strategies in different domains, and this hypothesis is supported by the small-to-moderate correlation between the social and academic versions of the scale, which range between .30 and .50. Thus far, to my knowledge, defensive pessimism has been researched in academic (see Cantor & Norem, 1989; Cantor, Norem, Niedenthal, Langston, & Brower, 1987; Norem & Cantor, 1986b, 1990; Norem & Illingworth, 1993), social (Showers, 1988, 1992), and recreational or sports contexts (Spencer, 1993; Spencer & Norem, 1996) using appropriate versions of the DPQ. Health defensive pessimism has also been researched (see Kiehl, 1995; Norem & Crandall, 1991) using a somewhat different set of specifically focused items. The correlations between the domain-specific versions of the DPQ and other variables are likely to reflect the particular domain under study.

It is worth noting that the social version of the DPQ correlates somewhat higher with several other measures—for example, the Self-Handicapping scale, the Self-Clarity measure, the Impostor Phenomenon scale, and the RRQ–Rumination measure—than does the academic version. This may be because the Social DPQ, worded so that ratings are given for social situations, taps into a broader domain than the academic version, which presumably refers to a more restricted goal domain.

---

[1]The second scale of the RRQ is labeled *reflection*, and thus, it may seem as if it should correlate positively with the reflectivity items on the DPQ. The actual items of the RRQ-Reflection scale, however, focus primarily on the enjoyment of self-reflection, whereas the reflectivity of the defensive pessimist tends to be task-focused, motivated by anxiety, focused on negative possible outcomes, and thus not particularly enjoyable. In other words, people using defensive pessimism before a task are

EMPIRICAL RELATIONSHIP TO OTHER OPTIMISM AND PESSIMISM CONSTRUCTS

Theoretically, as noted above, defensive pessimism as a strategy is distinct from both trait optimism or pessimism, and from a pessimistic attributional style, and the correlations in Table 4.1 support the distinction among those constructs. Thus, although defensive pessimism is clearly related to trait optimism as it is measured by the Life Orientation Test (Scheier & Carver, 1985), the correlations are not high enough to suggest that they are measuring the same construct. Moreover, the domain-specificity evident in the correlations between the social and academic versions of the DPQ further distinguish it from trait optimism, which should affect expectations across different domains and situations.

Similarly, the DPQ does not correlate highly with the subscales of the Attributional Style Questionnaire (Peterson et al., 1982): Its highest correlation is with the Internality subscale ($r = .23$; Norem & Sellars, 1995), which fits other data suggesting that defensive pessimists make internal attributions. This contrasts with those people who have a depressogenic attributional style, however, in that defensive pessimists tend to make internal attributions (specifically, to both effort and ability) for both positive and negative outcomes relevant to the domain in which they use their strategy. In addition their attributions are not consistently global or to stable characteristics as is the case with people who have depressogenic attributional style.

RESEARCH AND ONGOING THEORETICAL DEVELOPMENTS

One of the most interesting developments in research on defensive pessimism has been elaboration of the role of reflectivity in the defensive pessimism strategy and the corresponding exploration of the role of avoidance of reflectivity in strategic optimism. In the following I review research that supports the contention that individuals using defensive pessimism set defensively low expectations and extensively reflect on possible outcomes prior to a performance to feel more "in control" and to keep their anxiety from interfering with their performance. This research also suggests that some individuals use strategic optimism: They do not feel particularly anxious prior to a performance, and they set high expectations. They then actively avoid reflecting on possible outcomes—even positive ones—because doing so would make them anxious and jeopardize their performance.

---

not reflective because they enjoy being reflective, they are reflective because it serves a vital function for them, even if it is somewhat aversive.

Most of the research on defensive pessimism has contrasted it with strategic optimism. People using defensive pessimism construe their goals in significantly different ways than do strategic optimists. Academic defensive pessimists report that academic goals are more stressful and more difficult than do strategic optimists, and they feel less in control and more anxious with respect to those goals—even though the performance histories of these two sets of participants are comparable. This is true whether one asks people to appraise goals they generate themselves and categorize as achievement related, to report on their daily affect in goal-relevant situations by using experience-sampling methods, or to report their feelings of anxiety and control prior to a specific performance such as an exam or an experimental task (Cantor & Norem, 1989; Cantor et al., 1987; Norem, 1987, 1989; Norem & Cantor, 1990; Norem & Illingworth, 1993).

Thus, defensive pessimists are, in an important psychological sense, facing a different set of situations than strategic optimists. They must figure out how to manage their anxiety so that they can approach their goal and how to keep their anxiety from interfering with their performance. The optimists' task, in contrast, is to avoid arousing anxiety by maintaining their positive outlook.

One of the ways to understand how processes unfold over time, as well as to highlight the functions of these particular strategies, is to interfere with them. Thus, in one of the first experiments on defensive pessimism, Norem and Cantor (1986b) interfered with the expectation-setting component of defensive pessimism by telling participants in an experiment that they should expect to do well. Defensive pessimists who were encouraged subsequently performed significantly more poorly on the experimental tasks than did those who were not encouraged (see also Rich & Dalheimer, 1989).

Norem and Illingworth (1993) also tested directly the anxiety management functions of the defensive pessimists' playing-through process, as well as the strategic optimists' avoidance of reflectivity prior to a task. They randomly assigned strategic optimists and defensive pessimists to either a thought-listing condition, in which they had to list their thoughts about an upcoming task in response to a series of probes, or to a distraction condition, in which they worked on a task that had nothing to do with their pending performance. The thought-listing condition was designed to mimic the typical reflectivity or playing-through process used by defensive pessimists prior to a performance, and the distraction condition was intended to simulate the typical preperformance behavior of strategic optimists, as well as to make reflecting on the upcoming task difficult.

As predicted, defensive pessimists were significantly more anxious in the condition in which they were prevented from reflecting prior to their performance (Norem & Illingworth, 1993, Study 1), and they performed significantly more poorly in that condition. Just as important, the optimists were significantly more anxious when they had to reflect about the upcoming task than when they could distract themselves as usual. Mediational analyses show that managing anxiety really is the key to these performance results. This account is further bolstered by physiological data from this study, showing that skin conductance readings illustrate the same interaction pattern as the self-report and performance data.

In a conceptual replication of this experiment, graduate nursing students participated in an experience-sampling study, in which half of them reported on their progress toward self-generated goals when they were randomly "beeped" to fill out emotion and activity reports (Norem & Illingworth, 1993, Study 2). We expected that asking them specifically about their progress would induce active reflection. Defensive pessimists who were prompted to report on their progress reported more positive mood, felt more in control, and found their life tasks easier over a 7-day period than did defensive pessimists who were not prompted. On a follow-up questionnaire, the prompted defensive pessimists also reported more progress toward their goals. In contrast, optimists who were induced to be reflective by this method reported more negative affect, found their tasks more difficult, and reported less overall progress than did optimists who were not prompted to reflect.

I have used the metaphor *harnessing anxiety* to describe how the defensive pessimists' strategy works to allow them to do what they want to do, without being debilitated by their anxiety and negative affect. Defensive pessimism appears to function as a "do-it-yourself" cognitive therapy for anxiety; indeed, it resembles the worst-case analysis and mental rehearsal techniques often used by cognitive therapists (Beck, 1976; Ingram, 1986; Ingram & Hollon, 1986). In contrast, the optimists seem able to avoid becoming anxious by focusing away from thoughts about the upcoming task. If they are forced to think about possible outcomes, though, they do become anxious and perform more poorly. Trying to impose a different strategy on either group disrupts performance, but each group does quite well when using its preferred strategy.

Further data extend the understanding of the role of reflectivity and avoidance of reflectivity for defensive pessimists and strategic optimists, respectively. For example, Spencer and Norem (1996) examined performance on a dart-throwing task as a function of strategy and different kinds of imagery. Strategic optimists and defensive pessimists were randomly assigned to one of three imagery conditions that were modeled after the guided-imagery techniques most commonly used by sports psychologists to help athletes control anxiety and "psych up" for their performances. *Coping imagery* involves imagining something going wrong during a performance or competition and then imagining fixing or recovering from whatever has happened. *Mastery imagery* involves imagining a perfect, flawless performance. *Relaxation*, in contrast to the other two techniques, involves focusing away from thoughts about the performance and focusing on relaxing completely. Conveniently, these techniques represent useful ways to operationalize different important facets of reflectivity. Specifically, coping imagery closely resembles defensive pessimists' reflectivity prior to an upcoming task or performance. Relaxation imagery, in contrast, is similar to what strategic optimists do, in that it involves avoidance of thoughts about performance. Mastery imagery is an especially interesting case, because it involves reflective thought, but only about positive outcomes, in contrast to the defensive pessimists' reflective thought about possible negative outcomes. Thus it is similar to the defensive pessimists' strategy because of the reflectivity involved, but also similar to the optimists' strategy because it avoids negative thinking.

We predicted that as in previous research both defensive pessimists and strategic optimists would perform best on the dart-throwing task when they were in the conditions that best matched their preferred strategies, that is, the coping imagery condition for the defensive pessimists and the relaxation condition for the strategic optimists. The results supported our hypothesis: Defensive pessimists performed significantly better in the coping imagery condition than in the other two conditions, and strategic optimists performed significantly better in the relaxation condition than in the other two conditions. Both groups performed worst in the mastery condition—which did not fit either group's strategy—and, as in previous experimental studies, there were no overall differences in performance between defensive pessimists and strategic optimists. Thus, both groups were relatively debilitated in the conditions that did not fit their strategies, and both groups did relatively well in the conditions that matched their strategies.

Sanna (1996, 1998) also has shown that the content and consequences of pre- and posttask cognition for defensive pessimists and strategic optimists are very different. Congruent with earlier research, his results showed that defensive pessimists preferred upward "prefactuals" as they prepared for a performance. *Prefactual thinking* refers to mental simulation before the fact, and *upward prefactuals* are thoughts about how things might turn out better than expected (e.g., "If I weren't so anxious, my speech would go really well"). Strategic optimists, in contrast, preferred not to engage in prefactual thinking (or reflectivity). They also generated more downward counterfactuals (Sanna, 1996). *Counterfactuals* are mental simulations after the fact of outcomes that are different from actual outcomes. *Downward counterfactuals* focus on outcomes that are worse than the actual ones (e.g., "If I hadn't crammed at the last minute, I would really have bombed the test"). Sanna further showed that negative mood facilitates the defensive pessimists' preferred preparation and their subsequent performance, and positive mood interferes with it (Sanna, 1998). Conversely, positive mood facilitates the optimists' preferred strategy, and negative mood interferes with it and impairs performance. Norem and Illingworth (Illingworth, 1993; Norem & Illing-worth, 1999) also found that defensive pessimists performed best in a negative mood induction condition and worst in a positive mood induction condition, whereas strategic optimists performed best in a positive mood condition.

STRATEGY AND ADAPTATION

The research described earlier suggests that defensive pessimism and strategic optimism have important differences in costs and benefits and different potential risks. As Norem and Illingworth (1993) argued, results from experimental studies in the laboratory support the contention that both defensive pessimism and strategic optimism can work quite well: Across all the laboratory experiments reviewed here, strategic optimists and defensive pessimists perform equally well when they are in conditions that permit or facilitate use of their preferred strategy. Each strategy, however, leaves its user potentially vulnerable to different kinds of disruption (Sanna, 1998).

Thus, defensive pessimists seem to be vulnerable to positive mood because it interferes with their reflectivity prior to a task. It may at first seem counterintuitive that making anxious people feel good would disrupt their performance. Being in a good mood, however, may serve as a cue to stop preparation (Martin, Ward, Achee, & Wyer, 1993). For defensive pessimists, abandoning their anticipatory strategy may leave them signifi-cantly less prepared than they would otherwise be. Feeling good may then mean that they are even more vulnerable to the disruptive effects of anxiety that is re-aroused once they have to begin working on the task.

The performance of strategic optimists, in contrast, seems less vulnera-ble overall to mood inductions prior to a task, although their performance does suffer somewhat in negative mood conditions (Norem & Illingworth, 1999; Sanna, 1998; Showers, 1992). Manipulations that require the strategic optimists to reflect prior to a performance do disrupt their outcomes (Norem & Illingworth, 1993; Spencer & Norem, 1996). It may be that preperfor-mance mood has a less consistent effect than direct manipulation of thought content because being in a negative mood prompts attempts at mood repair that do not specifically involve reflecting about the upcoming task and do not generate anxiety about that task.

When looking at discrete actual performances, defensive pessimism and strategic optimism seem comparably successful for those who typically use them. There are other outcomes to consider, however. For example, defensive pessimists usually report being significantly less satisfied with their performances than do strategic optimists in experimental studies (Norem & Cantor, 1986a, 1986b; Norem & Illingworth, 1993). Similarly, in field studies, defensive pessimists typically report less satisfaction with both their past achievements and their current endeavors, and they also report more negative affect than strategic optimists (Cantor et al., 1987; Norem, 1987; Norem & Cantor, 1990; Norem & Illingworth, 1993). To the extent that one can consider affect an outcome of one's strategy, it appears that in this respect defensive pessimism is less effective than strategic optimism.

There are also some data suggesting that long-term outcomes for defensive pessimists may be worse than those for strategic optimists. Cantor and Norem (1989) reported that after 3 years in college, defensive pessimists reported slightly lower grade point averages and more physical and psychological symptoms than did strategic optimists. It is of interest to note that the worse outcomes were largely attributable to those students who used defensive pessimism in both social and academic domains. The interpersonal consequences of defensive pessimism are largely unstudied (Norem, 1991), but there are data suggesting that people react negatively to others' anxiety (Leary, Kowalski, & Bergen, 1988), as they do to others' depression (Coyne, 1976). To the extent that their strategy is visible to others, defensive pessimists may create negative impressions or annoy the people around them.[2]

Recall also that the correlation (Table 4.1) between social defensive pessimism and indicators of self-esteem difficulties were stronger than those for academic defensive pessimism. It may be that defensive pessimism is less effective as a strategy for social situations, in which success is more subjective and less clearly related to discrete performances for which one can prepare. (See chapters 12 and 16 in this volume for discussions of the cultural contexts influencing evaluation of pessimism and optimism.) Of course it may also be that social anxiety is more generally debilitating than anxiety about academic performance.[3]

Both the affect results and the long-term data suggest that there are significant costs to defensive pessimism. This does not mean, however, that there are no potential costs to strategic optimism. Given the experimental data suggesting that strategic optimists' performance may be disrupted by negative mood and by performance-related thoughts, it is reasonable to ask how they might fare in situations in which attention to negative information

---

[2]Female defensive pessimists list "boring" and "annoying" as characteristics of their feared possible selves more often than do strategic optimists, sugggesting that they may have some insight into the potential effects that their strategy may have on others.

[3]Frequently those hearing about defensive pessimism assume that its function is primarily impression management, that is, that the defensive pessimists are not really pessimistic, but are only trying to control the expectations of their audience or garner reassurance and praise. The available data, however, do not support this interpretation, at least not in its strong form. For example, the patterns of anxiety change as a function of strategy use or lack thereof that are observed in self-report data are repeated in skin conductance measures (Norem & Illingworth, 1993, Study 1). In addition, in Norem's research, defensive pessimists report lower expectations and higher anxiety regardless of whether those reports are made anonymously or publicly. Finally, defensive pessimism is correlated with lower scores on both the self-deception and impression management subscales of the BIDR (Paulhus, 1990).

might be important to future outcomes or to situations that are somehow unavoidable and anxiety arousing.

Kiehl (1995), for example, found that defensive pessimists saw AIDS-related risk behavior as more risky than did strategic optimists. Norem and Crandall (1991) found that defensive pessimists were more interested in receiving information about a fictitious disease that they might have contracted than were strategic optimists. These results are suggestive: If the strategic optimists' attempts to maintain their positive outlook include ignoring or discounting important information or the potential consequences of risky behavior, then this needs to be counted as a significant potential cost to the strategy (see also Weinstein, 1980, for work on the risk perceptions of unrealistic optimists).

Just as important, one must be cautious in evaluating any strategy solely by comparing it to an alternative strategy without consideration of the broader life context in which it is used. The effectiveness of a strategy should be assessed in terms of the goals or problems of those who use it. Strategy use in the real world is nonrandomly determined: Defensive pessimism is used by those who are anxious. They must manage their anxiety to perform well, in contrast to the strategic optimists, who are less troubled initially by anxiety. Defensive pessimism seems an excellent strategy for those who are anxious, precisely because it addresses their psychological reality: the need to control anxiety, which rarely simply goes away by wishful thinking. Although it is interesting to compare the outcomes of defensive pessimists and strategic optimists, one must also consider how the anxious defensive pessimists might fare without their strategy.

Sanna (1998) noted that in both the mental simulation and the coping literature there is a distinction between the preparative or self-improvement functions and the affective functions of simulation and coping strategies (Folkman & Lazarus, 1991; Markman, Gavanski, Sherman, & McMullen, 1993; Wood & Taylor, 1991). He argued that defensive pessimists seem to make more use of the preparative functions of mental simulation, whereas strategic optimists use the affective functions to maintain their positive outlook. I further suggest that defensive pessimism may be an especially useful strategy for self-improvement. In a study of social performance, participants made a 3-minute videotape in which they talked about themselves, ostensibly so that others could get to know them (similar to a dating service tape; Norem, 1991). Observers watched the tape and rated the performance on the same scales that the actors used to rate themselves. Overall, observers did not rate social defensive pessimists and strategic optimists differently.[4]

---

[4]It is important to note that observers only saw the actual performance in this study, not the preparation for the performance. If observers had watched or heard the anxious defensive pessimists as they prepared, they might have rated them less positively.

However, defensive pessimists rated themselves higher than did observers on a measure of how much they needed to improve their social self-presentation. In contrast, strategic optimists rated themselves lower on need for improvement than observers rated them. Participants in this study were given both negative and positive false feedback about their videotapes and then given a surprise recall test about that feedback later in the study. Overall, defensive pessimists were less accurate in their recall of the feedback, primarily because they recalled positive feedback as significantly less positive than it actually was; they were accurate in remembering the negative feedback. In contrast, optimists remembered the negative feedback as significantly less negative than it actually was, and they were more accurate in their recall of the positive feedback.

The defensive pessimists did not "feel good" relative to the strategic optimists in this study, nor were they particularly accurate overall; nevertheless, they clearly did pay attention to negative feedback, and they were focused on improving their performance. In the real world, negative feedback may be informative and helpful to one's attempts to improve oneself, even if it is unpleasant data to process. Defensive pessimists are clearly willing to "hear" that feedback, and thus, they would seem more likely than strategic optimists to benefit from it.

Further data specifically suggest that defensive pessimism may be useful for self-improvement and generally suggest that it is a useful strategy for those who are anxious. In a longitudinal study of female college students, I compared defensive pessimists, not only to strategic optimists, but also to highly anxious students who did not report using defensive pessimism (Norem, 1996). Those students using defensive pessimism were not significantly different from the others in the anxious group in levels of trait anxiety, in any of the "Big Five" personality traits, in SAT scores, in high school grade point average, or in self-esteem at the beginning of their first year of college. Both of the anxious groups initially reported lower self-esteem than did strategic optimists in the sample. Over their college years, however, the defensive pessimists showed significant increases in self-esteem. The anxious students who did not use defensive pessimism, in contrast, showed no significant increase in self-esteem through college. In addition, defensive pessimists achieved both higher grade point averages and greater subjective satisfaction than did other anxious students. Defensive pessimism, in this comparison, appears quite adaptive.

It is important to note, however, that although defensive pessimism may be helpful, those who use it do not necessarily become less anxious or generally more positive over time. Indeed, there may be self-perpetuating effects of the strategy (Sanna, 1998). Defensive pessimists are likely to recall their anxiety prior to any given success, and that is likely to color their anticipation of future endeavors. They are likely to recall their effort and to attribute their success to their effort. This internal attribution is positive in the sense that it suggests success is under one's control and replicable, but it also places emphasis on the necessity for hard work, and it has affectively different consequences than believing that success is relatively assured because of one's ability. Recalling the social performance study, if defensive pessimists typically recall or interpret positive feedback as less positive than it actually is, and if they focus particularly on negative feedback, then they are likely to maintain their sense of anxiety, their low expectations, and their focus on potential negative outcomes the next time they encounter a similar situation. Correspondingly, if the optimists pay relatively less attention to negative feedback or are more likely to remember it as positive, or if they simply remember positive feedback better than negative feedback, the next time they enter a similar situation, they are not likely to feel anxious or stressed.

Despite the potentially self-perpetuating affective cycle that might be associated with each strategy, however, strategies are hypothesized to be potentially changeable. Were there to be significant changes in construal of self, beliefs about the world, or appraisal of goals, one might expect corresponding strategy change. A spectacular failure, especially one that could be traced to lack of preparation for the unexpected, could induce more reflection among strategic optimists. Habituation to a particular situation might sufficiently decrease anxiety for the defensive pessimists so that they could anticipate without worry. Indeed, Martin (1999) found significant changes in strategy during the first 2 years of being at a university among Australian students. He showed that there was significantly more change in strategies than in other personality variables over this time, which fits with the theoretical conception of strategies as more mutable than traits or motives. In addition, he was systematically able to relate strategy change to significant changes in life circumstances. Specifically, those students who became more anxious about their academic work because of their experiences were more likely to change from using strategic optimism to using defensive pessimism. In contrast, those students who began to feel as if they were in control of their academic work were more likely to adopt a more optimistic strategy.

CONCLUSION AND FUTURE DIRECTIONS

Research on defensive pessimism and strategic optimism is relevant to other research on optimism and pessimism for several reasons. It is useful to note that pessimistic expectations can be merely defensive, that is, that they do not necessarily lead to self-fulfilling prophecies. Defensive pessimism, although perhaps in some sense a special case, suggests that personality places limits on the extent to which one can assume that positive thinking always leads to positive outcomes. More broadly, the research reviewed above points to the importance of considering expectations, or virtually any single trait or tendency, in the broader context of individuals' personalities and of their life contexts. This research shows that there are multiple paths that people may navigate toward their goals and that sometimes their goals reflect differences in their starting points. This consideration is important both to efforts to capture the texture of real life in psychological theories, as well as to attempts to apply the results of psychological research in therapeutic or other contexts. World outlooks are not "one size fits all" because people do not all live in the same world. Psychologists and educators do a disservice to the people they are trying to help if they ignore individual differences in temperament, history, and circumstance that make particular strategies more or less appropriate for specific individuals (see chap. 12 in this volume).

A number of important questions about defensive pessimism and strategic optimism await further research. As already discussed, there is relatively little work on the interpersonal consequences of defensive pessimism. It will be interesting to explore both short- and long-term reactions to individuals who use the strategy. One obvious question is whether one's own preferred strategies influence one's reactions to others' strategies, for example, do defensive pessimists get along better with other defensive pessimists than with strategic optimists?

The influence of both strategic optimism and defensive pessimism on decision making is also a potentially fruitful arena for further exploration. One might reasonably predict that defensive pessimists would be relatively averse to risk, whereas strategic optimists might take bigger risks. Alternatively, the defensive pessimists' extensive preparation might make them more willing to take some kinds of risks, for example, in cases in which extensive information is available. In a domain such as the stock market, the two strategies could lead to markedly different outcomes over time: The defensive pessimists might be expected both to have fewer large losses and fewer large gains than do the strategic optimists. More generally, relatively little research on these strategies outside of the academic domain, among people other than college students has been conducted.

One of the most important remaining questions about these strategies concerns their developmental origins. Although there are some data about the family environments of defensive pessimists and strategic optimists (Norem, 1987), there has been little systematic exploration of the factors that might influence who develops each strategy. Similarly, virtually nothing is known about when the strategies might emerge. Also little is known about how flexible individuals might be in their use of various strategies, which may prove to be very important to their adaptive value.

A pessimist might see the number and range of these questions as daunting, but let us reflect that although the pitfalls encountered as we continue this research may be considerable, the potential rewards in understanding are also great, and the journey itself should prove fascinating. A good defensive pessimist, then, would confront his or her anxiety and persevere.

REFERENCES

Adler, A. (1935/1979). Typology of meeting life problems. In H. L. Ansbacher & R. R. Ansbacher (Eds.), *Alfred Adler: Superiority and social interest* (pp. 66–71). New York: W. W. Norton.

Beck, A. T. (1976). *Cognitive therapy and the emotional disorders*. New York: International Universities Press.

Berglas, S. (1985). Self-handicapping and self-handicappers: A cognitive-attributional model of interpersonal self-protective behavior. In R. Hogan (Ed.), *Perspectives in personality* (Vol. 1, pp. 235–270). Greenwich, CT: JAI Press.

Caccioppo, J. T., Petty, R. E., & Kao, C. F. (1984). The efficient assessment of need for cognition. *Journal of Personality Assessment, 48,* 306–307.

Campbell, J. D., Trapnell, P. D., Heine, S. J., Lavalee, L. F., Katz, I. M., & Lehman, D. R. (1996). Self-concept clarity: Measurement, personality correlates, and cultural boundaries. *Journal of Personality and Social Psychology, 70,* 141–156.

Cantor, N., & Kihlstrom, J. F. (1987). *Personality and social intelligence*. Englewood Cliffs, NJ: Erlbaum.

Cantor, N., & Norem, J. K. (1989). Defensive pessimism and stress and coping. *Social Cognition, 7,* 92–112.

Cantor, N., Norem, J. K., Niedenthal, P. M., Langston, C. A., & Brower, A. M. (1987). Life tasks, self-concept ideals, and cognitive strategies in a life transition. *Journal of Personality and Social Psychology, 53,* 1178–1191.

Clance, P. R. (1985). *The impostor phenomenon: Overcoming the fear that haunts your success*. Atlanta, GA: Peachtree.

Costa, P. T., & McCrae, R. R. (1992). *Revised NEO Personality Inventory (NEO-PI-R) and NEO Five-Factor Inventory (NEO-FFI) professional manual*. Odessa, FL: Psychological Assessment Resources.

Coyne, J. (1976). Depression and the response of others. *Journal of Abnormal Psychology, 85,* 29–45.

Cuddihy, N., & Ronan, G. F. (1990, August). *Relationship between optimism, defensive pessimism and personal problem-solving*. Paper presented at the 98th Annual Convention of the American Psychological Association, Boston, MA.

Epstein, S., & Fenz, W. B. (1967). The detection of areas of emotional stress through variations in perceptual threshold and physiological arousal. *Journal of Experimental Research in Personality, 2,* 191–199.

Folkman, S., & Lazarus, R. S. (1991). Coping and emotion. In A. Monat & R. S. Lazarus (Eds.), *Stress and coping: An anthology* (3rd ed., pp. 207–227). New York: Guilford.

Hammontree, S. R., & Ronan, G. F. (1992, August). *Optimism, pessimism and defensive pessimism*. Paper presented at the 100th Annual Convention of the American Psychological Society, Washington, DC.

Higgins, R. L., & Harris, R. N. (1988). Strategic "alcohol" use: Drinking to self-handicap. *Journal of Social and Clinical Psychology, 6*, 191–202.

Illingworth, K. S. S. (1993). *Cognitive strategies and mood: The role of affect in the strategic use of optimism and defensive pessimism*. Unpublished doctoral dissertation, Northeastern University, Boston, MA.

Illingworth, K. S. S., & Norem, J. K. (1991). *Convergent and divergent correlates of optimism and defensive pessimism*. Paper presented at the Midwestern Psychological Association, Chicago, IL.

Ingram, R. E. (Ed.). (1986). *Information processing approaches to clinical psychology*. Orlando, FL: Academic Press.

Ingram, R. E., & Hollon, S. D. (1986). Cognitive therapy of depression from an information processing perspective. In R. E. Ingram (Ed.), *Information processing approaches to clinical psychology* (pp. 22–43). San Diego, CA: Academic Press.

Isaacowitz, D. M. & Seligman, M. E. P. (1998 August). Prevention of depression in older adults: Theory, methodology, and pitfalls. Invited paper presented in Opportunities and Pitfalls in Adult and Older Adult Prevention Research. Symposium at the annual meeting of the American Psychological Association, San Francisco, CA.

John, O. P., Donahue, E. M., & Kentle, R. L. (1991, July). *The "Big Five" Inventory— versions 4a and 54* (Tech. Rep. No. 10). Berkeley, CA: University of California at Berkeley, Institute of Personality and Social Research.

Jones, E. E., & Rhodewalt, F. (1982). *Self-Handicapping Scale*. Unpublished scale. Princeton University, NJ.

Kiehl, E. (1995). *Attitudes towards AIDS among unrealistic optimists, health optimists, and health defensive pessimists*. Unpublished honors thesis. Psychology Department, Wellesley College, Wellesley, MA.

Leary, M. R., Kowalski, R. M., & Bergen, D. J. (1988). Interpersonal information acquisition and confidence in first encounters. *Personality and Social Psychology Bulletin, 14*, 68–77.

Markman, K. D., Gavanski, I., Sherman, S. J., & McMullen, M. N. (1993). The mental simulation of better and worse possible worlds. *Journal of Experimental Social Psychology, 29*, 87–109.

Martin, A. (1999). *Self-handicapping and defensive pessimism: Predictors and consequences from a self-worth motivation perspective*. Unpublished doctoral dissertation, University of Western Sydney, Sydney, Australia.

Martin, L. L., Ward, D. W., Achee, J. W., & Wyer, R. S. (1993). Mood as input: People have to interpret the motivational implications of their moods. *Journal of Personality and Social Psychology, 64*, 317–326.

Neuberg, S. L., & Newsom, J. T. (1993). Personal need for structure: Individual differences in the desire for simple structure. *Journal of Personality and Social Psychology, 65*, 113–131.

Norem, J. K. (1987). *Strategic realities: Optimism and defensive pessimism.* Unpublished doctoral dissertation, University of Michigan, Ann Arbor.

Norem, J. K. (1989). Cognitive strategies as personality: Effectiveness, specificity, flexibility, and change. In D. M. Buss & N. Cantor (Eds.), *Personality psychology: Recent trends and emerging issues* (pp. 45–60). New York: Springer-Verlag.

Norem, J. K. (1991, May). *Self-enhancement and self-deception: Some costs of optimism and defensive pessimism.* Paper presented at the Midwestern Psychological Association, Chicago, IL.

Norem, J. K. (1996, August). *Cognitive strategies and the rest of personality.* Paper presented at the Annual Meeting of the American Psychological Association, Toronto, Canada.

Norem, J. K. (1998). Should we lower our defenses about defense mechanisms? *Journal of Personality, 66*, 895–917.

Norem, J. K., & Cantor, N. (1986a). Anticipatory and post hoc cushioning strategies: Optimism and defensive pessimism in "risky" situations. *Cognitive Therapy and Research, 10*, 347–362.

Norem, J. K., & Cantor, N. (1986b). Defensive pessimism: Harnessing anxiety as motivation. *Journal of Personality and Social Psychology, 51*, 1208–1217.

Norem, J. K., & Cantor, N. (1990). Cognitive strategies, coping and perceptions of competence. In R. J. Sternberg & J. J. Kolligian (Eds.), *Competence considered* (pp. 190–204). New Haven, CT: Yale University Press.

Norem, J. K., & Crandall, C. S. (1991, June). *Defensive pessimism and repression-sensitization show discriminant validity.* Paper presented at the 3rd Annual Convention of the American Psychological Society, Washington, DC.

Norem, J. K., & Illingworth, K. S. S. (1993). Strategy-dependent effects of reflecting on self and tasks: Some implications for optimism and defensive pessimism. *Journal of Personality and Social Psychology, 65*, 822–835.

Norem, J. K., & Illingworth, K. S. S. (1999). *Mood and performance among strategic optimists and defensive pessimists.* Unpublished manuscript. Department of Psychology, Wellesley College. Wellesley, MA.

Norem, J. K., & Sellars, R. (1995). Unpublished correlation matrix. University of Virginia, Charlottesville.

Paulhus, D. L. (1990). Measurement and control of response bias. In J. P. Robinson, P. Shaver, & L. Wrightsman (Eds.), *Measures of personality and social psychological attitudes* (pp. 17–60). San Diego, CA: Academic Press.

Pelham, B. W., & Swann, W. B., Jr. (1989). From self-conceptions to self-worth: On the sources and structure of global self-esteem. *Journal of Personality and Social Psychology, 57*, 672–680.

Peterson, C., Semmel, A., von Baeyer, C., Abramson, L. Y., Metalsky, G. I., & Seligman, M. E. P. (1982). The Attributional Style Questionnaire. *Cognitive Therapy and Research, 6*, 287–299.

Rich, A. R., & Dalheimer, D. (1989). The power of negative thinking: Irrational cognitions. *Journal of Cognitive Psychotherapy: An International Quarterly, 3*, 15–30.

Sanna, L. J. (1996). Defensive pessimism, optimism, and simulating alternatives: Some ups and downs of prefactual and counterfactual thinking. *Journal of Personality and Social Psychology, 71*, 1029–1036.

Sanna, L. J. (1998). Defensive pessimism, and optimism: The bitter-sweet influence of mood on performance and prefactual and counterfactual thinking. *Cognition and Emotion, 12*, 635–665.

Scheier, M. F., & Carver, C. S. (1985). Optimism, coping and health: Assessment and implications of generalized outcome expectancies. *Health Psychology, 4*, 219–247.

Showers, C. (1988). The effects of how and why thinking on perceptions of future negative events. *Cognitive Therapy and Research, 12*, 225–240.

Showers, C. (1992). The motivational and emotional consequences of considering positive or negative possibilities for an upcoming event. *Journal of Personality and Social Psychology, 63*, 474–483.

Showers, C., & Ruben, C. (1990). Distinguishing defensive pessimism from depression: Negative expectations and positive coping mechanisms. *Cognitive Therapy and Research, 14*, 385–399.

Spencer, S. M. (1993). *Defensive pessimism and strategic optimism in the athletic domain: An evaluation of performance outcomes and health-related aspects.* Unpublished doctoral dissertation, Northeastern University, Boston, MA.

Spencer, S. M., & Norem, J. K. (1996). Reflection and distraction: Defensive pessimism, strategic optimism, and performance. *Personality and Social Psychology Bulletin, 22*, 354–365.

Taylor, S. E., & Brown, J. D. (1988). Illusion and well-being: A social psychological perspective on mental health. *Psychological Bulletin, 103*, 193–210.

Trapnell, P. D., & Campbell, J. D. (1999). Private self-consciousness and the five-factor model of personality: Distinguishing rumination from reflection. *Journal of Personality and Social Psychology, 76*, 305–319.

Watson, D., & Friend, R. (1969). Measurement of social-evaluative anxiety. *Journal of Consulting and Clinical Psychology, 33*, 448–457.

Weinstein, N. D. (1980). Unrealistic optimism about future life events. *Journal of Personality and Social Psychology, 39*, 806–820.

Wood, J. V., & Taylor, S. E. (1991). Serving self-relevant goals through social comparison. In J. Suls & T. A. Wills (Eds.), *Social comparison: Contemporary theory and research* (pp. 23–49). Hillsdale, NJ: Erlbaum.

5

OPTIMISM AND HOPE CONSTRUCTS: VARIANTS ON A POSITIVE EXPECTANCY THEME

C. R. SNYDER, SUSIE C. SYMPSON, SCOTT T. MICHAEL, AND JEN CHEAVENS

In recent years, the effects of positive thinking have received growing attention by psychologists and health professionals (Snyder & McCullough, 2000). Since the late 1950s, increasing numbers of physicians have acknowledged the benefits of thoughts and feelings characterized by hope (Frankl, 1963; Pelletier, 1977; Schmale, 1972; Siegel, 1986; Simonton, Matthew-Simonton, & Creighton, 1978). As early as 1959, for example, Karl Menninger called on his colleagues to rediscover the power of hope. His sentiments were echoed in a 1975 commencement address in which Jerome Frank acknowledged that Cartesian dualism, embraced by the world of medicine, resulted in practitioners ignoring the hope and faith of their clients. He went on to suggest that hope was crucial for the course of treatment (see Snyder, Michael, & Cheavens, 1999). These pioneers in the general area of positive thinking would be pleased to see that the advantages long thought to be associated with a positive mental attitude are being confirmed by recent psychological researchers (Scheier & Carver, 1985, 1992; Snyder, 1994, 2000a, 2000b; Snyder, Irving, & Anderson, 1991). As psychology has embraced the importance of a positive mental attitude, a number of theoretical approaches have been proposed. In this chapter, we examine two of these approaches: optimism and hope.

In the seminal introductory article on their concept, Scheier and Carver (1985) defined *optimism* as the stable tendency to "believe that good rather than bad things will happen" (p. 219). Their Life Orientation Test (LOT) was revised nearly a decade later (LOT–R; Scheier, Carver, & Bridges, 1994). For a more thorough description of the LOT, see the methodological introduction (chap. 9, this volume).

A cognitive model of *hope* has been proposed as another explanation for the positive thinking process (Snyder, 1989, 1994, 2000a; Snyder, Irving, et al., 1991). Although most people may think of an optimist as "being hopeful," the two concepts as described in this chapter have similarities, as well as some differences. In the following sections, we present Snyder's model of hope and the measures developed to assess individual differences in levels of hope. Then the similarities and differences between hope and optimism are discussed. Research findings relevant to hope also are addressed. Finally, brief statements are made about the major distinction and fundamental shared characteristic between the concepts of optimism and hope.

HOPE THEORY

Snyder and his colleagues (Snyder, Harris, et al., 1991; Snyder, Irving, et al., 1991) conceptualized hope as a cognitive set that is directed at goal attainment. Hope is seen as having two interrelated components that are reciprocal. First, one must have a perception of successful agency regarding one's goals. Agency involves a sense of successful use of energy in the pursuit of goals in one's past, present, and future. Thus, *agency* is the mental motivation that one uses to initiate and sustain movement toward a goal (Snyder, 1994, 2000a). The second component necessary to this conception of hope is the perceived ability to generate successful routes or pathways to attain one's goals. In other words, *pathways thinking* is the perceived capability of imagining ways to reach a given goal, including the formation of subgoals along the way (Snyder, 1994, 2000a). Thus, *hope* is formally defined as "a positive motivational state that is based on an interactively derived sense of successful (a) agency (goal-directed energy), and (b) pathways (planning to meet goals)" (Snyder, Irving, et al., 1991, p. 287).

According to hope theory, successful movement toward one's goals requires both agency and pathways thinking. In this regard, one may have known people who profess to have the requisite agency thinking to propel them toward a future destination, yet they lack the perceived ability to plan effective strategies (pathways) to get there. On the other hand, one also may be familiar with those people who have thought of numerous ways to achieve their goals, but they seem to lack the agency to implement these plans. These people may appear to be idle dreamers, or they even may be labeled as just plain lazy. In our model, we suggest that the person lacking either agency or pathways thinking also lacks hope. In this regard, Snyder and his colleagues (Snyder, Harris, et al., 1991) argued that "to sustain movement toward the goals in one's life . . . both the sense of agency and the sense of pathways must become operative. That is, both agency and pathways are necessary, but neither is sufficient to define hope" (p. 571).

In Figure 5.1 we see that one's dispositional agency and pathways (at the far left, "learning history") provide the starting point for any potential goal-pursuit activity. For detailed discussions of the developmental processes that produce agency and pathways thought, see Snyder (1994, chap. 3), Snyder (2000a), and Snyder, McDermott, Cook, and Rapoff (1997).

The next step in the hope model is an appraisal of a goal outcome value, such that a goal must be of sufficient magnitude to command sustained

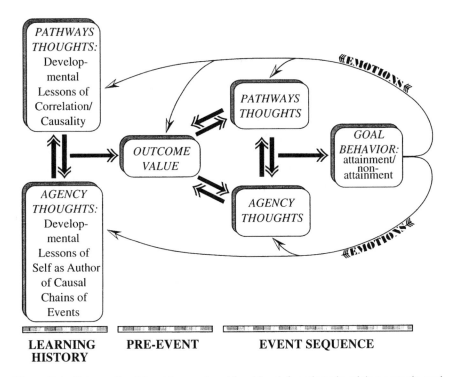

Figure 5.1. Schematic of feed-forward and feed-back functions involving agentic and pathways goal-directed thoughts in hope theory.

attention (see the "pre-event" stage in Figure 5.1). Assuming that the goal is of sufficient value, the "event sequence" begins with the agency and pathways components iterating so as to enhance each other. That is to say, the agency and pathways components are continually affecting and being affected by each other. Thus, there is a reciprocal action between the belief that one can attain one's goals and the perception that there are effective strategies to attain those goals.

Based on the iterative agency and pathways cognitive analysis, the person moves toward the goal and either does or does not attain it (see "goal behavior" in Figure 5.1). As can be seen in the boldface arrows that run left to right, a person's goal-directed thinking advances, but with the possibility of feedback within the major components (observe arrows going both ways). After the goal attainment or nonattainment, there are feedback processes that reflect the impact of the resulting goal engagement on the other components of the hope model (see regular weight arrows moving from right to left). "Riding" on these feedback lines, the person's emotional reaction is being fed back to the components in the system. In hope theory, positive emotions are hypothesized to result from perceived successful goal attainment; conversely, negative emotions reflect a perceived impeded or unattained goal outcome. Thus, in hope theory, perceptions about one's success in goal pursuits drive emotion (see Snyder et al.,1996, for empirical support). Overall we have posited an interrelated system of teleological thinking that permits modifying feedback at various points in the temporal sequence of our hope model. Accordingly, through the feedback process, an individual's level of hope is sustained or changed over time.

Optimism, as defined by Scheier and Carver (1985) and hope, as defined by Snyder and his colleagues (1991) are constructed within an expectancy-value framework to motivation; moreover, both are conceptualized as relatively stable characteristics that reflect general expectations about the future. These concepts differ, however, in how the expectancies are conceptualized to influence behaviors. Although they propose that outcome expectancies are the most important element that is related to predicting goal-directed behaviors, Scheier and Carver (1985) placed relatively less emphasis on the bases of these expectancies. Scheier and Carver intentionally de-emphasized the role of personal efficacy in optimism. On this point they wrote,

> Our own theoretical approach emphasizes a person's expectancies of good or bad outcomes. Most of the current measures that might otherwise be seen as adequate measures of optimism have confounded these *outcome* expectancies with a host of related variables such as morale, meaningfulness, well-being, and most notably, attributions of causes for the expectancies. It is our position that outcome expectancies per se are the best predictors of behavior rather than the bases from which

those expectancies were derived. A person may hold favorable expectancies for a number of reasons—personal ability, because the person is lucky, or because he is favored by others. The result should be an optimistic outlook—expectations that good things will happen. (Scheier & Carver, 1985, p. 223)

The hope model involves two types of expectancies: agency and pathways. The agency component is analogous to an efficacy expectancy, a belief in one's ability to successfully begin and maintain movement toward one's goals. As we have described in the hope model, one's perceived agency is based on previous goal-pursuit experience and feedback in a given goal pursuit (Snyder, Irving, et al., 1991). Agency interacts with the perceived ability to generate strategies that can be used to achieve those goals (i.e., the pathways component of hope); further, it is the continuous interaction of these two cognitive components that results in an outcome expectancy related to goal pursuits. Thus, in the Scheier and Carver model of optimism, it appears to be implicitly assumed that the pathways-related expectations in relation to goals are being tapped, whereas in hope theory, there is an explicit emphasis on the pathways component. To highlight this distinction, the optimism model rests on agency-like expectancies regarding goal attainment, whereas in the hope model, the pathways component of goal-directed thought is added.

Although optimism as measured by the LOT does not explicitly tap the pathways component, it should be acknowledged that from the earliest (e.g., Scheier & Carver, 1985) to most recent papers (e.g., Carver & Scheier, 1999), there are indications that optimists implicitly may use such planful thought. That is to say, the optimists, as measured by the LOT, exhibit elevated problem-focused coping (Scheier, Weintraub, & Carver, 1986; Strutton & Lumpkin, 1992) and planfulness (Fontaine, Manstead, & Wagner, 1993; Friedman et al., 1992). Therefore, the positive goal-directed expectancies as tapped by responses to the LOT and LOT–R may capture pathways-related thinking. In this regard, hope theory and related measurement devices for children (Snyder, Hoza, et al., 1997) and adults (Snyder, Harris, et al., 1991; Snyder, Sympson, et al., 1996) explicitly build in the pathways component. On this point, because items directly tapping pathways are not on the LOT or the LOT–R, it is not surprising that the pathways component of the Hope Scale has been found to be orthogonal to items on the LOT in a factor analysis (Magaletta & Oliver, 1999). How the Hope Scale with its explicit pathways component can provide unique predictive variance in relation to the LOT will be discussed subsequently.

In keeping with the two-component definition of hope, a scale was developed to assess individual differences in levels of dispositional hope. The Hope Scale (Snyder, Harris, et al., 1991) contains both the agency and pathways components of hope, and it is the focus of the next section.

As shown in Appendix 5.1, the Hope Scale contains four items tapping agentic thought, four items tapping pathways thought, and four filler items. The respondent uses an 8-point response continuum to rate the personal applicability of each item, with total Hope Scale scores ranging from a low of 8 to a high of 64. Additionally, for those people who may be interested in an ongoing, momentary index of hope, we have developed the State Hope Scale (Snyder, Sympson, et al., 1996), which can be seen in Appendix 5.2. This brief index has three pathways and three agency items, and people use the same response continuum as for the dispositional Hope Scale. Unlike the dispositional Hope Scale, the items on the State Hope Scale reflect ongoing goal-related thoughts, and the person is asked to respond while thinking about the "here and now." Total State Hope Scale scores can range from a low of 6 to a high of 48.

COMPARING THE DISPOSITIONAL HOPE SCALE AND THE LOT

The Hope Scale (Snyder, Harris, et al., 1991), and the LOT/LOT–R (Scheier & Carver, 1985; Scheier et al., 1994) have many things in common. Fundamentally, both stem from an expectancy-value approach to motivation, both were designed to assess individual differences in what are thought to be stable characteristics reflecting general expectations about the future, and both have been submitted to considerable validational procedures and used in a number of studies.

Factor Structure

Although both the LOT and the Hope Scale have been found to have two factors, Scheier and Carver (1985) described the factors of the LOT as positive and negative views of the same concept ("I'm always optimistic about my future" and "I rarely count on good things happening to me"). In the validation studies of the subsequently developed LOT–R, Scheier, Carver, and Bridges (1994) found one factor, which they labeled "optimism." In another analysis, Affleck and Tennen (1996) suggested that the LOT contains optimism and pessimism as two orthogonal (independent) constructs; moreover, confirmatory factor analyses have revealed that the LOT consists of separate optimism and pessimism factors (Robinson-Whelen, Kim, MacCallum, & Kiecolt-Glaser, 1997).

Factor analytic procedures have shown that the Hope Scale has two distinct factors that correspond with the theoretical model. Four agency items tap individuals' sense of successful determination in relation to their goals. Of these, one item refers to the past ("I've been pretty successful in life"), two items refer to the present ("I energetically pursue my goals" and "I meet the goals that I set for myself"), and one item refers to the future ("My past experiences have prepared me well for my future"; Snyder, Harris, et al., 1991). The second factor consists of the four items assessing an individual's belief in his or her ability to generate the pathways to goals and overcome any obstacles that may be encountered (e.g., "I can think of many ways to get out of a jam. Even when others get discouraged, I know I can find a way to solve the problem"; Snyder, Harris, et al. 1991). Although factor analyses of the Hope Scale support the existence of the two separate components, the agency and pathways components are positively correlated with each other (typical magnitudes of $rs = .40$). Thus, although agency and pathways are related, they are not measuring the same thing (Snyder, Harris, et al., 1991). Furthermore, confirmatory factor analytic procedures have shown that the Hope Scale indeed reflects an overarching hope construct that is undergirded by the agency and pathways components (Babyak, Snyder, & Yoshinoba, 1993).

In light of the conflicting findings regarding the factor structure of the LOT/LOT–R, additional studies would be enlightening. One such possible study would involve giving a large sample of research participants both the LOT–R and Hope Scale. We hypothesize that factor analysis on all the items would show that the optimism items of the LOT–R and the agency items of the Hope Scale load on one factor. Another means of investigating a similar question would be to examine the subscale patterns of correlations. In this regard, the LOT–R optimism items should relate more strongly to the agency than the pathways subscales of the Hope Scale. These predicted findings would support our speculation that hope may add predictive power beyond optimism in that both the agentic and pathways components are explicitly tapped by the Hope Scale. The only reported study related to the aforementioned point was a factor analysis conducted by Magaletta and Oliver (1999), who found that the pathways component in the Hope Scale was orthogonal to LOT items.

Internal Consistency

Any scale should demonstrate that the items are internally consistent (i.e., items relate together so as to measure the same concept, such as optimism or hope). Numerous studies have yielded Cronbach's alpha coefficients (a statistical procedure for corroborating the internal cohesiveness of scale items with each other) within acceptable ranges for the overall Hope Scale, as well as the two subscales. In the initial scale development article including eight samples (Snyder, Harris, et al., 1991), the Hope Scale exhibited alpha coefficients ranging from .74 to .84 (with statistically significant item-remainder coefficients of .23 to .63). The four-item agency subscale had alpha coefficients ranging from .71 to .76 (significant item-remainder coefficients [the extent to which individual items correlate with the total of all other items when those individual item scores are subtracted] of .40 to .72), and the four-item pathways subscale had alpha coefficients ranging from .63 to .80 (significant item-remainder coefficients of .36 to .63). Subsequent studies routinely have produced alpha coefficients ranging in the high .70s to the high .80s (Snyder, Sympson, et al., 1996).

Scheier and Carver (1985) reported a Cronbach alpha coefficient of .76 for the LOT; similarly, Scheier, Carver, and Bridges (1994) reported a Cronbach alpha coefficient of .78 for the LOT–R. Thus, both the LOT/LOT–R and the Hope Scale have acceptable internal reliabilities.

Temporal Stability

Because the Hope Scale was developed as a dispositional index, one would expect an individual's scores to remain stable across time. Different samples of college undergraduates have produced significant test–retest correlations: $r = .85$ over a 3-week interval (Anderson, 1988); $r = .78$ over a 4-week interval (Sympson, 1993); $r = .73$ over an 8-week interval (Harney, 1989); and $rs = .76$ and .82, respectively, over a 10-week interval in two studies (Gibb, 1990; Yoshinobu, 1989).

Scheier and Carver (1985) found a test–retest correlation of .79 over a 4-week interval for the LOT. Additionally, for the LOT–R, Scheier, Carver, and Bridges (1994) reported acceptable test–retest correlations for 4 months ($r = .68$), 12 months ($r = .60$), 24 months ($r = .56$), and 28 months ($r = .79$). These correlations, taken together, indicate that the Hope Scale, the LOT, and the LOT–R all exhibit both short- and long-term temporal stability. That is to say, the score on any one of the scales derived at one point in time is similar to the score when the same test is taken again at a later time.

Convergent and Discriminant Validity

To demonstrate the concurrent validity of a new instrument, researchers need to examine the correlation of responses on the new scale with responses to selected existing scales. Measures that are designed to gauge similar constructs should yield positive relationships by way of correlations, and scales evaluating conceptually opposed processes are expected to yield negative correlations. This is the essence of convergent validity. Likewise, no significant correlations should be found between scores on a new scale and scores on those measures supposedly tapping unrelated concepts, which is the core idea of discriminant validity. In this regard, both the Hope Scale and the LOT/LOT–R have been evaluated in relation to a number of other measures. The results of identical comparisons are reviewed next.

As would be expected, both the LOT and Hope Scale scores were positively correlated with Rosenberg's (1965) Self-Esteem Scale. The LOT exhibited a correlation of .48 (Scheier & Carver, 1985), and the Hope Scale correlation was .58 (Snyder, Harris, et al., 1991). In reflecting on the theoretical underpinnings of these constructs, we think that these results are understandable. Although the authors of the LOT acknowledge that "most optimists probably derive their sense of optimism from a history of successes, in which they have demonstrated their personal mastery," they also believed that "there exists a substantial minority of people for whom a sense of optimism derives from external" causes (Scheier & Carver, 1985, p. 221). In comparison, hope theory focuses on the experiences that people have had that contribute to their belief in future events. Furthermore, individuals with higher levels of hope would be expected to have an enhanced sense of self-esteem both because of past successes and because of their beliefs that workable routes to future goal pursuits are likely.

Both Hope Scale and LOT scores have correlated positively with scores on the Generalized Expectancy for Success Scale (GESS; Fibel & Hale, 1978). The GESS assesses expectancies for attaining goals across a variety of situations, and it has exhibited positive correlations of .54 and .55 with the Hope Scale in two separate studies (Gibb, 1990; Holleran & Snyder, 1990). The correlation of the GESS with the LOT was .56 in a study reported by Smith, Pope, Rhodewalt, and Poulton (1989).

Those people who have higher levels of hope and optimism also should score lower on measures of hopelessness and depression. When LOT and Hope Scale scores were correlated with scores on the Hopelessness Scale (Beck, Weissman, Lester, & Trexler, 1974) and the Beck Depression Inventory (BDI; Beck, Ward, Mendelsohn, Mock, & Erbaugh, 1961), the expected inverse relationships were observed. Hope correlated –.51 with the Hopelessness Scale, and –.42 with depression as measured by the BDI (Gibb, 1990), whereas the LOT correlated –.47 and –.49, respectively, with the hopelessness and depression indices (Scheier & Carver, 1985).

In assessing the discriminant validity of each scale, their respective authors used the same three measures and found similar results. The Marlowe–Crowne Social Desirability Scale (Crowne & Marlowe, 1960) correlated .30 with the Hope Scale and .26 with the LOT. This correlation was explained by Snyder and colleagues as reflecting a slight positive self-presentational style that is part of adaptive coping (Snyder, Harris, et al., 1991; Snyder et al., 2000b). In that light, that a modest relationship exists between social desirability and other positive constructs such as hope and optimism is not surprising. On the other hand, the public and private self-consciousness subscale scores from the Self-Consciousness Scale (Fenigstein,

Scheier, & Buss, 1975) yielded nonsignificant correlations of .06 and −.03, respectively, with the Hope Scale (Snyder, Harris, et al., 1991), and correlations of −.04 and −.05 with the LOT (Scheier & Carver, 1985). These latter findings, lending discriminant validity support to each scale, were predicted on the grounds that there was no theoretical reason to believe that the optimism and hope constructs should be related to consciousness about oneself.

The aforementioned results demonstrate the convergent and discriminant validity of both the Hope Scale and the LOT, yet they tell little about the differences between these two indices. In the following section we attempt to illustrate these differences more clearly.

Discriminant Utility

One reason for examining the correlations between a new and an existing scale is to determine whether there is a need for a new measure or whether it is merely replicating already existent indices. Although positive correlations between scales measuring similar constructs are important, ideally the new scale should account for additional predictive variance in relation to scores produced by these related constructs. In other words, there should be significant and unique variance explained by the new scale beyond that variance accounted for by the existent measures. Previously, we described this as *discriminant utility* (Snyder, Harris, et al., 1991).

There has been some controversy in this field of research about the possibility that many of the relatively new concepts proposed to explain and predict behaviors are, in reality, tapping neuroticism (Smith et al., 1989; Smith & Rhodewalt, 1991; Watson & Pennebaker, 1989). In this regard, Smith and his colleagues (Smith et al., 1989; Smith & Rhodewalt, 1991) have suggested that optimism, as measured by the LOT, is one construct that has a "problem of incomplete construct validation" (Smith & Rhodewalt, 1991, p. 743). They argued that traditional procedures for evaluating convergent and discriminant validity require more stringent application than those used by Scheier and Carver (1985, 1987). Citing Campbell and Fiske (1959), Smith and Rhodewalt (1991) maintained that

> convergent validity is demonstrated by a large correlation between two measures of a given trait, while discriminant validity is demonstrated by correlations between two measures of separate traits that are smaller than the correlations between the measures of a single trait. (p. 743)

In three samples, Smith and his colleagues (1989) found the LOT to be significantly correlated at .56 with the GESS (Fibel & Hale, 1978) and correlated at −.62 with measures of neuroticism (Eysenck & Eysenck, 1964) and negative affect (Watson & Clark, 1984). Citing these results as clearly indicating a lack of discriminant validity, they contended that it is possible that "the LOT is simply an inversely scored measure of neuroticism" (Smith & Rhodewalt, 1991, p. 744). They went on to report that significant correlations between coping and the LOT were largely eliminated when neuroticism was controlled through partial correlation (a statistical procedure for removing the common shared variance that a third variable displays in regard to the relationship of two other variables); conversely, controlling for optimism did not eliminate the significant relationships between neuroticism and coping.

Scheier and Carver (1992) responded to this criticism with two counterarguments. First, they pointed out that the domain-specific focus of the GESS (Fibel & Hale, 1978) makes it less than optimal as an alternative measure to the LOT, which focuses on generalized optimism. Their second response follows:

> It is important to keep in mind that neuroticism is a multifaceted construct which consists partly (though not entirely) of pessimism. Its broad scope means that it confounds pessimism with other qualities, such as emotional ability and worry. Thus, to ask whether an effect of pessimism is really an effect of neuroticism begs the question of whether all facets of neuroticism are important in producing the effect, or only that part of neuroticism which is pessimism. (Scheier & Carver, 1992, p. 216)

They then make the same argument regarding trait anxiety. In an attempt to discount the notion that the effects of optimism or pessimism can be better understood in terms of neuroticism, Scheier and his colleagues reported that they are attempting factor analyses of the items of the LOT and traditional measures of neuroticism (see Scheier & Carver, 1992, for more details; see also Lucas, Diener, & Suh, 1996). In later research, Scheier et al. (1994) have provided substantiating evidence that optimism is a viable construct that differs from neuroticism. In answer to the previous criticisms, Scheier, Carver, and Bridges (1994) reestablished the convergent and discriminant validity of the LOT, demonstrating its predictive validity beyond alternative explanations such as neuroticism, trait anxiety, self-mastery, and self-esteem; furthermore, in the same study, they validated a revised, shorter version of the LOT, known as the LOT–R, that exhibited psychometric standards equaling those found for the original scale.

We share some of Scheier and Carver's concerns regarding the role of negative affectivity as a counterexplanation. Because those people with higher levels of hope should be less likely to have high levels of negative affect, Hope Scale scores should correlate negatively with measures of negative affect. Indeed, in a correlational study (Holleran & Snyder, 1990), Hope Scale scores were significantly and negatively correlated with the

Taylor Manifest Anxiety scale (TMAS; Taylor, 1953), $r = -.47$, $p < .001$, and the State–Trait Anxiety Inventory, trait form (STAI–T, Spielberger, Gorsuch, & Luchene, 1970), $r = -.58$, $p < .001$. To examine whether the effects of hope were explained by negative affect, hierarchical regression analyses were performed. (These hierarchical regression analyses enable one to ascertain any unique or special predictive power that a given scale may have over other predictor scales in regard to a target or criterion variable of interest.) Using the Problem-Focused Coping subscale from the revised Ways of Coping Checklist (Folkman & Lazarus, 1985) as the criterion variable and forcing the TMAS and the STAI–T into the equation at Step 1 ($R^2 = .06$, $p < .01$), the prediction was significantly augmented when Hope was entered at Step 2 ($R^2 = .03$, $p < .05$). When Hope Scale scores were entered first ($R^2 = .09$, $p < .001$), however, the TMAS and STAI–T entered at Step 2 yielded no additional variance. Thus, these analyses reveal that negative affect cannot account for the relationship of hope to problem-focused coping (Snyder, Harris, et al., 1991).

Two additional studies (Sigmon & Snyder, 1990a, 1990b) tested the discriminant utility of the Hope Scale in relation to both positive and negative affect. In both studies, the Hope Scale correlated negatively with the negative affect items of the Positive and Negative Affect Schedule (PANAS; Watson, Clark, & Tellegen, 1988) as expected ($r = -.18$). In one study (Sigmon & Snyder, 1990b), Hope Scale scores correlated positively with the PANAS positive affect items ($r = .30$). The Active Coping and Planning subscales of the COPE (Carver, Scheier, & Weintraub, 1989) were administered along with the PANAS and the Hope Scale. When active coping was used as the criterion variable in hierarchical multiple regressions, negative affect entered at Step 1 did not yield significant results ($R^2 = .01$), whereas positive affect entered at Step 2 ($R^2 = .075$, $p < .01$) and Hope Scale scores entered at Step 3 ($R^2 = .09$, $p < .001$) both significantly augmented the predictions. When the steps were reversed, Hope Scale scores predicted active coping ($R^2 = .15$, $p < .001$) at Step 1, and positive affect augmented the prediction at Step 2 ($R^2 = .03$, $p < .05$), but negative affect entered at Step 3 did not augment the prediction. When planning was utilized as the criterion variable, neither positive affect nor negative affect significantly predicted planning; however, Hope Scale scores entered at Step 3 significantly augmented the prediction ($R^2 = .032$, $p < .05$). Again, when the order in which the variables were entered was reversed, neither positive nor negative affect augmented the significant prediction by hope. Thus, there is support for the predictive power of Hope Scale scores over affect measures.

Sigmon and Snyder (1990a) examined the relationship between hope and overall well-being. Study participants completed the Hope Scale, the PANAS, the STAI–T, and the Mental Health Inventory (Veit & Ware, 1983). Using hierarchical regression analyses with overall well-being as the criterion variable, Hope Scale scores significantly augmented the prediction even when it was entered at Step 4 ($R^2 = .01, p < .05$) after entering anxiety, negative affect, and positive affect at Steps 1, 2, and 3, respectively. These results indicate that hope accounts for unique variance (albeit very small) over and above that of negative affect and positive affect in overall well-being.

In yet another study, we were interested in the predictive capabilities of hope in relation to depression (see Snyder, Lapointe, Crowson, & Early, 1998). In two experiments, research participants first completed the Hope Scale and the Beck Depression Inventory (BDI; Beck et al., 1961). We then examined the preferences of these research participants for listening to short, recorded statements that were either affirming ("I can do this") or disaffirming ("I can't do this") in content. This preference choice was accomplished by having the research participant move a toggle switch that activated either the affirming or disaffirming statements (received auditorally via headphones); accordingly, we could measure the percentage of time that people spent listening to each tape. Results revealed that the Hope Scale scores significantly predicted the choice of listening to more affirming than disaffirming statements, and this effect remained when the shared variance related to depression was removed by way of statistical procedures; conversely, however, depression scores did not predict the choice of these tapes when the variance related to Hope Scale scores was removed. Thus, hopeful thoughts proved more powerful than depressive feelings in guiding preferences for affirming information. In the degree to which the ongoing self-talk of people may guide the actual conduct of their lives, it appears that hope may be related uniquely to the choice of more positive content for such internal dialogues.

The studies described previously provide evidence that negative and positive affectivity do not provide viable alternative explanations for the relationship between the Hope Scale and well-being, active coping, or planning. One additional research finding sheds light on the discriminant utility of the Hope Scale in relation to the LOT. As noted earlier, the LOT correlated positively with the Hope Scale in a study conducted by Holleran and Snyder (1990). In that study, participants also completed the Problem-Focused Coping index of the Revised Ways of Coping Checklist (Folkman & Lazarus, 1985) along with the LOT, the GESS, and the Hope Scale. When using a hierarchical regression with problem-focused coping as the criterion variable, our results suggested that Hope Scale scores were a some-what better predictor than were either the GESS or the LOT scores. When the LOT was forced into the equation at Step 1, $R^2 = .04, p < .05$; when the GESS was forced into the equation at Step 2, it augmented the prediction ($R^2 = .04, p < .05$); finally, when Hope Scale scores were forced into the equation at Step 3, they augmented the prediction further ($R^2 = .03$,

$p < .05$). Conversely, in the same study when Hope Scale scores were forced into the equation at Step 1, $R^2 = .085$, $p < .001$; subsequently, neither the LOT entered at Step 2 ($R^2 = .005$) nor the GESS entered at Step 3 ($R^2 = .015$) augmented the prediction (Holleran & Snyder, 1990). Overall, therefore, these results indicate that the Hope Scale was able to predict uniquely the problem-focused coping beyond the positive expectancies as tapped by the LOT and the GESS.

These results, taken together, suggest that the two-component aspect of hope theory, as well as the combining of the agency and pathways components in the measurement instrument provide an increase in the ability to understand and predict coping markers beyond that which can be obtained through the LOT scores. Obviously, other studies are needed to explore the relative predictive utility of the Hope Scale and the LOT in relation to a variety of outcome measures. Given the theoretical relationship between the LOT and the agency subscale component of the Hope Scale, we would expect relatively strong relationships between these indices in predicting outcomes. When the pathways component scores are added to the agency component to yield the full Hope Scale, however, we expect that the Hope Scale may provide enhanced variance (i.e., discriminant utility) in relation to LOT scores in predicting a variety of outcome markers.

POSITIVE SEQUELAE OF HOPE

Since Snyder (1989) first proposed a new model of hope roughly a decade ago, studies have found a positive relationship among hope and benefits related to psychological adjustment, achievement, problem solving, and health-related outcomes. In the following section we discuss each of these issues.

Psychological Adjustment

Hope is related to psychological adjustment in several ways. Research has shown that there is a positive correlation between hope and belief in one's capabilities, as well as between hope and feelings of self-worth. In one study, hope was positively correlated with children's perceptions of scholastic competence ($rs = .35–.59$), social acceptance ($rs = .23–.43$), athletic ability ($rs = .26–.35$), and physical appearance ($rs = .00–.46$; Snyder et al., 1997). Therefore, hopeful thinking in children is related to their beliefs about having the necessary abilities to accomplish specified goals. Hope also relates to the presence of positive feelings toward oneself. Hopeful thinking is associated with an increased feeling of self-worth in children ($rs = .23–.55$; Snyder et al., 1997), as well as adults ($rs = .35–.75$; Curry, Snyder, Cook,

Ruby, & Rehm, 1997; Snyder et al., 1996). In adults, hope has a significant positive correlation with self-esteem (Gibb, 1990). Further, higher hope is associated with lower levels of depression in children (Snyder, Hoza, et al., 1997). This latter relationship may be due, in part, to the different attributional styles of individuals with high and low hope scores (see chap. 3 in this volume on attributional styles). The pessimistic attributional style is one in which a person makes more internal, stable, and global explanations for bad events, and external, stable, and global explanations for good events (Kaslow, Tanenbaum, & Seligman, 1978). Children who score high on hope scales tend to have internal, stable, and global attributions for positive events, and external, stable, and global attributions for negative events (Snyder, Hoza, et al., 1997).

Thus, hope appears to have an inverse relationship with the typical pessimistic attributional style. That is to say, children with higher hope scores are less likely to make characteristically pessimistic explanations for their bad outcomes (e.g., "It's my fault, it's always my fault, and it's this way in all parts of my life"). Other research supports this finding, showing a significant inverse relationship between the BDI scores (Beck et al., 1961) and hope ($r = -.42$; Gibb, 1990).

Positive thinking and affect also have been found to relate to hope. Research has shown that hope, as measured by the State Hope Scale, is positively related to state measures of positive affect ($rs = .55-.65$) and negatively related to state measures of negative affect ($rs = -.47--.50$; Snyder, 1996). In addition, higher hope scores are related to ongoing states involving more positive thinking. The State Hope Scale correlated positively with the ratings of positive thoughts and negatively with the ratings of negative thoughts. Together, this evidence suggests that individuals whose scoring indicates higher hope both feel and think more positively on a day-to-day basis than do other individuals. This finding is further corroborated by evidence indicating that college students scoring high on hope measures as compared to those scoring low report feeling more inspired, confident, energized, eager, and challenged by their goals (Snyder, Harris, et al., 1991). Last, scores of higher hope have been described as becoming especially important to people experiencing loss of a loved one, job, and so forth (see Snyder, 1996; Snyder, 1998; Snyder, in press). Indeed, hope appears to be critical for goals involving successful interpersonal relationships (see Snyder, Cheavens, et al., 1997).

Achievement

Individuals possessing high hope also have increased performances in the achievement arenas. Hope has related positively to achievement in children even after variance associated with self-worth has been controlled statistically (Snyder, Hoza, et al., 1997). Additionally, college students with high—as compared to low—hope indicators demonstrate increased success in the academic realm (Snyder, Wiklund, & Cheavens, 1999). In a longitudinal study spanning 6 years, Hope Scale scores taken at the beginning of college predicted both subsequent cumulative grade point average and graduation status, as well as whether a student was dismissed from school in poor academic standing. The relationships between hope and both grade point average and graduation status remained after partialling out the variance due to ACT scores, suggesting that "high hope" is related to collegiate achievement beyond one's previous high school knowledge base. Previous studies with children (Snyder, Hoza, et al., 1997) and adults (Snyder, Harris, et al., 1991) have shown that hope exhibits very small and statistically nonsignificant ($rs < .10$) relationships to scores on standardized tests of intelligence.

Achievement in athletics also appears to be related to levels of hope. Curry et al. (1997) found that the combination of dispositional and state Hope Scale scores accounted for 56% of the variance related to track meet performance for female collegiate athletes. Furthermore, measures of confidence, self-esteem, and mood did not significantly augment the prediction of performance. Results also showed that Hope Scale scores provided additional predictive information about performance beyond natural ability, as rated by coaches. In summary, hope appears to be an independent factor with predictive utility in the achievement realms involving academics and sports.

Problem Solving

Research also supports the contention that hope is positively related to problem solving. These findings should come as no surprise given that the pathways component is a major part of hope theory. In studies designed to validate the dispositional Hope Scale, a number of findings emerged that support this contention (see Snyder, Harris, et al., 1991, for a review). As previously noted, Holleran and Snyder (1990) found that hope is a significant, unique predictor of problem-focused coping (i.e., the Problem-Focused Coping subscale of the revised Ways of Coping Checklist; Folkman & Lazarus, 1985) when controlling for optimism (as measured by the LOT) and negative affectivity (PANAS; Watson et al., 1988), and that neither optimism nor negative affectivity added any significant unique predictive value above that of hope. Following from hope theory, this finding is taken as an indication that the pathways component of hope reflects problem-solving thinking in regard to goal achievement.

In another study directly related to hope and coping (Sigmon & Snyder, 1990b), hope predicted both active coping (i.e., taking steps to overcome effects of stressors in a direct and effortful manner) and planning (i.e., producing strategies to cope with stressors), as measured by the Active Coping and Planning subscales of the COPE (Carver et al., 1989) when controlling for both positive and negative affectivity (PANAS). Thus, the effects of hope on coping and problem solving cannot be explained by the mediating effects of affectivity or optimism. As suggested earlier, we propose that it is the explicit pathways component of hope theory that helps to contribute the additional predictive power in explaining variance related to problem solving.

Health-Related Concerns

Research suggests that hope confers advantages to people in coping with illness-related problems. There are three reported studies relating hope to health, all of which suggest that there are benefits accruing for those with higher levels of hope. First, in the recovery process following spinal cord injury, higher levels of hope were related to better coping and to less depression (Elliott, Witty, Herrick, & Hoffman, 1991). Second, in a study of nurses working in a high-pressure hospital unit, those with higher levels of hope were less likely to report burnout (Sherwin et al., 1992). Third, higher hope levels in adolescent burn survivors correlated with engaging in fewer behaviors that would undermine recovery (Barnum, Snyder, Rapoff, Mani, & Thompson, 1998). These burn survivors also had a greater number of successful interactions with others, and a higher level of global self-worth.

Hope also appears to play an important role in coping with potentially life-threatening diseases. In a recent research project, college women scoring high on hope levels demonstrated greater knowledge about cancer and increased hope-specific coping responses to an imagined task of coping with cancer than did college women scoring low on hope levels, even when controlling for academic achievement, experience with cancer (in family or friends), and negative affectivity (Irving, Snyder, & Crowson, 1998). This relationship seemed to prevail as the research participants projected their reactions throughout the imagined course of the disease. Thus, hope may facilitate adjustment across the various stages of coping with illnesses.

A growing body of research is illuminating the role of finding benefits in adversity as a means of coping with health-related problems (see Affleck & Tennen, 1996; Tennen & Affleck, 1999, for reviews). Hope appears to play an important role in such benefit finding. In their review article, Affleck and Tennen (1996) discussed findings from an ongoing study concerning the psychological adjustment of individuals with fibromyalgia, a chronic disease that involves high levels of pain. Participants with high hope levels reported finding more benefits from their experience with the disease than did those with low hope levels, even when researchers controlled for optimism. The authors suggested that hope is an important factor in making positive appraisals of adverse situations. Affleck and Tennen proposed that reminding oneself about the benefits one accrues through the experience of adversity serves as an active coping strategy. In this study involving patients with fibromyalgia, Affleck and Tennen found that the correlation between "benefit finding" and "benefit reminding" was not significant when the pathways component of hope was partialled out. Thus, the hope component of planning routes to goals based on finding benefits in adversity plays a crucial role in the use of benefit reminding as a coping strategy. Again, this latter result highlights the importance of adding the pathways thinking component to that of agency in order fully to tap hope. Overall, hopeful thought appears to play a useful role in coping with health-related matters.

Summary of Positive Sequelae

The preceding research demonstrates the benefits of higher levels of hope for children and adults and how hope relates to coping in a variety of arenas, including academics, sports, problem-solving ability, and health. Moreover, in comparison to optimism, as well as negative affectivity, positive affectivity, locus of control, mood, depression, athletic aptitude, cognitive or intellectual aptitude, and helplessness, the hope scales have provided unique and augmenting variance in predicting outcomes. Thus, hope appears to be a good predictor of positive adjustment and coping, and this predictive utility cannot be explained by other individual differences indices that would reflect counterexplanations (see Snyder, Cheavens, & Michael, 1999, for a review).

CONCLUSION

The major difference in the models of optimism and hope is that the former emphasizes agentic goal-related thinking, whereas the latter emphasizes the mutual contribution of agentic and pathways goal-directed thoughts. Although we point out some differences in the optimism and hope theories, there are many important shared aspects of these two theories, thus the subtitle, "Variants on a Positive Expectancy Theme."

REFERENCES

Affleck, G., & Tennen, H. (1996). Construing benefits from adversity: Adaptational significance and dispositional underpinnings. *Journal of Personality, 64,* 899–922.

Anderson, J. R. (1988). *The role of hope in goal-setting, expectancy about success, and coping.* Unpublished doctoral dissertation, University of Kansas, Lawrence.

Babyak, M. A., Snyder, C. R., & Yoshinoba, L. (1993). Psychometric properties of the Hope Scale: A confirmatory factor analysis. *Journal of Research in Personality, 27,* 154–159.

Barnum, D. D., Snyder, C. R., Rapoff, M. A., Mani, M. M., & Thompson, R. (1998). Hope and social support in the psychological adjustment of children who have survived burn injuries and matched controls. *Children's Health Care, 27,* 15–30.

Beck, A. T., Ward, C. H., Mendelson, M., Mock, J., & Erbaugh, J. (1961). An inventory for measuring depression. *Archives of General Psychology, 4,* 53–63.

Beck, A. T., Weissman, A., Lester, D., & Trexler, L. (1974). The measurement of pessimism: The Hopelessness Scale. *Journal of Consulting and Clinical Psychology, 42,* 861–865.

Campbell, D. T., & Fiske, D. W. (1959). Convergent and discriminant validation by the multitrait–multimethod matrix. *Psychological Bulletin, 56,* 81–105.

Carver, C. S., & Scheier, M. F. (1999). Optimism. In C. R. Snyder (Ed.), *Coping: The psychology of what works* (pp. 182–204). New York: Oxford.

Carver, C. S., Scheier, M. F., & Weintraub, J. K. (1989). Assessing coping strategies: A theoretically based approach. *Journal of Personality and Social Psychology, 56,* 267–283.

Crowne, D. P., & Marlowe, D. (1960). A new scale of social desirability independent of psychopathology. *Journal of Consulting and Clinical Psychology, 24,* 349–354.

Curry, L. A., Snyder, C. R., Cook, D. L., Ruby, B. C., & Rehm, M. (1997). The role of hope in academic and sport achievement. *Journal of Personality and Social Psychology, 73,* 1257–1267.

Elliott, T. R., Witty, T. E., Herrick, S., & Hoffman, J. T. (1991). Negotiating reality after physical loss: Hope, depression, and disability. *Journal of Personality and Social Psychology, 61,* 608–613.

Eysenck, H. J., & Eysenck, S. B. G. (1964). *Manual for the Eysenck Personality Inventory.* London: University Press.

Fenigstein, A., Scheier, M. F., & Buss, A. H. (1975). Public and private self-consciousness: Assessment and theory. *Journal of Consulting and Clinical Psychology, 43,* 522–527.

Fibel, B., & Hale, W. D. (1978). The Generalized Expectancy for Success Scale—A new measure. *Journal of Consulting and Clinical Psychology, 46,* 924–931.

Folkman, S., & Lazarus, R. S. (1985). If it changes it must be a process: Study of emotion and coping during three stages of college examination. *Journal of Personality and Social Psychology, 48,* 150–170.

Fontaine, K. R., Manstead, A. S. R., & Wagner, H. (1993). Optimism, perceived control over stress, and coping. *European Journal of Personality, 7,* 267–281.

Frank, J. D. (1975). The faith that heals. *The Johns Hopkins Medical Journal, 137,* 127–131.

Frankl, V. (1963). *Man's search for meaning.* New York: Washington Square Press.

Friedman, L. C., Nelson, D. V., Baer, P. E., Lane, M., Smith, F. E., & Dworkin, R. J. (1992). The relationship of dispositional optimism, daily life stress, and domestic environment to coping methods used by cancer patients. *Journal of Behavioral Medicine, 15,* 127–141.

Gibb, J. (1990). *The Hope Scale revisited: Further validation of a measure of individual differences in the hope motive.* Unpublished master's thesis, University of Illinois at Urbana-Champaign.

Harney, P. (1989). *The Hope Scale: Exploration of construct validity and its influence on health.* Unpublished master's thesis, University of Kansas, Lawrence.

Holleran, S., & Snyder, C. R. (1990). *Discriminant and convergent validation of the Hope Scale.* Unpublished manuscript, University of Kansas, Lawrence.

Irving, L. M., Snyder, C. R., & Crowson, Jr., J. J. (1998). Hope and coping with cancer by college women. *Journal of Personality, 66,* 195–214.

Kaslow, N. J., Tanenbaum, R. L., & Seligman, M. E. P. (1978). *The KASTAN-R: A children's attributional style questionnaire (KASTAN-R-CASQ).* Unpublished manuscript, University of Pennsylvania, Philadelphia.

Lucas, R. E., Diener, E., & Suh, E. (1996). Discriminant validity of well-meaning measures. *Journal of Personality and Social Psychology, 73,* 616–628.

Magaletta, P. R., & Oliver, J. M. (1999). The hope construct, will and ways: Their relative relations with self-efficacy, optimism, and general well-being. *Journal of Clinical Psychology, 55,* 539–551.

Menninger, K. (1959). The academic lecture on hope. *The American Journal of Psychiatry, 109,* 481–491.

Pelletier, K. R. (1977). *Holistic medicine: From stress to optimum health.* New York: Delacorte Press/Seymore Lawrence.

Robinson-Whelen, S., Kim, C., MacCallum, R. C., & Kiecolt-Glaser, J. K. (1997). Distinguishing optimism from pessimism in older adults: Is it more important to be optimistic or not be pessimistic? *Journal of Personality and Social Psychology, 73,* 1345–1353.

Rosenberg, M. (1965). *Society and adolescent self-image.* Princeton, NJ: Princeton University Press.

Scheier, M. F., & Carver, C. S. (1985). Optimism, coping, and health: Assessment and implications of generalized outcome expectancies. *Health Psychology, 4,* 219–247.

Scheier, M. F., & Carver, C. S. (1987). Dispositional optimism and physical well-being: The influence of generalized outcome expectancies. *Journal of Personality, 55,* 169–210.

Scheier, M. F., & Carver, C. S. (1992). Effects of optimism on psychological and physical well-being: Theoretical and empirical update. *Cognitive Therapy and Research, 16,* 201–228.

Scheier, M. F., Carver, C. S., & Bridges, M. W. (1994). Distinguishing optimism from neuroticism (and trait anxiety, self mastery, and self-esteem): A reevaluation of the Life Orientation Test. *Journal of Personality and Social Psychology, 67*, 1063–1078.

Scheier, M. F., Weintraub, J. K., & Carver, C. S. (1986). Coping with stress: Divergent strategies of optimists and pessimists. *Journal of Personality and Social Psychology, 51*, 1257–1264.

Schmale, A. H. (1972). Giving up as a final common pathway to changes in health. *Advances in Psychosomatic Medicine, 28*, 714–721.

Sherwin, E. D., Elliott, T. R., Rybarczyk, B. D., Frank, R. G., Hanson, S., & Hoffman, J. (1992). Negotiating the reality of care giving: Hope, burnout, and nursing. *Journal of Social and Clinical Psychology, 11*, 129–139.

Siegel, B. D. (1986). *Love, medicine, and miracles: Lessons learned about self-healing from a surgeon's experience with patients.* New York: Harper & Row.

Sigmon, S. T., & Snyder, C. R. (1990a). *The independent contributions of positive and negative affect and hope in predicting psychological health.* Unpublished manuscript, University of Kansas, Department of Psychology, Lawrence.

Sigmon, S. T., & Snyder, C. R. (1990b). *Positive and negative affect as a counter-explanation for the relationship between hope and coping strategies.* Unpublished manuscript, University of Kansas, Department of Psychology, Lawrence.

Simonton, O. C., Matthew-Simonton, S., & Creighton, J. L. (1978). *Getting well again.* New York: Bantam Books.

Smith, T. W., Pope, M. K., Rhodewalt, F., & Poulton, J. L. (1989). Optimism, neuroticism, coping, and symptom reports: An alternative interpretation of the Life Orientation Test. *Journal of Personality and Social Psychology, 56*, 640–648.

Smith, T. W., & Rhodewalt, F. (1991). Methodological challenges at the social/clinical interface. In C. R. Snyder & D. R. Forsyth (Eds.), *Handbook of social and clinical psychology: The health perspective* (pp. 739–756). Elmsford, NY: Pergamon Press.

Snyder, C. R. (1989). Reality negotiation: From excuses to hope and beyond. *Journal of Social and Clinical Psychology, 8*, 130–157.

Snyder, C. R. (1994). *The psychology of hope: You can get there from here.* New York: Free Press.

Snyder, C. R. (1996). To hope, to lose, and hope again. *Journal of Personal and Interpersonal Loss, 1*, 1–16.

Snyder, C. R. (1998). A case for hope in pain, loss, and suffering. In J. H. Harvey, J. Omarzu, & E. Miller (Eds.), *Perspectives on loss: A sourcebook* (pp. 63–79). Washington, DC: Taylor & Francis.

Snyder, C. R. (2000a). Genesis: Birth and growth of hope. In C. R. Snyder (Ed.), *Handbook of hope: Theory, measures, and applications* (pp. 25–54). San Diego, CA: Academic Press.

Snyder, C. R. (2000b). Hypothesis: There is hope. In C. R. Snyder (Ed.), *Handbook of hope: Theory, measures, and applications* (pp. 3–21). San Diego, CA: Academic Press.

Snyder, C. R. (in press). The hope mandala: Coping with the loss of a loved one. In J. Gillham (Ed.), *Optimism and hope*. Radnor, PA: Templeton Foundation.

Snyder, C. R., Cheavens, J., & Michael, S. T. (1999). Hoping. In C. R. Snyder (Ed.), *Coping: The psychology of what works* (pp. 205–231). New York: Oxford University Press.

Snyder, C. R., Cheavens, J., & Sympson, S. C. (1997). Hope: An individual motive for social commerce. *Group Dynamics: Theory, Research, and Practice, 1*, 107–118.

Snyder, C. R., Harris, C., Anderson, J. R., Holleran, S. A., Irving, L. M., Sigmon, S. T., Yoshinobu, L., Gibb, J., Langelle, C., & Harney, P. (1991). The will and the ways: Development and validation of an individual-differences measure of hope. *Journal of Personality and Social Psychology, 60*, 570–585.

Snyder, C. R., Hoza, B., Pelham, W. E., Rapoff, M., Ware, L., Danovsky, M., Highberger, L., Rubinstein, H., & Stahl, K. J. (1997). The development and validation of the children's hope scale. *Journal of Pediatric Psychology, 22*, 399–421.

Snyder, C. R., Irving, L., & Anderson, J. R. (1991). Hope and health: Measuring the will and the ways. In C. R. Snyder & D. R. Forsyth (Eds.), *Handbook of social and clinical psychology: The health perspective* (pp. 285–305). Elmsford, NY: Pergamon Press.

Snyder, C. R., Lapointe, A. B., Crowson, Jr., J. J., & Early, S. (1998). Preferences of high- and low-hope people for self-referential input. *Cognition and Emotion, 12*, 807–823.

Snyder, C. R., & McCullough, M. (2000). A positive psychology field of dreams: "If you build it, they will come. . ." *Journal of Social and Clinical Psychology, 19*, 151–160.

Snyder, C. R., McDermott, D., Cook, W., & Rapoff, M. (1997). *Hope for the journey*. Boulder, CO: Westview.

Snyder, C. R., Michael, S., & Cheavens, J. (1999). Hope as a psychotherapeutic foundation for nonspecific factors, placebos, and expectancies. In M. A. Huble, B. Duncan, & S. Miller (Eds.), *Heart and soul of change* (pp. 179–200). Washington, DC: American Psychological Association.

Snyder, C. R., Sympson, S. C., Ybasco, F. C., Borders, T. F., Babyak, M. A., & Higgins, R. L. (1996). Development and validation of the State Hope Scale. *Journal of Personality and Social Psychology, 70*, 321–335.

Snyder, C. R., Wiklund, C., & Cheavens, J. (1999, August). *Hope and success in college*. Paper presented at the American Psychological Association, Boston.

Spielberger, C. D., Gorsuch, R. L., & Luchene, R. E. (1970). *The State-Trait Anxiety Inventory*. Palo Alto, CA: Consulting Psychologists Press.

Strutton, D., & Lumpkin, J. (1992). Relationship between optimism and coping strategies in the work environment. *Psychological Reports, 71*, 1179–1186.

Sympson, S. C. (1993). *Construction and validation of a state hope measure: A month in the lives of college students*. Unpublished master's thesis, University of Kansas, Lawrence.

Taylor, J. A. (1953). A personality scale of manifest anxiety. *Journal of Abnormal and Social Psychology, 48,* 285–290.

Tennen, H., & Affleck, G. (1999). Finding benefits in adversity. In C. R. Snyder (Ed.), *Coping: The psychology of what works* (pp. 279–304). New York: Oxford Press.

Veit, C. V., & Ware, J. E. (1983). The structure of psychological stress and well-being in general populations. *Journal of Consulting and Clinical Psychology, 51,* 730–742.

Watson, D., & Clark, L. A. (1984). Negative affectivity: The disposition to experience negative emotional states. *Psychological Bulletin, 96,* 465–490.

Watson, D., Clark, L. A., & Tellegen, A. (1988). Development and validation of brief measures of positive and negative affect: The PANAS scales. *Journal of Personality and Social Psychology, 54,* 1063–1070.

Watson, D., & Pennebaker, J. W. (1989). Health complaints, stress, and distress: Exploring the central role of negative affectivity. *Psychological Review, 96,* 233–253.

Yoshinobu, L. (1989). *Construct validation of the Hope Scale: Agency and pathways components.* Unpublished master's thesis, University of Kansas, Lawrence.

APPENDIX 5.1: THE ADULT TRAIT HOPE SCALE

Directions: Read each item carefully. Using the scale shown below, please select the number that best describes you and put that number in the blank provided.

> 1 = *Definitely False*
> 2 = *Mostly False*
> 3 = *Somewhat False*
> 4 = *Slightly False*
> 5 = *Slightly True*
> 6 = *Somewhat True*
> 7 = *Mostly True*
> 8 = *Definitely True*

_____ 1. I can think of many ways to get out of a jam.
_____ 2. I energetically pursue my goals.
_____ 3. I feel tired most of the time.
_____ 4. There are lots of ways around any problem.
_____ 5. I am easily downed in an argument.
_____ 6. I can think of many ways to get the things in life that are important to me.
_____ 7. I worry about my health.
_____ 8. Even when others get discouraged, I know I can find a way to solve the problem.
_____ 9. My past experiences have prepared me well for my future.
_____ 10. I've been pretty successful in life.
_____ 11. I usually find myself worrying about something.
_____ 12. I meet the goals that I set for myself.

Note. Administers of the scale should refer to it as "The Future Scale." The agency subscale score is derived by summing item nos. 2, 9, 10, and 12; the pathways subscale score is derived by adding item nos. 1, 4, 6, and 8. Items 3, 5, 7, and 11 are fillers and are ignored for scoring purposes. The total Hope Scale score is derived by summing the four agency and the four pathways items. From "The Will and the Ways: Development and Validation of an Individual Differences Measure of Hope," by C. R. Snyder, C. Harris, et al., 1991, *Journal of Personality and Social Psychology, 60,* p. 585. Copyright 1991 by the American Psychological Association. Reprinted with permission.

APPENDIX 5.2: THE ADULT STATE HOPE SCALE

Directions: Read each item carefully. Using the scale shown below, please select the number that best describes *how you think about yourself right now* and put that number in the blank before each sentence. Please take a few moments to focus on yourself and what is going on in *your life at this moment.* Once you have this "here and now" mindset, go ahead and answer each item according to the following scale:

1 = *Definitely False*
2 = *Mostly False*
3 = *Somewhat False*
4 = *Slightly False*
5 = *Slightly True*
6 = *Somewhat True*
7 = *Mostly True*
8 = *Definitely True*

_____ 1. If I should find myself in a jam, I could think of many ways to get out of it.
_____ 2. At the present time, I am energetically pursuing my goals.
_____ 3. There are lots of ways around any problem that I am facing now.
_____ 4. Right now, I see myself as being pretty successful.
_____ 5. I can think of many ways to reach my current goals.
_____ 6. At this time, I am meeting the goals that I have set for myself.

Note. The agency subscale score is derived by summing the three even-numbered items; the pathways subscale score is derived by adding the three odd-numbered items. The total State Hope Scale score is derived by summing the three agency and the three pathways items. Scores can range from a low of 6 to a high of 48. Administers of the State Hope Scale should refer to it as the "Goals scale for the present." From "Development and Validation of the State Hope Scale," by C. R. Snyder, S. C. Sympson, et al., 1996, *Journal of Personality and Social Psychology, 65,* p. 335. Copyright 1996 by the American Psychological Association. Reprinted with permission.

II

Physical–Biological Factors

6

OPTIMISM AND PHYSICAL WELL-BEING

CHRISTOPHER PETERSON AND LISA M. BOSSIO

In 1991, we published *Health and Optimism*, a book that described what at the time was characterized as the new psychology of optimism. We focused on the implications of emerging theory and research for understanding physical health. What was our conclusion at that time? Thinking "good" is linked to feeling "well," an assertion consistent with many people's common sense, yet until recently lacking solid scientific support. Since then, psychologists have continued to study the association between optimism and health. The original findings have been repeated and extended, and we now know more about this intriguing topic. Our purpose here is to take another look at the psychology of optimism and what it tells us about physical well-being.

As in our original discussion, we inform this chapter with what the evidence actually shows. We explain why it can be difficult to arrive at definitive conclusions about psychological influences on physical health, and thus, why the relevant research literature deserves to be taken seriously. We draw boundaries around these influences. For example, optimism is *one* of the determinants of physical health, but not the only one, and in some cases, not even a major one. We note what still remains to be learned about optimism and health. Finally, we stress that optimism per se does not have an automatic effect on health. If it did, smiley buttons could replace antibiotics, seat belts, and latex condoms (Peterson & Stunkard, 1989). Positive thinking is powerful only when it sets into motion a complex cascade of processes—biological, psychological, and social—that themselves lead to good health.

ESTABLISHING THE OPTIMISM–HEALTH LINK

Before we describe the research in support of the link between optimism and physical well-being, we need to address definition, measurement, and research design. None of these matters is cut and dried, and the validity of our conclusions rests on the convergence of studies that resolved these issues in somewhat different ways.

What Is Health?

Physical health and illness prove as difficult to define and thus to measure as the most fuzzy psychological constructs. Our belief is that no single and simple definition of physical well-being is adequate. Rather, a number of factors count toward our judgment of whether an individual is ill, but most are neither necessary nor sufficient:

- General complaints about feeling ill
- Specific symptoms such as shortness of breath
- Identifiable damage to the body
- Presence of germs
- Impairment of daily activities
- A short—as opposed to a long—life

These factors may disagree with one another. Someone might feel fine but harbor all sorts of germs. Someone else might be free of germs but feel poorly. Or yet a third individual might live a long but impaired life, or a short but vigorous one.

In making sense of health psychology research, we must understand just how physical health and illness are measured. There is a tendency, perhaps, to regard "hard" measures of health and illness, that is, those based on physical tests, as the most valid, but this bias is not warranted. Biological measures of illness, such as the presence of germs, are no more basic than psychological measures, such as a person's general sense of well-being or the degree to which he or she can lead an active life.

What Is Optimism?

In our review, we focus on *explanatory style:* how an individual habitually explains the causes of bad events (Peterson & Seligman, 1984). This
cognitive personality variable is sometimes described as pessimistic (when
bad events are explained with stable, global, and internal causes) versus
optimistic (when bad events are explained with unstable, specific, and external causes). Explanatory style is a distant influence on the specific expectation that one's behaviors are related (or not) to important outcomes (Abramson, Seligman, & Teasdale, 1978). A pessimistic explanatory style encourages
individuals to believe that they are helpless, that nothing they do matters,
whereas an optimistic explanatory style encourages individuals to believe
that their behaviors do affect outcomes. The expectation of helplessness
versus efficacy is the theoretically critical link between explanatory style
and outcomes such as physical well-being, but most research in this tradition
does not measure this intervening variable.

Explanatory style took off as its own line of research when measures
of this individual difference were developed. Several such measures now
exist (Reivich, 1995), but a caveat is in order. The relationships of the
different explanatory style measures to one another have not been extensively investigated. They presumably measure the same characteristic and
should converge impressively. Studies to date show a range of convergence,
and in some cases, alternative measures are almost independent of one
another (Peterson, Bettes, & Seligman, 1985; Peterson & Park, 1997). At
the same time, the different measures of explanatory style invariably are
correlated in theoretically predicted ways with such outcomes as physical
well-being.

Taken together, these results are paradoxical, implying that measures
of explanatory style have better validity than reliability. A possible resolution
is that each measure taps explanatory style at a somewhat different level of
abstraction and distance from the actual causal attributions people offer for
events that occur. Future researchers need to use all of the available measures
of explanatory style in the same investigation, to test this speculation.

Attributional Style Questionnaire

As explained elsewhere (see chap. 3, this volume), explanatory style
is usually measured with the Attributional Style Questionnaire (ASQ; Peterson et al., 1982). Because the earliest version of the ASQ had—at best—
modest reliability (Tennen & Herzberger, 1986), researchers fell into the
practice of using composites formed by averaging different attributional
dimensions. The effect was twofold. On the one hand, reliabilities were
typically increased because that many more items were used to estimate
someone's explanatory style. But on the other, researchers were not able to

investigate the roles assigned by the helplessness reformulation to the specific attributional dimensions (Carver, 1989). When researchers use lengthier (and thus more reliable) versions of the ASQ (Peterson & Villanova, 1988), they usually find that stability and globality are more related to health outcomes than is internality. This pattern makes theoretical sense in that stability and globality, as opposed to internality, directly influence the expectation of helplessness, determining when it is projected over time and generalized across situation (Abramson, Metalsky, & Alloy, 1989).

Content Analysis of Verbatim Explanations

As noted by Gillham and colleagues (see chap. 3, this volume) a second popular way of measuring explanatory style is a flexible content analysis method: the Content Analysis of Verbatim Explanations (CAVE; Peterson, Schulman, Castellon, & Seligman, 1992). Potential research participants neither able nor willing to participate in typical research can be studied with the CAVE technique, as long as they have left behind suitable material containing causal explanations about themselves. To date, the CAVE technique has been used with psychotherapy transcripts, interviews, open-ended questionnaires, political speeches, sports stories, religious texts, and song lyrics (see Lee & Peterson, 1997). The greatest methodological virtue of this approach to studying explanatory style is that it allows researchers to conduct longitudinal research retrospectively. If suitable verbal material can be located from early in the lives of individuals whose long-term fate is known, then the CAVE technique allows researchers to complete very quickly studies that nonetheless span decades. For obvious reasons, studies of explanatory style and physical well-being have frequently relied on the CAVE (Peterson, Seligman, & Vaillant, 1988).

Cognates of optimism

As previous chapters in this volume have made clear, explanatory style is not the only conceptualization of optimism in the research literature. Accordingly, we touch on studies that look at the related constructs of

- *dispositional optimism*: the general expectation that good events will be plentiful (or not) in the future (Scheier & Carver, 1985); and
- *self-efficacy*: the belief that one can (or cannot) enact a specific behavior leading to a desired outcome (Bandura, 1986).

Dispositional optimism is usually measured with a brief self-report questionnaire called the Life Orientation Test (LOT), described earlier (see Introduction and chap. 2, this volume). Self-efficacy is usually measured by asking an individual to indicate his or her confidence, using a percentage estimate, that the behavior of concern can be performed.

A number of investigations concerned with how people perceive their relative risk for specific illnesses also exist, and we describe some of these studies as well. Most measure these expectations with a single item, asking respondents to provide a percentage estimate that they will someday contract an illness or to provide a comparison to peers (*less likely, equally as likely, more likely*) that they will do so. A robust finding in this literature is that people underestimate their risks: The average individual sees him- or herself as below average in risk for a variety of maladies, which of course cannot be. This phenomenon is identified as an *optimistic bias* (Weinstein, 1989), and it is decried because it may lead people to neglect the basics of health promotion and maintenance. Later in this chapter, we will discuss the optimistic bias further because it seems to contradict our thesis that optimism is healthy.

What Is the Optimal Research Design?

The ideal investigation of the psychological precursors of illness, including, of course, optimism and pessimism, should satisfy procedural criteria such as these:

1. *The research design must be longitudinal.* Research participants must be followed over time. Merely showing a contemporaneous association between psychological states and physical well-being leaves unanswered the direction of the implied effect. Perhaps illness or health determines psychological state, or perhaps another factor gives rise to both the psychological state and health status.

2. *The longitudinal design must span enough time for changes in health to take place.* This may require several years or even decades. Because we are exploring new territory, we are not sure what should be the right time frame. We must, therefore, be leery of researchers who report "no results" from their studies trying to link psychological states with health and illness. Perhaps there really is no link to be found, and the researchers were indeed on a wild goose chase. But perhaps the optimal time span was not chosen.

3. *The initial health status of the research participants must be known when the investigation begins.* There is no point in finding that sick people stay sick, while healthy people stay healthy. Many researchers start with people's current health status and then try to work backward to reconstruct what they were like in

the first place. This is a reasonable procedure if the distant past can be reconstructed with fidelity, but that is not always the case. People distort their past, innocently or otherwise, and may retrospectively make better sense of what ensued than the facts warrant. Sick people may tell a story that rationalizes their sickness, and healthy people may rationalize their health. When we see a story about a centenarian, the person always attributes his or her longevity to something: eating yogurt, drinking cranberry wine, staying busy, whatever. These are pleasing accounts but hardly scientific explanations.

4. *An adequate number of research participants must be studied.* Links between psychological states and illness, if and when they exist, are apt to be subtle in nature and modest in strength. Only with a large number of research participants can patterns be discerned and potential confounds ruled out. Case studies of single individuals, no matter how striking, can be ambiguous precisely on this score.

5. *The psychological states of interest must be well-defined and measurable in a reliable and valid fashion.* Researchers should avoid in particular measures that are contaminated by a person's health status, which means that they end up using one aspect of his or her health to predict another aspect. The result, of course, is that these aspects will be related but that this convergence proves nothing. This has been a problem in stress research, for instance, where "illness" is considered a stressful life event that ends up being related to subsequent illness.

   Along these lines, some critics argue that optimism measures such as the LOT can be confounded by neuroticism, which also influences health measures that rely on respondents' self-reports (Costa & McCrae, 1987). A general inclination to complain may produce misleading correlations between pessimism and illness. A study that independently measures and controls for neuroticism (depression, dysphoria, whatever) is preferable to one that does not.

6. *Objective measures of health and illness must be made at the time that an investigation begins, during the study, and at its end.* Health and illness may seem easy for a researcher to ascertain, but remember our previous discussion of the fuzziness of health status. Knowing that no criterion of well-being is foolproof, researchers nonetheless must settle on a strategy for measuring it. As already emphasized, the various criteria of illness do not perfectly agree. One of the best established findings in 20th-century epidemiology is that morbidity and mortality do not

line up perfectly once we look separately at men and women: Women have more illnesses than men, but they also live longer (Verbrugge, 1989).

How Should We Think About This Research?

Several general points need to be made concerning how best to explain the influence of psychological factors on health and illness. First, Western science has for centuries made too strict a distinction between what is categorized as "mind" and what is categorized as "body." However, psychological factors and biological factors are mutually influential. This mutual influence is particularly important when our focus is on health and illness.

Second, despite the possible relevance of psychological factors to illness, we must not conclude that these are the only influences or even the most important ones. We all carry with us vulnerabilities and resiliencies as part of our genetic inheritance. One of the best predictors of longevity, for example, is how long our ancestors have lived.

Third, although most psychologists believe that psychological factors influence physical health and illness, there is considerable disagreement about the specificity of this influence. Do certain psychological states or traits make given illnesses more or less likely, or do they simply exert a general influence on well-being? Over the years theorists have proposed that angry people are at risk for heart disease, hopeless people for cancer, and so on. However, research suggests that such highly specific links usually do not exist (H. S. Friedman & Booth-Kewley, 1987). Still, a case can be made for studying how psychological factors influence a particular illness. Such a strategy holds constant many factors that potentially confound broader investigations of general well-being, such as sociodemographic and environmental risk factors for a specific illness, treatments, and the like (Schulz, Bookwala, Knapp, Scheier, & Williamson, 1996).

EMPIRICAL STUDIES OF OPTIMISM AND HEALTH

To date, there exist several dozen studies that have attempted to establish a correlation between optimism, rendered as explanatory style (measured with the ASQ or the CAVE) or dispositional optimism (measured with the LOT), and physical well-being.[1] Taken together, these studies

---

[1]If space permitted, we would survey research into the relatives of optimism and their link to physical health, constructs such as health locus of control (Wallston & Wallston, 1978), hardiness (Kobasa, 1979), sense of coherence (Antonovsky, 1985), positive illusions (Taylor, 1989), and so on. Suffice it to say that in each line of investigation, there is empirical support for the conclusion that positive thinking is correlated with good health, and negative thinking with poor health (Peterson, 1999).

converge impressively (see reviews by Carver, Spencer, & Scheier, 1998; Michaels, Michaels, & Peterson, 1997; Peterson, 1995, 1999, 2000; Peterson & Bossio, 1991, 1993; Peterson, Maier, & Seligman, 1993; Peterson & Seligman, 1987; Scheier & Bridges, 1995; Scheier & Carver, 1985, 1987, 1992).

Confirming Studies

Optimism predicts good health measured in a number of ways, from self-report, to physician ratings of general well-being, to doctor visits, to survival time following a heart attack, to immunological efficiency, to successful completion of rehabilitation programs to longevity. How strong is the association between optimism and good health? Most relevant studies report correlation coefficients in the .20–.30 range, which are moderate in size and typical of correlations in psychological research. Research participants included adults across the life span, some initially healthy and others initially quite ill. Many of these studies were longitudinal, spanning mere weeks to almost 5 decades. And at least some of these longitudinal studies statistically controlled for initial levels of health and potential confounds involving tendencies to complain.

Optimism apparently impacts health at a number of junctures. It can make the initial onset of illness less likely; it can minimize the severity of illness; it can speed recovery; and it can make relapse less likely. Most of the relevant studies, by virtue of rather stark correlational designs, do not allow conclusions about when health is impacted. Perhaps the cognates of optimism affect different aspects of physical well-being. Future investigations of a more fine-grained nature are indicated.

Studies of self-efficacy are usually more specific, focusing on how people respond once health is compromised in a given way. The following is a good summary of the relevant research:

> The evidence taken as a whole is consistent in showing that people's perceptions of their own efficacy are related to different forms of health behavior. In the realm of substance abuse, perceived self-regulatory efficacy is a reliable predictor of who will relapse and the circumstances of each person's first slip. Strong percepts of efficacy to manage pain increase pain tolerance . . . [Perceived efficacy with regard to] . . . eating and weight predicts who will succeed in overcoming eating disorders. Recovery from the severe trauma of myocardial infarction is tremendously facilitated by the enhancement of the patients' and their spouses' judgments of their physical and cardiac capabilities. And self-efficacy to affect one's own health increases adherence to medical regimens. . . . While specific procedures may differ for different domains, the

general strategy of assessing and enhancing self-percepts of efficacy to affect health ... has substantial general utility. (O'Leary, 1985, pp. 448–449)

So, the belief that one can cope appropriately with a given malady predicts successful rehabilitation or recovery.

Disconfirming Studies

Some studies fail to confirm the optimism–health association. In some cases, the procedural criteria discussed earlier for an optimal research design were not met. For example, Dua and Plumer (1993) found no association between explanatory style and the general health of nursing students, but only 27 research participants were included. This investigation had insufficient power to detect the hypothesized correlation (Peterson, Villanova, & Raps, 1985; Robins, 1988). For another example, Lin and Peterson (1990) found no association between explanatory style and recovery time from colds among mostly healthy college students, but their investigation spanned only a few weeks. A more adequate study would have looked at *patterns* in recovery from repeated episodes of minor illness over months or years.

Other studies deserve more attention because they imply that "positive" thinking may at times preclude good health. For example, *John Henryism* is a personality characteristic reflecting the degree to which someone believes that important life outcomes can be controlled if only sufficient effort is exerted. Among those African-American males in the lower class who lack the resources to make their belief in control a reality, John Henryism is linked to elevated blood pressure and presumably to all of the negative cardiac outcomes that result from hypertension (James, Hartnett, & Kalsbeek, 1983). Along these lines, the Type A coronary-prone behavior pattern seems to involve exaggerated beliefs about what the individual can make happen, and this style, again, has been linked to cardiac morbidity and mortality (M. Friedman & Rosenman, 1974).

The resolution suggested here is that optimism leads to good health when this belief is at least in principle veridical. What makes optimism an intriguing psychological variable is precisely that although it may be at odds with the initial facts (Taylor, 1989), it can be self-fulfilling. If circumstances do not allow an optimistic belief to be translated into a good outcome, then this belief is irrelevant at best and health-damaging at worst because it leads the individual to pursue impossible goals.

When unrealistic optimism is more a trait than a (transient) state, a person's life is compromised. Consider such problematic styles of behaving as hostility, perfectionism, risk taking, and narcissism; these can be recast in terms of unrealistic optimism (Peterson, 1999). Although not all these styles have been examined with respect to physical well-being, our strong sense is that they are indeed unhealthy.

The pervasive optimistic bias in risk perception is unrealistic and thus potentially hazardous. People who evidence the optimistic bias are Pollyannas—foolishly optimistic—and should not be confused with people who have an optimistic explanatory style. The positive expectations these latter individuals entertain are entwined with a sense of efficacy.

As Bandura (1986) emphasized, self-efficacy, although not identical with reality, is nonetheless influenced by the facts of the matter. Efficacy expectations ("I can perform this behavior") are advantageous only when coupled with veridical outcome expectations ("And this behavior has these consequences"). The optimistic bias in risk perception is the result of incorrect outcome expectations. However, the bias is reduced or eliminated to the degree that individuals have first-hand experience with or extensive knowledge about a given illness or injury and its risk factors (e.g., DeJoy, 1989; Kulik & Mahler, 1987; O'Hare, 1990; van der Velde, van der Pligt, & Hooykaas, 1994).

QUESTIONS ABOUT THE HEALTH–OPTIMISM LINK

Can a lifetime of good health be encouraged by the early cultivation of optimism? Gillham, Reivich, Jaycox, and Seligman (1995) have begun an intervention program that involves teaching grade school children to be more optimistic. Results to date suggest that optimism training makes subsequent episodes of depression less likely. Perhaps studies of physical well-being can be piggy-backed onto this ongoing investigation (see Buchanan, Gardenswartz, & Seligman, 1999).

We can similarly ask if optimistic ways of thinking acquired once an individual falls ill will boost good health. Again, studies of optimism and depression suggest that this question is worth pursuing. Cognitive therapy that targets negative ways of thinking alleviates depression and prevents its recurrence (Seligman et al., 1988). By implication, cognitive therapy for the seriously ill might pay health dividends.

Certainly, the most basic question that arises from research into optimism and health involves the mechanisms linking the two. In our earlier writing, we suggested that the link is overdetermined, and we sketched a number of plausible routes (Peterson & Bossio, 1991).

For example, there may be an immunological pathway. Kamen-Siegel, Rodin, Seligman, and Dwyer (1991) showed that optimism is positively correlated with the vigor with which the immune system responds to an antigen challenge. Several other researchers have looked at how explanatory style is linked to the progression of AIDS. Results here are mixed, but there are hints that optimism predicts survival time and that this effect is mediated in part by immunological factors (e.g., Blomkvist et al., 1994; Caumartin, Joseph, & Gillespie, 1993; Rabkin, Remien, Katoff, & Williams, 1993; but see Bofinger, Marguth, Pankofer, Seidl, & Ermann, 1993; Chuang, Jason, Pajurkova, & Gill, 1992; Tomakowsky, Lumley, Markowitz, & Frank, 1996).

There may also be an emotional pathway between optimism and health. An extensive research literature has shown optimism to be incompatible with depression (Sweeney, Anderson, & Bailey, 1986), and other studies have linked depression to poor health and early death. At least part of this latter path may be immunological (Schleifer, Keller, Siris, Davis, & Stein, 1985), and we begin to see the complexity involved in explaining why optimism and health are associated.

There are probably several cognitive pathways between optimism and health as well. Optimism is not an isolated belief but rather part of a complex knowledge system that can impact physical well-being in numerous ways. Dykema, Bergbower, and Peterson (1995), for example, showed that individuals with an optimistic explanatory style see the world as less filled with hassles than do their pessimistic counterparts; this tendency is in turn linked to better health.

Peterson and de Avila (1995), for another example, found that an optimistic explanatory style is associated with the belief that good health can be "controlled" (i.e., maintained and promoted). Indeed, in their research, Peterson and de Avila showed that an optimistic explanatory style is positively correlated with what we have been discussing as an optimistic bias in risk perception. However, this correlation was accounted for by the belief that one was able to do things to reduce risk.

Another explanation of why optimistic thinking is related to physical well-being points to a social pathway. People with a pessimistic explanatory style are often socially isolated (Anderson & Arnault, 1985), and social isolation is a consistent predictor of poor health (Cobb, 1976).

In general terms, the individual's social context can set the stage for the optimism–health link. Sagan (1987) put forth the intriguing argument that the dramatic increase in life expectancy in the Western world over the centuries was due not to breakthroughs in medical or public health practices but instead to cultural diffusion of the originally radical notion that an individual is a discrete self able to have an effect on the world. Once the idea of individual agency was invented, legitimized, and disseminated, the findings we have been discussing here became possible.

Although we believe that the link between optimism and health is complexly determined, the most typical and most robust mechanism is a mundane behavioral pathway. Self-efficacy research consistently attests to the beneficial behavior that efficacy expectations set into motion. Indeed,

Bandura (1977) developed the self-efficacy construct as part of a theory of behavior change. Similarly, Scheier and Carver's (1985) research on dispositional optimism emerged from a concern with self-regulation: how people align their behaviors with their goals and values. People who are dispositionally optimistic have better health because they act differently than do people who are dispositionally pessimistic; they cope differently, by persisting as opposed to giving up (Carver et al., 1993; Scheier et al., 1989; Strack, Carver, & Blaney, 1987). Individuals who are pessimistic about contracting AIDS sometimes engage in riskier sexual behavior, an example of a self-fulfilling prophecy if ever there were one (Kok, Ho, Heng, & Ong, 1990).[2]

Our own research on explanatory style similarly attests to the critical role of behavior in producing the optimism–health link. Peterson (1988) found that an optimistic explanatory style was associated with a variety of "healthy" practices: exercising, drinking in moderation, avoiding fatty foods, and the like. Peterson, Colvin, and Lin (1992) similarly found that people with an optimistic explanatory style were more likely than those with a pessimistic explanatory style to respond to colds with appropriate actions: resting and consuming more of Mom's chicken noodle soup.

Our most recent study of optimistic explanatory style and physical well-being looked at more than 1,000 individuals over almost 50 years (Peterson, Seligman, Yurko, Martin, & Friedman, 1998). Pessimistic individuals had an increased likelihood of an early death, and the large sample size made it further possible for us to investigate associations between explanatory style and death due to different causes. We expected that death by cancer and perhaps death by cardiovascular disease would be especially linked to a pessimistic way of thinking. However, we found that pessimistic individuals were most likely to die accidental or violent deaths. This effect was particularly pronounced for men.

Deaths like these are not random. "Being in the wrong place at the wrong time" may be the result of an incautious and fatalistic lifestyle entwined not only with pessimism but also with the male gender role. This study did not tell us what our deceased research participants were doing when they died accidentally or violently, but we strongly suspect that their behavior was somehow implicated, if only by affecting the settings they

---

[2]This result may not be a typical finding. Several studies have found that optimism is linked to behaviors that place one at risk for AIDS (e.g., Bahr et al., 1993; Perkins, Leserman, Murphy, & Evans, 1993), and still other investigations have discovered no association at all (e.g., Fontaine, 1994; Taylor et al., 1992). Perhaps both extreme pessimism *and* extreme optimism may be risk factors. The need to ground optimism in reality before deeming it healthy or unhealthy is underscored.

habitually entered (Buss, 1987). How does that old joke go? "I broke my nose in two places." "Oh, yeah? If I were you, I'd stay out of those places."

CONCLUSION

Optimistic thinking is linked to good health, but two important conditions must be satisfied. First, a person's optimism must lead him or her to act in a vigorous and sustained fashion: Behavior is a critical link in the process of attaining and sustaining physical well-being. Second, the behavior encouraged by optimism must have a realistic link to health. A casual reading of the popular literature on health and optimism might lead one to conclude that good health is all in a person's mind, but thoughts and beliefs must be situated within the person, and the person must be situated within the world (see Chopra, 1993; Cousins, 1981; Peale, 1952; Siegel, 1988).

It is no wonder that consumers are attracted to pop psychology. Americans are justifiably confused about health. The scientific establishment must bear considerable responsibility for this state of affairs. Citizens are deluged with information about health risks yet provided with no guidance about how to think about this information. For example, absolute risks should be stressed along with relative risks. It is ludicrous to debate whether mosquitoes or dentists can transmit AIDS if we overlook the role played by sexual practices.

Furthermore, modern medical practice has become so specialized and so narrowly biological that patients feel dealt out of the process of maintaining their own health. No wonder alternative medicine is thriving in the United States today (Eisenberg et al., 1993), just as it did about a century ago when conventional medicine was in a similar crisis (Weil, 1988). Alternative approaches address the whole person: thoughts, feelings, and behaviors. They allow the person to exercise choice. They sustain hope. Conventional medicine, in contrast, dismisses the role of psychological factors in health as placebo (that is, not real).

Finally, many health professionals, including ourselves in our own research, tend to focus on the quantity of life: how long people live and the degree to which they are free from disease. The quality of life—how people live for as long or as short as they do—is surely as important. Living well is sometimes referred to as wellness, a concept that cannot be captured by longevity or freedom from disease (Barsky, 1988). Wellness involves a zest for ongoing life, a fulfilling career, and satisfactory relationships with family members and friends. When we think about psychological influences on health, we should consider how psychology can add to the quality of life (Seeman, 1989).

REFERENCES

Abramson, L. Y., Metalsky, G. I., & Alloy, L. B. (1989). Hopelessness depression: A theory-based subtype of depression. *Psychological Review, 96*, 358–372.

Abramson, L. Y., Seligman, M. E. P., & Teasdale, J. D. (1978). Learned helplessness in humans: Critique and reformulation. *Journal of Abnormal Psychology, 87*, 49–74.

Anderson, C. A., & Arnault, L. H. (1985). Attributional style and everyday problems in living: Depression, loneliness, and shyness. *Social Cognition, 3*, 16–35.

Antonovsky, A. (1985). The sense of coherence as a determinant of health. In J. D. Matarazzo, S. M. Weiss, J. A. Herd, N. E. Miller, & S. M. Weiss (Eds.), *Behavioral health: A handbook of health enhancement and disease prevention* (pp. 114–129). New York: Wiley.

Bahr, G. R., Sikkema, K. J., Kelly, J. A., Fernandez, M. I., Stevenson, L. Y., & Koob, J. J. (1993). Attitudes and characteristics of gay men who remain at continued risk for contracting HIV infection. *International Conference on AIDS, 9*, 697.

Bandura, A. (1977). Self-efficacy: Toward a unifying theory of behavioral change. *Psychological Review, 84*, 191–215.

Bandura, A. (1986). *Social foundations of thought and action.* Englewood Cliffs, NJ: Prentice-Hall.

Barsky, A. J. (1988). *Worried sick: Our troubled quest for wellness.* Boston: Little, Brown.

Blomkvist, V., Theorell, T., Jonsson, H., Schulman, S., Berntorp, E., & Stiegendal, L. (1994). Coping style in relation to the consumption of factor concentrate in HIV-infected hemophiliacs during the years after their infection became known. *Psychotherapy and Psychosomatics, 61*, 205–210.

Bofinger, F., Marguth, U., Pankofer, R., Seidl, O., & Ermann, M. (1993). Psychosocial aspects of longterm-surviving with AIDS. *International Conference on AIDS, 9*, 878.

Buchanan, G. M., Gardenswartz, C. A. R., & Seligman, M. E. P. (1999, December 21). Physical health following a cognitive-behavioral intervention. *Prevention and Treatment, 2*, Article 10. Available on the World Wide Web: http://journals.apa.org/prevention/volume2/pre0020010a.html

Buss, D. M. (1987). Selection, evocation, and manipulation. *Journal of Personality and Social Psychology, 53*, 1214–1221.

Carver, C. S. (1989). How should multi-faceted personality constructs be tested? Issues illustrated by self-monitoring, attributional style, and hardiness. *Journal of Personality and Social Psychology, 56*, 577–585.

Carver, C. S., Pozo, C., Harris, S. D., Noriega, V., Scheier, M. F., Robinson, D. S., Ketcham, A. S., Moffat, F. L., & Clark, K. C. (1993). How coping mediates the effect of optimism on distress: A study of women with early stage breast cancer. *Journal of Personality and Social Psychology, 65*, 375–390.

Carver, C. S., Spencer, S. M., & Scheier, M. F. (1998). Optimism, motivation, and mental health. In H. S. Friedman (Ed.), *Encyclopedia of mental health* (Vol. 3, pp. 41–52). San Diego, CA: Academic Press.

Caumartin, S. M., Joseph, J. G., & Gillespie, B. (1993). The relationship between social participation and AIDS survival in the Chicago MACS/CCS cohort. *International Conference on AIDS, 9*, 886.

Chopra, D. (1993). *Ageless body, timeless mind.* New York: Harmony Books.

Chuang, H. T., Jason, G. W., Pajurkova, E. M., & Gill, M. J. (1992). Psychiatric morbidity in patients with HIV infection. *Canadian Journal of Psychiatry, 37*, 109–115.

Cobb, S. (1976). Social support as a moderator of life stress. *Psychosomatic Medicine, 38*, 300–314.

Costa, P. T., & McCrae, R. R. (1987). Neuroticism, somatic complaints, and disease: Is the bark worse than the bite? *Journal of Personality, 55*, 299–316.

Cousins, N. (1981). *The anatomy of an illness.* New York: Norton.

DeJoy, D. M. (1989). The optimism bias and traffic accident perception. *Accident Analysis and Prevention, 21*, 333–340.

Dua, J., & Plumer, G. (1993). Relationship between attributional style, individualized attributional style, and health. *Psychological Reports, 72*, 913–914.

Dykema, J., Bergbower, K., & Peterson, C. (1995). Pessimistic explanatory style, stress, and illness. *Journal of Social and Clinical Psychology, 14*, 357–371.

Eisenberg, D. M., Kessler, R. C., Foster, C., Norlock, F. E., Calkins, D. R., & Delblanco, T. L. (1993). Unconventional medicine in the United States: Prevalence, costs, and patterns of use. *New England Journal of Medicine, 328*, 246–252.

Fontaine, K. R. (1994). Effects of dispositional optimism on comparative risk perceptions for developing AIDS. *Psychological Reports, 74*, 843–846.

Friedman, H. S., & Booth-Kewley, S. (1987). The "disease-prone personality": A meta-analytic view of the concept. *American Psychologist, 42*, 539–555.

Friedman, M., & Rosenman, R. (1974). *Type A behavior and your heart.* New York: Knopf.

Gillham, J. E., Reivich, K. J., Jaycox, L. H., & Seligman, M. E. P. (1995). Prevention of depressive symptoms in schoolchildren: Two-year follow-up. *Psychological Science, 6*, 343–351.

James, S. A., Hartnett, S. A., & Kalsbeek, W. D. (1983). John Henryism and blood pressure differences among black men. *Journal of Behavioral Medicine, 6*, 259–278.

Kamen-Siegel, L., Rodin, J., Seligman, M. E. P., & Dwyer, J. (1991). Explanatory style and cell-mediated immunity. *Health Psychology, 10*, 229–235.

Kobasa, S. C. (1979). Stressful life events, personality, and health: An inquiry into hardiness. *Journal of Personality and Social Psychology, 37,* 1–11.

Kok, L. P., Ho, M. L., Heng, B. H., & Ong, Y. W. (1990). A psychosocial study of high risk subjects for AIDS. *Singapore Medical Journal, 31,* 573–582.

Kulik, J. A., & Mahler, H. I. (1987). Health status, perceptions of risk, and prevention interest for health and nonhealth problems. *Health Psychology, 6,* 15–27.

Lee, F., & Peterson, C. (1997). Content analysis of archival data. *Journal of Consulting and Clinical Psychology, 65,* 959–969.

Lin, E. H., & Peterson, C. (1990). Pessimistic explanatory style and response to illness. *Behaviour Research and Therapy, 28,* 243–248.

Michaels, C. E., Michaels, A. J., & Peterson, C. (1997). Motivation and health. In P. Pintrich & M. Maeher (Eds.), *Advances in motivation and achievement* (Vol. 10, pp. 339–374). Greenwich, CT: JAI Press.

O'Hare, D. (1990). Pilots' perception of risks and hazards in general aviation. *Aviation Space and Environmental Medicine, 61,* 599–603.

O'Leary, A. (1985). Self-efficacy and health. *Behaviour Research and Therapy, 23,* 437–451.

Peale, N. V. (1952). *The power of positive thinking.* Englewood Cliffs, NJ: Prentice-Hall.

Perkins, D. O., Leserman, J., Murphy, C., & Evans, D. L. (1993). Psychosocial predictors of high-risk sexual behavior among HIV-negative homosexual men. *AIDS Education and Prevention, 5,* 141–152.

Peterson, C. (1988). Explanatory style as a risk factor for illness. *Cognitive Therapy and Research, 12,* 117–130.

Peterson, C. (1995). Explanatory style and health. In G. M. Buchanan & M. E. P. Seligman (Eds.), *Explanatory style* (pp. 233–246). Hillsdale, NJ: Erlbaum.

Peterson, C. (1999). Personal control and well-being. In D. Kahneman, E. Diener, & N. Schwarz (Eds.), *Well-being: The foundations of hedonic psychology* (pp. 288–301). New York: Russell Sage Foundation.

Peterson, C. (2000). The future of optimism. *American Psychologist, 57,* 44–55.

Peterson, C., Bettes, B. A., & Seligman, M. E. P. (1985). Depressive symptoms and unprompted causal attributions: Content analysis. *Behaviour Research and Therapy, 23,* 379–382.

Peterson, C., & Bossio, L. M. (1991). *Health and optimism.* New York: Free Press.

Peterson, C., & Bossio, L. M. (1993). Healthy attitudes: Optimism, hope, and control. In D. Goleman & J. Gurin (Eds.), *Mind/body medicine: How to use your mind for better health* (pp. 351–366). Yonkers, NY: Consumer Reports Books.

Peterson, C., Colvin, D., & Lin, E. H. (1992). Explanatory style and helplessness. *Social Behavior and Personality, 20,* 1–14.

Peterson, C., & de Avila, M. E. (1995). Optimistic explanatory style and the perception of health problems. *Journal of Clinical Psychology, 51,* 128–132.

Peterson, C., Maier, S. F., & Seligman, M. E. P. (1993). *Learned helplessness: A theory for the age of personal control.* New York: Oxford University Press.

Peterson, C., & Park, C. (1997). *Implicit and explicit explanatory styles in the lifecourse of college-educated women.* Unpublished manuscript, University of Michigan, Ann Arbor.

Peterson, C., Schulman, P., Castellon, C., & Seligman, M. E. P. (1992). CAVE: Content analysis of verbatim explanations. In C. P. Smith (Ed.), *Motivation and personality: Handbook of thematic content analysis* (pp. 383–392). New York: Cambridge University Press.

Peterson, C., & Seligman, M. E. P. (1984). Causal explanations as a risk factor for depression: Theory and evidence. *Psychological Review, 91,* 347–374.

Peterson, C., & Seligman, M. E. P. (1987). Explanatory style and illness. *Journal of Personality, 55,* 237–265.

Peterson, C., Seligman, M. E. P., & Vaillant, G. E. (1988). Pessimistic explanatory style is a risk factor for physical illness: A thirty-five year longitudinal study. *Journal of Personality and Social Psychology, 55,* 23–27.

Peterson, C., Seligman, M. E. P., Yurko, K. H., Martin, L. R., & Friedman, H. S. (1998). Catastrophizing and untimely death. *Psychological Science, 9,* 127–130.

Peterson, C., Semmel, A., von Baeyer, C., Abramson, L. Y., Metalsky, G. I., & Seligman, M. E. P. (1982). The Attributional Style Questionnaire. *Cognitive Therapy and Research, 6,* 287–299.

Peterson, C., & Stunkard, A. J. (1989). Personal control and health promotion. *Social Science and Medicine, 28,* 819–828.

Peterson, C., & Villanova, P. (1988). An expanded Attributional Style Questionnaire. *Journal of Abnormal Psychology, 97,* 87–89.

Peterson, C., Villanova, P., & Raps, C. S. (1985). Depression and attributions: Factors responsible for inconsistent results in the published literature. *Journal of Abnormal Psychology, 94,* 165–168.

Rabkin, J. G., Remien, R., Katoff, L., & Williams, J. B. (1993). Resilience in adversity among long-term survivors of AIDS. *Hospital and Community Psychiatry, 44,* 162–167.

Reivich, K. (1995). The measurement of explanatory style. In G. M. Buchanan & M. E. P. Seligman (Eds.), *Explanatory style* (pp. 21–47). Hillsdale, NJ: Erlbaum.

Robins, C. J. (1988). Attributions and depression: Why is the literature so inconsistent? *Journal of Personality and Social Psychology, 54,* 880–889.

Sagan, L. A. (1987). *The health of nations: True causes of sickness and well-being.* New York: Basic Books.

Scheier, M. F., & Bridges, M. W. (1995). Person variables and health: Personality predispositions and acute psychological states as shared determinants for disease. *Psychosomatic Medicine, 57,* 255–268.

Scheier, M. F., & Carver, C. S. (1985). Optimism, coping, and health: Assessment and implications of generalized outcome expectancies. *Health Psychology, 4,* 219–247.

Scheier, M. F., & Carver, C. S. (1987). Dispositional optimism and physical well-being: The influence of generalized outcome expectancies on health. *Journal of Personality, 55*, 169–210.

Scheier, M. F., & Carver, C. S. (1992). Effects of optimism on psychological and physical well-being: Theoretical overview and empirical update. *Cognitive Therapy and Research, 16*, 201–228.

Scheier, M. F., Matthews, K. A., Owen, J. F., Magovern, G. J., Lefebvre, R. C., Abbott, R. A., & Carver, C. S. (1989). Dispositional optimism and recovery from coronary artery bypass surgery: The beneficial effects on physical and psychological well-being. *Journal of Personality and Social Psychology, 57*, 1024–1040.

Schleifer, S. J., Keller, S. E., Siris, S. G., Davis, K. L., & Stein, M. (1985). Depression and immunity. *Archives of General Psychiatry, 42*, 129–133.

Schulz, R., Bookwala, J., Knapp, J. E., Scheier, M. F., & Williamson, G. M. (1996). Pessimism, age, and cancer mortality. *Psychology and Aging, 11*, 304–309.

Seeman, J. (1989). Toward a model of positive health. *American Psychologist, 44*, 1099–1109.

Seligman, M. E. P., Castellon, C., Cacciola, J., Schulman, P., Luborsky, L., Ollove, M., & Downing, R. (1988). Explanatory style change during cognitive therapy for unipolar depression. *Journal of Abnormal Psychology, 97*, 13–18.

Siegel, B. S. (1988). *Love, medicine, and miracles.* New York: Perennial.

Strack, S., Carver, C. S., & Blaney, P. H. (1987). Predicting successful completion of an aftercare program following treatment for alcoholism: The role of dispositional optimism. *Journal of Personality and Social Psychology, 53*, 579–584.

Sweeney, P. D., Anderson, K., & Bailey, S. (1986). Attributional style in depression: A meta-analytic review. *Journal of Personality and Social Psychology, 50*, 974–991.

Taylor, S. E. (1989). *Positive illusions.* New York: Basic Books.

Taylor, S. E., Kemeny, M. E., Aspinwall, L. G., Schneider, S. G., Rodriguez, R., & Herbert, M. (1992). Optimism, coping, psychological distress, and high-risk sexual behavior among men at risk for acquired immunodeficiency syndrome (AIDS). *Journal of Personality and Social Psychology, 63*, 460–473.

Tennen, H., & Herzberger, S. (1986). Attributional Style Questionnaire. In D. J. Keyser & R. C. Sweetland (Eds.), *Test critiques* (Vol. 4, pp. 20–30). Kansas City, KS: Test Corporation of America.

Tomakowsky, J., Lumley, M. A., Markowitz, N., & Frank, C. (1996). *The relationships of optimistic explanatory style and dispositional optimism to health in HIV-infected men.* Unpublished manuscript, Wayne State University, Detroit, MI.

van der Velde, F. W., van der Pligt, J., & Hooykaas, C. (1994). Perceiving AIDS-related risk: Accuracy as a function of differences in actual risk. *Health Psychology, 13*, 25–33.

Verbrugge, L. M. (1989). Recent, present, and future health of American adults. *Annual Review of Public Health, 10*, 333–361.

Wallston, K. A., & Wallston, B. S. (1978). Locus of control and health: A review of the literature. *Health Education Monographs, 6,* 107–117.

Weil, A. (1988). *Health and healing* (Rev. ed.). Boston: Houghton Mifflin.

Weinstein, N. D. (1989). Optimistic biases about personal risks. *Science, 246,* 1232–1233.

7

OPTIMISM, PESSIMISM, AND DAILY LIFE WITH CHRONIC ILLNESS

GLENN AFFLECK, HOWARD TENNEN, AND ANDREA APTER

Dispositional optimism has become a new focal point of theory and research on adaptation to adversity and stressful events. Nowhere has this formidable resource been inspiring more investigation than in the literature on coping with illness and other medical stressors. Health problems and their treatment offer an excellent opportunity to evaluate whether a generalized expectancy for positive outcomes (Scheier & Carver, 1985) confers both short- and long-term benefits for both emotional and physical well-being. In this vein, people characterized as dispositional optimists have been shown to display superior psychosocial adaptation to a host of medical stressors, including coronary artery bypass surgery (Fitzgerald, Tennen, Affleck, & Pransky, 1993; Scheier et al., 1989); childbirth (Carver & Gaines, 1987);

The authors' studies described in this chapter were funded by the National Institute of Arthritis, Musculoskeletal, and Skin Diseases, the American Lung Association of Connecticut, and the University of Connecticut General Clinical Research Center. For their assistance with these studies, we thank co-investigators Susan Urrows, Pamela Higgins, Judith Fifield, Richard ZuWallack, and Micha Abeles.

147

failed in vitro fertilization (Litt, Tennen, Affleck, & Klock, 1992); bone marrow transplantation (Curbow, Somerfield, Baker, Wingard, & Legro, 1993); arthritis (Tennen, Affleck, Urrows, Higgins, & Mendola, 1992); tinnitus and hearing impairment (Andersson, 1996a); HIV-positive status (Taylor et al., 1992); pregnancy termination (Cozzarelli, 1993); and cancer in oneself (Carver et al., 1994); or in one's loved ones (Given et al., 1993).

In two reviews of the consequences of dispositional optimism for *physical* well-being, Scheier and Carver (1987, 1992) summarized effects from the appearance of physical symptoms in healthy individuals to milestones of physical recovery from coronary artery bypass surgery, and of mediators such as optimists' better health habits, more positive mood, coping strategies, competent immune functioning, and diminished cardiovascular reactivity to stress.

Vexing theoretical questions about the mechanisms by which dispositional optimism can prevent illness, foster recovery, and assist adaptation to health-related stressors remain, and many methodological problems in this research area require creative solutions. This chapter offers some conceptual refinements and methodological innovations for investigation of the *daily* consequences and constituents of optimism. Because few prospective studies of daily experience on dispositional optimism have been published, we draw heavily on the methods and empirical findings of our own research program on daily life with chronic illness. Before summarizing this work as it relates to literature on optimism, we review some of the theoretical and methodological advantages of a daily-process paradigm for research on optimism and on other personal dispositions and traits.

PERSONALITY AND THE STUDY OF EVERYDAY LIFE

Two decades ago, Lazarus (1978), Epstein (1979), and Csikszentmihalyi, Larson, and Prescott (1977) challenged personality psychologists to study intensively people's thoughts, feelings, and behaviors over time. Lazarus believed that for the field to advance, investigators needed to shift from examining a single individual difference on an isolated occasion to exploring processes and patterns of relations that unfold in time. Epstein (1983) argued that defining *personality* as relatively stable reaction tendencies that distinguish individuals from one another obliges us to inspect "responses of multiple individuals on multiple measures over multiple occasions" (p. 91). Csikszentmihalyi and colleagues (Csikszentmihalyi & Larson, 1987) initiated studies of daily experience in which individuals recorded their momentary thoughts, feelings, and behavior in response to signals from radio-controlled beepers. The "experience sampling method" presented a new perspective on everyday behavior and revealed the benefits of studying psychological processes in their natural context.

This call to study people over time and across occasions has had a growing impact on the way personality research is conducted (Tennen, Suls, & Affleck, 1991). Larsen (1990) surveyed articles appearing in three leading personality journals that employed intensive time-sampling methods, most of which took the day as their unit of analysis. The number of articles employing these methods increased nearly threefold between 1976 and 1988, a trend that we suspect has continued at an accelerating pace. This methodology has also been rapidly gaining popularity in the literature of health psychology and behavioral medicine (Affleck & Tennen, 1996; Stone & Shiffman, 1994). The compatibility of daily-process methods for research on personality and health should also accelerate this specific area of investigation.

Tennen et al. (1991) identified several ways in which a daily-process paradigm can advance research on personality, especially research at the intersection of personality and health. The first promise of such a paradigm lies in its giving personality theorists the ability to ask and answer the traditional questions of interest in creative new ways. For example, do people evidence consistency in their behavior and experience, or is daily variation the norm? A long-standing debate among personality theorists is the extent to which behavior is tied to its context and the extent to which it reflects traits. In response to this debate, Epstein (1977) argued that because traits refer to broad action tendencies, their adequate measurement requires aggregating data over time and across situations, a procedure executed best in the context of people's everyday activities and experiences. This issue remains relatively unstudied in the literature on optimism. Is optimism stable across time and situations when time intervals and situations flow from the rhythms and events of everyday life? Although individuals might differ in the "mean levels" of optimism across days and daily experiences, the deviations from the mean may represent an important "state" component of optimism, with its unique antecedents and consequences. The ebb and flow of symptoms in chronically ill individuals, for example, might track state variations in general optimism.

A second promise of studying daily life is that it will provide the capability to test new models of how major events influence health and well-being. It has been argued, for example, that major life events assume some of their adaptational consequences by influencing everyday affairs (Kanner, Coyne, Schaefer, & Lazarus, 1981; Zautra, Affleck, & Tennen, 1994). Thus, the death of a spouse is not only a significant loss, but also a disruption of established recreational patterns, formerly shared responsibilities, and day-to-day social relations. A key question for future research is whether optimism could buffer individuals from the disruption in everyday activities that typically stems from major life changes.

A third and most alluring promise is that studying people intensively may allow us to address questions that can *only* be answered by studying individuals on a daily basis. For example, do daily stressors affect mood beyond the day of their occurrence? Although Stone and Neale (1984a) reported that daily events affect mood only on the day they occur, Bolger, DeLongis, Kessler, and Schilling (1989) found that mood was actually brighter on a day following a stressful event than on stress-free days. The relation between fleeting events and vacillating emotions is undoubtedly complex and difficult to capture, and this complexity demands that we study individuals daily or even more intensively. Such studies could document the ability of optimism to modify the strength—or even direction—of the dynamic relations between events and emotions.

Another question that can only be addressed by studying daily experiences is whether certain emotions or symptoms co-occur within the same individual. For example, when people are depressed, are they also anxious? Are they also angry? That depression, anxiety, and hostility are positively correlated across individuals (e.g., Gotlib, 1984; Watson & Clark, 1984) has no bearing on these questions. Rather, this positive correlation shows that individuals who are less anxious than their peers are also less angry and less depressed (see Epstein, 1986). Intraindividual correlations over time and circumstances, which address these questions directly, actually reveal that when someone is sadder than usual, she or he is *less* angry (Epstein, 1983) and *less* anxious (Larsen & Ketelaar, 1991). To best understand the emotional and other processes related to psychological and physical well-being, we need to examine them as they unfold. Would the modest between-person relation between optimism and pessimism (e.g., Marshall, Wortman, Kusulas, Hervig, & Vickers, 1992) be replicated at the within-person level of the day-to-day covariation in the state components of these constructs? Individual differences in this association might be fertile territory for investigation.

These are only some of the questions that demand intensive time sampling. Another set of questions relate to the study of patterns in experience and behavior. For example, the daily experience paradigm allows us to address prospectively the duration of emotional distress (Epstein, 1983) and physical symptoms (Larsen & Kasimatis, 1991). It provides a context in which to study when and how individuals habituate to events (Bolger et al., 1989), and to study who is more likely to do so. It encourages us to examine the frequency of change in our adaptation to events (Larsen, 1987) and individual differences in reactivity to events (Affleck, Tennen, Urrows, & Higgins, 1994; Bolger & Schilling, 1991). Most clearly, it forces us to consider "time" as a psychological variable. Might optimistic people be distinguished by their ability to interrupt periods of distress? Might they recover more quickly from illness episodes? Might they be better able to limit the number of consecutive days in which their chronic illness symptoms are unusually severe?

The promise of a daily-process paradigm for research on optimism remains largely unmet. We are aware of only three published studies on optimism that used prospective daily measures for any purpose. Shifren and Hooker (1995) examined the characteristics of a "state" version of the Life Orientation Test (LOT; Scheier & Carver, 1985) in a sample of 30 spouse caregivers of individuals with probable Alzheimer's disease. Both the state LOT and mood were assessed daily for 30 days. The authors demonstrated significant day-to-day variability in state optimism. For approximately one third of the participants, state optimism changes were linked with changes in positive and negative affect from day to day. Shifren (1996) followed this up with a small study of patients with Parkinson's disease, who for 70 consecutive days completed the state version of the LOT and reported indicators of disease severity. For 3 of the 12 patients studied, heightened levels of optimism on a given day predicted declines the next day in perceived severity of the illness. More optimistic individuals, that is, those individuals who scored higher in average daily optimism, also saw themselves as less in need of assistance with activities of daily living.

Tennen et al. (1992) examined how dispositional optimism and finding benefits in adversity relate to one another and figure in the aggregate levels of daily symptoms, mood, and functioning of individuals with rheumatoid arthritis. After completing the LOT and measures of perceived control over and benefits from their chronic pain drawn from the Inventory of Perceived Control Beliefs (Mendola, 1990), research participants reported their pain intensity, mood, and pain-related activity limitations (e.g., missing work, cutting back on planned social activities) each day for 75 consecutive days. Those participants scoring higher on the LOT were significantly more likely to construe benefits from their illness, and they also reported significantly higher levels of average positive daily mood and fewer pain-related activity limitation days.

The study by Tennen et al. (1992) reports a few findings from our broader research program and sets the stage for summarizing many other effects of optimism or pessimism on prospective accounts of daily life with chronic illness. We begin an overview of our work with a more comprehensive look at the daily correlates of optimism and pessimism in our diary study of patients with rheumatoid arthritis. We then review selected findings from a full "idiographic–nomothetic" analysis of the effects of dispositional optimism and pessimism on daily life with participants experiencing either fibromyalgia or asthma. We close with an exploration of a possible constituent of optimism in daily life with chronic illness: the expectation of symptom changes from day to day.

OPTIMISM, PESSIMISM, AND DAILY LIFE WITH ARTHRITIS

Our first attempt to document the daily consequences of dispositional optimism or pessimism was in a prospective study of the daily life experiences of individuals with rheumatoid arthritis (RA), a chronic and painful disease. The 75 patients recruited for this study began their participation by completing questionnaire measures of optimism and pessimism with the LOT and a host of other background characteristics, including neuroticism, depressive symptoms, social support, pain appraisals, pain coping strategies, and catastrophizing responses to pain. Then, for 75 consecutive days, within 1 hour of bedtime they completed a structured diary that they returned to us by mail the next morning. The diary measures included the intensity of pain in 20 joints, the quality of the previous night's sleep, positive and negative mood reported on the POMS-B (Lorr & McNair, 1982), desirable and undesirable events reported with the Daily Life Experience Checklist (Stone & Neale, 1982), and the extent of pain-related daily limitations in work, child care, social and household responsibilities.

Aggregating these daily measures afforded an uncommonly reliable picture of patients' average days. As we have documented elsewhere (Affleck & Tennen, 1996), recall errors can be expected in retrospective accounts of events, symptoms, mood, and appraisals. More important than inaccuracy per se is the source of the error. We need to be concerned not only with random error, but especially with systematic error in the recall of pain, mood, and events. Individuals who differ on other study variables (or more important, in key ways not measured) may report differentially accurate data or use different cognitive heuristics to assist their recall (Linton, 1991).

The correlations presented in Table 7.1 taught us two lessons about the role of generalized outcome expectancies in daily life with RA. First was the independence of pessimism as a predictor of negative experiences. Regardless of their level of optimism, the more pessimistic patients reported more negative daily mood, more pain-related activity limitations, more negative daily events, and poorer sleep. Of interest is that the only pessimism-adjusted daily correlate of optimism was its association with positive mood.

These findings underscore the value of a two-factor model of generalized expectancies and daily life, evidenced especially by the parallelism between pessimism and negative experiences. They also reinforce the desirability of treating optimism and pessimism as separate constructs, instead of as opposite

Table 7.1.
Statistically Significant Correlates of Dispositional Optimism or Pessimism
in 75 Patients With Rheumatoid Arthritis

	Optimism	Pessimism
Education		−.23*
		(−.35**)
Neuroticism	−.45***	.58***
	(−.39***)	(.53***)
Depression symptoms	−.31**	.42***
	(−.21)	(.38***)
Perceived social support	.27*	−.35**
	(.23*)	(−.31**)
Personal control over pain	.43***	
	(.39***)	
Perceived efficacy of pain coping		−.25*
		(−.28*)
Pain catastrophizing	−.24*	.38***
	(−.16)	(.36**)
Perceived pain-related benefits	.28**	
	(.26*)	
Pain-coping strategies		
Positive self-statements	.29**	
	(.28**)	
Prayer and hope	.27*	
	(.24*)	
Distraction	.33**	
	(.27*)	
Reinterpret pain sensations	.25*	
	(.21)	
Daily diary aggregates		
Pain-related activity limitations		.23*
		(.23*)
Undesirable events		.30**
		(.28*)
Negative mood		.38***
		(.33**)
Positive mood	.46***	−.38***
	(.40***)	(−.31**)
Sleep quality		−.29**
		(−.23*)

Note. Nonparenthesized correlations are unpartialled; parenthesized correlations with optimism partial the effects of pessimism, parenthesized correlations with pessimism partial the effects of optimism.
* $p < .05$. ** $p < .01$. *** $p < .001$.

ends of a bipolar continuum. There is compelling evidence that optimism, at least as measured by total scores on the LOT, is not a unitary construct. Instead, the LOT appears to measure two relatively orthogonal constructs: optimism *and* pessimism (Chang, D'Zurilla, & Maydeu-Olivares, 1994; Robinson-Whelen, Kim, MacCallum, & Kiecolt-Glaser, 1997). Our findings agree with those establishing that optimism and pessimism may not have equivalent relations with other personality and adaptational outcome measures (e.g., Marshall et al., 1992; Mroczek, Spiro, Aldwin, Ozer, & Bosse, 1993).

Other correlations appearing in Table 7.1 taught us a second lesson, this one concerning the specificity of these findings. Optimism and pessimism were correlated with other person and situation variables that themselves figure in the quality of daily life. Once again, the more pessimistic individuals differed in other negative traits (neuroticism) and states (depression, poor social support) regardless of their level of optimism, and the more optimistic individuals were more likely to report cognitive coping strategies, good social support, and more personal control over their pain, regardless of their level of pessimism. The critical issue, which is more conceptual than statistical, concerns the status of these variables in the relation to generalized expectancies and daily experiences. Are they to be viewed as potential confounds or as mediators? If the former, they need to be controlled statistically. If the latter, they need to be incorporated as explanatory variables in fuller models, as has been accomplished in research on coping strategies as mediators of the relation between optimism and adaptation to health problems (Scheier & Carver, 1992).

A controversial point concerns the shared variance between the personality trait of neuroticism and that of optimism or pessimism. Smith, Pope, Rhodewalt, and Poulton (1989) were among the first to advocate partialling the effects of neuroticism from relations between optimism or pessimism and assessments of physical and psychological well-being. Scheier, Carver, and Bridges (1994) countered this argument with two observations. First, whereas the relation between optimism or pessimism and adaptational outcomes can often be "explained" by neuroticism, other important mediating variables linking personality and well-being, for example, coping behaviors, appear to be independently related to optimism or pessimism. Second, the construct of neuroticism itself consists partly of a pessimistic orientation, introducing a conceptual overlap between the two constructs. This complicates the interpretation of neuroticism-adjusted associations between optimism or pessimism and other adaptational processes and outcomes. Furthermore, Marshall et al. (1992) found that when optimism and pessimism are treated as independent constructs, only pessimism is a correlate of neuroticism.

The findings just summarized from our RA daily experience study fail to take full advantage of the variation in the person–day data set. By aggregating the daily reports, we lost information about the within-person relations between the daily-process variables. When both differences between persons and differences within persons over time are considered in a mixed "idiographic–nomothetic" design, one can use powerful statistical methods and draw stronger inferences about the role of optimism in the dynamics of daily life (Affleck & Tennen, 1996; Epstein, 1983; Larsen & Kasimatis, 1991).

EXAMINING RELATIONS WITHIN AND ACROSS INDIVIDUALS: MIXED IDIOGRAPHIC–NOMOTHETIC DESIGN

The dominant tradition in behavioral research is the *nomothetic approach,* which asks whether there are lawful relations among variables across individuals. The *idiographic approach* examines relations among variables *within* an individual, across time or situations in that individual's life. The combination of these approaches in the mixed idiographic–nomothetic design enables investigators to ask: *Are there relations between variables within individuals over time that generalize across individuals or that relate to differences between individuals?* Answering this question requires that we first examine relations among variables over time for each individual we study. We must then return to the population level in two ways: by determining if the within-person relations generalize across persons, and by discerning how they relate to differences between individuals. As we demonstrate next, relating within-person associations to between-person differences yields rich insights into the processes by which optimism and pessimism are expressed in the dynamics of daily life.

Daily Life With Chronic Illness: An Idiographic–Nomothetic Analysis

The two prospective daily studies we describe below were conducted with adult patients with asthma and women with primary fibromyalgia syndrome (PFS). The asthma sample consisted of 48 individuals with moderate-to-severe asthma who were taking inhaled steroids for disease management. The PFS sample comprises 89 women who experienced pain in all body quadrants of at least 3 months' duration, pain in 11 of 18 tender point sites upon moderate digital pressure exerted by a clinical examiner, and the absence of other musculoskeletal pain disorders that could cause secondary fibromyalgia (e.g., rheumatoid arthritis).

The intensive self-monitoring methods used in these studies were nearly identical. For 30 days (fibromyalgia) or 21 days (asthma) participants filled out paper-and-pencil diaries before retiring to sleep. Variables measured in the nightly booklet included a rating of that day's perceived control over illness symptoms; a rating of the perceived efficacy of that day's strategies of coping with symptoms; and a checklist of pain or asthma symptom coping strategies adapted from the Daily Coping Inventory (Stone & Neale, 1984b); and for fibromyalgia patients only, a checklist of undesirable and desirable daily events culled from the Inventory of Small Life Events (Zautra, Guarnaccia, Reich, & Dohrenwend, 1988).

Pain, asthma symptoms, and mood are likely to change over the course of a day, so even end-of-day summaries may be contaminated by systematic retrospection errors in subjective averaging (Hedges, Jandorf, & Stone, 1985). To gather within-day reports more reliably, we employed an "electronic interviewer" (ELI) modeled on Shiffman's (Shiffman et al., 1994) innovative procedure for "ecological momentary assessment" (Stone & Shiffman, 1994). Participants carried Psion Organizer II palm-top computers (Psion Corporation, Concord, MA), which were programmed to request, and then time stamp, information about their previous night's sleep quality once a day after awakening, and to request and then time stamp their symptoms, mood, and the extent to which their attention was focused on their symptoms three times a day, at randomly selected times during the morning, afternoon, and evening. (For further procedural details and other findings from our ELI studies, see Affleck et al., 1998; Affleck, Urrows, Tennen, Higgins, & Abeles, 1996; Apter et al., 1997).

The analyses summarized below concern the ability of dispositional optimism or pessimism to predict (a) mean levels of daily symptoms; attention to symptoms, mood, daily events, coping strategies, and symptom-related cognitions; and (b) variation in the within-person relations of changes in symptom severity with other measures, that is, "symptom-reactivity," and within-person relations of changes in undesirable events with other measures, that is, "stress-reactivity."

Statistical modeling of nomothetic–idiographic relations requires solutions that partition the dual sources of variance in person–day data sets. For our analyses we have adopted a simultaneous multilevel modeling (MLM) strategy. MLM treats both day-level and person-level observations as random sampling units so that inferences can be made to both days and persons from whom the sample was drawn. It allows estimation of the random effects for each person of one daily variable on another and then models the random effects of person attributes that may "modify" the strength and direction of within-person relations.

The specific MLM technique we use here is Hierarchical Linear Modeling (Bryk & Raudenbush, 1992). The vernacular of HLM calls daily observations "Level 1" variables that are nested within persons, the differences between whom are called "Level 2" variables (e.g., differences in personal attributes and instable situational factors). Level 2 variables can be used to simultaneously model individual differences in intercepts (means) of the level variables and to model their slopes, that is, the relations between Level 1 variables.

Table 7.2.

HLM Level 2 Analysis of Effects of Dispositional Optimism or Pessimism on Daily Variable Intercepts for 89 Fibromyalgia and 48 Asthma Patients

Daily variable	Fibromyalgia		Asthma	
	Optimism	Pessimism	Optimism	Pessimism
Intensity of pain/asthma symptoms	−.227	.513	−.213	.184
Attention to pain/asthma symptoms	−.067	.069	−.005	.049
Pleasant mood	.207***	−.156*	.148*	−.171*
Unpleasant mood	−.194**	.138*	−.071	.059
Personal control of pain/asthma symptoms	.000	−.026	.109	.009
Perceived efficacy of pain/asthma symptoms coping				
For pain/symptom improvement	.030	−.038	.609	−.014
For mood enhancement	.094*	−.073	.313	−.343
Desirable daily events	.321*	−.194	—	—
Undesirable daily events	−.010	−.028	—	—
Coping strategies to contend with pain/symptoms				
Take more medication	−.016	−.004	−.025*	.005
Behavioral action to reduce pain/symptoms	−.005	.005	−.008	.008
Relaxation	−.003	.003	−.024	.034*
Distraction	−.001	.003	−.015	.010
Redefinition	.011	.002	.012	.000
Vent emotions	−.001	−.004	−.009	.010*
Seek spiritual comfort	.027*	−.029*	.022*	.005
Seek emotional support	−.002	.002	−.010	.011*

Note. Tabular values are unstandardized maximum likelihood estimates.
* $p < .05$. ** $p < .01$. *** $p < .001$.

Optimism or Pessimism and Within-Person Intercepts

The ability of our Level 2 measures of optimism and pessimism to predict observation-level intercepts (means) was evaluated first. Table 7.2 presents the findings.

Unexpectedly, dispositional optimism and pessimism played no direct role in individuals' intercepts for momentary pain or asthma symptoms. Neither did it predict attention to pain or asthma symptoms or perceived control over pain or asthma symptoms. It did predict the daily moods of participants in both studies. In both groups, optimism predicted pleasant daily mood, and among those participants with fibromyalgia, so did lower levels of pessimism. Among those participants with fibromyalgia, pessimism was also a predictor of unpleasant mood and optimism a predictor of the frequency of desirable daily events.

Patients differing in levels of optimism or pessimism also used certain daily coping strategies to a greater or lesser extent. The more optimistic asthma patients were less likely to take extra medication to contend with that day's symptoms, and the more pessimistic asthma patients were more likely to seek emotional support and to vent distressing emotions. A more consistent finding across samples concerned differences in seeking spiritual comfort through prayer and other devotional activities. The more optimistic, or the less pessimistic, their general orientation, the more participants sought spiritual comfort as a way of coping with that day's pain or asthma symptoms. Optimistic participants also tended more to view their coping strategies as "mood regulators"; they were more likely to conclude that their day's coping efforts helped to improve their mood.

Optimism or Pessimism and Within-Person Slopes

Our next set of analyses answers the general question: Do optimists and pessimists differ in their unique within-person relations between one daily-process measure and another? We examined first those linkages expressing each person's symptom-reactivity, including the relation between symptom change and changes in mood, attention to symptoms, perceived control over symptoms, and perceived efficacy of coping strategies to improve symptoms. Only one of these relations could be predicted by levels of optimism or pessimism: Asthma patients who were more optimistic were significantly *less* likely to pay attention to their symptoms when they increased in severity ($b = -.02$; $t = -2.42$; $p = .02$), and this was true even when their degree of pessimism was taken into account in the Level 2 analysis.

We also examined in the sample composed of patients with fibromyalgia the within-person assessment of "daily stress reactivity" (Affleck et al., 1994), as evidenced by the magnitude of the within-person relation between changes in undesirable daily events and in mood, pain, and attention to pain. Again, there was an optimism-associated difference involving attentional processes. Greater optimism was linked with a significantly weaker association between a rise in undesirable events and an increase in attention to pain ($b = -.01$; $t = -2.80$; $p = .006$). This was the case even when the extent of pessimism was incorporated in the Level 2 analysis.

Discussion

In a review of research on the effects of dispositional optimism on psychological and physical well-being, Scheier and Carver (1992) concluded that "compared to pessimists, optimists manage difficult and stressful events with less subjective distress and less adverse impact on their physical well-being" (p. 224). They add that "in part, this 'optimistic advantage' seems due to differences between optimists and pessimists in the manner in which they cope with stress" (p. 224).

The findings of our two prospective daily studies of patients with fibromyalgia or asthma support this conclusion concerning the advantages of optimism for psychological well-being but not for physical well-being. In neither sample was dispositional optimism or pessimism a predictor of physical symptoms recorded three times a day across 30 or 21 days. In a broader conception of psychological well-being, the link between optimism and the experience of more desirable daily events by patients with fibromyalgia is noteworthy. In both groups, there were predictable effects of an optimistic or pessimistic orientation on daily mood. We also confirmed with daily reports of coping with pain or asthma symptoms that optimists and pessimists use some coping strategies to a greater or lesser degree. The tendency for optimists to rely more on spiritual or religious coping with chronic illness symptoms has not been found or addressed previously.

Are the daily mood differences associated with optimism and pessimism mediated by differences in coping strategy use (Scheier & Carver, 1992)? When we examined the within-person relations between those coping strategies associated with optimism or pessimism and mood the following day, there were no significant findings. Thus, we could find no strong evidence that the more positive mood of optimists, or the more negative mood of pessimists, was due to differences in their daily coping attempts. The mechanisms linking dispositional optimism or pessimism with daily mood are unclear from our data. That this relation is due to shared variance with neuroticism (Smith et al., 1989), an important facet of which is emotional distress across time and situations, remains a tenable conclusion until specific mediators are identified.

The ability of dispositional optimism or pessimism to explain individual differences in the within-person relations between daily-process variables was examined in the context of symptom reactivity and stress reactivity. *Symptom focus*, operationalized as the extent to which participants were "attending" to their symptoms during the half-hour before they were signalled by the electronic interviewer, was implicated in the only significant findings emerging from these analyses. Optimistic asthma patients were less likely to focus on their symptoms when they were worsening, and optimistic fibromyalgia patients were less likely to focus on their symptoms when they were experiencing undesirable events. This diminished attentional focus on symptoms when symptoms worsen or when undesirable events occur is likely an adaptive stress response associated with optimism. It extends to the dynamics of daily life with illness the conclusion that optimists are advantaged by their reluctance to dwell on problems or stressors (Carver et al., 1993). And, as our findings demonstrate, it is the presence of optimism, not the absence of pessimism, which confers this advantage.

In each of these studies, we explored yet another way in which optimism and pessimism might be expressed in daily life with chronic illness. This concerns the expectation that tomorrow will be a better (or worse) day than today. The findings summarized below reveal an "optimistic bias" underlying the expectation of tomorrow's pain or asthma symptoms.

DAILY SYMPTOM EXPECTANCIES: WILL TOMORROW BE A BETTER DAY?

Included in the nightly booklets completed by both fibromyalgia and asthma patients was a 0–10 rating (0 = *much worse than today*; 5 = *same as today*; 10 = *much better than today*) of how severe they expected tomorrow's pain (or asthma symptoms) to be. The mean on the 0–10 expectancy scale was 5.54 (*SD* = 1.85) for the fibromyalgia sample and 5.78 (*SD* = 1.68) for the asthma sample (recall that a value greater than 5 would be in the direction of expecting a better day tomorrow). There were nearly two times as many optimistic evenings (37.4%) as pessimistic evenings (19.0%) when fibromyalgia participants predicted tomorrow's pain, and more than three times as many optimistic (35.8%) as pessimistic (9.9%) evenings when asthma patients predicted tomorrow's symptoms. Optimistic days exceeded the number of pessimistic days in 62.9% of the fibromyalgia participants and in 72.9% of the asthma participants. For further analyses, we identified an *optimistic day* as a score of 6 or greater on the symptom expectancy scale and a *pessimistic day* as a score of 4 or less.

Do Symptom Expectancies Predict Next-Day Symptoms?

Is the prediction of a better or worse day tomorrow borne out by the *actual* change in tomorrow's symptoms? It was for those participants with fibromyalgia, but not those with asthma. This was disclosed by an HLM Level 1 analysis that modeled the next day's pain from the previous day's actual pain along with the previous day's prediction of the next day's pain. A more painful day today predicted a more painful day tomorrow (b = .309; $p < .001$); but in addition so did a pessimistic prediction about tomorrow's pain (b = 1.12; $p < .01$). Similarly, an optimistic prediction today predicted an improvement in tomorrow's pain when compared with today's pain (b = −.87; $p < .01$). We have identified only one other variable in our daily data set that is able to predict the change in pain from one day to the next; namely, the judgment that today's coping strategies were effective in reducing pain. Yet even when this variable is taken into account, the ability of pain expectancies to predict pain changes from day to day remains statistically significant. Because symptom expectancies did not predict next-day asthma symptoms, more study is needed to evaluate the generalizability of these findings across the spectrum of chronic illness.

Does Dispositional Optimism Predict Daily Symptom Expectancies?

The possibility that daily pain or symptom expectancies might be shaped in part by dispositional optimism or pessimism was examined through an HLM Level 2 analysis of intercepts for symptom expectancies. Neither optimism nor pessimism predicted daily symptom expectancies.

Within-Person Predictors of Symptom Expectancies

If optimism or pessimism had no direct effect on daily symptom expectancies, they could still have an indirect effect through their effects on other daily processes that might shape symptom expectancies. HLM analyses of the within-person correlates of optimistic and pessimistic days were conducted at the day level (Level 1). Table 7.3 summarizes these results for that day's pain or symptom severity, that day's mood, that day's perceived control over pain or symptoms, and that day's judgment of the efficacy of coping efforts to reduce pain or symptoms.

Thus far we have uncovered no description of a given day that appears to predict an optimistic outlook for the next day's symptoms. More can be

Table 7.3.
HLM Analysis of Level 1 Covariates of Optimistic and Pessimistic Expectancies for Tomorrow's Pain or Symptoms in Fibromyalgia Patients (N = 8010 days) and Asthma Patients (N = 1008 days)

Daily variable	Fibromyalgia patients		Asthma patients	
	Optimistic expectancy	Pessimistic expectancy	Optimistic expectancy	Pessimistic expectancy
Intensity of pain/asthma symptoms	−.001	.005*	−.003	.011*
Attention to pain/asthma symptoms	.012	.022	.018	.048*
Pleasant mood	.009	−.005	−.001	.003
Unpleasant mood	−.002	.007	.001	−.008
Personal control of pain/asthma symptoms	−.001	−.006	.019	−.032**
Perceived efficacy of pain/asthma symptoms coping				
For pain/symptom improvement	.005	−.014*	.006	−.033*
For mood enhancement	.009	−.004	.019	.001

Note. Tabular values are unstandardized maximum likelihood estimates.
* $p < .05$. ** $p < .01$. *** $p < .001$.

said about the same-day processes that are linked with a pessimistic forecast. For both the group of patients with asthma and that of patients with fibromyalgia, a day with more severe pain or symptoms predicted a pessimistic outlook for the next day's symptoms. A pessimistic expectation was also more likely for those patients with fibromyalgia when they judged that day's coping to be less effective in reducing their pain. For asthma patients, a pessimistic prediction was also more likely when they had perceived less personal control over that day's symptoms, as well as when they had paid more attention to that day's symptoms.

A multivariate analysis of the significant Level 1 predictors of fibromyalgia pain expectancies showed that almost 7% of the day-to-day variation in pessimistic expectancies could be explained by that day's pain severity and perceived coping efficacy, although neither was an independent predictor of a pessimistic day. Approximately 20% of the within-person variance in pessimistic expectancies for tomorrow's asthma symptoms was due to that day's symptom severity, perceived control over symptoms, and attention to symptoms. Both perceived control and symptom attention, but not symptom severity, remained significant variables in a day's pessimistic expectancy when all three were considered together in a multivariate HLM analysis.

Discussion

Just as general optimism colors people's expectations of the future, so does it color the outlook for the next day's symptoms in individuals living with either of two chronic illnesses. These individuals generally expressed a more optimistic than pessimistic outlook. In fact, optimistic daily forecasts outnumbered pessimistic ones by a ratio of 2:1 for fibromyalgia patients and 3:1 for asthma patients. Whereas asthma patients' expectancies did not predict what tomorrow would actually bring, fibromyalgia patients were as a group significantly more likely to experience the change they predicted for tomorrow's symptoms, whether they were optimistic or pessimistic.

It was surprising that neither dispositional optimism nor dispositional pessimism was implicated in patients' 24-hour expectancies. While puzzling, this lack of association between situational expectancies and generalized expectancies replicates the findings of both Scheier et al. (1989) and Fitzgerald, Tennen, Affleck, and Pransky (1993), who found that domain-specific and generalized expectancies were inconsistently related among patients undergoing coronary bypass surgery. The channels through which situational expectancies might be altered by experiences unrelated to dispositional optimism and the unique and overlapping contributions of situational and generalized expectancies require closer scrutiny, particularly because some investigators have demonstrated that situational expectancies account for the majority of variance in adjustment (e.g., Bandura, 1977), and others have demonstrated that it depends on the context and the adaptational outcome selected (Scheier et al., 1989).

We find it noteworthy that an optimistic anticipation of tomorrow's symptoms could not be predicted by the severity of today's symptoms, today's mood, or today's perception of control or coping efficacy. At the same time, several of these daily processes could predict a pessimistic forecast. Negative appraisals of today's ability to achieve personal control over symptoms *and* the perception that today's coping was ineffective led patients to expect tomorrow's symptoms to be even worse. Thus, whereas personal traits may not predict symptom expectancies, there are cognitive processes related to personal agency that figure in the waxing and waning of a pessimistic outlook. These processes, however, could not themselves be predicted by either dispositional optimism or pessimism.

CONCLUSION AND FUTURE DIRECTIONS

Andersson's (1996b) meta-analysis of 56 studies using the LOT found consistent effects of dispositional optimism on the reporting of physical symptoms, coping strategies, and negative affect. The new analyses presented here are the first to consider the effects of dispositional optimism on each of these processes when they are measured on a daily basis to better capture their fluctuations and moments of change. We conclude, as did Andersson, that emotional states are the most reliable consequence of optimism and pessimism. This was replicated in our studies of rheumatoid arthritis, asthma, and fibromyalgia and suggests that pessimism is mainly a predictor of daily sadness and optimism a predictor of daily happiness. The mood-regulatory function of optimism was evidenced as well in optimistic fibromyalgia patients' day-to-day judgments of the efficacy of their pain-coping strategies: Although optimists were not more likely than pessimists to find these strategies successful in alleviating their pain, they were more likely to find them helpful in improving their mood.

The major departure of our findings from those that have been generated in the larger optimism literature was the lack of association with momentary pain or symptom reports. We suspect that this discrepancy is due in part to the considerable difficulty that individuals display in recalling their illness symptoms and the possibility that optimism and pessimism are sources of systematic bias in symptom recall. Perhaps optimists recall the past more favorably than is warranted and pessimists less favorably than is deserved. Future research should combine retrospective with prospective daily reports to shed light on the role that optimism and pessimism might play in shaping recall heuristics.

Our idiographic–nomothetic design allowed us to assess the effects of optimism and pessimism on dynamic bivariate relations that measure the daily processes of "symptom reactivity" and "stress reactivity" at the within-person level. The yield from these analyses was not great, suggesting that individual differences other than levels of optimism and pessimism might underlie these processes. We did find two dynamic effects of optimism and pessimism, however, that add substantial support to the hypothesis that optimists cope better with adversity than do pessimists because they are less likely to dwell on their problems. Despite the fact that optimists and pessimists did not differ in their overall levels of attention to their symptoms, they did differ in the likelihood that they would be more focused on them *when* they worsened or when they were experiencing undesirable events. This Person × Situation interaction concerning attention deployment merits more study in other samples and with other contextual variables.

Finally, we introduced another construct for optimism research in the form of daily expectations for symptom change, which were unrelated to generalized outcome expectancies. Pessimistic expectations were fewer in number but could be predicted by negative daily experiences. The days on which our participants were optimistic about tomorrow's symptoms, on the other hand, could not be predicted. Extending the construct of daily expectancies to other samples and elaborating it with the anticipation of other daily experiences should occupy more attention in future research on optimism and pessimism.

REFERENCES

Affleck, G., & Tennen, H. (1996). Daily processes in coping with chronic pain: Methods and analytic strategies. In M. Zeidner & N. S. Endler (Eds.), *Handbook of coping* (pp. 151–180). New York: Wiley.

Affleck, G., Tennen, H., Urrows, S., & Higgins, P. (1994). Person and contextual features of stress reactivity: Individual differences in relations of undesirable daily events with mood disturbance and chronic pain intensity. *Journal of Personality and Social Psychology, 66,* 329–340.

Affleck, G., Tennen, H., Urrows, S., Higgins, P., Hall, C., Abeles, M., Newton, C., & Karoly, P. (1998). Fibromyalgia and women's pursuit of personal goals: A daily process analysis. *Health Psychology, 17,* 40–47.

Affleck, G., Urrows, S., Tennen, H., Higgins, P., & Abeles, M. (1996). Sequential daily relations of sleep, pain intensity, and attention to pain among women with fibromyalgia. *Pain, 68,* 363–368.

Andersson, G. (1996a). The role of optimism in patients with tinnitus and patients with hearing impairment. *Psychology and Health, 11,* 696–707.

Andersson, G. (1996b). The benefits of optimism: A meta-analytic review of the Life Orientation Test. *Personality and Individual Differences, 21,* 719–725.

Apter, A., Affleck, G., Reisine, S., Tennen, H., Barrows, E., Willard, A., & ZuWallack, R. (1997). Perception of airways obstruction in asthma: Sequential daily analyses of symptoms, PEFR, and mood. *Journal of Allergy and Clinical Immunology, 99,* 605–612.

Bandura, A. (1977). Self-efficacy: Toward a unifying theory of behavioral change. *Psychological Review, 84,* 191–215.

Bolger, N., DeLongis, A., Kessler, R. C., & Schilling, E. A. (1989). Effects of daily stress on negative mood. *Journal of Personality and Social Psychology, 57,* 808–818.

Bolger, N., & Schilling, E. A. (1991). Personality and the problems of everyday life: The role of neuroticism in exposure and reactivity to daily stressors. *Journal of Personality, 59,* 335–386.

Bryk, A. S., & Raudenbush, S. W. (1992). *Hierarchical linear models.* Newbury Park, CA: Sage Publications.

Carver, C. S., & Gaines, J. G. (1987). Optimism, pessimism, and post-partum depression. *Cognitive Therapy and Research, 11,* 449–462.

Carver, C., Pozo, C., Harris, S. D., Noriega, V., Scheier, M. F., Robinson, D. S., Ketcham, A. S., Moffat, F. L., Jr., & Clark, K. C. (1993). How coping mediates the effect of optimism on distress: A study of women with early stage breast cancer. *Journal of Personality and Social Psychology, 65,* 375–390.

Carver, C., Pozo-Kaderman, C., Harris, S. D., Noriega, V., Scheier, M. F., Robinson, D. S., Ketcham, A. S., Moffat, F. L., Jr., & Clark, K. C. (1994). Optimism versus pessimism predicts the quality of women's adjustment to early stage breast cancer. *Cancer, 73,* 1213–1220.

Chang, E. C., D'Zurilla, T. J., & Maydeu-Olivares, A. (1994). Assessing the dimensionality of optimism and pessimism using a multi-measure approach. *Cognitive Therapy and Research, 18,* 143–160.

Cozzarelli, C. (1993). Personality and self-efficacy as predictors of coping with abortion. *Journal of Personality and Social Psychology, 65,* 1224–1236.

Csikszentmihalyi, M., & Larson, R. (1987). The experience sampling method: Toward a systematic phenomenology. *Journal of Nervous and Mental Disease, 175,* 526–536.

Csikszentmihalyi, M., Larson, R., & Prescott, S. (1977). The ecology of adolescent experience. *Journal of Youth and Adolescence, 6,* 281–294.

Curbow, B., Somerfield, M. R., Baker, F., Wingard, J. R., & Legro, M. W. (1993). Personal changes, dispositional optimism, and psychological adjustment to bone marrow transplantation. *Journal of Behavioral Medicine, 16,* 423–443.

Epstein, S. (1977). Traits are alive and well. In D. Magnusson & N. S. Endler (Eds.), *Personality at the crossroads: Current issues in interactional psychology* (pp. 83–98). Hillsdale, NJ: Erlbaum.

Epstein, S. (1979). The stability of behavior, I: On predicting most of the people much of the time. *Journal of Personality and Social Psychology, 37,* 1097–1126.

Epstein, S. (1983). A research paradigm for the study of personality and emotions. In M. M. Page (Ed.), *Nebraska Symposium on Motivation: Vol. 1. Personality— Current theory and research* (pp. 91–154). Lincoln: University of Nebraska Press.

Epstein, S. (1986). Does aggregation produce spuriously high estimates of behavior stability? *Journal of Personality and Social Psychology, 50,* 1199–1210.

Fitzgerald, T. E., Tennen, H., Affleck, G., & Pransky, G. S. (1993). Quality of life after coronary artery bypass surgery: The importance of initial expectancies and control appraisals. *Journal of Behavioral Medicine, 16,* 25–43.

Given, C. W., Stommel, M., Given, B., Osuch, J., Kurtz, M. E., & Kurtz, J. C. (1993). The influence of cancer patients' symptoms and functional states on patients' depression and family givers' reaction and depression. *Health Psychology, 12,* 277–285.

Gotlib, I. H. (1984). Depression and general psychopathology in university students. *Journal of Abnormal Psychology, 90,* 521–530.

Hedges, S. M., Jandorf, L., & Stone, A. A. (1985). Meaning of daily mood assessments. *Journal of Personality and Social Psychology, 48,* 428–434.

Kanner, A. D., Coyne, J. C., Schaefer, C., & Lazarus, R. S. (1981). Comparison of two modes of stress measurement: Daily hassles and uplifts versus major life events. *Journal of Behavioral Medicine, 4,* 1–39.

Larsen, R. J. (1987). The stability of mood variability: A spectral analytic approach to daily mood assessments. *Journal of Personality and Social Psychology, 52,* 1195–1204.

Larsen, R. J. (1990, June). Second-order consistency: Patterns of change as units of personality. In J. K. Norem (Chair), *Modern units of personality research and their implications for the issue of consistency.* Symposium presented at the meeting of the American Psychological Society, Dallas, TX.

Larsen, R. J., & Kasimatis, M. (1991). Day-to-day physical symptoms: Individual differences in the occurrence, duration, and emotional concomitants of minor daily illnesses. *Journal of Personality, 59,* 387–424.

Larsen, R. J., & Ketelaar, T. (1991). Personality and susceptibility to positive and negative emotional states. *Journal of Personality and Social Psychology, 61,* 132–140.

Lazarus, R. S. (1978). A strategy for research on psychological and social factors in hypertension. *Journal of Human Stress, 4,* 35–40.

Linton, S. J. (1991). Memory for chronic pain intensity: Correlates of accuracy. *Perceptual and Motor Skills, 72,* 1091–1095.

Litt, M. D., Tennen, H., Affleck, G., & Klock, S. (1992). Coping and cognitive factors in adaptation to in vitro fertilization failure. *Journal of Behavioral Medicine, 15,* 119–126.

Lorr, M., & McNair, D. M. (1982). *Profile of Mood States-B.* San Diego, CA: Educational and Industrial Testing Service.

Marshall, G. N., Wortman, C. B., Kusulas, J. W., Hervig, L. K., & Vickers, R. R. (1992). Distinguishing optimism from pessimism: Relations to fundamental dimensions of mood and personality. *Journal of Personality and Social Psychology, 62*, 1067–1074.

Mendola, R. A. (1990). *Coping with chronic pain: Perceptions of control and dispositional optimism as moderators of psychological distress.* Unpublished doctoral dissertation, University of Connecticut, Storrs.

Mroczek, D. K., Spiro, A., Aldwin, C. M., Ozer, D. J., & Bossé, R. (1993). Construct validation of optimism and pessimism in older men: Findings from the normative aging study. *Health Psychology, 12*, 406–409.

Robinson-Whelen, S., Kim, C., MacCallum, R. C., & Kiecolt-Glaser, J. K. (1997). Distinguishing optimism from pessimism in older adults: Is it more important to be optimistic or not to be pessimistic? *Journal of Personality and Social Psychology, 73*, 1345–1353.

Scheier, M. F., & Carver, C. S. (1985). Optimism, coping, and health: Assessment and implications of generalized outcome expectancies. *Health Psychology, 4*, 219–247.

Scheier, M. F., & Carver, C. S. (1987). Dispositional optimism and physical well-being: The influence of generalized outcome expectancies on health. *Journal of Personality, 55*, 169–210.

Scheier, M. F., & Carver, C. S. (1992). Effects of optimism on psychological and physical well-being: Theoretical overview and empirical update. *Cognitive Therapy and Research, 16*, 201–228.

Scheier, M. F., Carver, C. S., & Bridges, M. W. (1994). Distinguishing optimism from neuroticism (and trait anxiety, self-mastery, and self-esteem): A reevaluation of the Life Orientation Test. *Journal of Personality and Social Psychology, 67*, 1063–1078.

Scheier, M. F., Matthews, K. A., Owens, J. F., Magovern, G. J., Sr., Lefebvre, R. C., Abbot, R. A., & Carver, C. S. (1989). Dispositional optimism and recovery from coronary artery bypass surgery: The beneficial effects on physical and psychological well-being. *Journal of Personality and Social Psychology, 57*, 1024–1040.

Shiffman, S., Fischer, L. A., Paty, J. A., Gnys, M., Hickcox, M., & Kassel, J. D. (1994). Drinking and smoking: A field study of their association. *Annals of Behavioral Medicine, 16*, 203–209.

Shifren, K. (1996). Individual differences in the perception of optimism and disease severity: A study among individuals with Parkinson's Disease. *Journal of Behavioral Medicine, 19*, 241–271.

Shifren, K., & Hooker, K. (1995). Stability and change in optimism: A study of spouse caregivers. *Experimental Aging Research, 21*, 59–76.

Smith, T. W., Pope, M. K., Rhodewalt, F., & Poulton, J. L. (1989). Optimism, neuroticism, coping, and symptom reports: An alternative interpretation of the Life Orientation Test. *Journal of Personality and Social Psychology, 56*, 640–648.

Stone, A. A., & Neale, J. M. (1982). Development of a methodology for assessing daily experiences. In A. Baum & J. E. Singer (Eds.), *Advances in environmental psychology, environment and health* (Vol. 4, pp. 49–83). New York: Erlbaum.

Stone, A. A., & Neale, J. M. (1984a). The effects of "severe" daily events on mood. *Journal of Personality and Social Psychology, 46,* 137–144.

Stone, A. A., & Neale, J. M. (1984b). New measure of daily coping: Development and preliminary results. *Journal of Personality and Social Psychology, 46,* 892–906.

Stone, A. A., & Shiffman, S. (1994). Ecological momentary assessment (EMA) in behavioral medicine. *Annals of Behavioral Medicine, 16,* 199–202.

Taylor, S. E., Kemeny, M. E., Aspinwall, L. G., Schneider, S. G., Rodriguez, R., & Herbert, M. (1992). Optimism, coping, psychological distress, and high-risk sexual behavior among men at risk for acquired immunodeficiency syndrome (AIDS). *Journal of Personality and Social Psychology, 63,* 460–473.

Tennen, H., Affleck, G., Urrows, S., Higgins, P., & Mendola, R. (1992). Perceiving control, construing benefits, and daily processes in rheumatoid arthritis. *Canadian Journal of Behavioral Science, 24,* 186–203.

Tennen, H., Suls, J., & Affleck, G. (1991). Personality and daily experience: The promise and the challenge. *Journal of Personality, 59,* 313–338.

Watson, D., & Clark, L. A. (1984). Negative affectivity: The disposition to experience aversive emotional states. *Psychological Bulletin, 96,* 465–490.

Zautra, A. J., Affleck, G., & Tennen, H. (1994). Assessing life events among older adults. In L. M. Powell, J. A. Teresi, (Eds.), *Annual review of gerontology and geriatrics: Focus on assessment techniques. Annual Review of gerontology and geriatrics,* Vol. 14 (pp. 324–352). New York: Springer.

Zautra, A. J., Guarnaccia, C. A., Reich, J. W., & Dohrenwend, B. P. (1988). The contribution of small events to stress and distress. In L. H. Cohen (Ed.), *Life events and psychological functioning* (pp. 123–148). Newbury Park, CA: Sage Publications.

8

OPTIMISM AND PESSIMISM: BIOLOGICAL FOUNDATIONS

MARVIN ZUCKERMAN

Thinking rosy futures is as biological as sexual fantasy. Optimistically calculating the odds is as basic a human action as seeking food when hungry or craving fresh air in a dump. Making deals with uncertainty marks us [as a species] as plainly as bipedalism.

(L. Tiger, 1979, p. 35)

Recently there was a lottery drawing with an extraordinary payoff of many millions of dollars. As I drove home I noticed long lines of people standing outside of newsstands. My first thought was that some momentous world event had occurred, and they were lining up to buy newspapers. Only later did I realize they were all buying lottery tickets. The odds of anyone winning were more than those of being struck by lightning. In fact if the bettors responded pessimistically to the shorter odds of getting struck by lightning, they would never leave their houses when it was raining. This tells us something about the biological value of optimism as contrasted with pessimism. Optimism leads to action with a possibility of reward no matter how remote the possibility, but pessimism results in inaction and paralysis in the necessary jobs of life, whether hunting woolly mammoths or starting a new business. "Nothing ventured, nothing gained" is the motto of capitalism and perhaps it is "wired in" to our species.

Tiger's quotation may be startling to many people who think of optimism as a purely learned attitude conditioned by the outcomes of events in life. Tiger speculates that an optimistic attitude had adaptive value in the struggles for life of our hominid ancestors over the million or so years of evolution. Seligman (1991) has shown that it still is an advantage for success in current life, whether in politics, business, or sports. Risk taking in novel or unpredictable situations is a necessity for exploration. A species such as *homo sapiens*, which came out of Africa and colonized the entire globe within the relatively short time span of 100,000 years, needed an optimistic outlook for success in adaptation to sometimes hostile new environments. A pessimistic species would have stayed in one locale, gathering fruit and nuts and hunting small animals until exhaustion of their food resources led to their extinction. They would have avoided the dangers of seeking mates outside of their own group and hastened their demise as a species through the deleterious effects of inbreeding.

The evolutionary hypothesis suggests that something genetic underlies the trait that is selected, but it does not guarantee that variations in the genetic structure are strong factors in variation in the trait among current members of the species (heritability). Negative outcomes of life experiences, particularly uncontrollable outcomes, reinforce a pessimistic attitude (Seligman, 1991). Those people strongly disposed toward optimism, however, seem to rebound quickly after the worst experiences. Voltaire's character, Candide, is a caricature of optimism created by his cynical, pessimistic author. Seligman (1991) has pointed out that normal, happy optimists are less realistic in their expectations than are depressed pessimists. However, if they persist long enough, "optimists" do get reinforced, unlike the pessimists who attempt nothing and therefore miss many rewards.

Of course one could argue that because optimism fosters risky choices and pessimism often leads to caution (rather than complete inaction) the pessimist would be more likely to survive in a risky, hostile environment. The optimist takes on the sabre-toothed tiger, while the pessimist runs for the safety of the cave. It would seem that an optimal balance between optimism and pessimism that is sensitive to the odds of risk would probably be the best strategy for survival. Fortunately, as with most traits, optimism and pessimism are normally distributed in the population. The extremes within a group may provide a balance in group decision making.

Evolutionary psychology provides explanations for distal causes of the general characteristics of a species relative to other species in terms of the environmental challenges faced by the species and of their physical capabilities in dealing with those challenges. Novel open environments are generally aversive to species such as rats, often used for an animal model of human behavior. This is understandable in terms of the dangers from predators both in the air and on the ground when the rat is out of its burrow. But rats must forage to survive, so they do so with caution. We find marked variations in the relative balance between exploratory activity and fearful freezing between subspecies of rats and mice when they are placed in an open field (Plomin, DeFries, McClearn, & Rutter, 1997). Similar problems were faced by our hominid ancestors, but unlike rodents, they did not hide in burrows but freely roamed the savannahs of Africa and the tundras of the Arctic pursuing large, dangerous game.

Evolutionary psychology is addressed to the general, if not universal, characteristics of a species. But this approach does not necessarily tell us much about the sources of individual differences within a species. To understand what biological factors might explain the variations in optimism and pessimism in the current members of our species, we must turn to fields such as behavior genetics, neuropsychology, and neuropharmacology. I attempt to do that in this chapter.

Tiger (1979) and Gould (1981) tend to denigrate psychology's attempt to operationally define and measure traits such as intelligence in humans. Without quantification of traits and related behavior one cannot begin to study the phenomena in any meaningful manner. In this respect, psychology is not different than any other science. One can question the reliability and construct validity of our measures, but these are scientific questions capable of answer, not imponderables only approachable from the philosopher's armchair. The first measures of personality and intellectual ability traits emerged in this century, and improved methods will undoubtedly be developed in the future. But our current measures have already provided some answers to the nature–nurture questions, even at the level of molecular genetics.

Personality traits such as optimism and pessimism may be studied at many levels, from the generalized trait level to their foundations in the DNA, or genetic level (Zuckerman, 1991, 1993). In between are other levels: of behavioral expression, and of learning and cognition, physiology, biochemistry, and neurology. In the section of this chapter discussing "traits," I attempt to place optimism and pessimism within the context of personality and emotional trait models. I will illustrate this placement with data from a recent study (Zuckerman, Joireman, Kraft, & Kuhlman, 1999). From the top (traits) I go directly to the bottom (genetics). In that section I will describe two studies of the genetics of optimism and pessimism traits.

Certain forms of psychopathology represent abnormal extremes of normal traits. Anxiety disorders, for instance, can be regarded as extreme expressions of the general trait of neuroticism. Optimism and pessimism find their most extreme expressions in the bipolar and unipolar mood disorders.

Although optimism is usually a healthy attitude in normally functioning people, in those experiencing mania it is expressed in wild, impulsive, and risky behavior and grandiose schemes. In the depressive phase of the bipolar disorder or in the episodic depressions of the unipolar mood disorder, we see a severe kind of pessimism expressed in a generalized hopelessness. Some of the genetics and biochemistry of these disorders may be relevant to the biological bases of optimism and pessimism.

In the next part of the chapter, I deal with the normal range of personality traits. A general discussion of the psychobiology of personality (see Zuckerman, 1991) is beyond the scope of this chapter; however, I will suggest the relatedness of pessimism to the biological traits underlying neuroticism, and the shared biological foundations of optimism with those for extraversion, impulsivity, and sensation seeking traits.

THE TRAITS

The reader may have noticed that I use the conjunction *and* when referring to optimism and pessimism rather than using a hyphen. Because optimism and pessimism are grammatical antonyms it has been assumed that they constitute a bipolar trait, similar to extraversion–introversion or dominance–submission. Of course, the nonpsychologist thinks in terms of types, so that a person is either an optimist or a pessimist, and they betray this type of thinking when they ask the question: "What proportion of the population are optimists?" But like most traits, optimism *and* pessimism are continuously and normally distributed. What was not expected is that they are distributed on two different, even if correlated, dimensions (Chang, D'Zurilla, & Maydeu-Olivares, 1994). Ball and Zuckerman (1990) developed the Generalized Reward and Punishment Expectancy Scales (GRAPES) by factor analyzing items designed to assess generalized reward expectancy and other items for generalized punishment expectancies. The analysis yielded two factors rather than a bipolar factor. Torrubia, Avila, Moltó, and Grande (1995) developed scales for susceptibility to cues for punishment (SP) and susceptibility to cues for reward (SR) based on Gray's (1982) model for personality. The scales assess short-term motivational and expectational effects of such cues. The two scales are uncorrelated.

Traits that are originally conceived of as bipolar (such as positive and negative affect), but turn out to be distinct and separate factors require a new conceptualization because what they measure, in terms of behavioral expressions and their biological and social origins, may be different. One explanation for their relative independence may be that they are situation-specific, rather than general traits, so that an individual may be optimistic in one class of situations, such as social interactions, but pessimistic in another, such as financial outcomes. There is certainly some specificity in these traits, but their good internal reliabilities also suggest there is a latent trait across situations. Another possibility is that these traits are subtraits of broader ones, such as extraversion–introversion and neuroticism, which are independent dimensions.

These are the kinds of questions that led us to an examination of the factorial relationships among personality, motivational, cognitive, and affect traits (Zuckerman, Joireman, Kraft, & Kuhlman, 1999). The personality traits included extraversion, neuroticism, and psychoticism from the Eysenck Personality Questionnaire-Revised (EPQ-R; Eysenck, Eysenck, & Barratt, 1985) and sociability, neuroticism, impulsive sensation seeking, aggression, and activity from the Zuckerman–Kuhlman Personality Questionnaire (ZKPQ; Zuckerman, Kuhlman, Joireman, Teta, & Kraft, 1993).

The GRAPES scales (Ball & Zuckerman, 1990) are optimism and pessimism scales similar to those in the LOT scale (Scheier & Carver, 1985). An example of a generalized reward expectancy or optimism item is: "I expect I will rise to the top of any field of work I am or will be engaging in." A punishment expectancy item is: "It is likely that most of us will have a serious car accident at some point in our lives."

The GRAPES assesses general expectancies of outcomes in the distant future. Torrubia et al.'s (1995) SP and SR scales represent immediate expectancies and their motivational effects. For instance, "Do you often do things to be praised?" (SR), or "Do you often refrain from doing something because you are afraid of it being illegal?" (SP).

The affect traits assessed by the Multiple Affect Adjective Check List-Revised (MAACL-R; Lubin & Zuckerman, 1999; Zuckerman & Lubin, 1985) includes three negative affects (anxiety, depression, hostility) and two positive affects (positive affect and sensation seeking, a kind of active or surgent type of positive affect).

The personality, cognitive, motivational, and affect traits were intercorrelated and factor analyzed in one sample and then subjected to a Procrustes rotation in a replication sample.[1] The results in the Procrustes rotation are shown in Table 8.1. Three factors were derived and labeled in terms of the personality factors defining them: Neuroticism (N), Extraversion (E), and Psychoticism-Impulsive Unsocialized Sensation Seeking (P-ImpUSS). The last factor has been previously obtained in factor analyses using three-factor solutions (Zuckerman, Kuhlman, & Camac, 1988; Zuckerman, Kuhlman, Thornquist, & Kiers, 1991). It includes the EPQ's Psychoticism, and the ZKPQ's Impulsive Sensation Seeking and Aggression–Hostility scales.

---

[1] A Procrustes rotation is one that is constrained by conditions established in advance so that the loadings of variables on the factors cannot exceed the maximum amounts set beforehand.

Table 8.1.
Factor Analysis and Procrustes Rotation of Personality, Cognitive, Motivational, and Affect Traits

Variables	N-Anxiety	E-Sociability	P-ImpUSS	VCC
EPQ: Neuroticism	**.81**	−.02	.34	.99
EPQ: Extraversion	−.17	**.87**	−.04	1.00
EPQ: Psychoticism	−.36	.10	**.76**	.98
ZKPQ: Neuroticism/Anxiety	**.75**	.01	.25	.98
ZKPQ: Sociability	−.01	**.68**	−.13	1.00
ZKPQ: Impulsive SS	−.35	**.41**	**.54**	.99
ZKPQ: Aggression/Hostility	.13	.23	**.60**	1.00
ZKPQ: Activity	−.07	**.37**	−.02	.82
Gen. Punishment Expectancy	**.65**	.02	.13	.95
Gen. Reward expectancy	−.38	**.55**	−.14	.93
Sens. signals of punishment	**.78**	−.30	.15	.99
Sens. signals of reward	.19	**.59**	.37	.98
MAACL: Anxiety	**.74**	−.08	.44	.96
MAACL: Depression	**.53**	−.32	**.56**	.97
MAACL: Hostility	**.46**	.02	**.66**	.91
MAACL: Positive Affect	−.25	**.44**	**−.57**	.99
MAACL: SS (Surgent) Affect	−.21	**.83**	.05	.95
FCC/TCC	.97	.98	.97	.97

Note. N = neuroticism; E = extraversion; P-ImpUSS = psychoticism-impulsive unsocialized sensation seeking; EPQ = Eysenck Personality Questionnaire; ZKPQ = Zuckerman-Kuhlman Personality Questionnaire; Gen. = Generalized; Sens. = Sensitivity to; MAACL = Multiple Affect Adjective Check List-Revised; SS = Sensation Seeking; VCC = variable congruence coefficient; FCC = factor congruence coefficient; TCC = total congruence coefficient. Boldface numbers indicate the primary loadings of variables on one or two of the three factors.

The GRAPES punishment expectancy (pessimism) and the Torrubia et al. (1995) susceptibility to punishment scales had strong relationships with the Neuroticism factor (N), and the GRAPES reward expectancy (optimism) and the susceptibility to reward scales had moderate relationships with the Extraversion factor. The MAACL-R negative affects, anxiety in particular, were strongly related to the N factor, whereas the positive affect scales, particularly the active, surgent type of positive affect (SSPA; e.g., adventurous, daring, enthusiastic, energetic, wild), were highly related to the E factor.

Because only one of the tests in the study, the ZKPQ, measured five personality factors, the factor analysis was able to produce only three significant factors. Table 8.2, however, shows the correlations between the Generalized Reward and Punishment Expectancy scales and all of the other personality and affect trait scales in the derivation and replication samples. Only the replicated correlations are described below. In both samples generalized reward expectancy correlated positively with EPQ extraversion; ZKPQ activity; MAACL positive and sensation-seeking (surgent) affects; and negatively with EPQ and ZKPQ measures of neuroticism, and MAACL anxiety and

Table 8.2.
Correlations Between Generalized Reward and Punishment Expectancy Scales and Personality and Affect Trait Scales

Expectancy	Reward expectancy		Punishment expectancy	
	Sample 1	Sample 2	Sample 1	Sample 2
EPQ: Extraversion	.38*	.48*	−.03	−.14
EPQ: Neuroticism	−.31*	−.37*	.45*	.50*
EPQ: Psychoticism	.03	.04	−.09	−.07
ZKPQ: Sociability	.18	.19	−.07	−.11
ZKPQ: Neuroticism-Anxiety	−.44*	−.28*	.41*	.39*
ZKPQ: Impulsive Sensation Seeking	.17	.26*	−.16	−.13
ZKPQ: Aggression-Hostility	.00	−.04	.08	.25*
ZKPQ: Activity	.32*	.30*	−.06	−.05
MAACL: Anxiety	−.23*	−.29*	.21*	.41*
MAACL: Depression	−.23*	−.39*	.22*	.40*
MAACL: Hostility	−.05	−.15	.12	.31*
MAACL: Positive Affect	.31*	.44*	−.13	−.21*
MAACL: Sensation Seeking Affect	.41*	.45*	−.19	−.10

Note. EPQ = Eysenck Personality Questionnaire; ZKPQ = Zuckerman-Kuhlman Personality Questionnaire; MAACL: Multiple Affect Personality Questionnaire-Revised. Sample 1, *n* = 188; sample 2, *n* = 135
*p < .0001.

depression. Generalized punishment expectancy correlated positively with EPQ and ZKPQ measures of neuroticism and with MAACL measures of anxiety and depression in both samples.

Thus cognitive, motivational, and affect traits are organized primarily within the two major and independent personality factors E and N. The relative independence of the GRAPES reward and punishment expectancy scales (they correlated −.28) and susceptibility to reward and punishment scales ($r = .05$) resembles the relative independence of optimism and pessimism scales found by Chang et al. (1994). The generalized reward expectancy scale is positively associated with extraversion and positive affects and negatively associated with neuroticism and the negative affects of anxiety and depression. Generalized punishment expectancy is positively associated with neuroticism and the negative affects of anxiety and depression. The associations of optimism and pessimism with personality dimensions of E and N and positive and negative affect traits suggest that these attitudinal dimensions may share some of the genetic and other biological factors with E and N.

GENETICS OF OPTIMISM AND PESSIMISM

Although personality dimensions such as E and N have been subjected to genetical analyses in many twin and adoption studies, only two twin studies have been published on the genetics of optimism and pessimism. Genetic-twin studies compare similarities or differences of a trait for identical and fraternal twins. Identical twins raised in the same families have all their genes in common and also share the same family environment. Fraternal twins also share the same family environment but have, on average, only half of their genes in common. The difference in similarity, as expressed in correlations, should control for the effects of shared environments, age, and gender (if only same-gendered fraternal twins are used). If genetic effects play no role relative to that for shared environment, then the correlations should be the same in identical and fraternal twins, but if genetic effects are significant, then the correlation should be significantly higher in identical twins than in fraternal twins. The ratio of the correlation of identical twins to that of fraternal twins should be about 2:1 if only polygenetic additive effects are involved, but the ratio may be more than 2:1 if other types of genetic mechanisms, such as dominance or epistasis (unique combinations of genes rather than simple additive effects) are involved in the trait. *Heritability* of a trait is the proportion of variance that can be attributed to genetic factors alone.

Schulman, Keith, and Seligman (1993) gave the Attributional Style Questionnaire (ASQ; Peterson et al., 1982) to 115 pairs of identical and 27 pairs of fraternal twins. On a composite score summing reactions to positive and negative events, the correlations were .48 for identical and 0 for fraternal twins. The difference between correlations indicates a substantial hereditary effect, but the 0 correlation in fraternal twins either indicates that the trait is entirely epistatic in genetic mechanism or that the correlation of the fraternal twins is unreliable because of the low number of participants in this group. The latter interpretation is more likely, but another anomalous finding emerged when the good and bad event scales were analyzed separately. For positive events, the analysis also showed a moderate correlation of .50 for identical twins, but the correlation for fraternal twins was nearly as high (.41), which would ordinarily indicate a substantial effect for shared environment. In contrast, the scale for bad events showed the same pattern as the composite scale, with correlations of .43 for identical and −.03 for fraternal twins. Schulman et al. (1993) note that the optimism score for positive events is more responsive to environmental experience and that it is the respondents' attributions about negative events that affect their behavior more. They suggest that optimism is not directly heritable and that the heritable component is a function of other traits, such as intelligence, attractiveness, or certain temperament traits, which are more heritable and affect the amount of failure or success in life experience. The actual outcomes of events then determine the generalized attitudes of optimism or pessimism toward future events. In another study, Seligman and his colleagues (Seligman et al., 1984) found that children's optimistic or pessimistic styles for interpreting bad events were correlated ($r = .39$) with their mothers' styles, but not with their fathers' styles. A relationship with the mother's style and not the father's is not readily explainable in terms of genetics unless a major gene involved is on the X chromosome. In that case boys could only inherit it from their mothers.

The twin study by Plomin et al. (1992) used the LOT scale, which is scored separately for optimism and pessimism. Unlike earlier studies in which the negative correlations between the two scales were moderate, optimism and pessimism scales were uncorrelated ($r = .02$). In addition to substantial numbers of identical (126) and fraternal (146) twins raised together, the study also included substantial groups of identical (72) and fraternal (178) twins raised apart. The correlations for identical twins raised apart constitute direct measures of heritability because heredity is presumably the only factor that could make them alike. These correlations were .28 for LOT optimism and .41 for LOT pessimism. However estimates of heritability based on all twins in the study using a model-fitting method yielded heritability values of .23 for LOT optimism and .27 for LOT pessimism. Some evidence of nonadditive types of genetic variance and shared environmental influences were found for optimism but not for pessimism.

Heritabilities for optimism and pessimism were lower than those typically found for personality traits such as extraversion and neuroticism, which average about .40 in recent studies and .50 in older studies (Bouchard, 1993; Loehlin, 1992). They are closer to those found for nonreligious social attitude items (Bouchard, Lykken, McGue, Segal, & Tellegen, 1990).

The lower heritabilities of optimism and pessimism suggest that their heritability may be indirect, as suggested by Schulman et al. (1993). Based on our previous analyses of our own measures of optimism and pessimism (GRAPES), I would suggest that optimism is partly based on the genetic bases for extraversion, and that pessimism is partly a function of genes for neuroticism. The influence of some effects of nonadditive genetic mechanisms and shared environmental effects for optimism is interesting in view of the findings in two studies of twins raised together and those raised apart in which there was evidence of nonadditive genetic effects and shared environments for extraversion but not for neuroticism (Pederson, Plomin, McClearn, & Friberg, 1988; Tellegen et al., 1988).

But even if there is some evidence for shared environmental effects in "learned optimism" (Seligman, 1991), the larger source of optimism is in the nonshared environment or the people and experiences that affect one twin but not the other. This is generally true for broader personality traits as well. Particular life experiences of loss and disappointment in relationships or at work may attenuate optimism and increase pessimism for future events. The effects of such events are probably influenced by temperament. It takes many and severe bad happenings to discourage optimists like Candide and Don Quixote for whom it always remains "the best of all possible worlds."

PSYCHOPATHOLOGY

Optimism and pessimism have not been studied directly in terms of their biological correlates. In a literature search of the psychological abstracts by database, I found few conjunctions of the terms *optimism* or *pessimism* with biological terms. Therefore, nearly all of what is to be said about the topic of this chapter depends on extrapolation from studies of mood and anxiety disorders in which the attitudes are found in extreme forms. Of course such extrapolation is dangerous, because even within the disorders, there is a great deal of variation in these cognitive phenomena. The biological factors underlying the disorders may not be the same as those influencing the attitudes of optimism and pessimism. Despite this limitation there is ample evidence of a close relationship between the disorders and the attitudes toward the future. When the depression is gone the pessimistic attitude usually disappears with it.

Nearly all forms of psychopathology involve genetically influenced vulnerabilities and stressful life experiences (Zuckerman, 1999). The drugs that are effective for treating certain disorders provide us with clues to the biological bases of the disorders and their prominent symptoms. Antipsychotic drugs reduce the hallucinations and delusions of schizophrenia, and antidepressant drugs reduce the depressive cognitive outlook of the severely depressed patient. The actions of these drugs in the brain may help us understand some symptoms of the disorders.

Optimism and pessimism are important cognitive traits in many disorders, but are particularly salient symptoms in the mood disorders. The short-term unrealistic optimism of the grandiose and impulsive manic episode can be transformed within days or hours to the pessimism and hopelessness of the depressive phase in patients with the rapid cycling bipolar (manic–depressive) disorder (Cutler & Post, 1982). Changes in the biochemistry during such mood shifts illustrate how the central neurochemical balances may affect mood and cognition.

Bipolar disorder is highly heritable (Gershon, 1990; Kendler, Pederson, Johnson, Neale, & Mathe, 1993). All of the primary brain monoamine neurotransmitters (norepinephrine, dopamine, and serotonin) have been implicated in some studies of the bipolar disorder (Goodwin & Jamison, 1990). The catecholamines (norepinephrine and dopamine) have been implicated in the switches from depression to mania in rapid cycling cases, although it is not clear whether these are causes or effects of the activity changes going from one state to the other. However drugs that increase activity in these systems can precipitate the switch in state. One of the factors that may be important in the stability or lability of these systems, particularly dopamine, is the general level of the enzyme monoamine oxidase (MAO). This enzyme regulates the level of monoamines by catabolic reduction of the neurotransmitter within the neuron. MAO-B is low in the blood platelets of patients with bipolar disorders, where they are in the ill or the well state. The association of MAO with bipolar disorder is interesting in view of the similar association of the sensation seeking trait with bipolar disorder and MAO (Zuckerman, 1985).

People with bipolar disorder tend to score high on the Sensation Seeking Scale whether they are in the manic, normal, or even depressed states. MAO levels are low in high sensation seekers and are also low in people whose behaviors and habits are associated with the trait of sensation seeking, such as tobacco, drug, and heavy alcohol use; gambling; and criminality (Zuckerman, 1994; Zuckerman, Buchsbaum, & Murphy, 1980). Low MAO levels are also found in patients with other disorders characterized by disinhibition, such as those with borderline and antisocial personalities and drug abuse disorders. MAO is nearly totally heritable and a gene for the B type has been located on the X chromosome.

Just as the manic state is associated with optimism, the depressive state is accompanied by pessimism. One of Beck's (1972) three major depressive schemas is "negative views of the future," or hopelessness. Abramson, Metalsky, and Alloy (1989) describe a *hopelessness depression* characterized by retarded behavior, lack of energy, apathy, lack of motivation, sleep disturbance, difficulty in concentration, negative cognitions, sad affect, and suicidal preoccupation. Hopelessness is regarded as the proximal cause of depression, whereas attributional styles, such as attribution of negative events to internal, stable, and global causes are conceived of as the predisposing causes for hopelessness and depression. It must be emphasized that the hopelessness or extreme pessimism of depressed individuals is a state that accompanies the mood change, and does not precede the depression, and usually dissipates when the depression is in remission. The attribution styles, however, may be more traitlike, and there is evidence that they remain elevated after treatment (Eaves & Rush, 1984).

Unipolar major depression, particularly that of the more severe hopelessness or melancholic type, shows substantial heritability, but that of the milder or neurotic type shows little or no evidence of heritability (Nurnberger & Gershon, 1992; Zuckerman, 1999). Deficits in brain norepinephrine (NE) or serotonin have been suggested as underlying the pathology of major depression (Maes & Meltzer, 1995; Schatzberg & Schildkraut, 1995). Drugs that activate either NE, serotonin, or both systems have been efficacious in the treatment of depression (Burke & Preskorn, 1995). Some patients respond more to NE-potentiating drugs, whereas others respond better to serotonin-selective drugs, suggesting that there may be two types of etiology for depression.

Neuroticism and anxiety traits are related negatively to reward expectancy, and they are related positively to punishment expectancy, as shown in Tables 8.1 and 8.2, therefore, anxiety disorders would be expected to show a similar relationship to generalized expectancies. Like depressive disorders, anxiety disorders are characterized by negative expectations for the future. People suffering from panic disorder believe that there will be harmful physical consequences of their panic attacks (McNally, 1990), and people with agoraphobia expect to have panic attacks if they venture outside of their homes. Patients with generalized anxiety disorder spend nearly every day worrying about possible dire events. In the specific phobias the expectations of negative consequences are less generalized and are confined to specific situations but play a prominent role in the avoidance patterns that develop out of the fearful expectations. These people are pessimistic about their abilities to cope with the feared situation and about what will happen to them if they enter into the situation or encounter the feared object.

Heritabilities for most of the anxiety disorders estimated from twin studies are modest (about 23–39%) but are even lower if not absent for general anxiety disorder and situational specific phobias (Kendler, Neale, Kessler, Heath, & Eaves, 1992a, 1992b). Panic disorder and phobic panic reactions in the phobic situations are mediated through a system in which norepinephrine is the principal neurotransmitter. At low levels of activity, this system mediates the sensitivity to signals of punishment (Gray, 1982) or short-term negative expectancies of punishment triggered by immediate cues in the environment. The system has also been described as an "alarm system" (Redmond, 1987). At high levels of activity, the system plays a role in panic attacks. Drugs that cause sudden increases in the activity of the system precipitate panic attacks in persons with panic disorders, and drugs that reduce activity in the system reduce anxiety (Price, Goddard, Barr, & Goodman, 1995). However other drugs, such as sodium lactate, that do not potentiate the noradrenergic system have the capacity to elicit panic reactions in patients with panic disorders. It is also interesting that drugs such as the benzodiazepines that inhibit the noradrenergic neurons by potentiating the GABA-inhibitory system are of benefit in generalized anxiety disorders but of little help in panic disorders. On the other hand, drugs that activate the serotonergic system have been efficacious in treating panic disorder, mixed anxiety and depression, and obsessive–compulsive disorder (Shader & Greenblatt, 1995).

Most of the drugs that have strong effects on panic disorder do not show these effects in normal control participants or in patients suffering most other types of anxiety disorders. Whatever is responsible for the initial spontaneous panic attacks, later attacks could be triggered by anything that causes arousal of autonomic activity and bodily cues associated with panic attacks. Expectations of attacks may be a self-fulfilling prophecy based on conditioning of external and internal cues associated with the initial attacks.

PERSONALITY

Extraversion, activity, sensation seeking, and impulsivity all may involve a general approach mechanism (Gray, 1982, 1987; Zuckerman, 1984, 1995), whereas neuroticism and anxiety are aspects of a behavioral inhibition mechanism (Gray, 1982). Theory and comparative research with non-human species have linked the approach mechanism to activity of the mesolimbic dopaminergic system involved in reward effects in the brain. At the cognitive level, the tendency to approach, or the relative balance between approach and inhibition, might be optimism and pessimism in terms of generalized expectancies of outcomes. This is particularly true in reaction to novel stimuli or situations where there has been no previous experience that could be used to predict outcomes. In this case one would have to fall back on generalized expectancies of outcomes in the decision to approach or enter into the situation. Reactivity of the dopaminergic system might be what underlies optimism as a trait or state. Of course previous experience in stressful situations where there was unavoidable stress may produce the pessimistic attitude of "learned helplessness" (Seligman, 1975) and a weakened approach and powerful inhibition mechanism. To the extent that the strengths of the approach and inhibition mechanisms depend upon genetically influenced brain systems, they may influence the generalized expectancies of reward and punishment. However, data from the two studies of the genetics of optimism and pessimism suggest only weak heritability influence relative to that in the personality traits. Some shared environmental influences were suggested for optimism, but not for pessimism. This could indicate that although parents and life experiences influence optimism, only life experiences outside of the family (nonshared) and the genetic predisposition affect pessimism.

The genetic component of pessimism may be shared with that for neuroticism, just as the genetic component of optimism is a joint function of shared genetic influences from extraversion and neuroticism. Plomin et al. (1992) chose not to control for neuroticism in their multivariate genetic analyses because it so lowly correlated with optimism and pessimism, but correlations in our study are much higher. If we can assume that the same biological factors influence pessimism as influence neuroticism, this would be the place to start if there is really a biology of pessimism. Neuroticism and trait anxiety are so closely related that they cannot be distinguished at the phenomenal level. The biological mechanisms involved in state anxiety are a best clue to those in trait anxiety, because a trait is more or less the summation of states over time (Zuckerman, 1976).

The central organizing structure for fear in the brain is the amygdala. This structure receives input from systems at all levels, from primary sensory signals to polymodal centers of organization in the thalamus and higher cortical centers, and it probably assigns significance to the stimuli (LeDoux, 1987). The output of the amygdala to the central gray, hypothalamus, trigeminal factor motor nucleus, locus coeruleus, and frontal cortex results in the typical autonomic arousal, facial expressions, startle, freezing of behavior, and increased vigilance associated with the emotion of fear (Davis, 1986; Davis, Hitchcock, & Rosen, 1987). The noradrenergic ascending bundle from the locus coeruleus carries the arousal to all areas of the cortex in a positive feedback loop. Individual differences in the sensitivity or reactivity of any parts of this system may underlie individual differences in the proneness to experience anxiety and to develop conditioned fear responses.

This kind of analysis of fear at the biological level does not minimize the role of life experiences and associated cognitive mechanisms, such as pessimism, on mood. But individuals having the same kind of negative experiences do not necessarily transform those experiences into a long-lasting expectation of future harm. Some of the differences in reactions to stressful experience may depend on the genetic or biological factors involved in individual differences.

Risk appraisal is a central mechanism in pessimism. If an activity is perceived as risky, this perception implies a pessimistic attitude toward outcome of that activity. Experience in particular activities is a factor in developing optimistic or pessimistic expectations for future outcomes. If no harm has resulted from the experience, then risk appraisal is reduced. But a harmful experience may increase risk appraisal and decrease the likelihood of repeating that experience if there is any choice. Personality disposition may predispose toward risk appraisal even for activities that were experienced. Sensation seeking is a trait that correlates highly with risk appraisal for novel situations never before experienced; low sensation seeking individuals tend to rate such situations as riskier than high sensation seeking individuals (Zuckerman, 1979). Neuroticism and extraversion were not related to the general risk appraisal tendency.

Impulsivity is another factor related to the tendency to enter into novel but potentially risky situations. However, impulsivity is often a result of a lack of appraisal of potential outcomes rather than of an inherently optimistic appraisal of situations. The impulsive person sometimes acts and thinks about the possible negative outcomes only after the act if ever. It is possible to be a cautious sensation seeker as is the mountain climber who plans his or her ascent very carefully, seeking to minimize all foreseeable risks. Sensation seekers have an optimistic bias in their beliefs in their own capacities to deal with the risks involved. But it is the unforeseen risks that are often fatal.

However, extraversion more so than sensation seeking is associated with general reward expectancy (see Tables 8.1 and 8.2). Extraverts are not necessarily risk takers or impulsive about activities with physical risks, but they probably do take more social risks than do introverts. The biological basis of extraversion is not as clear as that for neuroticism-anxiety. Extraversion, like sensation seeking, probably has a strong dopaminergic reactivity to novel situations or people. There may also be a lack of strength in inhibitory mechanisms. Both sensation seekers and extraverts have a tendency to become easily disinhibited in social situations. Of course, alcohol is a pharmacological agent widely used to promote disinhibition of behavior at social occasions. Extraverts and sensation seekers need less of it, and sometimes act as if they had reached an optimal level of intoxication when they have actually consumed very little alcohol. Alcohol or other drugs at moderate doses may increase optimism and decrease pessimism, although I have not seen any experimental studies of this effect. Gamblers who drink too much become recklessly optimistic in their betting, ignoring the reality of odds and bluffing their way to bankruptcy.

Mood, Arousal, and Arousability

Earlier in this book (see chap. 6, this volume) Peterson and Bossio reviewed the findings linking optimism and pessimism to physical well-being and outcomes of illness. Although there is some evidence that these attitudes show correlations with the immune system functions, these authors conclude that the major mechanism linking optimism and health is a "mundane behavioral pathway." Strangely, it is the pessimists who tend to engage in unhealthy behavior and neglect the possible ways of coping with an illness. It is as if they are resigned to their fate. The optimists, in contrast, tend to be confident that they can avoid illness through proper diet and health measures, and if they do become ill, that they can recover through appropriate treatment.

There is another way that pessimism may have deleterious effects on physical health. Like anxiety, pessimism is associated with negative moods, such as anxiety and depression, and these moods are associated with chronic arousal, that could be expressed in elevated blood pressure. One study recorded ambulatory blood pressures over a 3-day period with periodic assessments of mood (Räikkönen, Matthews, Flory, Owens, & Gump, 1999). Pessimists, particularly those low on optimism, had higher blood pressure over the 3 days of the experiment than did optimists, whereas the optimists' blood pressures only increased during negative mood states. The same findings were obtained for anxiety, but analysis showed independent effects of anxiety and optimism or pessimism. The results suggest a chronic elevation of blood pressure in pessimists even though only participants in the normal range of blood pressure (BP) were used in the study. In contrast, the optimists showed elevations of BP only during periods of negative mood states, perhaps an expression of attempts at coping. If chronic, nonadaptive elevations in blood pressure are characteristic of pessimists and anxious persons, it could predispose them to certain types of health problems, particularly those involving the cardiovascular system.

CONCLUSIONS

An optimistic attitude may be an adaptive trait selected in evolution for our species. But, as with personality and intellectual traits, there is wide individual variation in both optimism and pessimism. Heritability measures of the sources of this individual variation suggest a low (relative to personality traits) but significant heritability for optimism and pessimism. Some of this heritability may be due to the association of these cognitive traits with broader personality traits: optimism with extraversion and pessimism with neuroticism. Some of the same genes involved in the personality traits may influence the genetic part of the tendency to optimism and pessimism. Optimism is also influenced by shared familial factors and nonshared life events, but pessimism seems to be primarily learned by events outside of the shared family environment.

Optimism and pessimism play an important role in many disorders, particularly the mood disorders, where they appear to be state dependent. When in a depressed state, the patient tends to have a pessimistic outlook for the future, whereas during manic states, an unrealistic optimism prevails. Drug treatments can change these generalized expectancies, showing some dependency of optimism and pessimism on the biological states underlying the clinical conditions. But for less severe states of depression, cognitive and other therapies can also change the expectancy attitudes.

Pessimism may affect health through the chronic arousal associated with anxiety and helplessness in the pessimist. Optimism is adaptive because it encourages attempts to cope and achieve, whereas pessimism is nonadaptive because it discourages such attempts and tends to lead to passivity in the face of stress or challenge. Whatever is "wired in" to our species is probably due to the survival and mating skills of optimists among our early hominid ancestors. However, the pessimist also has certain values contributing to the survival of the species, such as avoiding excessive risks that could lead to premature extinction. Much of the biological bases of these traits are probably shared with that for the associated personality and mood traits.

Most of the inferences about the biological bases of optimism and pessimism come from their associations with better-researched personality and mood traits. However, this kind of indirect inference is not reliable. More research is needed on the direct associations between optimism and pessimism and biological traits. Experimental research is needed on the biological effects of failure and success. To what extent do these effects vary as a function of trait optimism and pessimism? What are the effects of drugs on these attitudes? Although psychobiological research on human attitudes is difficult, I am optimistic about the future for such research.

If optimism is a vital factor in health, it must work through biological mechanisms. We must learn what these mechanisms are and how they work.

REFERENCES

Abramson, L. Y., Metalsky, G. I., & Alloy, L. B. (1989). Hopelessness depression: A theory-based subtype of depression. *Psychological Review, 96*, 358–372.

Ball, S. A., & Zuckerman, M. (1990). Sensation seeking, Eysenck's personality dimensions and reinforcement sensitivity in concept formation. *Personality and Individual Differences, 11*, 343–353.

Beck, A. T. (1972). *Depression: Causes and treatment.* Philadelphia, PA: University of Pennsylvania Press.

Bouchard, T. J., Jr. (1993). Genetic and environmental influences on adult personality: Evaluating the evidence. In J. Hettema & I. J. Deary (Eds.), *Foundations of personality* (pp. 15–44). Dordrecht, Netherlands: Kluwer Academic Publishers.

Bouchard, T. J., Jr., Lykken, D. T., McGue, M., Segal, N. L., & Tellegen, A. (1990). Sources of human psychological differences. *Science, 250*, 223–228.

Burke, M. J., & Preskorn, S. H. (1995). Short-term treatment of mood disorders with standard anti-depressants. In F. E. Bloom & D. J. Kupfer (Eds.), *Psychopharmacology: The fourth generation of progress* (pp. 1053–1065). New York: Raven Press.

Chang, E. C., D'Zurilla, T. J., & Maydeu-Olivares, A. (1994). Assessing the dimensionality of optimism and pessimism using a multimeasure approach. *Cognitive Therapy and Research, 18*, 143–160.

Cutler, N. R., & Post, R. M. (1982). State related dyskinesias in manic-depressive illness. *Journal of Clinical Psychopharmacology, 2*, 350–354.

Davis, M. (1986). Pharmacological and anatomical analysis of fear conditioning using the fear-potentiated startle paradigm. *Behavioral Neuroscience, 100*, 814–824.

Davis, M., Hitchcock, J. M., & Rosen, J. B. (1987). Anxiety and amygdala: Pharmacological and anatomical analysis of the fear-potentiated startle paradigm. In

G. H. Bower (Ed.), *The psychology of learning and motivation* (Vol. 21, pp. 263–305). New York: Academic Press.

Eaves, G., & Rush, A. I. (1984). Cognitive patterns in institutionalized and remitted major depression. *Journal of Abnormal Psychology, 93,* 31–40.

Eysenck, S. B. G., Eysenck, H. J., & Barratt, P. (1985). A revised version of the psychoticism scale. *Personality and Individual Differences, 6,* 21–29.

Gershon, E. S. (1990). Genetics. In F. K. Goodwin & K. R. Jamison (Eds.), *Manic depressive illness* (pp. 369–401). New York: Oxford University Press.

Goodwin, F. K., & Jamison, K. R. (1990). *Manic-depressive illness.* New York: Oxford University Press.

Gould, S. (1981). *The mismeasure of man.* New York: Norton Press.

Gray, J. A. (1982). *The neuropsychology of anxiety: An enquiry into the functions of the septohippocampal system.* New York: Oxford University Press.

Gray, J. A. (1987). The neuropsychology of emotion and personality. In S. M. Stahl, S. D. Iverson, & E. C. Goodman (Eds.), *Cognitive neurochemistry* (pp. 171–190). Oxford: Oxford University Press.

Kendler, K. S., Neale, M. C., Kessler, R. C., Heath, A. C., & Eaves, L. J. (1992a). The genetic epidemiology of phobias in women. *Archives of General Psychiatry, 49,* 273–281.

Kendler, K. S., Neale, M. C., Kessler, R. C., Heath, A. C., & Eaves, L. J. (1992b). Major depression and generalized anxiety disorder: Same genes (partly) different environments? *Archives of General Psychiatry, 49,* 716–722.

Kendler, K. S., Pederson, N., Johnson, L., Neale, M. C., & Mathe, A. A. (1993). A pilot Swedish twin study of affective illness, including hospital- and population ascertained subsamples. *Archives of General Psychiatry, 50,* 699–706.

LeDoux, J. E. (1987). Emotion. In F. Plum (Ed.), *Handbook of physiology: The nervous system* (Vol. 5, pp. 419–459). Bethesda, MD: American Physiological Society.

Loehlin, J. C. (1992). *Genes and environment in personality development.* Newbury Park, CA: Sage Publications.

Lubin, B., & Zuckerman, M. (1999). *Manual for the Multiple Affect Adjective Check List-Revised (MAACL-R).* San Diego, CA: Educational and Industrial Testing Service.

Maes, M., & Meltzer, H. Y. (1995). The serotonin hypothesis of major depression. In C. E. Bloom & D. J. Kupfer (Eds.), *Psychopharmacology: The fourth generation of progress* (pp. 933–944). New York: Raven Press.

McNally, R. J. (1990). Psychological approaches to panic disorder: A review. *Psychological Bulletin, 108,* 403–419.

Nurnberger, J. I., Jr., & Gershon, E. S. (1992). Genetics. In E. S. Paykel (Ed.), *Handbook of affective disorders* (pp. 131–148). New York: Guilford.

Pederson, N. L., Plomin, R., McClearn, G. E., & Friberg, L. (1988). Neuroticism, extraversion and related traits in adult twins reared apart and reared together. *Journal of Personality and Social Psychology, 55,* 950–957.

Peterson, C., Semmel, A., von Baeyer, C., Abramson, L. Y., Metalsky, G. I., & Seligman, M. E. P. (1982). Attributional Style Questionnaire. *Cognitive Therapy and Research, 6,* 287–299.

Plomin, R., DeFries, J. C., McClearn, G. E., & Rutter, M. (1997). *Behavioral genetics.* New York: W. H. Freeman.

Plomin, R., Scheier, M. F., Bergeman, C. S., Pederson, N. L., Nesselroade, J. R., & McClearn, G. E. (1992). Optimism, pessimism and mental health: A twin/adoption analysis. *Personality and Individual Differences, 13,* 921–930.

Price, L. H., Goddard, A. W., Barr, L. C., & Goodman, W. K. (1995). Pharmacological challenges in anxiety disorders. In F. E. Bloom & D. J. Kupfer (Eds.), *Psychopharmacology: The fourth generation of progress* (pp. 1311–1324). New York: Free Press.

Räikkönen, K., Matthews, K. A., Flory, J. D., Owens, J. F., & Gump, B. B. (1999). Effects of optimism, pessimism, and trait anxiety on ambulatory blood pressure and mood during everyday life. *Journal of Personality and Social Psychology, 76,* 104–128.

Redmond, D. E., Jr. (1987). Studies of locus coeruleus in monkeys and hypotheses for neuropsychopharmacology. In H. Y. Meltzer (Ed.), *Psychopharmacology: The third generation of progress* (pp. 967–975). New York: Raven Press.

Schatzberg, A. F., & Schildkraut, J. J. (1995). Recent studies on norepinephrine systems in mood disorders. In F. E. Bloom & D. J. Kupfer (Eds.), *Psychopharmacology: The fourth generation of progress* (pp. 911–920). New York: Raven Press.

Scheier, M. F., & Carver, C. S. (1985). Optimism, coping, and health assessment and implications of generalized outcome expectancies. *Health Psychology, 5,* 219–247.

Schulman, P., Keith, D., & Seligman, M. E. P. (1993). Is optimism heritable? A study of twins. *Behavior Research and Therapy, 31,* 569–574.

Seligman, M. E. P. (1975). *Helplessness: On depression, development and death.* New York: Freeman.

Seligman, M. E. P. (1991). *Learned optimism.* New York: Knopf.

Seligman, M. E. P., Peterson, C., Kaslow, N. J., Tannenbaum, R. L., Alloy, L. B., & Abramson, L. Y. (1984). Attribution style and depressive symptoms among children. *Journal of Abnormal Psychology, 93,* 235–238.

Shader, R. I., & Greenblatt, D. J. (1995). The pharmacotherapy of acute anxiety: A mini-update. In F. E. Bloom & D. J. Kupfer (Eds.), *Psychopharmacology: The fourth generation of progress* (pp. 1341–1348). New York: Free Press.

Tellegen, A., Lykken, D. T., Bouchard, T. J., Wilcox, K., Segal, N., & Rich, A. (1988). Personality similarity in twins reared together and apart. *Journal of Personality and Social Psychology, 54,* 1031–1039.

Tiger, L. (1979). *Optimism: The biology of hope.* New York: Simon & Schuster.

Torrubia, R., Avila, C., Moltó, J., & Grande, I. (1995). Testing for stress and happiness: The role of the behavioral inhibition system. In C. D. Spielberger, I. G. Sarason, J. M. T. Brebner, E. Greenglass, P. Laungani, & A. M. O'Roark

(Eds.), *Stress and emotion: Anxiety, anger, and curiosity* (Vol. 15, pp. 191–211). Washington, DC: Taylor and Francis.

Zuckerman, M. (1976). General and situation-specific traits and states: New approaches to assessment of anxiety and other constructs. In M. Zuckerman & C. D. Spielberger (Eds.), *Emotions and anxiety: New concepts, methods, and applications* (pp. 133–174). Hillsdale, NJ: Erlbaum.

Zuckerman, M. (1979). Sensation seeking and risk-taking. In C. E. Izard (Ed.), *Emotions in personality and psychopathology* (pp. 163–197). New York: Plenum.

Zuckerman, M. (1984). Sensation seeking: A comparative approach to a human trait. *Behavioral and Brain Sciences, 7,* 413–471.

Zuckerman, M. (1985). Sensation seeking, mania, and monoamines. *Neuropsychobiology, 13,* 121–128.

Zuckerman, M. (1991). *Psychobiology of personality.* Cambridge, UK: Cambridge University Press.

Zuckerman, M. (1993). Personality from the top (traits) to bottom (genetics) with stops at each level between. In J. Hettema & I. J. Deary (Eds.), *Foundations of personality* (pp. xx–xx). Dordrecht, The Netherlands: Kluwer.

Zuckerman, M. (1994). *Behavioral expressions and biosocial bases of sensation seeking.* New York: Cambridge University Press.

Zuckerman, M. (1995). Good and bad humors: Biochemical bases of personality and its disorders. *Psychological Science, 6,* 325–332.

Zuckerman, M. (1999). *Vulnerability to psychopathology: A biosocial model.* Washington, DC: American Psychological Association.

Zuckerman, M., Buchsbaum, M. S., & Murphy, D. L. (1980). Sensation seeking and its biological correlates. *Psychological Bulletin, 88,* 187–214.

Zuckerman, M., Joireman, J., Kraft, M., & Kuhlman, D. M. (1999). Where do motivational and emotional traits fit within three factor models of personality? *Personality and Individual Differences, 26,* 487–504.

Zuckerman, M., Kuhlman, D. M., & Camac, C. (1988). What lies beyond E and N? Factor analyses of scales believed to measure basic dimensions of personality. *Journal of Personality and Social Psychology, 54,* 96–107.

Zuckerman, M., Kuhlman, D. M., Joireman, J., Teta, P., & Kraft, M. (1993). A comparison of three structural models for personality: The big three, the big five, and the alternative five. *Journal of Personality and Social Psychology, 65,* 757–768.

Zuckerman, M., Kuhlman, D., Thornquist, M., & Kiers, H. (1991). Five (or three) robust questionnaire scale factors of personality without culture. *Personality and Individual Differences, 12,* 929–941.

Zuckerman, M., & Lubin, B. (1985). *Manual for the Multiple Affect Adjective Check List-Revised (MAACL-R).* San Diego, CA: Educational and Industrial Testing Service.

III

Psychological Factors

9

OPTIMISM, PESSIMISM, AND PSYCHOLOGICAL WELL-BEING

MICHAEL F. SCHEIER, CHARLES S. CARVER,
AND MICHAEL W. BRIDGES

For the past several years, we and a number of other psychologists who are interested in issues concerning stress, coping, and health have been exploring the potential benefits of an optimistic orientation to life. The primary purpose of this chapter is to present an overview of the research that has accumulated on this issue. By design, our review is limited to effects on psychological well-being. Evidence linking optimism to physical well-being is reviewed elsewhere in this book.

This chapter is organized as follows. We begin by commenting on a distinction between two ways of assessing optimism and pessimism. Then we review some of the empirical evidence linking positive thinking to well-being. Our review focuses primarily on studies that are prospective in design,

Preparation of this chapter was facilitated by support from the National Cancer Institute (CA64710, CA62711, and CA78995) and the National Heart, Lung, and Blood Institute (HL65111, PR0HL65112, HL 65112, and PR0HL65111).

because of their superior methodological rigor. Having reviewed the literature, we go on to consider *why* optimism might confer benefits, arguing that the benefits are due, in part, to the way in which optimists and pessimists cope with problems. We close by asking whether the effects of optimism are always good and whether the effects of pessimism are always bad.

VARIATIONS IN CONCEPTIONS AND ASSESSMENT OF OPTIMISM

Expectancies are pivotal in contemporary theories of optimism, but as suggested by the opening chapters of this volume, there are at least a couple of ways to think about expectancies and how to measure them. One approach measures expectancies directly, asking people to indicate the extent to which they believe that their future outcomes will be good or bad. This is the approach we've taken in our work, as reflected in people's responses to the Life Orientation Test (LOT; Scheier & Carver, 1985) or to the briefer Life Orientation Test-Revised (LOT-R; Scheier, Carver, & Bridges, 1994), which we currently use. Expectancies that are generalized—expectancies that pertain more or less to the individual's entire life space—are what we mean when we use the terms *optimism* and *pessimism* (cf. Armor & Taylor, 1998).

The other approach to assessing optimism is more indirect. It assesses expectancies by examining *attributional style*, the characteristic manner in which a person explains prior events (Peterson & Seligman, 1984; Seligman, 1991; see also chap. 3, this volume). Attributions for bad outcomes that are explained in terms of causes that persist into the future, influence a broad range of events, and involve an aspect of the self are seen as pessimistic in nature. They are pessimistic because they carry the implication that negative outcomes will continue to occur in the future. The opposite attributional style, explaining negative events in terms of causes that are more time limited, narrow in their effects, and external to the self, is thought to reflect a more optimistic orientation. Although in principle attributional style can be assessed with respect to both negative and positive prior events, in practice, assessment is usually limited to negative outcomes.

These two approaches to conceptualizing and measuring optimism have led to their own research literatures, each of which sheds light on the nature and function of optimism and pessimism (see also Snyder et al.'s discussion of hope, another variant in this general line of theories, in chap. 5, this volume). In what follows, we focus mostly on optimism as operationalized by Scheier and Carver (Scheier & Carver, 1985; Scheier & Carver, 1992; Scheier et al., 1994)—that is, in terms of self-reported generalized expectancies.

EFFECTS OF OPTIMISM AND PESSIMISM
ON PSYCHOLOGICAL WELL-BEING

When people confront adversity or difficulty in their lives, they experience a variety of emotions, ranging from excitement and eagerness, to anger, anxiety, and depression. The balance among these feelings appears to relate to people's degree of optimism or pessimism. Optimists are people who expect to have positive outcomes, even when things are difficult. This confidence should yield a mix of feelings that is relatively positive. Pessimists expect negative outcomes. This doubt should yield a greater tendency toward negative feelings—anxiety, guilt, anger, sadness, or despair (Carver & Scheier, 1998; Scheier & Carver, 1992).

Over the past decade or so, researchers have examined relationships between optimism and distress in groups of people facing difficulty or adversity. The range of stressors involved in the research is very broad. For example, researchers have examined the experiences of students entering college (Aspinwall & Taylor, 1992); employees of businesses (Long, 1993); and survivors of missile attacks (Zeidner & Hammer, 1992). Researchers have measured the responses of people caring for medical patients of one type or another (Given et al., 1993; Hooker, Monahan, Shifren, & Hutchinson, 1992; Shifren & Hooker, 1995). Researchers have examined experiences of people dealing with medical procedures, such as childbirth (Carver & Gaines, 1987; Park, Moore, Turner, & Adler, 1997); abortion (Cozzarelli, 1993); coronary artery bypass surgery (Fitzgerald, Tennen, Affleck, & Pransky, 1993; Scheier et al., 1989); attempts at in vitro fertilization (Litt, Tennen, Affleck, & Klock, 1992); and bone marrow transplantation (Curbow, Somerfield, Baker, Wingard, & Legro, 1993). Yet other researchers have looked at how people deal with a diagnosis of cancer (Carver et al., 1993; Friedman et al., 1992); and the progression of AIDS (Taylor et al., 1992).

Some of these studies are more limited than are others. In some projects, the researchers assessed optimism and distress at the same point in time, usually after the negative event occurred. What's known from these cross-sectional studies is that people considered pessimists tended to report more distress than those considered optimists. What is not known is whether the pessimists may have been more distressed even before the event occurred. Additionally, cross-sectional studies make it difficult to tease apart causation. The presumption in the studies is that the casual arrow runs from optimism to distress, but the opposite possibility cannot be ruled out.

Given these inherent limitations of cross-sectional studies, it is far more useful to conduct prospective studies—to see how levels of distress shift and change over time and circumstance. Of course, it's sometimes difficult to recruit participants before the occurrence of the event in which you're interested (e.g., it's hard to know when a hurricane will occur, so it's hard to recruit people 2 weeks beforehand). But even in cases where participants were not recruited before the event, it's useful to examine the process of adaptation to the event across an extended period. Some of the studies that make up this literature on stress and well-being did assess participants at multiple time points, and we will focus on the studies here (for a representative sampling of cross-sectional research, see Table 9.1).

The roots of current research on optimism can be traced back to earlier work within the field of health psychology. For this reason, it is perhaps not surprising that much of what we know about the effects of optimism on psychological well-being comes from research conducted in health-related contexts.

Pregnancy and Childbirth

One early study of the effect of optimism on emotional well-being (Carver & Gaines, 1987) examined the development of depressed feelings after childbirth. Women in this study completed the LOT and a depression scale in the last third of their pregnancy. They then completed the depression measure again 3 weeks after their babies were born. Optimism was related to lower depression symptoms at the initial assessment. More important, optimism predicted lower levels of depressive symptoms postpartum, even when researchers controlled for the initial levels. Thus optimism seemed to confer a resistance to the development of depressive symptoms after having a baby.

A similar point is made by two more recent studies. As did Carver and Gaines, Fontaine and Jones (1997) administered the LOT and a measure of depression to women before and after childbirth. Optimism was once again associated with fewer depressive symptoms, both during pregnancy and 2 weeks postpartum. Park et al. (1997) also examined the effects of optimism on psychological adjustment during pregnancy. Women completed the LOT during their first prenatal clinic visit. During the last trimester of their pregnancy, the women's anxiety was assessed, as well as the extent to which they were maintaining positive states of mind. Optimism was a significant predictor of both. The predictive association of optimism with anxiety was negative, whereas the association with positive states of mind was positive.

Another medical situation that has been studied with respect to optimism effects is infertility—a problem that causes a good deal of unhappiness to a good many people (Stanton & Dunkel-Schetter, 1991). A procedure called in vitro fertilization is one way to circumvent fertility problems, but it doesn't always work. In this study, researchers focused on people whose attempts were unsuccessful (Litt et al., 1992). Approximately 8 weeks before

Table 9.1.

Cross-Sectional Studies Documenting Benefits of Optimism on Psychological Well-Being

Author(s)	Sample	Association With LOT scores
Ausbrooks, Thomas, & Williams, 1995	College students (N = 720)	Less chronic anger/less anger suppression
Barron, Foxall, von Dollen, Shull, & Jones, 1992	Elderly low-vision women (N = 56)	Less loneliness
Blankstein, Flett, & Koledin, 1991	College students (N = 408)	Fewer perceived hassles/more positive psychological adjustment
Chang, 1998b	College students (N = 388)	Less stress, fewer depressive symptoms/ higher satisfaction with life
Chang, 1998a	College students (N = 726)	Less depression/higher satisfaction with life
Curbow et al., 1993	Bone marrow transplant patients (N = 135)	Less negative mood/higher satisfaction with life
Desharnais, Godin, Jobin, Valois, & Ross 1990	Post-MI patients (N = 158)	Less perceived susceptibility/less fear
Dunn, 1996	Amputation patients (N = 138)	Less depression/higher self-esteem
Fontaine & Seal, 1997	Female adults (N = 101)	Fewer mood-related symptoms
Friedman et al., 1992	Mixed cancer patients (N = 954)	Lower levels of daily stress
Given et al., 1993	Cancer patient caregivers (N = 196)	Lower levels of depression
Guarnera & Williams, 1987	Elderly adults (N = 92)	Less external locus of control/more internal locus of control
Hooker et al., 1992	Alzheimer's disease spouse caregivers (N = 51)	Less stress, less depression/greater positive well-being
Khoo & Bishop, 1997	Adult Singaporeans (N = 126)	Less stress/greater positive well-being
Lauver & Tak, 1995	Patients experiencing breast cancer symptoms (N = 135)	Less anxiety in seeking care
Long, Kahn, & Schutz, 1992	Female business managers (N = 192)	Lower anxiety/higher job satisfaction
Long & Sangster, 1993	Rheumatoid arthritis patients (N = 107)	Better adjustment
Marshall & Lang, 1990	Professional women (N = 192)	Less depression
Nelson, Karr, & Coleman, 1995	College students (N = 241)	Fewer daily hassles
Neverlien & Backer, 1991	10–12-year-old dental patients (N = 163)	Less clinical dental anxiety
O'Brien, VanEgeren, & Mumby, 1995	Undergraduates (N = 131)	Lower stress levels
Schuller, 1995	College students (N = 75)	Lower trait anxiety
Sumi, Horie, & Hayakawa, 1997	Female Type A Japanese college students (N = 144)	Lower anxiety
Sweetman, Munz, & Wheeler, 1993	Male and female attorneys (N = 80)	Greater general well-being
Zeidner & Hammer, 1992	Victims of missile attacks (N = 261)	Lower anxiety, less depression, less fear

Note. MI = myocardial infarction.

the attempt, the researchers measured optimism, specific expectancies for fertilization success, coping strategies, distress levels, and the impact of the infertility on participants' lives. Later, 2 weeks after notification of a negative pregnancy test, distress was assessed. Neither demographics, obstetric history, marital adjustment, nor the rated effect of infertility on participants' lives predicted this Time 2 distress—but pessimism did. When Time 1 distress was controlled, pessimism was the strongest predictor of Time 2 distress.

Yet another study examined the influence of optimism on adjustment to abortion (Cozzarelli, 1993). Women completed measures of optimism, self-esteem, self-mastery, self-efficacy, and depression 1 hour prior to an abortion. Their depression and psychological adjustment were assessed 30 minutes after the abortion and again 3 weeks later. Optimists had less preabortion depression, better postabortion adjustment, and better 3-week adjustment than did pessimists. The authors of the study concluded that optimism relates to psychological adjustment both directly and also indirectly through a sense of personal efficacy.

The importance of optimism in adjusting to abortion has recently been reaffirmed in research by Major, Richards, Cooper, Cozzarelli, & Zubek (1998). Major et al. were interested in examining personal resources that might protect women from the distress due to an abortion. Optimism was identified in their research as a key component in a style of personal resilience that facilitated postabortion adjustment.

Coronary Artery Bypass Graft Surgery

Other research investigated the reactions of men who were undergoing and recovering from coronary artery bypass surgery (Scheier et al., 1989). Patients completed questionnaires the day before surgery, 6–8 days after surgery, and 6 months postsurgery. Prior to surgery, optimists reported lower levels of hostility and depression than did pessimists. A week after surgery, optimists reported feeling more relief and happiness, greater satisfaction with their medical care, and greater satisfaction with the emotional support they had received from friends. Six months after surgery, optimists reported higher quality of life than did pessimists. In a follow-up of the same patients 5 years after surgery (cited in Scheier & Carver, 1992), optimists continued to experience greater subjective well-being and general quality of life compared with pessimists. All these differences remained significant when medical factors were statistically controlled.

Another study on optimism and quality of life after coronary artery bypass surgery (Fitzgerald et al., 1993) assessed participants 1 month prior to surgery and 8 months after surgery. Analysis revealed that optimism was negatively related to presurgical distress. Furthermore, when the researchers controlled for presurgical life satisfaction, optimism was positively related to postsurgical life satisfaction. Further analysis revealed that the general sense of optimism appeared to operate on feelings of life satisfaction through a more focused sense of confidence about the surgery. That is, the general sense of optimism about life seems to have been funneled into a specific kind of optimism regarding the surgery, and from there to satisfaction with life. All of the effects involving optimism reported by Fitzgerald et al. (1993) were found to be independent of disease severity.

Similar salutary effects of optimism have been observed in a group of women undergoing coronary artery bypass surgery (King, Rowe, Kimble, & Zerwic, 1998). In this study, data were collected at 1 week, and 1, 6, and 12 months after surgery. At all points of time, optimism demonstrated significant adaptive relationships with positive mood, negative mood, and satisfaction with life. More importantly, optimism assessed at 1 week was associated with more positive mood and less negative mood at 1 month independent of initial levels of positive and negative mood.

Cancer

Optimism has also been studied in the context of adjusting to the diagnosis and treatment for cancer. One study examined the effect of optimism on psychological adaptation to treatment for early-stage breast cancer (Carver et al., 1993). Diagnosis and treatment for breast cancer is a traumatic experience, and cancer is a life-threatening disease. However, prognosis for persons with early-stage cancer is relatively good. This experience thus provides sufficient ambiguity about what will happen in the future to permit individual differences in optimism to be readily expressed. Patients in this study were interviewed six times: at the time of diagnosis, the day before surgery, 7–10 days after surgery, and 3, 6, and 12 months later. Optimism was assessed (using the LOT) at the time of diagnosis and was used to predict distress levels at the subsequent time points.

Optimism inversely predicted distress over time, above and beyond the effect of relevant medical variables and beyond the effects of earlier distress. That is, the prediction of distress at 3, 6, and 12 months after surgery was significant even when the immediately prior level of distress was controlled. Thus, optimism predicted not just lower initial distress, but also resilience to distress during the year following surgery.

In another study involving cancer patients, Johnson (1996) demonstrated the beneficial effects of optimism among a group of men receiving radiation therapy for prostate cancer. Optimism was assessed using the LOT prior to the first radiation treatment. Mood was assessed throughout the treatment period and 2 weeks, 1 month, and 3 months following the end

of treatment. Optimism was a strong predictor of patients' emotional responses both during and after treatment, with less optimistic patients being
particularly vulnerable to negative moods.

Also relevant here is a study by Christman (1990), which examined
adjustment among a group of patients undergoing radiotherapy for a variety
of cancers. Patients were enrolled into the project at one of three points
in time, on the first day of treatment, on the 15th day of treatment, and
on the last day of treatment. Multiple assessments were made on those
patients who were enrolled prior to the conclusion of their treatment.
Optimism was negatively related to adjustment problems at all three assessment points, as well as to illness uncertainty at the first and second assessment
points. These associations involving optimism could not be accounted for
in terms of differences between optimists and pessimists in their preferences
for health-related locus of control.

Other Health-Related Contexts

Still further evidence of the association between optimism and psychological well-being was found by Taylor et al. (1992) among a cohort of
gay and bisexual men at risk of developing Acquired Immunodeficiency
Syndrome (AIDS). Among those men who were seropositive (HIV+) as
well as those who were seronegative (HIV−) greater optimism was associated
with lower levels of subsequent psychological distress as measured by a
composite index of negative affect and by specific worries and concerns
about AIDS.

In a somewhat different medical population, Chamberlain, Petrie, and
Azaria (1992) demonstrated the beneficial effects of optimism among a
group of patients undergoing joint replacement surgery and rehabilitation.
Data were collected before surgery, the third day following surgery, and
approximately 6 weeks following surgery. Optimism assessed presurgically
was positively associated with follow-up levels of life satisfaction and positive
well-being, and negatively associated with psychological distress and pain.

Not only does optimism have a positive effect on the psychological
well-being of people dealing with medical conditions, but it also influences
the psychological well-being of people who are acting as caregivers to patients. In one project supporting this conclusion, researchers studied a group
of cancer patients and their caregivers and found that caregivers' optimism
related to a number of caregiver well-being variables (Given et al., 1993).
Optimism was related to lower symptoms of depression, less impact of caregiving on physical health, and less impact on caregivers' daily schedules.
Caregiver optimism thus predicted caregiver reactions to the burdens of
caring for a family member with cancer, and did so independent of patient variables.

Similar results have been found in research on caregivers of Alzheimer's patients (Hooker et al., 1992; Shifren & Hooker, 1995) and caregivers of patients suffering from stroke (Tompkins, Schulz, & Rau, 1988). In each case, optimism was associated with lower levels of depression and higher levels of psychological well-being.

Non Health-Related Contexts

Although much of the evidence for the relationship between optimism and psychological well-being comes from people facing health threats and people caring for seriously ill relatives, other researchers have looked at groups of people undergoing events that are difficult but far less extreme. For example, the start of a person's college years is a difficult and stressful time. Researchers have examined students making the adjustment to their first semester of college (Aspinwall & Taylor, 1992). Optimism, self-esteem, and a number of other variables were assessed when the students first arrived on campus. Measures of psychological and physical well-being were obtained at the end of the semester. Higher levels of optimism upon entering college predicted lower levels of psychological distress at the end of the semester. The relationship was independent of effects due to self-esteem, locus of control, desire for control, and baseline mood.

Another study of adjustment to college life (cited in Scheier & Carver, 1992) included some additional variables, such as perceived stress and loneliness. This project assessed most of the adjustment variables both at the beginning of the semester and at the end of the semester (rather than just at the end), and looked at changes in these measures over time. The data revealed that optimists became less stressed, less depressed, less lonely, and more socially supported over the semester, compared with their pessimistic counterparts.

In a similar vein, Stewart et al. (1997) examined adjustment among a group of first-year medical students. Students were surveyed prior to the beginning of their medical training. Two months later, students who initially reported high baseline levels of anxiety and low levels of optimism were more likely to develop symptoms of depression and anxiety.

In a study involving first-year law students, Segerstrom, Taylor, Kemeny, and Fahey (1998) assessed dispositional optimism and mood disturbance prior to the beginning of classes. The same measures were readministered at midsemester, approximately 8 weeks later. Baseline optimism was associated with fewer mood disturbances at follow-up. Relevant to our discussion here, this relation remained significant even after controlling for initial level of mood disturbance.

Among a community population of middle-age adults, Räikkönen, Matthews, Flory, Owens, and Gump (1999) assessed ambulatory blood pressure for 3 days and asked participants to keep a concurrent diary of daily moods and daily stressful events. In examining the average rating of mood across the three assessment days, the authors found that optimism (assessed before monitoring began) was significantly associated with lower negative mood and higher positive mood. Käikkönen et al. also found that optimists rated the stressfulness of the day's most negative event as less stressful than did pessimists.

In another study involving a middle-aged sample, Bromberger and Matthews (1996) focused on women approaching menopause. Optimism, depressive symptoms, and life stress were assessed at baseline and again 3 years later. Women with a more pessimistic orientation at baseline were at higher risk for symptoms of depression at follow-up. This effect was particularly pronounced among women who reported experiencing an ongoing stressor at the time at which pessimism was assessed. All of these effects remained significant after baseline depression was statistically controlled.

Finally, Cohen (1990) examined the effects of optimism on psychological well-being in a study of community nurse executives. Participants initially completed a survey that included the LOT. Later, these participants were scheduled for an interview and were asked to provide information regarding psychological symptoms. Optimism proved to be a significant predictor of psychological well-being, and did so independent of the number of years participants spent in nursing.

OPTIMISM, PESSIMISM, AND COPING

Differences in Coping Responses

As the evidence reviewed in the previous section makes clear, optimists experience less distress than do pessimists when dealing with difficulties in their lives. Is this just because optimists are more cheerful than pessimists? Apparently not, because the differences often remain even when statistical controls are incorporated for previous levels of distress. There must be other explanations. Do optimists do anything in particular to cope that helps them adapt better than pessimists? Many researchers are now investigating this possibility as a potential mechanism through which optimism confers psychological benefits. In this section we consider the strategies that optimists and pessimists tend to use, as well as the broader meaning of these strategies.

In many respects, this discussion is a more detailed depiction of the broad behavioral tendencies we discussed in chapter 2 of this volume, where we described expectancy-value models of motivation. That is, people who are confident about the future exert continuing effort, even when dealing with serious adversity. People who are doubtful about the future are more likely to try to push the adversity away as though they can somehow escape its existence by wishful thinking. They are more likely to do things that provide temporary distractions but don't help solve the problem. Sometimes they even give up trying. Both the effort and the removal of effort can be expressed in a variety of ways, and those expressions—coping reactions and coping strategies—are the focus of this section.

Differences in coping methods used by optimists and pessimists have been found in a number of studies. In one early project, Scheier, Weintraub, and Carver (1986) asked undergraduates to recall the most stressful event that had happened to them during the previous month and complete a checklist of coping responses with respect to that event. Optimism related positively to problem-focused coping, especially when the stressful situation was perceived to be controllable. Optimism also related to the use of positive reframing and (when the situation was perceived to be uncontrollable) with the tendency to accept the reality of the situation. In contrast, optimism related negatively to the use of denial and the attempt to distance oneself from the problem.

These findings provided the first indication that optimists don't use just problem-centered coping. They also use a variety of emotion-focused coping techniques, including striving to accept the reality of difficult situations and putting the situations in the best possible light. These findings hint that optimists may enjoy a coping advantage over pessimists even in situations that cannot be changed.

Other researchers have studied differences in dispositional coping styles among optimists and pessimists (Billingsley, Waehler, & Hardin, 1993; Carver, Scheier, & Weintraub, 1989; Fontaine, Manstead, & Wagner, 1993). As with situational coping, optimists reported a dispositional tendency to rely on active, problem-focused coping, and they reported being more "planful" when confronting stressful events. Pessimism was associated with the tendency to disengage from the goals with which the stressor is interfering. Although optimists reported a tendency to accept the reality of stressful events, they also reported trying to see the best in bad situations and to learn something from them. In contrast, pessimists reported tendencies toward overt denial and substance abuse, strategies that lessen their awareness of the problem. Thus, in general terms, optimists appear to be active copers and pessimists appear to be avoidant copers.

Other projects studied relationships between optimism and coping strategies in specific contexts. For example, Strutton and Lumpkin (1992) studied coping in the work environment. They found that optimists used problem-focused coping (such as directed problem solving) more than pessimists. Pessimism was related to the use of avoidant coping (self-indulgent escapism including sleeping, eating, and drinking). Another study focusing on executive women (Fry, 1995) found that optimists reacted to daily hassles differently than did pessimists. Optimistic women expected gain or growth from stressful events and reported coping indicative of acceptance, expressiveness, and tension reduction. They also reported using their social support in stressful circumstances rather than withdrawing, distancing, or engaging in self-blame.

Finally, the study of AIDS patients described earlier (Taylor et al., 1992) provides information regarding coping. In general, optimism was associated with active coping strategies. Optimism predicted positive attitudes and tendencies to plan for recovery, seek information, and reframe bad situations so as to see their most positive aspects. Optimists made less use of fatalism, self-blame, and escapism, and they didn't focus on the negative aspects of the situation or try to suppress thoughts about their symptoms. Optimists also appeared to accept situations that they could not change, rather than trying to escape those situations.

It is important to realize that the various associations that have emerged between optimism and coping do not seem to be simply due to a difference in the manner in which optimists and pessimists appraise events. Chang (1998a), for example, examined the impact of optimism and appraisals on coping with an upcoming course exam. Optimists and pessimists did not differ in their primary appraisals of the event, but they did differ in terms of their secondary appraisals. That is, optimists perceived the exam to be more controllable and their efforts to cope with it more effective than did pessimists. On the other hand, significant differences still emerged between optimists and pessimists on several varieties of coping even after the effect of secondary appraisals on coping was statistically controlled.

Promotion of Well-Being

In describing the manner in which optimists and pessimists cope with adversity, we should note several other studies. These studies do not deal with coping per se, but they make points that are closely related to the points we have made regarding coping. Many of the studies involve reactions to particular health threats or illness episodes. As a group, these studies demonstrate that optimists are more likely than pessimists to face health threats head-on, and do whatever they can to improve the situation they are confronting. In this respect, the behavior seems to reflect a type of problem-focused coping, an attempt to engage in proactive processes that promote good health and well-being (Aspinwall, 1997; Aspinwall & Taylor, 1997).

In one study, researchers looking at the possibility of individual differences in health promotion followed a group of heart patients who were participating in a cardiac rehabilitation program (Shepperd, Maroto, &

Pbert, 1996). Optimism among participants was related to greater success in lowering levels of saturated fat, body fat, and global coronary risk. Optimism was also related to increases in level of exercise across the rehabilitation period. In another study (cited in Scheier & Carver, 1992), researchers investigated the lifestyles of coronary artery bypass patients 5 years after their surgery. This study found that optimists were more likely than pessimists to be taking vitamins, to be eating low-fat foods, and to be enrolled in a cardiac rehabilitation program.

Heart disease isn't the only aspect of health-related behavior that has been related to optimism. Another obvious health risk related to people's behavior is HIV infection. By avoiding certain sexual practices (e.g., sex with unknown partners), people reduce their risk of infection. One study of HIV-negative gay men revealed that optimists reported having fewer anonymous sexual partners than did pessimists (Taylor et al., 1992). In another study, the intentions of a group of sexually active inner-city minority adolescents to engage in unsafe sex were examined (Carvajal, Garner, & Evans, 1998). Optimists reported stronger intentions of avoiding unsafe sex. Taken together, these findings suggest that optimists were making efforts or intending to make efforts to reduce their risk, thereby safeguarding their health.

One final study is also relevant here. Friedman, Weinberg, Webb, Cooper, & Bruce (1995) examined health behavior and health behavior intentions among a group of hospital employees at risk for skin cancer. Optimists were significantly more likely than pessimists to report intentions to engage in skin cancer-relevant health prevention behaviors (e.g., regular sunscreen use). In addition, among those participants identified at screening with suspicious lesions, those who were more optimistic were more likely to comply with recommended follow-up care.

Other studies have examined the health-related habits reported by groups of people with no particular salient health concerns. At least two such projects found associations such that optimists reported more health-promoting behaviors than did pessimists (Robbins, Spence, & Clark, 1991; Steptoe et al., 1994). In sum, the various studies described here suggest that optimism is associated with behaviors aimed at promoting health and reducing health risk.

Consistent with this pattern is research showing conclusively that optimists are not simply people who stick their heads in the sand and ignore threats to their well-being. Rather, they display a pattern of attending selectively to risks—risks that are both applicable to them and related to serious health problems (Aspinwall & Brunhart, 1996). If the potential health problem is minor, or if it is unlikely to bear on them personally, optimists do not show this elevated vigilance. Only when the threat matters does it emerge. This pattern of selective vigilance fits the idea that optimists scan their surroundings for threats to their well-being, but save their active coping efforts for threats that are truly meaningful.

Coping Differences and the Link to Emotional Distress

The foregoing studies help to establish that optimists cope differently than do pessimists. However, these studies do not show that such differences in coping tendencies are responsible for those differences we see in psychological well-being. Fortunately, a number of the studies reviewed earlier in the section on optimism and distress contained measures of coping tendencies in addition to measures of well-being. This allowed those researchers to examine whether the differences they observed in well-being were mediated by differences in coping. We report on the results of those studies in the following paragraphs. Several other studies are relevant to the discussion as well.

One of the studies reviewed earlier assessed the use of attentional-cognitive strategies as ways of dealing with the experience of coronary artery bypass graft surgery (Scheier et al., 1989). Before surgery, optimists were more likely than pessimists to report that they were making plans for their future and setting goals for their recovery. Optimists, as compared to pessimists, also tended to report being less focused on the negative aspects of their experience—their distress emotions and physical symptoms. Once the surgery was past, optimists were more likely than pessimists to report seeking out and requesting information about what the physician would be requiring of them in the months ahead. Optimists were also less likely to report trying to suppress thoughts about their physical symptoms. Results from path analyses suggested that the positive impact of optimism on quality of life 6 months postsurgery occurred through the indirect effect of differences in coping.

Similarly, King et al. (1998) also assessed coping in their study of women undergoing coronary bypass graft surgery. Although their results were not entirely consistent across all of the assessment points in their study, King et al.'s optimists displayed more positive thinking during the week following surgery, engaged in more attempts at finding meaning at 1 month, and employed less escapism at 12 months. Mediational analyses demonstrated that finding meaning and escapism were responsible, at least in part, for the relation observed between optimism and negative mood.

The study of adaptation to failed in vitro fertilization described earlier (Litt et al., 1992) also examined coping. Although the researchers did not find a relationship between optimism and instrumental coping, they did find that pessimism related to escape as a coping strategy. Escape, in turn, related to greater distress after the fertilization failure. In addition, optimists were more likely than pessimists to report feeling that they benefited some-how from the failed fertilization experience (e.g., by becoming closer to their spouse).

Several studies have examined the relationship between optimism, coping, and distress among cancer patients. One study followed women undergoing breast biopsy (Stanton & Snider, 1993). Optimism, coping, and mood were assessed the day before biopsy in all women participating in the study. Women who received a cancer diagnosis were then reassessed 24 hours before surgery and 3 weeks after surgery. Women with a benign diagnosis completed a second assessment that corresponded to either the second or the third assessment of the cancer group. Pessimists used more cognitive avoidance in coping with the upcoming diagnostic procedure than did optimists. This contributed significantly to distress prior to biopsy, and also predicted postbiopsy distress among women with positive diagnoses.

Another study of cancer patients, mentioned earlier in the chapter, examined the ways women cope with treatment for early stage breast cancer during the first full year after treatment (Carver et al., 1993). Optimism, coping (with the diagnosis of cancer), and mood were assessed the day before surgery. Coping and mood were also assessed 10 days postsurgery, and at three follow-up points during the next year. Both before and after surgery, optimism was associated with a pattern of reported coping tactics that centered on accepting the reality of the situation, placing as positive a light on the situation as possible, trying to relieve the situation with humor, and (at presurgery only) taking active steps to do whatever there was to be done. Pessimism was associated with denial and behavioral disengagement (giving up) at each measurement point.

The coping tactics that related to optimism and pessimism also related strongly to the distress that participants reported. Positive reframing, accep-tance, and the use of humor all related inversely to self-reports of distress, both before and after surgery. Denial and behavioral disengagement were positively related to distress at all measurement points. At the 6-month point a new association emerged, such that distress was positively related to another kind of avoidance coping: self-distraction. Not unexpectedly, given the pattern of the correlations, further analyses revealed that the effect of optimism on distress was largely indirect through coping, particularly at postsurgery.

Other studies have been designed to examine the mediational role of coping in the relationship between optimism and psychological well-being. In the college adaptation study described earlier (Aspinwall & Taylor, 1992), optimistic students were more likely than pessimistic students to engage in active coping and less likely to engage in avoidance coping. Avoidance coping was associated with poorer adjustment, and active coping was (separately) associated with better adjustment. The paths from optimism to well-being through coping were significant. Thus, as in the health studies just reviewed, the beneficial effects of optimism in this context seemed to be operating at least in part through the differences in coping.

Similarly, in the study described earlier concerning adjustment to pregnancy (Park et al., 1997), optimistic women were more likely than pessimistic women to engage in constructive thinking (i.e., the tendency to think about and solve daily problems in an effective way). Furthermore, as with optimism, constructive thinking also correlated negatively with later anxiety and positively with later positive states of mind. Subsequent analyses revealed that the association between optimism and each of these markers of psychological adjustment was mediated through the tendency of optimists to engage in constructive thinking.

Finally, recall the study by Segerstrom et al. (1998) examining mood disturbances among students enrolled in law school. Additional data gathered from that study showed that optimists engaged in less avoidant coping than did pessimists. Mediational analyses demonstrated that the differences between optimists and pessimists in the degree of mood disturbance they experienced were at least partially due to the differences between them in their use of avoidant coping strategies.

In sum, these studies indicate that optimists differ from pessimists both in their stable coping tendencies and in the kinds of coping responses that they spontaneously generate when they are confronting stressful situations. Optimists also differ from pessimists in the manner in which they cope with serious disease and with concerns about specific health threats. In general (see Exhibit 9.1), findings from this research suggest that optimists tend to use more problem-focused coping strategies than do pessimists. When problem-focused coping is not a possibility, optimists turn to adaptive emotion-focused coping strategies such as acceptance, use of humor, and positive reframing. Pessimists tend to cope through overt denial and by mentally and behaviorally disengaging from the goals with which the stressor is interfering.

Exhibit 9.1.
Coping Tendencies of Optimists and Pessimists

Optimists	Pessimists
Information seeking	Suppression of thoughts
Active coping and planning	Giving up
Positive reframing	Self-distraction
Seeking benefit	Cognitive avoidance
Use of humor	Focus on distress
Acceptance	Overt denial

Acceptance, Overcoming Adversity, and Continued Goal-Engagement

It is particularly noteworthy to us that optimists turn toward acceptance in uncontrollable situations, whereas pessimists tend to turn toward the use of overt denial. Although both tactics seem to reflect emotion-focused coping, there are important qualitative differences between them that may, in turn, be associated with different qualities of outcomes. More concretely, denial (the refusal to accept the reality of the situation) means attempting to adhere to a worldview that is no longer valid. In contrast, acceptance implies a restructuring of one's experience so as to come to grips with the reality of the situation that one confronts. Acceptance thus may involve a deeper set of processes, in which the person actively works through the experience, attempting to integrate it into an evolving worldview.

The active attempt to come to terms with the existence of problems may confer special benefits to acceptance as a coping response. We want to be very clear here, however, about the sort of acceptance we are talking about. The kind of acceptance we have in mind is a willingness to admit that a problem exists or that an event has happened—even an event that may irrevocably alter the fabric of one's life. We are *not* talking about a stoic resignation, a fatalistic acceptance of the negative consequences to which the problem or event might lead, despite how likely those consequences might be. The latter kind of acceptance does not confer a benefit at all.

Consider, for example, someone diagnosed with an illness such as a terminal cancer or AIDS. The ultimate outcome in both cases may be death. Yet, the person can accept the fact that he or she is terminally ill without simultaneously succumbing to the feeling that he or she is "as good as dead." The latter sort of acceptance, or resignation, may well promote a kind of functional death, in which the person prematurely disengages from the opportunities of life. Consistent with this idea there are some findings to suggest that people who react to illness diagnoses with stoic resignation or passive acceptance of their own impending deaths, actually die sooner than do those people who exhibit less of these qualities (Greer, Morris, & Pettingale, 1979; Greer, Morris, Pettingale, & Haybittle, 1990; Pettingale, Morris, & Greer, 1985; Reed, Kemeny, Taylor, Wang, & Visscher, 1994; for further discussion of this issue, see Scheier & Carver, in press).

In contrast to resignation to the ultimate consequence of the diagnosis, limited acceptance of the diagnosis per se may have very different consequences. It may cause people to reprioritize their lives, to realistically revise and cut back on long-term goals, and to use what time they have left in constructive and optimal ways. By accepting the fact that life may be compromised (but not over), people may be impelled to develop a more adaptive set of guidelines within which to live the life they have left. Why is this revised outlook on life so important, and why should it lead to enhanced well-being?

To answer these questions fully, we need to revisit some of the ideas we introduced in chapter 2 of this volume, describing the theoretical underpinnings of optimism (see also Carver & Scheier, 1998). In particular, recall the central role that is played by goals in the theory discussed there. In that view, people live life by identifying goals for themselves and working and behaving in ways to attain those goals (see Figure 9.1, Loop 1). Obviously, the goals themselves can take a variety of forms (Carver & Scheier, 1998). Regardless of their nature, however, goals provide the structure that defines people's lives and imbues them with meaning, both in the short run and in the long run.

Two factors are important in keeping people goal-engaged. One is the person's ability to identify goals that are valued. People don't take up goals that don't matter to them, and if they did, they wouldn't persist at them very long when things got difficult. Valued goals provide the purpose for living. The second factor is the sensed attainability of the goal. If a goal seems unattainable at the outset, effortful behavior will never even begin. If people continually fail to make progress toward goals they've committed themselves to, they will begin to withdraw effort and start to perceive those goals as out of reach. In contrast, hope enables people to hold onto valued goals, remain engaged in the process of goal striving, and stay committed to the attempt to move forward (see Figure 9.1, Loop 2).

The final part of the overall picture is that the loss of engagement in a goal does not necessarily lead to a vacuum of "goallessness." Elsewhere, we have discussed the ebb and flow of engagement and disengagement in terms of competition among goals (Carver & Scheier, 1998). We suggested that disengagement from one goal may reflect a weakening of commitment to it. Because people usually have many goals at once, however, this weakening of commitment permits another goal to become prepotent and thus permits behavior to shift toward *its* pursuit. Thus, the loss of one goal is often followed directly by pursuit of another one.

Sometimes this means scaling back to a less ambitious goal in the same domain as the abandoned goal. By taking up an attainable alternative, the person remains engaged in goal pursuit and forward movement (see Figure 9.1, Loop 3). This is particularly important when the blocked path concerns a value that is central to the self. People need multiple paths to these core values (cf. Linville, 1985, 1987; Showers & Ryff, 1996; Wicklund & Gollwitzer, 1982). If one path is blocked, people need to be able to divert to another one.

Consider a young woman, diagnosed with breast cancer, who has a great personal investment in family ties and in her career. If chemotherapy

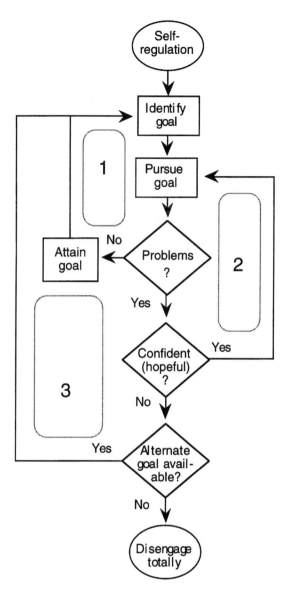

Figure 9.1. Successful self-regulation is a continuing process of identifying goals, pursuing them, attaining them, and identifying further ones (Loop 1). Given adversity, a step of evaluating chances of success may be added (Loop 2), but sufficient confidence places the person back into Loop 1. If confidence is low enough, the person may seek an alternative goal (Loop 3); if available, this loop returns the person to goal pursuit and attainment. If, however, the original goal is seen as unattainable and no alternative is available, the person may disengage completely. From *On the Self-Regulation of Behavior* (p. 349) by C. S. Carver and M. F. Scheier, 1998, New York: Cambridge University Press. Copyright 1998 by Cambridge University Press. Reproduced with permission.

destroys her ability to have children, positive family experiences can be obtained in other ways (cf. Clark, Henry, & Taylor, 1991). If her long-term career ambitions are threatened by the progression of the disease (e.g., by impending death), those ambitions might be realized in smaller ways in the time that remains. Alternatively, she might decide to reprioritize various aspects of her life and spend less time working and more time in close relationships.

In any case, it seems apparent that the ability to shift to a new goal, or to find a new path to a continuing goal, is a very important part of remaining goal-engaged. What happens if there is no alternative to take up? In such a case disengagement from an unattainable goal is not accompanied by a shift, because there is nothing to shift to. This is the worst situation, where there is nothing to pursue, nothing to take the place of what is seen as unattainable (cf. Moskowitz, Folkman, Collette, & Vittinghoff, 1996; Scheier & Carver, in press). If commitment to the unattainable goal remains, the result is great distress. If the commitment wanes, the result is emptiness. There is reason to suspect that such a state might also be implicated in premature death (Carver & Scheier, 1998).

IS OPTIMISM ALWAYS GOOD: IS PESSIMISM ALWAYS BAD?

The picture that we have painted throughout this chapter is one in which optimists are virtually always better off than are pessimists. The evidence we have reviewed indicates that they are less distressed when times are tough, they cope in ways that foster better outcomes for themselves, and are more proactive in their responses to adversity. Although there are certainly times and situations in which optimists are only minimally better off than pessimists, and there are probably cases where they have no advantage at all, remarkably little evidence exists that optimists are ever *worse* off than pessimists.

Several people have suggested the possibility that such situations may exist, that optimism may be potentially damaging (Schwarzer, 1994; Tennen & Affleck, 1987). And, indeed, there is logic behind this hypothesis. For example, too much optimism might potentially lead people to ignore a threat until it's too late, or might lead people to overestimate their ability to deal with an adverse situation, resulting in poorer outcomes.

Most of the data reviewed in the preceding sections indicate that this is generally not the case. On the other hand, there are a couple of studies that suggest the possibility that optimists may not always take action to enhance their future well-being. Goodman, Chesney, and Tipton (1995) studied the extent to which a group of adolescent girls at risk for HIV infection sought out information about HIV testing and agreed to have a test performed. Those scoring higher in levels of optimism were less likely to expose themselves to the information about HIV-testing, and were less likely to follow through with an actual test than were those who scored lower in levels of optimism (see also, Perkins, Leserman, Murphy, & Evans, 1993).

These findings contradict the bulk of evidence reviewed earlier. Why the findings diverge in this way is not clear. Goodman et al. (1995) noted that the average level of optimism among the adolescent girls they studied was substantially lower than the levels typically seen in other sample groups. This difference may somehow have played a role in the results. Alternatively, perhaps the results do not really contradict previous findings at all. Perhaps it seems so only because of the absence of other data that would render the findings more understandable. For example, no information was gathered in this study about the knowledge the girls had concerning the serostatus of their sexual partners. Perhaps optimists had gone to greater lengths than pessimists to verify that their partners were HIV-negative. If so, they would have had less need to seek out HIV-relevant information or have their HIV status tested.

In a similar vein, perhaps the adolescent girls in the Goodman et al. (1995) study took greater steps to avoid engaging in unsafe sex, and as a result of their cautiousness, had less need to pursue information about their HIV status. Consistent with this possibility are recent findings reported in a study by Carvajal et al. (1998), in which optimistic adolescent girls expressed stronger intentions to avoid unsafe sex than did their more pessimistic counterparts. Unfortunately, there was no evidence in the Goodman et al. (1995) study that optimistic participants were being any more cautious in actual sexual behavior. Moreover, Perkins et al. (1993) found that optimistic gay men were more likely than pessimistic gay men to report engaging in high-risk sexual behavior, results contradicting those of Carvajal et al. (1998). Obviously, more work is needed for these questions to be resolved.

The idea that optimists may fail to take steps to protect themselves against threats is one potential way in which optimism can work against a person. Another possibility worth considering is that the worldview of an optimist might be more vulnerable to the shattering impact of a traumatic event than that of a pessimist. Such an event is more consistent with the pessimist's worldview than with the optimist's. Given the diagnosis of metastatic cancer, the experience of a violent rape, or having one's home destroyed by fire or flood, who will react worse, the optimist or the pessimist? Will optimists be less able to rebuild the shattered assumptions of their lives? All these possibilities are legitimate. Any might occur. However, we are aware of no evidence that any of them systematically *does* occur.

Perhaps the lack of support for the idea that optimists respond worse to a shattering event reflects a more general lack of information about how qualities of personality relate to responses to trauma, or to experiences such as terminal illness. In reality, there is not a great deal of information on these questions. However, we do not expect optimists to respond adversely. Rather, we expect them to reset their sights on their changed realities, and to continue to make the best of the situations they are facing. Pessimists may find that their worldviews are confirmed by trauma or disaster, but we doubt that they will take much satisfaction in this confirmation. Rather, their experience will center on the anticipation of continued adversity, and on the feelings of distress to which such expectancies are attached.

CONCLUSION

Only relatively recently have researchers given rigorous attention to the possibility that an optimistic orientation to life is beneficial. But it does seem to be so. Put simply, optimists emerge from difficult circumstances with less distress than do pessimists. In part, this "optimistic advantage" is due to differences in the manner in which optimists and pessimists cope with the difficulties they confront. That is, optimists seem intent on facing problems head-on, taking active and constructive steps to solve their problems; pessimists are more likely to abandon their effort to attain their goals. When something cannot be changed, optimists try to cast the situation in the best way possible and accept its reality, rather than trying to will the event away. In contrast, pessimists are much more likely to engage in different varieties of avoidance coping.

The evidence obtained thus far provides an interesting window in how the worlds of the optimist and pessimist differ. On the other hand, the picture is not yet complete, or as clear as one might like. For example, although some forms of acceptance seem to promote well-being and health, the form that reflects resignation appears more detrimental. Systematic work needs to be done to understand the nature of the difference between these forms of acceptance, as well as to determine whether optimists use only one form and not the other. Additionally, we have speculated that a limited disengagement from goals can be helpful, in that it allows a person to remain goal-engaged in the same general life domain that was of interest initially. Future research should be sensitive to the fact that disengagement from goals is not always bad—indeed, is sometimes a necessity of living (Carver & Scheier, 1998; Wrosch, Scheier, Carver, & Schulz, 2000). This research should attempt to determine the conditions under which goal-engagement most adaptively gives way to disengagement in order to maximize outcomes and psychological health. Clearly, aspects of the puzzle linking optimism and pessimism to psychological well-being need further attention. In light of what has been revealed thus far, the challenge of refining and clarifying the picture would seem to be a worthwhile endeavor.

REFERENCES

Armor, D. A., & Taylor, S. E. (1998). Situated optimism: Specific outcome expectancies and self-regulation. In M. Zanna (Ed.), *Advances in experimental social psychology* (Vol. 30, pp. 309–379). San Diego, CA: Academic Press.

Aspinwall, L. G. (1997). Where planning meets coping: Proactive coping and the detection and management of potential stressors. In S. L. Friedman & E. K. Scholnick (Ed.), *The developmental psychology of planning: Why, how, and when do we plan?* (pp. 285–320). Mahwah, NJ: Erlbaum.

Aspinwall, L. G., & Brunhart, S. M. (1996). Distinguishing optimism from denial: Optimistic beliefs predict attention to health threats. *Personality and Social Psychology Bulletin, 22,* 993–1003.

Aspinwall, L. G., & Taylor, S. E. (1992). Modeling cognitive adaptation: A longitudinal investigation of the impact of individual differences and coping on college adjustment and performance. *Journal of Personality and Social Psychology, 63,* 989–1003.

Aspinwall, L. G., & Taylor, S. E. (1997). A stitch in time: Self-regulation and proactive coping. *Psychological Bulletin, 121,* 417–436.

Ausbrooks, D. P., Thomas, S. P., & Williams, R. L. (1995). Relationships among self-efficacy, optimism, trait anger, and anger expression. *Health Values, 19,* 46–54.

Barron, C. R., Foxall, M. J., von Dollen, K., Shull, K. A., & Jones, P. S. (1992). Loneliness in low-vision older women. *Issues in Mental Health Nursing, 13,* 387–401.

Billingsley, K. D., Waehler, C. A., & Hardin, S. I. (1993). Stability of optimism and choice of coping strategy. *Perceptual and Motor Skills, 76,* 91–97.

Blankstein, K. R., Flett, G. L., & Koledin, S. (1991). The brief College Student Hassles Scale: Development, validation and relation with pessimism. *Journal of College Student Development, 32,* 258–264.

Bromberger, J. T., & Matthews, K. A. (1996). A longitudinal study of the effects of pessimism, trait anxiety, and life stress on depressive symptoms in middle-aged women. *Psychology and Aging, 11,* 207–213.

Carvajal, S. C., Garner, R. L., & Evans, R. I. (1998). Dispositional optimism as a protective factor in resisting HIV exposure in sexually active inner-city minority adolescents. *Journal of Applied Social Psychology, 28,* 2196–2211.

Carver, C. S., & Gaines, J. G. (1987). Optimism, pessimism, and postpartum depression. *Cognitive Therapy and Research, 11,* 449–462.

Carver, C. S., Pozo, C., Harris, S. D., Noriega, V., Scheier, M. F., Robinson, D. S., Ketcham, A. S., Moffat, F. L., & Clark, K. C. (1993). How coping mediates the effect of optimism on distress: A study of women with early stage breast cancer. *Journal of Personality and Social Psychology, 65,* 375–390.

Carver, C. S., & Scheier, M. F. (1998). *On the self-regulation of behavior.* New York: Cambridge University Press.

Carver, C. S., Scheier, M. F., & Weintraub, J. K. (1989). Assessing coping strategies: A theoretically based approach. *Journal of Personality and Social Psychology, 56*, 267–283.

Chamberlain, K., Petrie, K., & Azaria, R. (1992). The role of optimism and sense of coherence in predicting recovery following surgery. *Psychology and Health, 7*, 301–310.

Chang, E. C. (1998a). Dispositional optimism and primary and secondary appraisal of a stressor: Controlling for confounding influences and relations to coping and psychological and physical adjustment. *Journal of Personality and Social Psychology, 74*, 1109–1120.

Chang, E. C. (1998b). Does dispositional optimism moderate the relation between perceived stress and psychological well-being? A preliminary investigation. *Personality and Individual Differences, 25*, 233–240.

Christman, N. J. (1990). Uncertainty and adjustment during radiotherapy. *Nursing Research, 39*, 17–20, 47.

Clark, L. F., Henry, S. M., & Taylor, D. M. (1991). Cognitive examination of motivation for childbearing as a factor in adjustment to infertility. In A. L. Stanton & C. Dunkel-Schetter (Eds.), *Infertility: Perspectives from stress and coping research* (pp. 157–180). New York: Plenum Press.

Cohen, J. H. (1990). Community nurse executives' psychologic well-being: Relationships among stressors, social support, coping, and optimism. *Public Health Nursing, 7*, 194–203.

Cozzarelli, C. (1993). Personality and self-efficacy as predictors of coping with abortion. *Journal of Personality and Social Psychology, 65*, 1224–1236.

Curbow, B., Somerfield, M. R., Baker, F., Wingard, J. R., & Legro, M. W. (1993). Personal changes, dispositional optimism, and psychological adjustment to bone marrow transplantation. *Journal of Behavioral Medicine, 16*, 423–443.

Desharnais, R., Godin, G., Jobin, J., Valois, P., & Ross, A. (1990). Optimism and health-relevant cognitions after a myocardial infarction. *Psychological Reports, 67*, 1131–1135.

Dunn, D. S. (1996). Well-being following amputation: Salutary effect of positive mean, optimism and control. *Rehabilitation Psychology, 41*, 285–302.

Fitzgerald, T. E., Tennen, H., Affleck, G., & Pransky, G. S. (1993). The relative importance of dispositional optimism and control appraisals in quality of life after coronary artery bypass surgery. *Journal of Behavioral Medicine, 16*, 25–43.

Fontaine, K. R., & Jones, L. C. (1997). Self-esteem, optimism, and postpartum depression. *Journal of Clinical Psychology, 53*, 59–63.

Fontaine, K. R., Manstead, A. S. R., & Wagner, H. (1993). Optimism, perceived control over stress, and coping. *European Journal of Personality, 7*, 267–281.

Fontaine, K. R., & Seal, A. (1997). Optimism, social support, and premenstrual dysphoria. *Journal of Clinical Psychology, 53*, 234–247.

Friedman, L. C., Nelson, D. V., Baer, P. E., Lane, M., Smith, F. E., & Dworkin, R. J. (1992). The relationship of dispositional optimism, daily life stress, and domestic environment to coping methods used by cancer patients. *Journal of Behavioral Medicine, 15,* 127–141.

Friedman, L. C., Weinberg, A. D., Webb, J. A., Cooper, H. P., & Bruce, S. (1995). Skin cancer prevention and early detection intentions and behavior. *American Journal of Preventive Medicine, 11,* 59–65.

Fry, P. S. (1995). Perfectionism, humor, and optimism as moderators of health outcomes and determinants of coping styles of women executives. *Genetics, Social, and General Psychology Monographs, 121,* 211–245.

Given, C. W., Stommel, M., Given, B., Osuch, J., Kurtz, M. E., & Kurtz, J. C. (1993). The influence of cancer patients' symptoms and functional states on patients' depression and family caregivers' reaction and depression. *Health Psychology, 12,* 277–285.

Goodman, E., Chesney, M. A., & Tipton, A. C. (1995). Relationship of optimism, knowledge, attitudes, and beliefs to use of HIV antibody test by at-risk female adolescents. *Psychosomatic Medicine, 57,* 541–546.

Greer, S., Morris, T., & Pettingale, K. W. (1979). Psychological response to breast cancer: Effect on outcome. *Lancet, 2,* 785–787.

Greer, S., Morris, T., Pettingale, K. W., & Haybittle, J. L. (1990). Psychological response to breast cancer and 15-year outcome. *Lancet, 1,* 49–50.

Guarnera, S., & Williams, R. L. (1987). Optimism and locus of control for health and affiliation among elderly adults. *Journal of Gerontology, 43,* 594–595.

Hooker, K., Monahan, D., Shifren, K., & Hutchinson, C. (1992). Mental and physical health of spouse caregivers: The role of personality. *Psychology and Aging, 7,* 367–375.

Johnson, J. E. (1996). Coping with radiation therapy: Optimism and the effect of preparatory interventions. *Research in Nursing and Health, 19,* 3–12.

Khoo, S., & Bishop, G. D. (1997). Stress and optimism: Relationships to coping and well-being. *Psychologia: An International Journal of Psychology in the Orient, 40,* 29–40.

King, K. B., Rowe, M. A., Kimble, L. P., & Zerwic, J. J. (1998). Optimism, coping, and long-term recovery from coronary artery bypass in women. *Research in Nursing and Health, 21,* 15–26.

Lauver, D., & Tak, Y. (1995). Optimism and coping with a breast cancer symptom. *Nursing Research, 44,* 202–207.

Linville, P. (1985). Self-complexity and affective extremity: Don't put all of your eggs in one cognitive basket. *Social Cognition, 3,* 94–120.

Linville, P. (1987). Self-complexity as a cognitive buffer against stress-related illness and depression. *Journal of Personality and Social Psychology, 52,* 663–676.

Litt, M. D., Tennen, H., Affleck, G., & Klock, S. (1992). Coping and cognitive factors in adaptation to *in vitro* fertilization failure. *Journal of Behavioral Medicine, 15,* 171–187.

Long, B. C. (1993). Coping strategies of male managers: A prospective analysis of predictors of psychosomatic symptoms and job satisfaction. *Journal of Vocational Behavior, 42,* 184–199.

Long, B. C., Kahn, S. E., & Schutz, R. W. (1992). Causal model of stress and coping: Women in management. *Journal of Counseling Psychology, 39,* 227–239.

Long, B. C., & Sangster, J. I. (1993). Dispositional optimism/pessimism and coping strategies: Predictors of psychosocial adjustment of rheumatoid and osteoarthritis patients. *Journal of Applied Social Psychology, 23,* 1069–1091.

Major, B., Richards, C., Cooper, M. L., Cozzarelli, C., & Zubek, J. (1998). Personal resilience, cognitive appraisals, and coping: An integrative model of adjustment to abortion. *Journal of Personality and Social Psychology, 74,* 735–752.

Marshall, G. N., & Lang, E. L. (1990). Optimism, self-mastery, and symptoms of depression in women professionals. *Journal of Personality and Social Psychology, 59,* 132–139.

Moskowitz, J. T., Folkman, S., Collette, L., & Vittinghoff, E. (1996). Coping and mood during AIDS-related caregiving and bereavement. *Annals of Behavioral Medicine, 18,* 49–57.

Nelson, E. S., Karr, K. A., & Coleman, P. K. (1995). Relationships among daily hassles, optimism and reported physical symptoms. *Journal of College Student Psychotherapy, 10,* 11–26.

Neverlien, P. O., & Backer, J. T. (1991). Optimism-pessimism dimensions and dental anxiety in children aged to 10 to 12 years. *Community Dental Oral Epidemiology, 6,* 342–346.

O'Brien, W. H., VanEgeren, L., & Mumby, P. B. (1995). Predicting health behaviors using measures of optimism and perceived risk. *Health Values, 19*(1), 21–28.

Park, C. L., Moore, P. J., Turner, R. A., & Adler, N. E. (1997). The roles of constructive thinking and optimism in psychological and behavioral adjustment during pregnancy. *Journal of Personality and Social Psychology, 73,* 584–592.

Perkins, D. O., Leserman, J., Murphy, C., & Evans, D. L. (1993). Psychosocial predictors of high-risk sexual behavior among HIV-negative homosexual men. *AIDS Education and Prevention, 5,* 141–152.

Peterson, C., & Seligman, M. E. P. (1984). Causal explanations as a risk factor for depression: Theory and evidence. *Psychological Review, 91,* 347–374.

Pettingale, K. W., Morris, T., & Greer, S. (1985). Mental attitudes to cancer: An additional prognostic factor. *Lancet, 1,* 750.

Räikkönen, K., Matthews, K. A., Flory, J. D., Owens, J. F., & Gump, B. B. (1999). Effects of optimism, pessimism, and trait anxiety on ambulatory blood pressure and mood during everyday life. *Journal of Personality and Social Psychology, 76,* 104–128.

Reed, G. M., Kemeny, M. E., Taylor, S. E., Wang, H. J., & Visscher, B. R. (1994). "Realistic acceptance" as a predictor of decreased survival time in gay men with AIDS. *Health Psychology, 13,* 299–307.

Robbins, A. S., Spence, J. T., & Clark, H. (1991). Psychological determinants of health and performance: The tangled web of desirable and undesirable characteristics. *Journal of Personality and Social Psychology, 61,* 755–765.

Scheier, M. F., & Carver, C. S. (1985). Optimism, coping and health: Assessment and implications of generalized outcome expectancies. *Health Psychology, 4,* 219–247.

Scheier, M. F., & Carver, C. S. (1992). Effects of optimism on psychological and physical well-being: Theoretical overview and empirical update. *Cognitive Therapy and Research, 16,* 201–228.

Scheier, M. F., & Carver, C. S. (in press). Adapting to cancer: The importance of hope and purpose. In A. Baum & B. L. Andersen (Eds.), *Psychosocial interventions for cancer.* Washington, DC: American Psychological Association.

Scheier, M. F., Carver, C. S., & Bridges, M. W. (1994). Distinguishing optimism from neuroticism (and trait anxiety, self-mastery, and self-esteem): A reevaluation of the Life Orientation Test. *Journal of Personality and Social Psychology, 67,* 1063–1078.

Scheier, M. F., Matthews, K. A., Owens, J. F., Magovern, G. J., Lefebvre, R. C., Abbott, R. A., & Carver, C. S. (1989). Dispositional optimism and recovery from coronary artery bypass surgery: The beneficial effects on physical and psychological well-being. *Journal of Personality and Social Psychology, 57,* 1024–1040.

Scheier, M. F., Weintraub, J. K., & Carver, C. S. (1986). Coping with stress: Divergent strategies of optimists and pessimists. *Journal of Personality and Social Psychology, 51,* 1257–1264.

Schuller, I. S. (1995). Cognitive style categorization width and anxiety. *Studia Psychologica, 37,* 142–145.

Schwarzer, R. (1994). Optimism, vulnerability, and self-beliefs as health-related cognitions: A systematic overview. *Psychology and Health, 9,* 161–180.

Segerstrom, S. C., Taylor, S. E., Kemeny, M. E., & Fahey, J. L. (1998). Optimism is associated with mood, coping, and immune change in response to stress. *Journal of Personality and Social Psychology, 74,* 1646–1655.

Seligman, M. E. P. (1991). *Learned optimism.* New York: Knopf.

Shepperd, J. A., Maroto, J. J., & Pbert, L. A. (1996). Dispositional optimism as a predictor of health changes among cardiac patients. *Journal of Research in Personality, 30,* 517–534.

Shifren, K., & Hooker, K. (1995). Stability and change in optimism: A study among spouse caregivers. *Experimental Aging Research, 21,* 59–76.

Showers, C. J., & Ryff, C. D. (1996). Self-differentiation and well being in a life transition. *Personality and Social Psychology Bulletin, 22,* 448–460.

Stanton, A. L., & Dunkel-Schetter, C. (Eds.). (1991). *Infertility: Perspectives from stress and coping research.* New York: Plenum Press.

Stanton, A. L., & Snider, P. R. (1993). Coping with breast cancer diagnosis: A prospective study. *Health Psychology, 12,* 16–23.

Steptoe, A., Wardle, J., Vinck, J., Tuomisto, M., Holte, A., & Wichstrøm, L. (1994). Personality and attitudinal correlates of healthy lifestyles in young adults. *Psychology and Health, 9,* 331–343.

Stewart, S. M., Betson, C., Lam, T. H., Marshall, I. B., Lee, P. W., & Wong, C. M. (1997). Predicting stress in first year medical students: A longitudinal study. *Medical Education, 3,* 163–168.

Strutton, D., & Lumpkin, J. (1992). Relationship between optimism and coping strategies in the work environment. *Psychology Reports, 71,* 1179–1186.

Sumi, K., Horie, K., & Hayakawa, S. (1997). Optimism, Type A behavior, and psychological well-being in Japanese women. *Psychological Reports, 80,* 43–48.

Sweetman, M. E., Munz, D. C., & Wheeler, R. J. (1993). Optimism, hardiness, and explanatory style as predictors of general well-being among attorneys. *Social Indicators Research, 29,* 153–161.

Taylor, S. E., Kemeny, M. E., Aspinwall, L. G., Schneider, S. G., Rodriguez, R., & Herbert, M. (1992). Optimism, coping, psychological distress, and high-risk sexual behavior among men at risk for Acquired Immunodeficiency Syndrome (AIDS). *Journal of Personality and Social Psychology, 63,* 460–473.

Tennen, H., & Affleck, G. (1987). The costs and benefits of optimistic explanations and dispositional optimism. *Journal of Personality, 55,* 377–393.

Tompkins, C. A., Schulz, R., & Rau, M. T. (1988). Post-stroke depression in primary support persons: Predicting those at risk. *Journal of Consulting and Clinical Psychology, 56,* 502–508.

Wicklund, R. A., & Gollwitzer, P. M. (1982). *Symbolic self-completion.* Hillsdale, NJ: Erlbaum.

Wrosch, C., Scheier, M. F., Carver, C. S., & Schulz, R. (2000). *The importance of goal disengagement in a positive psychology.* Unpublished manuscript, Carnegie Mellon University, Pittsburgh, PA.

Zeidner, M., & Hammer, A. L. (1992). Coping with missile attack: Resources, strategies, and outcomes. *Journal of Personality, 60,* 709–746.

10

UNDERSTANDING HOW OPTIMISM WORKS: AN EXAMINATION OF OPTIMISTS' ADAPTIVE MODERATION OF BELIEF AND BEHAVIOR

LISA G. ASPINWALL, LINDA RICHTER,
AND RICHARD R. HOFFMAN III

A clear picture of the mental and physical health benefits associated with optimism has emerged in the past 15 years. With few exceptions, people considered "optimists" appear to achieve better outcomes in a wide range of situations, including adjustment to life-threatening and chronic illnesses (e.g., cancer, AIDS) and major life transitions (e.g., moving from home to college, from one country to another; see Scheier, Carver, & Bridges, chap. 9, this volume; Taylor & Aspinwall, 1996, for reviews). However, optimistic beliefs do not appear to be associated with intelligence,

Lisa G. Aspinwall was supported in part by a grant from NSF (SBR-9709677) and by the Department of Psychology, University of Maryland. Linda Richter was supported in part by a National Research Service Award from NIMH (1F31 MH11240-01).

academic achievement, wealth, or other characteristics that might convey advantages in life (see, e.g., Epstein & Meier, 1989). How, then, are optimistic beliefs translated into good outcomes in such a wide range of life domains? That is, what do optimists think and do when encountering threatening, challenging, or novel situations that may account for these good outcomes? This chapter addresses the question: How does optimism work?

Throughout the chapter we use the term *optimist* and the phrase *high in optimism* to denote research participants whose scores on standardized measures of optimism are one standard deviation or more above the mean in their respective samples. The term *pessimist* and the phrase *low in optimism* denote participants whose scores are one standard deviation or more below the sample mean. Most of the research described here assesses optimism through Scheier and Carver's Life Orientation Test (LOT; 1985) of dispositional optimism (see the Introduction of this volume and Scheier, Carver, & Bridges, 1994, for more detail). Related frameworks, such as Snyder's (1994) work on hope and Armor and Taylor's (1998) examination of domain-specific optimistic beliefs, are also discussed.

We begin by reviewing what is known about how optimistic beliefs are associated with good outcomes. Next, we examine some intriguing recent evidence demonstrating greater flexibility in the cognitive processing and behavior of optimists that may explain their ability to adapt successfully to new situations, especially those situations that are negative or threatening. In particular, optimists seem to be more able than pessimists to vary their beliefs and behavior to match important features of the situation at hand. We will discuss the potential adaptational benefits of being able to moderate one's behavior in this way and identify some future research directions that might elucidate the mechanisms that account for such moderation.

POTENTIAL MEDIATORS OF OPTIMISTS' GOOD OUTCOMES: ACTIVE COPING AND THE SELF-FULFILLING PROPHECY

There is strong evidence that the link between optimism and good psychological adjustment may be explained by the different ways optimists and pessimists cope with stress (see Taylor & Aspinwall, 1996, for review; see Scheier et al., chap. 9, this volume). In their study of a large sample of freshmen college students, Aspinwall and Taylor (1992) found that optimists were more likely than pessimists to report active ways of coping (such as problem-solving efforts), and they were less likely than pessimists to report avoidant ways of coping (such as attempts to stop thinking about the problem or substance use). These ways of coping, in turn, predicted better self-reported psychological adjustment to college for these optimistic students 3 months later. Similar findings have been reported in a number of other contexts, ranging from emigration from East to West Germany (Jerusalem, 1993) to coping with surgery for breast cancer (Carver et al., 1993).

With respect to physical health,[1] there is evidence that optimists may take better care of themselves, either in response to illness or in order to prevent it. For example, Taylor et al. (1992) found that among gay men who were HIV-seropositive, those who were optimistic reported greater efforts to maintain their health through diet and exercise. Similar findings have been obtained in a study of residents of public housing in New Jersey, in which project residents who were optimistic were more likely to take actions to protect their personal health and also to improve conditions in their neighborhood (Greenberg, 1997). Such efforts at self-care represent one important pathway through which optimists are likely to fare better over time.

Thus far, the picture that emerges from studies of coping and health is that optimists report better adjustment to a wide range of stressors because they tend to cope actively instead of avoidantly. In other words, optimists tend to respond to difficulty with continued efforts to solve their problems, instead of denying the problems or wishing they would go away. Optimists are also more likely to take constructive steps to safeguard their health. This pattern of results may be understood as a sort of self-fulfilling prophecy: *Optimists*, by definition, are people with favorable expectations about the future. Such expectations should make success on a given problem seem more likely and should thereby promote continued problem-solving efforts, resulting in better outcomes (Carver & Scheier, 1990).

If all life problems and transitions were amenable to improvement through one's efforts, we would have a complete explanation of the benefits of optimism. However, many situations involve negative information and events largely outside our control, such as a diagnosis of life-threatening illness. In situations in which our problems cannot be solved or are not entirely amenable to our own efforts, it would be reasonable to predict that optimists' tendencies to cope actively would work against them, such that they might expend a great deal of energy trying to solve the unsolvable and thus expose themselves to disappointment, frustration, and failure. Interestingly, however, optimists appear to be more likely than people low in optimism to report disengaging from intractable situations and working to accept them. In the next section, we review evidence from naturalistic studies of stress and coping and from a laboratory study of persistence that suggests that optimists are more—rather than less—likely to disengage from uncontrollable stressors.

---

[1]There is accumulating evidence that optimism is associated with enhanced immunocompetence and other health benefits among people under stress (such as first-year law students) and among people managing serious illnesses (such as HIV infection). A review of this literature is beyond the scope of this chapter. Please see Taylor, Kemeny, Reed, Bower, and Gruenewald (2000).

OPTIMISTS' RESPONSES TO UNCONTROLLABLE STRESSORS: PARADOXES OF DISENGAGEMENT AND ACCEPTANCE

Evidence From Studies of Stress and Coping

The first evidence that optimists appear to be able to moderate their coping behavior based on whether a stressor is perceived to be controllable came from two studies by Scheier, Weintraub, and Carver (1986). As described previously (see chap. 9, this volume), optimistic college students who were asked to describe a prior stressor or to imagine one reported that they would cope actively with problems that were perceived to be controllable, but would disengage from active problem-solving efforts and use coping strategies designed to manage their emotions for problems perceived to be uncontrollable. Similar findings were obtained by Carver and his colleagues (1993) in a study of women adjusting to surgery for breast cancer. Compared to pessimists, optimistic women were more likely to indicate that they had accepted the reality of having had surgery for breast cancer. Optimists also reported greater use of humor in coping, and they reported lower levels of both denial (refusing to believe the surgery had happened) and disengagement (giving up attempts to cope with the aftermath of the surgery). Each of these coping strategies was, in turn, related to lower psychological distress in the year following the surgery (see chap. 9, this volume for additional detail).

Such moderation of behavior—coping actively with controllable stressors (the aftermath of the surgery) and accepting uncontrollable ones (having had the surgery)—closely resembles the well-known Serenity Prayer. In the Serenity Prayer, people wish for the courage to change the things they can change, the serenity to accept the things they cannot change, and—most important—the wisdom to know the difference. Embodied in this prayer is the idea that the key to successful adaptation may lie in being able to moderate one's beliefs and behaviors to match important objective features of problems, such as whether these beliefs are amenable to personal control. If one's situation is indeed uncontrollable, disengagement from active problem-solving efforts and acceptance of the reality of the situation might be adaptive responses that preserve resources for future coping efforts and limit current negative outcomes (Aspinwall & Richter, 1999; Aspinwall & Taylor, 1997).

To date, most research on optimism has focused on the first part of the Serenity Prayer, that is, on changing the things one can change through active coping. However, we have begun to suspect that the last two, largely unexplored parts of the Serenity Prayer (accepting things one cannot change and distinguishing things one can change from those one cannot) may play an important role in optimists' good outcomes. Thus far, the findings linking optimism to greater acceptance of and disengagement from uncontrollable situations are not well understood. As noted earlier, most theoretical accounts identify factors such as favorable expectations, generalized self-efficacy beliefs (Schwarzer & Jerusalem, 1995), and more favorable control appraisals (Chang, 1998) as keys to optimists' success. However, if optimists are predisposed to see their problems as controllable and their likely outcomes as favorable, why would they be more, rather than less, likely to disengage from uncontrollable situations and accept negative realities? Carver et al. (1993) speculated that belief in a good future may make current problems easier to accept, and thereby, easier to deal with. This explanation may account for optimists' greater acceptance, but it does not seem to account for how and whether optimists are able to distinguish controllable from uncontrollable situations.

In trying to understand this phenomenon, we have conducted several studies to test how optimists respond to negative events and information of various kinds. As we will review, we find evidence in a number of domains consistent with the idea that optimists' beliefs and behaviors are responsive to meaningful variations in the situations or problems presented to them. We first describe a study of how optimists allocate effort to controllable versus uncontrollable problems, and then examine optimists' responsiveness to other kinds of information.

Experimental Study of Optimism and Responses to Unsolvable Problems

In an effort to create a laboratory analog to the kinds of situations described in the Serenity Prayer, we examined how college students responded to a challenging test of verbal intelligence in which some problems were solvable and some were unsolvable. We were especially interested in how participants would respond to an initial set of problems that could not be solved. Would those who were optimistic quickly identify the problems as unsolvable within the time limit and move on to the rest, or would they use most of their time trying to solve the unsolvable problems, thus compromising their performance on the other problems?

We created this situation by modifying the widely used "nonproductive persistence" paradigm. In a typical study, participants are given a set of anagrams or other puzzles that, unbeknownst to them, cannot be solved, and the time they spend working on these before giving up is measured. Because the problems are unsolvable, longer solution times are interpreted as *nonproductive persistence* and are said to represent maladaptive coping. There are several potential difficulties with this procedure and with the interpretation of greater persistence as maladaptive (see Aspinwall & Richter, 1999, for discussion). One problem is that it is usually reasonable to assume that a problem one has been given can be solved, especially if it is the only task one has been given and time has been allotted for one to work on it. A related problem is that there is nothing else to do in the experimental setting but work on the unsolvable task. Under such conditions, persistence cannot really be said to be maladaptive, because persistence on the unsolvable task does not compromise efforts on other tasks.

To provide a better test of whether people can disengage from unsolvable problems and devote their efforts to solvable ones, we told college student participants that they would be completing sets of anagram puzzles as a test of verbal intelligence.[2] Participants were given a 20-minute time limit and instructed to solve as many problems as possible. For all participants, the first seven anagrams were completely unsolvable. For some participants, the seven unsolvable anagrams were the only task they were given (no alternatives condition), but for other participants there were two additional sets of seven anagrams each, and these alternative sets contained solvable puzzles (although participants were not given any information about the solvability of any of the problems). Additionally, some participants were allowed to return to previously unsolved trials, whereas others were not allowed to do so.

The results were striking. In the absence of alternative sets of puzzles, all participants (regardless of their level of optimism) worked on the unsolvable problems virtually until the end of the time limit. In contrast, when alternative tasks were available, participants high in optimism who were not allowed to return to previous trials disengaged approximately 4 minutes sooner from the unsolvable anagrams than did participants low in optimism. Note that for participants who were not allowed to return to previous trials, moving on to the solvable anagrams required admitting that one could not solve the first seven consecutive problems in a test of verbal intelligence.

An additional finding of the study was that optimists tended to outperform participants low in optimism on the first set of subsequent solvable trials when these trials were presented as alternative ways of demonstrating high verbal intelligence. These results suggest that optimists are able to disengage from unsolvable tasks in order to allocate effort to solvable tasks and are somewhat more likely to be successful on the solvable tasks, perhaps because they have preserved physical resources (e.g., time) or emotional resources (e.g., positive mood) by spending less time on problems that cannot be solved.

These findings are potentially important because they suggest that optimists are able to recognize and disengage from unsolvable problems and to devote problem-solving efforts to aspects of a situation that are controlla-

---

[2]For ease of presentation, we have simplified the design and results of this study. Please see Aspinwall and Richter (1999) for a complete presentation.

ble or solvable. They also provide complementary evidence to studies of coping in naturalistic settings (Carver et al., 1993; Scheier et al., 1986). In self-report studies of coping, several alternative explanations for optimists' superior adjustment are always present, such as the possibility that optimists report better outcomes because their problems are objectively less serious than those of pessimists or that optimists' reports of superior adjustment reflect a positive response bias or denial (see Aspinwall & Brunhart, 1996, for discussion and evidence). The design of the anagram study allowed us to present exactly the same (although, admittedly, much less important, severe, or enduring) problems to all participants, and to obtain objective measures of variations in problem-solving effort and performance. We obtained results that are quite consistent with those of naturalistic studies of coping among optimists, namely, that optimists who are exposed to unsolvable tasks do not invariantly persist on them and instead allocate effort to alternatives when they are available. Again, such findings are intriguing because they cannot be explained solely by the more favorable expectations optimists typically hold, or by other documented tendencies, such as the tendency to appraise situations as more amenable to personal control.

ADDITIONAL EVIDENCE FOR OPTIMISTS' MODERATION OF BELIEFS AND BEHAVIOR

In the following sections, we review two additional kinds of evidence that suggest optimism is associated with the successful moderation of beliefs and behavior, depending on important features of a situation or problem, such as whether it is controllable. These findings suggest that optimists' greater ability to distinguish controllable from uncontrollable situations may be part of a larger pattern of successful moderation of belief and behavior in ways that correspond well to objective features of a situation, especially situations that present the possibility of threat or loss.

Situated Optimism and the Moderation of Optimistic Beliefs in Specific Domains

Additional evidence for the adaptive moderation of belief and behavior among optimists comes from research on more domain-specific, rather than general, optimistic beliefs. Armor and Taylor (1998) reviewed several ways in which the beliefs and behavior of people with favorable expectancies about specific tasks or outcomes appear to be responsive to real and important features of the situation. Specifically, they examined cases in which the well-documented optimistic bias—the tendency to believe that one is at lower risk than others for negative events or that one's chances of success are greater than those of others (Taylor & Brown, 1988; Weinstein, 1987)—appeared to be tempered by reality.

The degree to which optimistic beliefs are responsive to reality is a critical issue in understanding whether and how optimistic beliefs are adaptive, because the belief that one is at less risk than others for negative outcomes across the board may interfere with important precautions, such as prudent driving, safer sex, and other preventive health behaviors. Additionally, if optimists' beliefs about their abilities or outcomes were not responsive to reality, they would be in danger of entering situations for which they were unprepared and of suffering dramatic disconfirmations of their favorable expectations.

Armor and Taylor (1998) identified three major ways in which optimistic beliefs appear to be grounded or situated in reality. The first is that people do not appear to be indiscriminantly optimistic, but, similar to the dispositional optimists described earlier, seem to vary their beliefs depending on whether they perceive events to be controllable. For events perceived to be controllable, the optimistic bias is large and robust; that is, people say they are much less likely than other people like them to experience negative outcomes. However, for events perceived to be uncontrollable, the optimistic bias is reduced or eliminated. A second major finding of Armor and Taylor's review was that the magnitude of the optimistic bias seemed to depend on whether a participant's performance could be verified. Unlike height or income, some desired attributes are harder to define and measure (e.g., sense of humor or *savoir faire*). When performance can be easily measured, people tend to have realistic assessments of their abilities and prospects, that is, they do not inflate their assessments relative to those of other people. It is only when people can hold favorable beliefs that are less subject to disconfirmation that they rate themselves as especially wonderful. Finally, Armor and Taylor noted that although people seemed to be more optimistic than would be warranted, their beliefs were not so distant from reality as to get them into trouble.

These findings suggest that there is a strategic element to optimistic beliefs, that people are able to hold them (and enjoy their motivational benefits) when they will serve them well (situation is controllable) and when they will not get them into trouble (they cannot be disconfirmed), but people temper their optimistic beliefs when they may put them at risk (failure, disconfirmation, embarrassment). Consistent with this point, research on the role of optimistic beliefs at different points in making decisions and implementing goals suggests that people seem to use their optimism to fuel actions toward goals, but suspend it when they are making plans about how to meet their goals, an activity that requires a more realistic assessment of their capabilities and prospects (Taylor & Gollwitzer, 1995).

From their review, Armor and Taylor concluded that optimistic beliefs are *bounded* (i.e., they don't get too far out of line); *strategic* (i.e., they help people meet their goals and are used selectively, rather than indiscriminantly); and *responsive* (i.e., they are adjusted to match features of a situation). Consistent with our research on coping and problem solving, all three of these properties of optimistic beliefs suggest that optimists may be skilled in knowing which kinds of situations are amenable to change (and which are not) and in modifying their beliefs and behavior accordingly.

Optimism and the Moderation of Cognitive Processing of Information

A third kind of evidence in support of the idea that optimists are more flexible and adaptive in their consideration of information about potential problems and stressors comes from studies of optimists' processing of different kinds of information about threats to health and well-being (Aspinwall & Brunhart, 1996, in press). The results of these studies suggest that optimists differ from pessimists in two potentially important ways: (a) Optimists pay more attention to negative information, remember more of it, and show evidence of greater elaborative processing of it, and (b) rather than devoting attention to all of the information presented, optimists pay particularly close attention to the most useful information available. In contrast, pessimists often pay less attention to negative information, and they do not vary their attention to such information as a function of its relevance to the self or to other potentially important properties.

Before describing these studies, it may be useful to review the impetus for them. They were initially undertaken to test a common alternative interpretation of the finding that optimism is consistently associated with better reported adaptation to negative life events, namely, that optimists report better outcomes not because they are better adjusted, but because they deny the gravity of their situations. The present studies tested whether optimism functioned as does denial or other defensive processes by assessing the prospective relation of optimism to attention to threatening information as a function of increasing severity or self-relevance. If, as the information became more threatening, optimists' attention to such information decreased, such a finding would support the idea that optimism functions similarly to denial. In contrast, if optimists' attention increased as the information became more threatening, such a finding would provide evidence that optimism was potentially adaptive in confronting negative information.

In one of our first studies in this area, we presented college students with information about the risks and benefits of their own health behaviors. Participants selected for their practice of different health behaviors (vitamin use, UV exposure) were presented with a menu of information about the benefits and risks of these behaviors, as well as neutral information (Aspinwall & Brunhart, 1996). We measured reading time for each kind of information as a function of optimism and participants' practice of each behavior. Two findings were of interest. First, optimists paid more attention to risk information than to neutral or benefit information. Second, for vitamin use, optimists' attention to risk information (e.g., about vitamin overdoses) increased as a function of lifetime vitamin use. That is, the greater the optimists' reported use of vitamins, the greater their reading time for information about its potential risks. These results suggest that optimism predicts increased attention to risk information, and that it does so as a function of increasing self-relevance of the negative information presented. It is of interest that among participants who did not use vitamins, there was no relation of optimism to reading time for information about the risks of vitamin use.

These findings about optimists' selective processing of health information as a function of how relevant the information is to them have recently been replicated in two studies by Abele (1999). In Abele's studies, participants were exposed to information about the health-protective benefits of exercise as well as to neutral information and then asked to recall as much information as possible in a surprise recall test 1 week later. In her first study, Abele's participants all were regular exercisers, and optimists were more likely than pessimists to recall information about the health-protective benefits of exercise at the follow-up, as compared to neutral information. In her second study, Abele included students who were not regular exercisers in addition to those who were. The results show striking evidence for the moderation of recall for information about exercise as a function of its relevance to the participants. Among those participants who exercised regularly, the recall advantage for exercise information over neutral information among optimists was replicated at a 1-week follow-up. It is of interest that, among participants who did not exercise regularly, optimism predicted lower recall for information about exercise. That is, when the information was relevant to them, optimists remembered more of it than did pessimists, but when the information was not relevant to them, optimists remembered less of it than did pessimists. The results of this second study are especially important because they suggest that there is no main effect relation of optimism to outcomes, such that optimists *always* do a particular behavior (e.g., that they always remember more health-protective information). Instead, these results suggest that optimists direct their attention to whatever is more relevant to them, given their needs and the situation.

A final piece of evidence consistent with the idea that optimists are more likely than pessimists to moderate their attention to threatening information based on important features of the situation comes from a study of attention to information about the risks and benefits of UV exposure among young adult women who sunbathed or used tanning salons regularly (Aspinwall & Brunhart, in press). This study was conducted to address two major limitations of our previous work. First, it is not clear that elevated reading time among optimists can be interpreted to mean greater acceptance of the risk information; instead, it is possible that increased reading time may be in the service of generating counterarguments to refute the information and its negative implications for the self. To test this possibility, we conducted stimulated recall interviews with participants following their exposure to the threatening health information. The interview protocols were coded for statements consistent with the risk information presented (elaboration), for statements refuting the risk information (counterarguing), and for other statements downplaying the risk or its relevance to the self (downplaying).

A second limitation of our previous work was that the health threats used (e.g., risks of vitamin use) were not especially serious, nor were participants necessarily engaged in health-compromising behavior. In the present study, we recruited young women college students who reported moderate-to-high levels of weekly UV exposure, either through sunbathing or the use of tanning booths. To create an especially high level of threat for some participants, we experimentally manipulated the immediate relevance of the threatening information by telling half of the participants that the average melanoma patient was a 25-year-old woman (proximal threat condition). The other half was told that the average patient was a 55-year-old woman (distal threat condition). In this design, the proximal threat condition presents the greater threat to immediate well-being.

All participants were presented with a computerized menu of information about the medical and cosmetic benefits and risks of UV exposure, as well as neutral information. After participants had read as much information as they wished, they were shown a videotape of their on-line session and asked to describe what they were thinking at each point. An analysis of the interview protocols revealed that optimists in the proximal threat condition were more likely to elaborate on the risk information and how it related to them than were pessimists, whereas the reverse was true in the distal threat condition. For example, one optimist in the proximal threat condition said, "I didn't know that it [skin damage] was cumulative. That kind of scared me, because I tan a lot. So I got a little more information on that." Another participant remarked, "This is interesting, I thought, because it talks about when your tan fades, it [the effect or damage] stays there. Because I do tan a decent amount of time, so it made me think a little bit. You forget it's so risky because I am young now." It is important to note that there was no evidence in the protocols that optimists were counterarguing or downplaying the risk information in either condition. These results provide additional evidence that optimists do indeed elaborate, rather than counter-argue, threatening information about their own behavior, and that they do so as a function of whether the threat is said to be proximal or distal.

BENEFITS OF OPTIMISTS' MODERATION OF BELIEF, BEHAVIOR, AND COGNITIVE PROCESSING

Thus far, we have reviewed several lines of research suggesting a similar conclusion: Optimists seem to be able to moderate their beliefs and behavior (coping in naturalistic settings, problem solving in experimental settings, beliefs about themselves and their prospects, and processing of threatening health information) based on important features of the task, situation, or information. Note that this moderation of belief, behavior, and processing effort does not appear to represent a general tendency toward greater variability or creativity in responding, but rather a predictable correspondence of optimists' responses to useful features of the situation, such as whether negative events are controllable, self-relevant, and proximal.

The ability to moderate one's responses to match important features of current problems may confer several adaptational benefits. Specifically, one benefit of recognizing and accepting unchangeable negative realities rather than trying to change them is that one may save coping resources and prevent further disappointments. For example, the optimists in our anagram study who gave up on the first seven (unsolvable) tasks were able to go on to the solvable ones with sufficient time remaining. At the same time, they limited their exposure to unsolvable tasks and to the motivational and cognitive deficits working on such tasks can create. Disengagement from unsolvable problems may conserve other resources, such as money and time. For example, the college sophomore who recognizes after a few failing grades in organic chemistry that he or she is not meant to be a physician and changes his or her major has invested fewer resources in an unsuitable career path than does someone who waits until junior year to reach that realization. Finally, adaptive disengagement may have the long-term effect of preserving the favorable beliefs that appear to facilitate such behavior. Specifically, people may better retain their optimism about future outcomes by recognizing situations that are not amenable to effort and by allocating their effort to those that may be. Otherwise, if optimism predisposed people to nonproductive persistence, it would be difficult to imagine how such beliefs could be maintained over time.

Armor and Taylor's (1998) analysis of situated optimism suggests other benefits as well. Holding favorable beliefs about oneself and one's prospects strategically and selectively may reduce the chances that one's beliefs will lead one to behave in ways that lead to failure, embarrassment, or harm. For example, the person whose hopes and dreams are pinned on having the fastest time in the 100 meter race has chosen a desired outcome that is rare (only one person in the world can have this distinction) and disconfirmable because it can be obtained only through one particular outcome, whereas the person who aspires to be the most spirited, inspiring, or original runner has a lot more leeway in defining success and, therefore, has a much smaller chance of a crushing public or private disconfirmation of this dream.

Finally, one major way in which optimists' moderation of belief and behavior may prove beneficial is in the flexible and selective allocation of processing resources, such as attention and elaborative processing, to only the most useful, self-relevant information in an array. The ability to discern which kinds of situations and information require attention and which may be safely ignored allows one to (a) devote one's resources to the most pressing problems, and (b) avoid the discouragement and frustration that would result from devoting close attention to all kinds of problems, regardless of whether they are solvable, relevant to the self, or otherwise worth one's attention. By being selective, optimists may be able to get the facts, without letting the facts get to them (Taylor, Collins, Skokan, & Aspinwall, 1989).

THREE EXPLANATIONS OF OPTIMISTS' MODERATION OF BELIEFS AND BEHAVIOR

Our review suggests that optimists are less likely to persist on uncontrollable or unsolvable problems, that they modify their favorable beliefs to be in line with the situation, and that they selectively direct cognitive processing to useful, self-relevant information, even when that information is negative. We have suggested that many advantages may accrue from such moderations in behavior. An important next step for research on optimism is to understand how such moderations are achieved. That is, how do optimists know the difference between controllable and uncontrollable stressors; how do they adjust their beliefs and behaviors to match important features of a problem or task; and how do they selectively process only self-relevant or otherwise useful information? In this final section, we identify three sets of potential mechanisms that might underlie these effects.

Parallel Findings in the Study of Positive Mood, Cognition, and Behavior

We begin our discussion of the mechanisms underlying optimists' apparent moderation of beliefs and behavior by noting that there are striking parallels between the kinds of moderation we have described among optimists and those found among people in whom a positive mood has been induced (see Aspinwall, 1998, for a review). It is important to note from the outset that we are not suggesting all positive beliefs and states work in the same manner or that all the benefits of optimism may be attributable to positive mood. Instead, we suggest that there may be some common mechanisms that underlie adaptive patterns of moderation of belief and behavior among optimists and people who are in positive moods.

First, there is evidence that people in a positive mood are more sensitive to important features of tasks and situations, such as whether a particular decision is important, than are people in neutral moods, and that people in positive moods moderate their behavior accordingly (see Isen, 1993, for review). For example, studies by Isen and her colleagues show that people in a positive mood take more risks when a hypothetical or unimportant task is presented to them, but become more risk averse and conservative than neutral participants when the stakes are real and high (e.g., when they are gambling for money or for research participation credits; Isen & Geva, 1987; Isen, Nygren, & Ashby, 1988). Under such conditions, positive-mood participants report more thoughts about losing than do neutral participants (Isen & Geva, 1987). These findings suggest that when a situation poses real potential for loss, people in a positive mood carefully consider the potential negative consequences of their actions and moderate their behavior accordingly.

Second, several studies suggest that people who undergo a positive mood induction or who experience success on a prior, unrelated task show greater interest in and greater processing of negative information about the self. Of particular interest is the fact that these effects, like those found for optimism, have been found to increase as a function of increasing relevance of the domain to the self. Specifically, Trope and Pomerantz (1998) found that people who succeeded on a prior, unrelated task showed greater interest in reading diagnostic feedback about their personal liabilities as the importance of the problematic domain increased. In contrast, those who had failed indicated greater interest in reading about their personal strengths as opposed to their weaknesses. Reed and Aspinwall (1998) found similar results concerning more rapid orientation to self-relevant health-risk information and lower levels of recall for risk-disconfirming information among people who had just undergone a positive experience. These findings parallel those obtained for optimism, in that optimists appear to attend selectively to risk information that is self-relevant.

Based on our studies of optimism and our review of parallel findings concerning positive mood and experiences, we have identified three potential explanations of optimists' apparent moderation of belief and behavior. Compared to people low in optimism, optimists may (a) process negative information more successfully, (b) process information more thoroughly and flexibly, and (c) differ in the development and refinement of procedural knowledge and skills in coping and problem solving. It is important to note that these explanations are not mutually exclusive, either with each other or with traditional explanations of the benefits of optimism, such as its link to active coping and persistence. Instead, as we will suggest, these different processes may work in concert as optimists encounter negative events and information in ways that enable them to moderate their behavior to match important features of the situation at hand.

Optimism Facilitates Processing of Negative Information

As we have reviewed, several studies now suggest that optimism and other positive beliefs and states reliably predict increased, rather than decreased, attention to negative information, if that information is useful or relevant to the self in some way. Attention to negative information is a critical first step in coping, problem solving, preventive health behavior, self-improvement, and a host of other self-regulatory behaviors (see Aspinwall & Taylor, 1997, for a review). In such domains as education, health, work, and interpersonal relations, careful processing of information about the self and the environment, especially negative information, is essential to obtaining feedback about one's progress toward goals, to formulating appropriate performance standards, and to evaluating behavioral alternatives. Therefore, any state or belief that contributes to the ability to process such information is likely to have enormous benefits.

The ability of people in a positive mood or people with positive beliefs to pay more attention to negative information may account for the more successful moderation of behavior, belief, and processing effort that we have reviewed in this chapter. That is, to determine whether a problem is worth addressing with active coping methods or is something one must accept or disengage from, one must be able to attend to the problem closely and to process even unflattering, threatening, or discouraging information in an unbiased manner. Veridical processing of such information is likely to assist optimists in developing solutions that correspond well to the objective features of stressors and problems and to assist them in modifying their efforts accordingly (Aspinwall & Taylor, 1997).

One explanation for such effects is that positive mood or experiences may serve as resources that allow people to confront negative information (Aspinwall, 1998; see also Tesser, Crepaz, Collins, Cornell, & Beach, in press; Trope & Pomerantz, 1998). That is, the presence of a positive mood may be a signal that one's current resources are sufficient to deal with the task at hand. This perceived adequacy of resources may influence a person's primary motive for responding to negative information in the following ways: If resources are perceived to be inadequate, one may be motivated to preserve short-term well-being by denying or counterarguing the information. However, if resources are perceived to be sufficient, one may be able to process such information veridically. In the case of optimism, the belief that future events are likely to be good may provide a chronically high estimate of one's affective resources, leading to the belief that one can weather the costs of attention to negative information in most situations.

Positive Beliefs and States Give Rise to More Thorough and Flexible Cognitive Processing

There are several other processing differences associated with positive beliefs and states that may confer advantages in noticing and responding to information relevant to actual or potential stressors. Isen (1993, in press) has reviewed several processing advantages conferred by induced positive mood, including greater creativity and more flexible, thorough, and efficient decision making and problem solving. In an extension of this work, Isen and her colleagues have proposed that positive affect leads to increased flexibility in judgment and behavior because of increased dopamine in two specific areas of the frontal cortex (Ashby, Isen, & Turken, 1999). Increased dopamine levels, in turn, are associated with processing differences attributed to greater flexibility in the executive attention system, such as the ability to "switch set," or change one's understanding of a problem. If positive mood has similar effects, this dopamine-mediated mechanism might account for the more flexible and more appropriate problem solving and decision making as well as the richer view of the task context found among people in whom a positive mood has been induced. It is possible that similar benefits accrue to optimists because of their characteristically more favorable mood. If this is the case, optimists should be better able to adjust their understanding of situations and problems to reflect new information, a processing difference that would surely confer advantages in moderating one's behavior to match the features of the situation.

There are other processing differences that are associated with positive mood and optimism that may affect the amount and nature of people's attention to their surroundings. For example, positive mood seems to promote an external focus of attention (Sedikides, 1992), whereas negative mood has been reliably associated with increased self-focus and corresponding deficits in self-regulation (see Pyszczynski & Greenberg, 1987, for a review). An outward focus may be more likely to promote attention to useful features of situations. There may also be important differences in how situations themselves are processed. For example, Basso, Schefft, Ris, and Dember (1996) found that both positive mood and optimism were positively related to a global processing bias (processing the overall structure of a stimulus before that of its component elements), whereas negative states, such as depression and anxiety, were predictive of a local processing bias (processing the components before the overall structure). If, for some reason, positive beliefs and states are associated with a tendency to process the whole before the parts, such a tendency could also account for optimists' more successful moderation of belief, behavior, and effort in that they may be more likely to respond to the features of the entire situation, rather than to its isolated local elements. It will be important for extensions of this work to include a neutral comparison group to establish whether positive states promote a broader processing style (see Fredrickson, 1998), whether negative states create perceptual narrowing or other deficits (see Derryberry & Reed, 1994), or both.

Taken together, the increased ability to devote attention to the situation as opposed to oneself, to process the global features of situations, and to "switch set" or flexibly change one's understanding of a problem may confer advantages in formulating responses that correspond well to the problem at hand. Such processes, working together and in conjunction with the increased ability to process negative information, may well account for optimists' apparent ability to moderate their beliefs and behavior to match important features of a situation or task.

Optimism Promotes the Development of Procedural Knowledge About Coping and Problem Solving

Thus far, our discussion has emphasized differences in attention to negative information and several aspects of processing style as explanations for optimists' typically more adaptive ways of responding to negative events and information. We believe that these two processes are functionally related to a third, namely, the development of procedural knowledge and coping skills in the course of one's problem-solving efforts. In describing this final mechanism, we return to our earlier discussion of the relation of optimism to active coping. There is ample evidence across a wide range of stressors that optimists are more likely to engage in active coping and less likely to engage in avoidant coping. One benefit of active attempts to solve problems, even if such attempts are unsuccessful, is that they are likely to yield information about a problem or situation. For example, if a problem does not respond to one's efforts, one learns that certain kinds of problem solving may not be successful for particular kinds of problems, or that some kinds of problems may not be amenable to active coping of any kind. Optimists, and people with other beliefs that predispose them to more active forms of coping, such as beliefs in personal control, may be more likely to try active ways of coping in a wide range of situations. As a result, they may acquire greater procedural knowledge about coping strategies and about problems and situations (see Aspinwall & Taylor, 1997; Skinner, 1997, for discussion). This information may then allow them to moderate their behavior, based on the features of the situation.

Related formulations, such as Snyder's (1994; chap. 5, this volume) work on dispositional hope, also note that favorable beliefs about one's future and a sense that one knows how to meet one's goals go hand in hand. Specifically, Snyder describes hope as a combination of the *will* to act toward one's goals (agency) and a knowledge of the *ways* one might achieve them (pathways). In his framework, the will and the ways are reciprocally derived through successful problem-solving experience. In support of this idea, there is some evidence that people with high levels of hope have greater knowledge about specific ways of coping and meeting their goals. In a role-playing study of coping with cancer, women college students who were high in hope were more knowledgeable about cancer and reported greater knowledge of "superior" coping strategies for dealing with a potential diagnosis (Irving, Snyder, & Crowson, 1998). What is interesting here is that none of these women had actually received a diagnosis of cancer, yet the coping behaviors they reported they would engage in were those deemed by the researchers as likely to be successful. Findings like this may reflect greater knowledge about coping and problem solving that these women were able to apply to the cancer role-playing situation.

Such results are consistent with the present analysis. People who engage in actions directed toward influencing the environment learn from the results of those actions a more refined sense of the pathways to meet their goals and the contingencies that govern whether those actions are likely to be successful. Over time, then, people who are predisposed to active coping should acquire a highly refined sense of how to cope with different situations. Such knowledge should promote problem-solving efforts that correspond well to important features of particular problems and that should generalize to new problems. In these terms, the success of optimists may be seen as a sort of self-fulfilling prophecy, but, it is important to note, not as one that depends only on the success of optimists' active efforts, but also on the successful application of information and skills gained from the failure of previous efforts.

How These Potential Mechanisms May Work in Concert

Future research might profitably examine how the process of developing and refining procedural knowledge and coping skills through active coping may work in tandem with some of the information-processing differences associated with optimism. Behaving in ways that elicit information about one's capabilities, about different ways of coping, and about different kinds of problems will only be valuable to the extent that one is able to learn from such experiences. Deriving benefits from one's failed coping attempts may require quite a bit of attention to negative information, especially information that is self-relevant. To the extent that optimists are better able to process negative information, they may be more likely to profit from the information elicited by their attempts at active coping. Similarly, increased processing flexibility, the ability to "switch set," and the tendency to process global aspects of situations should also increase the informational gain from one's coping attempts. These processing differences may confer advantages in detecting and responding to task contingencies, in changing one's perspective on emerging or changing stressors, and in recognizing whether tasks or problems are worth continued problem-solving and coping effort.

Conversely, the adaptive value of being able to process negative information and modify one's understanding of it is likely to depend on the amount of information available. Some unique benefits of optimism may lie in the information about problems and stressors elicited by active coping attempts. Specifically, although we have suggested that optimism may share with positive mood a beneficial relation to the processing of negative information and to several different aspects of processing style, the unique benefit of optimism may lie in the active coping tendencies promoted by favorable expectations. Positive mood, in contrast, is associated with few action tendencies (see Fredrickson, 1998, for discussion). In other words, although positive mood and other positive beliefs may show similar linkages to attention to negative information, optimism has unique relations to more adaptive coping strategies, such as more active and less avoidant ways of coping, when concurrent positive mood is statistically controlled (Aspinwall & Taylor, 1992; see Scheier et al., 1994, for related evidence). Therefore, it is unlikely that the effects linked to optimism will be solely attributable to the association of optimism with positive mood. What is much more likely is that optimism "works" because optimists enjoy processing advantages that are linked to positive beliefs and states *and* because optimists are more likely to engage in active problem-solving and coping efforts. These sets of processes working together may underlie optimists' more successful moderation of behavior and, ultimately, better outcomes in a wide range of situations.

CONCLUSION

Several different kinds of evidence reviewed here suggest that the beliefs and behavior of optimists, unlike those of pessimists, seem to correspond well to the objective features of the situation, especially when the situation has the potential to pose a threat to health or well-being.

Although such variations in beliefs and behaviors are just beginning to be understood, they may prove to be an important piece of the puzzle in understanding the adaptive benefits of optimism. To the extent that optimists are simultaneously more likely to act in ways that elicit information about the environment and more successful in processing information generated by these attempts, they may be better able to respond appropriately to important features of tasks or problems, leading to more efficient and successful coping efforts. Continued examination of the mechanisms underlying optimists' and pessimists' responses to negative events and information is likely to provide a more complete account of how optimism "works."

REFERENCES

Abele, A. E. (1999). *Dispositional optimism, unrealistic optimism and memory for more or less self-relevant information.* Manuscript submitted for publication.

Armor, D. A., & Taylor, S. E. (1998). Situated optimism: Specific outcome expectancies and self-regulation. In M. P. Zanna (Ed.), *Advances in experimental social psychology* (Vol. 30, pp. 309–379). New York: Academic.

Ashby, F. G., Isen, A. M., & Turken, A. U. (1999). A neurological theory of positive affect and its influence on cognition. *Psychological Review, 106,* 529–550.

Aspinwall, L. G. (1998). Rethinking the role of positive affect in self-regulation. *Motivation and Emotion, 22,* 1–32.

Aspinwall, L. G., & Brunhart, S. M. (1996). Distinguishing optimism from denial: Optimistic beliefs predict attention to health threats. *Personality and Social Psychology Bulletin, 22,* 993–1003.

Aspinwall, L. G., & Brunhart, S. M. (in press). What I *do* know won't hurt me: Optimism, attention to negative information, coping, and health. In J. E. Gillham (Ed.), *Dimensions of optimism and hope.* Philadelphia, PA: Templeton Foundation.

Aspinwall, L. G., & Richter, L. (1999). Optimism and self-mastery predict more rapid disengagement from unsolvable tasks in the presence of alternatives. *Motivation and Emotion, 23,* 221–245.

Aspinwall, L. G., & Taylor, S. E. (1992). Modeling cognitive adaptation: A longitudinal investigation of the impact of individual differences and coping on college adjustment and performance. *Journal of Personality and Social Psychology, 63,* 989–1003.

Aspinwall, L. G., & Taylor, S. E. (1997). A stitch in time: Self-regulation and proactive coping. *Psychological Bulletin, 121,* 417–436.

Basso, M. R., Schefft, B. K., Ris, D. M., & Dember, W. N. (1996). Mood and global-local visual processing. *Journal of the International Neuropsychological Society, 2,* 249–255.

Carver, C. S., Pozo, C., Harris, S. D., Noriega, V., Scheier, M. F., Robinson, D. S., Ketcham, A. S., Moffat, F. L., Jr., & Clark, K. C. (1993). How coping mediates the effect of optimism on distress: A study of women with early stage breast cancer. *Journal of Personality and Social Psychology, 65,* 375–390.

Carver, C. S., & Scheier, M. F. (1990). Principles of self-regulation: Action and emotion. In E. T. Higgins & R. M. Sorrentino (Eds.), *Handbook of motivation and cognition* (Vol. 2, pp. 3–52). New York: Guilford Press.

Chang, E. C. (1998). Dispositional optimism and primary and secondary appraisal of a stressor: Controlling for confounding influences and relations to coping and psychological and physical adjustment. *Journal of Personality and Social Psychology, 74,* 1109–1120.

Derryberry, D., & Reed, M. A. (1994). Temperament and attention: Orienting toward or away from positive and negative signals. *Journal of Personality and Social Psychology, 66,* 1128–1139.

Epstein, S., & Meier, P. (1989). Constructive thinking: A broad coping variable with specific components. *Journal of Personality and Social Psychology, 57,* 332–350.

Fredrickson, B. L. (1998). What good are positive emotions? *Review of General Psychology, 2,* 300–319.

Greenberg, M. (1997). High-rise public housing, optimism, and personal and environmental health behaviors. *American Journal of Health Behavior, 21,* 388–398.

Irving, L. M., Snyder, C. R., & Crowson, J. J., Jr. (1998). Hope and coping with cancer by college women. *Journal of Personality, 66,* 195–214.

Isen, A. M. (1993). Positive affect and decision making. In M. Lewis & J. M. Haviland (Eds.), *Handbook of emotions* (pp. 261–277). New York: Guilford Press.

Isen, A. M. (in press). Positive affect and decision making. In M. Lewis & J. M. Haviland (Eds.), *Handbook of emotions* (2nd ed.). New York: Guilford Press.

Isen, A. M., & Geva, N. (1987). The influence of positive affect on acceptable level of risk: The person with a large canoe has a large worry. *Organizational Behavior and Human Decision Processes, 39,* 145–154.

Isen, A. M., Nygren, T. E., & Ashby, F. G. (1988). Influence of positive affect on the subjective utility of gains and losses: It is just not worth the risk. *Journal of Personality and Social Psychology, 55,* 710–717.

Jerusalem, M. (1993). Personal resources, environmental constraints, and adaptational processes: The predictive power of a theoretical stress model. *Personality and Individual Differences, 14,* 15–24.

Pyszczynski, T., & Greenberg, J. (1987). Self-regulatory perseveration and the depressive self-focusing style: A self-awareness theory of reactive depression. *Psychological Bulletin, 102,* 122–138.

Reed, M. B., & Aspinwall, L. G. (1998). Self-affirmation reduces biased processing of health-risk information. *Motivation and Emotion, 22,* 99–132.

Scheier, M. F., & Carver, C. S. (1985). Optimism, coping and health: Assessment and implications of generalized outcome expectancies. *Health Psychology, 4,* 219–247.

Scheier, M. F., Carver, C. S., & Bridges, M. W. (1994). Distinguishing optimism from neuroticism (and trait anxiety, self-mastery, and self-esteem): A re-evaluation of the Life Orientation Test. *Journal of Personality and Social Psychology*, 67, 1063–1078.

Scheier, M. F., Weintraub, J. K., & Carver, C. S. (1986). Coping with stress: Divergent strategies of optimists and pessimists. *Journal of Personality and Social Psychology*, 51, 1257–1264.

Schwarzer, R., & Jerusalem, M. (1995). Optimistic self-beliefs as a resource factor in coping with stress. In S. E. Hobfoll & M. W. deVries (Eds.), *Extreme stress and communities: Impact and intervention* (pp. 159–177). Boston: Kluwer Academic.

Sedikides, C. (1992). Mood as a determinant of attentional focus. *Cognition and Emotion*, 6, 129–148.

Skinner, E. A. (1997). Planning and perceived control. In S. Friedman & E. Scholnick (Eds.), *The developmental psychology of planning: Why, how, and when do we plan?* (pp. 263–284). Hillsdale, NJ: Erlbaum.

Snyder, C. R. (1994). *The psychology of hope: You can get there from here*. New York: Free Press.

Taylor, S. E., & Aspinwall, L. G. (1996). Mediating and moderating processes in psychosocial stress: Appraisal, coping, resistance and vulnerability. In H. B. Kaplan (Ed.), *Psychosocial stress: Perspectives on structure, theory, life-course, and methods* (pp. 71–110). San Diego: Academic Press.

Taylor, S. E., & Brown, J. D. (1988). Illusion and well-being: A social psychological perspective on mental health. *Psychological Bulletin*, 103, 193–210.

Taylor, S. E., Collins, R. L., Skokan, L. A., & Aspinwall, L. G. (1989). Maintaining positive illusions in the face of negative information: Getting the facts without letting them get to you. *Journal of Social and Clinical Psychology*, 8, 114–129.

Taylor, S. E., & Gollwitzer, P. M. (1995). The effects of mindset on positive illusions. *Journal of Personality and Social Psychology*, 69, 213–226.

Taylor, S. E., Kemeny, M. E., Aspinwall, L. G., Schneider, S. G., Rodriguez, R., & Herbert, M. (1992). Optimism, coping, psychological distress, and high-risk sexual behavior among men at risk for Acquired Immunodeficiency Syndrome (AIDS). *Journal of Personality and Social Psychology*, 63, 460–473.

Taylor, S. E., Kemeny, M. E., Reed, G. M., Bower, J. E., & Gruenewald, T. L. (2000). Psychological resources, positive illusions, and health. *American Psychologist*, 55, 99–109.

Tesser, A., Crepaz, N., Collins, J. C., Cornell, D., & Beach, S. R. H. (in press). Confluence of self-defense mechanisms: On integrating the self-zoo. *Personality and Social Psychology Bulletin*.

Trope, Y., & Pomerantz, E. M. (1998). Resolving conflicts among self-evaluative motives: Positive experiences as a resource for overcoming defensiveness. *Motivation and Emotion*, 22, 5372.

Weinstein, N. D. (1987). Unrealistic optimism about susceptibility to health problems: Conclusions from a community-wide sample. *Journal of Behavioral Medicine*, 10, 481–500.

11

GREAT EXPECTATIONS: OPTIMISM AND PESSIMISM IN ACHIEVEMENT SETTINGS

JONATHON D. BROWN AND MARGARET A. MARSHALL

(You've got to) accentuate the positive;
Eliminate the negative;
Latch on to the affirmative;
And don't mess with mister in between.

—Johnny Mercer, 1944

Johnny Mercer was not a psychologist, but his insights regarding the role of positive thinking in psychological life are penetrating and insightful. Mercer, who enjoyed great success as one of the premier lyricists of his day, suffered from depression. Allegedly, he wrote this song on the way home from his psychiatrist's office in an attempt to remind himself to focus on his perceived strengths rather than his perceived failings.

The research reported in this article was supported by a Presidential Young Investigator Award from the National Science Foundation (SBR-8958211).

Research during the past 20 years has added empirical weight to Mercer's observation. Across a variety of indicators, people who hold positive beliefs about (a) their personal attributes, (b) their ability to bring about desired outcomes, and (c) their future, are better off than those who are more realistic (Aspinwall & Taylor, 1992; Bandura, 1986, 1997; Carver et al., 1993; Scheier & Carver, 1985, 1987; Scheier et al., 1989; Taylor & Brown, 1988, 1994). These benefits seem to be most apparent in achievement and health-related settings (Brown, 1998).

Positive self-relevant beliefs are not always advantageous, however. Too much self-aggrandizement can create interpersonal and intrapersonal problems (Baumeister, 1989, 1997; Baumeister, Heatherton, & Tice, 1993; Baumeister, Smart, & Boden, 1996; Colvin & Block, 1994; Colvin, Block, & Funder, 1995). Indeed, under some conditions, inflated self-views have been linked to self-destruction and violence toward others (Baumeister et al., 1996). Understanding when positive self-views have favorable and unfavorable consequences is, therefore, an important topic for research.

In this chapter, we examine the manner in which expectancies of success affect task performance and people's emotional reactions to their performance outcomes. The issue under consideration is the following: Are people better served by undertaking achievement-related tasks with high expectancies of success or are they better off being more modest and realistic? Before addressing this question, we note that *expectancies* and *optimism* are closely related constructs. The two terms are often used interchangeably, and high expectancies of success are one component of optimism. As Scheier, Carver, and Bridges (1994) note, "optimists are people who tend to hold positive expectancies of their future; pessimists are people who tend to hold more negative expectations for the future" (p. 1063). Because of these parallels, the manner in which expectancies affect task performance is relevant to a volume devoted to the study of optimism and pessimism.

EXPECTANCIES AND PSYCHOLOGICAL RESEARCH

The study of expectancies has a rich legacy in the field of psychology. The construct figures prominently in self-efficacy theory (Bandura, 1986, 1997); self-regulation theory (Carver & Scheier, 1981); goal-setting theory (Locke & Latham, 1990); attribution theory (Weiner, 1985, 1986); theories of achievement motivation (Atkinson, 1964; Feather, 1982); and Lewin's work on level of aspiration (Lewin, Dembo, Festinger, & Sears, 1944). In general, this research indicates that high expectancies of success are beneficial. People who expect to succeed perform better than do those who are less optimistic. In large part, this is because people with high expectancies of success work harder and longer and adopt more effective problem-solving strategies than do those who are pessimistic about their expectancies of success. These findings fit well with evidence indicating that positive self-relevant beliefs generally have positive consequences (Brown, 1991, 1998; Taylor & Brown, 1988, 1994).

Although expectancies have been an active area of research, several issues remain unresolved. One such issue is the precise manner in which expectancies affect task performance. A search of the relevant literature revealed that previous research relating expectancies to performance has either, (a) examined only two levels of expectancy (high and low) or, (b) used a correlational approach. These analytic approaches leave unanswered the question of whether high expectancies facilitate performance, low expectancies undermine performance, or both of these effects occur. It may be, for instance, that low expectancies are a liability, but that medium and high expectancies are equally beneficial.

A related question has been raised with respect to the construct of optimism. Optimism is often viewed as a unitary construct, but it also can be divided into two correlated dimensions: the presence of an optimistic outlook and the absence of a pessimistic outlook (G. N. Marshall, Wortman, Kusulas, Hervig, & Vickers, 1992). This distinction is important because the presence of a pessimistic outlook seems to be more predictive of psychological well-being than is the absence of an optimistic outlook (Robinson-Whelen, Kim, MacCallum, & Kiecolt-Glaser, 1997; Schulz, Bookwala, Knappy, Scheier, & Williamson, 1996). If expectancies affect task performance in a similar manner, we should find that low expectancies of success are a better predictor of performance than are high expectancies of success.

The condition under which expectancies influence performance is another issue to consider. When examining the manner in which expectancies affect performance, prior researchers have not distinguished between easy and difficult tasks. This issue is important because expectancies might not have much of an effect when tasks are easy. Easy tasks, almost by definition, require little in the way of effort, concentration, and persistence. Consequently, the benefits high expectancies provide in these areas are largely irrelevant.

To summarize, previous research has not established whether the relation between expectancies and performance is (a) linear and (b) affected by task difficulty.

Study 1: Task Performance

We (M. A. Marshall & Brown, 1999) recently conducted an investigation to address the nature of the relation between expectancies and performance. During the first part of the investigation, college students were told they were about to take a test that measured an intellectual ability called integrative orientation. *Integrative orientation* was described as a problem-solving skill involving the ability to find creative and unusual answers to problems. After attempting to solve several practice problems (of varying difficulty), the students indicated how many of the 10 problems they expected to solve on the upcoming test. After recording their expectancies, they took the test. Half of the participants were given a set of easy problems to solve; the other half were given a set of difficult problems to solve.

To determine the manner in which expectancies affected performance, we divided the students into 3 groups: those who expected to solve few of the 10 problems ($M = 2.57$); those who expected to solve about half of the problems ($M = 5.24$); and those who expected to solve most of the problems ($M = 8.40$). We then analyzed task performance as a function of expectancies of success and problem difficulty.

A 3×2 (Expectancies × Problem Difficulty) analysis of variance (ANOVA) on these data revealed a significant two-way interaction.[1] Inspection of the data shown in Figure 11.1 reveals two effects that are particularly noteworthy. First, expectancies had very little effect in the easy problem condition, but a sizable effect in the difficult problem condition. Second, in the difficult problem condition, low expectancies were associated with poor performance, but medium and high expectancies were equally beneficial.

These findings clarify several issues regarding the nature of the relationship between expectancies and performance. As noted earlier, correlational approaches or two-group studies (high vs. low expectancies) have obscured the manner in which expectancies affect performance. Our data show (a) that expectancies do not affect performance when problems are easy and (b) that low expectancies are associated with poor performance when problems are difficult, but that medium and high expectancies are equally effective.

Study 2: Emotional Reactions to Performance Outcomes

One conclusion to be drawn from these findings is that low expectancies are a liability and that high expectancies are not. This conclusion is premature, however, because we have yet to examine the manner in which expectancies influence emotional reactions to performance outcomes. Conceivably, low expectancies might soften the emotional impact of a negative performance.

William James (1890) appears to be the first psychologist to have considered this issue. In an oft-quoted passage, James argued that

> our self-feeling in this world depends entirely on what we *back* ourselves
> to be and do. It is determined by the ratio of our actualities to our

---

[1]Prior to analyzing the data, we performed a log transformation to stabilize the variances among the experimental conditions.

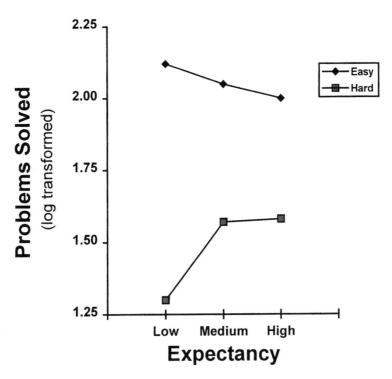

Figure 11.1. Task performance as a function of problem difficulty and expectancies of success: Study 1.

supposed potentialities; a fraction of which our pretensions are the denominator and the numerator our successes; thus, Self-esteem = Success/Pretensions. (p. 310)

Although James's use of the term *pretensions* was not entirely consistent (see Brown, 1998), he often used the term to refer to a person's aspiration level:

So we have the paradox of a man shamed to death because he is only the second pugilist or the second oarsman in the world. That he is able to beat the whole population of the globe minus one is nothing; he has pitted himself to beat that one; and as long as he doesn't do that nothing else counts. Yonder puny fellow, however, whom every one can beat, suffers no chagrin about it, for he has long ago abandoned the attempt to 'carry that line' as the merchants say, of self at all. (James, 1890, pp. 310–311)

James's point here is that how a person feels about an attained outcome is not simply a function of the outcome itself—it depends on the standards the person uses for gauging success and failure. Expectancies of success are one determinant of aspiration level. All else being equal, a student who expects to get an "A" in a course should be less satisfied with a "B" than a student who expects to get a "C."

In more general terms, it would seem that James believed expectancies and positive emotional reactions to performance outcomes are inversely related: The higher our expectancies, the less satisfied we are with a good performance and the more dissatisfied we are with a poor performance. We aren't aware of any research that has directly tested this assumption, but it does have important implications. It holds that high expectancies are a liability: They lessen positive emotional reactions to success and deepen negative emotional reactions to failure.

The opposite would seem to hold true for low performance expectancies. According to James, setting our sights low should magnify our positive emotional reactions to success and minimize our negative emotional reactions to failure. This seems to be what James (1890) had in mind when he wrote:

> [Self-esteem] may be increased as well by diminishing the denominator as by increasing the numerator. To give up pretensions is as blessed a relief as to get them gratified. . . . Everything added to the Self is a burden as well as a pride . . . our self-feeling is in our power. As Carlyle says: "Make thy claim of wages a zero, then hast thou the world under thy feet." (p. 311)

We conducted a second study to examine the manner in which expectancies affect people's emotional reactions to success and failure (M. A. Marshall & Brown, 1999). The procedures were similar to those used in Study 1, with two exceptions. After taking the test, the participants received feedback regarding their performance (i.e., they were told how many problems they solved). The participants then indicated how proud, pleased with themselves, humiliated, and ashamed of themselves they felt (1 = not at all; 7 = very much). These emotions were selected for study because they are explicitly concerned with how people feel about themselves when they succeed or fail (see Brown & Dutton, 1995; Brown & Marshall, 1998; Dutton & Brown, 1997). After reversing the scoring for the negative emotions, we averaged the four items to derive a single emotion score.

As in our earlier study, the number of problems each participant solved was analyzed using a 3 × 2 (Expectancy × Problem Difficulty) ANOVA. Replicating the results of our earlier study, the two-way interaction was significant. Figure 11.2 reveals that, once again, expectancies had virtually no effect in the easy problem condition, but a substantial effect in the difficult problem condition. Moreover, in the difficult problem condition, low expectancies were linked with poor performance, but medium and high expectancies were equally effective.

To determine how expectancies affected participants' emotional reactions to success and failure, we performed a similar ANOVA on the emotion

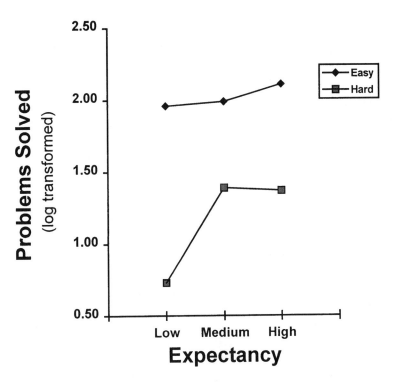

Figure 11.2. Task performance as a function of problem difficulty and expectancies of success: Study 2.

ratings. Analysis of these data produced a single main effect of task difficulty. Inspection of Table 11.1 shows that participants who received the easy set of problems felt better about themselves (M = 5.52) than did those who received the difficult set of problems (M = 4.50), and this effect did not depend on how many problems the participants expected to solve. Substantively, this finding means that expectancies did not influence emotional responses to success and failure, as James (1890) had hypothesized.

Table 11.1.
Emotion as a Function of Expectancies of Success and Problem Difficulty: Study 2

| Problem difficulty | Expectancies | | |
	Low	Medium	High
Hard	4.17	4.60	4.74
Easy	5.60	5.47	5.49

Note. Values could range from 1–7; higher numbers = more positive emotional reactions.

Table 11.2.
Emotion as a Function of Expectancies of Success and Task Performance: Study 2

Task performance	Expectancies		
	Low	Medium	High
Low	3.84	4.04	4.80
Medium	4.80	5.00	4.72
High	6.00	5.93	5.83

Note. Values could range from 1–7; higher numbers = more positive emotional reactions.

It might be argued that the data in Table 11.1 do not provide a fair test of James's (1890) hypothesis. Ideally, one would want to examine the match between the number of problems participants expected to solve and the number of problems they actually did solve. Table 11.2 presents data of this nature. If James is right, we should find that, at every level of task performance, those with low expectancies of success experienced more positive emotions than did those with high performance expectancies. The data in Table 11.2 provide very little support for this hypothesis. A 3 × 3 (Task Performance × Expectancy) ANOVA produced only a single main effect of task performance: Independent of their performance expectancies, participants found that the more problems they solved, the better they felt about themselves.

The means in the medium performance condition are especially informative. These participants solved between four to seven problems. Yet, among these participants, those who expected to solve more than seven problems and fell short of their expectations (high expectancy group) felt just as proud of themselves as did those who expected to solve less than four problems and exceeded their expectations (low expectancy group).

In summary, the results from the two preceding studies suggest that low performance expectancies are not beneficial. They undermine performance when difficult problems are encountered, and they do not soften the pain of failure when performances are poor. It appears, therefore, that "making thy claim of wages a zero" does not, as James opined, diminish the disappointment of failure.

Study 3: An Experimental Approach to Task Performance

At this point, the above-mentioned conclusion should be regarded as tentative. Expectancies were not experimentally manipulated in the two previous studies. People who expect to succeed are quite different from those who expect to fail, and these differences are associated with people's emotional lives. The effect is such that people who hold higher expectancies of success generally feel better about themselves than do those who are more pessimistic (Smith, Pope, Rhodewalt, & Poulton, 1989). These preexisting differences could obscure the manner in which expectancies influence people's emotional reactions to success and failure.

We conducted a third study to examine the influences of these preexisting differences (M. A. Marshall & Brown, 1999). In this study, we experimentally manipulated expectancies of success. This was accomplished by giving participants a pretest before they performed the target test. Using random assignment to conditions, one third of the participants were given a set of very difficult problems; one third were given a set of moderately difficult problems; and one third were given a set of easy problems. These variations were used to manipulate expectancies on the target test.

The target test was the same as the one used in our previous studies. And, as before, approximately half of the participants received an easy set of problems and half received a difficult set of problems.

Figure 11.3 shows the number of problems participants solved in each of the six experimental conditions (after using a log transformation). The data pattern is highly similar to the one observed in Studies 1 and 2.

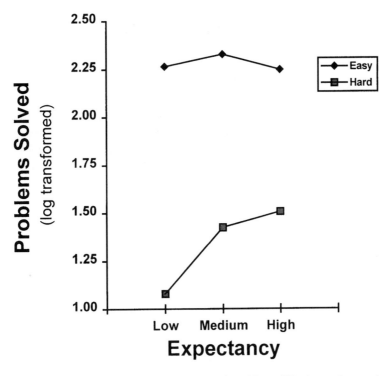

Figure 11.3. Task performance as a function of problem difficulty and expectancies of success: Study 3.

Table 11.3.
Emotion as a Function of Pretest Performance and Problem Difficulty:
Study 3

	Pretest performance		
Problem difficulty	Poor	Medium	Good
Hard	3.02	2.78	2.63
Easy	4.05	4.14	4.23

Note. Values could range from 1–5; higher numbers = more positive emotion.

Expectancies had little effect in the easy problem condition, but a substantial effect in the difficult problem condition. Further analyses within the difficult problem revealed that participants with low expectancies solved fewer problems than did those with medium and high expectancies, and that the medium and high expectancy groups did not differ. These findings mirror the results from our two earlier studies.

Table 11.3 shows participants' emotional reactions to their performance on the second test. It is clear that expectancies again had little effect on these emotional reactions. Instead, participants' emotional reactions were entirely a function of how they performed on the target task. Participants who succeeded felt better than those who failed, and this effect did not depend on how well the participants expected to do. These results are essentially the same as those in Study 2.

In summary, the results from Study 3 replicate and extend the results of Study 2. For easy problems, expectancies had virtually no effect; for difficult problems, low expectancies were a liability and moderate and high expectancies were equally advantageous. Furthermore, low expectancies did not cushion the pain of failure, and high (and moderate) expectancies did not diminish the pleasure of success.

Study 4: Application of These Effects in the Real World

Thus far, the data we have collected suggest that low expectancies of success are of little benefit. They are linked with poor performance at difficult tasks, and they do not lighten the blow of failure or brighten the glow of success. It is important to note, however, that the studies we have reported here have been conducted in laboratory settings. Furthermore, participants were performing a novel task that measured a fictitious ability, and their expectancies were apt to be held with only limited certainty. Each of these aspects calls into question the external validity of our findings. Accordingly, we conducted a final investigation to see whether our findings extend to real-world situations.

The participants were 132 University of Washington undergraduates who were enrolled in an upper division psychology course. Immediately prior to taking a midterm exam, students indicated how many of the 35 exam problems they expected to solve. Four days later, immediately after receiving their exam scores, the students rated their current emotional states.

Prior to analyzing the data, we divided the students into groups on the basis of their expectancies of success and exam performance. Students who expected to solve 29 or fewer problems were classified as having low expectancies ($M = 26.22$; $N = 32$); those who expected to solve 30 or 31 problems were classified as having medium expectancies ($M = 30.22$; $N = 60$), and those who expected to solve 32 or more problems were classified as having high expectancies ($M = 33.10$; $N = 40$). A similar procedure was used to further divide students into groups on the basis of their actual exam performance. Students who solved 29 or fewer problems were placed into the low performance condition ($M = 26.65$; $N = 51$); those who solved 30 or 31 problems were placed into the medium performance condition ($M = 30.44$; $N = 32$), and those who solved 32 or more problems were placed into the high performance condition ($M = 33.35$; $N = 49$).

A 3×3 (Expectancy $\times$ Task Performance) ANOVA was performed on students' emotional reactions to their task performance.[2] The ANOVA revealed a single main effect of task performance. Inspection of Table 11.4 shows that students who did very well on the test felt better about themselves ($M = 4.22$) than did those whose performance was moderate ($M = 3.59$), and students who performed at a moderate level felt better about themselves

Table 11.4.
Emotion as a Function of Expectancies of Success and Exam
Performance: Study 4

Exam performance	Expectancies		
	Low	Medium	High
Low	2.86	2.76	2.50
Medium	3.88	3.47	3.46
High	3.94	4.38	4.35

Note. Values could range from 1–5; higher numbers = more positive emotion.

[2]Because the difficulty of the exam problems was not randomly varied in this study, we did not examine the manner in which expectancies affected task performance (as we have done in the previous studies reported in this chapter).

than did those whose performance was rather poor (M = 2.71). Students' expectancies did not affect these emotional reactions.

DISCUSSION

When people undertake an achievement-related task, they usually have an idea how they will perform. Some people are optimistic. They have confidence in their ability and expect to do well. Others are less sanguine. They doubt their ability and fear the worst. Although pessimism can have positive consequences under some conditions (Cantor & Norem, 1989; Norem & Cantor, 1986), optimism seems to be more beneficial. People who hold positive beliefs about their ability generally fare better than do those who are pessimistic.

In this chapter, we have explored the manner in which expectancies of success (a construct quite similar to optimism) affect task performance and people's emotional reactions to their task performance. Several assumptions guided our inquiry into these issues.

Expectancies and Task Performance

First, we predicted that expectancies are important only when people confront difficult tasks. This prediction derives from the fact that expectancies affect performance by influencing how hard (vigor) and how long (persistence) people try. An easy task requires little in the way of vigor and persistence, so it makes sense to assume that expectancies are not important in this context.

We also predicted that although low expectancies of success are a liability when difficult tasks are confronted, moderate or high expectancies are equally effective. Our thinking here was more tentative, as previous research did not provide a firm basis for making this prediction. Research has, however, suggested that pessimism might be a more important psychological variable than optimism (G. N. Marshall et al., 1992; Robinson-Whelen et al., 1997; but see also Scheier et al., 1994). These findings suggested to us that expecting to fail is detrimental when difficult tasks are encountered, but it isn't necessary to think one is definitely going to succeed. More modest or moderate expectancies can also be effective.

The research reported in this chapter supported both of these predictions. Expectancies did not affect performance at easy tasks, but they did affect performance at difficult tasks. Moreover, when difficult problems were encountered, low expectancies were a liability, but moderate and high expectancies were equally advantageous. To cast these findings in more colloquial terms, it seems that "when the going gets tough, the pessimistic stop going."

Expectancies and Emotional Reactions to Task Performance

The present research also examined people's emotional reactions to their task performances. William James (1890) suggested that high expectancies are a burden. They lead people to be less satisfied with success and more dissatisfied with failure. We found no evidence to support this claim. People who expected to succeed were not more devastated when they failed than were people who expected to fail, and people who expected to fail were not more pleased with themselves when they succeeded than were those who expected to do well. Instead, expectancies had very little effect on people's emotional reactions to their task performances.

The attributions people make for performance outcomes may explain why we failed to find support for James's (1890) claim. Weiner and his associates (see Weiner, 1985, 1986 for reviews) have shown that people's emotional reactions to performance outcomes depend not only on their level of accomplishment, but also on the attributions they make for their performance. People who attribute success to high ability feel greater pride than do those who attribute success to good luck or help from others. Similarly, people who attribute failure to low ability feel greater shame and humiliation than do those who blame failure on bad luck or hindrance from others (Brown & Weiner, 1984).

Attributions are also thought to influence expectancies. People's attributions to ability are thought to be more likely when their performance matches expectancies (Miller & Ross, 1975). If so, people with high expectancies should be more apt to attribute success to high ability than those with low expectancies, and people with low expectancies should be more likely to attribute failure to low ability than would those with high expectancies.

Figure 11.4 outlines the nature of these presumed relations. The constellation of factors shown suggests that, under some circumstances, pessimistic expectancies of success can have negative, not positive, emotional consequences. They are associated with increased feelings of shame following failure and diminished feelings of pride following success. These associations oppose James's claim that "making thy claim of wages a zero" has positive emotional consequences, and provide a fruitful topic for future research.

CONCLUSION

In addition to clarifying the manner in which expectancies operate in achievement-related settings, our findings also bear on Taylor and Brown's (1988) work on positive illusions. After surveying a great deal of literature, Taylor and Brown concluded that positive self-relevant beliefs are generally

Expectancies	Outcome	Attribution	Emotion

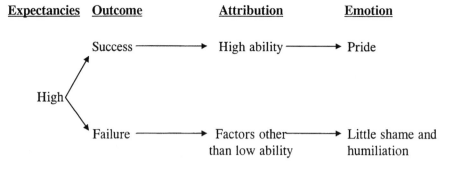

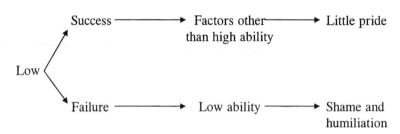

Figure 11.4. Schematic representation of the manner in which expectancies and attributions interact to affect emotional reactions to success and failure.

beneficial. Our findings offer a refinement of this position. Although negative thinking clearly offers no benefits in the situations we studied, a person may not need to be excessively optimistic either. In the data we collected, moderate and high expectancies of success were equally advantageous.

This point can, perhaps, best be conveyed by reconsidering Johnny Mercer's advice to "accentuate the positive, eliminate the negative, and don't mess with mister in between." In support of Mercer's claim, one should clearly "eliminate the negative" when difficult tasks are encountered. Under these conditions, negative thinking (a) leads to poor performance and (b) does not cushion the blow of failure. Mercer's recommendation to accentuate the positive also seems sound. Optimistic expectancies are linked with superior performance on difficult tasks, and do not diminish the luster of success or exacerbate the pain of failure. Whether one needs to avoid "messing with mister in between" is less clear, however. People's moderate performance expectancies functioned very similarly to high performance expectancies. These moderate expectancies were linked with superior performance at difficult problems, and they did not reduce positive emotional reactions to success. In this sense, then, they were just as effective as were positive expectancies. It appears, therefore, that those people who wish to mess with mister in between may do so with impunity.

REFERENCES

Aspinwall, L. G., & Taylor, S. E. (1992). Modeling cognitive adaptation: A longitudinal investigation of the impact of individual differences and coping on college adjustment and performance. *Journal of Personality and Social Psychology*, 63, 989–1003.

Atkinson, J. W. (1964). *An introduction to motivation*. Princeton, NJ: Van Nostrand.

Bandura, A. (1986). *Social foundations of thought and action*. Englewood Cliffs, NJ: Prentice-Hall.

Bandura, A. (1997). *Self-efficacy: The exercise of control*. New York: W. H. Freeman.

Baumeister, R. F. (1989). The optimal margin of illusion. *Journal of Social and Clinical Psychology*, 8, 176–189.

Baumeister, R. F. (1997). *Evil: Inside human violence and cruelty*. New York: W. H. Freeman.

Baumeister, R. F., Heatherton, T. F., & Tice, D. M. (1993). When ego threats lead to self-regulation failure: Negative consequences of high self-esteem. *Journal of Personality and Social Psychology*, 64, 141–156.

Baumeister, R. F., Smart, L., & Boden, J. M. (1996). Relation of threatened egotism to violence and aggression: The dark side of high self-esteem. *Psychological Review*, 103, 5–33.

Brown, J. D. (1991). Accuracy and bias in self-knowledge. In C. R. Snyder & D. F. Forsyth (Eds.), *Handbook of social and clinical psychology: The health perspective* (pp. 158–178). New York: Pergamon Press.

Brown, J. D. (1998). *The self*. New York: McGraw-Hill.

Brown, J. D., & Dutton, K. A. (1995). The thrill of victory, the complexity of defeat: Self-esteem and people's emotional reactions to success and failure. *Journal of Personality and Social Psychology*, 68, 712–722.

Brown, J. D., & Marshall, M. A. (1998). *Self-esteem and emotion: Some thoughts about feelings*. Manuscript submitted for publication.

Brown, J. D., & Weiner, B. (1984). Affective consequences of ability versus effort attributions: Controversies, resolutions, and quandaries. *Journal of Educational Psychology*, 76, 146–158.

Cantor, N., & Norem, J. K. (1989). Defensive pessimism and stress and coping. *Social Cognition*, 7, 92–112.

Carver, C. S., Pozo, C., Harris, S. D., Noriega, V., Scheier, M. F., Robinson, D. S., Ketcham, A. S., Moffat, F. L., Jr., & Clark, K. C. (1993). How coping mediates the effects of optimism on distress: A study of women with early stage breast cancer. *Journal of Personality and Social Psychology*, 65, 375–390.

Carver, C. S., & Scheier, M. F. (1981). *Attention and self-regulation: A control-theory approach to human behavior*. New York: Springer-Verlag.

Colvin, C. R., & Block, J. (1994). Do positive illusions foster mental health? An examination of the Taylor and Brown formulation. *Psychological Bulletin, 116*, 3–20.

Colvin, C. R., Block, J., & Funder, D. C. (1995). Overly positive self-evaluations and personality: Negative implications for mental health. *Journal of Personality and Social Psychology, 68*, 1152–1162.

Dutton, K. A., & Brown, J. D. (1997). Global self-esteem and specific self-views as determinants of people's reactions to success and failure. *Journal of Personality and Social Psychology, 73*, 139–148.

Feather, N. T. (Ed.). (1982). *Expectations and action: Expectancy-value models in psychology*. Hillsdale, NJ: Erlbaum.

James, W. (1890). *The principles of psychology* (Vol. 1). New York: Holt.

Lewin, K., Dembo, T., Festinger, L., & Sears, P. S. (1944). Level of aspiration. In J. M. Hunt (Ed.), *Personality and the behavioral disorders* (pp. 333–378). New York: Holt.

Locke, E. A., & Latham, G. P. (1990). *A theory of goal setting and task performance*. Englewood Cliffs, NJ: Prentice-Hall.

Marshall, G. N., Wortman, C. B., Kusulas, J. W., Hervig, L. K., & Vickers, R. R., Jr. (1992). Distinguishing optimism from pessimism: Relations to fundamental dimensions of mood and personality. *Journal of Personality and Social Psychology, 62*, 1067–1074.

Marshall, M. A., & Brown, J. D. (1999). *Expectations and realizations: The role of expectancies in achievement situations*. Manuscript in preparation.

Miller, D. T., & Ross, M. (1975). Self-serving biases in the attribution of causality: Fact or fiction? *Psychological Bulletin, 82*, 213–235.

Norem, J. K., & Cantor, N. (1986). Anticipatory and post hoc cushioning strategies: Optimism and defensive pessimism in "risky" situations. *Cognitive Therapy and Research, 10*, 347–362.

Robinson-Whelen, S., Kim, C., MacCallum, R. C., & Kiecolt-Glaser, J. K. (1997). Distinguishing optimism from pessimism in older adults: Is it more important to be optimistic or not to be pessimistic? *Journal of Personality and Social Psychology, 73*, 1345–1353.

Scheier, M. F., & Carver, C. S. (1985). Optimism, coping, and health: Assessment and implications of generalized outcome expectancies. *Health Psychology, 4*, 219–247.

Scheier, M. F., & Carver, C. S. (1987). Dispositional optimism and physical well-being: The influence of generalized outcome expectancies on health. *Journal of Personality, 55*, 169–210.

Scheier, M. F., Carver, C. S., & Bridges, M. W. (1994). Distinguishing optimism from neuroticism (and trait anxiety, self-mastery, and self-esteem): A reevaluation of the life orientation test. *Journal of Personality and Social Psychology, 67,* 1063–1078.

Scheier, M. F., Matthews, K. A., Owens, J. F., Magovern, G. J., Sr., Lefebvre, R. C., Abbott, R. A., & Carver, C. S. (1989). Dispositional optimism and recovery from coronary artery bypass surgery: The beneficial effects on physical and psychological well-being. *Journal of Personality, 57,* 1024–1040.

Schulz, R., Bookwala, J., Knappy, J. E., Scheier, M., & Williamson, G. M. (1996). Pessimism, age, and cancer mortality. *Psychology and Aging, 11,* 304–309.

Smith, T. W., Pope, M. K., Rhodewalt, F., & Poulton, J. L. (1989). Optimism, neuroticism, coping, and symptom reports: An alternative interpretation of the Life Orientation Test. *Journal of Personality and Social Psychology, 56,* 640–648.

Taylor, S. E., & Brown, J. D. (1988). Illusion and well-being: A social psychological perspective on mental health. *Psychological Bulletin, 103,* 193–210.

Taylor, S. E., & Brown, J. D. (1994). Positive illusions and well-being revisited: Separating fact from fiction. *Psychological Bulletin, 116,* 21–27.

Weiner, B. (1985). An attributional theory of achievement motivation and emotion. *Psychological Review, 92,* 548–573.

Weiner, B. (1986). *An attributional theory of motivation and emotion.* New York: Springer.

IV

Social–Cultural Factors

12

CULTURAL INFLUENCES ON OPTIMISM AND PESSIMISM: DIFFERENCES IN WESTERN AND EASTERN CONSTRUALS OF THE SELF

EDWARD C. CHANG

To be uncertain is to be uncomfortable, but to be certain is to be ridiculous.
–Chinese Proverb

In recent years, psychologists have joined anthropologists, sociologists, and linguists in recognizing the role of culture in shaping human behavior (Brislin, 1993; Hofstede, 1980; Jahoda, 1982; Marsella, DeVos, & Hsu, 1985). As a consequence, psychologists are quickly learning that what were once universally held notions about human nature, such as the need for positive self-regard, are more valid for understanding the behaviors of Westerners, but are often less valid for understanding the behaviors of non-

I would like to acknowledge Chang Suk-Choon and Tae Myung-Sook for their encouragement and support throughout this project.

Westerners, particularly, of Asians (Heine, Lehman, Markus, & Kitayama, 1999). Accordingly, some psychologists have begun to urge researchers to appreciate the different cultural contexts in which human behavior is studied, distinguishing between those contexts that are individualistic and those that are collectivistic (U. Kim, Triandis, Kagitcibasi, Choi, & Yoon, 1994; Triandis, 1995). In general, Western cultures (e.g., those of Europe and North America) are considered individualistic, given their prevailing emphasis on attending to the needs of the self over others (Greenwald, 1980; Waterman, 1984). Thus, for most Westerners, the attainment of personal happiness, rather than of group happiness is highly regarded and sought after (Heine et al., 1999). Consequently, the self that emerges from such cultures is one that perceives itself as independent of others. As embodied in Descartes' famous notion of *cogito ergo sum*, the thinking organism (*res cogitans*) is detached from all external objects, including other organisms (*res extensa*).

In contrast, the traditional focus in Eastern cultures (e.g., that of many Asian countries) has been to foster a view of the self as fundamentally interrelated with others (Doi, 1973; U. Kim et al., 1994; Markus & Kitayama, 1991). Hence, attending to others, experiencing harmonious interdependence with them, and fitting in not only are valued, but also are often strongly expected among members of such cultures (Weisz, Rothbaum, & Blackburn, 1984; Yee, 1992). For example, consistent with the Confucian notion of *filial piety*, order, hierarchy, and duty are cultural elements that are often highly valued and reinforced in Asian families. Thus, many Asians and Asian Americans are raised to show unconditional respect and duty to their parents while they are living and continued vigilance even after they have long passed away. For another example, consider one of the Four Noble Truths of Buddhism, namely, that all existence entails suffering. To progress to a state of enlightenment, one must not only eliminate individual desires, but also become attuned to the immanent harmony that exists between all living things. Hence, in contrast to the Western self, the exemplary self that is projected here is one that views itself as interdependent with others (Markus & Kitayama, 1991; Roland, 1988). These noted differences between Eastern and Western cultures are believed to not only promote two relatively distinct construals of the self (viz., independent vs. interdependent, respectively), but also to materialize in the differences in the way individuals from such cultures respectively think, feel, and act (Markus & Kitayama, 1991).

Accordingly, this chapter focuses on the influence of Eastern and Western cultures on optimism and pessimism, and is organized in two sections. The first looks at some of the notable research findings associated with the examination of optimism and pessimism between Easterners (Asian people) and Westerners (White people). Specifically, this section reviews findings from Heine and Lehman's (1995) study on unrealistic optimism, and Lee and Seligman's (1997) study on explanatory style, and then examines in greater detail findings from Chang's (1996a) study on dispositional optimism. The second section includes some implications of these and other notable findings for assessment and intervention. In particular, Beck's (1976) cognitive model of psychological adjustment is used to consider culture-specific interventions for working with distressed Asian and White Americans, and some pitfalls of viewing pessimism as a key marker of depression in others are discussed in light of recent findings. Finally, this chapter concludes with a brief section on challenges and future directions for research.

STUDIES OF OPTIMISM AND PESSIMISM IN EASTERNERS VERSUS WESTERNERS

From a scientific standpoint, the question of whether differences between Eastern and Western cultures have a significant influence on optimism and pessimism is one that must be addressed empirically. In that regard, one of the first major investigations focusing on cultural influences was conducted by Heine and Lehman (1995), who looked at potential differences in the expression of unrealistic optimism. Weinstein (1980) defined *unrealistic optimism* as a general tendency to expect that negative events are more likely to occur to others than to oneself, and conversely, that positive events are more likely to occur to oneself than to others. Based on a series of studies, Weinstein (1980, 1984) found that college students consistently judged their own susceptibility to a variety of threatening events and problems (e.g., alcoholism, suicide, auto accident injury) to be less than average compared with someone like them, thus implying that such events were more likely to happen to others.

In their first study, Heine and Lehman (1995) examined the tendency to express unrealistic optimism in 196 Japanese college students and in 90 Canadian college students of European descent. Among the different measures administered, participants were asked to rate the likelihood that they would experience a number of positive and negative future life events. Consistent with previous findings and with the view that Westerners tend to be unrealistically optimistic, these investigators found that Canadian students expressed a greater tendency to believe that positive events (e.g., "You will enjoy your career") were more likely to happen to them, whereas negative events (e.g., "Sometime in the future you will have a nervous breakdown") were more likely to happen to others. In contrast, the opposite pattern was found for Japanese students. Specifically, Japanese students indicated that positive events were more likely to happen to others, whereas negative events were more likely to happen to them. Hence, the Japanese students exhibited what Heine and Lehman (1995) referred to as greater *unrealistic pessimism* for themselves, rather than unrealistic optimism. Noteworthy is the fact that these cultural differences were found to be significant both within each cultural group and between the two cultural groups. That is, Japanese students were significantly more unrealistic in their pessimism compared with Canadian students.

Nonetheless, as Heine and Lehman (1995) noted, their findings may have been unintentionally confounded with other factors. Specifically, most of the event items that were used focused on consequences that only involved the individual (i.e., had an individualistic focus). Given that Japanese students come from a culture that promotes an interdependent construal of the self, such items may not have been considered important. If event items that focused on important consequences to others had been used (i.e., had an interdependent focus), then Japanese students may have displayed a level of unrealistic optimism similar to that of Canadian students. To address this concern, these investigators conducted a second study.

In their second study, Heine and Lehman (1995) examined 105 Japanese college students and 110 Canadian college students of European descent. Similar to their first study, items that asked about the likelihood that certain events would occur compared with the likelihood they would occur to others. Unlike the first study, however, the list of events now included those that were "independent" (e.g., "After growing old, you will find out that you never realized your most important dreams") and "interdependent" (e.g., "In the future you will not be able to provide a decent standard of living for your family"). If the previous findings were due to the lack of interdependent event items on the questionnaire, the current findings should show Japanese students expressing as much unrealistic optimism for interdependent events as Canadian students would for independent events. However, Heine and Lehman (1995) did not find this to be the case. Rather, they found again significant cultural differences both within and between the two cultural groups, similar to findings from their first study. That is, Canadian students expressed a greater tendency to believe that negative (independent and interdependent) events were more likely to happen to others than to them, whereas the opposite pattern was found for Japanese students. Thus, the type of event made little difference in these results. Given that Japanese students compared with Canadian students consistently failed to express unrealistic optimism for themselves, Heine and Lehman (1995) argued that this "cultural difference suggests that the 'normality' of self-enhancing biases might be specific to Western culture" (p. 605).

Although Easterners may not exhibit strong self-enhancing tendencies, Heine and Lehman's (1995) findings raise the notion that Asians may express strong self-effacing tendencies (i.e., unrealistic pessimism) or the tendency to see themselves as more average than others (Mizuno & Yamaguchi, 1997). However, given the bipolar nature of their conceptualization of optimism and pessimism, Heine and Lehman's findings are ambiguous: It is impossible to tell if Asians are actually scoring low on self-enhancing tendencies (optimism), high on self-effacing tendencies (pessimism), or both (low optimism, high pessimism). To help address this issue, we now move to a study that assessed for optimism and pessimism separately.

OPTIMISTIC AND PESSIMISTIC EXPLANATORY STYLE IN ASIANS AND NON-ASIANS: IS HEIGHTENED PESSIMISM A KEY SENSIBILITY AMONG ASIANS?

Using an explanatory style framework (see chap. 3, this volume), Lee and Seligman (1997) looked at differences in expressions of optimism and pessimism between Easterners and Westerners. Specifically, these investigators studied the responses of 312 mainland Chinese, 44 Chinese Americans, and 257 White Americans on the Attributional Style Questionnaire (ASQ; Peterson et al., 1982). As noted earlier in the introduction to this volume, the ASQ provides separate scores for a pessimistic explanatory style (for negative events) and for an optimistic explanatory style (for positive events). By including separate measures of optimism and pessimism, findings from Lee and Seligman's (1997) study can help us discern whether Easterners are simply less optimistic, more pessimistic, or both compared with Westerners (see Heine & Lehman, 1995).

Beginning with results for specific optimistic explanatory style dimensions associated with attributions for positive events, Lee and Seligman (1997) found no significant difference between Chinese and White American students on internality. However, mainland Chinese students were found to have significantly lower internality scores than those of Chinese American and White American students. Chinese American students were not significantly different on stability compared with White American and mainland Chinese students. On the other hand, mainland Chinese were found to have significantly lower stability scores than did White American students. For globality, a similar pattern emerged. That is, Chinese American students were not found to be significantly different on globality compared with White American and mainland Chinese students. However, mainland Chinese students were found to have significantly lower scores than did White American students on this attributional dimension for positive events.

For specific pessimistic explanatory style dimensions associated with attributions for negative events, no significant difference between Chinese and White American students was found on internality. However, mainland Chinese students were found to have significantly lower scores on internality than did Chinese and White American students. For stability, again, no significant difference between Chinese American and mainland Chinese students was found. In contrast, White American students were found to have significantly lower scores on stability for negative events compared with scores of Chinese American and mainland Chinese students. For globality, Chinese American students were not found to be significantly different from mainland Chinese and White American students. However, mainland Chinese students were found to have significantly higher scores on globality than did White American students. Taken together, these findings provide a very interesting but also complex picture of how mainland Chinese, Chinese American, and White American students differ on specific attribution dimensions for positive and negative events.

Yet, as has increasingly become the convention in studies of explanatory style, another way to consider differences in optimism and pessimism between the three groups is to compare their general explanatory styles by using composite scores (sum of internal, stable, and global scores). There are at least two advantages for doing so. Namely, findings based on composite scores are likely to be more reliable, and findings based on composite scores are also easier to interpret than findings based on specific attribution dimensions. Therefore, we now consider Lee and Seligman's (1997) comparative findings for optimism and pessimism when composite explanatory style scores were used. For optimistic explanatory style, Lee and Seligman (1997) found no significant difference between Chinese and White American students. However, mainland Chinese students were found to have a significantly lower optimistic explanatory style than did Chinese and White American students. That is, Chinese American students appeared to be just as "optimistic" as White American students, whereas mainland Chinese students were less optimistic than both their Chinese and White American counterparts. It is noteworthy that, for pessimistic explanatory style, these investigators found no significant difference between mainland Chinese and Chinese American students. However, the pessimistic explanatory styles of mainland Chinese and Chinese American students were found to be significantly greater than those of White American students. Thus, Chinese American students appeared to be just as "pessimistic" as mainland Chinese students, whereas White American students were less pessimistic than both Asian groups. These noted findings, especially for general explanatory styles, offer a more useful picture of the differences in optimism and pessimism between Easterners and Westerners than previously presented (see Heine & Lehman, 1995). For example, Lee and Seligman's (1997) findings indicate that some Asian groups (viz., Asian Americans) are just as self-enhancing or optimistic as Westerners (e.g., White Americans).

Thus far, I have presented findings from recent studies that indicate group differences in optimism and pessimism between Easterners and Westerners. However, group differences tell us little about relational differences.

For example, even if elevations on optimism are comparable between Asian and White Americans as found in Lee and Seligman's (1997) study, this does not necessarily mean that optimism is related to other variables in the same manner for the two ethnic groups. Accordingly, we now move to a study that looked at the relations between optimism, pessimism, and other important variables (viz., coping and adjustment) between Asian and White Americans.

DISPOSITIONAL OPTIMISM AND PESSIMISM AMONG ASIAN AND WHITE PEOPLE: THE POWER OF PESSIMISTIC THINKING?

According to Scheier and Carver's dispositional model (1985), *optimism* and *pessimism*, defined as generalized positive and negative outcome expectancies, represent individual differences variables that promote or abate psychological and physical adjustment (see chaps. 2 & 9, this volume, for more detailed discussions of this dispositional model). Specifically, these researchers have argued that optimism is associated with adaptive coping efforts (e.g., problem solving, seeking social support) and leads to securing positive outcomes, whereas pessimism is associated with maladaptive coping efforts (e.g., problem avoidance, social withdrawal) and leads to incurring negative outcomes. Consistent with this view, numerous empirical studies have shown that optimists are psychologically and physically better adjusted than their more pessimistic counterparts (see chaps. 6 & 9, this volume). The consistency and robustness of such findings over the past 2 decades have resulted in an almost incontrovertible acceptance of the view that optimism is always good, and pessimism is always bad.

However, according to Chang and his associates (Chang, 1996a; Chang, D'Zurilla, & Maydeu-Olivares, 1994; Chang, Maydeu-Olivares, & D'Zurilla, 1997), at least two issues remain unresolved in Scheier and Carver's (1985) dispositional model of optimism and pessimism. First, there has been considerable debate and controversy over the dimensionality of optimism and pessimism. Scheier and Carver's (1985) conceptualization of optimism and pessimism as measured by their Life Orientation Test (LOT) represents these constructs as polar opposites on a unidimensional continuum. However, as noted in the introduction, a number of investigators have seriously challenged this unidimensional model, arguing that dispositional optimism and pessimism are better conceived as representing two partially independent dimensions.

A second, related issue involves the generalizability of previous findings about the study of dispositional optimism and pessimism for different cultural groups. As Chang (1996a) noted, because most of the published studies in psychology have been based on largely White samples, "we know very little about optimism and pessimism among different racial or ethnic groups and about how they and related variables such as the use of different coping strategies are associated with psychological and physical health outcome" (p. 113). To address these concerns, Chang (1996a) conducted a study that looked at cultural differences between Asian Americans and White Americans on optimism, pessimism, coping, and adjustment.

Chang's (1996a) study involved 111 self-identified Asian Americans who were matched on age and sex with a random sample of 111 self-identified White Americans. It is noteworthy that the responses provided by mainland Asian (or international) students were not included in this study (cf. Lee & Seligman, 1997). All participants completed a set of measures at two points in time. At Time 1, participants completed the Extended Life Orientation Test (ELOT; Chang et al., 1997) which provides separate measures of optimism and pessimism. As noted in the introduction to this volume, the ELOT is an extended measure of the original LOT, and is based on the same conceptual definition proposed by Scheier and Carver (1985). However, unlike the LOT, the ELOT is considered a bidimensional measure that provides separate scores for optimism and pessimism (Chang, 1998b; Chang et al., 1997).

At Time 2, approximately 6 weeks later, participants completed measures assessing psychological and physical adjustment. Specifically, psychological adjustment was assessed by the Beck Depression Inventory (BDI; Beck, Ward, Mendelson, Mock, & Erbaugh, 1961) and by the Symptoms Checklist-90-Revised (SCL-90-R; Derogatis, 1983). The BDI assesses for symptoms of depression (e.g., "I am so sad or unhappy that I can't stand it"), whereas the SCL-90-R assesses for general psychological symptoms (e.g., anxiety, hostility, obsession, and compulsion). Because optimism and pessimism have been found to be related to physical adjustment, the Pennebaker Inventory of Limbic Languidness (PILL; Pennebaker, 1982) also was included. The PILL assesses for physical symptoms (e.g., coughing, insomnia, upset stomach, and headaches).

In addition, because coping also has been linked to adjustment (Lazarus & Folkman, 1984), a measure of coping strategies also was included in Chang's (1996a) study. Specifically, coping was assessed with the Coping Strategies Inventory (CSI; Tobin, Holroyd, Reynolds, & Wigal, 1989). Consistent with other measures of coping strategies such as the Ways of Coping Checklist (Folkman & Lazarus, 1980), this measure provides an assessment of several engaged coping strategies (viz., problem solving, cognitive restructuring, expressing emotion, and seeking social support) and several disengaged coping strategies (viz., problem avoidance, wishful thinking, self-criticism, and social withdrawal). The CSI was administered with the ELOT at Time 1.

Several important questions were addressed in Chang's (1996a) study. First, would Asian Americans differ on optimism or pessimism from White Americans? Second, would optimism or pessimism predict psychological and physical adjustment among Asian Americans as among White Americans? If so, would optimism and pessimism account for a similar amount of the variance in adjustment across the two cultural groups? And third, would optimism and pessimism have the same relational pattern with coping and adjustment among Asian Americans as among White Americans?

Do Asian and White Americans Differ on Levels of Optimism and Pessimism?

Table 12.1 presents the results of t tests reported in Chang (1996a), which compared differences in optimism, pessimism, coping strategies, and psychological and physical adjustment between Asian Americans and White

Table 12.1.
Ethnic Group Differences in Optimism, Pessimism, Coping Strategy, and Health Outcome

| | Ethnic group | | | | | |
| | Asian | | White | | | |
Criterion	M	SD	M	SD	$t(1, 220)$	p
Outcome expectancy						
Optimism	21.33	3.62	22.20	3.41	−1.83	ns
Pessimism	25.88	6.36	21.14	6.58	5.45	< .000026
Coping strategies						
Problem solving	26.28	6.11	26.01	6.88	0.31	ns
Cognitive						
restructuring	26.48	6.44	26.51	7.46	−0.04	ns
Express emotions	24.41	6.49	23.59	8.29	0.81	ns
Social support	28.94	7.33	26.57	8.97	2.16	ns
Problem avoidance	21.42	5.33	17.19	5.29	5.94	< .0000026
Wishful thinking	26.30	7.14	24.36	8.05	1.90	ns
Self-criticism	22.53	8.71	18.66	9.49	3.17	ns
Social withdrawal	21.55	6.63	18.45	5.90	3.68	< .0013
Health outcome						
Depressive						
symptoms	10.13	8.02	7.62	7.41	2.42	ns
Psychological						
symptoms	76.83	53.74	53.41	45.49	3.51	< .0013
Physical symptoms	97.78	26.09	102.57	25.01	0.16	ns

Note. For both ethnic groups, $N = 111$. All criteria were assessed at Time 1, except for health outcome, which was assessed at Time 2. From "Cultural Differences in Optimism, Pessimism, and Coping: Predictors of Subsequent Adjustment in Asian American and Caucasian American College Students," by E. C. Chang, 1996, *Journal of Counseling Psychology, 43*, p. 118. Copyright 1996 by the American Psychological Association. Reprinted with permission.

Americans. As this table shows, Asian Americans were not found to be significantly lower in their levels of optimism. However, Asian Americans were significantly more pessimistic than White Americans. Note, these findings are consistent with Lee and Seligman's (1997) findings for optimistic and pessimistic explanatory style (based on use of composite scores) between Chinese and White Americans as mentioned previously.

As Table 12.1 also shows, Asian Americans used more problem avoidance and social withdrawal strategies to deal with stressful situations than did White Americans. On the other hand, no significant cultural differences were found in the use of the other coping strategies. In addition, compared with White Americans, Asian Americans reported significantly more psychological symptoms as measured by the SCL-90-R. It is of interest that no significant differences were found between the two cultural groups on depressive and physical symptom reports as measured by the BDI and the PILL, respectively. Thus, Asian Americans reported more general psychological problems, but not more depressive or physical problems, than did White Americans. Taken together, these findings suggest that there are important differences and similarities in the levels of optimism, pessimism, coping, and adjustment between Asian and White Americans.

Are Optimism and Pessimism Important Predictors of Adjustment in Asian and White Americans?

To address this question, Chang (1996a) conducted a series of regression analyses that sought to identify significant predictors of each adjustment measure for each ethnic group. However, in addition to optimism and pessimism scores, scores on each of the coping strategies (as well as on age and gender) were included to determine if coping strategies would be found to be more important predictors of adjustment than optimism and pessimism. Results of these analyses as reported in Chang (1996a) for Asian Americans and White Americans are presented in Tables 12.2 and 12.3, respectively.

As Table 12.2 shows, for Asian Americans, optimism, problem solving, and pessimism were the only significant predictors found for depressive symptoms. Lack of optimism was found to account for the largest amount of the variance in depressive symptoms (13%), followed by problem solving, and pessimism, respectively. The final regression model accounted for 20% of the variance in depressive symptoms. For general psychological symptomatology, social withdrawal and optimism were the only significant predictors found. Although social withdrawal was found to account for the largest amount of the variance in psychological symptoms, lack of optimism was found to account for almost as much additional variance (9%). The final model accounted for 20% of the variance in psychological symptoms. Last, for

Table 12.2.
Stepwise Regression Analyses Showing Amount of Variance
Accounted for by Significant Predictors of Each Outcome Measure for
Asian Americans

Outcome Measure	β	R	R^2	$F(1, 109)$
BDI				
Optimism	−.23**	.36	.13	15.94***
Problem solving	−.23**	.41	.04	4.85*
Pessimism	.22*	.45	.03	5.07*
SCL-90-R				
Social withdrawal	.30***	.34	.11	14.04***
Optimism	−.29***	.45	.09	12.24***
PILL				
Optimism	−.32***	.34	.12	14.53***
Problem solving	−.17*	.39	.03	4.13*

Note. $N = 111$. BDI = Beck Depression Inventory; SCL-90-R = Symptom Checklist-90-Revised; PILL = Pennebaker Inventory of Limbic Languidness. From "Cultural Differences in Optimism, Pessimism, and Coping: Predictors of Subsequent Adjustment in Asian American and Caucasian American College Students," by E. C. Chang, 1996, *Journal of Counseling Psychology, 43*, p. 118. Copyright 1996 by the American Psychological Association. Reprinted with permission.
*$p < .05$. **$p < .01$. ***$p < .001$.

physical symptoms, optimism and problem solving were the only significant predictors found. Lack of optimism was found to account for the largest amount of the variance in physical symptoms (12%), followed by lack of problem solving. The final model accounted for 15% of the variance in physical symptoms for Asian Americans.

For White Americans, the only significant predictors of depressive symptoms found were pessimism, wishful thinking, optimism, and self-criticism (see Table 12.3). Pessimism was found to account for the largest amount of the variance in depressive symptoms (17%), followed by the other three predictors in the order just listed. The final regression model accounted for 31% of the variance in depressive symptoms. The only significant predictors of general psychological symptomatology found were pessimism, self-criticism, gender, and social withdrawal. Again, pessimism was found to account for the largest amount of the variance in psychological symptoms (20%), followed by the other three predictors. The final model accounted for 35% of the variance in psychological symptoms. Last, for physical symptoms, gender was the only significant predictor found. The final model accounted for 9% of the variance in physical symptoms for White Americans. Thus, lack of optimism appeared to be a strong predictor of psychological and physical adjustment among Asian Americans, whereas pessimism appeared to be a strong predictor of psychological adjustment among White Americans. I will discuss the implications of these particular findings for working with Asians who are distressed shortly.

Table 12.3
Stepwise Regression Analyses Showing Amount of Variance Accounted
for by Significant Predictors of Each Outcome Measure for
White Americans

Outcome Measure	β	R	R^2	F
BDI				
Pessimism	.20*	.42	.17	22.73***
Wishful thinking	.21*	.50	.08	11.88***
Optimism	–.20*	.53	.03	4.04*
Self-criticism	.17*	.55	.03	4.02*
SCL-90-R				
Pessimism	.30***	.45	.20	27.37***
Self-criticism	.22**	.53	.08	11.98***
Gender	.20*	.56	.04	5.51*
Social withdrawal	.17*	.58	.03	4.26*
PILL				
Gender	.29*	.30	.09	10.90**

Note. $N = 111$. BDI = Beck Depression Inventory; SCL-90-R = Symptom Checklist-90-Revised; PILL = Pennebaker Inventory of Limbic Languidness. From "Cultural Differences in Optimism, Pessimism, and Coping: Predictors of Subsequent Adjustment in Asian American and Caucasian American College Students," by E. C. Chang, 1996, *Journal of Counseling Psychology, 43*, p. 119. Copyright 1996 by the American Psychological Association. Reprinted with permission.
*p < .05. **p < .01. ***p < .001.

Are There Important Differences in the Pattern of Associations Among the Study Variables Between Asian and White Americans?

It is noteworthy that Chang (1996a) found that the pattern of correlations between the various study measures for Asian Americans was different from the one found for White Americans (see Chang, 1996a, Table 1). Most striking was the difference in the direction of the associations between pessimism and two of the engagement coping strategies (viz., problem solving and expressing emotions) for Asian Americans compared with White Americans. Specifically, pessimism was found to be negatively associated with use of problem solving and expressing emotions for White Americans. In sharp contrast, pessimism was found to be associated positively with use of these coping strategies for Asian Americans.

Given that pessimism and two of the engaged coping strategies were found to be associated positively for Asian Americans, but not for White Americans, Chang (1996a) conducted 2×2 (high vs. low pessimism $\times$ Asian vs. White American) ANOVAs with each of the eight coping strategies from the CSI as dependent variables to assess for significant interactions. Results of these analyses indicated only one significant interaction after controlling for number of comparisons that involved problem solving, $F(1, 218) = 13.33$; $p < .0013$ (Figure 12.1). As the figure shows, for problem-solving coping, highly pessimistic White Americans were found to use this coping

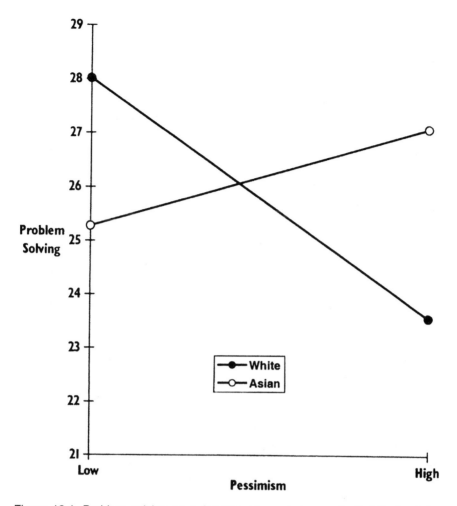

Figure 12.1. Problem solving as a function of pessimism and ethnicity for Asian Americans and White Americans. From "Cultural Differences in Optimism, Pessimism, and Coping: Predictors of Subsequent Adjustment in Asian American and Caucasian American College Students," by E. C. Chang, 1996, *Journal of Consulting Psychology,* 43, p. 119. Copyright 1996 by the American Psychological Association. Reprinted with permission.

strategy less frequently compared with less pessimistic White Americans. In contrast, highly pessimistic Asian Americans were found to use problem-solving coping more frequently than did less pessimistic Asian Americans. This finding is worth further consideration in relation to the heightened pessimism of Asians as noted earlier in Lee and Seligman's (1997) findings.

Are Asians defensive pessimists? Although a general self-effacing tendency among Easterners may help account for their heightened pessimism compared with Westerners (Heine & Lehman, 1995), this tendency does not help us answer why heightened pessimism would be maintained among Asians. One possibility may be that pessimism helps Asians incur positive consequences. Specifically, by anticipating the worst, Asians may paradoxically gain an immediate sense of certainty or control in their uncertainty about future outcomes (Chang, 1996b). This can be particularly advantageous for individuals who come from Eastern cultures and traditions that ascribe great value and importance to maintaining interpersonal connectedness and harmony. For example, by anticipating important negative interpersonal outcomes (e.g., shaming one's family, offending one's superior), Asians may be able to consider a greater range of preventive actions they can engage in to ensure more positive or acceptable outcomes.

Yet, considering greater options is not likely to provide a sufficient answer if changes in behavior do not occur. In that regard, Norem and Cantor's (1986) findings about defensive pessimism appear to be relevant. These researchers found that some high-achieving individuals use a "defensive pessimism" strategy that involves negative outcome expectancies, coupled with the use of active and engaged coping behaviors. According to Norem and Cantor (1986; see chap. 4, this volume), pessimism is not simply what people have because they are pessimists (similar to the notion of dispositional optimism or pessimism), but rather a reflection of what people do (e.g., using a particular way of thinking about certain things) in relation to a specific goal. Hence, consistent with Norem and Cantor's findings, Chang's (1996a) findings suggest that Asian Americans also may use their pessimism as a strategy to think about potential negative consequences and as a means to motivate themselves toward proactive behavior (e.g., problem solving). Thus, insofar as the link between pessimism and problem solving results in more positive rather than negative consequences, this can help explain why elevated pessimism scores are maintained among Asians.

USING BECK'S (1976) COGNITIVE MODEL OF PSYCHOLOGICAL DISTURBANCE TO WORK WITH ASIAN AND WHITE AMERICANS

The aforementioned findings, particularly those from Chang's (1996a) study, can have important implications for considering culture-specific interventions in working with distressed Asian compared with White Americans. Recall, Chang (1996a) found that (lack of) optimism was found to be one of the best, if not the best, predictors of depressive symptoms, psychological symptoms, and physical symptoms for Asian Americans, whereas pessimism was found to be a strong predictor of depressive symptoms and psychological symptoms for White Americans.

According to Beck's (1976) cognitive model of psychological disturbance, pessimism is presumed to play an important role in the development of depression. Chang's (1996a) findings for White Americans are consistent with this view. A key intervention used in changing how pessimistic thoughts lead to depressive symptoms is to refute or challenge evidence supporting such negative thoughts (Beck, Rush, Shaw, & Emery, 1979). For instance, after a client's negative beliefs (e.g., "I am a failure") have been translated to testable hypotheses (e.g., "I can't do anything right"), the practitioner can then help the distressed client focus on disconfirming these maladaptive beliefs by assisting in obtaining or introducing sufficient counterevidence (e.g., observing that the client successfully showed up for the appointment; Beck et al., 1979).

However, given that Chang (1996a) found lack of optimism, but not pessimism, predicted subsequent depressive symptoms in Asian Americans, a culture-specific intervention consistent with Beck's cognitive framework may focus distinctly on increasing optimistic thoughts in distressed Asian American clients rather than on decreasing their pessimistic thoughts. As noted by Chang (1996a), "by decreasing pessimism in Asian Americans, one could conceivably take away a major source of motivation that is related to adaptive and engaged coping behaviors such as problem solving" (p. 121). For instance, in working with Asian American clients who are dysphoric, the practitioner can help the client first identify untapped positive beliefs by referring to or obtaining supportive evidence (e.g., noting that the client has always shown up on time for his or her appointment). In sum, Chang's (1996a) findings suggest that in working with distressed Asian Americans, it may be particularly valuable to use interventions that focus on increasing their level of optimism, whereas for White Americans, it may be more valuable to use interventions that focus on decreasing their level of pessimism.

ASSESSING PSYCHOLOGICAL DISTURBANCE IN ASIAN AMERICANS: DISTINGUISHING PESSIMISM FROM DEPRESSION

Moreover, findings from Chang's (1996a) study also indicate a potential need for examining the clinical significance of various combinations of high and low optimism and pessimism within individual clients. That is, because Asians and Asian Americans may "normally" express elevated levels of pessimism (Lee & Seligman, 1997), as found in Chang's (1996a) study to be positively correlated with expressions of depressive, psychological, and physical symptoms, it would be important to distinguish between subgroups who do and do not express a concomitant level of optimism. For example, Asian Americans who express high levels of pessimism relative to White

Americans, but little optimism, may be particularly vulnerable to psychological disturbance and physical illness. In contrast, it may be that some Asians, despite their robust pessimism, express a "balance" of negative and positive thoughts (yin and yang) that functions adaptively for them. Therefore, in assessing for pessimism, it may be critical to also assess for expressions of optimism. In fact, by neglecting to assess for expressions of optimism, mental health professionals (especially those with little experience in working with Asians) may inaccurately construe Asian Americans' expression of pessimism as a sign of a depressive disorder.

Because pessimism is an important indicator of clinical depression (i.e., in expressions of hopelessness and helplessness; American Psychiatric Association, *Diagnostic and Statistical Manual of Mental Disorders; DSM-IV*, 1994), clinicians and counselors may need to exercise great caution when assessing Asian Americans to differentiate those who have depressive symptoms from those with nondepressive, but pessimistic thoughts. Findings from a recent set of studies conducted by Helweg-Larsen, Sadeghian, and Webb (1999) that looked at the stigma of being pessimistic strongly underscore this important and practical point.

In their first study, Helweg-Larsen et al. (1999) presented students with information describing an optimistic target (i.e., a hypothetical student who expressed that his health risks were lower than those of other students); a pessimistic target (a hypothetical student who expressed that his health risks were greater than those of other students); and a neutral target (a hypothetical student who expressed that his health risks were about the same as those of other students). After this presentation, students were then asked questions regarding how sad or happy, depressed or not depressed, and hopeless or not hopeless each of the targets appeared. In addition, students were also asked a set of questions that tapped their tendency to socially accept or reject the target (e.g., "fun to hang out with the person"). It is of interest to note that results from this study show that students were more likely to perceive the pessimistic target as being more sad, depressed, and hopeless, and less likely to be socially accepted. A second study was conducted to determine if these initial findings may have been due to people's lay perception that pessimists take more health risks, and thus account for pessimists' greater social rejection by others. It was surprising to note that results of the second study indicated the exact opposite. That is, the optimistic target student was perceived as more of a risk taker than was the pessimistic target student. Nevertheless, consistent with findings from the first study, social rejection was strongest for the pessimistic target student, who was again perceived as more sad, hopeless, and depressed.

In their final study, Helweg-Larsen et al. (1999) again presented students with pessimistic, optimistic, and neutral targets, but this time, students heard a tape recording of a hypothetical student who responded pessimistically, optimistically, or in a neutral manner to an interviewer asking about his chances of various health risks. However, before students had a chance to listen to these recordings, information regarding the mental state of the target student was manipulated by the researchers. Specifically, students were either given no information about the mental health of the target student, or given the information that the mental health of the target student was good (e.g., "person was happy and neither depressed nor hopeless"). Hence, for example, prior to hearing the target student express his pessimism about health risks, a student was told that the target student was mentally healthy. What these investigators found confirmed their earlier findings that people tend to associate pessimism with depression. Specifically, when no information was given about the target student, student-participants again perceived the pessimistic target as more sad, hopeless, and depressed, and in turn, were again more likely to reject him than to reject the optimistic target student. However, when information was given indicating that the target student was not dysphoric, students showed no difference in their ratings between optimistic and pessimistic targets on sadness, hopelessness, and depression. Moreover, students also showed no difference in their ratings between these target students on measures of social rejection.

In sum, Helweg-Larsen et al.'s research not only identified important social costs of being pessimistic, but also identified a critical source of people's prejudice and social rejection of pessimists, namely, the presumption that pessimists are depressed individuals. Therefore, given that Asian Americans are "normally" more pessimistic than White Americans (Chang, 1996a; Lee & Seligman, 1997), Asians may be at greater risk of being diagnosed for depressive disorders. That is, practitioners lacking experience or cultural competency in working with Asians may be quick to judge an Asian American's expression of heightened pessimism as a telltale sign of an underlying depression or enduring dysthymia. However, by assessing for expressions of both optimism and pessimism in evaluating Asians, as noted earlier, practitioners may be able to effectively disentangle Asian Americans' "normal" expression of pessimism from signs reflecting clinical depression or dysthymia (e.g., where expressions of optimism may be absent). In addition, given the subjective nature of social evaluations, Helweg-Larsen et al.'s (1999) findings also reinforce the value of using more objective (i.e., behavioral) techniques in the assessment of depression or dysthymia, which may be particularly useful when interacting with pessimistic Asians. No doubt, given that the studies conducted by Helweg-Larsen et al. (1999) mostly involved White participants and no Asians (M. Helweg-Larsen, personal communication, December 26, 1999), it would be interesting to see how Asians perceive expressions of optimism and pessimism in others.

CHALLENGES AND FUTURE DIRECTIONS FOR RESEARCH

Asian Americans as More Than a Single Ethnic Category

Just as it would be incorrect to say that all White Americans look or act the same, it is incorrect for researchers and mental health professionals to assume that Asian Americans are a homogenous population. Although genetically influenced features such as skin color may indicate that Asian Americans are more racially similar to each other compared with other racial groups, this should not be taken to suggest that they are all the same. In fact, when one considers factors such as language and cultural practices, Asian Americans begin to look and sound quite different (e.g., Sue & Morishima, 1982; Uba, 1994). They represent a very diverse population. According to Uba (1994), one can enumerate as many as 25 distinct Asian American ethnic groups living in the United States. Each of these ethnic groups differs across a number of important dimensions. For example, the history of different Asian American groups living in the United States varies considerably. Whereas Chinese and Japanese Americans are likely to have been members of American society for several decades (Daniels, 1988), Korean and Vietnamese Americans are likely to present as more recent immigrants (Takaki, 1989).

Nonetheless, although they share similar immigration histories, Chinese and Japanese Americans are not alike. As a tragic historical example, consider the treatments of Chinese and Japanese Americans in the United States during WWII. Unlike Chinese Americans, about 120,000 Japanese Americans, many of whom were US citizens, were transported to internment camps. This prejudicial treatment experienced by many Nisei (second generation) Japanese Americans has profoundly influenced Sansei (third generation) Japanese Americans. According to Nagata (1991), third-generation Japanese Americans not only struggle with the same problems their parents did, but also they struggle to believe and trust in American society. For such reasons, some researchers have argued that the term *Asian American* itself can be misleading and potentially harmful if such important differences between and within the different Asian ethnic groups are overlooked (Abe & Zane, 1990; Phinney, 1996). Therefore, it would be important to consider how optimism and pessimism may differ and relate to other important variables across the different Asian American ethnic groups.

Optimism and Pessimism in Predicting Adjustment in Asian Americans

Although optimism and pessimism have been found to be important predictors of adjustment, such findings are often based on studies that rarely compare the predictive power of these variables to other robust predictors of adjustment. For example, studies have shown that positive and negative affectivity are also strongly associated with psychological adjustment (e.g., Watson, Clark, & Carey, 1988; Watson, Clark, & Tellegen, 1988). Furthermore, Marshall, Wortman, Kusulas, Hervig, and Vickers (1992) have found that positive and negative affectivity map significantly onto optimism and pessimism, respectively. Therefore, it is not clear how important optimism and pessimism are in predicting adjustment beyond positive and negative affectivity, and in predicting adjustment between Asians and White people.

To address some of these issues, Chang (1999) examined the relative contributions of optimism and pessimism above those made by positive and negative affectivity in predicting scores on several commonly used measures of psychological disturbance in 92 Asian and 252 White Americans. After controlling for the variance accounted for by positive and negative affectivity in each of the outcomes (viz., measures assessing for trait anxiety, depression, hopelessness, psychological distress, and psychological symptoms), overall for White Americans, optimism and pessimism continued to account for a significant amount of additional variance in each outcome measure. In contrast, for Asian Americans, optimism and pessimism accounted for a significant amount of additional variance in only two of the outcomes (viz., trait anxiety and hopelessness) beyond what was accounted for by positive and negative affectivity. This is not to say that optimism and pessimism are not important variables associated with adjustment for Asians, but rather, that the influence of these variables on adjustment for Asians may be mediated by other important variables, such as mood.

For still another important predictor of psychological outcomes, consider perfectionism (Chang, 2000; Chang & Rand, 2000). Similar to findings for pessimism, findings for expression of perfectionism are greater for Asian Americans than for White Americans (Chang, 1998a; Kawamura, Frost, & Harmatz, 1999). Yet, we know little about how optimism and pessimism compare with perfectionism in predicting adjustment for Asians or for White people. Similarly, insofar as coping has been conceptualized and measured in many different ways (Chang, in press), there is still no definitive study of optimism, pessimism, and coping as predictors of adjustment in Asians and White people. No doubt, more studies are needed to compare optimism and pessimism to other robust predictors of adjustment.

Outcome Measures for Studying Asian People

Western researchers are becoming increasingly aware that when studying the culturally different, they must not only be careful to not impose their cultural values and biases in understanding non-Westerners, but also that they must appreciate those processes and outcomes that are most meaningful to such groups. It is noteworthy that some culture-bound disturbances reflecting symptoms of both anxiety and depression are particular to Asians. For example, *shenjing shuairuo* (or neurasthenia) refers to a condition observed among Asian people, including Asian Americans, where the expressed symptoms can be very similar to those typically presented in mood and anxiety disorders (*DSM-IV*, 1994). However, there has been little study of neurasthenia in Asian Americans (e.g., Lin, 1989; Yamamoto, 1992). Hence, we know very little about how optimism and pessimism predict culturally relevant outcomes such as neurasthenia among Asian Americans.

Also, because researchers have commonly focused on maladaptive outcomes, we know little about how variables such as optimism and pessimism relate to positive outcomes. Yet, what are the positive outcomes that should be considered? For example, Ryff (1989; Ryff & Keyes, 1995) has offered a useful conceptualization of subjective well-being composed of six relatively distinct dimensions. These dimensions are autonomy, environmental mastery, personal growth, positive relations with others, purpose in life, and self-acceptance. However, some of these dimensions tend to reflect attributes that are likely to be highly regarded by most Westerners, but not by most Easterners. Therefore, the consideration of culturally appropriate and meaningful outcome measures (both positive and negative) should be an important priority for researchers and practitioners who study or work with Asian populations (Okazaki, 1998).

CONCLUSION

Although the mechanisms by which optimism and pessimism develop and are maintained in different cultural groups have yet to be clearly understood, the present chapter makes it clear that any model of optimism and pessimism that ignores the influence of culture is likely to be incomplete. For example, E.-Y. Kim (1993) has noted that some Asian Americans (viz., Korean Americans) express effort optimism, a perception that with direct effort, anything is possible. Hence, despite findings indicating comparable elevations on expressions of optimism between Asian and White Americans (Chang, 1996a; Lee & Seligman, 1997), important differences may be uncovered when specific aspects of optimism are considered (e.g., optimism for engaging in successful behavior). Clearly, more studies are needed to address the many questions that remain to be considered in studying optimism and pessimism in groups of Easterners and Westerners. As I hope this chapter has impressed on the reader, the study of cultural influences on variables such as optimism and pessimism can be both fascinating and arduous. It will require researchers, scholars, and practitioners alike to take on the challenge of considering optimism and pessimism as much a function of the individual as of the person's social and cultural environment.

REFERENCES

Abe, J. S., & Zane, N. W. S. (1990). Psychological maladjustment among Asian and White American college students: Controlling for confounds. *Journal of Counseling Psychology, 37*, 437–444.

American Psychiatric Association. (1994). *Diagnostic and statistical manual of mental disorders* (4th ed.). Washington, DC: Author.

Beck, A. T. (1976). *Cognitive therapy and the emotional disorders*. New York: International Universities Press.

Beck, A. T., Rush, A. J., Shaw, B. F., & Emery, G. (1979). *Cognitive therapy of depression: A treatment manual*. New York: Guilford Press.

Beck, A. T., Ward, C. H., Mendelson, M., Mock, L., & Erbaugh, J. (1961). An inventory for measuring depression. *Archives of General Psychiatry, 4*, 561–571.

Brislin, R. (1993). *Understanding culture's influence on behavior*. Fort Worth, TX: Harcourt Brace and Jovanovich.

Chang, E. C. (1996a). Cultural differences in optimism, pessimism, and coping: Predictors of subsequent adjustment in Asian American and Caucasian American college students. *Journal of Counseling Psychology, 43*, 113–123.

Chang, E. C. (1996b). Evidence for the cultural specificity of pessimism in Asians versus Caucasians: A test of a general negativity hypothesis. *Personality and Individual Differences, 21*, 819–822.

Chang, E. C. (1998a). Cultural differences, perfectionism, and suicidal risk in a college population: Does social problem solving still matter? *Cognitive Therapy and Research, 22*, 237–254.

Chang, E. C. (1998b). Distinguishing between optimism and pessimism: A second look at the "optimism neuroticism hypothesis." In R. R. Hoffman, M. F. Sherrik, and J. S. Warm (Eds.), *Viewing psychology as a whole: The integrative science of William N. Dember* (pp. 415–432). Washington, DC: American Psychological Association.

Chang, E. C. (1999). *Cultural differences in psychological distress in Asian and Caucasian American college students: Examining the role of cognitive and affective concomitants*. Unpublished manuscript, University of Michigan, Ann Arbor.

Chang, E. C. (2000). Perfectionism as a predictor of positive and negative psychological outcomes: Examining a mediational model in younger and older adults. *Journal of Counseling Psychology, 47*, 18–26.

Chang, E. C. (in press). A look at the coping strategies and styles of Asian Americans: Similar and different? In C. R. Snyder (Ed.), *Coping and copers: Adaptive processes and people*. New York: Oxford University Press.

Chang, E. C., D'Zurilla, T. J., & Maydeu-Olivares, A. (1994). Assessing the dimensionality of optimism and pessimism using a multimeasure approach. *Cognitive Therapy and Research, 18*, 143–160.

Chang, E. C., Maydeu-Olivares, A., & D'Zurilla, T. J. (1997). Optimism and pessimism as partially independent constructs: Relations to positive and negative affectivity and psychological well-being. *Personality and Individual Differences, 23,* 433–440.

Chang, E. C., & Rand, K. L. (2000). Perfectionism as a predictor of subsequent adjustment: Evidence for a specific diathesis-stress mechanism among college students. *Journal of Counseling Psychology, 47,* 129–137.

Daniels, R. (1988). *Asian Americans: Chinese and Japanese in the United States since 1850.* Seattle: University of Washington Press.

Derogatis, L. R. (1983). *The SCL-90 R: Administration, scoring, and procedures manual II.* Baltimore, MD: Clinical Psychometric Research.

Doi, T. (1973). *The anatomy of dependence.* Tokyo: Kodansha.

Folkman, S., & Lazarus, R. S. (1980). An analysis of coping in a middle-aged community sample. *Journal of Health and Social Behavior, 21,* 219–239.

Greenwald, A. G. (1980). The totalitarian ego: Fabrication and revision of personal history. *American Psychologist, 35,* 603–618.

Heine, S. J., & Lehman, D. R. (1995). Cultural variation in unrealistic optimism: Does the West feel more invulnerable than the East? *Journal of Personality and Social Psychology, 68,* 595–607.

Heine, S. J., Lehman, D. R., Markus, H. R., & Kitayama, S. (1999). Is there a universal need for positive self-regard? *Psychological Review, 106,* 766–794.

Helweg-Larsen, M., Sadeghian, P., & Webb, M. S. (1999). *The stigma of being pessimistically biased.* Unpublished manuscript, Transylvania University, Lexington, KY.

Hofstede, G. (1980). *Culture's consequences.* Beverly Hills, CA: Sage Publications.

Jahoda, G. (1982). *Psychology and anthropology.* London: Academic Press.

Kawamura, K. Y., Frost, R. O., & Harmatz, M. G. (1999). *The relationship between parental harshness and perfectionism: A study of Asian-American and Caucasian college students.* Unpublished manuscript, University of Massachusetts at Amherst.

Kim, E.-Y. (1993). Career choice among second-generation Korean-Americans: Reflections of a cultural model of success. *Anthropology and Education Quarterly, 24,* 224–248.

Kim, U., Triandis, H. C., Kagitcibasi, C., Choi, S. C., & Yoon, G. (Eds.). (1994). *Individualism and collectivism: Theory, method, and applications.* Newbury Park, CA: Sage.

Lazarus, R. S., & Folkman, S. (1984). *Stress, appraisal, and coping.* New York: Springer.

Lee, Y.-T., & Seligman, M. E. P. (1997). Are Americans more optimistic than the Chinese? *Personality and Social Psychology Bulletin, 23,* 32–40.

Lin, T.-Y. (1989). Neurasthenia revisited: Its place in modern psychiatry. *Culture, Medicine and Psychiatry, 13,* 105–129.

Markus, H. R., & Kitayama, S. (1991). Culture and the self: Implications for cognition, emotion, and motivation. *Psychological Review, 98,* 224–253.

Marsella, A., DeVos, G., & Hsu, F. L. K. (1985). *Culture and self.* London: Tavistock.

Marshall, G. N., Wortman, C. B., Kusulas, J. W., Hervig, L. K., & Vickers, R. R., Jr. (1992). Distinguishing optimism from pessimism: Relations to fundamental dimensions of mood and personality. *Journal of Personality and Social Psychology, 62,* 1067–1074.

Mizuno, M., & Yamaguchi, S. (1997, August). *Reframing Japanese pessimism: I'm more typical than the average person.* Paper presented at the 2nd annual meeting of the Asian Association of Social Psychology, Kyoto, Japan.

Nagata, D. (1991). Transgenerational impact of the Japanese American internment: Clinical issues in working with children of former internees. *Psychotherapy, 28,* 121–128.

Norem, J. K., & Cantor, N. (1986). Defensive pessimism: Harnessing anxiety as motivation. *Journal of Personality and Social Psychology, 51,* 1208–1217.

Okazaki, S. (1998). Psychological assessment of Asian Americans: Research agenda for cultural competency. *Journal of Personality Assessment, 70,* 54–70.

Pennebaker, J. W. (1982). *The psychology of physical symptoms.* New York: Springer-Verlag.

Peterson, C., Semmel, A., von Baeyer, C., Abramson, L. Y., Metalsky, G. I., & Seligman, M. E. P. (1982). The Attributional Style Questionnaire. *Cognitive Therapy and Research, 6,* 287–299.

Phinney, J. (1996). When we talk about American ethnic groups, what do we mean? *American Psychologist, 51,* 918–927.

Roland, A. (1988). *In search of self in India and Japan: Toward a cross-cultural psychology.* Princeton, NJ: Princeton University Press.

Ryff, C. D. (1989). Happiness is everything, or is it? Explorations on the meaning of psychological well-being. *Journal of Personality and Social Psychology, 57,* 1069–1081.

Ryff, C. D., & Keyes, C. L. M. (1995). The structure of psychological well-being revisited. *Journal of Personality and Social Psychology, 69,* 719–727.

Scheier, M. F., & Carver, C. S. (1985). Optimism, coping, and health: Assessment and implications of generalized outcome expectancies. *Health Psychology, 4,* 219–247.

Sue, S., & Morishima, J. (1982). *The mental health of Asian Americans.* San Francisco: Jossey-Bass.

Takaki, R. (1989). *Strangers from a different shore: A history of Asian Americans.* Boston: Little Brown.

Tobin, L. D., Holroyd, K. A., Reynolds, R. V., & Wigal, J. K. (1989). The hierarchical factor structure of the Coping Strategies Inventory. *Cognitive Therapy and Research, 13,* 343–361.

Triandis, H. C. (1995). *Individualism and collectivism.* Boulder, CO: Westview Press.

Uba, L. (1994). *Asian Americans: Personality patterns, identity, and mental health.* New York: Guilford Press.

Waterman, A. S. (1984). *The psychology of individualism*. New York: Praeger.

Watson, D., Clark, L. A., & Carey, G. (1988). Positive and negative affectivity and their relation to anxiety and depressive disorders. *Journal of Abnormal Psychology, 97*, 346–353.

Watson, D., Clark, L. A., & Tellegen, A. (1988). Development and validation of brief measures of positive and negative affect: The PANAS scales. *Journal of Personality and Social Psychology, 54*, 1063–1070.

Weinstein, N. D. (1980). Unrealistic optimism about future life events. *Journal of Personality and Social Psychology, 39*, 806–820.

Weinstein, N. D. (1984). Why it won't happen to me: Perceptions of risk factors and susceptibility. *Health Psychology, 3*, 431–457.

Weisz, J. R., Rothbaum, R. M., & Blackburn, T. C. (1984). Standing out and standing in: The psychology of control in America and Japan. *American Psychologist, 39*, 955–969.

Yamamoto, J. (1992). Psychiatric diagnoses and neurasthenia. *Psychiatric Annals, 22*, 171–172.

Yee, A. H. (1992). Asians as stereotypes and students: Misperceptions that persist. *Educational Psychology Review, 4*, 95–132.

13

THE OPTIMISM–PESSIMISM INSTRUMENT: PERSONAL AND SOCIAL CORRELATES

WILLIAM N. DEMBER

My interest in the constructs of optimism and pessimism originated in a search for correlates of individual differences in susceptibility to the *Pollyanna principle*, the broad tendency for people to give priority to the positive in perception, memory, and language usage (see Dember, Martin, Hummer, Howe, & Melton, 1989; Dember & Penwell, 1980; Matlin & Stang, 1978). That tendency, manifested in group means on a variety of simple tasks, although widespread, is not universal. Some people conform strongly to the Pollyanna tendency, while a few show what might be called an "anti-Pollyanna" bias. For example, in a classroom demonstration, I often ask undergraduate students to write a list of 12 pairs of antonyms that might be used to describe a person, physically or psychologically (e.g., slim-fat; happy-sad). They then are asked to circle the member of each pair of adjectives that is the more complimentary or positive. The Pollyanna tendency is revealed in the greater than chance number of times that the first member of each pair (the one on the left, if written, or the first adjective uttered, if spoken) is assessed as the more positive, as would be the case with the two examples I have just given. In such demonstrations, the mean frequency comes out to be about 9, where chance is 6. The first time I ran that demonstration, I asked the students to score their own protocols and then announce the total, which could range from 0 to 12. I put the frequency distribution on the board as the numbers were called out. Sure enough, the scores were biased toward the high end (conformity to the Pollyanna principle), but there were some scores below 6, and one such low scoring participant asked what that might mean. I mumbled something to the effect that whatever score any particular individual achieved probably had no significance; it was the group tendency that mattered. I am not convinced that the student was satisfied with that brush-off, and I certainly was not ready to dismiss the notion that scoring low on a Pollyanna task might say something about the person. My initial thought was that low scoring participants might have strongly pessimistic personalities, just as those with very high scores might be unrealistically optimistic.

My desire to test that hypothesis led me on a search for a good measure of optimism and pessimism, assuming along with most everyone else at the time that optimism and pessimism lay at opposite poles of a single dimension. These events occurred in the late 1970s, and either out of a lack of diligence, or because there were no satisfactory measures yet in the literature, my search was unsuccessful. So I decided to create a questionnaire, the optimism–pessimism (OP) instrument for measuring optimism and pessimism. This chapter offers a progress report on that effort. It is not intended as a general review of the optimism-pessimism literature. Of the results that research with the OP instrument yielded, the most important, I believe, is that optimism and pessimism are partially independent constructs: They are only moderately negatively correlated (usually in the low-to-mid −.50s, although on occasion in the low −.60s) and in many, though by no means all, instances are differentially related to other variables.

CREATION OF THE OP INSTRUMENT

In developing the OP instrument, I followed the familiar strategy of creating items in the form of brief statements that the respondent could either endorse or reject by using a four-alternative, Likert-type format (*strongly agree, agree, disagree, strongly disagree*). To balance for response biases, such as yea-saying or nay-saying, I decided to have an equal number of items worded such that endorsement implied either an optimistic or a pessimistic orientation. It was my initial intent to combine the responses on the two subsets of items, reverse-scoring one set and adding the item values to get a total score. In addition to the relevant items, which had been prescreened for face validity by a panel of advanced graduate students, there were also to be a number of "filler" statements, hopefully to mask the intent of the instrument. I began the task of writing items with the aid of an undergraduate student. Part way through, a graduate student, Mary Newman (later Mary Hummer) took up the project for her master's thesis, where the focus was to be on basic psychometric issues such as item–test correlations and internal reliability. Of secondary concern at that point was the issue of validity.

One outcome of the initial analyses of the Newman (1983) data— obtained from 216 undergraduate students participating to fulfill a course requirement—was the deletion of 2 optimistic and 2 pessimistic items from initial sets of 20. As a result 18 items of each type were left along with the original 20 filler items.

With regard to the second, more important outcome, although it had been our intent to create a single OP scale, the data were nevertheless analyzed separately by item type, and it became apparent that we had two scales, that is, an 18-item O (optimism) scale and an 18-item P (pessimism) scale, which were only moderately correlated with one another ($r = -.52$ in this first study). Moreover, the value of Cronbach's alpha for each of the two scales was higher ($\alpha = .84$ for optimism and .86 for pessimism) than the canonical correlation (.74) between the two scales (Cronbach, 1951). That general finding has been replicated in numerous follow-up studies, with the value of r typically running in the low $-.50$s to the low $-.60$s. Even more dramatic is the finding that O and P scores were uncorrelated in a sample of Ethiopian international students, whereas that correlation for a sample of comparable non-Ethiopian Africans was $-.52$ (Bantirgu, 1995). Test–retest correlations over a 2-week interval were found to be .75 for optimism and .84 for pessimism (Dember & Brooks, 1989). Neither in those, nor in follow-up studies have we found any differences between men and women on level of O or P, on the magnitude of the correlation between them, or in correlations with other variables.

It is primarily on the basis of those modest correlations between optimism and pessimism that we routinely compute both an O score and a P score for each participant in our research and typically do not combine those scores into a composite optimism–pessimism value. However, in a recently completed experiment on the role of optimism and pessimism in vigilance performance (Helton, Dember, & Warm, 1999), it proved useful to create two extreme groups, High O–Low P and Low O–High P, with High and Low defined as above or below the group median. When so categorized, pessimistic participants showed a steeper decline over time in performance efficiency than did optimistic participants. Fischer & Leitenberg (1986) have also reported the non–bipolarity of optimism and pessimism based on an instrument they developed for use with children, suggesting that the surprisingly moderate correlation between O and P is not peculiar to the OP instrument.

Note that the content of the O and P items is quite varied. It was our intent not to restrict the substance of the statements to a single category (e.g., expectations about one's own future prospects or assessments of the present or future state of the world in general), but rather to cover a wide variety of domains. In that way, we hoped to have an instrument which would be related to a broad range of other measures, even at the cost of not being highly predictive of any single measure. For example, some items in the OP instrument are personally relevant, and some refer to universal, timeless "truths" (e.g., April showers bring May flowers). That heterogeneity of content shows up in factor analyses (e.g., Chang, D'Zurilla, & Maydeu-Olivares, 1994) that identify more than the intended two factors, optimism and pessimism, but it does not seem seriously to vitiate internal reliability.

CORRELATIONS WITH PERSONALITY MEASURES

As a first pass at examining construct validity of the O and P scales, Newman did obtain data from her participants on several other variables, including a rating on a 7-point scale in response to the question: "In general, how optimistic or pessimistic would you say you are?" A rating of 1 was associated with extreme optimism, and a rating of 7 with extreme pessimism. (In hindsight, we should have asked two questions: "How optimistic would you say you are" and "how pessimistic would you say you are?"). Those self-ratings were correlated with O at $r = -.55$ and with P at .53, about the same level as the correlation between O and P. Clearly, the scales and the self-ratings were tapping a common construct, but the self-ratings could not simply substitute for the scales. Those results lend support to the construct validity of the O and P scales, and at the same time indicate that they have potential use beyond that of the self-ratings. Of course, as single-item measures, the self-ratings are likely to have less than optimal reliability; it would be interesting to check out their test–retest reliability, as well as to ask the two questions alluded to above rather than just the one question we did ask, which assumes a unidimensional continuum running from highly optimistic at one end to highly pessimistic at the other. Asking both questions would also permit calculation of the correlation between responses to the optimism and the pessimism questions, just as we correlate the values on the O and P scales.

Data on additional single-item questions asked of Newman's participants have been reported in Dember et al. (1989). Especially interesting are responses to two questions designed to tap the extent to which a participant was committed to a religious or a political ideology. The expectation was that such commitment would be associated with high optimism or low pessimism on the grounds that the solace afforded by an ideological system fosters an upbeat attitude by helping the individual find meaning and direction in a complex, confusing, even chaotic world (see Dember, 1974, 1989). Moreover, political ideologies, such as communism and socialism, often promise a rosy future on this earth once those who oppress the downtrodden are removed, forcibly if necessary, from positions of power. Similarly, religious ideologies typically point to an afterlife, when, for true believers, the woes of our corporeal existence will be replaced by heavenly bliss. The data showed that for both politics and religion, those participants who answered "yes" to the question about commitment had significantly higher O scores than those who said "no," but the groups did not differ on P scores, an instance in which the O and P scales are differentially related to a criterion measure. Those findings with regard to religion were replicated by Dember and Brooks (1989), who also reported impressive correlations (high .50s, low .60s) between both O and P and happiness. Similar findings with regard to religious fundamentalism have also been reported by Sethi and Seligman (1993).

Because the results come from a correlational design, it is possible, of course, that optimistic people are attracted to an ideological system, rather than that adherents derive their elevated optimism from their commitment to the ideology. My preference at this point is for the latter interpretation. Indeed, I would expect that those people who are already highly optimistic would not need to seek comfort in a ready-made ideology; if that were indeed so, the difference in optimism scores that Newman found is all the more impressive, because the noncommitted group would contain a subset of people high in optimism independent of their political or religious affiliations. Responses to another single-item question about the imminent likelihood of nuclear war revealed a similar pattern, except in this instance only pessimism was predictive. That is, those people who believed that a nuclear war was likely by the year 2000 had significantly higher P scores than those who did not, but the two groups did not differ on O scores.

Participants were also asked to predict their grade-point average (GPA) for the coming quarter. In this case, both O and P were predictive, in the expected direction, with values of r at .21 and $-.28$, respectively. Incidentally, those low values of r, statistically significant by virtue of the large sample size, are fairly typical of the magnitude of correlations with O and P, as well as with other measures of optimism and pessimism, and with many of the variables investigated thus far. Moreover, as suggested by the last result, in both the Newman study and in subsequent research, the P scale tends to be more strongly related to other variables than the O scale, perhaps because P scores typically have a greater variance than O scores. At this point, there are neither sufficient empirical data nor sufficiently well-articulated theories to enable researchers to anticipate the kinds of variables (dispositional or behavioral) that are better predicted from one scale or the other, or to anticipate when the two will be equivalent in the strength of their relations with other variables.

In the remainder of this section, we summarize much of the evidence we do have on various "personality" correlates of O and P, including their relations with two other popular instruments for measuring optimism and pessimism, the Life Orientation Test (LOT; Scheier & Carver, 1985) and the Attributional Style Questionnaire (ASQ and its variant, the Expanded Attributional Style Questionnaire or EASQ; Peterson et al., 1982; Peterson & Villanova, 1988). (See Introduction, this volume for a brief discussion of the LOT, the ASQ, and other related instruments.) We also present some data on the relative predictive ability of the three instruments (OP, LOT, & EASQ) with regard to coping style and depression. These comparative data offer some encouragement that the OP instrument provides "value added" in this increasingly crowded domain. The article by Dember et al. (1989) alluded to above reports the results of both the Newman thesis and a subsequent thesis by Stephanie Martin (1986). The latter was concerned primarily with personality correlates of the O and P scales, in particular anxiety and defense (see Dember et al., 1989, for complete details). Here I want first to note that Martin's data, based on 228 participants and drawn, as were Newman's, from the Introductory Psychology pool of participants at the University of Cincinnati, very closely replicate the values Newman obtained for the level of optimism and pessimism, the correlation between the two scales, and their internal reliability. The consistency between the statistical properties of the two data sets is especially noteworthy given that the studies were run about 3 years apart.

Second, in addition to the OP, participants in the Martin study responded to the Repression–Sensitization Scale (RS; Byrne, Barry, & Nelson, 1963) and to the Defense Mechanisms Inventory (DMI; Ihilevich & Gleser, 1986). The latter is an objectively scorable instrument for assessing the extent to which the respondent uses each of five categories of defense mechanism, turning against self (TAS, an intrapunitive defense); reversal (REV, a repressive defense); principalization (PRN, an intellectualizing defense); turning against other (TAO, an aggressive defense); and projection (PRO, perceiving one's own unconscious motives and conflicts in others). The RS scale has embedded within it a measure of anxiety, the Welsh A (Welsh, 1956), and the correlation between RS scores and anxiety scores is very high (see, e.g., Watson & Clark, 1984). Hence, there is good reason to consider the RS a measure of anxiety rather than a measure, as originally conceived, of repressive tendencies or of their opposite, sensitizing tendencies.

With regard to RS scores and Welsh A scores, as expected, O was negatively correlated with both ($r = -.42$ and $-.34$, respectively), while P was correlated positively, and more strongly with both ($r = .65$ and $.60$, respectively).[1] It was further expected, and found, that O scores would correlate positively with REV ($r = .28$) and with PRN ($r = .19$). In addition, O scores were negatively related to TAS ($r = -.27$) and with PRO ($r = -.19$). P scores, as expected, correlated positively with TAS ($r = .29$) and with PRO ($r = .21$) and negatively with PRN and REV (in both cases, $r = -.32$). In three instances, the magnitude of the correlation with P was significantly greater than that with O, that is, with regard to PRN, RS, and A, although the latter two scales, as noted, are themselves so highly correlated (in this study, $r = .94$) as to constitute a single measure. In general, there was no instance in which a scale correlated more strongly with O than with P. Leaving aside the theoretical rationale for the expectations indicated above, it is clear that people's optimistic and pessimistic tendencies, as assessed by the OP, do relate, sometimes at respectable levels, to their levels of anxiety and to their preferences among the defense mechanisms tapped by the DMI. Correlations with measures of coping strategy, an alternative conception to that of defense mechanisms, follow the same general pattern, as summarized immediately below.

In a complex and highly ambitious unpublished doctoral dissertation, Raquel Natali-Alemany (1991) examined, among other things, the relation between O and P and the coping strategies tapped by the Constructive Thinking Inventory (CTI; Epstein & Meier, 1989). The latter is comprised of 10 scales, including a general factor called global constructive thinking (GCT). Although the individual scales yielded interesting results, for the sake of simplicity and brevity only data related to the GCT coping strategy will be reported here.

The participants were students enrolled in advanced undergraduate courses who volunteered for strictly altruistic reasons; all 115 filled out the OP and CTI questionnaires, but of those, only 81 also agreed to keep a daily log of their mood states over a 2-week period by way of the Positive and Negative Affect Schedule (PANAS; Watson, Clark, & Tellegen, 1988) and the Wessman & Ricks (1966) Elation-Depression scale (ED). In addition, they responded daily to a measure of control or lack of control (Harrigan, Kues, Ricks, & Smith, 1984) and a life events inventory (Zautra, Guarnaccia, & Dohrenwend, 1986). Again, for the sake of brevity, of those measures, only the data from the PANAS and the ED Scale will be presented here. The results reported are from the 81 participants who completed all

---

[1]Throughout, when reference is made to variables as correlated, *significantly* is implied when not explicitly stated; and for significantly, read $p < .05$.

of the measures. Note that the PANAS yields two independent scores, one for positive affect (PA) and one for negative affect (NA), whereas the Wessman and Ricks scale yields a score on a unidimensional scale, where high scores reflect high levels of positive mood.

There were significant, relatively high correlations between the GCT and both O ($r = .51$) and P ($r = -.67$). These correlations indicate that optimistic individuals as well as those who are low in pessimism tend to favor use of coping strategies that can be considered adaptive. Because, as in prior studies, O and P scores were significantly correlated ($r = -.37$; a seemingly low value, but not significantly lower than the values reported in Dember et al., 1989), it was deemed instructive to examine the correlations between O and P and GCT after partialling out the contribution of the other measure in order to determine the unique contribution of each to the zero-order correlations. Thus, when O with the P tendency statistically partialled out was related to GCT, the resulting partial correlation was reduced to .38, which nevertheless remained significant; similarly, the partial correlation between P and GCT was reduced to $-.60$, again still statistically significant. Thus, with regard to GCT, both O and P made unique contributions, with P seemingly the better predictor.

The participants' PANAS and E (Elation) scores were averaged over the 14 days during which they kept daily records. In general, these participants reported being high on PA and low on NA; similarly, their average E score (6.2 out of a maximum of 10) corresponded closely to the statement "Feeling pretty good; OK," which was associated with the scale value of 6.0.

O scores were correlated significantly with mean PA ($r = .32$) and with mean E scores ($r = .40$). P scores were significantly related only to E scores ($r = -.28$). When O and P scores were partialled out from one another, the partial correlation between O and PA was necessarily unchanged, treating the nonsignificant correlation between P and PA as though it had a value of zero. The partial correlation between O and E scores was reduced from .40 to .33, again still significant, and that between P and E was reduced from $-.28$ to $-.16$, not significant. Thus, in this instance, only O scores were uniquely predictive of mood, as assessed by way of both the PA and the E scales. Recall that it was P scores that made the greater unique contribution to GCT. Hence, in this study, it was clearly valuable to have both O and P measures because they operated differentially with regard to coping strategy and mood.

The Natali-Alemany dissertation was followed up in part and also extended in a project reported by Geers, Reilley, DeRonde, & Dember (1996). Reilley, Geers, Lindsay, Dember, and Schafer (1998) also provide data by way of self-reported physical health, which is best predicted by the O and P scales as compared with LOT and attribution style measures (ASQ and EASQ). More directly pertinent to issues of personality per se, three main concerns were addressed in the Geers et al. (1996) study: (a) The replicability of the findings by Natali-Alemany that O and P scores are related to the GCT scale on the CTI, a general measure of coping strategy; (b) the interrelations among three measures of optimism and pessimism, the OP, Scheier & Carver's (1985) LOT, and the ASQ (see the 48-item version in Seligman, 1990); and (c) the relative ability of those three measures to predict scores on both the GCT and the Beck Depression Inventory (BDI; Beck, Ward, Mendelson, Mock, & Erbaugh, 1961).

Participants were drawn from the Introductory Psychology participant pool at the University of Cincinnati. The number entering into the correlations fluctuated around 200 (for some scales, there were missing data because of failure of a few participants to complete all the instruments).

With regard to the GCT, the correlations between it and the O and P scales were both significant and highly similar in level and pattern to those reported by Natali-Alemany ($r = .54$ and $-.74$). Exactly as in the original Newman thesis, the correlation between O and P scores was $-.52$. Hence, partial rs were computed, yielding the following reduced values: For O with GCT, the partial $r = .35$, still statistically significant; for P, the partial $r = -.64$, again reduced, but still, of course, significant. Those partial r values are remarkably similar to those found by Natali-Alemany between GCT and O and P ($.38$ and $.60$, respectively). As before, it is P that seems to make the greater unique contribution to GCT.

Intercorrelations among O, P, ASQ, and the LOT are given in Table 13.1. With regard to the three instruments for measuring optimism or pessimism, the highest correlations are those between both O and P and the LOT. O and P also correlate with the ASQ, but more modestly and quite symmetrically. The correlation between the LOT and the ASQ is also modest. Clearly, and not unexpectedly, the instruments that share a common format, the OP and the LOT, yield scores that are the most highly related.

The table also shows that O, P, and LOT are more highly correlated with BDI than is the ASQ, and that O, P, and LOT correlate to about the

Table 13.1.
Intercorrelations Among Measures of Optimism and Pessimism

		1	2	3
1	O	—	—	—
2	P	−.52	—	—
3	LOT	.57	−.66	—
4	ASQ	.39	−.39	.29

Note: N = 204; all values of r are significant at p < .05. O = optimism; P = pessimism; LOT = Life Orientation Test; ASQ = Attributional Style Questionnaire. Data from "Optimism, Pessimism, Depression, and Coping," poster presented at the annual meeting of the American Psychological Society, San Francisco, CA, 1996. Adapted with permission.

same degree with BDI. Although not presented here, when the ASQ is decomposed into scores based only on "good" and "bad" scenarios, attribution scores from the bad scenarios are the more highly related to BDI scores.

Relations between O and P and GCT scores are presented in detail above. LOT and GCT are correlated at $r = .60$, a value intermediate between that for the O scale ($r = .54$) and that for the P scale ($r = -.74$). The correlation between ASQ and GCT scores is considerably lower ($r = .34$).

Two multiple regression analyses were performed, with O, P, LOT, and ASQ as predictor variables, and GCT and BDI as criterion measures. For GCT, the multiple R was .77; P was by far the strongest predictor ($\beta = -.56$), followed by O ($\beta = .17$) and LOT ($\beta = .13$), with ASQ scores making no unique contribution ($\beta = -.02$). For BDI, the multiple R was .54; again, P was the strongest predictor ($\beta = .29$), followed by O ($\beta = -.15$) and LOT ($\beta = -.12$, ns), with ASQ scores again making no unique contribution to the prediction of BDI scores ($\beta = .08$, ns). Given those outcomes, one might question the reliability or even the accuracy of scoring of the ASQ protocols, but note that ASQ scores do relate meaningfully, although not substantially, to all of the other measures. Finally, here as in prior studies, P seems to be the most useful of the several scales. O does make a unique, although weak, contribution to the prediction of both GCT and BDI, while the LOT contributes uniquely, and even more weakly, but only to the prediction of GCT scores.

SOCIAL INTERACTIONS

The above section focuses on progress to date in elucidating the relations of optimistic and pessimistic tendencies to various personality characteristics. Efforts to examine the impact of these tendencies on social interactions have only recently begun. I use the term *social interactions* somewhat loosely to cover disparate issues ranging from the friendship patterns of optimistic and pessimistic individuals to the optimistic or pessimistic tendencies of special populations, such as business leaders and Peace Corps volunteers.

Anyone at all familiar with the general literature is aware that an important venue for the application of measures of optimism and pessimism is the area of physical and mental health. Indeed, the earliest and most dramatic findings were those that emanated from the Seligman group. Perhaps the best known of those was a longitudinal study by Peterson, Seligman, and Vaillant (1988) on the physical health of a group of former Harvard undergraduates, elite students whose health had been followed over several decades. Through the use of a content analysis system (CAVE; content analysis of verbatim explanations) applied to essays these students had written while at Harvard about a prior wartime experience, it was possible to assign to each participant a number reflecting that person's explanatory style. The CAVE technique, in short, served as a surrogate for the ASQ. Physical health at the time the essays were written was controlled, and given this there was still a significant correlation between CAVE scores and a measure of physical health: The more "pessimistic" the attribution style in college, the poorer one's health in middle age. Various explanations for that relation have been offered, including one that directly implicated impaired immune function. For the present purpose, an especially intriguing hypothesis was offered by Peterson and Bossio (1991), who argued that pessimistic individuals have inadequate social support, which has been shown to put one at risk for poor health. Why should people with pessimistic attitudes have inadequate social support? Peterson and Bossio further argue that by virtue of their pessimism, such people simply do not make good company. Hence, pessimistic individuals have trouble maintaining friendships.

One implication of that line of thought is that pessimistic people will by default eventually end up with close friends who are equally pessimistic, that is, the best each member of a friendship dyad can do is to pair up with people who are no less pessimistic. Of course, in the real world, one does not have an infinite number of potential friends to choose from or be chosen by, nor is there time enough for the process to yield friendship pairs exactly equal in pessimism. In addition, there are other bases for friendship maintenance besides one's pessimistic orientation. Nevertheless, it might be expected that the pessimism scores of close friends would be significantly correlated.

We (Dember, Geers, Reilley, & Raisman, 1995) attempted to test that expectation by asking students in the Introductory Psychology participant pool at the University of Cincinnati to come to a room on campus along with a person they considered to be a close friend. The degree of friendship was assessed by way of a questionnaire given to both members of each dyad; based on a stringent criterion, the data from a few dyads were not used for failure to meet that criterion. One initial surprise was the large number of male–female friendship pairs. Because such mixed-gender pairs might have a very different basis for a close friendship than same-gender pairs, we decided to analyze the data separately for male–male, female–female, and male–female dyads. In addition to having the participants respond to the OP instrument, we also asked them to respond to the EASQ, and for another purpose entirely, to fill out a health questionnaire. Only the correlational data pertinent to the hypothesized relation between pessimism scores of close friends will be reported here.

In essence, no significant correlations were found for the male–female ($N = 20$) or female–female ($N = 40$) pairs on O, P, or EASQ scores. Indeed, the only significant correlations involving EASQ were with O and P (both in the low .20s; $N = 184$, $p < .01$). However, the O scores of the 20 male–male pairs were highly correlated ($r = .65$, $p < .05$). So, from these results, what seems to matter in friendship maintenance among male college students is their level of optimism, not their level of pessimism. In an effort to pin that finding down and to see whether there might be other personality variables on which friendships are founded (perhaps it is nothing more than "birds of a feather flocking together"), Sean Reilley conducted a second study (Reilley & Dember, 1996; see also Geers, Reilley, & Dember, 1998) following the same general logic, only this time omitting the EASQ and adding three other brief measures, the Self-Expression (Assertiveness) Scale (SES; Galassi, Delo, Galassi, & Bastien, 1974); the NYU Loneliness Scale (Rubenstein & Shaver, 1992); and the Sensation Seeking Scale II (SSS; Zuckerman, 1979). Again, dyads were categorized as male–female ($N = 31$), female–female ($N = 39$), and male–male ($N = 22$). As before, only the correlation between O scores was significant and only for the male–male pairs (again, $r = .65$, $p < .05$). With regard to the other measures, the only significant between-friends correlation was that for male–female dyads on the SSS ($r = .37$, $p < .05$). One can offer a reasonable interpretation of the last finding, but it is not pertinent to the theme of the present chapter. What does seem clear from these two studies is that although optimism does seem important as basis for friendship among male friends, there is no evidence of a role for pessimism. Why optimism works, and why only for male–male dyads is not clear.

It is possible that the results represent an artifact of the way that the students' friends were solicited for the study. We have speculated that optimistic and pessimistic individuals have several friends covering a range of optimism and pessimism values. Indeed, our data from the friendship questionnaire show that optimistic and pessimistic individuals have equal numbers of friends, although the length of their typical friendships differs, with optimists reporting friendships of longer duration. We assume that optimistic people will in general be more inclined to assent to participate in a study of this sort (with nothing in it for them except being able to help out a friend in need) than will pessimistic individuals. So, when an optimistic student turns, perhaps wittingly, to one of his or her optimistic friends with a request to participate, that overture is likely to be accepted; similar requests to pessimistic friends, should they occur, will generally be rejected. So optimists come to the study with friends who are also predominantly optimistic. By contrast, when pessimistic individuals solicit participation from among their friends, who may indeed be predominantly pessimistic, they may also turn initially to whatever optimistic friends they have, expecting them to accede. But, since their friends are predominantly pessimistic, some of whom may agree to participate, pessimistic individuals may come to the study with a mixture of optimistic and pessimistic friends. Such a scenario might explain why optimism worked in this study, but pessimism did not, although it is silent on why only for male–male pairs. In any case, it would seem worthwhile to find an alternative method of determining the optimism and pessimism levels of people's close friends to check the generality of the present results. In the meantime, the Peterson and Bossio speculation about pessimists' inadequate support networks has led us to some intriguing and puzzling findings as well as to further evidence for the non-bipolarity of optimism and pessimism.

The final two studies described below are a bit hard to categorize as involving either personality correlates of optimism and pessimism or social interactions. Perhaps it is best to think of them as concerned with social settings in which optimism and pessimism are implicated, either because the settings induce such orientations or because such orientations serve as screens for entry into those settings.

In the first study, one question, among others, was whether Peace Corps volunteers who had returned from service would show higher than usual levels of optimism, unusually low levels of pessimism, or perhaps both. Based on some pilot interviews, the critical variable seemed to be pessimism. And that is how it turned out. Peace Corps volunteers who had returned from their assignments filled out the OP along with other measures and participated in a lengthy interview (Gerety, 1996). Of interest here is the finding that this group ($N = 30$), although having a mean O score (54.90) not significantly different from that of a norm group (53.75) of 1,033 undergraduates who had served in four prior studies (Dember et al., 1989, Studies 1 and 2; Hummer, Dember, Melton & Schefft, 1992; Terezis, 1990), did have a significantly and substantially lower mean P score (norm group M = 37.1; Gerety M = 32.4; $t = 3.74$, $p < .001$). I need to note here that the norm group mean O score was incorrectly reported as 55.75 in a prior study (Lewis, Dember, Schefft, & Radenhausen, 1995) and used by Gerety as well as in the study below by Wunderley, Reddy, and Dember (1998). Use of that inflated norm group value had no impact on the Gerety et al. results, but it did lead to an erroneous conclusion by Wunderley et al. regarding the relative optimism level of the participants in their study.

As suggested above, it is not clear whether their unusually low level of pessimism is what made it easy for the Peace Corps volunteers to undertake this difficult assignment and, perhaps, made them attractive to the selection officers, or whether their success in the field lowered their initial level of pessimism. Of course, all of the above factors may have been implicated. It would be interesting to assess applicants for Peace Corps service for their O and P levels, but to keep those data from entering into the selection decision. In that way, one could examine both the O and P levels of applicants in general as well as the scores of those who had been selected.

It seems plausible that P scores would be lower than typical among the applicants and then would progressively decline through the selection and postservice phases.

A somewhat different outcome was found in the second study (Wunderley et al., 1998) on special groups, in this case 48 male business leaders and 197 (49 women, 148 men) of their "direct reports" or "constituents." These participants worked for mid- to large-size manufacturing firms in the greater Cincinnati area. Leaders as well as their constituents filled out the OP instrument along with two other measures: (a) The Kirton Adaption-Innovation Inventory (KAI; Kirton, 1976), which assesses one's tendencies to respond to challenge either simply by adapting to it or by initiating change through innovative strategies; and (b) the Leadership Practices Inventory (LPI; Kouzes & Posner, 1988). The latter instrument can be taken either from the perspective of one's own behavior (LPI-Self) or to characterize the leadership practices of someone else (LPI-Observer). In this study, the measure of interest was the LPI-Observer scores of constituents judging their particular leader, that is, a measure, on five factors (scales), of how the constituents viewed their leader. For purposes of feedback, the leaders filled out the LPI-Self, but those data were not analyzed, because the focus of the study was on leaders per se. For the sake of economy, the constituents did not fill out either the KAI or the LPI-Self. The five LPI scales are called Challenging the Process, Inspiring a Shared Vision, Enabling Others to Act, Modeling the Way, and Encouraging the Heart.

Both the leader group and the constituents had significantly and substantially lower mean P scores (leaders: $M = 31.35$, $t = 7.61$; constituents: $M = 32.57$, $t = 11.16$; in both cases, $p < .001$) than the norm group. Both groups also had significantly, although moderately, higher O scores than the norm group (leaders, $M = 56.38$, $t = 3.41$; constituents: $M = 55.65$, $t = 2.46$; in both cases, $p < .01$). Again, it seems that what differentiates these successful business leaders and their constituents, who are on a track toward leadership positions, from the norm group is their dramatically low P scores, although their O scores were also somewhat elevated. Indeed, it seems reasonable that excessively optimistic business leaders would seem naive and lack credibility, whereas very low levels of pessimism would be a virtue. In the Peace Corps study and in this one, the participants were older than members of the norm group, which might account for their low P scores. However, correlational analyses indicated that age per se probably does not account for the results obtained.

For the measure of innovativeness, the KAI, a significant, but very modest correlation was obtained with P scores ($r = -.27$, $p < .05$). That is, pessimistic leaders tend not to employ innovative problem-solving strategies. For the LPI-Observer measures, which assess the constituents' impressions of their leaders, the data were examined by first obtaining a mean value on each of the five scales of the ratings given by all of a given leader's constituents (typically, 5 or 6, but ranging from 3 to 9). As expected, all five scales were positively correlated with O and negatively with P, but of those correlations, only two were significant: Inspiring a Shared Vision and Encouraging the Heart, both of which correlated with O, again modestly, at $r = .27$ ($p < .05$). Thus, with regard to level, it was P that differentiated these participants from the norm group, and P that was predictive of problem-solving style, whereas O was predictive of the constituents' assessments of their leaders' ability to inspire and encourage. Once more, the results indicate that there is virtue in measuring O and P separately and not combining them into a single measure. Note also that the LPI-Observer scores are the first to correlate with an OP measure that does not emanate from self-report, that is, to tap the impact that one's optimism or pessimism has on close associates, lending what might be called "ecological validity" to the OP instrument.

CONCLUSION

What began as a search for correlates of individual differences in susceptibility to the Pollyanna principle has led to the development of an instrument for measuring optimism and pessimism as separate constructs. The OP instrument has thus far proven to have reasonable psychometric properties vis-à-vis internal consistency and test–retest reliability. It yields means that are quite consistent from study to study, except when special populations are investigated, such as returned Peace Corps volunteers and business leaders. Both of the latter two groups departed from normative values on pessimism, markedly so for the business leaders. The latter were also somewhat more optimistic than the normative population, although the Peace Corps volunteers were not.

Having a separate measure of each construct turns out to be not only psychometrically indicated, because O and P scores are usually only moderately correlated, but also to offer additional predictive use, because the two measures often correlate differentially with other variables.

O and P have been shown to correlate sensibly with both measures of defense mechanisms and of coping style as well as with a variety of personality traits and relevant single-item questionnaire responses. Although such correlations typically are only in the modest-to-moderate range, correlation coefficients in the .60s and .70s have been found between P and measures of anxiety and coping. The OP instrument yields reasonable correlations with other purported measures of optimism and pessimism, that is the LOT and the ASQ, but also contributes unique variance to the prediction of such variables as depression and coping style. Indeed, the P measure generally is the strongest predictor of those variables compared with O, LOT, and ASQ.

There is some evidence that close male friends have highly correlated O, but not P scores, a finding that probably reflects more than a simple like-seeks-like tendency. Why no between-friend correlations on O are found when a female is part of the dyad or when P is the measure being examined remain questions for further research. The developmental-genetic origins of differences in optimistic and pessimistic tendencies need to be further explored, as well as the extent to which O and P are subject to long-term change through success or failure in meeting formidable challenges. It would be instructive to examine optimism and pessimism in people for whom pessimism might be adaptive, such as commercial airline pilots. Finally, there is need for further clarification of the meaning of the two constructs, optimism and pessimism, some of which hopefully will emerge from the several chapters in this volume and some, undoubtedly, from the future work that the volume inspires. Most important, more highly sophisticated studies on the issue of the purported non-bipolarity of optimism and pessimism should be conducted. Additional research is also warranted on the moderating role of optimism and pessimism in the performance of both laboratory tasks and so-called real-world work assignments and especially on the impact of both negative and positive feedback on mood and subsequent performance of optimistic and pessimistic individuals.

REFERENCES

Bantirgu, T. (1995). *Psychological effects of prolonged stress on Ethiopian expatriates in the United States*. Unpublished doctoral dissertation, University of Cincinnati, Ohio.

Beck, A., Ward, C., Mendelson, M., Mock, J., & Erbaugh, J. (1961). An inventory for measuring depression. *Archives of General Psychiatry, 4*, 53–63.

Byrne, D., Barry, J., & Nelson, D. (1963). Relation of the revised repression-sensitization scale to measures of self-description. *Psychological Reports, 13*, 323–334.

Chang, E. C., D'Zurilla, T. J., & Maydeu-Olivares, A. (1994). Assessing the dimensionality of optimism and pessimism using a multi-measure approach. *Cognitive Therapy and Research, 18*, 143–161.

Cronbach, L. J. (1951). Coefficient alpha and the internal structure of tests. *Psychometrika, 16*, 297–335.

Dember, W. N. (1974). Motivation and the cognitive revolution. *American Psychologist, 29*, 161–168.

Dember, W. N. (1989). Cognition, motivation, and emotion: Ideology revisited. In R. R. Hoffman & D. S. Palermo (Eds.), *Cognition and the symbolic processes: Applied and ecological perspectives* (pp. 153–162). Hillsdale, NJ: Erlbaum.

Dember, W. N., & Brooks, J. (1989). A new instrument for measuring optimism and pessimism: Test-retest reliability and relations with happiness and religious commitment. *Bulletin of the Psychonomic Society, 27,* 365–366.

Dember, W. N., Geers, A. L., Reilley, S. P., & Raisman, S. (1995, May). *Optimism, pessimism, friendship, and health.* Poster presented at the annual meeting of the American Psychological Society, New York.

Dember, W. N., Martin, S. H., Hummer, M. K., Howe, S. R., & Melton, R. S. (1989). The measurement of optimism and pessimism. *Current Psychology: Research and Reviews, 8,* 109–119.

Dember, W. N., & Penwell, L. (1980). Happiness, depression, and the Pollyanna principle. *Bulletin of the Psychonomic Society, 15,* 321–323.

Epstein, S., & Meier, P. (1989). Constructive thinking: A broad coping variable with specific components. *Journal of Personality and Social Psychology, 57,* 332–350.

Fischer, M., & Leitenberg, H. (1986). Optimism and pessimism in school-aged children. *Child Development, 57,* 241–248.

Galassi, J. P., Delo, J. S., Galassi, M. D., & Bastien, S. (1974). The college self-expression scale: A measure of assertiveness. *Behavior Therapy, 5,* 165–171.

Geers, A. L., Reilley, S. P., & Dember, W. N. (1998). Optimism, pessimism, and friendship. *Current Psychology: Research and Review, 17,* 3–19.

Geers, A. L., Reilley, S. P., DeRonde, L., & Dember, W. N. (1996, July). *Optimism, pessimism, depression, and coping.* Poster presented at the annual meeting of the American Psychological Society, San Francisco, CA.

Gerety, C. A. (1996). *Admired figures, values and attitudes of returned Peace Corps volunteers.* Master's thesis, University of Cincinnati, Ohio.

Harrigan, J. A., Kues, J. R., Ricks, D. F., & Smith, R. (1984). Moods that predict coming migraine headaches. *Pain, 20,* 385–396.

Helton, W. S., Dember, W. N., & Warm, J. S. (1999). Optimism-pessimism and false failure feedback: Effects on vigilance performance and stress. *Current Psychology: Research and Review, 18,* 311–325.

Hummer, M. K., Dember, W. N., Melton, R. S., & Schefft, B. K. (1992). On the partial independence of optimism and pessimism. *Current Psychology: Research and Reviews, 11,* 37–50.

Ihilevich, D., & Gleser, G. C. (1986). *Defense mechanisms: Their classification, correlates and measurement with the Defense Mechanisms Inventory.* Owosso, MI: DMI Associates.

Kirton, M. (1976). Adaptors and innovators. *Journal of Applied Psychology, 61,* 622–629.

Kouzes, J. M., & Posner, B. Z. (1988). *The leadership practices inventory.* San Diego, CA: Pfeiffer.

Lewis, L. M., Dember, W. N., Schefft, B. K., & Radenhausen, R. A. (1995). Can experimentally induced mood affect optimism and pessimism scores? *Current Psychology: Developmental, Learning, Personality, Social, 14,* 29–41.

Martin, S. H. (1986). *Optimism, pessimism, and psychological defense.* Master's thesis, University of Cincinnati, Ohio.

Matlin, M. W., & Stang, D. J. (1978). *The Pollyanna principle.* Cambridge, MA: Schenkman.

Natali-Alemany, R. (1991). *Moods, coping, and perception of daily life events: Are these factors related to optimism and pessimism?* Doctoral dissertation, University of Cincinnati, Ohio.

Newman, M. K. (1983). *The measurement of optimism/pessimism.* Master's thesis, University of Cincinnati, Ohio.

Peterson, C., & Bossio, L. M. (1991). *Health and optimism.* New York: Free Press.

Peterson, C., Seligman, M. E. P., & Vaillant, G. E. (1988). Pessimistic explanatory style is a risk factor for physical illness: A thirty-five year longitudinal study. *Journal of Personality and Social Psychology, 55,* 23–27.

Peterson, C., Semmel, A., von Bayer, C., Abramson, L. Y., Metalsky, G. I., & Seligman, M. E. P. (1982). The Attributional Style Questionnaire. *Cognitive Therapy and Research, 6,* 287–299.

Peterson, C., & Villanova, P. (1988). An expanded Attributional Style Questionnaire. *Journal of Abnormal Psychology, 97,* 87–89.

Reilley, S. P., & Dember, W. N. (1996, July). *Correlations among friends' scores on optimism, pessimism, loneliness, assertiveness, and sensation seeking.* Poster presented at the annual meeting of the American Psychological Society, San Francisco, CA.

Reilley, S. P., Geers, A. L., Lindsay, D. L., Dember, W. N., & Schafer, J. C. (1998, May). *Disentangling the importance of different optimism-pessimism instruments: Research issues and implications.* Poster presented at the annual meeting of the American Psychological Society, Washington, DC.

Rubenstein, C. M., & Shaver, P. (1992). The experience of loneliness. In L. A. Peplau & D. Perlman (Eds.), *Loneliness: A source book of current theory, research, and therapy* (pp. 206–223). New York: Wiley.

Scheier, M. F., & Carver, C. S. (1985). Optimism, coping, and health: Assessment and implications of generalized outcome expectancies. *Health Psychology, 4,* 219–247.

Seligman, M. E. P. (1990). *Learned optimism.* New York: Knopf.

Sethi, S., & Seligman, M. E. P. (1993). Optimism and fundamentalism. *Psychological Science, 4,* 256–259.

Terezis, H. C. (1990). *Optimism and pessimism: Manipulation via musical mood induction.* Master's thesis, University of Cincinnati, Ohio.

Watson, D., & Clark, L. A. (1984). Negative affectivity: The disposition to experience aversive emotional states. *Psychological Bulletin, 96,* 465–490.

Watson, D., Clark, L. A., & Tellegen, A. (1988). Development and validation of brief measures of positive and negative affect: The PANAS. *Journal of Personality and Social Psychology, 54,* 1063–1070.

Welsh, G. S. (1956). Factor dimensions A and R. In G. S. Welsh & W. G. Dahlstrom (Eds.), *Basic readings on the MMPI in psychology and medicine* (pp. 264–281). Minneapolis, MN: University of Minnesota Press.

Wessman, A. E., & Ricks, D. F. (1966). *Mood and personality.* New York: Holt.

Wunderley, L. J., Reddy, W. B., & Dember, W. N. (1998). Optimism and pessimism in business leaders. *Journal of Applied Social Psychology, 28,* 751–760.

Zautra, A. J., Guarnaccia, C. A., & Dohrenwend, B. P. (1986). Measuring small life events effects. *American Journal of Community Psychology, 14,* 629–655.

Zuckerman, M. (1979). *Sensation seeking: Beyond the optimal level of arousal.* Hillsdale, NJ: Erlbaum.

V

Changes and Treatment

14

BUILDING OPTIMISM AND PREVENTING DEPRESSIVE SYMPTOMS IN CHILDREN

JANE E. GILLHAM, KAREN J. REIVICH, AND ANDREW J. SHATTÉ

Although adult depression is common (estimates are that as many as one in five of us will experience clinical depression in our lifetime), until relatively recently, it was believed that childhood depression was rare. Epidemiological studies indicate that between 2% and 5% of children and adolescents are clinically depressed (Anderson, Williams, McGee, & Silva, 1987; Kovacs, 1989) and as many as 30% of adolescents experience depressive symptoms at any given time (Angold, 1988; Rutter, 1986). Depression in young people seems to be on the rise. Recent findings indicate that as many as 20% of adolescents may experience an episode of clinical depression by the end of high school (Lewinsohn, Hops, Roberts, & Seeley, 1993). Many depressed youth experience a pervasive sense of hopelessness, which in the worst cases can lead to suicide. Each year, 8% of high school students attempt suicide and approximately 13 of every 100,000 adolescents in this country take their own lives (Centers for Disease Control, 1991). Clearly, it is crucial for researchers to increase our understanding of the origins of optimism and depression, and to develop interventions to treat and prevent depressive disorders in children.

Cognitive models of adult depression have been widely researched. In particular, as we discussed earlier, a large body of research indicates that a pessimistic explanatory style and dispositional pessimism are linked to depression in adults (see chap. 3, this volume; see also Beck, 1976; Robins & Hayes, 1995; Scheier & Carver, 1992). Cognitive–behavioral therapy, which targets these cognitive vulnerabilities, is effective in boosting explanatory style, increasing optimism, and treating depression in adults (Beck, Hollon, Young, Bedrosian, & Budenz, 1985; DeRubeis & Hollon, 1995; Ilardi, Craighead, & Evans, 1997; Seligman et al., 1988). In recent research, psychologists have begun to apply cognitive models and interventions to childhood and adolescent depression. In this chapter we review this research in three major sections. First, we provide a brief overview of the cognitive model and of cognitive–behavioral therapy for depression in adulthood. This overview focuses on the relationship of explanatory style and dispositional optimism to depression. Second, we review research on the development of optimism, explanatory style, and depression in children. Developmental and environmental risk factors are discussed, as well as research on the link between optimism and explanatory style and depression in children. In the final section, we describe interventions that may foster optimism and build resilience to depression in children and adolescents. As will be shown, research has not yet provided much knowledge about the origins of explanatory style or optimism, and we have a lot to learn about how to promote resiliency in children. Thus, this chapter outlines an area that is important and exciting for future research.

COGNITIVE MODELS OF DEPRESSION

Cognitive models of depression have in common the emphasis they place on the role of beliefs or interpretations in determining our emotional and behavioral reactions to events. Two types of beliefs that have been widely researched are explanatory style and optimism (for greater discussion of research on explanatory style and depression, see chap. 3, this volume). Briefly, a pessimistic explanatory style and pessimistic expectations are linked to depressive symptoms and depressive disorders in adults. There is some evidence that these variables increase the risk for subsequent depressive symptoms and episodes (Beck, 1976; Robins & Hayes, 1995; Scheier & Carver, 1992). According to the hopelessness theory of depression, explanations and expectations are closely connected (Abramson, Metalsky, & Alloy, 1989). Individuals who attribute setbacks to stable and global factors are more likely to experience pessimism and helplessness following negative life events. Such individuals will believe there is little they can do to change their circumstances and will expect problems to persist over time. According to the hopelessness theory, these individuals will be more vulnerable to developing depression than those with an optimistic explanatory style, particularly to developing a subtype of depression characterized by profound hopelessness and suicidal ideation.

Cognitive–behavioral therapy (CBT) targets the negative interpretations depressed clients often make for events in their lives. Typically, CBT involves two overlapping components: a cognitive-restructuring component and a skill-acquisition component. In the cognitive-restructuring component, clients learn to identify negative interpretations for events and to evaluate these interpretations by considering alternatives and evidence for them. The cognitive component helps individuals to see that setbacks they view as catastrophic are, in fact, often caused by factors that are temporary or changeable. The skill-acquisition component equips individuals with behavioral skills that allow them to more successfully accomplish their goals. Clients learn a variety of skills for coping with difficult emotions and day-to-day problems. Skills typically include relaxation, assertiveness, and procedures for breaking large tasks into manageable components. As clients apply these skills and are able to achieve desired outcomes, they may become increasingly confident and optimistic in their interpretations of events. Thus, both the cognitive restructuring and the behavioral skills appear to be important for boosting explanatory style and optimism.

CBT is effective at treating adult depression (Beck et al., 1985; DeRubeis & Hollon, 1995; Ilardi et al., 1997; Seligman et al., 1988), and has been found to be more effective than pharmacotherapy in preventing relapse (e.g., Evans, Hollon, DeRubeis, & Piasecki, 1992). This is important because recent research indicates that, for many people, depression is a recurrent disorder (Cicchetti & Toth, 1998). Long-term improvement following CBT has been attributed to CBT's focus on providing clients with cognitive and behavioral skills that can be used when problems are encountered in the future, long after therapy has ended. Improvement in explanatory style during cognitive therapy for depression is linked to successful outcome and maintenance of gains (DeRubeis & Hollon, 1995; Ilardi et al., 1997; Seligman et al., 1988). A recent study indicates that CBT can improve explanatory style and prevent depressive symptoms and anxiety in college students at risk for depression (Seligman, Schulman, DeRubeis, & Hollon, 1999).

DEVELOPMENT OF DEPRESSION, OPTIMISM, AND EXPLANATORY STYLE IN CHILDREN

Are cognitive models applicable to depression in children and adolescents? Over the past 15 years, researchers have begun to explore this question.

Before we can fully answer it, however, we need to know the age at which children can experience depression. Not surprisingly, there has been a great deal of debate on this topic (see Bemporad, 1994, for a review). Many psychodynamic theorists postulated that clinical depression required a fully developed superego and sense of self. Thus, depression could not be experienced until adolescence. However, research applying diagnostic criteria to children has revealed that children do experience depression before they reach adolescence. As many as 7–9% of children may experience an episode of depression before the age of 14 (Garrison, Schluchter, Shoenbach, & Kaplan, 1989). Depression in children under 10 appears to be quite rare (Rutter, 1986).

According to Bemporad (1994), depressive disorders rarely occur before middle-to-late childhood. Very young children may experience transient depressive reactions to stressful events, but these reactions subside after these events have ended and endure only when stressors are chronic. Beginning in middle childhood, depressive reactions become increasingly stable and independent of stressful life events. Research indicates that depression increases during the middle school years and is quite common by adolescence (Hankin, Abramson, Moffitt, Silva, & McGee, 1998; Kashani, Rosenberg, & Reid, 1989; Rutter, 1986; but see Nolen-Hoeksema, Girgus, & Seligman, 1992). Cognitive symptoms of depression are absent or rare in preschoolers, but become increasingly common during the elementary school years (Bemporad, 1994; Cicchetti & Toth, 1998). For example, McConville and colleagues found that children's depressive reactions were not characterized by low self-esteem until age 8. Hopelessness did not emerge as a symptom in children until closer to age 10 (McConville, Boag, & Purohit, 1973).

Cognitive Development and Explanatory Style and Optimism

Developmental research suggests that cognitive models of depression become increasingly applicable to children as they develop (Garber & Flynn, 1998). The transition to formal operations, and changes in self-concepts, causal thinking, and thinking about the future may make explanatory style and dispositional optimism especially relevant to depression in children by the beginning of the middle school years.

As children's thinking moves from the preoperational to the concrete operational, and finally, to the formal operational stage, it becomes increasingly governed by abstract schemas or rules (Bemporad, 1994; Inhelder & Piaget, 1958). Although there is considerable debate and inconsistency in research on the age at which formal operations is achieved, interpretations of events may be increasingly driven by cognitive styles such as explanatory style or dispositional optimism as children approach adolescence.

Self-Concepts

Children's self-concepts undergo a dramatic change with development. In preschool and early elementary school, their self-descriptions involve observable characteristics and behaviors (e.g., "I play the piano"). By late childhood, these descriptions are more stable and more likely to involve personality traits and social comparison information (e.g., "I'm a sensitive person, I'm more generous than most people"; Cicchetti & Schneider-Rosen, 1986; Damon & Hart, 1988), characteristics that are less tied to observable behaviors and, therefore, may be more prone to biases (Harter, 1990).

This shift toward more traitlike descriptions is not likely to be a problem for children with positive self-concepts. Unfortunately, however, there is some evidence that children evaluate their abilities more negatively as they move from early to late childhood (e.g., Frey & Ruble, 1987, 1990; Pintrich & Blumenfeld, 1985). For example, Ruble and colleagues (Ruble, Boggiano, Feldman, & Loebl, 1980) found that kindergartners' ratings of their ability were higher than the ratings of second and fourth graders following identical feedback. Pintrich and Blumenfeld (1985) found that second graders rated their academic ability and their behavioral conduct more positively than did sixth graders.

Children's concepts of ability may also change in ways that make their self-concepts more vulnerable. According to Dweck and Leggett (1988), young children tend to believe that ability is a malleable quality. Thus, practice and learning can make one smarter. Older children, in contrast, are more likely to believe ability is a stable quality that cannot change. Intelligence is perceived to be a fixed entity that is revealed through academic performance and achievement. Similarly, Langer and Park (1990) propose that young children are taught to attribute failure to precompetence ("I haven't learned this yet"), and older children are taught to attribute failure to incompetence ("I'm not able to do this").

The research on children's self-concepts and conceptions of ability has important implications for the development of explanatory style and optimism. It suggests that older children may be more likely than younger children to attribute problems to personality flaws that are stable and global. If this is true, positive outcomes will seem less likely and more difficult to attain.

Causal Attributions

Older children may be more prone than younger children to making causal attributions. Piaget (1926, 1959) reported that children under the age of 6 or 7 were rarely concerned with the causes of events, and frequently had difficulty expressing causal relationships. For example, in a 1926 study, he asked 6–10-year-old children to finish incomplete sentences that stopped at the word *because* (e.g., "The man fell off his bicycle because—"). Young children frequently had difficulty completing these sentences and tended to give responses involving expectations or predictions (e.g., "he broke his arm"; Piaget, 1926).

We do not yet know the ages at which explanatory style becomes stable or first can be measured. Children can complete paper-and-pencil measures of explanatory style beginning at about 8 years of age (Nolen-Hoeksema et al., 1992). Little research exists on explanatory style in younger children. Nolen-Hoeksema (1986) attempted to assess explanatory style in preschool children using interviews. Similar to Piaget's findings, the findings in her study revealed that preschoolers rarely gave causal explanations for events. Instead, they talked about solutions and expectations. It is interesting to note that a focus on solutions, rather than on causes, may protect young children from hopelessness and helplessness. Dweck and Leggett (1988) found that elementary school children who are prone to helplessness (who give up following failure) attribute their failures to stable and global causes (e.g., "I'm stupid"). In contrast, children who display persistence when challenged focus on solutions (e.g., "I need to try harder"). Thus, persistent children are less likely to describe causes for failure; although it can be argued that their solutions imply unstable and specific causes (e.g., "I didn't try hard enough").

Thinking About the Future

Thinking about the future becomes increasingly sophisticated as children approach adolescence. They are more able to think about long-term goals and to consider alternative possibilities for the future (Bemporad, 1994; Keating, 1980). Yet, Bemporad argues that adolescents don't have the life experience necessary to put negative events into context. Thus, they may frequently catastrophize, believing that consequences of negative events will endure through time. For example, a poor grade on a geometry exam may be taken as evidence that pursuing a career in math or science is hopeless. If a child's explanatory style becomes increasingly pessimistic with development, we should expect that his or her dispositional pessimism will also increase, because our predictions about the future in part stem from the causal attributions we make (Abramson et al., 1989). Consistent with this hypothesis, hopelessness has been found to be a common symptom of depression in adolescence (McConville et al., 1973).

Link Between Pessimistic Interpretive Styles and Depression

Recent research indicates that cognitive models are applicable to depression in children at least by late childhood. Children with depressive symptoms report lower self-esteem, greater hopelessness, and more pessimistic explanatory styles than do children who do not suffer from these symptoms (for reviews, see Garber, Quiggle, & Shanley, 1990; Gladstone & Kaslow, 1995; Joiner & Wagner, 1995a; Kaslow, Brown, & Mee, 1994). It is not yet clear whether pessimism and a pessimistic explanatory style are causes or simply covariates of depression. Nolen-Hoeksema and colleagues have found that explanatory style predicts future symptoms of depression (Nolen-Hoeksema, Girgus, & Seligman, 1986, 1992). However, Hammen and colleagues found that explanatory style did not predict depressive symptoms in children (Hammen, Adrian, & Hiroto, 1988; for reviews see Gladstone & Kaslow, 1995; Joiner & Wagner, 1995a). The relationship between explanatory style and depressive symptoms may change over time. In one longitudinal study of children as they moved from third through eighth grade, young children's depressive symptoms were predicted by life events alone (and not by explanatory style). Once children reached sixth grade, explanatory style began to predict depressive symptoms (Nolen-Hoeksema et al., 1992).

McCauley and colleagues studied explanatory style in children from ages 7–17 (McCauley, Mitchell, Burke, & Moss, 1988). Consistent with the predictions above, the study showed that explanatory style became increasingly pessimistic over this time period. In our research, we found that explanatory style grew increasingly pessimistic in a sample of children followed for 3 ½ years from the beginning of middle school to the beginning of high school (Gillham & Reivich, 1999a). Curiously, depressive symptoms did not increase significantly over this time period, although they have been found to increase in other studies (Kashani et al., 1989, Rutter, 1986). In contrast to our findings and to those reported by McCauley and colleagues, Garber and colleagues found no significant change in pessimistic interpretive styles from seventh through twelfth grade (Garber, Weiss, & Shanley, 1993).

Taken together, these findings suggest cognitive factors implicated in adult depression become increasingly relevant in children, especially as they approach adolescence. Early adolescence may be an important window during which to target explanatory style and optimism.

Environmental Risk Factors

Of course, as Cicchetti and Toth (1998) point out, depression cannot be explained by developmental changes alone. Although a substantial minority of adolescents will experience a depressive episode, most are resilient. A variety of environmental risk factors for depression have been proposed, including parental depression and psychopathology, marital conflict, poverty, and other life stressors (for reviews, see Cicchetti & Toth. 1998; Downy

& Coyne, 1990). All these factors are likely to affect children's explanatory style, levels of optimism, and, in turn, their depressive symptoms.

Little is known about the origins of optimism or explanatory style (see Garber & Flynn, 1998 for a recent review of literature on the origins of cognitive styles). Psychologists have suggested that children learn interpretive styles from the important adults in their lives. Parents may instill optimistic or pessimistic styles through modeling or through the way they habitually explain events in their children's lives (Seligman, Reivich, Jaycox, & Gillham, 1995). They may reinforce certain types of interpretations made by their children. Only a handful of studies have investigated the relationship between parents and children's styles for interpreting events. These have yielded conflicting findings. In some studies, parent and child explanatory styles converge. In others, no correlation is found (for a review, see Joiner & Wagner, 1995b). Dweck and colleagues have proposed that children may internalize the attributions made by their teachers regarding their failures and successes (Dweck, Davidson, Nelson, & Enna, 1978). These researchers found that girls gave more pessimistic explanations for their failures than did boys, and that this difference was consistent with a discrepancy in the attributions teachers gave for failure in male versus female students (Dweck et al., 1978).

Negative life events or stressors may also predispose children to a pessimistic explanatory style. Early helplessness experiments demonstrated that exposure to uncontrollable aversive events leads to passivity and depressive symptoms in humans and other animals. Conversely, control and mastery experiences protect against helplessness (e.g., Seligman, 1975). Children who grow up in poverty, who are exposed repeatedly to violence or intense marital conflict, or who are exposed to chronic parental mental illness, and who repeatedly experience failure may be more prone to developing a pessimistic explanatory style. Consistent with this hypothesis, pessimistic interpretive styles have been linked to previous experience of life stressors, including parental conflict (Nolen-Hoeksema, Girgus, & Seligman, 1986), maternal psychopathology (Garber & Robinson, 1997), and a history of child abuse (Gold, 1986; Kaufman, 1991).

PROMOTING OPTIMISTIC INTERPRETIVE STYLES AND PREVENTING DEPRESSIVE SYMPTOMS IN CHILDREN

Can interventions that promote optimism and reduce depression in adults be applied effectively to children? Are cognitive–behavioral therapies effective with children? In the remainder of this chapter, we explore these questions. We begin with a discussion of cognitive–behavioral interventions that have been used to treat helplessness and depression in children, including reattribution training and CBT. We then discuss the Penn Optimism Program, designed to prevent depressive symptoms in middle school children. Finally, we conclude with some speculations about other methods through which optimism and an optimistic explanatory style can be promoted, especially in younger children.

Attribution Retraining

Attribution retraining is a technique that has been used primarily to improve students' persistence following failure on academic tasks (Craske, 1985; Dweck, 1975; Fowler & Peterson, 1981; for reviews see Cecil & Medway, 1986; Forsterling, 1985). In the typical intervention, children are taught to attribute failure to lack of effort (an unstable and specific—or more optimistic—cause) rather than to lack of ability (a stable and global—or more pessimistic—cause). In some studies, adults model the new explanations, and in others, adults correct the pessimistic explanations and reward the optimistic explanations that children make. Attribution retraining has been found to increase children's persistence on math problems (Craske, 1988; Okolo, 1992) and on reading assignments (Fowler & Peterson, 1981). Attribution retraining has also been extended to other types of difficulties. For example, Aydin (1988) used attribution retraining to improve social competence in children. Children in the intervention group were taught to attribute social failures to a lack of effort, and members of this intervention group improved significantly in explanatory style and acceptance by peers. In contrast, there was no change in explanatory style or peer acceptance in members of a control group. Attribution retraining has also been used to improve athletic performance in adolescents (e.g., Miserandino, 1998).

Most attribution retraining interventions are much less cognitively demanding than the cognitive-restructuring component of CBT. Studies using this technique typically teach children to substitute one attribution ("I didn't try hard enough") for another ("I don't have the ability"). Children are not explicitly taught to rigorously evaluate the accuracy of their interpretations of events. One advantage of attribution retraining is that it may be accessible to younger children. It has been used with 8- and 9-year-olds (e.g., Dweck, 1975; Fowler & Peterson, 1981) and with children with mental retardation (Turner, Dofney, & Dutka, 1997). The technique may be fragile, however, because new beliefs are not necessarily more realistic than the ones they replace. Optimistic attributions may be hard to maintain if children are repeatedly confronted with evidence indicating these attributions are not accurate. Little is known about the long-term effects of attribution retraining programs or their effects on depressive symptoms.

Cognitive–Behavioral Therapy

The cognitive restructuring component of CBT is quite demanding and requires metacognition (thinking about thinking), consideration of alternative possibilities, and hypothesis testing—abilities that characterize formal operations (adolescent and adult thought; Inhelder & Piaget, 1958; Keating, 1980). It is perhaps not surprising then that CBT has been found to be effective in treating and preventing adolescent depression (e.g., Clarke et al., 1995; Clarke, Rohde, Lewinsohn, Hops, & Seeley, 1999; for reviews see Gillham, Shatté, & Freres, in press; Kaslow & Thompson, 1998). For example, Clarke and colleagues found that an intervention based on CBT significantly prevented depressive symptoms and depressive episodes in a sample of adolescents at risk for depression. It is impressive that the prevention effects lasted through 12 months of follow-up (Clarke et al., 1995).

Recent studies suggest that CBT also may be effective in reducing depressive symptoms in middle school age children (see Kaslow & Thompson, 1998). It is important to note that interventions used with younger children frequently place less emphasis on cognitive-restructuring techniques. Thus, positive effects of some interventions may be due to the acquisition of behavioral, rather than of cognitive, skills. Researchers need to evaluate the effectiveness of the individual components of these programs.

Penn Optimism Program

Given the evidence that depressive symptoms increase over the middle school years and then rise dramatically in high school (see Hankin et al., 1998; Rutter, 1986), we were interested in investigating whether CBT can prevent depressive symptoms before children reach high school. With this goal in mind, we developed the Penn Optimism Program (POP), a school-based program based on adult CBT. POP is a 12-session, manualized intervention. Children participate in POP in groups of approximately 8–12 students, either after school or during the school day. Groups are led by school teachers, guidance counselors, and advanced graduate students in clinical psychology. The program is described briefly below (for more detailed descriptions, see Seligman et al., 1995; Shatté, Gillham, & Reivich, in press).

Cognitive Restructuring

As in adult CBT, POP involves both cognitive restructuring and skill acquisition. Middle school students are (at least in theory) at the cusp of formal operations and are not as skilled as adolescents at tasks that require hypothesis testing and evaluation of their own thinking. Therefore, a variety of techniques are used to make the cognitive-restructuring techniques accessible and engaging. Skits, stories, role-plays and cartoons are used to introduce and emphasize concepts.

The cognitive-restructuring component begins with the cognitive model of emotion and behavior (Beck, 1976; Ellis, 1962). Students learn that feelings and behaviors are due in large part to the way they think about events that happen to them. The link between thoughts and feelings is introduced using cartoons. For example, in one set of worksheets, students are asked to generate the beliefs that would lead to a given behavioral or emotional consequence (see Figure 14.1). For homework, they write about situations in their own lives, using the cartoon format to illustrate their beliefs and the resulting feelings and behaviors.

POP then teaches children about optimistic versus pessimistic styles of interpreting events. Skits are used to illustrate the types of thoughts that characterize pessimistic and optimistic styles, and the consequences of these styles. For example, in one set of skits two characters, Gloomy Greg and Hopeful Holly, attend a school dance. Both children ask peers to dance with them, and both are rejected. However, they respond quite differently to this rejection. Greg attributes the event to stable, and global causes ("I'm a loser," "No one likes me") and makes pessimistic predictions (e.g., "No one will ever dance with me," "I'll never have any fun at dances"). Consequently, he feels dejected and hopeless. He sits down on the bench for the rest of the evening and has a miserable time. Holly, in contrast, attributes the event to causes that are more unstable and specific (e.g., "Maybe I

Figure 14.1. The link between thoughts and feelings.

wasn't polite enough," "Maybe he promised someone else this dance," "Maybe that boy doesn't like me"). The predictions she makes are more hopeful. She asks other peers to dance and, eventually, finds a partner and has fun at the party. In POP, children learn that pessimistic styles can make them feel sad and give up on goals, even when these goals are, in fact, achievable. Cartoon worksheets are also used to give children practice with the concept of interpretive styles. Children are given cartoons that depict pessimistic interpretations and are instructed to rewrite the cartoons with more optimistic attributions and predictions.

Although we focus on explanatory style and optimism, POP's goal is not simply to teach "positive thinking." The goal is realistic thinking. We have found that many children are reflexive pessimists; they habitually interpret events pessimistically and often this pessimism seems to exceed what is warranted given the situation. The third step in the cognitive-restructuring component, therefore, is to teach children a variety of techniques for thinking accurately about problems. Children learn to evaluate their beliefs by considering evidence for and against them. They learn to generate alternative interpretations, to evaluate these alternatives, and to identify those interpretations that are most accurate. We use a detective analogy to illustrate this process. Problems are compared to crimes. A good detective, like Sherlock Holmes, solves a crime by listing a variety of suspects (initial belief plus alternatives) and looking for clues (evaluates evidence) for each one. Bad detectives, in contrast, conclude that the first suspect they consider (initial belief) must be guilty, without evaluating the evidence. Once they understand the process, children practice this skill frequently during sessions and for homework over the course of the program.

Middle school and high school students with depressive symptoms often catastrophize about problems. That is, they believe that terrible outcomes are likely to occur following negative events and that these outcomes will endure. For example, after an embarrassing experience at school, a child may become convinced that she will be ridiculed by most of her peers for the remainder of the school year. She may imagine that even her closest friends will come to reject her, and that she will have no one to talk to or socialize with when she begins high school next year. This type of thinking process leads to considerable anxiety and hopelessness. The story of Chicken Little is useful for illustrating the consequences of catastrophic thinking, and "Don't be a Chicken Little" is a slogan that is used throughout the program. To counter catastrophic thinking, participants are taught to consider other possible outcomes of the situation. In the "worst-best-most likely" procedure, children first list the disastrous outcomes they fear. Then, they are encouraged to list the best possible outcomes they can imagine for the situation. These best outcomes are often equally unlikely and equally extreme. For example, a fantastic outcome for the above situation may be that other children in the school feel sympathetic toward the girl and, as a result, invite her to many parties. She becomes the most popular girl in the school and enters high school with everyone fighting to be her friend. Considering the positive extreme helps children realize that the disasters they imagine are also unlikely to occur. The next step in this process is for children to list several outcomes that are more likely, to evaluate these outcomes, and to select those that seem most realistic given the situation (e.g., Several of the girl's peers will tease her over the next week or so). Once they have identified the most likely outcomes, they are taught how to plan for and deal with the negative aspects of these outcomes.

Skill Acquisition

Although cognitive skills provide hope that problems will dissipate and that change is possible, they do not provide the skills required to effect that change. The second half of the program teaches skills that can be used to solve a variety of problems, including emotion-control techniques, relaxation, assertiveness and negotiation techniques, and a method for countering procrastination. In addition, students learn an approach to problem solving that involves generating a variety of possible solutions for problems they encounter and then evaluating these solutions and deciding between them. This process may be especially helpful in counteracting hopelessness, because children learn that usually there are a variety of paths through which positive outcomes can be achieved. As with the cognitive component, techniques are introduced through skits, stories, and cartoon characters (e.g., "Say-it-straight Samantha") that illustrate specific skills. Students are encouraged to role-play possible solutions in the group and to practice the skill for homework between sessions.

Research on POP

In our first study of POP, fifth and sixth graders were identified as at-risk for depression based on reports of parental conflict and current depressive symptoms. The 69 children who participated in the intervention were compared with a matched control group of children. Initial results indicated that POP significantly improved explanatory style and reduced depressive symptoms (Jaycox, Reivich, Gillham, & Seligman, 1994). These effects endured through a 2-year follow-up period (Gillham, Reivich, Jaycox, & Seligman, 1995). There was a dramatic reduction in reports of moderate-to-severe levels of depressive symptoms across the 2-year follow-up period. For example, at the 2-year follow-up, 44% of control participants reported moderate-to-severe levels of symptoms as compared with only 22% of POP participants. Mediational analyses suggested that improvements in explanatory style were, in part, responsible for the program's effect on depressive symptoms. It is important to note that data from 2½- and 3-year follow-ups indicate the prevention effect for depressive symptoms was no longer significant (Gillham & Reivich, 1999b), suggesting that booster sessions may be important for long-term prevention of depression.

This study had several methodological limitations, including the lack of random assignment to condition and reliance on self-report measures. In addition, there was no test of treatment specificity. Thus, it is possible that POP's effects were due to social support or other factors not specific to CBT. Research that addresses these limitations is currently underway. Gillham and Seligman (1999) recently completed a study in which children were randomly assigned to POP or a control group. The children participating in this study were followed for 12 months after POP groups ended. POP participants reported improvements in explanatory style and depressive symptoms following the intervention. There was some evidence that POP prevented depressive symptoms over the follow-up period. Although average levels of depressive symptoms were not significantly different at 6 or 12 months, peak levels of symptoms across the follow-up were significantly lower in POP participants than in participants of the control group. Current studies are underway to investigate POP's effectiveness relative to other interventions, the effects of POP on children's behavior as observed by parents and teachers, and POP's ability to prevent clinical diagnoses of depression.

Building the Foundation for an Optimistic Explanatory Style

CBT offers promise as a means of boosting optimism and explanatory style, and as a means of preventing depression in late childhood and adolescence. However, there are many other possible paths through which optimistic interpretive styles can be promoted, and these may be effective for young children as well. If children learn optimism and explanatory style from adults, a powerful intervention may be to boost explanatory style in parents and teachers. Children's explanatory style may benefit when their depressed parents participate in CBT, for example, or when their teachers are educated about the effects of attributing failure to lack of ability. If uncontrollable stressors breed pessimism, therapeutic and societal interventions that target violence, abuse, parental psychopathology, and poverty may promote optimistic styles in children. If repeated failure leads children to attribute events to permanent causes and to expect continued failure, they may benefit from interventions that improve their academic, athletic, artistic, social, and other skills. Finally, providing children with control and mastery experiences may help lay the foundation for an optimistic interpretive style. By facing challenges, struggling, and, eventually, succeeding, children may learn to view even large problems as temporary and changeable. All of these paths should increase children's resiliency.

SUMMARY AND CONCLUSION

In summary, analysis of recent research suggests that depressive symptoms and depressive disorders are common during middle school and rise dramatically during the high school years (Angold, 1988; Hankin et al., 1998; Lewinsohn et al., 1993). Cognitive vulnerabilities, such as a pessimistic explanatory style or dispositional pessimism, that are implicated in adult depression are relevant to childhood depression at least by the end of elementary school or beginning of middle school. Our interpretation of these findings suggests that the middle school years offer an important window for intervention programs. We are encouraged by recent research indicating that CBT techniques effective in treating adult depression can also be used to foster an optimistic explanatory style and prevent depressive symptoms in children. Despite these findings, researchers still know very little about the origins of optimistic interpretive styles or how to build these styles in children. It is likely that there are many pathways through which optimistic styles can be fostered in children. Discovering these pathways is an important and exciting area for future research.

REFERENCES

Abramson, L. Y., Metalsky, G. I., & Alloy, L. B. (1989). Hopelessness depression: A theory-based subtype of depression. *Psychological Review, 96*, 358–372.

Anderson, J., Williams, S., McGee, R., & Silva, P. A. (1987). The prevalence of DSM-III diagnoses in a large sample of pre-adolescent children from the general population. *Archives of General Psychiatry, 44*, 69–76.

Angold, A. (1988). Childhood and adolescent depression: I. Epidemiological and aetiological aspects. *British Journal of Psychiatry, 152*, 601–617.

Aydin, G. (1988). The remediation of children's helpless explanatory style and related unpopularity. *Cognitive Therapy and Research, 12*, 155–165.

Beck, A. T. (1976). *Cognitive therapy and the emotional disorders*. New York: International Universities Press.

Beck, A. T., Hollon, S. D., Young, J. E., Bedrosian, R. C., & Budenz, D. (1985). Treatment of depression with cognitive therapy and amitriptyline. *Archives of General Psychiatry, 42*, 142–148.

Bemporad, J. R. (1994). Dynamic and interpersonal theories of depression. In W. M. Reynolds & H. F. Johnson (Eds.), *Handbook of depression in children and adolescents* (pp. 81–95). New York: Plenum Press.

Cecil, M. A., & Medway, F. J. (1986). Attribution retraining with low achieving and learned helpless children. *Techniques, 2,* 173–181.

Centers for Disease Control. (1991). Attempted suicide among high school students—United States. 1990. *Morbidity and Mortality Weekly Report, 40,* 633–635.

Cicchetti, D., & Schneider-Rosen, K. (1986). An organizational approach to childhood depression. In M. Rutter, C. E. Izard, & P. B. Read (Eds.), *Depression in young people: Developmental and clinical perspectives* (pp. 71–134). New York: Guilford Press.

Cicchetti, D., & Toth, S. L. (1998). The development of depression in children and adolescents. *American Psychologist, 53,* 221–242.

Clarke, G. N., Hawkins, W., Murphy, M., Sheeber, L., Lewinsohn, P. M., & Seeley, J. (1995). Targeted prevention of unipolar depressive disorder in an at-risk sample of high school adolescents: A randomized trial of a group cognitive intervention. *Journal of the American Academy of Child and Adolescent Psychiatry, 34*(3), 312–321.

Clarke, G. N., Rohde, P., Lewinsohn, P. M., Hops, H., & Seeley, J. R. (1999). Cognitive-behavioral treatment of adolescent depression: Efficacy of acute group treatment and booster sessions. *Journal of the American Academy of Child and Adolescent Psychiatry, 38,* 272–279.

Craske, M. (1985). Improving persistence through observational learning and attribution retraining. *British Journal of Educational Psychology, 55,* 138–147.

Craske, M. (1988). Learned helplessness, self-worth motivation and attribution retraining for primary school children. *British Journal of Educational Psychology, 58,* 152–164.

Damon, W., & Hart, D. (1988). *Self-understanding in childhood and adolescence.* New York: Cambridge University Press.

DeRubeis, R. J., & Hollon, S. D. (1995). Explanatory style in the treatment of depression. In G. M. Buchanan & M. E. P. Seligman (Eds.), *Explanatory style* (pp. 99–112). Hillsdale, NJ: Erlbaum.

Downey, G., & Coyne, J. C. (1990). Children of depressed parents: An integrative review. *Psychological Bulletin, 108,* 50–76.

Dweck, C. S. (1975). The role of expectations and attributions in the alleviation of learned helplessness. *Journal of Personality and Social Psychology, 31,* 674–685.

Dweck, C. S., Davidson, W., Nelson, S., & Enna, B. (1978). Sex differences in learned helplessness: II. The contingencies of evaluative feedback in the classroom, and III. An experimental analysis. *Developmental Psychology, 14,* 268–276.

Dweck, C. S., & Leggett, E. L. (1988). A social-cognitive approach to motivation and personality. *Psychological Review, 95,* 256–273.

Ellis, A. (1962). *Reason and emotion in psychotherapy.* New York: Lyle Stuart.

Evans, M. D., Hollon, S. D., DeRubeis, R. J., & Piasecki, J. M. (1992). Differential relapse following cognitive therapy and pharmacotherapy for depression. *Archives of General Psychiatry, 49,* 802–808.

Forsterling, F. (1985). Attribution retraining: A review. *Psychological Bulletin, 98,* 495–512.

Fowler, J. W., & Peterson, P. L. (1981). Increasing reading persistence and altering attributional style of learned helpless children. *Journal of Educational Psychology, 73,* 251–260.

Frey, K. S., & Ruble, D. N. (1987). What children say about classroom performance: Sex and grade differences in perceived competence. *Child Development, 58,* 1066–1078.

Frey, K. S., & Ruble, D. N. (1990). Strategies for comparative evaluation: Maintaining a sense of competence across the life span. In R. J. Sternberg & J. Kolligian (Eds.), *Competence considered* (pp. 167–189). New Haven, CT: Yale University Press.

Garber, J., & Flynn, C. (1998). Origins of depressive cognitive style. In D. K. Routh & R. J. DeRubeis (Eds.), *The science of clinical psychology: Accomplishments and future directions* (pp. 53–93). Washington, DC: American Psychological Association.

Garber, J., Quiggle, N., & Shanley, N. (1990). Cognitions and depression in children and adolescents. In R. E. Ingram (Ed.), *Contemporary psychological approaches to depression* (pp. 87–115). New York: Plenum Press.

Garber, J., & Robinson, N. S. (1997). Cognitive vulnerability in children at risk for depression. *Cognition and Emotion, 11,* 619–635.

Garber, J., Weiss, B., & Shanley, N. (1993). Cognitions, depressive symptoms, and development in adolescents. *Journal of Abnormal Psychology, 102,* 47–57.

Garrison, C. Z., Schluchter, M. D., Schoenbach, V. J., & Kaplan, B. K. (1989). Epidemiology of depressive symptoms in young adolescents. *Journal of the American Academy of Child and Adolescent Psychiatry, 28,* 343–351.

Gillham, J. E., & Reivich, K. J. (1999a). Depressive symptoms through the middle school years. Unpublished manuscript, University of Pennsylvania, Philadelphia.

Gillham, J. E., & Reivich, K. J. (1999b). Prevention of depressive symptoms in school children: A research update. *Psychological Science, 10,* 461–462.

Gillham, J. E., Reivich, K. J., Jaycox, L. H., & Seligman, M. E. P. (1995). Prevention of depressive symptoms in schoolchildren: Two-year follow-up. *Psychological Science, 6,* 343–351.

Gillham, J. E., & Seligman, M. E. P. (1999). School-based prevention of depressive symptoms in children. Does including parents help? Unpublished manuscript, University of Pennsylvania, Philadelphia.

Gillham, J. E., Shatté, A. J., & Freres, D. R. (2000). Preventing depression: A review of cognitive-behavioral and family interventions. *Applied and Preventive Psychology, 9* 63–88.

Gladstone, T. R. G., & Kaslow, N. J. (1995). Depression and attributions in children and adolescents: A meta-analytic review. *Journal of Abnormal Child Psychology, 23,* 597–606.

Gold, E. R. (1986). Long-term effects of sexual victimization in childhood: An attributional approach. *Journal of Consulting and Clinical Psychology, 54,* 471–475.

Hammen, C., Adrian, C., & Hiroto, D. (1988). A longitudinal test of the attributional vulnerability model in children at risk for depression. *British Journal of Clinical Psychology, 27,* 37–46.

Hankin, B. L., Abramson, L. Y., Moffitt, T. E., Silva, P. A., & McGee, R. (1998). Development of depression from preadolescence to young adulthood: Emerging gender differences in a 10-year longitudinal study. *Journal of Abnormal Psychology, 107,* 128–140.

Harter, S. (1990). Developmental differences in the nature of self-representations: Implications for the understanding, assessment, and treatment of maladaptive behavior. *Cognitive Therapy and Research, 14,* 113–142.

Ilardi, S. S., Craighead, E. W., & Evans, D. D. (1997). Modeling relapse in unipolar depression: The effects of dysfunctional cognitions and personality disorders. *Journal of Consulting and Clinical Psychology, 65,* 381–391.

Inhelder, B., & Piaget, J. (1958). *The growth of logical thinking from childhood to adolescence.* New York: Basic Books.

Jaycox, L. H., Reivich, K. J., Gillham, J. E., & Seligman, M. E. P. (1994). Prevention of depressive symptoms in school children. *Behaviour Research and Therapy, 32,* 801–816.

Joiner, T. E., & Wagner, K. D. (1995a). Attributional style and depression in children and adolescents: A meta-analytic review. *Clinical Psychology Review, 15,* 777–798.

Joiner, T. E., & Wagner, K. D. (1995b). Parental, child-centered attributions and outcome: A meta-analytic review with conceptual and methodological implications. *Journal of Abnormal Child Psychology, 24,* 37–52.

Kashani, J. H., Rosenberg, R. K., & Reid, J. C. (1989). Developmental perspectives in child and adolescent depressive symptoms in a community sample. *American Journal of Psychiatry, 141,* 1397–1402.

Kaslow, N. J., Brown, R. T., & Mee, L. L. (1994). Cognitive and behavioral correlates of childhood depression: A developmental perspective. In W. M. Reynolds & H. F. Johnston (Eds.), *Handbook of depression in children and adolescents: Issues in clinical child psychology* (pp. 97–121). New York: Plenum Press.

Kaslow, N. J., & Thompson, M. P. (1998). Applying the criteria for empirically supported treatments to studies of psychosocial interventions for child and adolescent depression. *Journal of Clinical Child Psychology, 27,* 146–155.

Kaufman, J. (1991). Depressive disorders in maltreated children. *Journal of the American Academy of Child and Adolescent Psychiatry, 30,* 257–265.

Keating, D. P. (1980). Thinking process in adolescence. In J. Adelson (Ed.), *Handbook of adolescent psychology* (pp. 211–246). New York: Wiley & Sons.

Kovacs, M. (1989). Affective disorders in children and adolescents. *American Psychologist, 44*, 209–215.

Langer, E. J., & Park, K. (1990). Incompetence: A conceptual reconsideration. In R. J. Sternberg & J. Kolligian (Eds.), *Competence considered* (pp. 149–166). New Haven, CT: Yale University Press.

Lewinsohn, P. M., Hops, H., Roberts, R., & Seeley, J. (1993). Adolescent psychopathology: I. Prevalence and incidence of depression and other DSM-III-R disorders in high school students. *Journal of Abnormal Psychology, 102*, 110–120.

McCauley, E., Mitchell, J. R., Burke, P., & Moss, S. (1988). Cognitive attributes of depression in children and adolescents. *Journal of Consulting and Clinical Psychology, 56*, 903–908.

McConville, B. J., Boag, L. C., & Purohit, A. P. (1973). Three types of childhood depression. *Canadian Psychiatric Association Journal, 18*, 133–137.

Miserandino, M. (1998). Attribution retraining as a method of improving athletic performance. *Journal of Sport Behavior, 21*, 286–297.

Nolen-Hoeksema, S. (1986). Developmental studies of explanatory style and learned helplessness in children. Unpublished doctoral dissertation, University of Pennsylvania, Philadelphia.

Nolen-Hoeksema, S., Girgus, J. S., & Seligman, M. E. P. (1986). Depression in children of families in turmoil. Unpublished manuscript, University of Pennsylvania, Philadelphia.

Nolen-Hoeksema, S., Girgus, J. S., & Seligman, M. E. P. (1992). Predictors and consequences of childhood depressive symptoms: A five-year longitudinal study. *Journal of Abnormal Psychology, 101*, 405–422.

Okolo, C. M. (1992). The effects of computer-based attribution retraining on the attributions, persistence, and mathematics computation of students with learning disabilities. *Journal of Learning Disabilities, 25*, 327–334.

Piaget, J. (1926). *Judgment and reasoning in the child.* New York: Harcourt, Brace & World.

Piaget, J. (1959). *The language and thought of the child.* New York: Basic Books.

Pintrich, P. R., & Blumenfeld, P. C. (1985). Classroom experience and children's self-perceptions of ability, effort, and conduct. *Journal of Educational Psychology, 77*, 646–657.

Robins, C. J., & Hayes, A. M. (1995). The role of causal attributions in the prediction of depression. In G. M. Buchanan & M. E. P. Seligman (Eds.), *Explanatory style* (pp. 71–98). Hillsdale, NJ: Erlbaum.

Ruble, D. N., Boggiano, A. K., Feldman, N. S., & Loebl, J. H. (1980). Developmental analysis of the role of social comparison in self-evaluation. *Developmental Psychology, 16*, 105–115.

Rutter, M. (1986). The developmental psychopathology of depression. In M. Rutter, C. E. Izard, & P. B. Read (Eds.), *Depression in young people: Developmental and clinical perspectives* (pp. 3–30). New York: Guilford Press.

Scheier, M. F., & Carver, C. S. (1992). Effects of optimism on psychological and physical well-being: Theoretical overview and empirical update. *Cognitive Therapy and Research, 16,* 201–228.

Seligman, M. E. P. (1975). Helplessness: On depression, development, and death. San Francisco: W. H. Freeman & Co.

Seligman, M. E. P., Castellon, C., Cacciola, J., Schulman, P., Luborsky, L., Ollove, M., & Downing, R. (1988). Explanatory style change during cognitive therapy for unipolar depression. *Journal of Abnormal Psychology, 97,* 13–18.

Seligman, M. E. P., Reivich, K. J., Jaycox, L. H., & Gillham, J. (1995). *The optimistic child.* New York: Houghton-Mifflin.

Seligman, M. E. P., Schulman, P., DeRubeis, R. J., & Hollon, S. D. (1999). The prevention of depression and anxiety. *Prevention & Treatment, 2,* 8, journals.apa.org.

Shatté, A. J., Gillham, J. E., & Reivich, K. J. (in press). Promoting hope in children and adolescents. In J. E. Gillham (Ed.), *The science of optimism and hope: Essays in honor of Martin E. P. Seligman.* Radnor, PA: Templeton Foundation Press.

Turner, L. A., Dofny, E. M., & Dutka, S. (1997). Effect of strategy and attribution training on strategy maintenance and transfer. *American Journal on Mental Retardation, 98,* 445–454.

15

OPTIMISM, PESSIMISM, AND PSYCHOTHERAPY: IMPLICATIONS FOR CLINICAL PRACTICE

JAMES L. PRETZER AND CHAILLE A. WALSH

Art, a 43-year-old engineer who has never had a long-term romantic relationship, is anticipating an upcoming date. In discussing his anticipations with his therapist (the first author) he reports thinking, "What will I have to say? She'll think I'm boring. I don't have anything to offer." He feels anxious, discouraged, and depressed. When he has experienced these thoughts and feelings in the past he has typically postponed, canceled, or avoided social interactions, and this avoidance has prolonged his social anxiety and isolation.

Art is quite pessimistic regarding his upcoming date. In fact, his thinking regarding a wide range of social interactions is consistently pessimistic. This pessimism plays an important role in perpetuating Art's problems with relationships. Because he anticipates that social interactions will go badly and will accomplish little, he usually fails to initiate them and thus remains isolated. In addition, the growing body of research on the impact of optimism and pessimism in many areas of life (as discussed throughout this volume) suggests that Art's pessimism may have effects that extend far beyond his love life. Should Art's therapist focus narrowly on reducing his social anxiety and avoidance, address his pessimism as well, or is it more important to address his pessimism than to focus on specific concerns about social interactions? If his therapist chooses to address Art's pessimism to some extent, how can this be accomplished? How will the therapist effectively modify Art's pessimistic outlook? This chapter will address the question of whether it is useful to modify adults' positive and negative expectancies and will present a cognitive–behavioral approach to increasing optimism.

A number of cognitive–behavioral approaches to psychotherapy have emphasized the importance of negative thoughts in understanding and treating many forms of psychopathology. In particular, Beck's Cognitive Therapy (A. T. Beck, Rush, Shaw, & Emery, 1979) is known for its emphasis on identifying and modifying negative thoughts and has received substantial empirical support (see DeRubeis & Crits-Cristoph, 1998).[1] Seligman (1990) argues that the psychotherapeutic interventions used in cognitive therapy (CT) directly modify optimism and pessimism and asserts that CT is effective specifically because it decreases pessimism and increases optimism. Thus, the cognitive perspective on psychotherapy seems especially relevant.

OPTIMISM, PESSIMISM, AND PSYCHOPATHOLOGY: A COGNITIVE PERSPECTIVE

The Role of Negative Thinking in Psychopathology

Consider our case example. Art was thinking, "What will I have to say? She'll think I'm boring. I don't have anything to offer." He was feeling anxious, discouraged, and depressed, and he was inclined to avoid his upcoming date. How are we to understand Art's pessimistic outlook and its impact on his mood and his behavior?

The cognitive view of human functioning (Beck et al., 1979) emphasizes three aspects of cognition (see Figure 15.1). An individual's "automatic thoughts," his or her immediate, spontaneous appraisal of the situation, are seen as playing a central role in eliciting and shaping the individual's emotional and behavioral response to a situation. CT asserts that individuals automatically evaluate the many situations they encounter or anticipate

---

[1]A variety of cognitive and cognitive–behavioral approaches to psychotherapy have been developed in recent years. Although these approaches have much in common, there are important conceptual and technical differences among them. To minimize confusion, the specific approach developed by Aaron T. Beck and his colleagues will be referred to as *cognitive therapy* (CT), whereas the term *cognitive–behavioral* will be used as a collective term to refer to the full range of cognitive and cognitive–behavioral approaches.

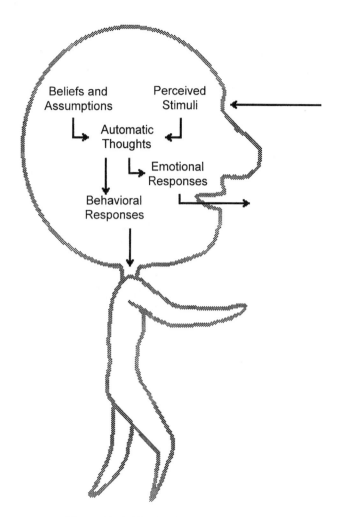

Figure 15.1. The basic cognitive model.

throughout the day and that the content of these evaluations has an important impact on their emotional and behavioral responses. If the individual's evaluation of the situation is realistic, his or her emotional and behavioral responses are likely to prove adaptive. If the evaluation of the situation is unrealistic, his or her emotional and behavioral responses are likely to prove dysfunctional.

Humans do not "start from scratch" in perceiving and interpreting each event or situation they encounter. Rather, in each situation, the individual's response is influenced by sets of interrelated concepts, beliefs, and assumptions, which CT therapists refer to as *schemas*. As the individual proceeds through daily life, relevant schemas are automatically activated and used in responding to the situations the individual encounters. For example, imagine that Art is proceeding through his busy day as an engineer. As he works on a new project, consults a reference book, or goes for a cup of coffee, his beliefs and assumptions about relationships are inactive because they are not relevant to the situation. Thus they have little impact on his mood or behavior. However, as he approaches the coffee pot and sees that a female colleague is standing there, his schemas related to male–female interactions are activated automatically and have an immediate impact. Art's schema for male–female interactions includes an assumption that women are repelled by "boring" men and are attracted to "cool" men. It also includes an unspoken assumption that he is boring. Thus, when this schema was activated in real-life situations, Art immediately attempted to appear cool, to monitor whether he was being successful in these attempts, and to monitor whether the woman seemed bored.

Because Art was alert for signs of disinterest or boredom, he was quick to recognize those occasions when others did, indeed, find him boring and, because he was not equally vigilant for times when others enjoyed their interactions with him, he developed a biased view of their reactions to him. Furthermore, when Art encountered an occasion on which a woman showed clear evidence of enjoying his company, he was inclined to discount the experience (i.e., "They don't really mean it," "They're only saying that to be nice," or "If they get to know me better they'll find out that I'm not as interesting as they think.") because this experience was inconsistent with his assumptions. In short, Art's vigilance for experiences that appeared to confirm his preconceptions and his tendency to discount experiences that were inconsistent with his worldview tended to confirm and perpetuate his assumptions about himself and others.

In addition to their beliefs and assumptions about "the way things are," individuals also hold beliefs and assumptions about how one should deal with various situations that might be termed *interpersonal strategies*. For example, Art believed that the way to be attractive to women was to act cool (i.e., to be sure that he did not appear anxious and to be careful not to show too much interest in the woman). His attempts to put this belief into practice had a major impact on his interpersonal relationships. Not only did his careful attempts to act cool result in his appearing stiff and awkward, but his self-consciousness also raised his level of anxiety and made it increasingly difficult for him to act cool. Because concealing any sign of anxiety was an important part of Art's strategy for appearing cool, he feared that it would become apparent to others and defeat his attempts. If he was not confident that he could conceal his anxiety, Art would become "flustered" and conclude that he had failed in his efforts to act cool. He had experienced many occasions on which his strategy of attempting to act cool had failed; however, he consistently attributed his failures to having not acted cool enough and, therefore, resolved to try harder the next time. It did not appear that he ever considered the possibility that this might be an ineffective strategy. (For a more detailed discussion of the role of schemas in psychopathology, see Pretzer & Beck, 1996.)

Another aspect of cognition that can contribute to persistent misperceptions of situations are systematic errors in reasoning, termed *cognitive distortions*. Human beings are prone to a variety of errors in logic, which can contribute to misinterpretations of events and amplify the impact of schemas (see Table 15.1). For example, Art manifested a strong tendency to focus selectively on his faults and shortcomings, and he tended to overlook his good points. This tendency strongly reinforced his negative outlook.

The cognitive view is that, given the complexity of daily life and the ambiguity of many interpersonal interactions, occasional misperceptions and misinterpretations of events are inevitable. However, isolated misperceptions and misinterpretations give rise to isolated maladaptive responses, which are easily corrected by subsequent experiences. For seriously maladaptive responses to develop, a systematic bias in perception, recall, or interpretation would be required. This would result in more persistent maladaptive responses than would result from "normal" misperceptions and misinterpretations. If it also distorted the feedback process, either by strongly biasing the interpretation of events or by influencing the responses of others, it could result in very persistent maladaptive responses.

Since the individual's schemas, beliefs, and assumptions have a major impact on the perception, recall, and interpretation of events, they are one possible source of such a systematic bias. However, they are not the only possible source of a systematic bias in the perception, recall, and interpretation of events. Despite CT's name, the model is not exclusively cognitive. Rather, the cognitive model focuses on the interplay between cognition, affect, and behavior in psychopathology (see Figure 15.2). The effect of Art's beliefs and assumptions on his perception of events and on his interpersonal behavior was discussed above, but the cycle does not end with the effects of cognition on behavior. A person's interpersonal behavior influences the responses of others, and their responses can, in turn, result in experiences that can influence that individual's beliefs and assumptions. For example, a number of Art's friends and family members responded to his anxiety, pessimism, and lack of success in relationships with advice that reinforced his tendency to attribute failures to inadequacies on his part. This advice also reinforced his assumption that he had to try to act cool (e.g., "Don't be so nervous, it will drive women away," "You have to be more confident," or "Don't say that, say _____ instead.").

Although the cognitive model assumes that the individual's interpretation of events shapes his or her emotional response to the situation, CT also argues that the individual's emotional state has important effects on cognition. A large body of research has demonstrated that affect tends to

Table 15.1.
Common Cognitive Distortions

Distortion	Definition
Dichotomous thinking	Viewing experiences in terms of two mutually exclusive categories with no "shades of gray" in between. For example, believing that one is *either* a success *or* a failure and that anything short of a perfect performance is a total failure.
Overgeneralization	Perceiving a particular event as being characteristic of life in general rather than as being one event among many. For example, concluding that an inconsiderate response from one's spouse shows that she doesn't care despite her having showed consideration on other occasions.
Selective abstraction	Focusing on one aspect of a complex situation to the exclusion of other relevant aspects of that situation. For example, focusing on the one negative comment in a performance evaluation received at work and overlooking the positive comments.
Disqualifying the positive	Discounting positive experiences that would conflict with the individual's negative views. For example, rejecting positive feedback from friends and colleagues on the grounds that "they're only saying that to be nice," rather than considering whether the feedback could be valid.
Mind reading	Assuming that one knows what others are thinking or how others are reacting despite having little or no evidence. For example, thinking, "I just know he thought I was an idiot!" despite the other person's having given no apparent indication of his reactions.
Fortune telling	Reacting as though expectations about future events are established facts rather than recognizing them as fears, hopes, or predictions. For example, thinking "He's leaving me, I just know it!" and acting as though this is definitely true.
Catastrophizing	Treating actual or anticipated negative events as intolerable catastrophes rather than seeing them in perspective. For example, thinking, "Oh my God, what if I faint!" without considering that although fainting may be unpleasant or embarrassing, it is not terribly dangerous.
Maximization and minimization	Treating some aspects of the situation, personal characteristics, or experiences as trivial and others as very important, independent of their actual significance. For example, thinking "Sure, I'm good at my job, but so what, my parents don't respect me."
Emotional reasoning	Assuming that one's emotional reactions necessarily reflect the true situation. For example, concluding that because one feels hopeless, the situation must really be hopeless.
"Should" statements	The use of "should" and "have to" statements that are not actually true to provide motivation or control over one's behavior. For example, thinking "I shouldn't feel aggravated. She's my mother, I have to listen to her."
Labeling	Attaching a global label to oneself rather than referring to specific events or actions. For example, thinking "I'm a failure!" rather than "Boy, I blew that one!"
Personalization	Assuming that one is the cause of a particular external event when, in fact, other factors are responsible. For example, thinking, "She wasn't very friendly today, she must be mad at me," without considering that factors other than one's own behavior may be affecting the other individual's mood.

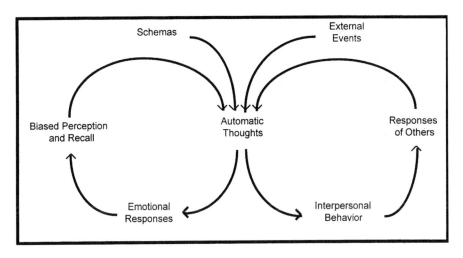

Figure 15.2. The role of cognition in psychopathology.

influence both cognition and behavior in mood-congruent ways (Isen, 1984). For example, even a mild, experimentally induced depressed mood biases perception and recall in a depression-congruent way (see Watkins, Mathews, Williamson, & Fuller, 1992 for a recent discussion). A depressed mood increases the likelihood that the individual will focus on negative aspects of the situation and preferentially recall negative past experiences. Although this phenomenon has not been investigated extensively for most other moods, it appears that many moods tend to bias perception and recall in a mood-congruent way. For example, as an individual's level of anxiety increases, attentional processes appear to be biased in favor of signs of threat (Watkins et al., 1992). This phenomenon lays the foundation for a potentially self-perpetuating cycle where the individual's automatic thoughts elicit a particular mood, the mood biases perception and recall in a mood-congruent way, and this increases the likelihood of additional mood-eliciting automatic thoughts, which elicit more of the mood in question, which further biases perception and recall, and so on, until the cycle is interrupted.

Affect can play an important role in an individual's functioning in another way as well. As Taylor and Rachman (1991, 1992) have noted, individuals may fear certain emotions and may strive to avoid the emotion itself; may seek to escape from experiencing the emotion as quickly as possible; or may attempt to avoid thoughts, memories, or situations that they expect to elicit the emotion. At the time when Art sought treatment, he frequently avoided situations, thoughts, and memories that led to his feeling anxious. In particular, he avoided interactions with women who he found attractive because he anticipated feeling anxious and because he was convinced that he would fail anyway. He also avoided thinking about social interactions because simply thinking about a conversation or an upcoming date elicited significant anxiety. This cognitive avoidance made it difficult for him to think effectively about his problems and find ways of overcoming them because he would have to tolerate anxiety in order to do so.

It is important to note that the cognitive model does *not* assert that cognition causes psychopathology. Cognition is viewed as an important part of the cycles through which human beings perceive and respond to events, and thus, is viewed as having an important role in pathological responses to events. As an important part of these cycles, cognition is also seen as a promising point for intervention, but not as the sole cause of psychopathology or as the sole point for effective intervention.

From Negative Thinking to Optimism or Pessimism

CT has traditionally focused on the impact of specific thoughts, beliefs, and cognitive distortions rather than emphasizing broad biases in cognition such as dispositional pessimism. Research into CT has focused on the question of whether it provides an effective treatment approach and whether particular thoughts and assumptions contribute to psychopathology. Relatively little attention has been focused on the question of whether persistent individual differences in optimism or pessimism are relevant to psychotherapy or the question of whether such individual differences can be modified. For example, a recent volume that provides a comprehensive review of research into cognitive factors that contribute to vulnerability to depression does not explicitly discuss optimism and pessimism (Ingram, Miranda, & Segal, 1998).

Only in recent years have a few investigators begun to consider optimism and pessimism from a cognitive or cognitive–behavioral perspective. However, if one understands optimism and pessimism in terms of generalized expectancies (Scheier & Carver, 1992); in terms of attributional style (Peterson & Seligman, 1984); or in terms of a consistent positive or negative bias in the interpretation of events (Riskind, Sarampote, & Mercier, 1996), it is not hard at all to conceptualize optimism and pessimism from a cognitive perspective.

One of the most widely known cognitive–behavioral perspectives on optimism and pessimism has been developed by Seligman (1990). In his research into what is termed *learned helplessness*, Seligman and his colleagues demonstrated that laboratory animals could learn either to passively tolerate negative events (electric shock) or to persistently seek to escape the electric shock. In subsequently exploring this phenomenon in human beings, he found that some individuals were quick to give up after a few negative experiences, while others persisted despite recurrent failures. In explaining this phenomenon, Seligman focused on the attributions these individuals made. He argues that individuals who believed that nothing they could ever do would change their situation became hopeless and depressed. Those who believed that they could influence the outcome remained optimistic and persisted in efforts to overcome misfortune.

From Seligman's perspective (1990), optimism and pessimism are a matter of the explanatory style that the individual acquires over the course of development. He emphasizes three aspects of individuals' explanatory style: personalization, pervasiveness, and permanence. Consider our case example. In it, Art consistently tended to attribute failures in social interactions to internal causes ("She doesn't like me because I'm boring."); his attributions regarding his failures were quite global ("This is the way I am."); and he attributed his failures to factors he saw as permanent ("This is the way I am going to be."). In theory, the results would be quite different for an individual who had the same experience of rejection but made different attributions. For example, one could attribute rejection to external causes (perhaps "I must not be her type," or "I guess she isn't interested in dating."). The attributions could be specific rather than general ("Sue's not interested, maybe Mary would like to go out."). Or responsibility for the rejection could be attributed to factors that are temporary rather than permanent (e.g., "I'll try again when she is in a better mood," or "Maybe I need to get better at asking women out."). Seligman argues that pessimism is a result of persistently attributing negative events to personal, pervasive, and permanent causes, whereas optimism results from attributing misfortune to temporary, specific, and external causes.

Riskind and his colleagues (Riskind et al., 1996) present a somewhat different cognitive perspective on optimism and pessimism. They note studies where the correlation between positive and negative thought content is low (Ingram & Wisnicki, 1988); where a decrease in negative thinking does not necessarily result in an increase in positive thinking (Watson, Clark, & Carey, 1988); and where the outcome of CT is more strongly correlated with increases in positive thinking than with decreases in negative thinking (Garamoni, Reynolds, Thase, Frank, & Fascizka, 1992). Consequently, they argue that pessimism is not simply the result of specific negative thoughts and that, to adequately understand pessimism and develop an effective intervention approach, the standard cognitive model needs additional development. They start from A. T. Beck's early suggestion (1967) that rigid, absolute schemas may lead to greater vulnerability to hopelessness and pessimism, and they argue that some individuals hold schemas that seem to promote pessimism or suppress optimism. Examples include beliefs such as "If I think too positively, I'll just be disappointed," "If I'm optimistic, I'll overlook something and fail," or "If I think positively, I'm just kidding myself."

Riskind and his colleagues point out that when optimism-suppressing schemas are present, successful treatment could result in a reduction in negative thinking without a concomitant rise in positive thinking. In a recent study, Stewart and colleagues (1993) found that a subgroup of depressed patients who did not believe that they could positively affect their own futures responded poorly to CT. Riskind et al. (1996) suggest that the impact of optimism-suppressing schemas may explain this finding and that interventions designed to address optimism-suppressing schemas and to increase the frequency of positive automatic thoughts might overcome the poor treatment response observed in such "demoralized" individuals. This perspective suggests that modifications to standard CT might significantly increase its effectiveness as an approach to decreasing pessimism and increasing optimism.

HOW CAN PSYCHOTHERAPISTS MODIFY OPTIMISM OR PESSIMISM?

Three Cognitive Approaches

In terms of intervention, Seligman's and his colleagues proposed methods for helping children develop into optimists rather than pessimists have been discussed in chapter 14 and are beyond the scope of this one. In discussing treatment of adults who have a pessimistic, depressogenic explanatory style, Seligman advocates CT as a treatment approach. In fact, he goes as far as to assert that the effectiveness of CT as a treatment of depression is due to its ability to reduce pessimism (Seligman, 1990, p. 91). Seligman seems to assume that all that a therapist needs to do to produce a lasting decrease in pessimism is to help the individual identify pessimistic thoughts and dispute them. He does not propose that therapists make any adaptations or adjustments to "standard" CT when the goal is to decrease pessimism *and* increase optimism.

Fresco and his colleagues (Fresco, Craighead, et al., 1995; Fresco, Sampson, et al., 1995) do not present a detailed theoretical discussion of optimism and pessimism but propose adapting standard cognitive–behavioral interventions to focus more directly on increasing optimism. The implicit assumption is that interventions that are explicitly directed toward increasing optimism will prove more efficient and effective than interventions that target negative thinking in the hopes of *indirectly* increasing optimism.

Riskind and his colleagues (Riskind et al., 1996) present the most extensive proposal regarding how to best modify standard CT to maximize its impact on optimism or pessimism. These authors argue that "standard" focuses on decreasing the amount of negative thinking, and this is not necessarily sufficient to produce increases in optimism. They advocate using cognitive techniques explicitly to challenge optimism-suppressing schemas, to enhance positive thinking, and to increase optimistic thought content as a way of increasing the effectiveness of CT. Regarding our case example, this perspective would suggest that interventions specifically intended to increase Art's optimism may be more effective than either interventions focused on decreasing his negative thinking and his pessimism or than interventions focused on decreasing his social anxiety and improving his social skills.

Toward an Integrative Approach

There are both commonalties and differences among the approaches to increasing optimism advocated by Seligman, by Riskind and his colleagues, and by Fresco and colleagues. Despite the differences between the approaches, they can be integrated into a more comprehensive approach toward increasing optimism. In doing so, it is important to note that the intervention approaches advocated by Seligman (1990) and Riskind and his colleagues (1996) are intended to be used in the context of ongoing CT and that, although the approach developed by Fresco and his colleagues (Fresco, Craighead, et al., 1995; Fresco, Sampson, et al., 1995) was designed as a self-administered treatment, the techniques used are equally appropriate in the context of ongoing CT. We propose integrating the three approaches toward increasing optimism within a more comprehensive approach to CT.

Foundations for Effective Intervention

Beck and other cognitive therapists (e.g., J. S. Beck, 1994; A. T. Beck et al., 1979; Freeman, Pretzer, Fleming, & Simon, 1990) have written extensively about structuring treatment to maximize the effectiveness of cognitive–behavioral interventions. For example, they have emphasized the idea that cognitive–behavioral interventions are more effective if they are applied in the context of a collaborative relationship between therapist and client, and they have argued that if a therapist and client are working together toward goals that the client values, this collaboration reduces resistance and increases the client's active involvement in therapy. The collaborative approach that Beck advocates goes beyond simply agreeing on mutually acceptable goals to include approaches such as "guided discovery," "collaborative empiricism," and "behavioral experiments," which are designed to structure therapy so that the client and therapist work together with the client playing an active role both in developing an understanding of the problems and in the change process.

Cognitive therapists have emphasized the importance of intervening flexibly based on a clear formulation of the client and his or her problems rather than applying invented techniques in a "cookbook" manner (A. T. Beck et al., 1979; Freeman et al., 1990; Persons, 1989). (For a more detailed discussion of these issues, see J. S. Beck, 1994; A. T. Beck et al., 1979; Freeman et al., 1990, & Persons, 1989.)

Increasing Motivation for Change

Some clients who enter treatment are strongly and consistently motivated to change from the outset. When this is the case, treatment can proceed directly to interventions designed to develop a better understanding of the individual's problems or to interventions designed to produce the desired changes. However, many individuals enter therapy without strong, consistent motivation to change. When this is the case, it can be important for treatment to include interventions designed to increase and consolidate motivation for change. One such intervention would involve helping the client to clearly identify the "costs" of his or her pessimism and the likely benefits of a more optimistic outlook. At this stage it can be important to check for any fears the client has regarding the consequences of change. If these fears present a significant impediment, it can be important to address them, both with cognitive interventions and behavioral experiments. When a client's lack of consistent motivation for change is a particular problem, the therapist can use the motivational interviewing approach developed by Miller and Rollnick (1991).

Identifying and Challenging Pessimistic Thoughts

As Seligman (1990) has suggested, a variety of "standard" CT interventions that focus on identifying and modifying dysfunctional thoughts can be used in an attempt to replace a client's pessimistic thinking with more optimistic thinking. Take our case example, where Art found himself in situations where he assumed that a particular woman would have no interest in him. His therapist helped him to look critically at his thoughts, to consider any indications that she was not interested as well as any indications of interest on her part, and to draw realistic conclusions about her likely level of interest. In many situations, Art did not have sufficient information to know whether the woman was likely to be interested in him, so his therapist presented the idea of initiating a conversation as a way of finding out. When Art tried this he was surprised to discover that several women showed interest in him.

Although this type of intervention approach was initially designed to modify people's dysfunctional cognitions believed to contribute to psychopathology, it is flexible enough to use without significant modification for increasing optimism. However, given the evidence that interventions that reduce the amount of negative thinking do not necessarily result in a corresponding increase in positive thinking, these interventions alone may not prove sufficient to produce lasting increases in optimism (see Watson, Clark, & Carey, 1988).

Identifying Alternatives to Pessimism

If individuals are to adopt less pessimistic outlooks, what sort of alternative view would be best? Clients often assume that the alternative the therapist has in mind is the polar opposite (i.e., instead of expecting a negative outcome, trying always to expect a positive outcome). Is this indeed the most promising alternative? Consider our case example: Art's tendency was to approach his date with a mindset such as "I'll be boring. She'll have a lousy time. She won't want to go out with me again. There's no point to trying." Do we, as therapists, want to try to get him to switch to the other extreme ("I'll be charming. She'll have a great time. We'll date for a few months and then get married and live happily ever after.")?

Certainly, if Art could believe this alternative view, it would make a big difference both in his mood and in his behavior. However, two problems are apparent. First, it is hard to imagine how Art could reach a point where he honestly believes this alternative view because it is so discrepant from his current view. Second, suppose Art was able to adopt this view, what would happen when he went on his date? It seems that there is a significant chance that his experiences on the date would disconfirm his "optimistic" view. It would appear that any increase in optimism that is based on Art's adopting such an extreme positive view will likely prove to be transitory.

There are a variety of other alternatives to Art's extreme pessimism that are worth considering (see Table 15.2). We advocate working collaboratively with the client to consider the alternatives and choose a promising one to try out in real life. Theoretically, it seems that the ideal alternative would be one that the client finds relatively easy to believe, that results in beneficial changes in the individual's mood and behavior, that is practical to implement in real-life situations, and that is likely to be supported by his or her experience in daily life.

To his therapist, Art appeared to be a fairly ordinary guy who was neither remarkably charming nor remarkably boring. Art and his therapist chose to combine the approaches labeled "adopt a mildly positive view" and "accept realistically negative aspects of the situation and plan how to cope with them" (i.e., "I'm an OK guy. Some women will be interested in me and some won't. I should try to meet women who like me the way I am rather than trying to look cool. If I get nervous, it is better to go ahead anyway than to avoid it."). This alternative worked well in real-life situations.

Table 15.2.
Alternatives to Pessimism in Approaching a Date

Alternative approach	Specific thoughts
Anticipate the best possible outcome	"I'll be charming. She'll have a great time. We'll get married and live happily ever after."
Adopt a less pessimistic view	"I probably won't be charming enough but I'll give it a try anyway. There's a chance that I could do OK."
Adopt a mildly positive view	"I'm a decent guy. If I don't get so anxious and pressured it will go OK. If I keep trying, I'll end up getting more comfortable with dating and it will go better."
Try to be realistic in anticipating likely outcomes	"I'll give it a good try but the odds are that I'll need to date a number of women before I find a relationship that works out."
Accept realistically negative aspects of the situation and plan how to cope with them	"When I get self-conscious, I tend to hold back and get tongue-tied. When I get involved in the conversation, it goes better. I'll make a point of speaking up."
Be mindful of negative emotions without letting them determine the outcome	"I'm nervous and self-conscious but that's just the way I react when dating. I'll go ahead and give it a good try anyway."
Focus on pursuing positive outcomes rather than on avoiding negative outcomes	"How can I approach it so that we both have a good time? I'll pick an activity that we both like."

Specific Cognitive and Behavioral Interventions

In addition to using "standard" CT interventions, therapists can tailor standard techniques to focus more specifically on optimism. Fresco and his colleagues (Fresco, Craighead, et al., 1995; Fresco, Sampson, et al., 1995) adapted the cognitive–behavioral techniques of self-monitoring and cognitive restructuring by combining them into a self-administered format and instructing participants to keep a "daily diary" in which they monitored both good and bad events and rated the causes of the events in terms of their stability, internality, and globality. He directed the research participants to then think of other possible causes of the events and to rate those causes on the same dimensions. In theory, tailoring "standard" interventions to address aspects of cognition that are directly related to optimism or pessimism should increase their impact.

It is also possible to design interventions that are specifically designed to decrease pessimism or increase optimism. One such technique, which Riskind et al. (1996) propose, consists of the therapist helping the client to identify and modify dysfunctional "optimism-suppressing" beliefs. Their assumption is that an individual who holds a belief such as "I don't deserve positive things or good outcomes" or "Happiness, positive thinking, and optimism are illusions" will be more prone to engage in optimistic thinking if the therapist can help him or her adopt an alternative view that supports optimism. In Art's case, he assumed that optimistic thinking was "dangerous" because an optimistic outlook would result in his attempting social interactions with attractive women who would then find him boring and reject him. As long as he believed that optimistic thinking would lead directly to rejection, he was reluctant to adopt this more positive outlook. After his therapist helped him examine these beliefs and adopt alternative views ("Avoiding rejection at all costs results in my being isolated. I can take small chances and cope with rejection if it happens. If I take small chances, I can find out if women react the way I anticipate and I can learn how to get relationships to go better."), he was more willing to approach interpersonal situations with a guardedly optimistic outlook.

A second intervention that Riskind et al. (1996) propose is termed *positive visualization*. In this technique, the therapist asks the client to choose a problematic situation and to visually rehearse attaining a positive outcome. The client is instructed to imagine the outcome he or she would like to achieve rather than visualizing the outcome he or she expects and to visualize the specific steps needed to achieve these results. The visualization can specifically target the challenges the client would be likely to encounter in real life. Thus, Art might be asked to visualize a casual conversation with an attractive acquaintance from beginning to end, to imagine encountering the problems which he would normally encounter in such a situation, to imagine coping successfully with each problem as it arises, and to imagine a successful outcome. In order for Art to be able to imagine coping successfully with the problems he encounters, the therapist would need to help him to identify these and to identify promising ways of coping with them.

Riskind et al. (1996) present two variations on the positive visualization technique. The first is the "story board" technique, where the client is instructed to visualize a series of discrete scenes that lead to a desired outcome. For example, a salesman who has difficulty making unsolicited calls might be asked to first visualize making calls to potential customers, then to visualize some of the calls resulting in appointments, and finally to visualize some of the appointments resulting in sales. At each step, the client would imagine coping with any difficulties that arise and would imagine a successful outcome, such as being pleased that he or she carried out the task. The second variation on the positive visualization technique is the "invulnerability training" technique, where the client would visualize feeling good about how he or she handled the situation when things *do not* turn out the way the client hoped they would. Riskind and his colleagues propose that when positive visualizations of these types are repeated across a variety of situations and different areas of life, there may be a point at which the effects of the visualizations generalize and have beneficial effects that are not confined to the specific situations visualized.

The "silver lining" technique (Riskind et al., 1996) is a simple process in which the client is assigned the task of taking a negative experience and identifying one genuinely positive element in it. The client's task is not simply to mouth positive platitudes but to identify genuinely positive aspects of the experience. Riskind argues that this simple exercise can have a significant impact. For example, at the outset of therapy, whenever Art had a social interaction that did not result in a date, he was inclined to declare it to have been a total failure. After identifying the realistic positive outcomes of some of these "failures" (i.e., "At least I got myself to try," "I'm getting less anxious about striking up a conversation," "She seems to be getting more comfortable too," or "I didn't get a date but she did show some interest.") he found it easier to persist long enough with his efforts to start getting some dates.

A fourth technique recommended by Riskind et al. (1996) is "pump priming," a technique based on the principle of cognitive priming. Events relevant to a particular cognitive construct or schema can increase the salience of the schema and increase the likelihood of its being spontaneously elicited by subsequent events. Riskind gives the example of an individual who reads an article about cats over coffee in the morning and subsequently throughout the day is more likely to think spontaneously about cats, to notice references to cats, and to recall memories of cats. He suggests that by having individuals intentionally attend to experiences relevant to a schema that they wish to encourage, to intentionally repeat relevant self-statements, or to visualize relevant stimuli, it may be possible to increase spontaneous attention to positive experiences, increase spontaneous use of an optimistic explanatory style, and so forth.

It is likely that a variety of other cognitive–behavioral interventions could be modified to more specifically address optimism and pessimism. For example, Burns's (1980) "antiprocrastination sheet" technique asks the client to record his or her anticipations about how difficult and how rewarding it will be to perform a particular task, and then, following completion of the task, to rate how difficult the task actually turned out to be and how rewarding it actually was to perform the task. This technique can easily be modified to target the specific expectancies that are relevant for decreasing an individual's pessimism or increasing their optimism.

The "antipessimism sheet" shown in Figure 15.3 is one possible way of doing this. Clients are asked to identify upcoming events that they are likely to approach with a pessimistic outlook and to list each event in the first column of the form. Before the event, the individual is asked to record the best they can foresee happening, the worst they can foresee happening, and the outcome that seems most likely. Following the event, they are asked

Upcoming Event	**Before** the event: The best I can foresee happening is:	The worst I can foresee happening is:	The outcome which seems most likely is:	**After** the event: The actual outcome was:

Figure 15.3. Antipessimism sheet.

to record the actual outcome. After a number of events have been recorded, therapist and client can examine the correspondence between the individual's anticipations and the actual outcome, the impact a pessimistic outlook has on the actual outcome, and what the client can do to influence the outcome.

The antipessimism sheet was not used with Art because it had not yet been developed. Instead, the same type of intervention was used in a less structured way. Art was asked to rate the level of anxiety he anticipated experiencing in upcoming interactions, the degree of interest he anticipated that the woman would display, and the level of satisfaction he expected to experience following the interaction. Following the interactions, he and his therapist discussed his actual experience, looked for consistent biases in his expectancies, and identified positive outcomes, which Art tended to overlook (i.e., decreases in his anxiety, opportunities to test his preconceptions, and improvements in his social skills). This process seemed to facilitate Art's recognizing that his anticipations were unduly negative and to increase his ability to appreciate the positive aspects of interactions that produced mixed results.

Relapse Prevention

When therapy has been successful, there remains a risk of relapse at some point in the future. Borrowing ideas from Marlatt and Gordon's (1985) work on relapse prevention in the treatment of substance abuse, a cognitive therapist at the conclusion of treatment typically helps the client identify "high-risk" situations where there is an increased risk of relapse, plan how to cope with these events if they occur, and practice the skills needed for the client to cope effectively. For example, as Art had his initial success in interpersonal relationships, he gradually accepted the idea that he was not inherently boring and began to believe that people could genuinely be interested in him once they got to know him. However, if he were to experience rejection in a relationship or if he were to encounter someone who accused him of being boring, he could easily revert to his original negative outlook, especially if he experienced several such experiences. Art's treatment concluded with his therapist helping him identify adaptive self-statements to use in coping with rejection (i.e., "Things didn't work out with her but I know from experience that other women can be interested in me.") and plan active steps for him to take in coping with rejection (i.e., "Avoiding rejection just makes things worse, I need to continue reaching out to others even if it is hard at first.").

CAN COGNITIVE–BEHAVIORAL INTERVENTIONS PRODUCE LASTING CHANGES IN OPTIMISM AND PESSIMISM?

Only a limited number of studies have directly examined the effectiveness of cognitive–behavioral interventions designed specifically to modify optimism or pessimism.[2] Fresco and colleagues combined the cognitive–behavioral techniques of self-monitoring and cognitive restructuring into a self-administered format and investigated the effects of 1 month of self-administered "optimism training" on pessimistic college students (Fresco, Craighead, et al., 1995; Fresco, Sampson, et al., 1995). Analysis of student participants' attributional styles before and after treatment indicated that 1 month of minimally supervised, self-guided intervention produced a greater reduction in pessimistic explanatory style than in a no-treatment approach in the control group of students.

Riskind and his colleagues (1996) compared the effects of three group treatments (standard cognitive therapy, optimism training, and cognitive priming) with progressive relaxation training (as a control group) in a sample of 83 college students. This study's results yielded promising initial support

---

[2] There is considerable evidence that CT and related cognitive–behavioral approaches are effective treatments for depression and, because interventions designed to reduce negative thinking play a prominent role in these intervention approaches, it is tempting to interpret this as providing evidence that CT increases optimism or decreases pessimism (see Seligman, 1990). However, this line of reasoning assumes that the efficacy of CT for depression is due to its effects on negative cognitions and that interventions that modify specific negative cognitions lead to lasting changes in levels of optimism or pessimism. Because neither assumption is beyond debate, research into the efficacy of CT as a treatment for depression is not directly relevant to the question of whether cognitive–behavioral interventions can be used to increase optimism.

for the effectiveness of the optimism training condition. The optimism training group had scores superior to those of the control group on four out of five measures. This included a significantly higher level of optimistic interpretations for negative events and a higher level of positive self-statements. It is interesting to note that optimism training's effects appeared to be specific to positive thinking. It did not demonstrate a significant effect on the level of negative self-statements. In this study, the other treatment approaches did noticeably less well. Standard cognitive therapy scores were superior to those of the control group on two out of five measures (positive self-statements and problem-solving self-efficacy), while the cognitive priming treatment was not significantly more effective than that of the control group (progressive relaxation training) on any of the measures.

The findings reported by these investigators are encouraging. Unfortunately, these studies have only been conducted with college undergraduates and have not yet been replicated, thus, their generalizability is severely limited. It goes without saying that more extensive research with a broader range of populations will be needed before we have grounds for drawing firm conclusions.

THE EFFECTS OF MODIFYING OPTIMISM AND PESSIMISM IN ADULTS

The association between optimism and a wide variety of positive outcomes (Scheier & Carver, 1992; see also chap. 9, this volume) makes it tempting to assume that interventions that increase an individual's optimism will produce manifold benefits. However, this proposition has not yet received extensive scrutiny. Fresco, Craighead, et al. (1995) found that, in a sample of 125 college undergraduates, 1 month of self-administered optimism training produced a significant increase in the use of an optimistic explanatory style, and a nonsignificant trend toward lower depression scores and health symptom scores. A hierarchical multiple regression analysis found that the cross-product of attributional style by life stress significantly predicted level of depression and health symptoms for control participants but not for participants who received the optimism training. These results were interpreted as suggesting that 1 month of optimism training may have moderated the effects of the diathesis–stress interaction in pessimistic college students. However, findings such as this provide encouragement rather than a convincing demonstration of the benefits of optimism training.

The authors' clinical experience is consistent with the research, which suggests that cognitive–behavioral interventions can produce significant changes in optimism and pessimism and that this can have substantial benefits. In Art's case, initial interventions led him to reevaluate his pessimism regarding relationships. After five sessions, he began initiating conversations and was surprised to find that some women responded positively. By Session 7, he had begun dating and experimenting with allowing himself to be genuine rather than trying to appear "cool." At that point in therapy, he was considering a sexual relationship and talked with his therapist about how to let his girlfriend know that he had an erectile dysfunction. He subsequently discussed his sexual dysfunction with his girlfriend, and they initiated a sexual relationship.

By Session 10, Art spontaneously expressed the opinion that "anyone can be interesting once you get to know them" and, as he did so, he seemed to be expressing an honest conviction that this applied to him as well as to others. After Session 11, Art reported that he felt comfortable while dating and while facing other social situations. He was dating actively and, although he was not completely satisfied with his primary romantic relationship, he expressed confidence that he could successfully pursue relationships on his own. Treatment was terminated by mutual agreement with the option of Art's resuming treatment in the future if he encountered difficulty.

ISSUES TO CONSIDER REGARDING OPTIMISM AND PESSIMISM IN PSYCHOTHERAPY

Should the Goal of Intervention Be Optimism, Realism, or Something Else?

When CT originated as a treatment for depression, there was a strong focus on decreasing the amount of negative thinking or on counteracting negative thoughts due to the hypothesized role of negative thinking in depression. As cognitive–behavioral investigators have begun considering optimism and pessimism, some seem to assume that optimism and pessimism are polar opposites and that, therefore, interventions that decrease negative thinking will necessarily increase positive thinking. However, the previously cited studies that found little correlation between positive and negative thought content, found that a decrease in negative thinking did not necessarily result in an increase in positive thinking, and found that therapeutic outcome was more strongly correlated with changes in positive thinking than with changes in negative thinking seem to present a strong challenge to this assumption (Garamoni et al., 1992; Ingram & Wisnicki, 1988; Watson et al., 1988).

Riskind et al. (1996) interpret these findings as showing the importance of working explicitly to enhance positive thinking and optimistic thought content rather than simply attempting to decrease negative thinking. However, a number of other perspectives have been presented. Kendall (1982) argued that the goal of intervention should be to increase the amount of "non-negative thinking" rather than attempting to increase positive thinking. The "states of mind model" asserts that one should focus on the balance between positive and negative cognitions rather than looking at either in isolation (Bruch, 1997; Schwartz & Garamoni, 1989). Fresco, Craighead, et al. (1995) suggest that realistic thinking might be a better alternative than either optimism or pessimism. Other, more radical alternatives include "acceptance" (Hayes, Jacobson, Follette, & Doucher, 1994; Wilson, 1996) or "mindfulness" (Linehan, 1993, pp. 144–147) as alternatives to either optimism or pessimism. Clearly this is a topic in need of further exploration.

Are Increases in Optimism Following Treatment a Side Effect of Decreased Depression?

The increase in optimism observed in depressed individuals following a successful course of CT has been interpreted as demonstrating that CT is effective as a means of increasing optimism (Seligman, 1990). However, an alternative hypothesis is that the decrease in pessimism or increase in optimism observed following successful treatment of depression is a result of the decrease in depression rather than a direct result of CT on the individual's levels of optimism or pessimism.

At this point, some empirical evidence appears to support this hypothesis. For example, in an empirical investigation of the proposed characteristics of "Depressive Personality Disorder" (see American Psychiatric Association, *Diagnostic and Statistical Manual of Mental Disorders; DSM-IV*, 1994), Hartlage, Arduino, and Alloy (1998) found that pessimism appeared to be a state-dependent concomitant of depression rather than an enduring personality characteristic which predisposed individuals to depression. However, other evidence suggests that an individual's level of optimism is not simply an artifact of the individual's level of depression and actually may protect the individual against the development of depression. For example, Carver and Gaines (1987) found that level of optimism measured during the third trimester of pregnancy predicted level of postpartum depression even after statistically controlling for initial level of dysphoria.

It appears that it will be important for researchers to design studies of the effectiveness of interventions intended to decrease pessimism or increase optimism so that it is possible to distinguish changes in these qualities that are a direct effect of the interventions from changes that are a side effect of changes in depression. It will be important for investigators to remember that viewing pessimism as an effect of depression and the hypothesis that optimism confers resistance to depression are not necessarily incompatible.

It is possible that pessimism is, to some extent, a result of depression, whereas optimism, to some extent, tends to reduce the likelihood of an individual becoming depressed.

Is Too Much Optimism Risky?

A number of authors suggest that optimism can be hazardous in some situations and that individuals should be cautious or selective in adopting an optimistic outlook. For example, Seligman (1990) suggests that one should *not* use an optimistic outlook in situations where the cost of failure would be high (p. 209). Similarly, Freeman and DeWolf (1992) assert that an overly optimistic outlook can contribute to poor decision making, failure to accept responsibility for one's actions, persisting with a maladaptive strategy, and other problems (pp. 84–90). If there are any significant risks to adopting a more optimistic approach to life, treatments designed to increase optimism will need to take them into account.

Scheier and Carver (1992) provide a good discussion of a variety of ways in which optimism, particularly unrealistic optimism, might have disadvantages. They conclude that, although the picture is still incomplete, optimism appears to have substantial advantages over pessimism. Some research does support the idea that there may be risks, as well as benefits, to optimism. For example, in a study of cognitions related to risk-taking behavior, Fromme, Katz, and Rivet (1997) found that positive outcome expectancies were more consistently associated with risk taking than were beliefs about potential negative consequences. Clearly, this is an issue that calls for further examination and that will need to be considered as approaches to increasing optimism are developed and tested.

Should Cultural Differences Be Considered?

Most available research on optimism and pessimism has been conducted on Caucasian American participants, and much of the authors' clinical experience has been with Caucasian American clients. However, there is reason to believe that attention to cultural differences may be important both in conducting research on this topic and in intervening clinically. Chang (1996) examined differences in optimism, pessimism, and coping between Asian American and Caucasian American college students. He found consistent differences between the two groups of subjects that suggested optimism may have an important influence on adjustment for Asian American students, and pessimism may be more important for Caucasian American students. In discussing the clinical implications of these findings Chang suggests that interventions designed to reduce pessimism may be appropriate for Caucasian Americans, and interventions designed to increase optimism may be more appropriate for Asian Americans. After practicing for some time in an ethnically diverse community, the authors' experience is consistent with the hypothesis that cultural differences can have an important impact on levels of optimism and pessimism. Further research will be needed to examine a broader range of cultures and to clarify the extent to which cultural differences are important. (For a more detailed discussion of cultural influences on optimism and pessimism, see chap. 12, this volume.)

Do the Benefits of Modifying Optimism and Pessimism Justify the Costs?

Given the assertions that researchers make regarding the manifold benefits of optimism and the potential for developing interventions that result in lasting increases in optimism, one could wax enthusiastic about such interventions. However, at a time when health care budgets face financial constraints and managed care organizations play an increasing role in determining which intervention approaches will receive financial reimbursement, it is increasingly important for investigators to go beyond examining the effectiveness of a given treatment approach to also consider whether it is cost effective. An intervention approach is likely to receive much greater acceptance by professionals, the public, and those who control the funding if it is clear that the benefits of intervention substantially outweigh the costs.

CONCLUSION

Shall we be optimistic and emphasize the great benefits which could potentially result from intervention approaches designed to increase dispositional optimism, or shall we be pessimistic and emphasize the unanswered questions and significant problems faced by investigators in this field? Perhaps we betray our own biases in advocating a "realistic" perspective. Interventions designed to increase optimism have potential to produce substantial benefits if they prove to be both effective and cost effective; however, they will need further development and investigation to reach that stage.

Significant challenges remain. In particular, it is clear that cognitive–behavioral interventions can be effective and efficient in producing short-term change in specific cognitions. It is not yet clear if these same intervention approaches can produce broad, long-term changes of the sort needed to produce persistent increases in dispositional optimism. Although some proponents are enthusiastic about the potential of cognitive–behavioral interventions to produce lasting changes (J. S. Beck, 1994; Pretzer & Beck,

1996; Seligman, 1990) the available research has focused much more attention on the immediate, specific effects of CT and less attention on the broad, long-term effects. It is ironic, perhaps, that those investigators who possess a high level of dispositional optimism are most likely to persist with their research in the face of the inevitable difficulties and setbacks to eventually provide us with an answer to this question.

REFERENCES

American Psychiatric Association. (1994). *Diagnostic and statistical manual of mental disorders* (4th ed., rev.). Washington, DC: American Psychiatric Association.

Beck, A. T. (1967). *Depression: Clinical, experimental, and theoretical aspects.* New York: Harper & Row. (Reprinted as *Depression: Causes and treatment.* Philadelphia: University of Pennsylvania Press, 1972).

Beck, A. T., Rush, A. J., Shaw, B. F., & Emery, G. (1979). *Cognitive therapy of depression.* New York: Guilford Press.

Beck, J. S. (1994). *Cognitive therapy: Basics and beyond.* New York: Guilford Press.

Bruch, M. A. (1997). Positive thoughts or cognitive balance as a moderator of the negative life events-dysphoria relationship: A reexamination. *Cognitive Therapy and Research, 21,* 25–38.

Burns, D. D. (1980). *Feeling good: The new mood therapy.* New York: William Morrow.

Carver, C. S., & Gaines, J. G. (1987). Optimism, pessimism, and postpartum depression. *Cognitive Therapy and Research, 11,* 449–462.

Chang, E. C. (1996). Cultural differences in optimism, pessimism, and coping: Predictors of subsequent adjustment in Asian American and Caucasian American college students. *Journal of Counseling Psychology, 43,* 113–123.

DeRubeis, R. J., & Crits-Cristoph, P. (1998). Empirically supported individual and group psychological treatments for adult mental disorders. *Journal of Consulting and Clinical Psychology, 66,* 37–52.

Freeman, A., & DeWolf, R. (1992). *The 10 dumbest mistakes smart people make and how to avoid them: Simple and sure techniques for gaining greater control of your life.* New York: Harper Collins.

Freeman, A., Pretzer, J. L., Fleming, B., & Simon, K. M. (1990). *Clinical applications of cognitive therapy.* New York: Plenum Press.

Fresco, D. M., Craighead, L. W., Sampson, W. S., Watt, N. M., Favell, H. E., & Presnell, K. E. (1995, March). *The effects of self-administered "optimism training" on attributional style, levels of depression, and health symptoms of pessimistic college students.* Poster presented at the annual meeting of the Eastern Psychological Association, Boston, MA.

Fresco, D. M., Sampson, W. S., Craighead, L. W., Clark, J., & Enns, C. (1995, November). *Self-administered optimism training: The process of lessening the impact of pessimistic explanatory style.* Poster presented at the annual meeting of the Association for Advancement of Behavior Therapy, Washington, DC.

Fromme, K., Katz, E. C., & Rivet, K. (1997). Outcome expectancies and risk-taking behavior. *Cognitive Therapy and Research, 21,* 421–442.

Garamoni, G. L., Reynolds, C. F., Thase, M. E., Frank, E., & Fascizka, A. L. (1992). Shifts in affective balance during cognitive therapy of major depression. *Journal of Consulting and Clinical Psychology, 60,* 260–266.

Hartlage, S., Arduino, K., & Alloy, L. B. (1998). Depressive personality characteristics: State dependent concomitants of depressive disorder and traits independent of current depression. *Journal of Abnormal Psychology, 107,* 349–354.

Hayes, S. C., Jacobson, N. S., Follette, V. M., & Doucher, M. J. (1994). *Acceptance and change: Content and context in psychotherapy.* Reno, NV: Context Press.

Ingram, R. E., Miranda, J., & Segal, Z. V. (1998). *Cognitive vulnerability to depression.* New York: Guilford Press.

Ingram, R. E., & Wisnicki, K. S. (1988). Assessment of positive automatic cognition. *Journal of Consulting and Clinical Psychology, 56,* 898–902.

Isen, A. M. (1984). Toward understanding the role of affect in cognition. In R. S. Wyer & T. K. Skrull (Eds.), *Handbook of social cognition* (pp. 179–236). Hillsdale, NJ: Erlbaum.

Kendall, P. C. (1982). Cognitive processes and procedures in behavior therapy. In C. M. Franks, G. T. Wilson, P. C. Kendall, & S. D. Hollon (Eds.), *Assessment strategies for cognitive behavioral intervention.* New York: Academic Press.

Linehan, M. M. (1993). *Cognitive-behavioral treatment of borderline personality disorder.* New York: Guilford Press.

Marlatt, G. A., & Gordon, J. M. (Eds.). (1985). *Relapse prevention: Maintenance strategies in the treatment of addictive behaviors.* New York: Guilford.

Miller, W. R., & Rollnick, S. (1991). *Motivational interviewing: Preparing people to change addictive behavior.* New York: Guilford.

Persons, J. B. (1989). *Cognitive therapy in practice: A case formulation approach.* New York: Norton.

Peterson, C., & Seligman, M. E. P. (1984). Causal explanations as a risk factor for depression: Theory and evidence. *Psychological Review, 91,* 347–374.

Pretzer, J. L., & Beck, A. T. (1996). A cognitive theory of personality disorders. In J. F. Clarkin & M. F. Lenzenweger (Eds.), *Major theories of personality disorder* (pp. 36–105). New York: Guilford.

Riskind, J. H., Sarampote, C. S., & Mercier, M. A. (1996). For every malady a sovereign cure: Optimism training. *Journal of Cognitive Psychotherapy: An International Quarterly, 10,* 105–117.

Scheier, M. F., & Carver, C. S. (1992). Effects of optimism on psychological and physical well-being: Theoretical overview and empirical update. *Cognitive Therapy and Research, 16,* 201–228.

Schwartz, R. M., & Garamoni, G. L. (1989). Cognitive balance and psychopathology: Evaluation of an information processing model of positive and negative states of mind. *Clinical Psychology Review, 9,* 271–294.

Seligman, M. E. P. (1990). *Learned optimism.* New York: A. A. Knopf.

Stewart, J. W., Mercier, M. A., Quitkin, F. M., McGrath, P. J., Nunes, E., Young, J., Ocepek-Welikson, K., & Trocamo, E. (1993). Demoralization predicts non-response to cognitive therapy in depressed outpatients. *Journal of Cognitive Psychotherapy, 7,* 105–116.

Taylor, S., & Rachman, S. J. (1991). Fear of sadness. *Journal of Anxiety Disorders, 5,* 375–381.

Taylor, S., & Rachman, S. J. (1992). Fear and avoidance of aversive affective states: Dimensions and causal relations. *Journal of Anxiety Disorders, 6,* 15–25.

Watkins, P. C., Mathews, A., Williamson, D. A., & Fuller, R. D. (1992). Mood-congruent memory in depression: Emotional priming or elaboration? *Journal of Abnormal Psychology, 101,* 581–586.

Watson, D., Clark, L. A., & Carey, G. (1988). Positive and negative affectivity and their relation to anxiety and depressive disorders. *Journal of Abnormal Psychology, 97,* 346–353.

Wilson, G. T. (1996). Acceptance and change in the treatment of eating disorders and obesity. *Behavior Therapy, 27,* 417–439.

VI

The Future

16

A VERY FULL GLASS: ADDING COMPLEXITY TO OUR THINKING ABOUT THE IMPLICATIONS AND APPLICATIONS OF OPTIMISM AND PESSIMISM RESEARCH

JULIE K. NOREM AND EDWARD C. CHANG

As much of the research discussed in this volume indicates, there is substantial evidence that optimism, in its many forms, is related to better outcomes (e.g., coping, satisfaction, well-being) measured in a variety of ways across a variety of contexts. This evidence makes it extremely tempting to conclude that optimism is always to be desired over pessimism, and further, that as educators, policy consultants, therapists, and parents we should do everything we can to promote optimism. Indeed, as we leave the century espousing the sentiments of Dale Carnegie and "Don't Worry, Be Happy," it seems churlish, as well as somewhat un-American, to dwell on caveats to that conclusion.

Nevertheless, we live in a culture where cautions about overgeneralization, misapplication, or limitations—all the carefully considered details written up in the presentation of original research—are easily lost in the rush for catchy sound bites, palatable self-help, and quick-fix policy. It thus becomes especially important that we clarify for ourselves, and for those who might be consumers of our research, the ways in which our theories and research present a picture that is more complicated—and much more potentially useful—than the simple phrases "optimism is good" and "pessimism is bad" suggest. Accordingly, in this chapter we review some complexities that seem important to consider both as we design our research, and as we disseminate it. Despite use of the term *complexity* in the title, the two-part message of the chapter is rather simple: (a) There are potential benefits *and* costs to both optimism and pessimism (as they are variously defined in the literature) that may be highly sensitive to context (broadly and variously defined); and thus, (b) our research designs, interpretations of results, advocacy, interventions, and teaching need to be sensitive to costs, benefits, and context.

WHAT IS CONTEXT?

The complexity referred to in the chapter title immediately arises when one considers the contexts that might be important to understanding the functions and consequences of optimism and pessimism. Without claiming to exhaust the list of possibilities under this heading, some of these important contexts that have implications for optimism and pessimism include

1. the specific kind of optimism and pessimism under scrutiny
2. the other personality characteristics of individuals who are optimistic and pessimistic (i.e., the intrapsychic context)
3. the particular outcome variables considered
4. the interpersonal and social contexts within a culture
5. the life-span developmental context
6. the larger cultural context.

Varieties of Optimism and Pessimism

As is clear from the table of contents for this volume, optimism and pessimism are used as "umbrella" terms within the field. They in fact refer to several distinct concepts, often require modifiers (e.g., "naive optimism") or are used as modifiers (e.g., "pessimistic attributional style"), and only sometimes correspond to everyday usage. Among the concepts included in the literature are dispositional optimism and pessimism (Scheier & Carver, 1985); optimistic and pessimistic attributional or explanatory styles (Peterson & Seligman, 1987); naive optimism (Epstein & Meier, 1989); optimistic biases or illusions (Taylor & Brown, 1988); neurotic and rational pessi-mism (Kelman, 1945); unrealistic optimism (Weinstein, 1980); unrealistic pessimism (Dolinski, Gromski, & Zawisza, 1987); realistic pessimism (Frese, 1992); and defensive pessimism and strategic optimism (Norem & Cantor, 1986a). That list does not even include terms that are strongly related, such as *hope* (as previously discussed by Snyder, Sympson, Michael, & Cheavens, chap. 5, this volume).

Of these concepts, dispositional optimism and pessimism—defined as the tendency to hold generally positive or negative expectations—probably best represent the lay or colloquial understanding of the terms (as discussed by Carver & Scheier, chap. 2, this volume, and Scheier, Carver, & Bridges, chap. 9, this volume). Even these concepts, however, are more complex than they seem at first glance, in that the initial assumption that optimism and pessimism are opposite ends of the same continuum has been questioned (as mentioned in the introduction to this volume). There is now reason to believe that they represent two unipolar dimensions: The opposite of opti-mism is the lack of optimism, which is distinguishable from the presence of pessimism (Marshall, Wortman, Kusulas, Hervig, & Vickers, 1992). Simi-larly, the opposite of pessimism is the lack of pessimism, which is distinguish-able from the presence of optimism (Robinson-Whelen, Kim, MacCallum, & Kiecolt-Glaser, 1997).

Distinctions among these constructs are more than semantic to the extent that the different constructs have different consequences. There is some evidence, for example, that lack of optimism may have different consequences than does the presence of pessimism. Chang (1998) found that pessimism among college students was related to physical symptom reports, whereas optimism was not. In another study of college students, Chang, Maydeu-Olivares, and D'Zurilla (1997) found that pessimism, but not optimism, was related again to dysphoric symptoms. Schulz, Bookwala, Knapp, Scheier, and Williamson (1996) found that optimism was unrelated to survival in cancer patients, but that pessimism was correlated with earlier death. Räikkönen, Matthews, Flory, Owens, and Gump (1999) found that pessimistic adults (as well as those who were dispositionally anxious) had higher ambulatory blood pressure and greater negative mood than did opti-mistic adults. When the optimistic participants were in a negative mood, however, their blood pressure was as high as the pessimistic participants'.

Obviously we should be cautious about basing an intervention on any one study. Nevertheless, the results of these studies illustrate some ways we need to be careful in thinking about intervention. To the extent that optimism and pessimism are stable dispositions, and assuming some potential for change at the disposition level, it may be that potential for change varies depending on whether one is trying to create an optimistic disposition, or to dampen a pessimistic one. Similarly, if one is designing an intervention, it may very well be that different techniques need to be developed for creating optimism and diminishing pessimism, and it will be important to determine which goal is most important: If pessimism alone is associated with survival, we should not expend resources trying to increase optimism (at least until it can be shown that this has some reciprocal effect on levels of pessimism). Although optimism was clearly associated with more positive outcomes in Räikkönen et al.'s (1999) study, it is not at all clear that trying to make people more optimistic would effect such important health indicators as blood pressure. That is, optimism in this study did not appear to have *protective* benefits as much as pessimism seemed to have significant costs. Of course, if blood pressure volatility is strongly moderated by mood, it may very well be that trying to increase optimism would help people to regulate their moods, which might, in turn, have desirable effects on blood pressure. Nevertheless, we do not want to waste resources increasing optimism if we might more efficiently focus on some other mood regulation strategies or biofeedback techniques.

Intrapsychic Context and Comparison of Outcomes

The results discussed above reinforce the importance of the very basic idea that the more we know about the mechanisms that underlie a given empirical association between optimism, pessimism, and any other variable, the more likely it will be that our interventions or applications will be effective. Clearly, however, as we learn more about what can be changed and how to change it, we also need to consider precisely *what* we might want to change, in which contexts. At this point, we know very little about how to either increase dispositional optimism, or decrease dispositional pessimism—and certainly many dispositional theorists would be pessimistic about change at this level. Other varieties of optimism and pessimism are theoretically more amenable to change, however. Seligman (1991) has argued strongly that optimism can be learned. He and his colleagues define *optimism* as a particular explanatory style in response to negative life events (as previously discussed by Gillham, Shatté, Reivich, & Seligman, chap. 3, this volume). Seligman is also a persuasive advocate of learning a more optimistic style. Yet, much of the research on "learned optimism" has been based almost entirely on studies of people's pessimistic attributions for negative events, not on their optimistic attributions for positive events (Peterson & Chang, in press). In that sense, it seems curious that so much has been said by so many theorists about teaching people to develop an optimistic explanatory style, when in fact, there have actually been very few direct studies showing that an optimistic explanatory style leads to positive adjustment. Taylor (1989; Taylor & Brown, 1988) also argues for the benefits of an optimistic bias as part of a set of "mild positive illusions" that are related to better adaptation, and that are, to some extent, malleable. However, the adaptiveness of positive illusions has been seriously questioned (Baumeister, 1989; Colvin & Block, 1994). Norem (1989; see also chap. 4, this volume) proposes that the cognitive strategies of defensive pessimism and strategic optimism are potentially changeable. We talk a little more about research on these strategies below.

As we consider what might be changed, however, there are further complexities that might influence our answers to the question of whether, or under what circumstances, we should try to change what we might be able to change. Optimism and pessimism—in all the ways they can be defined—do not exist in an intrapsychic vacuum. Instead, they are more or less integrated into personality and are strongly related to a variety of other personality characteristics, temperament, and past experiences. Park, Moore, Turner, and Adler (1997), for example, take care to distinguish between positive effects of optimism that are mediated by constructive thinking and the less sanguine effects of "naive optimism." Their results lead them to suggest that optimism may need to be "channeled" through effective thinking strategies if it is to lead to better coping and adjustment; in other words, they found little evidence that optimism in isolation was related to better coping.

The question of whether optimism and pessimism are truly discriminable from related constructs has plagued researchers in this area from the start (Scheier, Carver, & Bridges, 1994). Putting aside the psychometric complexities of this debate for the moment, we need to consider the following: Even if we can isolate the positive or negative statistical impact of a given kind of optimism or pessimism on a particular outcome variable, it does not follow that an application of research seeking to target pessimism or optimism in isolation will be able to do so. In addition, it does not necessarily follow that even if this research does target pessimism or optimism in isolation, that there will be the further intended effect on the outcome in question. Davidson and Prkachin (1997), in one of the few published attempts to disentangle the effects of dispositional optimism and unrealistic optimism, showed in two different studies that dispositional optimism and unrealistic optimism *interacted* to predict coronary heart disease (CHD) related outcomes. In the first study, optimism alone was unrelated to exercise over time, while unrealistic optimism was related to decreased exercise over time. Those participants who scored high on both optimism and unrealistic optimism showed the largest *decreases* in exercise over time, while those who scored high in optimism and low in unrealistic optimism showed the greatest *increases*. A similar pattern was found in a second study, when the outcome variable was knowledge of CHD prevention after classroom instruction. In both studies, unrealistic optimism and dispositional optimism were positively, although not strongly, correlated with each other. Davidson and Prkachin's (1997) results suggest that attempting to increase optimism without taking into account other psychological variables would be misguided: We might have little effect on outcome, if we only targeted optimism, or we might have the unintended, "collateral" effect of increasing unrealistic optimism. At the extreme, trying to increase the optimism of those people who are already unrealistically optimistic might have serious negative effects. We are not suggesting that anyone has tried to do this—only that it seems that relatively little thought is typically given to how potential changes in optimism might influence and be influenced by other aspects of personality. Interaction effects such as those found by Davidson and Prkachin need to be included in our assessment of the costs and benefits of different kinds of optimism and pessimism.

We also need to be cognizant that statistical identification of the effects of single variables may have questionable relevance to psychology in vivo. That is, just because we can control statistically for the relationship between optimism and other variables (e.g., extraversion, narcissism, etc.) does not mean that we can necessarily target optimism in ways that separate it from other characteristics of actual people.

There are other examples of the ways in which cost–benefit analyses of optimism and pessimism are influenced by intrapsychic context, as well as by the particular outcome variables one examines. As reviewed in chapter 4 of this volume, Norem and her colleagues have done considerable research on the cognitive strategies of defensive pessimism and strategic optimism (Cantor & Norem, 1989; Norem, 1989; Norem & Cantor, 1986a, 1986b, 1990; Norem & Illingworth, 1993; Spencer & Norem, 1996). Defensive pessimism refers to a strategy individuals may use to pursue important goals: These individuals set unrealistically low expectations and then, for a given situation, devote considerable energy to mentally playing through or reflecting on all the possible outcomes they can imagine. Researchers have typically contrasted defensive pessimism with strategic optimism. The latter refers to a strategy whereby individuals set optimistic expectations for their own performance and actively avoid extensive reflection.

Generally this research has shown that defensive pessimists perform as well as strategic optimists, and that both groups show performance decrements and increased anxiety when prevented from using their preferred strategies. Much of this research has also shown that strategic optimists tend to be more satisfied and in a better mood than defensive pessimists, and they may exhibit better health and better performance over the long term. Often, however, a much too simplistic picture emerges from quick comparisons of outcomes in this research. Three reasons for this that are relevant to this chapter come to mind. The first is that too little attention is given to the fact that the individuals using these strategies are facing *different* psychological situations as they approach their goals. The second is that this research, as with much of the research in the field, covers too restrictive a range of variables and may ignore subtle or hidden costs of each strategy. The third is that too much attention is paid to the particular contrast between the outcomes of strategic optimists and defensive pessimists, when there are other equally, or even more, relevant contrasts to consider.

People who use defensive pessimism are typically high in anxiety (on state, trait, and physiological measures; Norem & Cantor, 1986a, 1986b; Norem & Illingworth, 1993; Spencer & Norem, 1996)—and that aspect of intrapsychic context is fundamental to understanding the strategy. It is tempting to think that people using defensive pessimism need to be calmed down and reassured, and that the best thing for them is to help them become more optimistic. In contrast, however, research suggests that it is very important to understand the particular function of the pessimism exhibited by people using this strategy. Its meaning and its consequences are only seen when it is considered in conjunction with the problem that anxiety poses for individuals motivated to pursue performance goals. Defensive pessimism (low expectations coupled with extensive reflection) offers a solution to that problem. Defensive pessimists perform *better* when they are allowed to maintain their low expectations and reflect before a task; their performance is impaired (and they feel more anxious) if that reflective process is disrupted (Norem & Cantor, 1986b; Norem & Illingworth, 1993; Spencer & Norem, 1996).

Further arguing against the "let's cheer 'em up" approach to defensive pessimists, research shows that positive mood inductions impair the performance of defensive pessimists, even though they may be effective at making them feel better (Norem & Illingworth, 1999; Sanna, 1998). Finally, a longitudinal study has shown significant improvement in self-esteem, as well as better overall performance and adjustment among anxious women who use defensive pessimism, as compared with anxious women who do not use the strategy (Norem, 1996).

There may indeed be costs to using defensive pessimism, as well as to other forms of pessimism, especially when one considers social outcomes. In Western societies such as the United States, where self-enhancement appears to be the rule, rather than the exception, an individual's expressions of pessimism may be perceived as undesirable by more optimistic others. Consistent with Helweg-Larsen, Sadeghian, and Webb's (1999) findings, most Westerners tend to socially reject pessimists. The existence of costs for defensive pessimism, however, does not necessarily negate its advantages for those who use it in terms of anxiety-management and subsequent performance. In addition, the relative costs and benefits of both defensive pessimism and strategic optimism may vary significantly across culture and context. In Eastern cultures where self-effacement is normative, expressions of optimism might be considered incongruent with the expectations of most

Asian people. As Chang (1996) found, Asians have a tendency to be more pessimistic than non-Asians. Accordingly, in Eastern cultures, optimistic individuals might incur negative interpersonal reactions from more pessimistic others. Currently, as discussed below, there is relatively little research that has examined the potential social and personal costs of optimism.

In quick review, these results present a complex, yet coherent picture of the costs and benefits associated with these strategies, and they begin to suggest some problems that might be associated with trying to change the strategies individuals use. We clearly need to take into account the other aspects of personality and experience with which varieties of optimism and pessimism are intertwined, as well as the varieties of outcomes for which they might have implications, before drawing broad conclusions about what characteristics or strategies are most desirable.

Interpersonal and Social Context

We do not have the space in this chapter to consider all the important aspects of context that should influence how we think about applications of optimism and pessimism research. There are, however, some examples that we can use to illustrate briefly the importance of other aspects of context.

Both Taylor and Seligman suggest that there are particular decision-making contexts that benefit from the accurate, albeit negative, perspective associated with pessimism (Seligman, 1991; Taylor & Gollwitzer, 1995). Seligman in particular argues that there needs to be *flexibility* associated with an optimistic perspective for it to be adaptive (see also Norem, 1989, on the importance of flexibility in strategy use). Situations where the potential "downside" is either relatively likely or relatively serious would seem especially to call for a balance of pessimism and optimism.

Currently, almost no research exists on the extent to which individuals (or on *which* individuals) are able to achieve this kind of balance or flexibility. One of the things likely to influence whether individuals can be flexible in their optimism is the extent to which it may be maintained by inhibitory or defensive processes, such as denial, repression, and projection (Norem, 1998). If and when optimism persists because of unconscious processes, then the costs associated with those processes need to be added to our assessments of this trait and to our understanding of how difficult individual change is likely to be. There are at least two kinds of costs that may be associated with what might be called defensive optimism: (a) direct health costs, such as those associated with repression (e.g., Pennebaker, Hughes, & O'Heeron, 1987); and (b) indirect costs that may accumulate precisely because less accessible unconscious processes are likely to limit flexibility (Norem, 1998).

A number of person-perception and group process research studies suggest that optimism, as part of the constellation of characteristics associated with extraversion, is highly regarded in others, at least in the United States. This "high regard" may be a very important influence on the social outcomes of optimists and pessimists. Nevertheless, very little research has examined specifically the social interactions and social networks of optimistic and pessimistic people, especially as they evolve over time. Following from other research, however, there is reason to hypothesize that optimists may have broader, yet less intense social networks than do pessimists (Norem, 1987). Considerable research remains to be done to explore the potential costs and benefits of optimism and pessimism that may derive from differences in the interpersonal interactions of those possessing each characteristic. One specific and glaring absence in the literature concerns the potential differences in others' reactions to optimism and pessimism that might be related to gender—a question that goes beyond whether there are mean differences, to see if the correlates and outcomes of pessimism and optimism in different contexts vary by gender.

Though there is voluminous research suggesting the advantages of self-enhancing and optimistically biased self-perceptions (e.g., Taylor & Armor, 1996; Taylor & Brown, 1988), little has been done to examine the potential implications of these tendencies as they influence perception of other people.[1] One wonders whether a pervasive tendency to be optimistic about one's self—especially if it is related to self-enhancement and even denial—might lead to ignoring or denigrating others and their potential contributions (Weinstein & Lachendro, 1982). Seldom have we seen much discussion or research into those kinds of potential costs. In one such rare exception, Colvin, Block, and Funder (1995) examined the social and interpersonal costs of self-enhancement. In one set of studies, young men and women were rated by others at 18 years of age (Study 1) and rated again 5 years later (Study 2). Results from both studies indicated that expressions of self-enhancement were associated with negative evaluations as made by independent raters as well as by friends. For men, negative evaluations included impressions such as "is guileful and deceitful" and "hostile toward others," whereas for women, they included impressions such as "transfers or projects blame" and "keeps people at a distance." In a final study involving opposite-gender interactions (Study 3), these investigators found again that men and women who self-enhanced were negatively rated by their peers. The consistency of their findings led Colvin et al. (1995) to raise strong doubts about the benefits of positive illusions:

> The present analyses suggest that self-enhancement, while aiding one's self-esteem, is over the long term an ineffective interpersonal strategy with both friends and acquaintances and, therefore, the growth or

---

[1]One exception is research that suggests that enhancing and optimistic biases extend to close others.

development of self. A vicious cycle is generated whereby self-enhancement is rigidly and frequently used to maintain positive self-regard but
at a continual and cumulative cost of alienating one's friends and
discouraging new acquaintances. (p. 1161)

Most research focuses on variables having to do with individual outcomes, rather than with outcomes associated with larger social groups, which
is congruent with our societal focus on individual development and achievement. Consider Ryff and Keyes's (1995) model and measure of psychological
well-being measured across six different dimensions of adaptive functioning
(e.g., self-acceptance, personal growth). Although we consider their model
and measure very important given the dearth of positive outcome measures
available to researchers, it is unfortunate that only one of the six scales
explicitly assesses for outcomes that go beyond the immediate person (viz.,
Positive Relations With Others). It is our contention that just as individual
optimism may have benefits for society at large—such as might be reaped
from the "can-do" attitude of the stereotypical American—there might also
be costs to society associated with a lack of attention to potential negative
outcomes. (What might be saved if we more routinely asked ourselves and
others with whom we make decisions "What if we are wrong"?) It is much
more difficult, of course, to do research on those kinds of outcomes. It does
not follow, however, that they are necessarily less important to consider.

Let us briefly note another way in which the social aspect of optimism
and pessimism has been neglected. More than half a century ago, Sanford,
Conrad, and Franck (1946) studied facets of optimism associated with the
consequences of war. Since then, and despite Bandura's (1977, 1986) emphasis that expectancies tied to specific contexts are more likely to be linked
to behavior, researchers have remained slow to embrace notions of "situated"
optimism and pessimism. (Note that we are not referring to Armor &
Taylor's [1998] notion of situated optimism as previously discussed by
Aspinwall, Richter, & Hoffman, chap. 10, this volume.) Nonetheless, some
researchers have looked at optimism associated with college life and academic performance (Prola & Stern, 1984); love relationships (Carnelley &
Janoff-Bulman, 1992); mood regulation (Catanzaro, 1993); and risk for AIDS
(Taylor et al., 1992). We anticipate in the forthcoming decades more studies
involving "situated" optimism and pessimism.

Life-Span Developmental Context

As is common in personality and social psychology, college students
have provided a convenience sample for much of the research on optimism
and pessimism although there are significant exceptions to this generalization. There is research, however, that suggests that the costs and benefits

of optimism and pessimism may vary across the life span; accordingly, we need to be sensitive to this aspect of context as we think about research applications. Isaacowitz and Seligman (1998) report that among the elderly, a realistically pessimistic perspective is associated with *better* adaptation to negative life events, in contrast to the typical findings with younger participants in the sample groups. In a related manner, Robinson-Whelen et al. (1997) found little evidence for the "power of positive thinking" in predicting anxiety, stress, depression, and self-appraised health among an older aged group of people composed of caregivers and noncaregivers. In addition, it is worth noting that although dispositional optimism and pessimism have been found to be unidimensional in college student populations (Scheier & Carver, 1985), the relation between the two variables has consistently been lower, and in some cases nonsignificant, in samples of people from older populations (e.g., Mroczek, Spiro, Aldwin, Ozer, & Bossé, 1993; Robinson-Whelen et al., 1997). For example, in a sample of older Swedish adults, Plomin et al. (1992) found that dispositional optimism was unrelated to dispositional pessimism ($r = -.02$). It is difficult to make out what these correlational findings may mean, although they do suggest that age (or factors associated with age, such as life experiences) may be an important moderator of the dimensionality of optimism and pessimism. Because increasingly more people in America and in other parts of the world are living longer, we look forward to seeing more studies that help evaluate the costs and benefits of optimism and pessimism among the elderly population.

On the other hand, there has been a growing push to teach children to be more optimistic and less pessimistic (Seligman, Reivich, Jaycox, & Gillham, 1995). Again, this has been based on the seldom-challenged assumption that optimism is good and pessimism is bad. Although this trend has caught the attention of parents and teachers alike who are eager to find a quick and simple panacea for dealing with problematic children, we still know too little about the form and function of optimism and pessimism among children to even begin meaningfully considering the short- and long-term costs and benefits of such interventions.

Helping children think more optimistically may help them feel less sad at some particular point in time—or even over time. We do not know very much, however, about what other effects such efforts may have over time. In fact, similar to findings that have linked high self-esteem (another highly regarded attribute in the minds of most parents and teachers) with expressions of hostility and anger (see e.g., Baumeister, Smart, & Boden, 1996; Kernis, Grannemann, & Barclay, 1989), efforts to promote high optimism and to eliminate pessimism may produce negative outcomes later on. For example, in a study involving young adults, Kasser and Ryan (1993) found that optimism associated with one's ability to obtain financial success was *negatively* associated with self-actualization, vitality, and global functioning, and *positively* associated with anxiety and behavioral disorders (viz., oppositional and conduct disorders).

For another example, consider Taylor et al.'s (1992) finding that AIDS-related optimism was positively associated with risky sexual behaviors. Although Taylor et al.'s finding was based on the study of a very specific population (viz., gay men), we find it difficult to ignore the potential implications for adolescents and young adults who remain a high-risk group for HIV infection (see also Kiehl, 1994). Consistent with our notion of "balance" throughout this chapter, Schwartz (1992) argues that deviations in *either* direction from an optimal balance of positive and negative thoughts (e.g., optimism and pessimism, respectively), will result in sure and certain psychopathology. Hence, it may be just as maladaptive to be excessively optimistic as it can be to be excessively pessimistic. Accordingly, parents and teachers may want to exercise caution before running the risk of nurturing a generation of overly optimistic children who may be at high risk for disappointment and disturbance when faced later on with many of the hardships and realities of modern life (e.g., parental divorce, violence, illness, poverty). In fact, data suggests that the "power of positive thinking" can sometimes backfire under stressful life conditions.

According to Brown and McGill's (1989) identity disruption model, accumulation of life events inconsistent with one's self-concept or identity is believed to result in maladjustment (e.g., poor physical health). As expected, these investigators found that an accumulation of positive life events was associated with greater physical symptoms for those who held negative compared with positive self-schemas. In contrast to this model, Chang (1999a) set out to examine the relations among optimism, pessimism, negative life events, and adjustment in a sample of young adults. Considering the potential costs of optimism, Chang (1999a) predicted that the accumulation of negative life events may cause greater disturbance for optimists than for pessimists, and thus, poorer adjustment in the former than in the latter group. In contrast, it was expected that chronic expectations for negative outcomes would actually help pessimists abate the harmful influence of negative life events on adjustment. Consistent with expectations, results of this study indicated that the associations between negative life events and poor psychological and physical outcomes were exacerbated for optimists, but not for pessimists. In fact, for pessimists, experiencing greater negative life events was not even significantly related to outcomes. Hence, underscoring Tennen and Affleck's (1987) concerns about the potential costs of dispositional optimism, these findings indicate that when a lot of bad things happen, optimists indeed may be particularly vulnerable. However, because Chang's (1999a) study was based on a college student population, the generalizability of these findings to younger populations remains an open question.

In considering environmental influences further, we should not neglect the potential role of broad social factors on optimism. For example, Schutte, Valerio, and Carrillo (1996) found that for White Americans, the relation between socioeconomic status and dispositional optimism was positive and significant. In addition, more specific contexts also must be considered. For example, Burger and Palmer (1992) found that individuals who had recently experienced the 1989 California earthquake tended to express greater pessimism for being seriously hurt in a natural disaster than did a group of control participants who had not experienced the earthquake. However, the former group did not differ from the control group in expectancies concerning a variety of other traumatic life events unrelated to natural disasters (e.g., mugging, divorce, heart attack). Thus, environmental determinants of pessimism for one situation may not influence pessimism for others. In a more recent study that tracked responses to the 1994 California earthquake, similar findings were obtained for those people who had just experienced the earthquake (Helweg-Larsen, 1999). Particularly notable, however, was Helweg-Larsen's finding that for those people who directly experienced the earthquake, the specificity of their lack of optimism bias (e.g., believed that one's chances of getting seriously injured in a future earthquake was greater than the typical student) remained relatively unchanged across a 5-month period, compared with those who did not have such experiences. Hence, exposures to certain types of encounters (possibly those that are life-threatening and unpredictable), appear to have a specific and enduring influence on people's lack of optimism. However, it is unclear if such outcomes are adaptive, maladaptive, or a little bit of both.

As previously discussed by Zuckerman (see chap. 8, this volume), very few studies have looked at potential biological influences on optimism and pessimism. Moreover, of the conducted studies, very similar methodologies have been used, namely, comparing monozygotic and dyzygotic twins in their expressions of optimism and pessimism. Another way to explore underlying biological influences associated with the development of optimism and pessimism is to consider relations between biological parents and their children. In a recent study that focused on how optimism and pessimism moderated the link between perceived stress and adjustment in a sample of younger and older adults, the latter group was largely composed of biological parents of the former group (Chang, 1999b). Although not a central point of the study, dispositional optimism was found to be significantly, albeit very modestly, correlated between biologically related parents and their adult children ($r = .12$). Given that research in behavioral genetics indicates that a child typically obtains half of his or her genes from each biological parent, it is surprising that a more robust correlation was not found. Thus, these findings may suggest that environmental factors (and their interaction with biological factors) play a greater role in the development of optimism and pessimism. No doubt, we will have to wait for the results of studies using more rigorous methodologies, such as adoption studies, to better distinguish the influences of genetics, environment, and their interaction on optimism and pessimism. In general, as can be seen in this section much work remains to be done on the origins of kinds of optimism and pessimism, as well as on their development and their consequences across the life span.

Cultural Contexts

In a study of 31 countries where people were asked if the coming year would be better or worse than the present year, Michalos (1988) found that the average percentage of people who expressed optimism for the coming year across a 10-year period varied by country. For example, over a 7-year period, an average of 50% of Americans believed that the new year would be better compared with an average of 10% among Austrians. Cultural differences in optimism or pessimism also can be expressed in other ways. The first author recalls receiving voluminous mail from Eastern European Block countries requesting reprints of the first articles on defensive pessimism—evidence that the popularity of pessimism research might vary across cultures. Beyond interest in research, there is also good reason to believe that the implications and consequences of optimism and pessimism—their cultural meaning generally—vary across culture.

The United States is widely perceived as a notably optimistic society by people in other countries. Beyond this stereotype, there has been much theorizing about aspects of American culture that promote and value optimism, such as high social mobility and an emphasis on individualism (e.g., Murphy, 1947). It would not be surprising if the costs and benefits of optimism and pessimism also varied depending on cultural context. Zane, Sue, Hu, and Kwon (1991) found that Asian Americans had higher scores in pessimism in some domains, but their scores were less optimistic than White Americans in other domains, and that the particular patterns of optimism and pessimism were consistent with differences in cultural values. Chang (1996) also found that Asian Americans were significantly more pessimistic than were White Americans, but not significantly less optimistic. In addition, although pessimism was negatively associated with problem solving and with expressing emotion coping strategies for White Americans, it was positively associated with use of these coping strategies for Asian Americans. He interprets these data in terms of the different cultural sensibilities of the two groups, and notes that, much as with defensive pessimists, negative outcome expectancies are correlated with active coping among

Asian Americans. Chang's research suggests that we be extremely cautious about trying to adapt research findings from groups composed of White American populations.

This research also points to the potential for cultural clashes as people of different backgrounds try to work together, as is a common part of American life. For example, Helweg-Larsen et al.'s (1999) findings indicating that pessimistic target participants are more likely than optimistic target participants to be socially rejected because of people's common assumption that pessimists are depressed, may suggest significant social and psychological costs for many Asian Americans, who typically do express heightened pessimism (as previously discussed by Chang, chap. 12, this volume). Therefore, to the extent that optimism and pessimism are differently valued and interpreted by individuals from different cultural backgrounds, one would expect significant misunderstanding and confusion in clinical, educational, work-related, and other settings, concerning efforts to impress an optimistic viewpoint. A bolder vision and model that respects differences and similarities between people is needed if a culturally pluralistic society such as ours is to thrive and flourish (Epps, 1974).

Cultural contexts may also influence the malleability of optimism and pessimism. Dispositional optimism and pessimism may be especially difficult to change in a cultural context where these qualities are perceived to be unchangeable. Choi, Nisbett, and Norenzayan (1999) have noted that, whether from Eastern or Western cultural backgrounds, people almost universally appear to make dispositional attributions (e.g., "Jane is smiling because she is a happy person"). Yet, according to Choi et al., most Asians, unlike most Westerners, appear to perceive dispositions as changeable and socially situated (e.g., "Jane is smiling because she is a happy person ever since she successfully completed her doctoral defense"). In a similar vein, research has shown that the American tendency to believe that math ability is fixed, permanent, and strongly gender-related may impede efforts to decrease the differences between scores of males and females on standardized math tests. In contrast, in some countries (e.g., China), math ability is believed to be primarily a function of effort, and there is no gender difference in math performance (Halpern, 1992). The implications of these findings are too numerous to consider in the present context, but at least two relevant points come to mind. First, efforts to change dispositional optimism and pessimism may be more effective among those who perceive dispositions as malleable (e.g., Easterners), than among those who may perceive dispositions as immutable (e.g., Westerners). Second, we speculate that the negative consequences of dispositions (or explanatory style) may be most harmful for those who believe that dispositions, in general, are unchangeable and unaffected by situational factors. Hence, the view that optimism is always good and pessimism is always bad may be moderated by whether one believes that "once an optimist always an optimist" or "once a pessimist always a pessimist."

Finally, beyond our recognition of the influences of a Westernized culture that typically pushes Americans to see themselves better off than others (Taylor & Brown, 1988), we hope to keep things in perspective, and suggest another important concomitant, dare we say cause, of Americans' noted optimism. For many immigrants, coming to America has often been associated with visions of attainable prosperity, that is, of obtaining means to live a substantially better life for oneself and for one's family (Roger, 1990). Hence, it should not be a great surprise if some of the most optimistic people on earth have come to make America their home. By the same token, recall the heightened pessimism of Asians discussed earlier. In Japan where long work hours are the rule rather than the exception, people have suffered from cardiovascular attacks and in some cases died due to *karoshi*, extreme work overload (e.g., Nakagawa & Sugita, 1994; Uehata, 1991). Thus, for some Asians, pessimism may be a realistic reflection of the demanding conditions of their lives.

SUMMARY AND CONCLUSION

We hope it is clear that the point of this chapter is not to refute the voluminous literature that relates optimism to good outcomes. Rather, our point is simply to suggest that we embrace the complexity in that literature and recognize the gaps in our knowledge, especially in any attempt to apply research findings in "real life." As researchers who have focused on pessimism as well as on optimism, we are perhaps especially sensitive to the zeitgeist that tends to present optimism as uniquely and completely rose-colored. We feel strongly that, in fact, the picture is multicolored. The benefits and costs of optimism and pessimism depend on individual personality; the kind of optimism or pessimism about which one speaks; the kinds of outcomes one focuses on; and the particular social, cultural, and life span contexts. Thorough and thoughtful consideration of these aspects of context ought to lead to more insightful research into the costs and benefits of optimism and pessimism, as well as to more effective applications of that research for the betterment of all people.

REFERENCES

Armor, D. A., & Taylor, S. E. (1998). Situated optimism: Specific outcome expectancies and self-regulation. In M. P. Zanna (Ed.), *Advances in experimental social psychology* (Vol. 30, pp. 309–379). New York: Academic Press.

Bandura, A. (1977). Self-efficacy: Toward a unifying theory of behavioral change. *Psychological Review, 84,* 191–215.

Bandura, A. (1986). *Social foundations of thought and action: A social cognitive theory.* Englewood Cliffs, NJ: Prentice-Hall.

Baumeister, R. F. (1989). The optimal margin of illusion. *Journal of Social and Clinical Psychology, 8,* 176–189.

Baumeister, R. F., Smart, L., & Boden, J. M. (1996). Relations of threatened egotism to violence and aggression: The dark side of high self-esteem. *Psychological Review, 103,* 5–33.

Brown, J. D., & McGill, K. L. (1989). The cost of good fortune: When positive life events produce negative health consequences. *Journal of Personality and Social Psychoogy, 57,* 1103–1110.

Burger, J. M., & Palmer, M. L. (1992). Changes in and generalization of unrealistic optimism following experiences with stressful events: Reactions to the 1989 California earthquake. *Personality and Social Psychology Bulletin, 18,* 39–43.

Cantor, N., & Norem, J. K. (1989). Defensive pessimism and stress and coping. *Social Cognition, 7,* 92–112.

Carnelley, K. B., & Janoff-Bulman, R. (1992). Optimism about love relationships: General vs specific lessons from one's personal experiences. *Journal of Social and Personal Relationships, 9,* 5–20.

Catanzaro, S. J. (1993). Mood regulation expectancies, anxiety sensitivity, and emotional distress. *Journal of Abnormal Psychology, 102,* 327–330.

Chang, E. C. (1996). Cultural differences in optimism, pessimism, and coping: Predictors of subsequent adjustment in Asian American and Caucasian American college students. *Journal of Counseling Psychology, 43,* 113–123.

Chang, E. C. (1998). Distinguishing between optimism and pessimism: A second look at the "optimism neuroticism hypothesis." In R. R. Hoffman, M. F. Sherrik, & J. S. Warm (Eds.), *Viewing Psychology as a whole: The integrative science of William N. Dember* (pp. 415–432). Washington, DC: American Psychological Association.

Chang, E. C. (1999a). *Optimism, pessimism, negative life events, and psychological and physical adjustment: When expecting the best, but experiencing the worst, is associated with negative outcomes.* Unpublished manuscript, Department of Psychology, University of Michigan, Ann Arbor.

Chang, E. C. (1999b). *Optimism-pessimism and stress appraisal in younger and older adults: Testing a cognitive interactive model of psychological adjustment.* Unpublished manuscript, Department of Psychology, University of Michigan, Ann Arbor.

Chang, E. C., Maydeu-Olivares, A., & D'Zurilla, T. J. (1997). Optimism and pessimism as partially independent constructs: Relations to positive and negative affectivity and psychological well-being. *Personality and Individual Differences, 23,* 433–440.

Choi, I., Nisbett, R. E., & Norenzayan, A. (1999). Causal attribution across cultures: Variation and universality. *Psychological Bulletin, 125,* 47–63.

Colvin, C. R., & Block, J. (1994). Do positive illusions foster mental health? An examination of the Taylor and Brown formulation. *Psychological Bulletin, 116,* 3–20.

Colvin, C. R., Block, J., & Funder, D. C. (1995). Overly positive self-evaluations and personality: Negative implications for mental health. *Journal of Personality and Social Psychology, 68,* 1152–1162.

Davidson, K., & Prkachin, D. (1997). Optimism and unrealistic optimism have an interacting impact of health-promoting behavior and knowledge changes. *Personality and Social Psychology Bulletin, 23,* 617–625.

Dolinski, D., Gromski, W., & Zawisza, E. (1987). Unrealistic pessimism. *Journal of Social Psychology, 127,* 511–516.

Epps, E. G. (1974). *Cultural pluralism.* Berkeley, CA: McCutchan Publishing.

Epstein, S., & Meier, P. (1989). Constructive thinking: A broad coping variable with specific components. *Journal of Personality and Social Psychology, 57,* 332–350.

Frese, M. (1992). A plea for realistic pessimism: On objective reality, coping with stress, and psychological dysfunction. In L. Montada, S.-H. Filipp, & M. J. Lerner (Eds.), *Life crises and experiences of loss in adulthood* (pp. 81–94). Hillsdale, NJ: Erlbaum.

Halpern, D. F. (1992). *Sex differences in cognitive abilities.* Hillsdale, NJ: Erlbaum.

Helweg-Larsen, M. (1999). (The lack of) optimistic biases in response to the 1994 Northridge earthquake: The role of personal experience. *Basic and Applied Social Psychology, 21,* 119–129.

Helweg-Larsen, M., Sadeghian, P., Webb, M. S. (1999). The stigma of being pessimistically biased. Unpublished manuscript, Transylvania University, Lexington, KY.

Isaacowitz, D. M., & Seligman, M. E. P. (1998). *Prevention of depression in older adults: Theory, methodology and pitfalls.* Invited paper presented in Opportunities and Pitfalls in Adult and Older Adult Prevention Research. Symposium at the Annual Meeting of the American Psychological Association, San Francisco, CA.

Kasser, T., & Ryan, R. M. (1993). A dark side of the American dream: Correlates of financial success as a central life aspiration. *Journal of Personality and Social Psychology, 65,* 410–422.

Kelman, H. (1945). Neurotic pessimism. *Psychoanalytic Review, 32,* 419–448.

Kernis, M. H., Grannemann, B. D., & Barclay, L. C. (1989). Stability and level of self-esteem as predictors of anger arousal and hostility. *Journal of Personality and Social Psychology, 56,* 1013–1022.

Kiehl, E. (1994). *Attitudes towards AIDS among unrealistic optimists, health optimists, and health defensive pessimists.* Unpublished honors thesis. Psychology Department, Wellesley College, Wellesley, MA.

Marshall, G. N., Wortman, C. B., Kusulas, J. W., Hervig, L. K., & Vickers, R. R., Jr. (1992). Distinguishing optimism from pessimism: Relations to fundamental dimensions of mood and personality. *Journal of Personality and Social Psychology, 62*, 1067–1074.

Michalos, A. C. (1988). Optimism in thirty counties over a decade. *Social Indicators Research, 20*, 177–180.

Mroczek, D. K., Spiro, A., Aldwin, C. M., Ozer, D. J., & Bossé, R. (1993). Construct validation of optimism and pessimism in older men: Findings from the normative aging study. *Health Psychology, 12*, 406–409.

Murphy, G. (1947). *Personality: A biosocial approach to origins and structure.* New York: Harper & Brothers.

Nakagawa, T., & Sugita, M. (1994). Life style changes and psychosomatic problems in Japan. *Homeostasis in Health and Disease, 35*, 180–189.

Norem, J. K. (1987). *Strategic realities: Optimism and defensive pessimism.* Unpublished doctoral dissertation, University of Michigan, Ann Arbor.

Norem, J. K. (1989). Cognitive strategies as personality: Effectiveness, specificity, flexibility, and change. In D. M. Buss & N. Cantor (Eds.), *Personality psychology: Recent trends and emerging issues* (pp. 45–60). New York: Springer-Verlag.

Norem, J. K. (1996, August). *Cognitive strategies and the rest of personality.* Paper presented at the Annual Meeting of the American Psychological Association, Toronto, Canada.

Norem, J. K. (1998). Should we lower our defenses about defense mechanisms? *Journal of Personality, 66*, 895–917.

Norem, J. K., & Cantor, N. (1986a). Anticipatory and post hoc cushioning strategies: Optimism and defensive pessimism in "risky" situations. *Cognitive Therapy and Research, 10*, 347–362.

Norem, J. K., & Cantor, N. (1986b). Defensive pessimism: Harnessing anxiety as motivation. *Journal of Personality and Social Psychology, 51*, 1208–1217.

Norem, J. K., & Cantor, N. (1990). Cognitive strategies, coping and perceptions of competence. In R. J. Sternberg & J. J. Kolligian (Eds.), *Competence considered* (pp. 190–204). New Haven, CT: Yale University Press.

Norem, J. K., & Illingworth, K. S. S. (1993). Strategy-dependent effects of reflecting on self and tasks: Some implications for optimism and defensive pessimism. *Journal of Personality and Social Psychology, 65*, 822–835.

Norem, J. K., & Illingworth, K. S. S. (1999). *Mood and performance among strategic optimists and defensive pessimists.* Unpublished manuscript, Department of Psychology, Wellesley College, Wellesley, MA.

Park, C. L., Moore, P. J., Turner, R. A., & Adler, N. E. (1997). The roles of constructive thinking and optimism in psychological and behavioral adjustment during pregnancy. *Journal of Personality and Social Psychology, 73*, 584–592.

Pennebaker, J. W., Hughes, C. F., & O'Heeron, R. C. (1987). The psychophysiology of confession: Linking inhibitory and psychosomatic processes. *Journal of Personality and Social Psychology, 52,* 781–793.

Peterson, C., & Chang, E. C. (in press). Optimism and flourishing. To appear in C. L. M. Keyes (Ed.), *Flourishing: The positive person and the good life.* Washington, DC: American Psychological Association.

Peterson, C., & Seligman, M. E. P. (1987). Explanatory style and illness. *Journal of Personality, 55,* 237–265.

Plomin, R., Scheier, M. F., Bergeman, C. S., Pedersen, N. L., Nesselroade, J. R., & McClearn, G. E. (1992). Optimism, pessimism and mental health: A twin/adoption analysis. *Personality and Individual Differences, 13,* 921–930.

Prola, M., & Stern, D. (1984). Optimism about college life and academic performance in college. *Psychological Reports, 55,* 347–350.

Räikkönen, K., Matthews, K. A., Flory, J. D., Owens, J. F., & Gump, B. B. (1999). Effects of optimism, pessimism and trait anxiety on ambulatory blood pressure and mood during everyday life. *Journal of Personality and Social Psychology, 76,* 104–113.

Robinson-Whelen, S., Kim, C., MacCallum, R. C., & Kiecolt-Glaser, J. K. (1997). Distinguishing optimism from pessimism in older adults: Is it more important to be optimistic or not to be pessimistic? *Journal of Personality and Social Psychology, 73,* 1345–1353.

Roger, D. (1990). *Coming to America: A history of immigration and ethnicity in American life.* New York: HarperCollins.

Ryff, C. D., & Keyes, C. L. M. (1995). The structure of psychological well-being revisited. *Journal of Personality and Social Psychology, 69,* 719–727.

Sanford, R. N., Conrad, H. S., & Franck, K. (1946). Psychological determinants of optimism regarding the consequences of war. *Journal of Psychology, 22,* 207–235.

Sanna, L. J. (1998). Defensive pessimism and optimism: The bitter-sweet influence of mood on performance and prefactual and counterfactual thinking. *Cognition and Emotion, 12,* 635–665.

Scheier, M. F., & Carver, C. S. (1985). Optimism, coping, and health: Assessment and implications of generalized outcome expectancies. *Health Psychology, 4,* 219–247.

Scheier, M. F., Carver, C. S., & Bridges, M. W. (1994). Distinguishing optimism from neuroticism (and trait anxiety, self-mastery, and self-esteem): A reevaluation of the Life Orientation Test. *Journal of Personality and Social Psychology, 67,* 1063–1078.

Schulz, R., Bookwala, J., Knapp, J. E., Scheier, M., & Williamson, G. M. (1996). Pessimism, age, and cancer mortality. *Psychology and Aging, 11,* 304–309.

Schutte, J. W., Valerio, J. K., & Carrillo, V. (1996). Optimism and socioeconomic status: A cross-cultural study. *Social Behavior and Personality, 24,* 9–18.

Schwartz, R. M. (1992). State of mind model and personal construct theory: Implications for psychopathology. *International Journal of Personal Construct Psychology*, *5*, 123–143.

Seligman, M. E. P. (1991). *Learned optimism*. New York: Knopf.

Seligman, M. E. P., Reivich, K., Jaycox, L. H., & Gillham, J. (1995). *The optimistic child*. Boston: Houghton-Mifflin.

Spencer, S. M., & Norem, J. K. (1996). Reflection and distraction: Defensive pessimism, strategic optimism, and performance. *Personality and Social Psychology Bulletin*, *22*, 354–365.

Taylor, S. E. (1989). *Positive illusions: Creative self-deception and the healthy mind*. New York: Basic Books.

Taylor, S. E., & Armor, D. A. (1996). Positive illusions and coping with adversity. *Journal of Personality*, *64*, 873–898.

Taylor, S. E., & Brown, J. D. (1988). Illusion and well-being: A social psychological perspective on mental health. *Psychological Bulletin*, *103*, 193–210.

Taylor, S. E., & Gollwitzer, R. M. (1995). The effects of mindset on positive illusions. *Journal of Personality and Social Psychology*, *69*, 213–226.

Taylor, S. E., Kemeny, M. E., Aspinwall, L. G., Schneider, S. G., Rodriguez, R., & Herbert, M. (1992). Optimism, coping, psychological distress, and high-risk sexual behavior among men at risk for acquired immunodeficiency syndrome (AIDS). *Journal of Personality and Social Psychology*, *63*, 460–473.

Tennen, H., & Affleck, G. (1987). The costs and benefits of optimistic explanations and dispositional optimism. *Journal of Personality*, *55*, 376–393.

Uehata, T. (1991). Long working hours and occupational stress-related cardiovascular attacks among middle-aged workers in Japan. *Journal of Human Ergology*, *20*, 147–153.

Weinstein, N. D. (1980). Unrealistic optimism about future life events. *Journal of Personality and Social Psychology*, *39*, 806–820.

Weinstein, N. D., & Lachendro, E. (1982). Egocentrism as a source of unrealistic optimism. *Personality and Social Psychology Bulletin*, *8*, 195–200.

Zane, N. W. S., Sue, S., Hu, L., & Kwon, J. (1991). Asian-American assertion: A social learning analysis of cultural differences. *Journal of Counseling Psychology*, *38*, 63–70.

AUTHOR INDEX

Abbott, R. A., *144, 167, 215, 255*
Abe, J. S., 274, *277*
Abele, A. E., 226, *236*
Abeles, M., 156, *164*
Abramson, L. Y., 54, 55, 56, 57, 59, 60, 63, 66, 69, *72, 73, 74*, 87, 100, 129, 130, *140*, 179, *185, 187*, *279*, 298, 302, 304, 306, *315*, *318*
Achee, J. W., 91, 98
Adler, A., 80, 97
Adler, N. E., 191, *214*, 351, *365*
Adrian, C., 57, 67, 71, 307, *318*
Affleck, G., 106, 117, *118, 123*, 147, 148, 149, 150, 152, 155, 156, 158, 162, *164, 165, 166, 168*, 191, 208, *212, 213, 216*, 358, *367*
Ahrens, A. H., 63, *70*
Akhavan, S., 69
Aldwin, C. M., 154, *167*, 357, *365*
Allen, G. W., 27, 28
Alloy, L. B., 54, 57, 69, *74*, 130, *140*, 179, *185, 187*, 302, *315*, 341, *345*
Allport, G., 4, *11*
American Psychiatric Association, 272, *277*, 341, *344*
Amirkhan, J. H., 67, 69
Anderson, C. A., 137, *140*
Anderson, J., 301, *315*
Anderson, J. R., *12*, 102, 108, *119, 122*
Anderson, K., 137, *144*
Andersson, G., 148, 163, *164, 165*
Angold, A., 301, *315*
Antonovsky, A., 133, *140*
Apter, A., 156, *165*
Arduino, K., 341, *345*
Armor, D. A., 40, *49*, 190, *211*, 218, 223, 224, 225, *236*, 355, 356, *362, 367*
Arnault, L. H., 137, *140*
Ashby, F. G., 230, 232, *236, 237*
Aspinwall, L. G., 67, 69, *144, 168*, 191, 197, 200, 201, 203, *211, 216*, 217, 218, 220, 221, 222, 223,

225, 226, 227, 229, 230, 231, 233, 235, 236, *237, 238*, 240, *253*, 367
Atkinson, J. W., 240, *253*
Ausbrooks, D. P., 193, *211*
Austin, J. T., 34, 35, 49
Avila, C., 172, *187*
Aydin, G., 309, *315*
Azaria, R., 196, *212*

Babyak, M. A., 107, *119, 122*
Backer, J. T., 193, *214*
Baer, P. E., *120, 212*
Bahr, G. R., 138, *140*
Bailey, J., 4, 8, *11*
Bailey, S., 137, *144*
Baker, F., 148, *165*, 191, *212*
Ball, S. A., 172, 173, *185*
Bandura, A., 130, 136, 138, *140*, 162, 240, *253*, 356, *363*
Bantirgu, T., 283, *296*
Barclay, L. C., 357, *364*
Barnum, D. D., 117, *119*
Barr, L. C., 180, *187*
Barratt, P., 173, *186*
Barron, C. R., 193, *211*
Barrows, E., *165*
Barry, J., 286, *296*
Barsky, A. J., 139, *140*
Basso, M. R., 232, *236*
Bastien, S., 292, *297*
Bates, J. E., 57, 69
Baumeister, R. F., 240, *253*, 351, 357, *363*
Beach, S. R. H., 231, *238*
Beck, A. T., 85, 89, 97, 109, 113, 115, *119*, 179, *185*, 259, 271, *277*, 289, *296*, 302, 303, 311, *315*, 322, 325, 329, 331, 332, 343, *344, 345*
Beck, J. S., 331, 332, 343, *344*
Bedrosian, R. C., 302, *315*
Belongia, C., 60, *71*
Bemporad, J. R., 304, 306, *315*
Bennet, D. S., 57, 69
Benson, H., xx, *xxi*

Bergbower, K., 137, *141*
Bergeman, C. S., *73, 187, 366*
Bergen, D. J., 92, 98
Bergin, A. E., xvii, xx, *xxi*
Berglas, S., 80, 97
Berntorp, E., *140*
Betson, C., *216*
Bettes, B. A., 56, *73*, 129, *142*
Bible, xix, xx, *xxi*
Billingsley, K. D., 199, *211*
Bishop, G. D., 193, *213*
Blackburn, T. C., 65, *74*, 258, *280*
Blaney, P. H., 138, *144*
Blankstein, K. R., 193, *211*
Block, J., 240, *254*, 351, 355, *364*
Blomkvist, V., 137, *140*
Blumenfeld, P. C., 305, *319*
Boag, L. C., 304, *319*
Boden, J. M., 240, *253*, 357, *363*
Bofinger, F., 137, *140*
Boggiano, A. K., 305, *319*
Bolger, N., 150, *165*
Bookwala, J., 133, *144*, 241, *255*, 349, *366*
Booth-Kewley, S., 133, *141*
Borders, T. F., *122*
Bossé, R., 154, *167*, 357, *365*
Bossio, L. M., 58, *73*, 134, 136, *142*, 291, *298*
Bouchard, T. J., Jr., 177, *185, 187*
Bower, J. E., 219, *238*
Bradbury, T. N., 59, *71*
Bradley, C. F., 59, *72*
Brehm, J. W., 42, 44, 46, *49, 51*
Brickman, P., 65, 69
Bridges, M. W., 6, *12*, 41, *50*, 102, 106, 108, 111, *120*, 134, *143*, 154, *167*, 190, 215, 218, *237*, 240, *254*, 351, *366*
Brislin, R., 257, *277*
Bromberger, J. T., 198, *211*
Brooks, J., 283, 285, *297*
Brower, A. M., 86, *97*
Brown, C., 44, *49*
Brown, J. D., 81, *100*, 224, 238, 240, 241, 243, 244, 247, 251, *253*, *254, 255*, 349, 350, 355, 358, *362, 363, 367*
Brown, R. T., 307, *318*
Bruce, S., 201, *213*
Bruch, M. A., 341, *344*

Brunhart, S. M., 201, *211*, 223, 225, 226, *227, 236*
Bryk, A. S., 156, *165*
Buchanan, G. M., 54, 56, 58, 69, *70*, 136, *140*
Buchsbaum, M. S., 179, *188*
Budenz, D., 302, *315*
Burger, J. M., 359, *363*
Burke, M. J., 179, *185*
Burke, P., 307, *319*
Burnett, J. W., 67, *70*
Burns, D. D., 336, *344*
Burns, M. O., 65, *70*
Buss, A. H., 110, *119*
Buss, D. M., 139, *140*
Byrne, D., 286, *296*

Cacciola, J., *144*
Cacioppo, J. T., 85, *97*
Calkins, D. R., *141*
Camac, C., 173, *188*
Campbell, D. T., 110, *119*, xx, *xxi*
Campbell, J. D., 85, 86, *97, 100*
Camus, A., 4, *11*
Cantor, N., 77, 81, 86, 88, 91, 92, *97*, 99, 250, *253, 254*, 270, *279*, 349, 352, 353, *363, 365*
Carey, G., 275, *280*, 329, 333, *346*
Carnelley, K. B., 356, *363*
Carrillo, V., 359, *366*
Carvajal, S. C., 201, 209, *211*
Carver, C. S., 4, 6, *12*, 34, 35, 36, 37, 38, 39, 40, 41, 42, 43, 45, 48, *49*, *50*, 53, 54, 59, 60, 63, 64, 67, 68, *70*, *73, 74*, 85, 87, *100*, 102, 104, 105, 106, 108, 109, 110, 111, 112, 117, *119*, *120, 121*, 130, 134, 138, *140, 141, 143*, *144*, 147, 148, 151, 154, 158, 159, *165, 167*, 173, *187*, 190, 191, 192, 194, 195, 197, 199, 201, 203, 205, 206, 207, 208, 210, *211, 212, 215, 216*, 218, 219, 220, 221, 223, 236, *237*, *238*, 240, *253, 255*, 263, 264, *279*, 286, 289, *298*, 302, *320*, 328, 339, 341, 342, *344, 345*, 348, 351, 357, *366*
Castellon, C., 7, *12*, 130, *143, 144*
Catanzaro, S. J., 356, *363*
Caumartin, S. M., 137, *141*

Cecil, M. A., 309, *316*
Centers for Disease Control, 301, *316*
Chamberlain, K., 196, *212*
Chang, E. C., 6, *11*, 62, 66, *70*, 153, *165*, 172, 175, *185*, 193, 200, *212*, 221, *237*, 259, 263, 264, 265, 266, 267, 268, 269, 270, 271, 273, 275, 276, 277, *278*, 284, 296, 342, 344, 349, 350, 354, 358, 359, 360, *362*, *363*, *366*
Cheavens, J., 101, 115, 116, 118, *122*
Chesney, M. A., 208, *213*
Chiara, A., 69
Choi, I., 361, *364*
Choi, S. C., 258, *278*
Chopra, D., 139, *141*
Christman, N. J., 196, *212*
Chuang, H. T., 137, *141*
Cichetti, D., 303, 304, 305, 307, *316*
Clance, P. R., 84, 85, *97*
Clark, H., 201, *215*
Clark, J., *344*
Clark, K. C., *49*, *141*, *165*, 211, 236, 253
Clark, L. A., 63, 66, *70*, *74*, 110, 112, *123*, 150, *168*, 275, 280, 286, 298, 299, 329, 333, 346
Clark, L. F., 208, *212*
Clarke, G. N., 310, *316*
Cleiren, M., 42, *49*
Coates, D., 69
Cobb, S., 137, *141*
Cochran, S., 54, 60, *71*
Cohen, J. H., 198, *212*
Cohn, E., 69
Cole, D. A., 61, *74*
Coleman, P. K., 193, *214*
Collette, L., 208, *214*
Collins, J. C., 231, *238*
Collins, R. L., 229, *238*
Colvin, C. R., 240, *254*, 351, 355, *364*
Colvin, D., 138, *142*
Conrad, H. S., 356, *366*
Cook, D. L., 114, *119*
Cook, W., *122*
Cooper, H. P., 201, *213*
Cooper, M. L., 194, *214*
Cornell, D., 231, *238*
Cornette, M., 69
Costa, P. T., 85, *97*, 132, *141*

Cousins, N., 139, *141*
Coyne, J. C., 92, 97, 149, *166*, 308, *316*
Cozzarelli, C., 148, *165*, 191, 194, *212*, *214*
Craighead, E. W., 57, *71*, 302, *318*
Craighead, L. W., 330, 331, 334, 338, 339, 341, *344*
Crandall, C. S., 84, 86, 93, 99
Craske, M., 309, *316*
Creighton, J. L., 101, *121*
Crepaz, N., 231, *238*
Crits-Cristoph, P., 322, *344*
Crofton, A., 63, *72*
Cronbach, L. J., 283, *296*
Crowne, D. P., 109, *119*
Crowson, Jr., J. J., 113, 117, *120*, *122*, 234, *237*
Csikzentmihalyi, I. S., 65, *70*
Csikzentmihalyi, M., 65, *70*, 148, *165*
Cuddihy, N., 81, *97*
Curbow, B., 148, *165*, 191, 193, *212*
Curry, L. A., 114, 116, *119*
Cutler, N. R., 178, *185*
Cutrona, C. E., 59, 65, *70*

Dalheimer, D., 88, *100*
Damon, W., 305, *316*
Daniels, R., 274, *278*
Danovsky, M., *122*
Davidson, K., 351, *364*
Davidson, P. O., 59, *72*
Davidson, R. J., 39, *49*
Davidson, W., 308, *316*
Davis, K. L., 137, *144*
Davis, M., 182, *185*
de Avila, M. E., 58, *73*, 137, *142*
DeFries, J. C., 171, *187*
DeJoy, D. M., 136, *141*
Delblanco, T. L., *141*
Delo, J. S., 292, *297*
DeLongis, A., 150, *165*
Dember, W. N., 7, *11*, 232, 236, 281, 283, 284, 285, 286, 288, 291, 292, 293, *296*, *297*, 298, 299
Dembo, T., 240, *254*
Derogatis, L. R., 264, *278*
DeRonde, L., 288, *297*
Derryberry, D., 233, *237*
DeRubeis, R. J., 57, 60, *70*, *71*, *74*, 302, 303, *316*, *317*, 320, 322, *344*
Descartes, R., 14, 15, 28

Deshavnais, R., 193, *212*
DeVos, G., 257, *279*
DeWolf, R., 342, *344*
Diener, E., 66, *72*, 111, *120*
Dixon, W. A., 67, *70*
Dofney, E. M., 309, *320*
Dohrenwend, B. P., 156, *168*, 287, *299*
Dolinski, D., 349, *364*
Donahue, E. M., 85, 98
Doucher, M. J., 341, *345*
Downing, R., *144*
Downy, G., 307, *316*
Dua, J., 135, *141*
Dunkel-Schetter, C., 192, *215*
Dunn, D. S., 193, *212*
Dutka, S., 309, *320*
Dutton, K. A., 244, *253*, *254*
Dweck, C. S., 34, *49*, 58, *70*, 305, 306,
    308, 309, *316*
Dworkin, R. J., *120*, *212*
Dwyer, J., 136, *141*
Dykema, J., 137, *141*
Dykman, B. M., 63, 69
D'Zurilla, T. J., 6, *11*, 62, 66, *70*, 153,
    165, 172, *185*, 263, *277*, 284,
    296, 349, *363*

Early, S., 113, *122*
Eaves, G., 179, *186*
Eaves, L. J., 180, *186*
Edelman, R. E., 63, *70*
Eisenberg, D. M., 139, *141*
Elliott, E. S., 34, *49*
Elliott, T. R., 117, *119*, *121*
Ellis, A., 311, *316*
Emery, G., 271, *277*, 322, *344*
Engel, G. L., 9, *11*
Engel, R. A., 60, *71*
Enna, B., 308, *316*
Enns, C., *344*
Epps, E. G., 361, *364*
Epstein, S., 85, 86, *97*, 148, 149, 150,
    155, *165*, *166*, 218, *237*, 287,
    297, 348, *364*
Erbaugh, J., 109, *119*, 264, *277*, 289, *296*
Ermann, M., 137, *140*
Evans, D. D., 57, *71*, 302, *318*
Evans, D. L., 138, *142*, 209, *214*
Evans, M. D., 303, *317*
Evans, R. I., 201, *211*

Eysenck, H. J., 110, *119*, 173, *186*
Eysenck, S. B. G., 110, *119*, 173, *186*

Fahey, J. L., 197, *215*
Fascizka, A. L., 329, *345*
Favell, H. E., *344*
Feather, N. T., 61, *71*, 240, *254*
Feinstein, S. B., 63, *72*
Feldman, N. S., 305, *319*
Fenigstein, A., 109, *119*
Fenz, W. B., 85, 86, 97
Fernandez, M. I., *140*
Festinger, L., 240, *254*
Fibel, B., 109, 110, 111, *119*
Fincham, F. D., 59, *71*
Fischer, L., *167*
Fischer, M., 283, *297*
Fiske, D. W., 110, *119*
Fitzgerald, T. E., 147, 162, *166*, 191, 194,
    195, *212*
Fleming, B., 331, *344*
Flett, G. L., 193, *211*
Flory, J. D., 183, *187*, 197, *214*, 349, *366*
Flynn, C., 304, 308, *317*
Folkman, S., 93, *98*, 112, 113, 116, *119*,
    208, *214*, 264, *278*
Follette, V. M., 67, *71*, 341, *345*
Fontaine, K. R., 105, *119*, 138, *141*, 192,
    193, 199, *212*
Forsterling, F., 309, *317*
Foster, C., *141*
Fowler, J. W., 309, *317*
Foxall, M. J., 193, *211*
Franck, K., 356, *366*
Frank, C., 137, *144*
Frank, E., 329, *345*
Frank, J. D., 101, *119*
Frank, R. G., *121*
Frankl, V. E., 4, *11*, 101, *120*
Fredrickson, B. L., 233, 235, *237*
Freeman, A., 331, 332, 342, *344*
Freres, D. R., 310, *317*
Fresco, D. M., 330, 331, 334, 338, 339,
    341, *344*
Frese, M., 349, *364*
Freud, S., 24, 25, 26, 28, 29
Frey, K. S., 305, *317*
Friberg, L., 177, *186*
Friedman, H. S., 133, 138, *141*, *143*
Friedman, L. C., 105, *120*, 191, 193, 201,
    212, *213*

Friedman, M., 135, *141*
Friend, R., 84, 85, *100*
Frijda, N. H., 37, *49*
Fromme, K., 342, *345*
Frost, R. O., 275, *278*
Fry, P. S., 200, *213*
Fuller, R. D., 327, *346*
Funder, D. C., 240, *254*, 355, *364*

Gaines, J. G., 59, *70*, 147, *165*, 191, 192, 211, 341, *344*
Galanter, E., 33, *50*
Galassi, J. P., 292, *297*
Galassi, M. D., 292, *297*
Garamoni, G. L., 329, 340, 341, *345, 346*
Garber, J., 67, *71*, 304, 307, 308, *317*
Gardenswartz, C. A. R., 58, 69, 136, *140*
Garner, R. L., 201, *211*
Garrison, C. Z., 304, *317*
Gates of Prayer, xix, *xxi*
Gavanski, I., 93, *98*
Geers, A. L., 288, 289, 291, 292, *297, 298*
Gerety, C. A., 293, *297*
Gershon, E. S., 178, 179, *186*
Geva, N., 230, *237*
Gibb, J., *12*, 108, 109, 115, *120, 122*
Gill, M. J., 137, *141*
Gillespie, B., 137, *141*
Gillham, J. E., 57, 60, 63, 68, *71*, 74, 130, *141*, 307, 308, 310, 313, 314, *317, 318*, 320, 357, *367*
Girgus, J. S., 68, *72*, 304, 307, 308, *319*
Given, B., *166, 213*
Given, C. W., 148, *166*, 191, 193, 196, *213*
Gladstone, T. R. G., 57, *71*, 307, *318*
Gleser, G. C., 286, *297*
Gnys, M., *167*
Goddard, A. W., 180, *187*
Godin, G., 193, *212*
Gold, E. R., 68, *71*, 308, *318*
Goldney, R. D., 57, *74*
Golin, S., 57, *71*
Gollwitzer, P. M., 206, *216*, 224, *238, 354, 367*
Goodman, E., 208, 209, *213*
Goodman, W. K., 180, *187*
Goodwin, F. K., 178, *186*
Gordon, J. M., 337, *345*

Gorsuch, R. L., 112, *122*
Gotlib, I. H., 150, *166*
Gould, S., 171, *186*
Grande, I., 172, *187*
Grannemann, B. D., 357, *364*
Gray, J. A., 172, 180, 181, *186*
Greenberg, J., 232, *237*
Greenberg, M., 219, *237*
Greenblatt, D. J., 180, *187*
Greenwald, A. G., 258, *278*
Greer, S., 205, *213, 214*
Gromski, W., 349, *364*
Gruenewald, T. L., 219, *238*
Guarnaccia, C. A., 156, *168*, 287, *299*
Guarnera, S., 193, *213*
Gump, B. B, 183, *187*, 197, *214*, 349, *366*

Haaga, D. A., 63, *70*
Halberstadt, L. J., 56, 66, *72*
Hale, W. D., 109, 110, 111, *119*
Hall, C., *164*
Halpern, D. F., 361, *364*
Hammen, C., 54, 60, 67, *71*, 307, *318*
Hammen, C. L., 57, *71*
Hammer, A. L., 191, 193, *216*
Hammontree, S. R., 81, *98*
Hankin, B. L., 304, 310, 315, *318*
Hanson, S., *121*
Hansson, R., 42, *50*
Hardin, S. I., 199, *211*
Hardin, T. S., 56, *72*
Harmatz, M. G., 275, *278*
Harney, P., *12*, 108, *120, 122*
Harrigan, J. A., 287, *297*
Harris, C., *12*, 102, 103, 105, 106, 107, 109, 110, 112, 115, 116, *122, 124*
Harris, R. N., 80, *98*
Harris, S. D., *49, 141*, 165, *211*, 236, *253*
Hart, D., 305, *316*
Harter, S., 305, *318*
Hartlage, S., 341, *345*
Hartnett, S. A., 135, *141*
Hawkins, W., *316*
Hayakawa, S., 193, *216*
Haybittle, J. L., 205, *213*
Hayes, A. M., 57, 66, *73*, 302, *319*
Hayes, S. C., 341, *345*
Heath, A. C., 180, *186*

Heatherton, T. F., 240, *253*
Hedges, S. M., 156, *166*
Hegel, G. W. F., 19, 20, 21, *29*
Heidegger, M., 3, 4, *11*
Heine, S. J., 97, 258, 259, 260, 261, 262, 269, *278*
Helton, W. S., 283, *297*
Helweg-Larsen, M., 272, 273, *278*, 353, 359, 361, *364*
Heng, B. H., 138, *142*
Henry, S. M., 208, *212*
Heppner, P. P., 67, *70*
Herbert, M., *144*, *168*, 216, 238, *367*
Herrick, S., 117, *119*
Hervig, L. K., 6, *11*, 41, *50*, 150, *167*, 241, *254*, 275, *279*, 349, *364*
Herzberger, S., 129, *144*
Hickcox, M., *167*
Higgins, E. T., 38, *49*
Higgins, P., 148, 150, 156, *164*, *168*
Higgins, R. L., 80, 98, *122*
Highberger, L., *122*
Hilsman, R., 67, *71*
Hiroto, D., 57, 67, *71*, 307, *318*
Hitchcock, J. M., 182, *185*
Hjelle, L., 60, 63, *71*
Ho, M. L., 138, *142*
Hoffman, J. T., 117, *119*, *121*
Hofstede, G., 257, *278*
Hogan, M. E., 69
Holleran, S. A., *12*, 109, 111, 113, 114, 116, *120*, *122*
Hollon, S. D., 57, *70*, *74*, 89, 98, 302, 303, *315*, *316*, *317*, *320*
Holroyd, K. A., 264, *279*
Holte, A., 216
Hooker, K., 151, *167*, 191, 193, 197, *213*, *215*
Hooykaas, C., 136, *144*
Hops, H., 301, 310, *316*, *319*
Horie, K., 193, 216
Houston, D. M., 67, *71*
Howe, S., 7, *11*
Howe, S. R., 281, *297*
Hoza, B., 105, 115, 116, *122*
Hsu, F. L. K., 257, *279*
Hu, L., 360, *367*
Hughes, C. F., 354, *365*
Hume, D., 18, *29*
Hummer, M. K., 7, *11*, 281, 293, *297*
Hutchinson, C., 191, *213*

Ihilevich, D., 286, *297*
Iliardi, S. S., 57, *71*, 302, 303, *318*
Illingworth, K. S. S., 84, 86, 88, 91, 92, 98, 99, 352, 353, *363*, *365*
Ingram, R. E., 89, 98, 328, 340, *345*
Inhelder, B., 304, 310, *318*
Irving, L. M., *12*, 102, 105, 117, *120*, *122*, 234, *237*
Isaacowitz, D. M., 98, 357, *364*
Isen, A. M., 230, 232, 236, *237*, 327, *345*

Jacobson, N. S., 67, *71*, 341, *345*
Jahoda, G., 257, *278*
James, S. A., 135, *141*
James, W., 27, *29*, 242, 243, 244, 245, 246, 251, *254*
Jamison, K. R., 178, *186*
Jandorf, L., 156, *166*
Janoff-Bulman, R., 356, *363*
Jason, G. W., 137, *141*
Jaycox, L. H., 57, 68, *71*, *74*, 136, *141*, 308, 313, *317*, *318*, 320, 357, *367*
Jerusalem, M., 219, 221, *237*, *238*
Jobin, J., 193, *212*
John, O. P., 85, 98
Johnson, J. E., 195, *213*
Johnson, J. G., 63, *72*
Johnson, L., 178, *186*
Joiner, T. E., 56, 57, 68, *72*, 307, 308, *318*
Joireman, J., 171, 173, *188*
Jones, E. E., 84, 85, 98
Jones, L. C., 192, *212*
Jones, P. S., 193, *211*
Jones, R. D., 65, *70*
Jonsson, H., *140*
Joseph, J. G., 137, *141*

Kagitcibasi, C., 258, *278*
Kahn, S. E., 193, *214*
Kalsbeek, W. D., 135, *141*
Kamen, L. P., 60, 63, *72*
Kamen-Siegel, L., 136, *141*
Kanner, A. D., 149, *166*
Kant, I., 18, 19, *29*
Kao, C. F., 85, 97
Kaplan, B. K., 304, *317*
Karr, K. A., 193, *214*
Kashani, J. H., 304, 307, *318*

Kasimatis, M., 150, 155, *166*
Kaslow, N. J., 56, 57, *71, 72, 74,* 115, *120, 187,* 307, 310, *318*
Kassel, J., *167*
Kasser, T., 357, *364*
Katoff, L., 137, *143*
Katz, E. C., 342, *345*
Katz, I. M., *97*
Kaufman, J., 68, *72,* 308, *318*
Kaurza, Jr., J., 69
Kawamura, K. Y., 275, *278*
Keating, D. P., 306, 310
Keith, D., 68, *74,* 176, *187*
Keller, R. R., xvii, *xxi*
Keller, S. E., 137, *144*
Kelly, J. A., *140*
Kelman, H., 349, *364*
Kemeny, M. E., *144, 168,* 197, 205, *214, 215, 216,* 219, *238, 367*
Kendall, P. C., 341, *345*
Kendler, K. S., 178, 180, *186*
Kentle, R. L., 85, *98*
Kernis, M. H., 357, *364*
Kessler, R. C., *141,* 150, *165,* 180, *186*
Ketcham, A., *165*
Ketcham, A. S., *49, 141, 165,* 211, *236, 253*
Ketelaar, T., 150, *166*
Keyes, C. L. M., 276, *279,* 355, *366*
Khoo, S., 193, *213*
Kidder, L., 69
Kiecolt-Glaser, J. K., 106, *120,* 153, *167, 241, 254,* 349, *366*
Kiehl, E., 86, 93, *98,* 358, *364*
Kiers, H., 173, *188*
Kihlstrom, J. F., 77, *97*
Kim, C., 106, *120,* 153, *167,* 241, *254, 349, 366*
Kim, E.-Y., 276, *278*
Kim, U., 258, *278*
Kimble, L. P., 195, *213*
King, K. B., 195, 202, *213*
Kirton, M., 294, *297*
Kitayama, S., 258, *278*
Klinger, E., 42, *49*
Klock, S., 148, *166,* 191, *213*
Knapp, J. E., 133, *144,* 349, *367*
Knappy. J. E., 241, *255*
Kobassa, S. C., 133, *142*
Kok, L. P., 138, *142*
Koledin, S., 193, *211*

Koob, J. J., *140*
Kouzes, J. M., 294, *297*
Kovacs, M., 301, *319*
Kowalski, R. M., 92, 98
Kraft, M., 171, 173, *188*
Kues, J. R., 287, *297*
Kuhlman, D. M., 171, 173, *188*
Kukla, A., 42, 44, 46, *49*
Kulik, J. A., 136, *142*
Kurtz, J. C., *166, 213*
Kurtz, M. E., *166, 213*
Kusulas, J. W., 6, *11,* 41, *50,* 150, *167,* 241, *254,* 275, *279,* 349
Kwon, J., 360, *367*

Lachendro, E., 355, *367*
Lam, T. H., *216*
Lane, M., *120, 212*
Lang, E. L., 193, *214*
Langelle, C., *12, 122*
Langer, E. J., 305, *319*
Langston, C. A., 86, *97*
Lapointe, A. B., 113, *122*
Larsen, R., 149, *166,* 150, 155
Larson, D., xx, *xxi*
Larson, R., 148, *165*
Larson, S., xx, *xxi*
Latham, G. P., 240, *254*
Lauver, D., 193, *213*
Lavalee, L. F., *97*
Lazarus, R. S., 93, *98,* 112, 113, 116, *119,* 148, 149, *166,* 264, *278*
Leary, M. R., 92, *98*
LeDoux, J. E., 182, *186*
Lee, F., 130, *142*
Lee, P. W., *216*
Lee, Y.-T., 259, 261, 262, 263, 264, 266, 269, 271, 273, 276, *278*
Lefebvre, R. C., *144, 167, 215, 255*
Leggett, E. L., 305, 306, *316*
Legro, M. W., 148, *165,* 191, *212*
Lehman, D. R., *97,* 258, 259, 260, 261, 262, 269, *278*
Leibniz, G., 16, *29*
Leitenberg, H., 283, *297*
Leserman, J., 138, *142,* 209, *214*
Lester, D., 109, *119*
Levin, J. S., xx, *xxi*
Lewin, K., 240, *254*
Lewinsohn, P. M., 301, 310, 315, *316, 319*

Lewis, L. M., 293, 298
Lin, E. H., 135, 138, *142*
Lin, T.-Y., 276, *278*
Lindsay, D. L., 288, *298*
Linehan, M. M., 341, *346*
Linton, S. J., 152, *166*
Linville, P., 206, *213*
Lips, B. J., 67, *70*
Litt, M. D., 148, *166*, 191, 192, 202, *213*
Locke, E. A., 240, *254*
Loebl, J. H., 305, *319*
Loehlin, J. C., 177, *186*
Long, B. C., 191, 193, *214*
Lorr, M., 152, *166*
Lovinger, R. J., xvii, *xxi*
Lubin, B., 173, *186*, *188*
Luborsky, L., *144*
Lucas, R. E., 66, *72*, 111, *120*
Luchene, R. E., 112, *122*
Lumley, M. A., 137, *144*
Lumpkin, J., 105, *122*, 199, *216*
Lykken, D. T., 177, *185*, *187*

MacCallum, R. C., 106, *120*, 153, *167*,
        241, *254*, 349, *366*
MacKay, D. M., 33, *50*
Maes, M., 179, *186*
Magaletta, P. R., 105, 107, *120*
Magovern, G. J., Sr., *144*, *167*, *215*, *255*
Mahler, H. I., 136, *142*
Maier, S. F., 134, *143*
Major, B., 194, *214*
Mani, M. M., 117, *119*
Manly, P. C., 59, *72*
Manstead, A. S. R., 105, *119*, 199, *212*
Marcel, G., 4, *11*
Marguth, U., 137, *140*
Markman, K. D., 93, *98*
Markowitz, N., 137, *144*
Markus, H. R., 258, *278*
Marlatt, G. A., 337, *345*
Marlowe, D., 109, *119*
Maroto, J. J., 200, *215*
Marsella, A., 257, *279*
Marshall, G. N., 6, *11*, 41, *50*, 150, 154,
        167, 193, *214*, 241, 250, *254*,
        275, *279*, 349, *364*
Marshall, I. B., *216*
Marshall, M. A., 241, 244, 247, *253*, *254*
Martin, A., 80, 84, 95, *98*
Martin, L. L., 91, *98*

Martin, L. R., 138, *143*
Martin, S. H., 7, *11*, 281, 286, 297, *298*
Maslow, A., 4, *12*
Mathe, A. A., 178, *186*
Mathews, A., 327, *346*
Matlin, M. W., 281, *298*
Matthew-Simonton, S., 101, *121*
Matthews, K. A., *144*, *167*, 183, *187*,
        197, 198, *211*, *214*, *215*, *255*,
        349, *366*
Maydeu-Olivares, A., 6, *11*, 62, 66, *70*,
        153, *165*, 172, *185*, 263, *277*,
        284, *296*, 349, *363*
McCauley, E., 307, *319*
McClearn, G. E., 73, 171, 177, *186*, *187*
McConville, B. J., 304, 306, *319*
McCrae, R. R., 85, *97*, 132, *141*
McCullough, M., 101, *122*
McDermott, D., *122*
McGee, R., 301, 304, *315*, *318*
McGill, K. L., 358, *363*
McGrath, P. J., *346*
McGue, M., 177, *185*
McLearn, G. E., *366*
McMahon, R. J., 59, *72*
McMullen, M. N., 93, *98*
McNair, D. M., 152, *166*
McNally, R. J., 180, *186*
Medway, F. J., 309, *316*
Mee, L. L., 307, *318*
Meier, P., 218, *237*, 287, *297*, 348, *364*
Melton, R. S., 7, *11*, 281, 293, *297*
Meltzer, H. Y., 179, *186*
Mendelson, M., 109, *119*, 264, *277*, 289,
        296
Mendola, R. A., 148, 151, *167*, *168*
Menninger, K., 101, *120*
Mercier, M. A., 328, *345*, *346*
Merleau-Ponty, M., 4, *12*
Metalsky, G. I., 54, 56, 57, 66, 69, *72*,
        73, 87, 100, 130, *140*, 179, *185*,
        279, *298*, 302, *315*
Michael, S. T., 101, 118, *122*
Michaels, A. J., 134, *142*
Michaels, C. E., 134, *142*
Michalos, A. C., 360, *365*
Miller, D. T., 251, *254*
Miller, G. A., 33, *50*
Miller, L., xvii, *xxi*
Miller, W. R., 332, *345*
Miranda, J., 328, *345*

Miserandino, M., 309, *319*
Mitchell, J. R., 307, *319*
Mizuno, M., 260, *279*
Mock, J., 109, *119*, 289, 296
Mock, L., 264, *277*
Moffat, F. L., Jr., 49, *141*, *165*, *211*, 236, 253
Moffitt, T. E., 304, *318*
Moltó, J., 172, *187*
Monahan, D., 191, *213*
Monahan, J., 58, *73*
Moore, P. J., 191, *214*, 351, *365*
Morishima, J., 274, *279*
Morris, T., 205, *213*, *214*
Moskowitz, J. T., 208, *214*
Moss, S., 307, *319*
Mroczek, D. K., 154, *167*, 357, *365*
Mumby, P. B., 193, *214*
Munz, D. C., 193, *216*
Murphy, C., 138, *142*, 209, *214*
Murphy, D. L., 179, *188*
Murphy, G., 360, *365*
Murphy, M., *316*

Nagata, D., 274, *279*
Nakagawa, T., 362, *365*
Natali-Alemany, R., 287, 289, *298*
Neale, J., 150, 152, 156, *168*
Neale, M. C., 178, 180, *186*
Needles, D. J., 63, 69, *72*
Nelson, D., 286, 296
Nelson, D. V., *120*, *212*
Nelson, E. S., 193, *214*
Nelson, S., 308, *316*
Nesselroade, J. R., *73*, *187*, *366*
Nesser, J., 60, *71*
Neuberg, S. L., 85, 99
Neverlien, P. O., 193, *214*
Newman, M. K., 283, 284, *298*
Newsom, J. T., 85, 99
Niedenthal, P. M., 86, 97
Nietzsche, F., 22, 23, 24, 29
Nisbett, R. E., 361, *364*
Nolen-Hoeksema, S., 58, 68, *72*, 74, 304, 306, 307, 308, *319*
Norem, J. K., 77, 78, 79, 81, 84, 85, 86, 88, 91, 92, 93, 94, 97, 98, 99, 100, 250, 253, 254, 270, *279*, 349, 351, 352, 353, 354, 355, 363, *365*, *366*
Norenzayan, A., 361, *364*

Noriega, V., 49, *141*, *165*, *211*, *236*, *253*
Norlock, F. E., *141*
Nunes, E., *346*
Nunn, K. P., 62, 65, *72*
Nurnberger, J. I., Jr., 179, *186*
Nygren, T. E., 230, *237*

O'Brien, W. H., 193, *214*
Ocepek-Welikson, K., *346*
O'Hare, D., 136, *142*
O'Heeron, R. C., 354, *365*
Okazaki, S., 276, *279*
Okolo, C. M., 309, *319*
O'Leary, A., 135, *142*
Oliver, J. M., 105, 107, *120*
Ollove, M., *144*
Ong, Y. W., 138, *142*
Orbuch, T. L., 42, *50*
Osuch, J., *166*, *213*
Owens, J. F., *144*, *167*, 183, *187*, 197, *214*, *215*, 255, 349, *366*
Ozer, D. J., 154, *167*, 357, *365*

Pajurkova, E. M., 137, *141*
Palmer, M. L., 359, *363*
Pankofer, R., 137, *140*
Pargament, K. I., *xvii*, xx, xxi
Park, C., 129, *143*
Park, C. L., 191, 192, 204, *214*, 351, *365*
Park, K., 305, *319*
Paty, J. A., *167*
Paulhus, D. L., 92, 99
Pbert, L. A., 201, *215*
Peale, N. V., 139, *142*
Pederson, N. L., *73*, 177, 178, *186*, *187*, 366
Pelham, B. W., 85, 99
Pelham, W. E., *122*
Pelletier, K. R., 101, *120*
Pennebaker, J. W., 110, *123*, 264, *279*, 354, *365*
Penwell, L., 281, *297*
Peregoy, P. L., 44, *50*
Perkins, D. O., 138, *142*, 209, *214*
Perloff, J. M., 64, *72*
Persons, J. B., 64, *72*, 332, *345*
Pervin, L. A., 34, 35, *50*
Peterson, C., 7, *12*, 56, 57, 58, 62, 63, 64, *73*, *74*, 85, 87, *100*, 128, 129, 130, 133, 134, 135, 136, 137, 138, *141*, *142*, *143*, 176,

Peterson, C., *continued*
    187, 190, *214*, 261, *279*, 286,
    290, *298*, 328, *345*, 348, 350,
    366
Peterson, P. L., 309, *317*
Petrie, K., 196, *212*
Pettingale, K. W., 205, *213, 214*
Petty, R. E., 85, *97*
Pham, L. B., 40, *51*
Phinney, J., 274, *278*
Piaget, J., 304, 305, 310, *318, 319*
Piasecki, J. M., 303, *317*
Pintrich, P. R., 305, *319*
Plomin, R., 68, *73*, 171, 177, 181, *186,
    187*, 357, 366
Plumer, G., 135, *141*
Pomerantz, E. M., 230, 231, *238*
Pope, A., 15, 16, *29*, 154, *167*
Pope, M. K., 66, *74*, 109, *121*, 247, 255
Posner, B. Z., 294, *297*
Post, R. M., 178, *185*
Poulton, J. L., 66, *74*, 109, *121*, 154,
    167, 247, 255
Powers, W. T., 35, *50*
Pozo, C., 49, *141, 165*, 211, 236, 253
Pozo-Kaderman, C., *165*
Pransky, G. S., 147, 162, *166*, 191, *212*
Prescott, S., 148, *165*
Preskorn, S. H., 179, *185*
Presnell, K. E., *344*
Pretzer, J. L., 325, 331, 343, *344, 345*
Pribram, K. H., 33, *50*
Price, L. H., 180, *187*
Prkachin, D., 351, 352, *364*
Prola, M., 356, *366*
Purohit, A. P., 304, *319*
Pyszczynski, T., 232, *237*

Quiggle, N., 307, *317*
Quitkin, F. M., *346*

Rabinowitz, V. C., *69*
Rabkin, J. G., 137, *143*
Rachman, S. J., 327, *346*
Radenhausen, R. A., 293, *298*
Räikkönen, K., 183, *187*, 197, *214*, 349,
    350, 366
Raisman, S., 291, *297*
Rand, K. L., 275, *278*
Rapoff, M. A., 117, *119, 122*
Raps, C. S., 135, *143*

Rau, M. T., 197, *216*
Raudenbush, S. W., 156, *165*
Reddy, W. B., 293, *299*
Redmond, D. E., Jr., 180, *186*
Reed, G. M., 205, *214*, 219, 238
Reed, M. A., 233, *237*
Reed, M. B., 230, *237*
Rehm, M., 115, *119*
Reich, J., 156, *168*
Reid, J. C., 304, *318*
Reilley, S. P., 288, 291, 292, *297*, 298
Reisine, S., *165*
Reivich, K. J., 56, 57, 58, 68, *71*, 73, 74,
    129, 136, *141, 143*, 307, 308,
    310, 313, 314, *317, 318, 320*,
    357, 367
Remien, R., 137, *143*
Rettew, D., 58, *73*
Reynolds, C. F., 329, *345*
Reynolds, R. V., 264, *279*
Rhodewalt, F., 66, *74*, 84, 85, 98, 109,
    121, 121, 154, *167*, 247, 255
Rich, A., 177, *187*
Rich, A. R., 88, *100*
Richards, C., 194, *214*
Richards, P. S., xvii, xx, *xxi*
Richter, L., 220, 221, 222, *236*
Ricks, D. F., 287, *297*, 299
Ris, D. M., 232, *236*
Risinger, R. T., 67, *69*
Riskind, J. H., 328, 329, 330, 331, 334,
    335, 336, 338, 340, *345*
Rivet, K., 342, *345*
Robbins, A. S., 201, *215*
Roberts, R., 301, *319*
Robins, C. J., 57, 66, *73*, 135, *143*, 302,
    319
Robinson, D. S., 49, *141, 165*, 211, 236,
    253
Robinson, N. S., 308, *317*
Robinson-Whelen, S., 106, *120*, 153,
    167, 241, 250, 254, 349, 357,
    366
Rodin, J., 136, *141*
Rodriguez, R., *144, 168*, 216, 238, 367
Roger, D., 362, *366*
Rogers, C., 4, *12*
Rohde, P., 310, *316*
Roland, A., 258, *279*
Rollnick, S., 332, *345*
Ronan, G. F., 81, *97*, 98

Roseman, I. J., 38, *50*
Rosen, J. B., 182, *185*
Rosenberg, M., 109, *120*
Rosenberg, R. K., 304, *318*
Rosenman, R., 135, *141*
Ross, A., 193, *212*
Ross, M., 251, *254*
Rothbaum, F. M., 65, *74*, 258, *280*
Rowe, M. A., 195, *213*
Ruben, C., 81, *100*
Rubinstein, C. M., 292, *298*
Rubinstein, H., *122*
Ruble, D. N., 305, *317*, *319*
Ruby, B. C., 115, *119*
Rush, A. I., 179, *186*
Rush, A. J., 271, *277*, 322, *344*
Russell, D., 65, *70*
Rutter, M., 171, *187*, 301, 304, 307, 310, *320*
Ryan, R. M., 357, *364*
Rybarczyk, B. D., *121*
Ryff, C. D., 206, *215*, 276, *279*, 355, *366*

Sadeghian, P., 272, *278*, 353, *364*
Sagan, L. A., 137, *143*
Sampson, W. S., 330, 331, 334, 338, *344*
Sanford, R. N., 356, *366*
Sangster, J. I., 193, *214*
Sanna, L. J., 90, 91, 93, 94, *100*, 353, *366*
Sarampote, C. S., 328, *345*
Sartre, J.-P., 4, *12*
Satterfield, J. M., 58, 59, *73*
Schaefer, C., 149, *166*
Schaeffer, D. E., 57, *71*
Schafer, J. C., 288, *298*
Schatzberg, A. F., 179, *187*
Schefft, B. K., 232, 236, 293, *297*
Scheier, M. F., 4, 6, *12*, 34, 35, 36, 37, 38, 39, 40, 41, 42, 43, 45, 46, 48, *49*, *50*, 53, 54, 59, 60, 63, 67, 68, *73*, *74*, 85, 87, *100*, 102, 104, 105, 106, 108, 109, 110, 111, 112, *119*, *120*, *121*, 130, 133, 134, 138, *141*, *143*, *144*, 147, 148, 151, *154*, 158, 159, 162, 163, *165*, *167*, 173, *187*, 190, 191, 194, 197, 199, 201, 202, 205, 206, 207, 208, 210, *211*, *212*, *215*, 216, 218, 219, 220, 223, 235, 236, 237, 238, 240, 241, 250, 253, 255, 263,

264, *279*, 286, 289, 298, 302, *320*, 328, 339, 342, *345*, 348, 349, 351, 357, *366*
Schildkraut, J. J., 179, *187*
Schilling, E. A., 150, *165*
Schleifer, S. J., 137, *144*
Schluchter, M. D., 304, *317*
Schmale, A. H., 101, *121*
Schneider, S. G., *144*, *168*, 216, *238*, *367*
Schneider-Rosen, K., 305, *316*
Schoenbach, V. J., 304, *317*
Schopenhauer, A., 21, *29*
Schuller, I. S., 193, *215*
Schulman, P., 7, *12*, 57, 58, 68, *74*, 130, *143*, *144*, 176, 177, *187*, 303, *320*
Schulman, S., *140*
Schulz, R., 133, *144*, 197, 210, 216, 241, *255*, 349, *366*
Schutte, J. W., 359, *366*
Schutz, R. W., 193, *214*
Schwartz, R. M., 341, 346, 358, *366*
Schwarzer, R., 208, *215*, 221, *238*
Seal, A., 193, *212*
Sears, P. S., 240, *254*
Sedikides, C., 232, *238*
Seeley, J., 301, *319*
Seeley, J. R., 310, *316*
Seeman, J., 139, *144*
Segal, N. L., 177, *185*, *187*
Segal, Z. V., 328, *345*
Segerstrom, S. C., 197, 204, *215*
Seidl, O., 137, *140*
Self, E. A., 44, 46, *49*
Seligman, M. E. P., 4, 7, *12*, 53, 54, 56, 57, 58, 59, 60, 65, 68, 69, 70, 71, 72, 73, 74, 75, 87, *100*, 115, *120*, 129, 130, 136, 138, *140*, *141*, *142*, *143*, *144*, 170, 176, 177, 181, *187*, 190, *214*, *215*, 259, 261, 262, 263, 264, 266, 269, 271, 273, 276, 278, 279, 285, 290, *298*, 302, 303, 304, 307, 308, 310, 313, 314, *317*, *318*, *319*, *320*, 322, 328, 329, 330, 331, 332, 338, 341, 342, 344, *345*, 346, 348, 350, 354, 357, *364*, *366*, *367*
Sellars, R., 87, *99*
Semmel, A., 56, *73*, *74*, 87, *100*, 279, *298*

Sethi, S., 285, 298
Shader, R. I., 180, *187*
Shanley, N., 307, *317*
Shatté, A. J., 310, *317*
Shaver, P., 292, 298
Shaw, B. F., 271, *277*, 322, *344*
Sheeber, L., *316*
Shepperd, J. A., 200, *215*
Sherman, S. J., 93, 98
Sherwin, E. D., 117, *121*
Shiffman, S., 149, 156, *167*, *168*
Shifren, K., 151, *167*, 191, 197, *213*, *215*
Showers, C. J., 81, 82, 86, 91, *100*, 206, *215*
Shull, K. A., 193, *211*
Siegel, B. D., 101, *121*
Siegel, B. S., 139, *144*
Sigmon, S. T., *12*, 112, 116, *121*, *122*
Sikkema, K. J., *140*
Silva, P. A., 301, 304, *315*, *318*
Simon, K. M., 331, *344*
Simonton, O. C., 101, *121*
Siris, S. G., 137, *144*
Skinner, E. A., 233, *238*
Skokan, L. A., 229, *238*
Smart, L., 240, *253*, 357, *363*
Smart, N., xx, *xxi*
Smith, F. E., *120*, *212*
Smith, R., 287, *297*
Smith, T. W., 66, *74*, 109, 111, *121*, *121*, 154, 159, *167*, 247, *255*
Snider, P. R., 203, *215*
Snyder, C. R., 8, *12*, 101, 102, 103, 104, 105, 106, 107, 108, 109, 110, 111, 112, 113, 114, 115, 116, 117, 118, *119*, *120*, *121*, *122*, 124, 125, 218, 234, *237*, *238*
Somerfield, M. R., 148, *165*, 191, *212*
Spence, J. T., 201, *215*
Spencer, S. M., 86, 89, 91, *100*, 134, *141*, 352, 353, *363*
Spielberger, C. D., 112, *122*
Spiro, A., 154, *167*, 357, *365*
Stahl, K. J., *122*
Stang, D. J., 281, 298
Stanton, A. L., 192, 203, *215*
Stein, M., 137, *144*
Steptoe, A., 201, *216*
Stern, D., 356, *366*
Stevenson, L. Y., *140*
Stewart, I. N., 44, *50*

Stewart, J. W., 330, *346*
Stewart, S. M., 197, *216*
Stiegendal, L., *140*
Stommel, M., *166*, *213*
Stone, A. A., 149, 150, 152, 156, *166*, 168
Strack, S., 138, *144*
Stroebe, M. S., 42, *50*
Stroebe, W. S., 42, *50*
Strutton, D., 105, *122*, 199, *216*
Stunkard, A. J., 128, *143*
Sue, S., 274, *279*, 360, *367*
Sugita, M., 362, *365*
Suh, E., 66, *72*, 111, *120*
Suls, J., 149, *168*
Sumi, K., 193, *216*
Swann, W. B., Jr., 85, 99
Sweeney, P. D., 57, *71*, 137, *144*
Sweetman, M. E., 193, *216*
Swickert, R. J., 67, 69
Sympson, S. C., 105, 106, 108, *122*, 125

Tak, Y., 193, *213*
Takaki, R., 274, *279*
Tannenbaum, R. L., 56, *72*, *74*, 115, *120*, *187*
Tassoni, C. J., 60, *71*
Taylor, D. M., 208, *212*
Taylor, J. A., 112, *123*
Taylor, S. E., 40, 49, *51*, 67, 69, 81, 93, *100*, 135, 138, *144*, 148, *168*, 190, 191, 196, 197, 200, 201, 203, 205, *211*, *214*, *215*, *216*, 217, 218, 219, 220, 223, 224, 225, 229, 231, 233, 235, 236, *238*, 240, 241, 251, *253*, *255*, 327, 346, 349, 350, 354, 355, 356, 358, 362, *367*
Teasdale, J. D., 54, 69, 129, *140*
Tellegen, A., 112, *123*, 177, *185*, *187*, 275, *280*, 287, 299
Tennen, H., 106, 117, *118*, *123*, 129, *144*, 147, 148, 149, 150, 151, 152, 155, 156, 162, *164*, *165*, *166*, *168*, 191, 208, *212*, *213*, *216*, 358, *367*
Terezis, H. C., 293, 298
Tesser, A., 47, *51*, 231, *238*
Teta, P., 173, *188*
Thase, M. E., 329, *345*
Theorell, T., *140*

Thom, R., 44, *51*
Thomas, S. P., 193, *211*
Thompson, M. P., 310
Thompson, R., 117, *119*
Thornquist, M., 173, *188*
Thornton, K. M., 58, *74*
Thornton, N., 58, *74*
Tice, D. M., 240, *253*
Tiger, L., 169, 171, *187*
Tiggemann, M., 57, 61, 67, *71, 74*
Tillich, P., 4, *12*
Tipton, A. C., 208, *213*
Tobin, L. D., 264, *279*
Tomakowsky, J., 137, *144*
Tompkins, C. A., 197, *216*
Torrubia, R., 172, 173, 174, *187*
Toth, S. L., 303, 304, 307, *316*
Trapnell, P. D., 85, 86, 97, *100*
Trexler, L., 109, *119*
Triandis, H. C., 258, *278, 279*
Trocamo, E., *346*
Trope, Y., 230, 231, *238*
Tuomisto, M., *216*
Turken, A. U., 232, *236*
Turner, J. E., 61, *74*
Turner, L. A., 309, *320*
Turner, R. A., 191, *214*, 351, *365*

Uba, L., 274, *279*
Uehata, T., 362, *367*
Urrows, S., 148, 150, 156, *164, 168*

Vaillant, G. E., 58, *73*, 130, *143*, 290, *298*
Valerio, J. K., 359, *366*
Vallacher, R. R., 36, *51*
Valois, P., 193, *212*
van der Pligt, J., 136, *144*
van der Velde, F. W., 136, *144*
Vancouver, J. B., 34, 35, *49*
VanEgeren, L., 193, *214*
Veit, C. V., 112, *123*
Verbrugge, L. M., 133, *144*
Vickers, R. R., Jr., 6, *11*, 41, *50*, 150, *167*, 254, 275, *279*, 349, *364*
Villanova, P., 7, *12*, 56, *73*, 130, 135, *143*, 286, *298*
Vinck, J., *216*
Visscher, B. R., 205, *214*
Vittinghoff, E., 208, *214*
Voltaire, F., 16, 17–18, *30*

von Baeyer, C., 12, 56, *73, 74*, 87, *100*, *279, 298*
von Dollen, K., 193, *211*

Waehler, C. A., 199, *211*
Wagner, H., 105, *119*, 199, *212*
Wagner, K. D., 57, 68, *72*, 307, 308, *318*
Wallston, B. S., 133, *145*
Wallston, K. A., 133, *145*
Wang, H. J., 205, *214*
Ward, C. H., 109, *119*, 264, 277, 289, *296*
Ward, D. W., 91, *98*
Wardle, J., *216*
Ware, J. E., 112, *123*
Ware, L., *122*
Warm, J. S., 283, *297*
Waterman, A. S., 258, *280*
Watkins, P. C., 327, *346*
Watson, D., 63, 66, 70, *74*, 84, 85, *100*, 110, 112, 116, *123*, 150, *168*, 275, 280, 286, *298, 299*, 329, 333, 340, *346*
Watt, N. M., *344*
Webb, A. D., 201, *213*
Webb, M. S., 272, *278*, 353, *364*
Wegner, D. M., 36, *51*
Weil, A., 139, *145*
Weinberg, A. D., 201, *213*
Weiner, B., 240, 251, *253, 255*
Weinstein, N. D., 93, *100*, 131, *145*, 224, *238*, 259, *280*, 349, 355, *367*
Weintraub, J. K., 105, 112, *119*, 121, 199, *212, 215*, 220, *238*
Weiss, B., 307, *317*
Weissman, A., 109, *119*
Weissman, A. N., 57, *74*
Weisz, J. R., 65, *74*, 258, *280*
Welsh, G. S., 286, *299*
Wessman, A. E., 287, *299*
Wheeler, R. J., 193, *216*
Whitehouse, W. G., *69*
Wichstrøm, L., *216*
Wicklund, R. A., 206, *216*
Wigal, J. K., 264, *279*
Wiklund, C., 116, *122*
Wilcox, K., 177, *187*
Willard, A., *165*
Williams, J. B., 137, *143*
Williams, R. L., 193, *211, 213*

Williams, S., 301, *315*
Williamson, D. A., 327, *346*
Williamson, G. M., 133, *144*, 241, *255*, 349, *366*
Wilson, G. T., 341, *346*
Winefield, A. H., 57, *74*
Winefield, H. R., 57, *74*
Wingard, J. R., 148, *165*, 191, *212*
Wisnicki, K. S., 340, *345*
Witty, T. E., 117, *119*
Wong, C. M., *216*
Wood, A., 19, *30*
Wood, J. V., 93, *100*
Wortman, C. B., 6, *11*, 41, 42, 44, 46, *50*, *51*, 150, *167*, 241, *254*, 275, *279*, 349, *364*
Wright, R. A., 44, *51*
Wrosch, C., 210, *216*
Wunderley, L. J., 293, 294, *299*
Wyer, R. S., 91, *98*

Yamaguchi, S., 260, *279*
Yamamoto, J., 276, *280*

Ybasco, F. C., *122*
Yee, A. H., 258, *280*
Yoon, G., 258, *278*
Yoshinobu, L., *12*, 107, 108, *119*, *122*, *123*
Young, J., *346*
Young, J. E., 302, *315*
Yurko, K. H., 138, *143*

Zane, N. W. S., 274, *277*, 360, *367*
Zautra, A. J., 149, 156, *168*, 287, *299*
Zawisza, E., 349, *364*
Zeidner, M., 191, 193, *216*
Zerwic, J. J., 195, *213*
Zubek, J., 194, *214*
Zuckerman, M., 171, 172, 173, 178, 179, 181, 182, *185*, *186*, *188*, 292, *299*
Zullow, H. M., 54, 59, 60, 61, 63, 65, *75*
ZuWallack, R., *165*

SUBJECT INDEX

Abortion, 194
Absurdity of existence, 22
Acceptance, 203
    of the inevitable, 219–221
    of meaninglessness of life, 22
    psychological well-being linked to,
       205–206
    as resignation, 210
Achievement
    emotional response to performance
       outcomes, 242–246, 251
    expectancy effects, 240, 242,
       250–253
    explanatory style linkage, 57–58, 59
    hope and, 115–116
    optimism outcomes, 217–218
Action
    goals and, 35–36
    optimism–pessimism and, 169–170
    outcome expectancies, *vs.* inaction,
       61
Action-identification theory, 36
Adaptive behavior
    disengagement as, 42–43, 228
    evolutionary value of optimism, 170,
       184–185
    information processing in optimists,
       225–228, 229, 234–236
    life-span development context,
       356–357
    moderation of goals, 228–229
    response to uncontrollable situa-
       tions, 219–225, 228
    strategies of optimists, 228
    target of therapy, 350–351
Affective functioning
    adjustment predictors, 275
    co-occurring emotions, 150
    cognitive model of psychopathology,
       322–323, 325–328
    in cognitive strategies, 79–80
    emotional response to performance
       outcomes, 242–246, 249–250, 251
    feedback control processes, 37–39
    health–optimism linkage, 137
    in hope measurement, 111–112

in hope theory, 104, 115
    positive and negative affectivity,
       65–66
Agency, 234
    in hope theory, 102, 104–105
    measurement, 106–107
    See also Control; Self-efficacy beliefs
Aggression, 24, 25
Allocation of effort/resources, 221–223,
    228, 231–232
Alternative medicine, 139
Alzheimer's disease, 197
Amygdala, 182
Antipessimism sheet, 336–337
Anxiety
    co-occurring emotions, 150
    defensive pessimism and, 80, 84, 87,
       88, 89, 93
    expectancies in anxiety disorders,
       180–181
    measurement, 286
    in strategic optimism, 87–88
    trait correlates, 174–175
Appollinian impulse, 22–23
Arthritis, 152–155
Asian culture, 353–354, 360–361
    adjustment predictors, 266–267,
       274–275
    assessment considerations, 271–273,
       274
    attributional style, 261–263
    concept of self, 258
    defensive pessimism in, 269–270
    depression assessment, 273
    depression intervention, 270–271,
       272
    diversity of, 274
    optimism and pessimism in, 259–
       261, 265–270, 342–343
    outcome measures, 275–276
Aspirations, 243–244
Assessment
    cultural differences, 270, 271–273
    depression, 270
    See also Measurement
Asthma, 155–162

Attentional processes
    of optimists and pessimists, 226–227,
        229, 231
    processing of negative information,
        231–232
Attribution Style Questionnaire, 286,
    289–290
Attributional retraining, 309
Attributional style
    cognitive intervention, 338–339
        with children, 309, 311–312,
            314–315
    conceptualization of optimism–
        pessimism and, 62, 63, 190
    consistency over time and situations,
        65
    control and, 64
    coping and, 67
    cultural differences, 261–263
    depression and, 57
    depression-associated, 302–303
    depression risk in children, 304, 307
    developmental origins, 67–68,
        305–306
    diathesis–stress model, 66–67
    dimensions of measurement, 63–64
    dispositional optimism and, 59
    emotional response to performance
        outcomes, 251
    empirical studies of health linkage,
        133–136
    expectancies and, 59–61, 251
    genetic factors, 68
    hope and, 115
    hopelessness theory, 55
    intergenerational transmission, 308
    learned helplessness, 328–329
    marital satisfaction and, 58–59
    measurement, 7, 56, 129–130, 190
    optimistic, 53–54, 129, 190
    performance and achievement link-
        age, 57–58, 59
    pessimistic, 129, 190
        vs. defensive pessimism, 81, 87
    physical health and, 58, 135, 136–
        137, 138
    for positive vs. negative events,
        62–63
    preventive intervention, 10
    reformulated learned helplessness the-
        ory, 54–55

research opportunities, 68–69
    as target of therapy, 350–351
    well-being linkage, 66–67
Attributional Style Questionnaire, 7, 56,
    129–130
    Defensive Pessimism Questionnaire
        and, 87
Automatic thoughts, 322–323
Avoidance behaviors
    affect-creating feedback loops in, 38
    brain function, 39
    coping style of pessimists, 199,
        203–204
    cultural differences, 266
    discrepancy-enlarging feedback loops
        in, 34
    reflectivity avoidance, in strategic op-
        timists, 88–90

Balance of optimism and pessimism, 11
    evolutionary advantage, 170
    group distribution, 170
    for psychological well-being, xvii
    in religious traditions, xvii–xx
    social functioning and, 354–356
Beck Depression Inventory, 289–290
Biology
    of information processing, 232
    of mood disorders, 178–181
    of personality traits, 181–183,
        184–185
    research base, 178
    research needs, 359–360
    See also Brain function
Biopsychosocial approach, 9
Bipolar disorder, 171–172, 178
    biological basis, 178–179
Brain function
    amygdala role, 182
    in approach–avoidance behaviors, 39
    information processing style, 232
Buddhism, 258, xviii

Cancer, 195–196, 203
Caregivers, 196–197
Catastrophe theory, 8, 44–48
Catastrophic thinking, 306
Change processes
    client motivation, 332
    cognitive therapy, 322

creating optimism *vs.* diminishing pessimism, 349–350
cultural differences, 361
intrapsychic effects of changes in optimism and pessimism, 350–353
learned optimism, 350–351
Childbirth, 192
Children, 10
attribution retraining, 309
attributional style, 305–306, 307
cognitive–behavioral therapy, 310–315
control and mastery experiences, 308
hope and well-being in, 114–115
outcomes of optimism interventions, 357–358
self-concepts, 305
suicide risk, 301
Children, depression in
cognitive risk factors, 304–307
developmental capacity and, 303–304
environmental risk factors, 307–308
epidemiology, 301
leading to suicide, 301
predictors, 306–307
preventive interventions, 308–315
Children's Attributional Style Questionnaire, 56
Christianity, xix–xx
Cognitive priming, 336
Cognitive styles
depression-associated, 302–303
depression predictors, 271
depression risk in children, 304–307
negative thinking in psychopathology, 322–328
of optimists, 225–235
response to unsolvable problems, 221–223, 228
See also Strategies, cognitive
Cognitive Styles Questionnaire, 56
Cognitive therapy
automatic thoughts in, 322–323
conceptualization of optimism–pessimism in, 328–330
model of psychopathology, 322–328
modification of optimism or pessimism, 330–340
outcomes, 341–342

rationale, 322
relapse prevention, 337–338
therapeutic relationship, 331
treatment goals, 340–341
Cognitive–behavioral therapy
conceptualization of optimism–pessimism in, 328–330
for depression, 302, 303
for depression in children, 308–315
modification of optimism or pessimism, 338–339
outcome studies, 343–344
skill-acquisition component, 303, 313
College students
generalizability of research, 356–357
stress response, 197, 203–204
Confidence
affect-creating feedback loops in, 37–38, 39–40
behavioral consequences, 41–42, 43–44
catastrophe theory of behavior, 45–46, 47–48
in expectancy–value model of motivation, 32
in generalized outcome expectancies, 41
Confucianism, xviii–xix
Constructive thinking, 204
Constructive Thinking Inventory, 287–289
Content Analysis of Verbatim Explanations, 56, 130, 290–291
Control
in defensive pessimism strategy, 77
development of explanatory style, 308, 314–315
maladaptive beliefs, 65
optimism–pessimism and, 5, 64–65, 224
response to uncontrollable stressors, 219–225, 228, 229
Coping
active forms, 233
advantages of optimism, 210
confidence and doubt effects, 42
cultural differences, 264, 265, 266–270
defensive pessimism and, 81
explanatory style linkage, 67

Coping, *continued*
    hope and, 113–114, 117–118
    with illness. *See* Coping with
        chronic illness
    information processing style,
        233–234
    methods of optimists and pessimists,
        198–204, 218–219
    optimism–health linkage, 9,
        205–208
    optimism–pessimism effects, 67,
        192–198
    predictors of adjustment, 266–267
    response to uncontrollable stressors,
        219–225
Coping with chronic illness, 195–197
    acceptance, 205–206
    daily life with arthritis, 152–155
    daily symptom expectancies, 160–
        163, 164
    hope and, 117–118
    idiographic–nomothetic analysis,
        155–157
    optimism–pessimism effects on daily
        coping, 157–160, 163–164
Coronary artery bypass surgery, 194–195,
    201, 202
Coronary heart disease, 351–352
Cost of care, 343
Cost–benefit analysis of change, 362
    cultural context, 360–362
    intrapsychic context, 352–354
    life-span development context,
        356–360
    social context, 354–356
Counterfactual thinking, 90

Daily functioning
    in coping with arthritis, 152–155
    duration of stress effects on mood,
        148–149
    idiographic–nomothetic analysis of
        coping with illness, 155–157
    mediation of expectancies in chronic
        illness, 160–163
    optimism research, 149–152
    optimism–pessimism effects on cop-
        ing with illness, 157–160
    research rationale, 148–149
Dasein, 3–4
Death, acceptance of, 205–206

Defense Mechanisms Inventory, 286, 287
Defensive pessimism, 8, 351
    anxiety management, 80, 84, 87, 88,
        89, 93
    change in strategy, 95
    characteristic behaviors, 77–78
    as cognitive strategy, 78–81
    contextual factors, 353
    cost–benefit analysis of treatment,
        352–354
    counterfactual thinking in, 90
    cultural differences, 269–270
    decision making style, 96
    definition, 77
    developmental origins, 96
    distinguishing characteristics, 80–81,
        82
    goal construal in, 88
    implications for future research,
        95–97
    interpersonal consequences, 92, 96
    long-term outcomes, 92
    measurement, 81–86
    mood induction effects, 90–91
    potential costs, 91–93, 94–95
    prefactual thinking in, 90
    as process, 79
    reflectivity component, 82–84,
        87–90
    self-awareness in use of, 79
    self-esteem and, 86, 94
    self-improvement outcomes, 93–94
    as self-perpetuating, 94–95
    self-satisfaction and, 91–92
    strategic optimism and, 80, 87–88
    trait optimism and, 87
    treatment outcomes, 352–353
    vs. pessimistic attributional style, 81,
        87
    vs. realistic pessimism, 84
    vs. self-handicapping, 80
    vs. trait pessimism, 81, 87
Defensive Pessimism Questionnaire, 8,
    82–84, 87
Definitions, 31–32
    optimism, 5, 53, 102
    pessimism, 5
    physical well-being, 128
    types of optimism and pessimism,
        348–349
Denial, 203, 205, 220

Depression
    attributional style, 57, 59, 302–303
    in children. *See* Children, depression
        in
    co-occurring emotions, 150
    cognitive models, 302–303
    cognitive therapy, 330, 341–342
    cognitive–behavioral therapy, 302,
        303
    cultural differences, 266, 267, 270–
        271, 272, 273
    diathesis–stress model, 66–67
    expectancies in, 302–303
    hope and, 113, 115
    hopelessness theory, 55, 179,
        302–303
    increase in optimism as treatment ef-
        fect, 341–342
    neurophysiology, 179–180
    pessimism and, 271
    physical well-being and, 137
    postpartum, 192
    relapse, 303
    trait correlates, 174–175
Descartes, René, 14–15
Desire, Buddhist conceptualization, 258,
        xviii
Development, 10
    attributional style, 305–306
    depression risk in children, 303–308
    explanatory style and, 67–68
    future beliefs, 306
    life-span analysis of optimism and
        pessimism, 356–360
    origins of cognitive strategies, 96
    self-concept, 305
Diathesis–stress model
    explanatory style and well-being link-
        age, 66–67
    optimism–pessimism linkage, 67
Difficult tasks, 241–242, 246–248, 250
Dionysian impulse, 22–23
Discrepancy-enlarging feedback loop, 34
    in affectual processes, 38
Discrepancy-reduction feedback loop,
        32–34
    in affectual processes, 37–38
Disengagement, 203
    as adaptive behavior, 42–43, 228
    as change in goal engagement, 206–
        208, 210

coping style of pessimists, 199
as doubt effect, 42
in maintenance of self-efficacy be-
    liefs, 228–229
from uncontrollable stressors,
    219–223
Dopaminergic system, 178–179, 181, 232
Doubt
    affect-creating feedback loops in,
        37–38, 39–40
    behavioral consequences, 41–42,
        43–44
    catastrophe theory of behavior, 45–
        46, 47–48
    expectancy–value model of motiva-
        tion, 32
    in generalized outcome expectancies,
        41

Easy tasks, 241–242, 246–248, 250
Elation-Depression Scale, 287–288
Escape strategy, 202–203
Evolutionary psychology
    adaptive value of optimism, 170,
        184–185
    explanatory power, 170–171
Expanded Attributional Style Question-
    naire, 7, 56
Expectancies
    assessment of likelihood of outcome,
        39–40, 64
    attributional style and, 251
    cognitive interventions to modify,
        336–337
    cognitive restructuring with chil-
        dren, 312–313
    current conceptualization, 240–241
    daily symptom expectancies in
        chronic illness, 160–163, 164
    in defensive pessimism strategy, 79,
        81–82, 95–96
    in defining optimism and pessimism,
        31–32
    depression and, 302–303
    development in children, 306
    effect on performance, 240, 250–253
    emotional response to performance
        outcomes and, 242–246
    explanatory style and, 59–61
    hope theory, 104–105
    hopelessness theory, 55

Expectancies, *continued*
   learned helplessness theory, 55
   measurement, 190
   mechanisms of influencing perfor-
     mance, 241
   memory role in, 39–40, 41
   optimism and, 240
   perception of control and, 64–65
   predictors of performance, 241
   task difficulty and, in performance
     outcomes, 241–242, 246–248,
     250
   variations in breadth of, 40–41
   See also Generalized expectancy out-
     comes
Expectancy–value model of motivation,
   32, 198–199
   goal hierarchy and, 36–37
   hope theory, 104–105
   measurement, 106
Explanatory style. *See* Attributional style
Extended Life Orientation Test, 6–7, 264
Extraversion–introversion
   biological basis, 181–183, 183
   trait correlates, 173, 174–175, 183
Eysenck Personality Questionnaire-
   Revised, 173, 174–175

Failure, emotional response to, 242–246
Family-of-origin, explanatory style in,
   67–68
Fatalism, 23–24
Fear, 182
Feedback loops
   in affectual processes, 37–39
   discrepancy-enlarging, 34
   discrepancy-reducing, 32–34
   goals and, 34–35
   hierarchical organization of, 35
   in hope theory, 104
   in self-regulation, 32–34
Fibromyalgia, 155–162
Freud, Sigmund, 24–27

Gender differences
   internalization of attributions, 308
   research needs, 355
   social relations, 291–292, 296
Generalized Expectancy for Success
   Scale, 109–111
Generalized outcome expectancies, 4
   in anxiety disorders, 180–181

   cognitive therapy conceptualization,
     328
   confidence and doubt in, 41
   cultural differences, 259–261,
     263–266
   in daily coping with arthritis,
     152–155
   daily symptom expectancies in
     chronic illness, 162–163
   measurement, 6–7, 173, 190
   purpose, 40–41
   trait correlates, 173–175, 182–183
   See also Expectancies
Generalized Reward and Punishment Expectancy Scales, 172, 173, 174,
   175
Genetic factors, 170
   dispositional optimism–pessimism,
     68
   explanatory style, 68
   in optimism and pessimism, 175–
     178, 184
Giving up
   as adaptive behavior, 42–43
   catastrophe theory and, 44–48
   importance of activity and, 47
Goals
   action and, 35–36
   attainability, 206
   behavioral significance, 35
   changes in commitment to, as cop-
     ing strategy, 206–208, 224–225
   conditions for engagement, 206, 210
   construal in cognitive strategies, 78–
     79, 88
   in expectancy–value model of behav-
     ior, 36–37
   feedback loops and, 34–35
   hierarchical organization, 35, 36–37
   hope theory, 102–104
   level of abstraction, 35, 37
   moderation of, in optimists, 228–229
Great Chain of Being, 15–16
Guided-imagery techniques, 89–90

Happiness, 19
   Freud's conceptualization of social re-
     lations, 24–25
   James's conceptualization of social re-
     lations, 27
   in worst possible world, 21–22

Health. *See* Physical well-being; Psychological well-being
Heart surgery, 194–195, 201, 202
Hegel, Wilhelm Friedrich, 19–21
HIV/AIDS, 196, 200, 201, 208–209, 358
Hope
    achievement and, 115–116
    assessment, 105–106
    cognitive model, 102–106
    coping with illness and, 117–118
    depression and, 113, 115
    dispositional requirements, 102–103
    expectancy characteristics, 104–105
    overall well-being and, 112–113, 114, 118
    problem-focused coping and, 113–114
    problem solving and, 116–117, 234
    psychological adjustment and, 114–115
    research trends, 101–102
Hope Scale, 8, 105–106, 124–125
    correlation with other measures, 106–114
Hopelessness
    in children, 306
    control and, 64–65
    depression theory, 55, 179, 302–303
    developmental capacity for, 304
    diathesis–stress model, 66
Hostility
    co-occurring emotions, 150
Human suffering
    Buddhist thought, 258
    Hegelian philosophy, 19–20
    Voltaire's response to philosophical optimism, 16–18
Hume, David, 18
Humor, as coping strategy, 203, 220
Hysterisis, 44–46, 47

Ideological commitment, 284–285
Illusory glow optimism, 81
Immunological function, 136–137
Importance of activity or events, 60–61
    hope theory, 103–104
    moderation of behavior according to, 230
    motivation and, 47
Impulsivity, 182–183
Infertility, 192–193, 202–203

Information processing style, 225–228, 235–236
    cognitive distortions, 325
    cognitive theory of psychopathology, 322–328
    global/local bias, 232–233
    inward/outward focus, 232
    in moderation of belief and behavior, 229–231
    neurophysiology, 232
    problem-solving, 233–234
    processing of negative information, 230, 231–232, 234–235
    schemas, 324–325, 329–330
Inhibition, 181
Intelligence, 217–218
Interpersonal relations. *See* Social relations
Islamic thought, xix

James, William, 27–28
Judaism, xix

Leadership positions, 294–295
Learned helplessness, 4, 328–329
    control and, 64–65
    as diathesis–stress model, 66
    explanatory style in, 54–55
Learned optimism, 350–351
Leibniz, Gottfried, 16
Life Orientation Test, 6–7, 102, 105, 153–154
    correlation with other measures, 106–114
    Optimism–Pessimism Instrument and, 286

Marital satisfaction, 58–59
Meaning of being, 3–4, 206
    acceptance of meaningless of life, 22
    Nietzschean conceptualization, 22–23
Measurement
    attributional style, 7, 56, 190
    current state, 5–6
    defensive pessimism, 81–86
    expectancies, 190
    explanatory style, 129–130
    generalized outcome expectancies, 6–7, 173
    hope, 105–106

Measurement, *continued*
    popular instruments, 6–8
    social interaction, 290–295
    trait research, 171–172
    See also Assessment; *specific instrument*
Memory, 226
    in shaping expectancies, 39–40, 41
Menopause, 198
Methodology
    daily process research rationale,
        148–151
    idiographic–nomothetic analysis,
        154–156
    outcome measurement in Asian populations, 275–276
    research on health–psychology linkage, 131–133
Moderation of beliefs and behavior
    mechanisms of, 229–235
    strategies of optimists, 228–229
Monoamine oxidase, 179
Mood
    dispositional optimism as predictor
        of, 157, 159, 163
    disruption of cognitive strategies by,
        90–91
    duration of daily stress effects, 150
    information processing and, 232–
        233, 235
    in moderation of belief, 230
    neurophysiology, 178–181
    positive, optimism and, 229–231
    in processing negative information,
        231–232
    psychological well-being in medical
        events, 195–196
Moral reasoning, 18–19
Motivation
    affect-creating feedback loops in,
        38–39
    assessment of likelihood of outcome
        and, 39–40
    for change, 332
    disengagement as adaptive response,
        42–43
    expectancy–value model, 32
    expectations and, 61
    explanatory style and, 61
    perception of control and, 64–65
    pessimism and, 9

qualities of hope, 102
    sense of task importance in, 47
Multiple Affect Adjective Check List-
    Revised, 173, 174–175

Negative effects of optimism, 135–136,
    208–210, 240, 342, 356
Neurasthenia, 276
Neuroticism
    biological basis, 181–182
    discriminant validity of measures
        and, 110–111, 154
    trait correlates, 173, 174–175
Nietzsche, Friedrich, 22–24
Nonproductive persistence, 221
Norepinephrine, 178, 179

Older persons, 10, 357
Optimism, generally
    defined, 5, 31–32, 53, 102, 348–349
    potential negative effects, 135–136,
        208–210, 240, 342, 356
Optimism–Pessimism Instrument, 7–8
    construct validity, 284
    contents, 284
    correlations with personality measures, 284–290, 295–296
    creation and development, 281–284
    findings, 281
    psychometric properties, 295
    relation of optimism and pessimism
        in, 283–284
    social interaction findings, 290–295,
        296

Panic disorders, 180–181
Parent–child relations, and depression
    risk in children, 307–308
Pathways thinking, 102–105
Penn Optimism Program, 310–314
Perfectionism, 275
Pessimism
    advantages of, 8–9, 78
    generally defined, 5, 31–32, 348–349
Philosophical conceptualizations
    evolution in modern period, 13,
        14–28
    forms of reasoning in expectations,
        13–14
    optimism–pessimism in meaning of
        being, 3–4

Physical well-being
    caregiver stress, 196–197
    current conceptualization of optimism effects, 127–128, 133
    daily-process paradigm, 149–150
    definition, 128, 139–140
    depression and, 137
    design of psychological linkage research, 131–133
    empirical studies of optimism linkage, 133–136, 147–148
    explanatory style and, 58, 135, 138
    health benefits of optimism, 9, 53, 59, xvii
    health-promoting behaviors, 200–201
    information processing style for health protection, 225–226
    mechanism of optimism effects, 134–135, 136–139, 148, 183, 219
    mechanism of pessimism effects, 183–184
    perceived risk of illness, 131
    potential negative effects of optimism, 135–136
    psychological well-being during medical stress, 192–197, 202–203, 205–208
    public perception and attitudes, 139
    self-efficacy beliefs and, 134–135, 137–138
    See also Coping with chronic illness
Political beliefs/actions, 285
Pollyanna principle, 281–282
Pope, Alexander, 15–16
Positive and Negative Affect Schedule, 287–288
Positive illusions, 80–81, 251–252, 350–351, 355–356
Postpartum depression, 59
Potentiality of being, 3–4
    Freud's conceptualization, 24
    philosophical conceptualizations of early modern period, 15–16, 19–20
Prefactual thinking, 90
Pregnancy, 192, 204
Preventive interventions
    depression in children, 308–315
    health-related behaviors of optimists and pessimists, 200–202

promoting resiliency in children, 10
    See also Relapse prevention
Problem-focused coping, 113–114, 199
Problem solving
    cultural differences in coping strategies, 266–267, 268–269
    hope and, 116–117, 234
    information processing style, 233–234
Psychological well-being
    biological basis of psychopathology, 178
    cognitive model of psychopathology, 322–328
    coping tendencies of optimists and pessimists, 198–204, 218–219
    cultural considerations in outcomes measurement, 275–276
    explanatory style linkage, 66–67
    during health-related stress events, 192–197, 205–208
    hope and, 112–113, 114–118
    mechanism of optimism–pessimism effects, 205–208
    optimism and, 9, 53, 59, 189–190, 191, 210, xvii
    optimism and pessimism in psychopathology, 171–172
    pessimism and, 191, 210
    research design, 191–192
Psychopathology
    optimism and pessimism in psychopathology, 178–181
Psychoticism, 173

Reflectivity, 82–84
    in defensive pessimism construct, 87–90
Reframing, 203
Reinforcement of optimism and pessimism, 170
Relapse prevention
    cognitive intervention, 337–338
    depression, 303
Religion and spirituality, 10
    balance of optimism and pessimism as themes of, xvii–xx
    correlations in Optimism–Pessimism Instrument, 284–285
    early modern philosophical conceptualizations, 16, 18–19

Religion and spirituality, *continued*
    Freud's conceptualization of human
        development, 25–26
    psychological well-being and, xx
Repression–Sensitization Scale, 286, 287
Resignation, 210
Risk
    information processing, 226–227,
        230
    perceived risk of illness, 131
    sensation seeking, 173, 174, 181, 182
Rumination, 61

Schemas, 323–324, 329–330
Schopenhauer, Arthur, 21–22
Science, human happiness and, 25–26,
    27, 28
Self-awareness, in defensive pessimism,
    79
Self-concept
    aspiration level and, 243–244
    cultural factors, 257–258
    development in children, 305
    expectancy effects on response to
        performance, 244–245, 249–250
    Hegelian philosophy, 20
    identity disruption model, 358
    optimism–pessimism and, 5, 240
    processing of negative information
        about self, 230
    sense of independence, 258
Self-efficacy beliefs
    depression prevention in children,
        314–315
    depression risk in children, 308
    disengagement from unsolvable prob-
        lems in maintenance of, 228
    hope theory, 102–105, 114
    measurement, 107, 130
    optimistic bias, 135, 224
    physical well-being and, 134–135,
        137–138
Self-esteem
    defensive pessimism and, 86, 94
    hope and, 114–115
    self-handicapping strategies to pro-
        tect, 80
Self-handicapping, 80
Self-regulation of behavior, 8
    feedback control processes, 32–34
    goals in, 34–35, 41

hierarchical organization of feedback
    loops in, 35–36
Sensation seeking
    biological basis, 181
    trait correlates, 173, 174, 182
Serenity Prayer, 220
Serotonoergic system, 178, 179–180
Sexuality and sexual behavior, 24–25
Silver lining technique, 336
Situated optimism, 356
Skepticism, 18
Social intelligence theory, 78
Social relations
    attribution retraining in children,
        309
    cognitive model, 324–325
    culturally-mediated concept of self,
        258
    defensive pessimism strategy and, 92,
        96
    Freud's conceptualization of human
        development, 24–27
    health–optimism linkage, 137
    Hegelian concept of human develop-
        ment, 20–21
    learned helplessness model, 329
    optimism–pessimism and, 273, 290–
        295, 321–322, 354–356, 361
Social–cognitive theory, 78
Sociocultural context, 9–10
    adjustment predictors, 274–275
    attributional style, 261–263
    clinical significance, 276
    concept of self, 257–258
    coping strategies, 264, 265, 266
    cost–benefit analysis of optimism,
        360–361, 362
    cultural differences in coping strate-
        gies, 266–270
    depression assessment and interven-
        tion, 270–271, 273
    implications for assessment, 271–
        273, 274
    outcome measures, 275–276
    perceived malleability of optimism–
        pessimism, 361–362
    self-efficacy, 137
    significance of optimism–pessimism,
        4–5
    studies of optimism and pessimism,
        259–261, 263–264

treatment considerations, 342–343
treatment outcomes, 353–354
Strategic optimism, 351
    anxiety control, 87–88
    change in strategy, 95
    decision making style, 96
    defensive pessimism and, 80, 87–88
    definition, 80
    developmental origins, 96
    distinguishing features, 80–81
    measurement, 84–86
    mood induction effects, 90–91
    potential costs, 91, 92–93
    reflectivity component, 88–90
    related constructs, 80–81
    self-improvement outcomes, 93–94
    as self-perpetuating, 94–95
    treatment outcomes, 352–353
Strategies, cognitive
    affective component, 79–80
    evaluation of effectiveness, 93
    malleability, 78–79, 95
    mood induction effects, 90–91
    reflectivity component, 87–90
    user's awareness of, 79
    See also Cognitive styles; Defensive
        pessimism; Strategic optimism
Substance use, 183
Suicidal behavior/ideation, among chil-
    dren, 301

Summum bonum, 19
Surgery, 194–195, 196

Therapeutic relationship in cognitive
    therapy, 331
Threat, information processing in re-
    sponse to, 226–227, 235
Type A behavior pattern, 135

Unsolvable problems, 221–223, 228

Values
    advantages of pessimism, 8–9
    cultural diversity, 9
    in expectancy–value model of moti-
        vation, 32
    in feedback control processes, 33–34
    Kantian view of optimism, 19
    optimism–pessimism in, 5
Virtue, 19
Visualization techniques, 335–336
Voltaire, 16–18

Will, 234
    as blind striving, 21–22

Zuckerman–Kuhlman Personality Ques-
    tionnaire, 173, 174–175

ABOUT THE EDITOR

Edward C. Chang, PhD, is an assistant professor of clinical psychology at the University of Michigan. He received his PhD in 1995 from the State University of New York at Stony Brook after completing a clinical internship at Bellevue Hospital Center–New York University Medical Center. Dr. Chang previously taught at Northern Kentucky University, where he received the Outstanding Junior Faculty Award in the College of Arts and Sciences and served as a chapter president of Sigma Xi. He is on the editorial boards of several journals, including the *Journal of Personality and Social Psychology*, *Cognitive Therapy and Research*, and the *Journal of Social and Clinical Psychology*. He has published numerous articles and chapters on optimism and pessimism, social problem solving, perfectionism, and cultural influences on behavior.

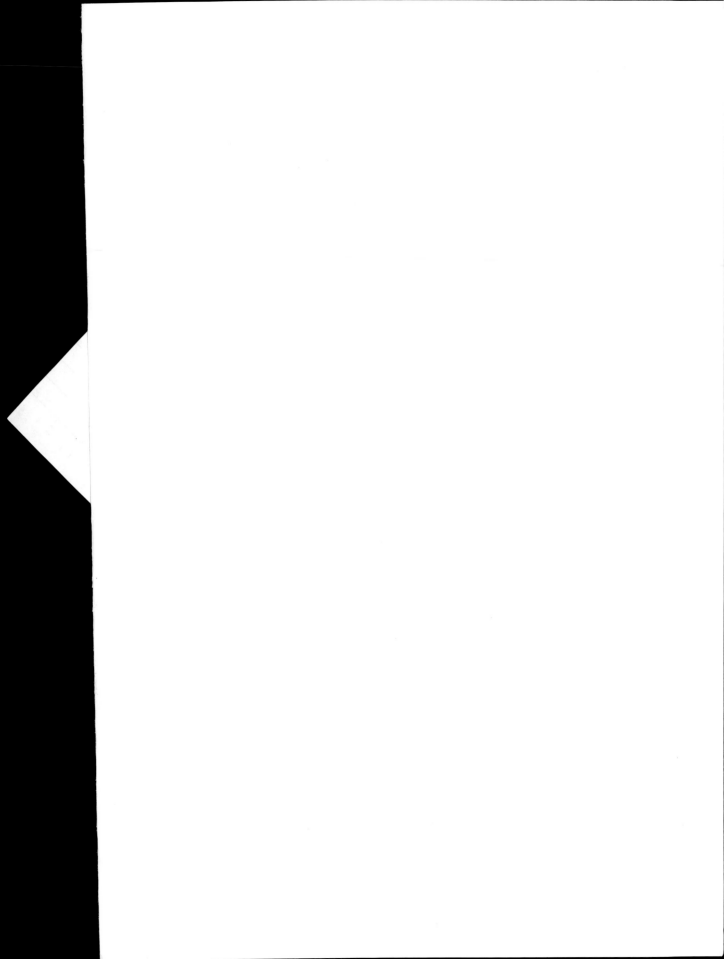

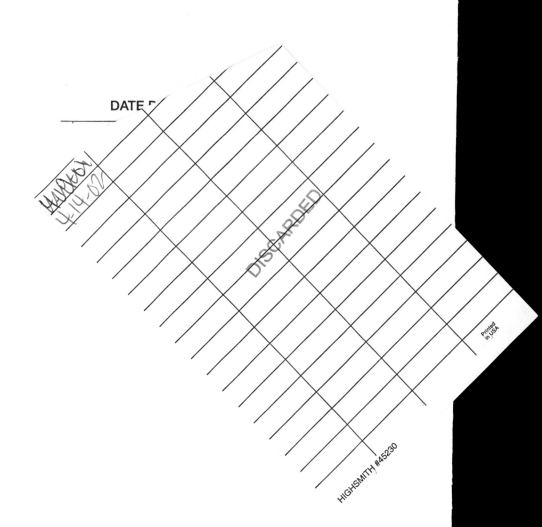

DATE

DISCARDED

HIGHSMITH #45230

Printed in USA